My

Personal

BOOK

2,567
+ 8,623
11,190

MACMILLAN/McGRAW-HILL

Mathematics in Action

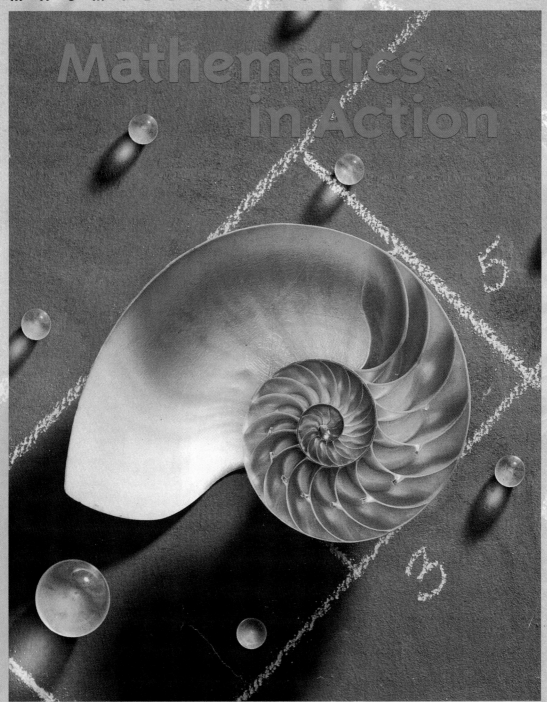

Audrey L. Jackson   Martin L. Johnson   Steven J. Leinwand
Richard D. Lodholz   Gary L. Musser   Walter G. Secada

MACMILLAN/McGRAW-HILL SCHOOL PUBLISHING COMPANY
New York   Columbus

CONSULTANTS

MULTICULTURAL AND EDUCATIONAL CONSULTANTS

Rim An

Marcia Ascher

Elsie Babcock

Vicki Chan

Dr. Alejandro Gallard

Zelda Gold

Jerilyn Grignon

Earlene Hall

Susan Lair

Dr. Barbara Merino

Carol Mitchell

James R. Murphy

Gail Lowe Parrino

Yolanda Rodriguez

Claudia Zaslavsky

ASSESSMENT CONSULTANT

Michael Priestley

COOPERATIVE LEARNING CONSULTANT

Liana Nan Graves

ACKNOWLEDGMENTS

The publisher gratefully acknowledges permission to reprint the following copyrighted material:

"Major Parties' Popular and Electoral Vote for President," and "Professional Basketball Arenas," from THE WORLD ALMANAC, 1989. Copyright © Newspaper Enterprise Association. New York, N.Y. 10166. Used by permission.

COVER DESIGN Designframe Inc. **COVER PHOTOGRAPHY** Pete McArthur

ILLUSTRATION Doran Ben-Ami; 144, 145 • Dianne Bennett; 199 • Marty Blake; 196, 197 • Alex Bloch; 332, 333 • Hal Brooks; 408, 409 • Taylor Bruce; 328, 329, 516 • Circa 86, Inc.; 507 • Ira Cook; 6, 7 • Clare Courtney; 402 • Margaret Cusack; 448, 449 • Deborah Danilla; 34, 236, 452 • Jim Delapine; 94, 154, 202, 232, 278, 490, 500 • Daniel DelValle; 363, 404, 436 • Eldon Doty; 370, 371 • Ted Enik; 208 • Richard Erickson; 310, 311, 512, 513 • David FeBland; 340 • Barbara Friedman; 292 • Simon Galkin; 70, 71, 116, 117, 184, 185, 323 • Donald Gambino; 125, 213, 261, 299, 383, 423, 461, 501 • Doreen Gay-Kassel; 104, 105 • Myron Grossman; 324, 325 • Meryl Henderson; 73 • Al Hering; 284, 285 • Marc Herman; 68, 246, 248, 249, 250 • Chris Hill; 69 • Pamela Johnson; 52, 53, 138, 139, 396, 461 • Rosanne Kakos; 160, 161 • Terry Kovalcik; 26, 148, 149, 318, 319, 414, 488, 489 • Mike Kowalski; 320, 321, 400, 401 • Lingta Kung; 140 • Akio Matsuyoshi; 549, 550, 551, 552, 553, 554 • Bill Mayer; 22, 23 • Michael McNally; 314 • Richard McNeel; 62, 63 • MKR Design; Handmade props • James Needham; 92, 93, 118 • Jeff Nishinaka; 1 • Michael O'Reilly; 200, 201, 242, 243, 290, 454 • Hima Pamoedjo; 374, 403, 492 • Robert Pasternak; 28, 29, 66, 67, 210, 476, 480, 481 • Susan Pizzo; 2, 3 • Lisa Pomerantz; 13, 192, 193, 244 • Rodica Prato; 8, 9, 64 • Marcy Dunn Ramsey; 511 • Roger Roth; 4, 5 • Ed Sauk; 49 • S.D. Schindler; 351 • Bob Shein; 378, 379 • Terry Sirrell; 526, 527 • Joel Snyder; 271, 547 • Susan Spellman; 58, 59 • April Blair Stewart; 260, 312, 365 • Marc Taffet; 114, 190, 191, 228, 484 • Vantage Art; 433 • Rhonda Voo; 152, 153 • Josie Yee; 146, 147, 166, 280, 356, 373, 376, 377, 402, 416, 442 • Rusty Zabransky; 12, 13, 19, 24, 28, 32, 72, 76, 148, 165, 203, 208, 211, 228, 232, 238, 258, 296, 297, 338, 380, 420, 458, 498, 534 • Ron Zalme; 240, 241 • Maggie Zander; 212, 274, 275 • Jerry Zimmerman; 50, 51, 110, 111, 180, 382 • **CONTENTS:** Don Baker

PHOTOGRAPHY After Image, Inc./Charles Feil, 368 • Allsport USA/Scott Halleran, 254 • Allstock/Randy Wells, 112 • American Museum of Natural History, 10-11 • Ancient Art & Architecture Collection, 225BL • Art Resource, Inc., 422B; Giraudon, 272T; Scala/Museo d'America, Madrid, 136-137M; SEF, 352-353 • The Bettmann Archive, 178-179 • Black Star/Bart Bartholomew, 142; Carol Bernson, 237M; Stern, 178TL • Lee Boltin Picture Library, 106ML, TR, B, 322 • Bruce Coleman Inc./B. Burch, 189; Jane Burton, 76T, B; Dan DeWilde, 456-457; Keith Gunnar, 327; E. Hosking, 77R; John Shaw, 102BL • Comstock/Cameron Davidson, 395B • Bob Daemmrich Photos, 74B • DRK Photo/John Gerlach, 103 • Focus On Sports, 227 • FPG International/Gerald Clyde, 422T • The Granger Collection, 90-91, 143 • Grant Heilman Photography/Larry Lefever, 413, 459T • Scott Harvey for MMSD, 70, 71 • Michal Heron, 124, 157, 287 • The Image Bank/Anthony Barboza, 60; Garry Gay, 211R; Bill Plummer, 434-435 bkgnd; Toby Rankin, 459B • The Image Works/Bob Daemmrich, 207; NASA, 67 • Index Stock, 66 • International Stock Photography Ltd./Elliott Varner Smith, 48 • J. Gerard Smith Photography, 30, 31, 61, 150, 151, 186, 187, 256, 257, 282, 295, 407, 446, 486, 487, 496, 525, 532 • Ken Karp for MMSD, 158, 159, 235, 456-457, 460L, 524-525 • Justin Kerr, 137BR • Bill Kontzias, 537 • Leo De Wys, Inc./Kim McHugh, 46-47; George Munday, 369 • Lockheed Aircraft Corp., 167T • Magnum/Erich Hartmann, 237T, B • Masterfile/© Imtek Imagineering, 224M • David Muench Photography, 472-473 • Museum & Library of Maryland History, 394-395 • Odyssey/Robert Frerck, 106MR, 352; E.S. Curtis, 473B • Stephen Ogilvy, 54, 55, 74, 98, 99, 125, 230, 231, 334, 339, 341, 398, 410, 417, 475, 494, 495 • Omni-Photo Communications, Inc./Ken Karp, 16, 18, 35, 56, 57, 78, 79, 101, 108, 123, 156, 204, 205, 213, 253, 261, 288, 299, 326, 330, 331, 340, 380, 381, 423, 474, 494, 501, 520, 521, 522, 534; John Lei, 33, 164, 165, 286, 316, 317, 383, 411, 438, 514, 515 • Photo Researchers/Toni Angermayer, 76; Biophoto Associates, 100T, B; Dr. Tony Brain/Science Photo Library, 483M; Brian Brake/Rapho, 272-273; CNRI/Science Photo Library, 483B; Dan Guravich, 182; George Holton, 136-137 bkgnd; Paolo Koch, 189; Susan McCarthy, 96; NASA/Science Source, 15; K.R. Porter, 483T; Gary Retherford, 24B; Jacana Sci, 77; Phototake/Al Lamme, 100T • Photri, 167B, 523 • The Picture Cube/John Coletti, 238 • Research Plus/Kurt Anderson, 513, 535; Franklin Avery, 11, 33, 311, 339; Laurence Bartone, 123, 165, 179, 211, 259, 273, 297, 353, 381, 499; Lawrence Migdale, 459; Karen Rantzman, 421 • Joseph Sachs, 258, 259, 296, 297, 420, 421, 458, 459, 495, 498, 499 • John Running, 234T, M, B • Silver Image/Richard Hobbs, 102TL, TR • Smithsonian Institution, 434-435 • Southwest Museum Collection, 472T • Stock Boston/Owen Franken, 90BL • The Stock Market/Al Assid, 211L; Wayne Eastep, 536M; Edgeworth Productions, 162; K. Iwasaki, 14; J.T. Miller, 447; Lewis Portnoy, 189; Will Ryan, 107; © 1991 Joe Towers, 224-225 bkgnd • Superstock, 10 • Tom Stack & Associates/Dave Watts, 536T, B • TSW-Click/Chicago/David Schultz, 289 • U.S. Postal Service, 395T • Viesti Associates/Reed Kaestner, 418; Ginny Ganong Nichols, 21, 419, 497, 533; Joe Viesti, 226, 406 • Regelm Vlaleverd III (Ruiters), 460R • Uniphoto/Everett C. Johnson, 394-395 • Malcolm Varon, 91 • Bill Waltzer, 339 • Westlight/M. Angelo, 106TL; Warren Morgan, 277; Bill Ross, 276 • **CONTENTS:** Franklin Avery, vi • Lawrence Bartone, vii • Richard Haynes, Inc., vB • Ken Karp, iii • Scott Harvey for MMSD, viii • Tina Mucci, vT, ixB • Ginny Ganong Nichols, x • Omni Photo Communications Inc./Ken Karp, v • Ginny Ganong Nichols, Viesti Associates, Inc., ixT

Macmillan/McGraw-Hill School Division
10 Union Square East
New York, New York 10003

Printed in the United States of America
ISBN 0-02-109267-2 / 6
1 2 3 4 5 6 7 8 9 RRW 99 98 97 96 95 94 93

3 USING MULTIPLICATION: WHOLE NUMBERS, DECIMALS

MATH *CONNECTIONS:* AREA • VOLUME

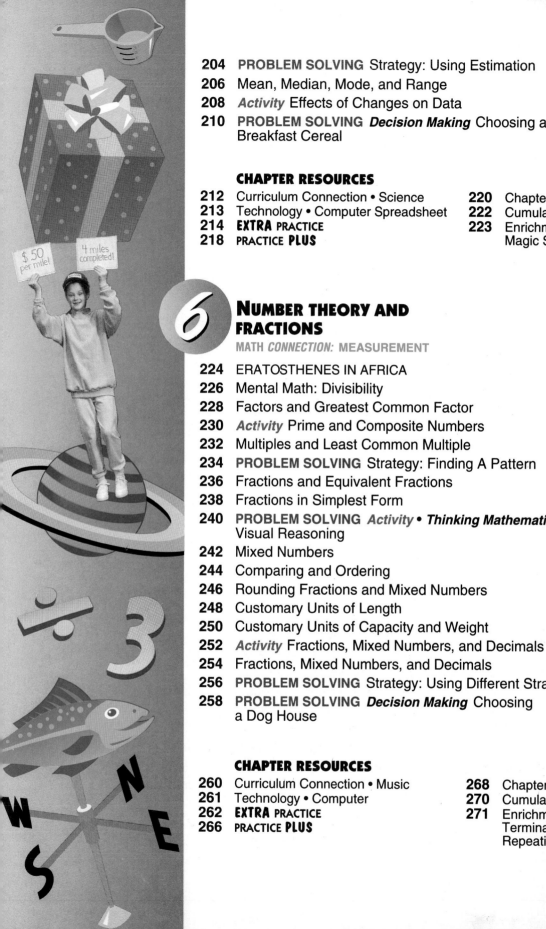

6 NUMBER THEORY AND FRACTIONS

MATH *CONNECTION:* MEASUREMENT

7 ADDING AND SUBTRACTING FRACTIONS AND MIXED NUMBERS

8 MULTIPLYING AND DIVIDING FRACTIONS AND MIXED NUMBERS

MATH *CONNECTIONS:* MEASUREMENT • AREA

9 GEOMETRY

10 RATIO, PROPORTION, AND PERCENT

MATH *CONNECTIONS:* ALGEBRA • MEASUREMENT

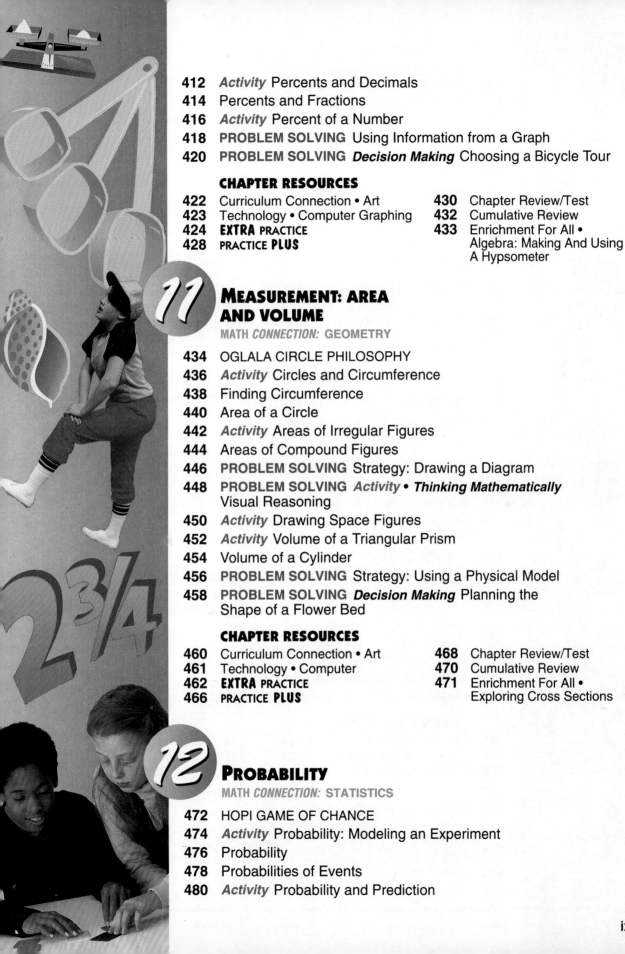

11 MEASUREMENT: AREA AND VOLUME

MATH *CONNECTION:* GEOMETRY

12 PROBABILITY

MATH *CONNECTION:* STATISTICS

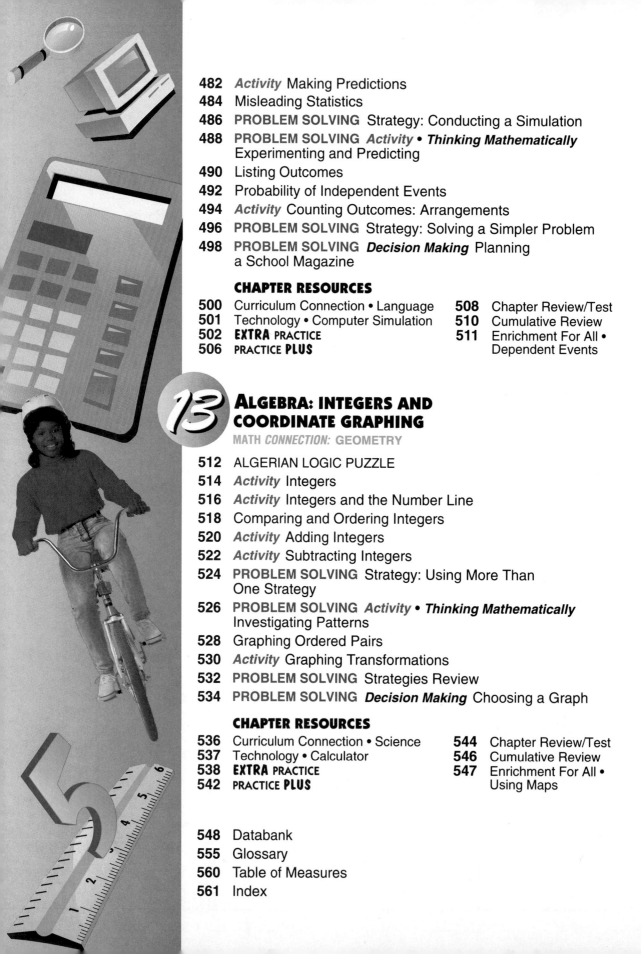

13 ALGEBRA: INTEGERS AND COORDINATE GRAPHING

MATH *CONNECTION:* GEOMETRY

GETTING STARTED

THINKING
MATHEMATICALLY

Mathematics is more than just numbers! Some mathematics problems do not use numbers at all. They use pictures, drawings, maps, or even cartoons. What do they have in common then? Every mathematics problem asks you to use a logical approach to find a solution. In these opening pages, you will be introduced to just a few of the ways that you can think mathematically.

Of course, thinking mathematically will help you with your math homework; but the benefits do not stop there. It can help you in *all* of your schoolwork, as well as in your everyday life. You will learn how to approach problems creatively. In fact, the word *mathematics* comes from a Greek word meaning "what is learned." So try the games and puzzles on these pages, have fun, and think about what (and how) you are thinking!

Audrey Jackson

Steve Leinwand

Martin Johnson

Gary L Musser

Richard Lodholz

Walter G. Secada

Shop 'til You Stop

GET BACK TO SCHOOL IN STYLE!

Shirts
Regularly $8.99
SALE PRICE $6.99

Sweaters
Were $12.99
Now $9.99

Jeans
Originally $21.99
On sale for $15.99

Sneakers
Once: $35.99
TODAY ONLY: $27.99

Socks
Usually $1.99
Price slashed to 99 cents!!

ALL SALES TAX INCLUDED IN OUR LOW LOW PRICES!!!

Applying Mathematics

Suppose you have $50. You want to buy 2 shirts and a pair of jeans.

1. How much will they cost? *$13.98*

2. How much will you save compared to the original prices? *$14.00*

3. How much will you have left if you started with $50? *36.02*

4. What else could you buy with your remaining money? *Another 1 pair of jeans, Another shirt, 1 sweater, 3 pairs of socks*

Suppose this is your back-to-school shopping list:

Sneakers
3 Pairs of Socks
Sweater
2 Pairs of Jeans

06.93

5. Will $100 be enough? How can you tell quickly? *yes By estimating*

6. How much will you spend on your shopping? *72.93*

7. How much will you save because you bought the items on sale? *$ 26.00*

Suppose you have $100 to spend at this sale.

8. What is the least number of items you could buy to spend the greatest amount of your money? *3+1=4 4*

9. By purchasing no more than 2 of each item, how close can you come to spending exactly $100? *Don't know*

Think about the prices in the sale. You can use the fact that every price ends in .99 to help you solve some problems.

10. If you purchase one item, the amount spent will end in $.99. What will the amount end in if you purchase two items? three items? *2-.98 4-.96 3-.97 5:*

Use the pattern you discover to help you solve these problems.

11. Rita spent $10.98 on clothing from the sale. What did she buy? How do you know? *a sweater & a pair of socks*

12. Sam spent $26.94 on clothing. What did he buy? *pair of jeans, 1shirt 4 pairs of socks*

13. Make up some other problems based on this back-to-school sale. Have others solve your problems. Check to see if their solutions are correct.

BSHY

Back and Forth and Back Again

WAS IT A CAT I SAW?

Investigating Patterns

A palindrome is anything that reads the same forward and backward. For example, these words are all palindromes:

DAD	MOM	ANNA	BOB
LEVEL	DID	TOT	NOON

This sentence is a palindrome:

Was it a cat I saw?

Palindromes can also be numbers. For example:

44   676   80,508   99,044,144,099

1. Copy this chart. It shows all of the 2-digit numbers. Which 2-digit numbers are palindromes? Where do they appear on this chart? Color them in red.

10	(11)	12	13	14	15	16	17	18	19
20	21	(22)	23	24	25	26	27	28	29
30	31	32	(33)	34	35	36	37	38	39
40	41	42	43	(44)	45	46	47	48	49
50	51	52	53	54	(55)	56	57	58	59
60	61	62	63	64	65	(66)	67	68	69
70	71	72	73	74	75	76	(77)	78	79
80	81	82	83	84	85	86	87	(88)	89
90	91	92	93	94	95	96	97	98	(99)

You can make a palindrome from any number. Take a number. Add its reverse.

For example: Begin with: 12
                 Reverse it: + 21
                 Add: 33   A palindrome!

It takes only one step to form a palindrome using the number 12. Some numbers take more than one step.

Begin with: 19
Reverse it: + 91
Add: 110   Not a palindrome yet
Reverse it: + 011
Add again: 121   A palindrome!

The number 19 is a 2-step palindrome.

2. Complete this chart and look for patterns. Once you have found where to place 12, you can also place 21. Why?

If you do not get a palindrome for a number in 6 steps, you can stop and write that number in the last column.

2-DIGIT NUMBERS

Palindromes	1 step	2 steps	3 steps	4 steps	5 steps	6 steps	more than 6 steps
11 22 33	12	19					

3. Now look at the number chart you copied from page 4. Use six other colors to represent each column on the chart above. What pattern do you find?

WHAT ARE PENTOMINOES?

Visual Reasoning

A. Pentominoes are a set of 12 shapes that are used in puzzles. Each shape is made up of 5 squares. Each pentomino follows these rules:

- The squares are the same size.
- Each square touches at least one other square.
- When squares touch, their sides match completely.

Here are 3 pentominoes:

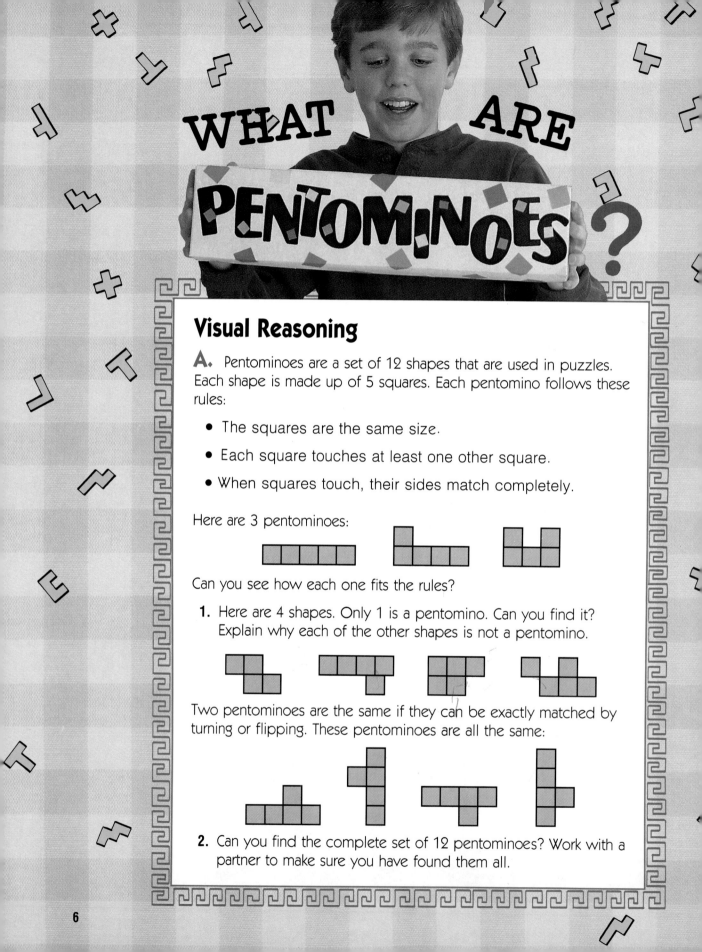

Can you see how each one fits the rules?

1. Here are 4 shapes. Only 1 is a pentomino. Can you find it? Explain why each of the other shapes is not a pentomino.

Two pentominoes are the same if they can be exactly matched by turning or flipping. These pentominoes are all the same:

2. Can you find the complete set of 12 pentominoes? Work with a partner to make sure you have found them all.

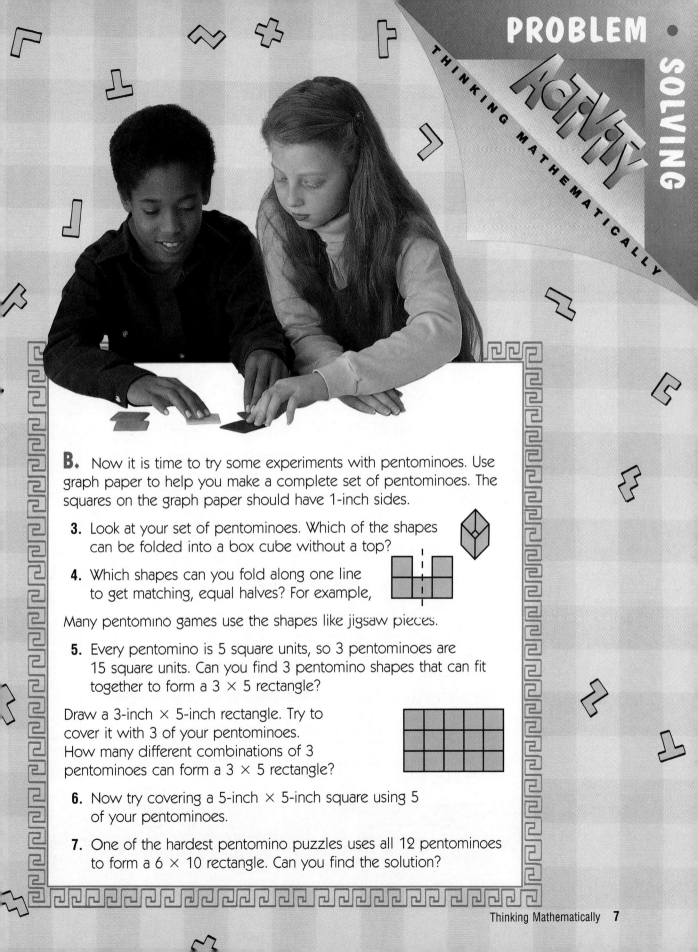

B. Now it is time to try some experiments with pentominoes. Use graph paper to help you make a complete set of pentominoes. The squares on the graph paper should have 1-inch sides.

3. Look at your set of pentominoes. Which of the shapes can be folded into a box cube without a top?

4. Which shapes can you fold along one line to get matching, equal halves? For example,

Many pentomino games use the shapes like jigsaw pieces.

5. Every pentomino is 5 square units, so 3 pentominoes are 15 square units. Can you find 3 pentomino shapes that can fit together to form a 3 × 5 rectangle?

Draw a 3-inch × 5-inch rectangle. Try to cover it with 3 of your pentominoes. How many different combinations of 3 pentominoes can form a 3 × 5 rectangle?

6. Now try covering a 5-inch × 5-inch square using 5 of your pentominoes.

7. One of the hardest pentomino puzzles uses all 12 pentominoes to form a 6 × 10 rectangle. Can you find the solution?

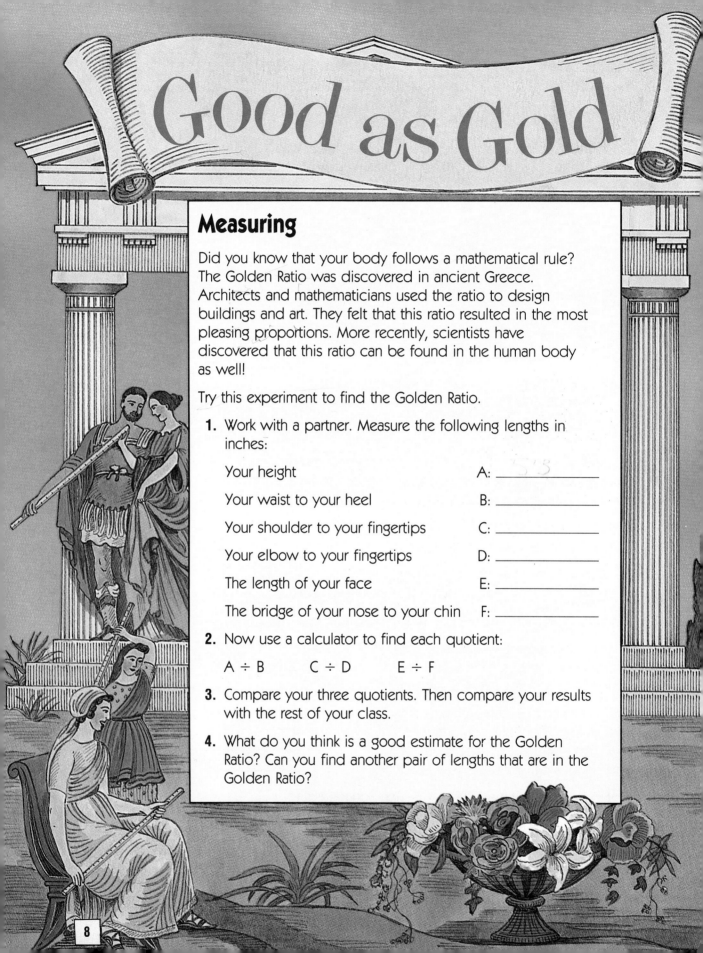

Good as Gold

Measuring

Did you know that your body follows a mathematical rule? The Golden Ratio was discovered in ancient Greece. Architects and mathematicians used the ratio to design buildings and art. They felt that this ratio resulted in the most pleasing proportions. More recently, scientists have discovered that this ratio can be found in the human body as well!

Try this experiment to find the Golden Ratio.

1. Work with a partner. Measure the following lengths in inches:

   Your height   A: _____55_____

   Your waist to your heel   B: _____

   Your shoulder to your fingertips   C: _____

   Your elbow to your fingertips   D: _____

   The length of your face   E: _____

   The bridge of your nose to your chin F: _____

2. Now use a calculator to find each quotient:

   A ÷ B   C ÷ D   E ÷ F

3. Compare your three quotients. Then compare your results with the rest of your class.

4. What do you think is a good estimate for the Golden Ratio? Can you find another pair of lengths that are in the Golden Ratio?

In Other Words

Collecting and Interpreting Data

It has been estimated that there are over 4,000 languages in the world. Amazingly, more than half the people in the world speak one of the eight languages in this table.

Language	Number of Speakers
Chinese	800,000,000
English	410,000,000
Hindi	290,000,000
Spanish	280,000,000
Russian	270,000,000
Arabic	170,000,000
Bengali	160,000,000
Portuguese	150,000,000

1. What kind of graph could you use to show this data? Would you use the exact data? Choose one style and create a graph.

2. Do you find the graph or the table more helpful? What are the advantages of each form?

You might be surprised at how many languages are represented by students in your class and their families. Conduct a survey to find out.

3. First guess how many languages are spoken by the students, their parents, and grandparents.

4. Next design a survey. What questions will you ask? How will you gather your information? Gather your data using the survey you designed.

5. Organize your data in a table and a graph.

6. Discuss the results of your survey. How accurate was your original guess? What other information did you get?

7. Do you think the survey accurately represents your class? Why or why not? What might you do differently next time you take a survey?

THE INCA

The Inca Empire existed in South America about 500 years ago. Local administrators for the head of the Inca state kept many detailed records.

The records were kept on connected sets of colored cords called *quipus* (KEY-poos). Each *quipu* had a main cord from which other cords were hung. Knots were made in the hanging cords to represent numbers in a base-ten system. Usually, each hanging cord contained one number. Clusters of knots were separated by spaces and placed one above the other. Each cluster represented a higher power of ten.

The number on each *quipu* cord is read from the point where it is attached to the main cord down to its free end. First, the knots in the cluster closest to the main cord are counted. For a 3-digit number, this cluster stands for hundreds. The middle cluster represents tens, and the bottom cluster, ones. No knots in a place stands for zero in that place.

Quipu cords can have different colors. The different colors represent different kinds of information. For instance, if the population of an Inca village were being recorded, a red cord might have been used for men, yellow for women, and green for children. Then, for recording the numbers from a second village, a second set of cords with the same colors would have been used.

QUIPU

MATH CONNECTION: Statistics

UNDERSTANDING NUMBERS:
WHOLE NUMBERS, DECIMALS

1. What numbers are represented in the drawing on page 10?

2. Work with a partner. Use different colors to draw a *quipu*. How would you record information such as how many desks and chairs are in the classroom on your *quipu*?

3. If you counted the desks and chairs in two classrooms, how would you record this information on your *quipu*? How many cords would you need? How many different colors would you use?

ACTIVITY

Frequency Tables and Diagrams

Georgia asked her classmates to write the names of their favorite sports on slips of paper. Which sport was named most often?

WORKING TOGETHER

1. How can you organize the data to solve the problem? *Use a diagram or a frequency Table*

2. Which sport is the most popular? How do you know? *Swimming, Ilooket*

3. List other information you can get from your organized data.

This is how two students organized the data. Jason made a **frequency table**. He made a tally mark each time a sport was named. Debbie made a **frequency diagram** by drawing a dot each time a sport was named.

FAVORITE SPORTS		
SPORT	TALLY	FREQUENCY
swimming	‖‖ ||	7
bicycling	|||	3
baseball	‖‖		6
fishing	||	2
skiing	‖‖	5
horseback riding			1

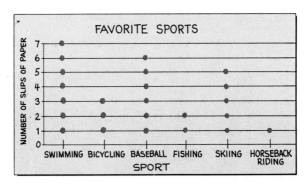

SHARING IDEAS

4. How many students took part in the survey?

5. Use Jason's table to name the third most popular sport.

6. Use Debbie's diagram to name the 3 least popular sports.

7. How does the way you organized the data compare with the frequency table or diagram?

8. How might a sporting goods store use this information? Why might a store want to gather more data?

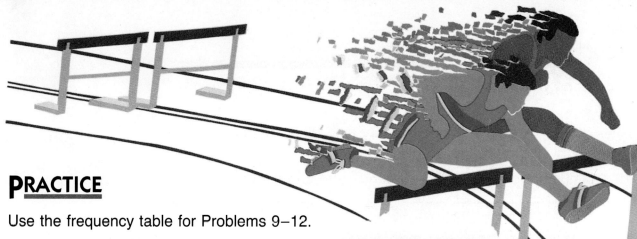

PRACTICE

Use the frequency table for Problems 9–12.

9. Which size team has the highest frequency? 28

10. How many teams have more than 30 students? 3

11. How many teams are there in the league? 24

12. Which two team sizes have a frequency of 4? 29, 31

NUMBER OF STUDENTS ON TRACK TEAMS IN LEAGUE

Number of Students	Number of Teams	
	Tally	Frequency
28	ЖІ ІІІ	8
29	ІІІІ	4
30	ЖІ	5
31	ІІІІ	4
32	ІІ	2
33	І	1

Make a frequency table or frequency diagram for the data.

13. **POINTS SCORED BY BASKETBALL TEAM**

75	70	68	68	57	62	63
77	68	76	69	72	37	61
68	66	72	70	68	66	60
61	68	70	66	64	62	63

14. **COACHES' CHOICES OF BRANDS OF BASEBALL BATS**

A	A	B	B	B	C	A	A	B	A
A	B	B	B	A	A	C	A	B	C
B	A	C	D	B	A	B	C	A	D
A	B	C	C	B	C	A	B	C	A

15. Conduct a survey. Collect information about sports, hobbies, TV shows, books, food, people, school subjects, colors, music, or whatever else interests you. Show the results of the survey in a frequency table or diagram.

Critical Thinking

The ad at the right appeared in a newspaper.

16. What important information is missing without a frequency table or diagram?

17. Would you buy this product? Why?

Most Coaches Recommend Brand X Footballs

Whole Numbers

A. The planet Saturn is a very long distance from the Sun.

You can use the **place-value chart** below to help read the number of kilometers between Saturn and the Sun.

Billions Period			Millions Period			Thousands Period			Ones Period		
H	T	O	H	T	O	H	T	O	H	T	O
		1	4	1	9	4	2	4	0	0	0

Standard form: 1,419,424,000

Short word name: 1 billion, 419 million, 424 thousand

Read: one billion, four hundred nineteen million, four hundred twenty-four thousand

1. How do the names of the periods help you read the numbers?

2. Why are there commas in a number with more than three digits?

3. Which digit is in the tens place of the millions period?

4. How would you write the standard form of three thousand, nine?

B. You can write a number in **expanded form** to show the value of each digit.

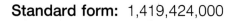

$39,830 = (3 \times 10,000) + (9 \times 1,000) + (8 \times 100) + (3 \times 10) + (0 \times 1)$
$\qquad\qquad\quad$ **30,000** $\qquad\quad$ **9,000** $\qquad\quad$ **800** $\qquad\quad$ **30** $\qquad$ **0**

5. In which place does the digit 3 have a greater value?

6. How does the value of each place change as you move from right to left in the place-value chart?

TRY OUT Write each number in three different ways.

7. three thousand, two hundred

8. $(9 \times 1,000) + (0 \times 100) + (9 \times 10) + (8 \times 1)$

_320,001_

PRACTICE

Write the short word name.

9. 72,854,103,983
_12 billion, 854 million, 103
thousand, 983 hundred_

10. 107,064,004 _107 million,
64 thousand, four_

11. 7,000,426,000

Write in standard form.

12. 16 billion, 4 thousand

13. 100 million, 43

14. 235 billion

15. sixteen thousand, twelve

16. thirty-seven billion, four million, fifty

17. $(2 \times 10,000) + (5 \times 1,000) + (0 \times 100) + (7 \times 10) + (6 \times 1)$

18. $(6 \times 100,000) + (4 \times 10,000) + (0 \times 1,000) + (3 \times 100) + (0 \times 10) + (5 \times 1)$

Name the place value of the digit 7 in the number.

19. 567,241,055

20. 270,316,998,400

21. 609,711,432

Write the short word name for the digit 5 in the number.

22. 459,630,000

23. 570,400,000,000

24. 23,530,000

Write in expanded form.

25. 87,204

26. 163,477,013

27. 91,042,007,672

Write each number in two different ways.

28. The diameter of the Earth at the equator is about twelve thousand, seven hundred eighty-five kilometers.

29. Mercury is the closest planet to the Sun. Its distance from the Sun is about 58,100,000 km.

30. The closest the Moon comes to the Earth is about three hundred fifty-four thousand, three hundred forty kilometers.

Critical Thinking

31. Is a thousand million greater than a billion? Why or why not?

32. Is a billion tens greater than ten billion? Why or why not?

33. Olivia read the number 1,000,800 as "1 thousand, 8 hundred." What was her mistake? What is the correct answer?

Decimals

A. Gina is making a mosaic with 100 tiles. So far she has cemented 32 tiles. How would you write a decimal to show how much of the mosaic is covered?

Gina writes 32 out of 100 as the fraction $\frac{32}{100}$; 32 hundredths is the same as 3 tenths and 2 hundredths.

You can show this in a place-value chart.

Gina has covered 0.32 of the mosaic.

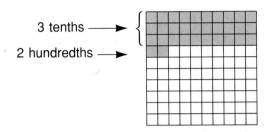

3 tenths
2 hundredths

ones		tenths	hundredths
0	.	3	2

decimal point

B. You can use a place-value chart to read decimals.

tens	ones		tenths 0.1	hundredths 0.01	thousandths 0.001	ten-thousandths 0.0001	hundred-thousandths 0.00001
2	0	.	2	4	6	4	1

Standard form: 20.24641

Short word name: 20 *and* 24 thousand, 641 hundred-thousandths

Read: twenty *and* twenty-four thousand, six hundred forty-one hundred-thousandths

Expanded form: (2 × 10) + (0 × 1) + (2 × 0.1) + (4 × 0.01) + (6 × 0.001) + (4 × 0.0001) + (1 × 0.00001)

1. The digit 4 appears in two places. In which place does it have the greater value? hynndredths

2. How does the place value of the last digit help you read a decimal?

C. Decimals that name the same amount are called **equivalent decimals**.

$$\frac{5}{10} = \frac{50}{100} = \frac{500}{1,000}$$

So 0.5 = 0.50 = 0.500

3. What happens to a decimal if zeros are added to the right?

4. four hundred seventy-six
hundred-thousandths *.00476*
   a. 0.0476   **c.** 476,000
   (b.) 0.00476 **d.** 0.47600

5. three hundred and forty-one
thousandths *.341*
   (a.) 0.341   **c.** 300.041
   b. 341,000 **d.** 341

6. Which is equivalent to 2.56?
   a. 2.50   **b.** 2.566 *(c.)* 2.560   **d.** 2.5606

PRACTICE

Write the short word name.

7. 3.8 *three and eight tenths*   **8.** 12.18 *twelve and eighteen hundredths*   **9.** 5.12348 *five and twelve thousand three hundred forty eight hundred thousandths*   **10.** 0.0681 *six hundred eighty one ten-thousandths*

Write in standard form.

11. 27 and 5 tenths *27.5*

12. 9 ten-thousandths *.0009*

13. seven and five hundredths *7.05*

14. one hundred and six thousandths *100.006*

15. $\frac{376}{100,000}$ *.00376*   **16.** $28\frac{53}{1,000}$ *28.053*   **17.** $(7 \times 0.1) + (5 \times 0.01) + (3 \times 0.001)$

18. $(7 \times 1) + (0 \times 0.1) + (2 \times 0.01) + (4 \times 0.001) + (4 \times 0.0001) + (8 \times 0.00001)$

Write the value of the digit 6 in each number.

19. 46.203   **20.** 27.164   **21.** 0.13476   **22.** 0.80962

Write in expanded form.

23. 26.52   **24.** 0.8732   **25.** 0.07503   **26.** 6.0109

Write as a fraction or a mixed number.

27. 0.003   **28.** 8.27   **29.** 2.0957   **30.** 0.06027

Which two decimals are equivalent?

31. 0.0603
0.00603
0.06030

32. 0.017
0.01700
0.00170

33. 1.00080
1.0080
1.008

34. 5.01
5.0010
5.01000

Write the number in standard form.

35. There are sixty-two thousand, five hundred two pieces of art in the museum.

36. The length of one of the floors of the museum is seventeen and nine hundredths meters.

Comparing and Ordering

A. At the Lincoln School track meet, Martinez ran the 200-m dash in 25.6 seconds. Johnson ran the race in 25.8 seconds. Who ran the faster race?

You can think of a number line to compare their times.

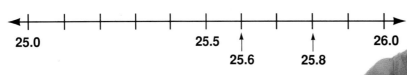

The number line shows 25.6 comes before 25.8. So 25.6 < 25.8.

Or you can compare the numbers without a number line.

Step 1	**Step 2**
Line up the decimal points. Starting at the left, find the first pair of digits that are not equal.	Compare the digits.

2 5 . 6
2 5 . 8

Think: 6 < 8
25.6 < 25.8

Martinez ran the faster race.

1. Compare 25.8 and 25.3. Which is greater? How do you know?

B. You can order numbers by comparing them first.

2. Who had the longest jump? the shortest jump? How do you know?

3. Arrange the lengths in order from least to greatest.

LONG JUMP

Chen	5.62 m
Mason	5.39 m
Wyatt	5.50 m

TRY OUT Write the letter of the correct answer.

4. Which number is least?   **a.** 0.230   **b.** 1.032   **c.** 0.023   **d.** 0.232

5. Which number is greatest?   **a.** 0.0076   **b.** 0.052   **c.** 0.009   **d.** 0.3

PRACTICE

Complete. Write >, <, or =.

6. 213,458 ● 213,454   **7.** 0.031 ● 0.310   **8.** 5 ● 4.8   **9.** 15 ● 15.000

10. 10,020 ● 100,200   **11.** 2.7 ● 2.699   **12.** 90 ● 9.8   **13.** 0.8 ● 0.08

Order from least to greatest.

14. 84,923; 84,932; 87,239; 84,329   **15.** 219,370; 69,993; 219,392; 291,370

16. 12.001, 1.2, 1.23, 12.1   **17.** 0.908, 9, 0.8, 0.809

Solve.

18. If 3.7■6 < 3.756, what numbers can ■ stand for?

19. If 8.0■ > 8.047, what numbers can ■ stand for?

20. Name two whole numbers between 26.1 and 28.1.

21. Name two decimals between 4.77 and 4.78.

Critical Thinking

22. Rosita is comparing 2.6 and 2.47. She thinks, "6 is less than 47, so 2.6 is less than 2.47." Is she right? Why or why not?

Mixed Applications

23. It is estimated that 15,500,000 people watched a recent Super Bowl on television. Write the short word name for this number.

24. Zina won the high-jump event with a jump of one and forty-two hundredths meters. Write the number in standard form.

LOGICAL REASONING

Decimals A, B, C, D, and E are shown at the right.

- A is greater than C.
- A is less than D.
- B and E have the same digit in the thousandths place.
- B is the least of the decimals.

Which decimal is A? B? C? D? E?

4.318
4.752
0.4752
0.47052
0.4301

PROBLEM SOLVING

✓ UNDERSTAND
✓ PLAN
✓ TRY
✓ CHECK
✓ EXTEND

Using the Five-Step Process

Study how the five-step process is used to solve this problem.

Claudio and David made a table that showed what they had earned during their summer vacation. Which student earned more during the summer?

Jobs	Claudio's Earnings	David's Earnings
Mowing lawns	$170	$180
Baby-sitting	160	170
Delivering papers	130	140
Collecting cans	60	70

UNDERSTAND

What do I know?
What do I need to find out?

I know how much each student earned.
I need to find out who earned more during the summer.

PLAN

What can I do?

I can compare the amounts that each boy earned from doing the same job.

TRY

Let me try my plan.

David earned more from each job than Claudio did. So David must have earned more during the summer than Claudio did.

CHECK

Have I answered the question?
Does my answer make sense?

Yes. David earned more than Claudio.
Yes. If the numbers in one addition problem are greater than the numbers in another, the first sum will be greater than the second.

EXTEND

What have I learned?

I have learned that I can sometimes tell which of two sums will be greater by comparing the numbers to be added. I may not have to do the actual addition.

PRACTICE

Apply what you have learned about the
five-step process to solve the problem. Use
mental math, a calculator, or paper and
pencil. You may need to use data from the
table on page 20 to solve the problem.

> **Remember:**
> What do I know?
> What do I need to find out?
> What can I do?
> Did I answer the question?
> What have I learned?

1. Which student earned less from delivering papers and
   collecting cans? *Claudio*

2. Which student earned more from mowing lawns and
   baby-sitting? How much more? *David $20.00 more*

3. Claudio spent $20 of his earnings on supplies for the new
   school year and $70 on new clothes. How much less did he
   spend on school supplies than on clothes? *$50.00 less*

4. David spent $20 on school supplies, $70 on clothes,
   and $30 on video games. How much of his earnings
   did he have left after buying these items? *$440.00*

5. David put $55 into a savings account in June. In July *David-155*
   he put in $40, and in August he put in another $60.
   Claudio put $75, $50, and $65 into his savings *Claudio-190*
   account. Which student saved more of his earnings?

6. In the fall Claudio bought a used bicycle with some of
   his savings. He made 3 equal payments of $30 each.
   How much did the bicycle cost? *$90.00*

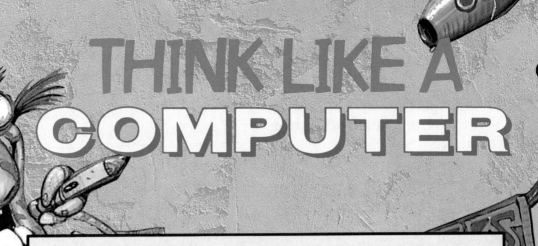

THINK LIKE A COMPUTER

Using Number Concepts

A. You might have heard that computers can play games. In fact, some of them play very well! They play by following a set of strategy rules exactly. Think about your own strategies as you learn to play Number Monster.

There can be two to four players. To play Number Monster, you need two sets of cards numbered 0 to 9. You will have 20 cards in all. You also need paper and pencil.

To begin, each player should draw a gameboard like the one below.

A	B	C	D

Shuffle the cards. Then the first player takes the top card and writes that digit in any one of his or her four squares. The card is placed face up next to the deck. The next player picks the next top card and writes the digit in a square. Play continues until every player has written a complete 4-digit number. The player with the greatest number is the winner.

The first two moves of a sample game are shown below. Remember: 0 □ □ □ will not give a 4-digit number.

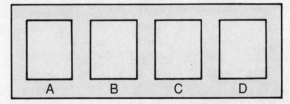

PLAYER 1	PLAYER 2
Picks 7 [ ][7][ ][ ]	Picks 3 [ ][ ][ ][3]
Picks 2 [ ][7][ ][2]	Picks 8 [8][ ][ ][3]

1. Play several rounds of Number Monster. Think about how you decide to place each digit. Do you follow any rules of your own as you play?

2. Suppose the first number you pick is a 9. Where will you put it? What if it is a 0?

3. You can also try a variation in which the winner is the player with the least 4-digit number. How would this change the way you play?

B. How could a computer play Number Monster? It would have to have a set of complete directions to follow about every possible turn.

Think about the first turn of play. There are ten possible digits. For the first card, a computer might follow a strategy like this:

> If the number is 8 or 9, place it in A.
> If the number is 5, 6, or 7, place it in B.
> If the number is 2, 3, or 4, place it in C.
> If the number is 0 or 1, place it in D.

4. Can you devise a computer strategy for an entire game of Number Monster? Remember to include every possibility. In the second turn, you will have to account for the fact that one square is already filled. You might write: Second card—If the number is 0 or 1, place it in D. If D is filled, place it in C.

5. Now match your "computer" against that of another student. Play several rounds of the game, following your computer strategy exactly. Does one strategy win more often? Could you change your strategy to improve it?

6. Think about other factors that you have not included in your computer program. Do you think a human player has a better chance of winning than the computer? Why or why not?

Rounding Whole Numbers and Decimals

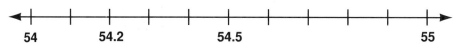

A. In 1980 there were 54.2 people per square mile in Texas. A 1987 estimate of population showed there were about 62.5 people per square mile. How would you complete the newspaper headline?

Indira decided to use **rounded numbers.** She thought of a number line to round 54.2 to the nearest whole number.

```
    54        54.2          54.5                    55
```

She said, "54.2 is between 54 and 55. It is nearer to 54 than to 55, so I'll round down. Rounded to the nearest whole number, 54.2 is 54."

The population was about 54 people per square mile in 1980.

1. **What if** the population had been 54.8 people per square mile? Should she have rounded up or down? Why?

B. Here is how Peter rounded 62.5 to the nearest whole number.

Step 1

Find the place to which you are rounding.

6 2 . 5

Step 2

Look at the digit to the right.
If it is 5 or greater, round up.
If it is less than 5, round down.

6 2 . 5   *Think:* The digit is 5 so round up.

So 62.5, rounded to the nearest whole number, is 63. The headline would read: "63 people per square mile, up from 54 people in 1980."

2. Rounding money is similar to rounding decimals. Round $25.49 to the nearest dollar and the nearest dime.

TRY OUT Round:

3. 12.827 to the nearest hundredth.

4. 3.8771 to the nearest thousandth.

PRACTICE

Round 713,657,508.96513 to the place named.

5. millions

6. hundred millions

7. ten millions

8. billions

9. thousands

10. hundred thousands

11. thousandths

12. hundredths

13. tenths

Round $8,752.97 to the place named.

14. $1,000

15. $10

16. $1

17. $.10

Write the place to which the number was rounded.

18. 181,412 to 180,000

19. 5.073 to 5.07

20. 27.90102 to 28

21. 43,500 to 44,000

22. 0.0605 to 0.061

23. 1.9999 to 2.0

To which whole number is the calculator display close?

24. $\boxed{2.497}$

25. $\boxed{9.31}$

26. $\boxed{0.79}$

27. $\boxed{99.7513}$

Solve.

28. What is the greatest whole number that, when rounded to the nearest thousand, is 7,000?

29. What is the least whole number that, when rounded to the nearest hundred, is 1,500?

Using a rounded number write a headline for the statement.
You may need to use the Databank on page 549.

30. A mystery novel sold 1,845,013 copies.

31. The planet Mercury travels 29.73 miles per second.

32. The U.S. male population is expected to be about ■ by the year 2000.

33. The number of people 65 and over will be 36,246,000 by the year 2000.

34. A telemarketing company spent $211,857,112 on phone calls.

35. School enrollment increased by 13.58 percent.

Critical Thinking

Would you round or use the exact number in the newspaper headline?

36. RECORD 38.7 INCHES OF RAIN!

37. 39,679,315 GO TO POLLS

38. MANUTE BOL TALLEST PLAYER IN NBA AT 7 ft $6\frac{3}{4}$ in.

39. 224,372,599,000 HOURS OF TV WATCHED IN U.S. IN 1 YEAR

Reading and Interpreting Bar Graphs

In a survey students in the sixth grade were asked to rate their likes and dislikes on a scale of 1 to 7. (The more they liked an activity, the higher the rating.) Adults were asked to use the same scale to rate what they thought were students' likes and dislikes. The mean, or average, scores are shown in the **double-bar graph.**

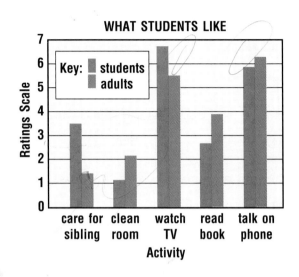

WHAT STUDENTS LIKE

Key: ■ students ■ adults

Ratings Scale

Activity: care for sibling, clean room, watch TV, read book, talk on phone

1. What activity do students like best?

2. What do adults think students like best?

Look at how students rate "care for sibling." Note that the bar is about halfway between 3 and 4. You can say that students rate "care for sibling" at about 3.5 on the scale.

3. Which activity do adults rate about 3.9?

4. About what rating do students give to reading a book?

5. Why is it necessary to include a **key** on a double-bar graph?

6. Which activity do students and adults rate the closest? For which activity are the ratings farthest apart? Why?

TRY OUT

7. The table to the right shows the data from the double-bar graph, rounded to the nearest tenth. Which of Problems 1–6 could have been answered more easily using the table? For which problems was the graph more helpful? Why?

WHAT STUDENTS LIKE

Activity	Students	Adults
care for sibling	3.5	1.4
clean room	1.1	2.1
watch TV	6.7	5.5
read book	2.7	3.9
talk on phone	5.9	6.2

PRACTICE

8. What is the subject of the single-bar graph at the right? *# of books read during summer vacation*

9. What information is shown on the vertical axis? on the horizontal axis? *# of books; student*

10. What does the tallest bar show? *Who read the Most + how Many books that person read*

11. How many books did Kim read during the summer vacation? *15*

12. About how many books did Joi read? *18*

13. Who read about twice as many books as Kweku? *Carmen*

14. Starting with the person who read the most books, list the names in order of the number of books read. *Carmen, Joi, Kim, Kweku, + Dave*

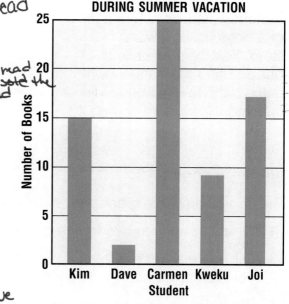

NUMBER OF BOOKS READ DURING SUMMER VACATION

The double-bar graph at the right shows the results of a survey that was taken in a small school district.

15. What kinds of data are being compared? *age + gender*

16. Why are the horizontal bars broken between 0 and 16?

17. Do the people surveyed watch more or less TV as they get older? *less*

18. In which age groups do males watch more TV than females? *15-18 + 12-14*

19. In which age group do males and females watch TV for about the same number of hours? *12-14*

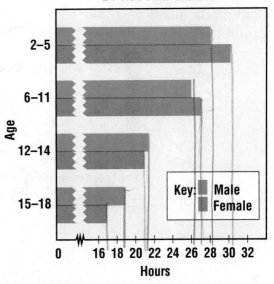

AVERAGE WEEKLY TV VIEWING BY AGE AND GENDER

Critical Thinking

Look at the double-bar graph above.

20. What additional information would you need about the data?

21. Would the results have been about the same if all young people in the United States had been surveyed? Why or why not?

ACTIVITY

Making Bar Graphs

Pretend you are the manager of a computer software store. You want to make a bar graph of the data shown in the table to use at a sales meeting. How would you do it?

Game	July Sales	August Sales
Pac Kid	$658.90	$838.60
Pong	$449.25	$569.05
Trivia	$599.00	$688.85
Arcade	$1,048.25	$1,198.00
Checkmate	$539.10	$628.95

WORKING TOGETHER

Before you draw the graph, you must make a few decisions.

1. What title will you use for the graph?

2. What scale will you use?

3. Will you make a single- or double-bar graph?

4. Will you round the amounts? If so, to what place?

5. Will the bars run vertically or horizontally?

6. How will you label each axis?

Pam made this double-bar graph to display the data.

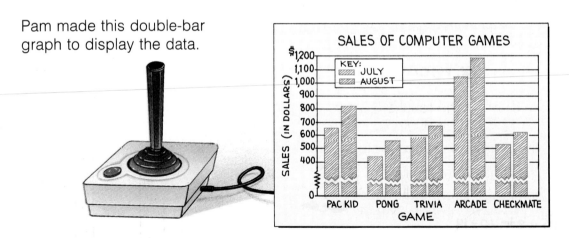

SHARING IDEAS

7. How is Pam's graph like yours? How is it different?

8. What scale did Pam use? What scale did you use? Why?

9. Pam drew jagged lines to show that she had left out part of the scale and each bar. Why did she do that?

10. Write three statements that you can use at the sales meeting.

11. Name another way you could have presented the data.

PRACTICE

Choose two of the three tables of data.
Make a bar graph for each.

12.

AVERAGE
COMPUTER USE BY
STUDENTS

Week	Hours
1	3.5
2	4.2
3	5.8
4	6.9
5	7.1
6	7.0

13.

PERCENT OF WORKERS WITH
DESKTOP COMPUTERS

Type of Job	Year	
	1985	1990 (estimated)
technical	55.9	76.2
managerial	36.5	64.4
medical	23.6	48.7
clerical	25.0	38.5
retail	16.6	32.7

14.

PROFIT ON SALE OF COMPUTERS
(in millions of dollars)

Brand	1986	1987	1988	1989
Mark 360	3.9	7.5	9.8	11.1
Pear IIW	2.9	5.7	8.9	12.5

Choose one of the following. Make a
bar graph to show the results of your
survey. Write your conclusions.

15. Take a survey of the most popular
brands of computers in your area.
Ask students and adults which
kind of computer they own or
would like to own.

16. Take a survey to find how
frequently electronic appliances
are used by young people. Make
the following list: TV, home
computer, VCR, stereo, radio, and
cassette player. Ask your friends
to rank each by how often it is
used. Your graph should show
whether there is a difference in the
rankings made by boys and girls.

PROBLEM SOLVING

Strategy: Conducting an Experiment

Which of the vowels *a*, *e*, *i*, *o*, or *u* is used most frequently?

You can make a guess, but you would still need to test your guess. The best way to solve a problem of this kind is to conduct an experiment.

Plan your experiment.

Work with another student. Get a newspaper. Cut out the first two paragraphs of an article. Do not include part of a headline. Then guess which vowel is used most often, second most often, and so on. Record your guesses.

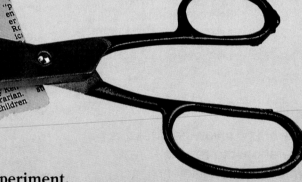

Try your experiment.

1. Find the number of *a*s, *e*s, *i*s, *o*s and *u*s in the paragraphs that you cut out. Record your results in a table.

2. Order the vowels from most frequently used to least frequently used.

3. Compare your guesses with the results of your count. Were your guesses close?

4. Compare your guesses and results with those of others in your class. Are they similar?

5. **What if** you counted vowels in one column of your local telephone directory? Would your results be the same?

Letter	Number in Paper
a	
e	
i	
o	
u	

PRACTICE

Conduct an experiment to solve the problem.

6. In which season do the greatest number of students have their birthdays? Make a guess and record it. Then conduct an experiment by asking all the students in your class. Record your results and display them in a bar graph.

7. If you toss a paper cup in the air 50 times, how many times will it land right side up? upside down? on its side? Guess the results. Record your guess. Then conduct an experiment. Show your results in a frequency diagram.

8. How often does a toothpick that you drop 20 times on notebook paper land on a line of the paper? First make a guess. Then conduct an experiment. Drop a toothpick 20 times from one foot above a sheet of notebook paper. Display your results in a table.

9. Which hair color do you find most frequently and least frequently in your class? Conduct an experiment and record your results in a table. Make a bar graph to show your results.

10. In a paper bag there are a red crayon, a blue crayon, a green crayon, and a yellow crayon. All are the same size. If you reach into the bag 30 times, how many times will you pick the yellow crayon? (All four crayons are in the bag each time you pick.) Make a guess before you start. Record your results in a table.

11. How good are people at guessing how long it takes ten seconds to pass? Conduct an experiment with 15 students. Use a watch or a clock with a second hand. Have each student tell you when he or she thinks ten seconds is up. Keep a record of how many seconds really have passed when they say "Now." Make a table to show your results.

DECISION MAKING

Problem Solving: Planning a Class Trip

SITUATION

The sixth grade has decided to go to a theme park for its spring class trip. The park must not be more than 2 hours away. The trip must cost less than $25 per student. The school will pay for the bus. There are 28 students in the class. The planning committee has collected the information below.

PROBLEM

Which theme park should the committee recommend?

DATA

	BAR–K RANCH	ADVENTURE PARK	WATER WORLD
Travel Time	1½ hours	2 hours	1 hour
Admission (per student)	$16.00	$12.00	$20.00 ($15.00 for groups of 20 or more)
Free Attractions	• Hay Ride • Access to barns and stables • Old West show and Sing-Along	• All rides, except Cyclone City • Magic show	• Pool, slides, tidal wave tank, chute-to-chute • Dolphin show
Food	Picnic lunch included	$2.25 – $6.00 per person	$3.00 to $6.00 per person
Other Information	horseback riding: $20.00 per hour All students are guaranteed trail rides, but there may be a wait. Inside arcades and waiting areas.	Cyclone City: $3.00 per ride Waiting time may be more than an hour for most rides. Inside arcades and waiting areas.	U-Drive power boats: $6.00 per hour No waiting time. No inside arcades or waiting areas.

USING THE DATA

What is the total cost of admission and of the least expensive lunch at each theme park?

1. Bar-K Ranch 16.00   **2.** Adventure Park 14.25   **3.** Water World 18.00

What is the total cost of admission and of the most expensive lunch at each theme park?

4. Bar-K Ranch 16.00   **5.** Adventure Park 18   **6.** Water World 21

MAKING DECISIONS

7. At which park would they spend the least for admission and lunch? Adventure Park

8. *What if* they wanted to go on added attractions? At which park would they be able to go on the least number?

9. The planning committee is very concerned about the possibility of rain. Which park should they not recommend?

10. *What if* the following numbers of students in the class have already visited these parks? How would this information affect the committee's decision?
Bar-K Ranch: 9   Adventure Park: 24   Water World: 6

11. *Write a list* of other things the committee needs to think about when planning the trip.

12. Which theme park would you choose? Why?

Math and Social Studies

About 4,000 years ago in Babylonia, people wrote in soft clay with an instrument called a *stylus*. The stylus made a wedge-shaped dent in the clay. The clay was then baked to make it hard. The numbers from 1 to 9 are shown at the right.

When the number 10 was written, the stylus was turned on its side. So ⟨ ∨ meant 11.

Babylonians used the number 60 as a base for number representation. Beginning with the number 60, Babylonians put the mark to the left of those from 1 to 59. In this 60s place, each mark meant 60 times what it meant in the column to the right, just as our numbers in the tens place are 10 times the number in the ones place.

What if a mark in the 60s place were turned on its side? How would you read the number?

Think: Start at the right. There are 3 ones and 2 tens. The next mark is 60. The last mark on the left means 10 times 60, or 600. The number reads 683.

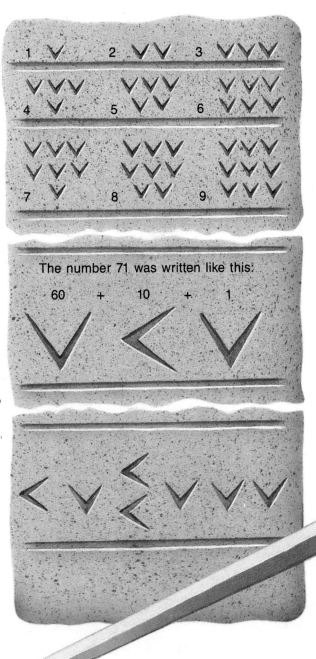

The number 71 was written like this:

60 + 10 + 1

ACTIVITIES

1. Read about another ancient counting system. What base was used? What marks represented the numbers? Make a chart explaining the system.

2. Find out about recording systems or calculating devices. You might research the abacus, "Napier's bones," or Pascal's adding machine. Write a brief report for the class.

Computer Spreadsheet Algebra: Functions

The figures below show the first three terms of a sequence. Each is built using cubes. Study the pattern and then use cubes to find the next two terms of the sequence by counting the total number of cubes in each new figure.

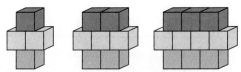

A table can be completed that shows the relationship between the number of the term in the sequence and the total number of cubes in the figure for that term. This relationship is called a **function**. A function can often be described by a rule for producing exactly one number from another.

You can use the computer spreadsheet program NEXT TERM to explore the above sequence.

AT THE COMPUTER

1. Enter the number 1 on the first line of the NUMBER OF TERM column. Check that the value for the NUMBER OF CUBES matches what you found above. Repeat the process for the next four terms of the sequence.

2. Predict the values for the number of cubes for the sixth and seventh terms. Use the computer to check the values.

3. Look at the spreadsheet table. What do you notice about the cube totals for consecutive terms? Check the pattern by entering any other group of consecutive term numbers.

4. For each term rearrange the cubes in rows of three. What do you notice?

5. Write a function rule that describes the relationship between the number of cubes in a figure and the number of the term.

6. Use your function rule to find the total number of cubes for the twentieth term. Then use the computer to check your answer and find other terms of the sequence.

EXTRA PRACTICE

Frequency Tables and Diagrams, page 13

1. Make a frequency table or frequency diagram for the data. Then use your frequency table for Questions 2–4.

Daily Average Temperatures (°C) in Summerville in July
17 19 18 18 19 20 20 21 18 19 21 20 19 21 22 22
20 21 20 21 21 20 21 21 22 22 20 21 21 22 22

2. What was the lowest average temperature in July?

3. The average temperature in Summerville in July is most often ▪.

4. What is the frequency of 20°C?

Whole Numbers, page 15

Write the short word name.

1. 82,561,204,973   2. 870,604,050   3. 8,000,564,000

Write in standard form.

4. 25 billion, 3 thousand   5. 10 million, seven   6. 43 billion, 32 thousand

7. $(8 \times 100,000) + (6 \times 10,000) + (4 \times 1000) + (0 \times 100) + (2 \times 10) + (4 \times 1)$

Write in expanded form.

8. 36,207   9. 254,098,176   10. 5,230,080,005

Decimals, page 17

Write the short word name.

1. 5.6   2. 22.15   3. 17.4301

Write in standard form.

4. 67 and 3 tenths   5. 6 ten-thousandths   6. 14 thousandths

7. six and 5 thousandths   8. two hundred and one thousandth   9. $\frac{435}{10,000}$

10. $(8 \times 0.1) + (0 \times 0.01) + (4 \times 0.001) + (3 \times 0.0001) + (2 \times 0.00001)$

Write in expanded form.

11. 52.3649   12. 4.067   13. 0.08054

EXTRA PRACTICE

Comparing and Ordering, page 19

Complete. Write >, <, or =.

1. 456,718 ● 456,717
2. 200,300 ● 20,030
3. 283,456 ● 238,465
4. 687,534 ● 687,345
5. 50,200 ● 500,200
6. 783,267 ● 783,269
7. 0.081 ● 0.810
8. 3.8 ● 4
9. 35.00 ● 35
10. 6.788 ● 6.8
11. 0.7 ● 0.08
12. 50 ● 5.8
13. 1.658 ● 1.6580
14. 89 ● 89.03
15. 34,035 ● 34.035

Order from least to greatest.

16. 34,813; 34,831; 36,828; 34,829
17. 56,825; 56,805; 56,815; 56,518
18. 331,470; 31,482; 331,462; 331,481
19. 27,879; 27,789; 27,878; 27,782
20. 18, 1.8, 18.002, 1.83, 18.1
21. 21, 2.1, 21.005, 2.18; 21.8
22. 0.107, 1, 0.2, 0.207
23. 28.2, 2.8, 28, 28.001, 2.85
24. 4.756, 4.7, 4.765, 4.8
25. 0.809, 8, 0.8, 0.807

Problem Solving Strategy: Using the Five-Step Process, page 21

Use the five-step process to solve the problem.

1. Lena bought a camera in September for $70. She made 5 equal payments to pay for the camera. How much was each payment?

2. Rico spent $30 for a skateboard, $20 for a backpack, and $13 for a shirt. How much less did he spend on a shirt than on a skateboard?

3. Rico can earn $136 in 8 weeks from delivering newspapers. He can earn $75 in 4 weeks from mowing lawns. In 8 weeks can Rico earn more from mowing lawns or delivering papers?

4. Lena took 4 rolls of film to the camera store to be developed. She received 31, 23, 36, and 24 photographs. How many photographs did Lena receive?

5. For 3 days Lena took pictures of Rico riding his skateboard. In all she shot 48 pictures. If Lena took 18 photographs on Monday and 15 on Tuesday, how many did she take on Wednesday?

EXTRA PRACTICE

Understanding Numbers: Whole Numbers and Decimals **37**

EXTRA PRACTICE

Rounding Whole Numbers and Decimals, page 25

Round 827,135,069.87416 to the place named.

1. hundred millions
2. thousands
3. ten millions
4. tenths
5. hundreds
6. hundredths
7. billions
8. ten-thousandths
9. ones

Round $6,592.48 to the place named.

10. $1,000
11. $10
12. $1
13. $.10

Write the place to which the number was rounded.

14. 541,074 to 500,000
15. 285,172 to 290,000
16. 6,752 to 6,750
17. 87,542 to 88,000
18. 2.8777 to 2.878
19. 0.0755 to 0.1
20. 3.999 to 4.00
21. 87.1019 to 87
22. 9,874,162 to 10,000,000
23. 476 to 500
24. 0.23846 to 0.2385
25. 9.6 to 10

Reading and Interpreting Bar Graphs, page 27

1. What is the subject of the graph on the right?

2. What information is shown on the vertical axis? the horizontal axis?

3. What does the longest bar show?

4. What was the population of Philadelphia in 1970?

5. What was the population of Detroit in 1980?

6. Which cities show an increase in population between 1970 and 1980?

7. Which city shows the greatest drop in population?

8. Which city's population has changed the least?

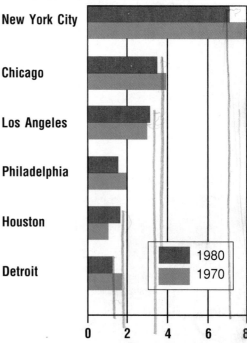

POPULATION OF SELECTED CITIES

Making Bar Graphs, page 29

Make a bar graph for each table of data.

1.

NUMBER OF STUDENTS IN AFTER-SCHOOL ACTIVITIES

Activity	Drama	Sports	Computer Club	Creative Writing	Art	Music
1st Semester	213	325	178	123	78	54
2nd Semester	168	251	206	165	104	87

2.

SEEBROOK MOVIE ATTENDANCE

Time	Sun.	Mon.	Tues.	Wed.	Thurs.	Fri.	Sat.
Afternoon	561	164	211	342	175	231	674
Evening	1,071	982	871	1,120	1,001	1,315	1,472

Problem Solving Strategy: Conducting an Experiment, page 31

Conduct an experiment to solve.

1. Which eye color do you find most frequently in your class? Conduct an experiment and record your results in a table. Make a bar graph to show your results. Which color occurs most frequently? least frequently?

2. How many other students are the oldest child in their family? Make a guess and record it. Then conduct an experiment by surveying your class. Record your results in a table. Are more girls the oldest in their family? or are boys?

3. If you throw a number cube 30 times, how many times will the number 4 appear on top? First make a guess. Then ask ten other students to make a guess. Next, conduct an experiment. Keep a tally of how many times the number 4 appears on top. Which student made the best guess?

4. If you toss a quarter in the air 50 times, how many times will it land face side up? Guess the result for 50 tosses. Record your guess. Then conduct an experiment. Keep a tally of how the coin lands. Show your results in a frequency diagram.

Practice PLUS

KEY SKILL: Comparing and Ordering (Use after page 19.)

Level A

Compare. Write >, <, or =.

1. 32,156 ● 32,152   **2.** 200,100 ● 20,010   **3.** 5.9 ● 6   **4.** 25.00 ● 25

Order from least to greatest.

5. 14,824; 14,842; 14,819; 14,829   **6.** 22.07; 22.7; 22.71; 22

7. Last year 12,235 bicycles were sold at Bike World. This year 12,215 bicycles were sold. During which year were more sold?

Level B

Compare. Write >, <, or =.

8. 113,331 ● 113,313   **9.** 456,034 ● 456,043   **10.** 15,019 ● 150,190

11. 3,789 ● 3.9   **12.** 0.07 ● 0.7   **13.** 80 ● 8.8

Order from least to greatest.

14. 817,429; 87,402; 817,402; 871,024   **15.** 572,014; 572,140; 572,041; 57,078

16. 0.8; 8; 0.871; 0.87   **17.** 15.003; 1.5; 1.56; 15.3

18. Terry jumped 1.23 m, Jill jumped 1.05 m, Juan jumped 1.32 m, and Janelle jumped 1.30 m. Write their names in order from the greatest amount jumped to the least.

Level C

Compare. Write >, <, or =.

19. 609,609 ● 609,609   **20.** 1,584,629 ● 1,548,692   **21.** 1,000,346 ● 791,346

22. 0.1086 ● 10.1086   **23.** 2.334 ● 2.3343   **24.** 8.8228 ● 8.8282

Order from least to greatest.

25. 96,012; 96,010; 96,032; 96,023   **26.** 17,098; 17,039; 17,095; 17,093

27. 0.00175; 0.0175; 0.0875; 0.00875   **28.** 1,023; 102.3; 1.023; 10.23

29. Melanie solved a math puzzle in 1.5 minutes, Jim in 12 minutes, Bill in 1.75 minutes, and Barbara in 12.5 minutes. Write their names in the order they finished.

PRACTICE PLUS

KEY SKILL: Rounding Whole Numbers and Decimals (Use after page 25.)

Level A

Round 23,761,085.24378 to the place named.

1. tenths **2.** ones **3.** ten-thousandths

4. tens **5.** thousandths **6.** thousands

7. hundreds **8.** hundredths **9.** ten millions

10. A new car that John is thinking of buying has a sticker price of $11,582.68. What is the cost of the car to the nearest hundred dollars?

Level B

Round 617,852,340.68541 to the place named.

11. hundreds **12.** millions **13.** tenths

14. ten-thousandths **15.** ten thousands **16.** hundredths

17. thousandths **18.** ones **19.** hundred millions

20. Elizabeth has $1,625.89 in a savings account. She said, "I have about $2,000 in the bank." What place did she round to?

Level C

Round 999,879,674.98794 to the place named.

21. millions **22.** tenths **23.** thousandths

24. hundredths **25.** tens **26.** hundred millions

27. ten thousands **28.** thousands **29.** ones

30. George said, "The amount of money I have in the bank rounded to the nearest ten thousand dollars is $10,000." What is the greatest amount of money that he can have in the bank?

CHAPTER REVIEW/TEST

LANGUAGE AND MATHEMATICS

Complete the sentences. Use the words in the chart on the right.

1. Data are organized to show the number of *frequency* times each item of data occurred in a(n) ■. *diagram*

2. To show the place value of each digit in a standard number, you can write the number in its ■. *expanded form*

3. Decimals that name the same amount are called ■. *equivalent decimals*

4. Replacing an exact number with a number that is easier to use is called ■ the number. *rounding*

> **VOCABULARY**
>
> expanded form
> rounding
> frequency diagram
> equivalent decimals
> bar graph

CONCEPTS AND SKILLS

5. Write the short word name for 91.287.

6. Write two billion, four hundred in standard form. *2,000,000,400*

Name the place value of the digit 0 in each number.

7. 305,652,196

8. 20,237,955,817

9. 2.056

Order from least to greatest.

10. 0.743; 0.706; 0.918; 0.7302

Complete. Write >, <, or =.

11. 6 billion, 520 million ■ 6,520,000

Round 15.3752 to the nearest:

12. whole number   13. hundredth

Round 7,230,648,507 to the nearest:

14. 100,000,000   15. 1,000,000

Use the frequency table to answer Questions 16–18.

16. Which amount has the highest frequency?

17. Which amount has the next highest frequency?

18. Make a frequency diagram from the table.

WEEKLY EARNINGS FOR SIX MONTHS

Amount	$4.00	$4.25	$4.50	$4.75
Tally	ＨＨＴ I	IIII	ＨＨＴ ＨＨＴ	IIII
Frequency	6	4	10	4

Use the bar graph to answer Questions 19–21.

19. What information is shown on the horizontal axis?

20. Which grade rated smoking most dangerous before viewing the film?

21. On which grade did the film have the greatest effect?

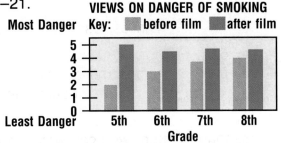

VIEWS ON DANGER OF SMOKING

Most Danger   Key: ▮ before film ▮ after film

Least Danger   5th   6th   7th   8th
Grade

Critical Thinking

22. Which is the *least* whole number that rounds to 1,000?

23. List all whole numbers between 18.704 and 23.998.

Mixed Applications

24. Tania has four kinds of birdseed to put in an outside feeder. She wants to conduct an experiment to see which kind the birds like best. How would you conduct the experiment and record your results?

25. Andrew made a tally of how far, in yards, he jumped in 17 tries. Here is his tally: 3.0, 3.1, 3.3, 3.3, 3.4, 3.5, 3.4, 3.4, 3.4, 3.3, 3.4, 3.0, 3.5, 3.4, 3.0, 3.1. Make a frequency table of his data.

PERFORMANCE ASSESSMENT

Work together with your group to solve this problem.

This table shows the consumption of four different vegetables in 1975 and 1990, according to the United States Department of Agriculture.

Make a double-bar graph that shows the change for each vegetable, rounded to the nearest pound, in 1975 and 1990.

YEARLY CONSUMPTION (POUNDS PER PERSON)

Vegetables	1975	1990
Carrots	9.9	11.8
Lettuce	24.1	22.7
Potatoes	119.9	118.7
Tomatoes	74.0	81.4

1. *Think about:*
   - how to round the numbers
   - how to organize and display the data in a double-bar graph

2. Write a few statements describing what the graph shows.

CUMULATIVE REVIEW

Choose the letter of the correct answer.

1. The standard form of five and six hundredths is ■.
   a. 5.6   c. 0.56
   b. 5.06   d. not given

2. Round 7.4862 to the nearest thousandth.
   a. 7.490   c. 7.486
   b. 7.49   d. not given

3. Which of these numbers is greater than 0.3?
   a. 0.04   c. 0.199
   b. 0.20   d. not given

4. What is the word name for 6.702?
   a. six and seven hundred and two
   b. six thousand, seven hundred and two
   c. six and seven hundred two thousandths
   d. not given

5. Which set of numbers is ordered from least to greatest?
   a. 19.0625; 19.625; 190.0005
   b. 19.625; 19.0625; 190.0005
   c. 19.0625; 190.0005; 19.625
   d. 190.005; 19.625; 19.0625

6. Which is the best way to display the amounts of snowfall for the last six months in two cities?
   a. single-bar graph
   b. double-bar graph
   c. frequency diagram
   d. frequency table

7. Choose the number for seven billion, twenty million, five.
   a. 7,020,000.5   c. 7,020,000,005
   b. 720 billion, 5   d. not given

8. Round 62.495 to the nearest whole number.
   a. 63   c. 62.5
   b. 62   d. not given

9. 6.03 ● 6.008
   a. >   c. =
   b. <   d. not given

10. Round 47,151,028 to the nearest ten million.
    a. 40,000,000   c. 50,151,028
    b. 47,000,000   d. not given

11. What is the place value of the digit 4 in the number 0.46?
    a. tenths   c. ones
    b. units   d. tens

12. Which is the best way to organize a tally of bowling scores?
    a. frequency table
    b. double-bar graph
    c. number line
    d. place-value chart

A frequency diagram shows which brand of sneakers most sixth graders wear.

13. Which data would *not* be shown?
    a. number of students surveyed
    b. how many brands were worn
    c. the most expensive brand
    d. the brand liked best

14. The data could also be shown in a ■.
    a. single-bar graph
    b. double-bar graph
    c. number line
    d. not given

BINARY NUMBERS

We use 10 digits to count. All numbers are based on combinations of the digits 0 through 9. Our numbers are *base-10 numbers.*

Computers use *binary numbers.* Binary numbers, or *base-2 numbers,* are represented by just 2 digits— 0 and 1. All binary numbers are based on combinations of 0 and 1.

Base 10	Base 2	Base 10	Base 2
0	0	6	110
1	1	7	111
2	10	8	1000
3	11	9	1001
4	100	10	1010
5	101	11	1011

Each system uses different numbers to refer to the same number.

$$4_{\text{base 10}} = 100_{\text{base 2}}$$
$$111_{\text{base 2}} = 7_{\text{base 10}}$$

The values of the places in a base-10 number are powers of 10.

1   10   100   1,000   10,000

The values of the places in a base-2 number are powers of 2.

1   2   4   8   16

You can rename a binary number as a base-10 number. Write $10110_{\text{base 2}}$ in base 10.

1	**0**	**1**	**1**	**0**
1×16	0×8	1×4	1×2	0×0

$$16 + 0 + 4 + 2 + 0 = 22$$

You also can rename a base-10 number as a binary number. Write $30_{\text{base 10}}$ in base 2.

Think: What powers of 2 will add up to 30?

$$30 = 1 \times 16 + 1 \times 8 + 1 \times 4 + 1 \times 2 + 0 \times 1$$
$$1 \qquad 1 \qquad 1 \qquad 1 \qquad 0$$

Rename the binary number in base 10.

1. 101 **2.** 11011

3. 111111 **4.** 110111

5. 101010 **6.** 1101101

Rename the base-10 number in base 2.

7. 9 **8.** 21

9. 39 **10.** 52

11. 62 **12.** 87

A Special ABACUS from RUSSIA

In many shops, department stores, and markets throughout Russia, salespeople calculate a customer's bill on a *schoty* (s-CHIO-tee). The *schoty* is a kind of abacus that can be adapted to add sums of money. In Russia, rubles and kopeks are units of money. People who are skillful on the *schoty* can move the beads along the wires to show amounts of rubles and kopeks as fast as, or faster than, they could use a calculator.

The *schoty* was introduced in France in the early 1800s after the French emperor Napoleon invaded Russia. Poncelet, one of Napoleon's officers, was impressed by the Russians' skill in using the *schoty*. He took an abacus back to France and introduced it into the schools as a way to teach students arithmetic. From France, a version of the *schoty* was exported to schools in Germany and the United States.

Here is a diagram of a horizontal *schoty* used to count money.

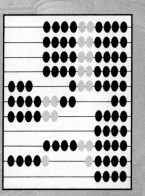

millions
hundred-thousands
ten-thousands
thousands
hundreds
tens
ones
decimal point
tenths
hundredths
fractions

The bottom wire can be used for calculating with the fractions $\frac{1}{4}$, $\frac{2}{4}$, and $\frac{3}{4}$. The fourth wire from the bottom can be used to separate rubles from kopeks.

1. Why do you think there are different-colored beads on the *schoty*?
2. The diagram above shows the number 386.05. Explain how the positions of the beads on the *schoty* show this number.

Mental Math: Adding and Subtracting

A. The New England Line makes 3 stops in Massachusetts, 24 stops in Connecticut, and 17 stops in New York. How many stops does it make in all?

You can use the properties of addition to make groups of 10.

$17 + (24 + 3) = 17 + (3 + 24)$ ← Commutative Property
$= (17 + 3) + 24$ ← Associative Property
$= 20 + 24$
$= 44$

The train makes 44 stops.

1. How would you add $13 + 25 + 47 + 35$ mentally?

B. You can also use **compensation** to add mentally.

Add: $296 + 28$

Think: $296 + 28$
$+ 4 \downarrow \quad \downarrow - 4$
$300 + 24 = 324$

So $296 + 28 = 324$.

2. Use compensation to add $197 + 136$ mentally.

C. You can use **equal additions** to subtract mentally.

Think: $235 - 197$
$+ 3 \downarrow \quad \downarrow + 3$
$238 - 200 = 38$

So $235 - 197 = 38$.

3. Use equal additions to subtract $214 - 96$ mentally.

TRY OUT Write the letter of the correct answer.

4. $29 + 8 + 2 + 1$ **a.** 30   **b.** 40   **c.** 11   **d.** 37

5. $498 + 26$ **a.** 524   **b.** 500   **c.** 526   **d.** 472

6. $456 - 198$ **a.** 256   **b.** 654   **c.** 656   **d.** 258

PRACTICE

Add or subtract mentally.

7.	8.	9.	10.	11.	12.
8 6 2 + 4	35 18 + 25	$182 67 + 18 267	25 48 + 175 248	$38 26 162 + 144 370	155 378 145 + 122 780

13.	14.	15.	16.	17.	18.
72 + 49	$34 + 38	54 + 27	299 + 176	499 + 599	1,743 + 497

19.	20.	21.	22.	23.	24.
64 − 28	83 − 57	65 − 47	483 − 299	1,375 − 399	$2,732 − 987

Critical Thinking

25. How could you use equal subtractions to subtract 712 − 203 mentally?

Mixed Applications

26. A freight train has 19 cars with lumber, 25 with corn, 15 with wheat, and 11 with oats. How many cars are there in all?

27. A train has 24 passengers in the first car, 32 in the second, and 46 in the last. How many tickets will the conductor need to punch?

28. The Denis Line carried 1.3 million passengers last year. The Clavey Line carried 2.28 million. Which line carried the most passengers?

29. *Write a problem* that involves mental math to add the number of tickets a train conductor punches in a week.

LOGICAL REASONING

You read **Roman numerals** from left to right. First find pairs of symbols that increase in value. Subtract the value of the smaller symbol from the value of the larger symbol. Then add from left to right.

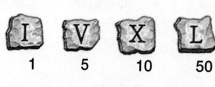

I 1   V 5   X 10   L 50

Example: D   C   X   L

500 + 100 + (50 − 10) = 640

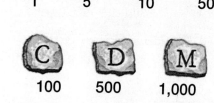

C 100   D 500   M 1,000

Write our standard form for the Roman numeral.

1. XXI   **2.** CVI   **3.** LXXIV   **4.** CDX   **5.** MMCDIX

Estimating Sums and Differences: Rounding

A. James wrote a short story and a newspaper article on his computer. The story had 15,981 characters and the article had 7,619 characters. Can James transfer these to a disk with 30,720 characters of storage?

An estimate may answer this question. Here are two methods:

Method 1
Round to the greatest place of the greater number.

$$
\begin{array}{r}
15,981 \rightarrow 20,000 \\
+\;\;\;7,619 \rightarrow +\,10,000 \\
\hline
30,000
\end{array}
$$

Method 2
Round to the greatest place of the lesser number.

$$
\begin{array}{r}
15,981 \rightarrow 16,000 \\
+\;\;\;7,619 \rightarrow +\;\;8,000 \\
\hline
24,000
\end{array}
$$

The documents can be stored on the disk.

1. Which estimate is closer to the exact answer? Why?

2. Estimate by rounding: 6,548 + 1,164. How can you make the estimate closer to the exact answer?

B. You can also estimate differences by rounding.

Estimate: 4,251 − 879

Method 1
$$
\begin{array}{r}
4,251 \rightarrow 4,000 \\
-\;\;\;879 \rightarrow -\,1,000 \\
\hline
3,000
\end{array}
$$

Method 2
$$
\begin{array}{r}
4,251 \rightarrow 4,300 \\
-\;\;\;879 \rightarrow -\;\;900 \\
\hline
3,400
\end{array}
$$

3. Which estimate is closer to the actual answer? Why?

4. Estimate: 6,751 − 379. Use both methods. Which rounding method is more useful? Why?

TRY OUT Write the letter of the correct answer. Estimate by rounding.

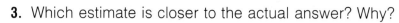

5. 5,234 + 945 + 3,894   **a.** 1,000   **b.** 10,000   **c.** 15,000   **d.** 20,000

6. 2,357 + 6,791 + 4,799   **a.** 14,000   **b.** 21,000   **c.** 28,000   **d.** 35,000

PRACTICE

Estimate by rounding.

7.	2,317 9,630 + 4,312 *16,059*	**8.**	15,125 9,738 + 3,244	**9.**	65,431 7,965 + 8,192	**10.**	53,438 6,219 + 7,358	**11.**	7,559 6,293 + 628
12.	29,306 − 7,253	**13.**	56,529 − 4,208	**14.**	1,873 − 465	**15.**	32,484 − 17,464	**16.**	5,493 − 724
17.	83,650 − 2,830	**18.**	79,018 13,275 + 34,741	**19.**	$83,257 − 9,368	**20.**	$4,207 3,582 611 + 508	**21.**	87,124 − 9,512
22.	58,738 − 3,424	**23.**	$104,322 94,311 + 22,563	**24.**	410,671 − 47,012	**25.**	238,152 28,171 + 11,586	**26.**	$298,812 − 43,734

27. 480,871 − 391,739   **28.** 328,548 + 28,958 + 946,585   **29.** 9,455 − 467

30. 256,678 − 146,987   **31.** $7,896 + $859,234 + $1,460   **32.** 35,365 − 112

Critical Thinking

33. Estimate: 1,243 − 895. Would rounding to the greatest place of the greater number give a useful estimate? Why or why not?

Mixed Applications

Solve. You may need to use the Databank on page 549.

34. Annette sells computers. Her monthly sales goal was $50,000. Her weekly amounts were $10,124; $15,800; $12,617; and $18,256. Did she reach her goal?

35. Garo has saved $3,200 for a computer. The computer he wants to buy sells for $3,615. How much more money does he need to save to buy the computer?

36. Janine cleared files from her computer that had these numbers of characters: 6,152; 5,876; 7,872; and 8,172. How many characters did she delete?

37. Write the names of the Computers R Us salespeople in order of their sales amounts. Begin with the person who sold the most.

Front-End Estimation: Sums and Differences

A. There are three horses being loaded onto a trailer. Their weights are 1,650 lb, 1,389 lb, and 1,105 lb. Is their combined weight at least 3,500 lb?

You can use **front-end estimation** to answer this question.

Step 1

Add the front digits.
Write zeros for the other digits.

```
  1,650
  1,389
+ 1,105
  3,000
```

Step 2

Adjust the estimate.

```
  1,650      Think: 650 + 389
  1,389             is about 1,000.
+ 1,105
  4,000      3,000 + 1,000 = 4,000
```

Their combined weight is at least 3,500 lb.

1. How does adjusting make the estimate closer to the exact answer?

2. How would you estimate 5,763 + 314 + 4,009?

B. You can also use front-end estimation to estimate differences.

Estimate: $8,082 − $5,769

Step 1

Subtract the front digits.
Write zeros for the other digits.

```
  $8,082
−  5,769
   3,000
```

Step 2

Adjust the estimate.

```
   $8,082     Think: 0 < 7
−   5,769            The exact answer is
  <$3,000            less than $3,000.
```

3. Estimate: 9,803 − 675. How does the adjusted estimate show that the exact answer is greater than 9,000?

TRY OUT Write the letter of the correct answer. Estimate. Use the front digits and adjust.

4. 2,167 + 3,412 + 2,527   **a.** 6,000   **b.** 8,000   **c.** 9,000   **d.** 10,000

5. 8,549 − 781   **a.** greater than 8,000   **b.** less than 8,000

PRACTICE

Estimate. Use the front digits and adjust.

6.	6,742 3,082 + 2,371	**7.**	3,572 4,112 + 517	**8.**	5,371 1,323 + 5,219	**9.**	$4,237 + 5,109	**10.**	91,737 30,421 + 59,155

11.	4,721 − 3,598	**12.**	$672 − 398	**13.**	78,251 − 3,254	**14.**	4,376 − 748	**15.**	8,721 − 6,598

16.	8,168 9,387 1,702 + 1,196	**17.**	45,121 23,894 + 2,316	**18.**	$12,097 − 3,254	**19.**	34,353 1,678 + 4,356	**20.**	67,314 − 14,165

Estimate to tell whether the statement is true or false.

21. $197 + 878 < 1,000$ **22.** $5,678 − 519 > 5,500$ **23.** $512 + 445 > 900$

Mixed Applications

Solve. You may need to use the Databank on page 549.

24. The most powerful tug, the *Smit Singapore,* can pull 378,000 lb. Can it pull barges weighing 128,120 lb; 98,890 lb; 68,620 lb; and 58,120 lb all together?

25. The XYZ Corporation pays $12,872 to have its garbage hauled away by a barge. The ABC Corporation pays $18,125. Can XYZ claim to save over $6,000?

26. Which passenger ship can carry more weight, the *Norway* or the *Canberra?*

27. The *Big Hulk* has a length of 226 ft. The *Sea Giant* has a length of 195 ft. Which tugboat is longer? About how much longer is it?

Mixed Review

Find the answer. Which method did you use?

MENTAL MATH
CALCULATOR
PAPER/PENCIL

28. $5.02 − $3.89   **29.** 6,182 + 6,019   **30.** $7.50 − $4.49

31. 85 + 95 + 73   **32.** 6,398 − 700   **33.** 8,541 − 7,509

Adding and Subtracting Whole Numbers

A. Monica and Steven made a chart of the tickets sold during the past year for the concerts in the park. What is the total number of tickets sold?

Monica used a calculator, and Steven used paper and pencil to add the numbers.

TICKET SALES FOR CLASSICAL MUSIC CONCERTS IN THE PARK

Concert	Tickets Sold
Beethoven	365,127
Mozart	287,674
Haydn	298,872
Chopin	326,412

<u>Monica</u>

365,127 (+) 287,674 (+) 298,872 (+) 326,412

(=) | *1278085.* |

<u>Steven</u>

```
  222 11
  365,127
  287,674
  298,872
+ 326,412
1,278,085
```

Both found the sum to be 1,278,085 tickets.

1. Is their answer reasonable? How do you know?

2. Why is a calculator the best method for this problem?

3. When would it be easier to use paper and pencil or mental math?

B. You can subtract money amounts as if they were whole numbers.

Subtract: $712 − $598

<u>Monica</u>

712 (−) 598 (=) | *114.* |

<u>Steven</u>

$712 − $598

$+ 2 \downarrow \qquad \downarrow + 2$

$714 − $600 = $114

4. How did Steven subtract mentally?

TRY **OUT**   Write the letter of the correct answer.

5. 147 + 608 + 253   **a.** 1,008   **b.** 1,080   **c.** 10,008   **d.** 188

6. 6,489 − 5,493   **a.** 1,996   **b.** 1,004   **c.** 996   **d.** 96

PRACTICE

Add or subtract. Use mental math, a calculator, or paper and pencil.

7. 7,654
        3,892
        4,597
      + 876

8. 3,471
          827
      + 129

9. 25,675
        38,127
        49,678
      + 27,512

10. 345,678
         245,712
         789,124
       + 78,092

11. 9,225,679
       + 8,787,321

12. $5,824
       − 1,899

13. 62,273
       − 39,998

14. 780,013
       − 32,728

15. 18,872
       − 16,742

16. 782,431
       − 98,789

17. 67,824 + 8,712 + 872 + 389

18. 49,821 − 8,942

19. 7,804 − 619

20. $281,898 + $3,224 + $89 + $12,639

21. 9 thousands − 27 tens

22. 43 ones + 12 tens + 8 hundreds

Critical Thinking

Without adding or subtracting to find the exact answer, how can you tell that the answer is incorrect?

23. 4,897 + 3,985 + 7,786 = 106,668

24. 5,301 − 430 = 1,001

Mixed Applications

25. Chopin was born in 1810 and played his first major concert in 1829. Mozart was born in 1756 and played his first major concert in 1762. Who was younger at his first concert?

26. On Saturday $138,386 was taken in for concert ticket sales. On Sunday $98,875 was taken in. How much more was taken in on Saturday than on Sunday?

MENTAL MATH

Here is a way to add whole numbers mentally.

23
35
+ 67

Think:
23 + 30 = 53
53 + 5 = 58
58 + 60 = 118
118 + 7 = 125

Use this zigzag method to find the sum.

1. 74 + 81 + 35 **2.** 56 + 13 + 42 **3.** 84 + 63 + 72

ACTIVITY

Algebra: Equations

How could you balance this scale?

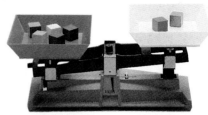

One way is to place 3 more blocks on the right side. This shows the **equality** 5 = 5.

WORKING TOGETHER

You can use cubes, a paper bag, and a balance scale to explore equalities. Take turns with a partner doing these activities.

Activity 1

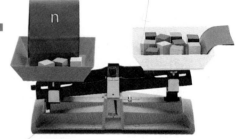

Step 1 The first student sets up an unbalanced scale in which the left side has more cubes than the right side. There should be cubes both inside and outside a bag on the left side.

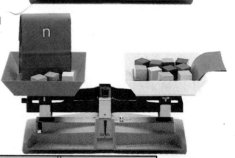

Step 2 The second student reaches into the bag and takes out cubes one at a time, until the scale is balanced. Then he or she tells how many cubes are in the bag and how this number was found. Record the results in a table like this:

Cubes Hidden in Bag on Left Side		Cubes You See on Left Side		Total Cubes on Right Side	"What is n?"
n	+	3	=	10	7

The number sentence $n + 3 = 10$ is an **equation**. n is a variable. A **variable** is a symbol used to represent a number or set of numbers.

Step 3 The first student writes an equation to show that the value for n is correct. Look at the example.

Example:
$$n + 3 = 10$$
$$7 + 3 = 10$$
$$10 = 10$$

Activity 2

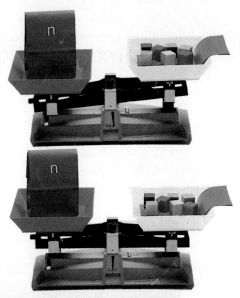

Step 1 The first student sets up an unbalanced scale in which the left side has more cubes than the right side. All the cubes on the left side should be hidden in a bag.

Step 2 The second student reaches into the bag and takes out cubes one at a time, until the scale is balanced. Then he or she tells how many cubes were in the bag at the start. The results are then recorded in a table.

Cubes Hidden in Bag on Left Side		Cubes Taken Away from Left Side		Total Cubes on Right Side	"What is *n*?"
n	−	2	=	7	9

Step 3 The first student then writes an equation to show that each answer for *n* is correct. Look at the example.

Example:
$$n - 2 = 7$$
$$9 - 2 = 7$$
$$7 = 7$$

SHARING IDEAS

1. How do your methods for finding *n* in each activity compare with those of others?

2. What other way could the unbalanced scale at the beginning of the lesson have been balanced?

ON YOUR OWN

Represent the problem using a balance scale, a paper bag, and cubes. Draw a picture.

3. 6 is added to a number. The sum is 13.

4. 7 is subtracted from a number. The difference is 4.

5. Joy gave Katie 3 coins from her coin collection. Joy now has 9 coins left. How many did she have to begin with?

6. Bob added 5 stamps to his stamp collection. He now has 15 stamps. How many stamps did he have before?

7. *Write a problem* of your own. Ask others to solve it using a balance.

Algebra: Solving Equations

A. Sam says, "I am thinking of a number. The sum of the number and 7 is 15. What is the number?"

1. Which of the following equations represents the picture?

   $n + 7 = 15$ $n - 15 = 7$

What number does the letter n stand for in $n + 7 = 15$?

John thinks: $8 + 7 = 15$; n stands for 8.
Susan thinks: $n = 15 - 7$; $n = 8$.

Both John and Susan found the value of n to be 8.

2. How did John solve the equation?

3. How did Susan use inverse operations to solve for n?

4. How can you check that the value of n is 8?

B. You can also solve equations that involve subtraction. Beth says, "I am thinking of a number. 14 less than the number is 32. What is the number?"

Solve: $n - 14 = 32$

John thinks: $46 - 14 = 32$; n stands for 46.
Susan thinks: $n = 32 + 14$; $n = 46$.

5. How did Susan use inverse operations to solve for n?

SHARING IDEAS

6. How could you express $n + 7 = 19$ as a number puzzle?

7. How could you use inverse operations to solve the equation from Problem 6?

2 13 ×3 61   3 17 ×5 80   17 +6

PRACTICE

Solve and check. Use mental math when you can.

8. $n + 5 = 12$ 7 **9.** $n + 4 = 13$ 9 **10.** $n + 9 = 17$ 8 **11.** $n + 7 = 15$ 8

12. $n - 6 = 4$ 10 **13.** $n - 8 = 8$ 16 **14.** $n - 7 = 9$ 16 **15.** $n - 9 = 6$ 15

16. $n + 17 = 93$ 10 **17.** $n - 38 = 25$ 63 **18.** $n + 41 = 105$ 64 **19.** $n - 16 = 163$ 179

20. $n - 7 = 96$ 103 **21.** $n + 39 = 78$ ▪ **22.** $n + 13 = 26$ 13 **23.** $n - 19 = 36$ 55

24. $n + 19 = 19$ 0 **25.** $n - 77 = 23$ 100 **26.** $n - 49 = 45$ 94 **27.** $n + 9 = 27$ 18

28. $n - 27 = 25$ 52 **29.** $n - 45 = 35$ 80 **30.** $n + 41 = 47$ 6 **31.** $n + 12 = 24$ 12

Does 6 solve the equation? Write *yes* or *no*.

32. $n + 5 = 11$ yes **33.** $n + 3 = 3$ NO **34.** $n - 3 = 3$ yes **35.** $n - 2 = 4$ yes

Does 24 solve the equation? Write *yes* or *no*.

36. $n - 5 = 2$ NO **37.** $48 - n = 24$ yes **38.** $n + 12 = 12$ NO **39.** $n + 6 = 30$ yes

Write an equation. Then solve for the missing number.

40. A number minus 8 equals 11. 19

41. A number plus 9 equals 15. 6

42. In 7 years Michael will be 16 years old. How old is Michael now? 9

43. Jane said, "I'm thinking of a number. The number plus 68 is equal to 129." 61

44. Luis said, "I'm thinking of a number. The number minus 250 equals 350." 600

45. **Write a problem** that involves solving an addition equation. Ask others to solve it.

LOGICAL REASONING

Christine is taller than Stephanie but shorter than Brian. Greg's height is between Brian's and Christine's. Meghan would be the shortest if it weren't for Joe. List the names of the students in order from shortest to tallest.

IMSCBB

PROBLEM SOLVING

Strategy: Using Estimation

A. Tonight 1,100 children are expected to attend the circus. The circus plans to give a kazoo to each child. Karen, the circus manager, has 545 red kazoos, 385 green kazoos, and 460 yellow kazoos.

Karen wants to make sure she has enough kazoos. So she decides to underestimate the number of kazoos she has by rounding down. Then she compares her underestimate to 1,100, the target number.

Think: **545 + 385 + 460**

Add: 500 + 300 + 400 = 1,200

Since 1,200 > 1,100, Karen knows there are enough kazoos.

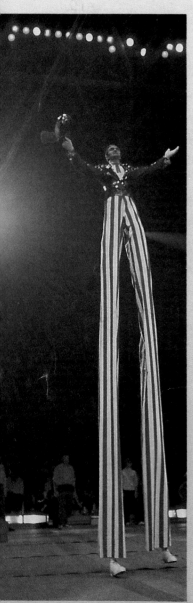

1. What if Karen had 345 red kazoos but still had the same number of green and yellow kazoos? What would her underestimate have been? Find the exact sum. Is the underestimate useful? Why?

2. What should you do when an underestimate is less than, but close to a target number?

B. The circus plans to give away posters to children attending the evening's performance. It has 785 clown posters, 540 animal posters, and 408 acrobat posters.

Karen knows that 2,000 children will be at the circus. She wants to find out if there will be enough posters. So she overestimates the number of posters the circus already has.

Think: **785 + 540 + 408**

Add: 800 + 600 + 500 = 1,900

Since 1,900 < 2,000, Karen knows she has to order more posters.

3. ***What if*** the circus had 608 acrobat posters? What would Karen's overestimate have been? Find the exact sum. Is the overestimate useful?

4. What should you do when an overestimate is greater than, but close to the target number?

PRACTICE

Use estimation to solve the problem. Did you overestimate or underestimate?

5. The fire-eater drank 1,000 cups of ice water the last time the circus was in town. He drank 325, 275, and 245 cups during the three weeks of this year's performances. Did he drink as many cups as he did last time?

6. The Big Top Circus is giving performances for charity. The circus hopes to raise $10,000. In four performances it raised $2,700; $3,450; $3,750; and $2,100. Did the circus meet its goal?

7. A circus has 365 red T-shirts, 635 green T-shirts, and 575 blue T-shirts to give away to senior citizens. If 1,500 senior citizens attend the show tonight, will there be enough T-shirts?

8. Last week the One Ring Circus sold 785, 883, 654, 597, and 726 tickets. The owners had hoped to sell 4,000 tickets. Did the owners sell as many tickets as they had hoped?

Strategies and Skills Review

Solve. Use estimation, mental math, a calculator, or paper and pencil.

9. Last year the circus made $300,050. This year's profits were $45,900 more. How much were this year's profits?

10. In the first six months of this year, the circus has bought 7.95 T of hay for the animals. About how many tons will be needed for the whole year?

11. The graph below shows how many people visited the circus each week last month to watch the lions and tigers being fed. In all, about how many people came to the feeding last month?

12. **_Write a problem_** that can be solved by using estimation. Solve your problem. Ask others to solve your problem.

ATTENDANCE AT FEEDING TIME

Fill 'Er Up

1 2 3   4 5 6   7 8 9

Using Number Concepts

A. Many puzzles ask you to place a set of digits so that they add up in a certain way. You may be tempted to just keep guessing until you find the right answer. But if you think about the problem, you can usually find a better method.

1. Fill in the boxes with the numbers 2 through 10 so that each row, column, and diagonal adds up to 18.

Think before you place! What do you need? You need sets of three numbers that add up to 18.

Example: 2 + 6 + 10 = 18

How many sets do you need? Just count. There are three horizontals, three verticals, and two diagonals. You need eight sets. Can you find the other seven?

Now look at your sets. Which number appears most frequently? Where do you think you will place that number? Which numbers appear secondmost frequently? Where will they go? Do you see how a careful approach helps you avoid random guessing?

2. Use the numbers 1–7 so that each vertical, horizontal, and diagonal has the same sum.

You may need to do a little guessing to solve this one, but you should still think logically. How many sets of numbers will you need? Which circle in the diagram is the most used? What number might you logically decide to place in that circle?

When you've solved this problem for numbers 1–7, try it again using the numbers 3–9. What rules can you follow to help you?

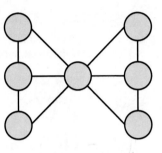

B. Try these problems. Remember— think before you start.

3. Use the numbers 1–9 so that each side of the triangle has the same sum.

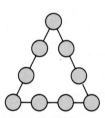

4. Use the numbers 1–9 to get a correct sum. Once you have found one solution, try it again! This one has over 300 possible answers. How are some of the answers related?

5. Place the numbers 1–9 so that you can count from 1 up to 9 by following the arrows.

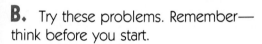

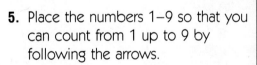

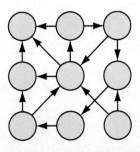

Estimating Decimal Sums and Differences

A. The post office is 0.19 miles from the drugstore. The drugstore is 5.26 miles from the library. The library is 7.81 miles from the mall. About how many miles would you have to drive from the post office to the mall?

You can estimate to solve the problem.

Rounding		Front-End

Rounding

Round to the greatest place of the greatest number.

0.19	0
5.26	5
+ 7.81	+ 8
	13

Round to the greatest place of the least number.

0.2
5.3
+ 7.8
13.3

Front-End

Add the front digits and adjust the sum.

0.19
5.26
+ 7.81
13

Think: 5 + 7 = 12
0.19 + 0.81 is about 1.
12 + 1 = 13

1. Which method is the easiest way of estimating? Why?

2. Which method is closer to the exact answer? Why?

B. You can also estimate differences of decimals.

Estimate: 9.16 − 0.586

Rounding

Round to the greatest place of the greater number.

9.16	9
− 0.586	− 1
	8

Round to the greatest place of the lesser number.

9.2
− 0.6
8.6

Front-End

Subtract the front digits and adjust the difference.

9.16
− 0.586
< 9.0

Think: 5 > 1
The exact answer is less than 9.0.

3. What is the advantage of estimating by rounding to the greatest place of the greater number?

4. What is the advantage of estimating by rounding to the greatest place of the lesser number?

TRY OUT Write the letter of the best estimate.

5. 5.22 + 7.33 + 0.54   **a.** 12   **b.** 13   **c.** 15   **d.** 17

6. 6.32 − 0.47   **a.** 6   **b.** 5.8   **c.** 5.1   **d.** 2

PRACTICE

Estimate the sum or difference by rounding.

7.	8.	9.	10.	11.
1.89	7.454	$8.40	2.69	1.69
0.49	0.43	3.20	0.89	2.29
+ 0.35	+ 0.872	+ .78	+ 0.79	3.67
				+ 0.59

12.	13.	14.	15.	16.
6.712	7.671	4.78	5.272	$3.26
− 0.501	− 2.645	− 2.72	− 0.89	+ 1.81

Estimate. Use the front digits and adjust.

17.	18.	19.	20.	21.
4.58	8.932	$8.25	5.83	2.14
0.33	0.22	2.67	8.23	3.65
+ 0.57	+ 0.14	+ .57	+ 0.16	+ 9.45

22.	23.	24.	25.	26.
4.621	3.899	3.42	$8.27	8.91
− .51	− 2.562	− 1.51	− 5.73	− 6.54

Use estimation to tell if the change from $5 will be more or less than $1.

27. $3.19 + $1.79

28. $2.39 + $1.19 + $.29

Mixed Applications

29. Mr. Chin drove his car 6.49 miles on one errand and 3.89 miles on another errand. Did he travel at least 10 miles?

30. Maria bicycled 2.55 miles, while Andie traveled 1.75 miles. Maria walked an additional 1.25 miles. How much farther did she travel?

31. In its first year after lift-off, a space probe traveled 13.72 million miles; in its second year, 14.99 million miles; and in its third year, 15.4 million miles. Write in standard form the total distance traveled.

32. *Write a problem* that can be solved by estimating the distance between two points on a map. Ask others to solve your problem.

Mixed Review

Find the answer. Which method did you use?

33. 198 + 443 + 897

34. 8,003 − 5,224

35. 7,500 + 3,400

36. 8,687 − 5,776

37. 65 + 25 + 15

38. 58,640 − 12,500

MENTAL MATH
CALCULATOR
PAPER/PENCIL

Adding and Subtracting Decimals

A. An astronaut's suit has a mass of 84.32 kg. The backpack has a mass of 56.9 kg. What is the total mass of the suit and backpack?

Kent used a calculator. Jody used paper and pencil.

Kent	Jody
84.32 ⊕ 56.9 ⊜ $\boxed{141.22}$	1 1 8 4 . 3 2 + 5 6 . 9 0 1 4 1 . 2 2

Both Kent and Jody found the total mass to be 141.22 kg.

1. Is 141.22 kg a reasonable answer? Why?

2. When might it be better to use a calculator to add decimals?

3. How can you check your answer?

B. An astronaut weighed 80 kg. He wanted to lose 1.5 kg. The next week he weighed 78.589 kg. Did he reach his goal?

Kent	Jody
80 ⊖ 78.589 ⊜ $\boxed{1.411}$	9 9 9 7 10 10 10 10 8 0 . 0 0 0 − 7 8 . 5 8 9 1 . 4 1 1

Since 1.411 < 1.5, the astronaut did not reach his goal.

4. How can you check the answer?

5. How could you have used addition to solve the problem?

TRY OUT   Write the letter of the correct answer.

6. 17.2549 + 3.21
   - **a.** 17.5759
   - **c.** 175.759
   - **b.** 20.4649
   - **d.** 204.649

7. 70 − 5.999
   - **a.** 1.001
   - **c.** 75.999
   - **b.** 10.01
   - **d.** 64.001

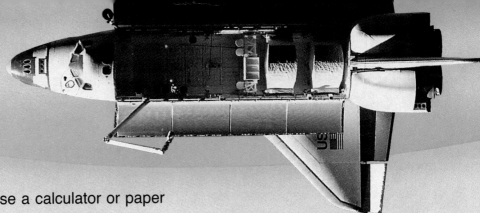

PRACTICE

Add or subtract. Use a calculator or paper and pencil.

8. $\overset{1}{1}27.07$
    $+\quad 3.02$
    $\overline{130.09}$

9. $\overset{11}{2}1.6312$
    $+\quad 8.921$
    $\overline{30.5522}$

10. 0.6244
     0.9332
     $+\ 2.64$
     $\overline{4.1976}$

11. $3.6\overset{1}{7}3$
     9.274
     $+\ 7.505$
     $\overline{20.452}$

12. $\overset{1\ 2}{7}.23$
     7.29
     5.871
     $+\ 3.445$
     $\overline{23.834}$

13. 3.67
     $-\ 2.2$
     $\overline{1.47}$

14. $\overset{4\,'2''}{5.32+''}$
     $-\ 0.974$
     $\overline{4.347}$

15. $\overset{1\,9\,9\,9}{2.0007}$
     $-\ 0.0825$
     $\overline{1.9182}$

16. $\overset{4\,9\ 12}{5.02}$
     $-\quad .59$
     $\overline{4.43}$

17. 9
     $-\ 2.6072$
     $\overline{7.6072}$

18. $3.21 + 6.7 + 1.23$

19. $2.51 - 0.6247$

20. $276.1 - 13.64$

21. $\$5,274.63 + \$1,999.84$

22. 432 thousandths − 141 thousandths

23. 16 hundredths + 3 tenths

24. 3 and 4 thousandths − 2 thousandths

25. 7 and 2 tenths − 9 tenths

Do only those exercises that will have an answer less than 10.

26. 29.072
     $-\ 19.9$

27. 6.432
     $+\ 2.8$

28. 7.892
     $+\ 2.341$

29. 32.721
     $-\ 23.5$

30. 60
     $-\ 50.72$

Mixed Applications

Solve. Which method did you use?

31. In 1989 NASA requested $10,897,500,000 for the space program. For 1991 NASA requested $13,274,100,000. How much more was requested for 1991?

32. An astronaut's suit and backpack have a total mass of 141.21 kg. The suit has a mass of 79.55 kg. What is the mass of the backpack?

33. It cost $2,000,000,000 to build the space shuttle *Atlantis.* The cost of a new space shuttle was projected at $2,300,000,000. Write the amounts using decimals and the word *billion.*

34. On Earth an astronaut's mass is 61.4 kg. On Jupiter her mass would be 159.64 kg. About how much greater would her mass be on Jupiter?

Metric Units of Length: Perimeter

A. These pictures will help you recall some metric units of length.

The wire has
a width of
1 millimeter (mm).

The paper clip has
a width of
1 centimeter (cm).

The casette has
a length of
1 decimeter (dm).

The door has
a width of
1 meter (m).

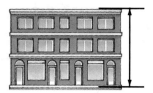

The height of the
three-story building
is 1 dekameter (dam).

The distance around
the baseball diamond is
about 1 hectometer (hm).

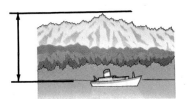

The height of Mt.
McKinley is about
6 kilometers (km).

The meter is the basic unit of length and distance in the metric system.

km	hm	dam	Basic Unit	dm	cm	mm
1,000 m	100 m	10 m	1 meter (m)	0.1 m	0.01 m	0.001 m

1. Why is it better to measure the length of a paper clip in millimeters instead of meters?

2. Why is it better to measure the height of a mountain in kilometers instead of millimeters?

3. What is the relationship between kilometers and meters? between meters and centimeters? between centimeters and millimeters?

B. Study this diagram showing a rectangle and two rulers.

4. What is the length in centimeters?

5. What is the width in centimeters?

6. What is the **perimeter**, distance around the rectangle?

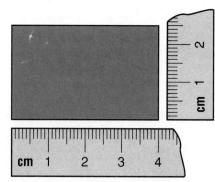

Use *mm, cm, dm, m,* or *km* to complete.

7. The height of a room is about 3 ■.

8. The length of a sofa is about 20 ■.

9. The width of this book is about 20 ■.

10. The width of the point of a sharp pencil is about 2 ■.

11. The perimeter of Colorado is about 1,900 ■.

PRACTICE

Match. Select the answer that seems reasonable.

12. length of a football field   **a.** 2 m

13. thickness of a quarter   **b.** 1 km

14. perimeter of a notebook   **c.** 100 m

15. width of a chair   **d.** 2 mm

16. height of a basketball player   **e.** 6 dm

17. distance you can walk in 10 minutes **f.** 100 cm

Mixed Applications

18. A tennis court measures 11 m by 24 m. On all sides there will be 2 m between the court and the fence. How many meters of fencing are needed?

19. The air distance from New York to Denver is 2,624 km. The distance from Denver to Los Angeles is 1,137 km. What is the distance from New York to Los Angeles?

20. A roll of vinyl-coated fence costs $41.39. A roll of steel fence costs $31.49. How much more does the roll of vinyl-coated fence cost?

21. **Write a problem** that involves finding the perimeter of an object. Use an object whose sides can be measured easily.

┌─ **LOGICAL REASONING** ─────────────────

Trace the square grid. Each side of the small squares is $\frac{1}{2}$ cm long. Separate the grid into five sections, each section with a perimeter of 4 cm. The five sections do not need to have the same shape.

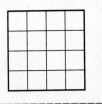

PROBLEM SOLVING

Strategy: Drawing a Diagram

Alan Yamada has taught his friends how to play the Japanese game *Go*. Alan, Betty, Carla, and David all want to play, but only two people can play at a time. Each one wants to play the other three. How many matches will they need to play?

You can use a diagram to understand the problem better. Represent each person with a dot. Label the dots with the first letter of each person's name. Draw lines from *A* to *B*, from *A* to *C*, and from *A* to *D* to represent the matches Alan will play.

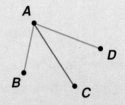

1. How many lines will you need to add to the diagram for Betty? Name the end points for the lines. (Remember: The diagram already shows a match between Betty and Alan.)

2. How many matches can still be played? Name the points on the line.

3. In all, how many matches will be played?

4. **What if** you put all the dots in a straight line like the one below?

A   B   C   D

Would this diagram be as easy to use as the first? Why or why not?

5. **What if** Ellen decides she wants to play each of the others? Draw a diagram to represent these matches.

PRACTICE

Draw a diagram to help you solve the problem.

6. Alan has organized a *Go* match for his friends. He has set up 4 game boards in 4 separate corners of his backyard. He wonders how many pathways there are from any one board straight to any other board. How many pathways are there?

7. Alan's sister, Tani, wants to arrange 4 different pictures she took of the match on her bulletin board. She must tack the 4 corners of each picture. The pictures can overlap a little at the sides. What is the least number of tacks Tani can use?

8. A flower garden in the Yamada's backyard is 4 m wide and 8 m long. A path 1.6 m wide goes around the outside edge of the garden, and a fence runs along the rim of the path. How long is the fence?

9. Alan, Tani, and Carla each want to play one match of *Go* with each of the following: Betty, David, and Ellen. How many matches will they need to play?

Strategies and Skills Review

Solve. Use estimation, mental math, a calculator, or paper and pencil.

10. Alan is on the high school track team. He earned $94 mowing lawns and $61.50 running errands. Use estimation to decide whether he has earned enough money to buy a pair of running shoes and a sweatsuit for $150.

11. Last year Alan's high school track team sold 266, 285, and 178 tickets to 3 of its meets. Use estimation to decide how many tickets the team should print this year for the 3 meets to be sure there will be enough tickets. Did you underestimate or overestimate? Why?

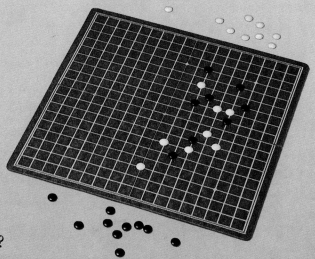

12. Alan wants to walk from home (*H*) to a sporting goods store (*S*) without any unnecessary walking. In how many ways could he do this?

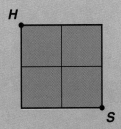

13. *Write a problem* that can be solved using a diagram. Solve your problem. Ask others to solve it.

Using Addition and Subtraction: Whole Numbers and Decimals   **71**

Reading and Interpreting Line Graphs

Jay is deciding whether to live in Roanoke, Virginia, or in Austin, Texas. He made a **double-line graph** of temperature data he had collected. Since none of the temperatures is below 45°F, Jay saved space by leaving out this part of the graph.

AVERAGE TEMPERATURES (°F)

Month	Roanoke	Austin
January	45.6	60.0
February	47.9	63.8
March	56.3	70.7
April	67.9	79.0
May	76.1	85.2
June	83.0	91.7
July	85.9	95.4
August	84.9	95.9
September	79.5	89.4
October	69.9	81.3
November	57.6	70.2
December	46.6	63.0

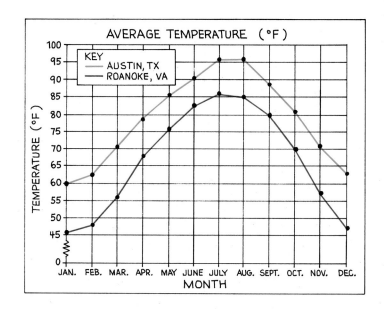

Some questions are easier to answer using a line graph, while others are easier using a table of numbers. Tables are a collection of data, but line graphs can be used to study trends. As you answer each of the following questions, decide whether it is easier to answer using a line graph or a table.

1. What was Roanoke's hottest month? Austin's?

2. What was Roanoke's coldest month? Austin's?

3. What was the average temperature in each city in May?

TRY OUT Use the table or graph to answer the question.

4. Which city reaches its hottest month earliest?

5. In which months was Austin's average temperature in the low 70s?

6. If Jay prefers a climate where the winters are no colder than 50°F, which city would he choose? If he prefers summers that are no warmer than 90°F?

PRACTICE

Use the graph to answer Problems 7–10.

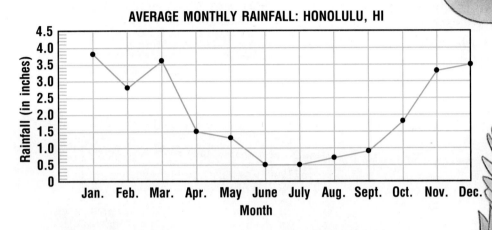

AVERAGE MONTHLY RAINFALL: HONOLULU, HI

7. Which are the two driest months?

8. Which are the three rainiest months?

9. In which months is there an average of about 3 in. of rain?

10. If you were planning a vacation, during which months would you go? Why?

Murray read a study about the average heights of boys and girls. The study contained this graph.

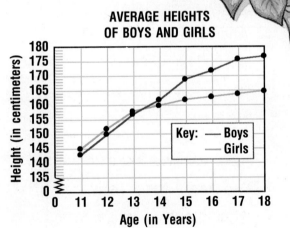

AVERAGE HEIGHTS OF BOYS AND GIRLS

11. About how much taller is the average girl than the average boy at age 11?

12. About what is the average height of girls at age 13?

13. At what age do boys begin to grow taller than girls?

Critical Thinking

Would you use a double-bar or double-line graph to display this information? Why?

14. the change in population of Orlando, Florida, and New York City from 1950–1990

15. tee-shirt sales and sweatshirt sales of Grades 5, 6, 7, and 8 in a fund-raising drive

ACTIVITY

Making Line Graphs

Imagine that you are the advertising director for a store called Sports Land. You want to make a line graph to show the data to the right at a sales meeting. How would you draw the graph?

SALES OF TRAC AND DUNK-EM SNEAKERS (IN DOLLARS)

Month	Trac	Dunk-Em
July	$39,772	$28,872
Aug.	$34,641	$32,619
Sept.	$42,512	$66,217
Oct.	$35,678	$43,721
Nov.	$28,172	$39,724
Dec.	$44,789	$68,712

WORKING TOGETHER

Before you draw your graph, you must make a few decisions.

1. What title will you use for the graph?

2. Why would you make a double-line graph to display this data?

3. What scale will you use?

4. Will you round the numbers? If so, to what place?

5. How will you label each axis?

Here is one way to draw the double-line graph:

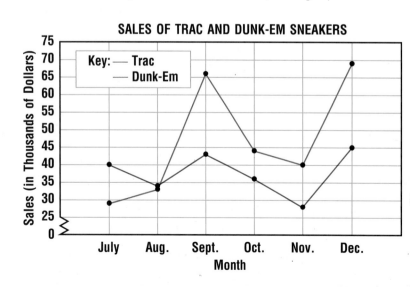

SALES OF TRAC AND DUNK-EM SNEAKERS

Key: — Trac
— Dunk-Em

Sales (in Thousands of Dollars)

Month

SHARING IDEAS

6. How is the graph similar to yours? How is it different?

7. Why is there a gap in the vertical axis?

8. To what place were the numbers rounded? Did you round to the same place?

PRACTICE

Make a single-line graph to display the data from one of the tables.

9. **JOGGING OUTFITS SOLD**

Year	Number of Outfits
1984	580
1985	633
1986	550
1987	794
1988	867
1989	899
1990	1,236

10. **CUSTOMERS WHO RETURNED PURCHASES**

Month	Number
July	15
August	12
September	17
October	9
November	18
December	30

Make a double-line graph to display the data from one of the tables.

11. **AQUA SWIMSUIT SALES (APRIL–SEPTEMBER)**

Month	Brand A	Brand X
April	$2,387	$2,432
May	$3,469	$2,651
June	$4,742	$3,921
July	$5,971	$3,921
August	$5,372	$4,021
September	$4,325	$5,724

12. **SHOPPERS WHO PURCHASED AT PRE-HOLIDAY SALE**

Day	Male	Female
Monday	800	487
Tuesday	912	759
Wednesday	775	800
Thursday	831	1,128
Friday	1,193	887
Saturday	2,000	1,094

Critical Thinking

Use the graph on page 74 to answer Problems 13 and 14.

13. What may have caused Dunk-Em's sales to increase sharply from August through September?

14. Predict the sales of the two brands of sneakers for January.

DECISION MAKING

Problem Solving: Choosing a Pet

SITUATION

The Luke family wants a pet. They live in a small apartment. They went to a pet store and found the information below.

PROBLEM

What kind of pet should they choose?

DATA

	Parakeet	Tropical Fish (10)	Hamster
Cost	$20	$10	$6
Annual cost of food	$50	$13	$25
One-time costs	Cage and accessories: $25	Aquarium and accessories: $82	Cage and accessories: $30

USING THE DATA

What is the initial cost of purchasing the pet and a home?

1. parakeet   **2.** tropical fish   **3.** hamster

What is the total first-year cost of owning the pet?

4. parakeet   **5.** tropical fish   **6.** hamster

MAKING DECISIONS

7. If they want to spend as little as possible at first, which pet should they choose?

8. If the Lukes want to spend $100 or less in the first year, which pet should they not choose?

9. How much could they save on annual food costs by getting tropical fish instead of a parakeet?

10. *What if* the pet will be alone for periods of time? Which pet might they choose?

11. *Write a list* of other factors the Luke family should take into consideration in choosing a pet.

12. Which pet would you choose? Why?

Math and Art

When an architect draws a map of a building, such as a house, it is called a *building plan*. A plan of a house shows the dimensions, or measurements, of the whole house and of each room. It also shows where the windows, doors, closets, and plumbing fixtures are. A building plan guides the construction of the house. It can also help the occupant of the house plan furniture arrangements.

The chart shows some common symbols used in building plans.

▬▬▬▬	wall
▬▬ ▭ ▬▬	window in wall
▬▬ ▬▬	entryway

Measurements are written in feet (') and inches ("). So 12'6" × 11'0" is read "twelve feet six inches by eleven feet."

What if you wanted to put the following furniture into the room shown at the right?

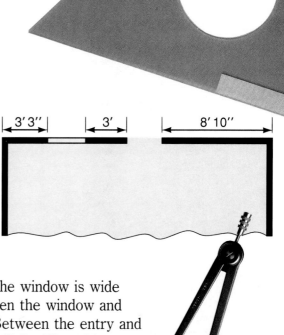

| 3'3" | 3' | 8'10" |

Couch—6'0"   Piano—5'0"
Bookcase—3'0"   Table—4'0"

Which furniture could you place against the wall where the entryway is without blocking either the entry or the window?

Think: The distance between the corner and the window is wide enough for one bookcase. The distance between the window and entry is also wide enough for one bookcase. Between the entry and the wall on the right, the couch or the piano will fit. The table and bookcase or the piano and bookcase will also fit there.

ACTIVITIES

1. Use graph paper to plan a room. On one sheet draw a room showing the dimensions. Cut another sheet into shapes that represent furniture. Try various arrangements.

2. With a partner, plan your "dream house." Don't forget to include the kitchen, bathrooms, halls, and closets. Display your "dream house" to the class.

Calculator: Build the Numbers

You can use your calculator to build decimals.
Use only the numbers 1, 0.1, 0.01, 0.001, 0.0001, 0.00001 and the
⊕ and ⊜ keys.

Follow these steps to build the number 2.342.

Enter	Calculator Display
1 ⊕ 1 ⊕	2.
0.1 ⊕ 0.1 ⊕ 0.1 ⊕	2.3
0.01 ⊕ 0.01 ⊕ 0.01 ⊕ 0.01 ⊕	2.34
0.001 ⊕ 0.001 ⊜	2.342

1. How would you build the number 1.0352? 0.30314?

Use your calculator to build each number. Use only the numbers
1, 0.1, 0.01, 0.001, 0.0001, 0.00001 and the ⊕ and ⊜ keys.

2. 1.3   3. 2.04   4. 1.002

5. 0.0422   6. 5.62   7. 3.0442

8. 0.115   9. 2.0213   10. 4.004

11. 6.142   12. 6.06   13. 0.00031

14. 2.5   15. 0.3332   16. 1.0114

USING THE CALCULATOR

17. Can you build the numbers in Questions 2 and 5 above by
    starting with places other than the ones place? Why or why not?
    Try building the numbers in Questions 2 and 5.

**Now try this. Use only the numbers 1, 0.1, 0.01, and 0.001, and
the ⊕, ⊖, and ⊜ keys to build each of the numbers.**

18. 0.9   19. 1.8   20. 1.98

21. 3.96   22. 2.09   23. 3.08

24. 2.119   25. 0.089   26. 1.009

27. 0.107   28. 3.278   29. 0.901

EXTRA PRACTICE

Mental Math: Adding and Subtracting, page 49 ....

Rewrite to solve each problem mentally.

1. $7 + 1 + 9 + 3$ **2.** $26 + 17 + 14$ **3.** $28 + 25 + 32$

4. $175 + 82 + 25$ **5.** $183 + 47 + 17$ **6.** $39 + 27$

7. $56 + 18$ **8.** $298 + 135$ **9.** $67 + 196$

10. $74 - 27$ **11.** $86 - 48$ **12.** $63 - 16$

13. $432 - 298$ **14.** $651 - 197$ **15.** $567 - 399$

Use mental math to find the sum or difference.

16. $17 + 25 + 13 + 15$ **17.** $288 + 64 + 12$ **18.** $84 - 36$

19. $325 - 199$ **20.** $297 + 146$ **21.** $651 - 395$

Estimating Sums and Differences: Rounding, page 51 ....

Estimate by rounding.

1.	**2.**	**3.**	**4.**	**5.**
$8{,}614$	$7{,}824$	$37{,}714$	$2{,}174$	$\$30.21$
$+\ 5{,}071$	$+\ \ \ 417$	$-\ 19{,}342$	$-\ \ \ 385$	$+\ \ \ 8.56$

6. $68{,}017 + 23{,}385 + 14{,}842$ **7.** $39{,}402 - 7{,}815$ **8.** $\$220{,}087 - \$57{,}916$

9. $75{,}129 + 63{,}871 + 5{,}614$ **10.** $3{,}452 - 736$ **11.** $588{,}719 - 47{,}815$

12. $879 + 94 + 614 + 303$ **13.** $\$2{,}524 - \$1{,}296$ **14.** $418 - 272$

Front-End Estimation: Sums and Differences, page 53 ....

Estimate. Use the front digits and adjust.

1.	**2.**	**3.**	**4.**	**5.**
$5{,}617$	$6{,}712$	$\$82{,}171$	$35{,}134$	$88{,}174$
$3{,}075$	$2{,}241$	$40{,}381$	$43{,}071$	$31{,}381$
$+\ 4{,}482$	$+\ \ \ 321$	$+\ 38{,}429$	$+\ \ 4{,}582$	$+\ \ 1{,}017$

6.	**7.**	**8.**	**9.**	**10.**
$8{,}841$	$5{,}271$	$7{,}813$	$\$14{,}197$	$87{,}214$
$-\ 7{,}699$	$-\ \ \ 912$	$-\ 5{,}698$	$-\ \ 5{,}345$	$-\ 24{,}831$

11.	**12.**	**13.**	**14.**	**15.**
$6{,}035$	$\$16{,}711$	$58{,}636$	$2{,}047$	$3{,}704$
$11{,}385$	$-\ \ 8{,}900$	$-\ 49{,}048$	$5{,}477$	$+\ 4{,}456$
$+\ 45{,}406$			$+\ 1{,}957$	

Adding and Subtracting Whole Numbers, page 55

Add or subtract.

1. 8,241
$+$ 935

2. 8,642
2,175
3,471
$+$ 917

3. 35,675
28,341
49,132
17,416

4. 7,143
2,619
$+$ 387

5. 387,124
28,549
2,104
$+$ 13,379

6. 7,914
$-$ 2,999

7. $82,341
$-$ 49,687

8. 790,012
$-$ 82,698

9. 7,117,079
$-$ 6,877,999

10. 68,721
$-$ 7,689

11. $87,124 + $7,819 + $685 + $289

12. 6,701 $-$ 597

13. 2,118,308 $-$ 1,102,381

14. 3,193 + 5,391 + 7,184

15. 895,568 + 4,193,185

16. 48,196 $-$ 5,965

Solving Equations, page 59

Solve and check. Use mental math whenever you can.

1. $n + 6 = 13$

2. $n - 5 = 9$

3. $n + 8 = 15$

4. $n - 9 = 7$

5. $n - 7 = 5$

6. $n - 14 = 14$

7. $n + 9 = 17$

8. $n + 32 = 68$

9. $n - 41 = 39$

10. $n + 25 = 90$

11. $n - 29 = 62$

12. $n + 38 = 72$

13. $n + 19 = 24$

14. $n + 58 = 103$

15. $n - 17 = 111$

16. $n - 88 = 157$

Problem Solving Strategy: Using Estimation, page 61

Use estimation to solve the problem. Did you underestimate or overestimate?

1. At the soccer game there were 187 children under thirteen, 692 teenagers, and 475 adults. Did at least 1,500 people attend the game?

2. James is a game warden and his goal is to tag 100 deer a day. On Wednesday he tagged 31 fawns, 53 does, and 22 bucks. Did James reach his goal on that day?

3. Ms. Ektal has $2,000 to spend on textbooks. She plans to spend $542 on math books, $478 on English books, and $743 on music books. Will Ms. Ektal have enough money to buy all the books?

4. The first class to collect 1,800 aluminum cans for recycling will receive a new globe. The sixth-grade class has collected 633, 519, 442, and 327 cans. Has the class collected enough cans?

EXTRA PRACTICE

Estimating Decimal Sums and Differences, page 65 ....

Estimate the sum or difference by rounding.

1. 5.812 − 0.714	**2.** 7.38 − 1.97	**3.** 0.84 7.43 + 0.58	**4.** $6.86 1.87 + .42	**5.** 8.787 − 0.713

Estimate Use the front digits and adjust.

6. 7.89 0.69 + 0.18	**7.** 5.682 0.374 + 3.125	**8.** $7.29 − 4.99	**9.** 0.64 4.76 + 8.38	**10.** 8.051 − 3.673

Adding and Subtracting Decimals, page 67 ....

Add or subtract.

1. 3.0009 − 0.0715	**2.** $3.01 − 0.79	**3.** 8 − 2.0174	**4.** 81.6387 + 9.2849	**5.** 6.87 3.42 2.974 + 2.445

6. $3,174.73 + $2,998.75   **7.** 8.41 + 7.2 + 3.14   **8.** 4.19 − 0.8276

9. 875.4 − 29.89   **10.** 7 − 3.1719   **11.** 3.21 + 4 + 0.0178

12. 5.186 + 4.3812   **13.** 6.1 + 3.1808 + 9   **14.** 2.5831 − 2.05

Metric Units of Length: Perimeter, page 69 ....

Match. Select the answer that seems reasonable.

1. the width of a nickel	**a.** 1.3 km
2. the length of a car	**b.** 1 mm
3. the length of the Golden Gate Bridge	**c.** 3.5 m
4. the width of a head of a pin	**d.** 1,255 km
5. the height of the Statue of Liberty	**e.** 2 cm
6. the distance from Denver to Dallas	**f.** 30 dam

Problem Solving Strategy: Drawing a Diagram, page 71 ....

Draw a diagram to help you solve the problem.

1. Mikio made a sandbox for his sister. The sandbox measured 4 m by 5 m. Then he decided to put a wooden border around the sandbox. The border is 0.75 m wide. What is the perimeter of the sandbox now?

2. A tennis tournament has 8 players. The first two players drawn will play each other. Then the winner will play the next player and so on. How many matches will be played to get a tournament winner?

Reading and Interpreting Line Graphs, page 73 ....

1. About how much more did Jamie earn baby-sitting than delivering papers the third week?

2. In which week was there the greatest difference in the amount of money earned?

3. About how much money did Jamie earn the 8th week

4. Jamie wants to work only one job. Which one should she choose? Why?

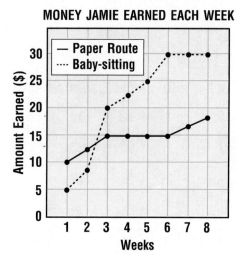

MONEY JAMIE EARNED EACH WEEK

Making Line Graphs, page 75 ....

Make a line graph to display the data.

1.

SALES OF RUNNING SHOES

Month	Sales
July	$28,872
August	$32,641
September	$42,512
October	$35,678
November	$28,172
December	$45,789

2.

TRAVELERS

Year	To U.S.	From U.S.
1984	26,913,000	34,388,000
1985	25,417,000	35,257,000
1986	25,359,000	37,595,000
1987	29,657,000	40,196,000
1988	33,736,000	41,045,000

Source: U.S. Travel Center, D.C.

Practice *PLUS*

KEY SKILL: Solving Equations (Use after page 59.)

Level A

Solve and check. Use mental math whenever you can.

1. $n + 5 = 11$
2. $n - 4 = 4$
3. $n + 6 = 13$
4. $n - 9 = 5$
5. $n - 8 = 4$
6. $n - 7 = 9$
7. $n + 8 = 13$
8. $n + 7 = 14$
9. $n + 7 = 10$
10. $n + 3 = 12$
11. $n - 5 = 9$
12. $n - 8 = 10$
13. $n + 3 = 9$
14. $n - 3 = 11$
15. $n + 1 = 8$
16. $n - 4 = 13$

17. A number minus 9 is 6. What is the number?

Level B

Solve and check. Use mental math whenever you can.

18. $n - 17 = 13$
19. $n + 18 = 25$
20. $n + 16 = 28$
21. $n - 21 = 10$
22. $n + 15 = 22$
23. $n - 22 = 19$
24. $n - 35 = 35$
25. $n + 19 = 23$
26. $n - 20 = 25$
27. $n + 25 = 41$
28. $n - 45 = 15$
29. $n + 75 = 100$
30. $n + 38 = 50$
31. $n - 15 = 30$
32. $n + 27 = 34$
33. $n - 44 = 8$

34. Don said, "I'm thinking of a number. The number plus 51 is equal to 100. What is the number?"

Level C

Solve and check. Use mental math whenever you can.

35. $n - 48 = 49$
36. $n - 55 = 28$
37. $n + 36 = 103$
38. $n + 67 = 121$
39. $n - 29 = 139$
40. $n + 42 = 131$
41. $n + 73 = 151$
42. $n - 84 = 141$
43. $n + 91 = 160$
44. $n - 64 = 61$
45. $n - 85 = 115$
46. $n + 77 = 142$
47. $n + 72 = 185$
48. $n - 57 = 46$
49. $n - 74 = 36$
50. $n + 34 = 213$

51. Seven years ago, the elephant was 29. How old is the elephant now?

KEY SKILL: Adding and Subtracting Decimals (Use after page 67.)

Level A

Add or subtract.

1.	2.	3.	4.	5.
26.38 + 18.14	8.72 − 3.5	52.471 + 8.75	$8.19 − .63	9.277 3.014 + 8.538

6. $41.75 + $23.83   **7.** 5.218 − 2.876   **8.** 7.56 − 5.29

9. Sue bought a notebook and pen. The total cost was $3.99. How much change did she receive from a $5 bill?

Level B

Add or subtract.

10.	11.	12.	13.	14.
31.878 + 9.834	8.61 − 2.741	3.073 − 0.872	2.197 + 7.9	25.493 15.024 + 42.5

15. $17.59 − $3.99   **16.** 5.678 + 3.356 + 9   **17.** 9.5 − 6.74

18. Bill weighs 53.1 kg, and Tom weighs 45.81 kg. How much more does Bill weigh than Tom?

Level C

Add or subtract.

19.	20.	21.	22.	23.
$87.49 15.89 25.98 + 10.59	7 − 2.871	82.7 − 59.874	387.5 67.814 0.87 + 87.2371	6.1 − 3.0579

24. 0.6174 + 0.92 + 5 + 0.875   **25.** 15 − 0.897   **26.** $251 − $189.75

27. A four-person relay team had these times: 1.027 minutes, 1.02 minutes, 1.1 minutes, and 0.97 minutes. What is the total time for the team?

CHAPTER REVIEW/TEST

LANGUAGE AND MATHEMATICS

Complete the sentences. Use the words in the chart on the right.

1. The distance around a closed figure is the ■. *perimeter*

2. A number sentence with an equal sign is a(n) ■. *equation*

3. The basic unit of length and distance in the metric system is a(n) ■ *meter*

4. Rounding numbers to the greatest place of the lesser number is one way to ■ a sum. *estimate*

CONCEPTS AND SKILLS

Estimate the sum or difference.

5. $5.37 + $6.52 + $1.61

6. 7.492 − 0.392

7. 11,623 − 7,535

Add or subtract.

8. $3,925.78 + $638.52 + $1,865.23

9. $583.24 − $495.68

10. 126,503 − 79,484

11. 6,925 + 362 + 981

Solve each equation for *n*.

12. $19 + n = 32$

13. $81 − n = 18$

14. $n − 75 = 11$

15. What is the length of the line in millimeters? _____

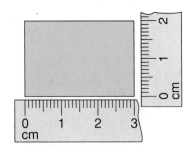

Complete.

16. The width of the rectangle is ■ cm.

17. The length of the rectangle is ■ cm.

18. The perimeter of the rectangle is ■ cm.

19. 1 cm = ■ mm.

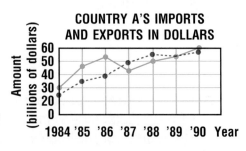

COUNTRY A'S IMPORTS AND EXPORTS IN DOLLARS

Use the line graph to answer Questions 20–21.

20. In which year were imports the highest?

21. How much were 1988 imports? 1988 exports?

----- Imports
—— Exports

22. The average monthly temperatures in degrees Fahrenheit for Oslo, Norway, in order from January to December are: 25°, 27°, 33°, 40°, 45°, 54°, 64°, 60°, 55°, 45°, 35°, 25°. Make a line graph to display this data.

Critical Thinking

23. Show how to use equal additions to subtract mentally.

   a. 322 − 94　　　　　　　　**b.** 56 − 19　　　　　　　　**c.** $622 − $296

Mixed Applications

24. A garden is in full bloom. There are 3,740 irises, 8,350 daisies, and 9,625 tulips. Does the garden have at least 20,000 flowers in bloom? Did you overestimate or underestimate?

25. A rug with a border is 6 m long and 3 m wide. The border is 0.5 m wide. What is the perimeter of the rug without the border? Draw a diagram.

PERFORMANCE ASSESSMENT

Work together with your group to solve this problem.

This table shows the average annual precipitation for six U.S. cities rounded to the nearest inch.

Make a double-line graph to display the data. Then summarize what the graph shows. Include addition and subtraction statements to compare the precipitation in the cities.

AVERAGE ANNUAL PRECIPITATION (INCHES)

City	Rain	Snow
Albany, NY	46	57
Columbus, OH	53	15
Salt Lake City, UT	11	48
Spokane, WA	20	50
Burlington, VT	42	68
Philadelphia, PA	36	14

1. *Think about:*
- how to present the precipitation data clearly in a double-line graph
- how you would use addition and subtraction to describe the changes shown in the graph

2. Write a paragraph explaining why a line graph is a good way to follow trends over a period of time. You may use your addition and subtraction statements to support your explanation.

CUMULATIVE REVIEW

Choose the letter of the correct answer.

1. Round 46,327.1329 to the nearest thousand.
   a. 46,327.133
   b. 46,000
   c. 50,000.132
   d. not given

2. Which is less than 86,074,813?
   a. 86,103,200
   b. 86,093,000
   c. 86,081,920
   d. not given

3. Solve: $n - 32 = 17$
   a. 15
   b. 51
   c. 49
   d. not given

4. Estimate the sum by rounding:
   48,261 + 18,352 + 10,795
   a. 80,000
   b. 75,000
   c. 70,000
   d. not given

5. Add: 9 + 17 + 3 + 2
   a. 35
   b. 31
   c. 32
   d. not given

6. The length of a crayon is about:
   a. 90 km.
   b. 90 m.
   c. 90 cm.
   d. not given

7. What is the perimeter of two rectangles each 5 cm by 2 cm?
   a. 14 cm
   b. 20 cm
   c. 28 cm
   d. not given

8. What is the frequency of Y?

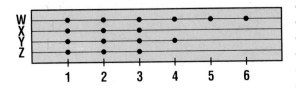

   a. 4
   b. 3
   c. 6
   d. not given

9. What is the place value of 4 in 0.0468?
   a. tens
   b. tenths
   c. hundredths
   d. not given

10. What is the difference between 6.96 and 2.385?
    a. 4.311
    b. 9.345
    c. 4.575
    d. not given

11. 1 m = ■ cm
    a. 100
    b. 1,000
    c. 10
    d. not given

12. A stuffed animal costs $16.95. Estimate the change from $20.
    a. $3.00
    b. < $3
    c. $4.00
    d. not given

Use the graph for Questions 13–14.

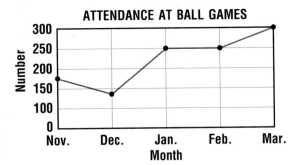

13. During which month was attendance highest?
    a. February
    b. November
    c. March
    d. not given

14. About how many attended the games in December?
    a. < 100
    b. > 100
    c. > 150
    d. not given

ENRICHMENT FOR ALL

ALGEBRA: VENN DIAGRAMS

To plan schedules the school needs to know how many students are in the computer club and in the chorus. Seven students are in the computer club only, 9 are in the chorus only, and 4 more students are in both clubs.

John used the **Venn diagram** at the right to show this information.

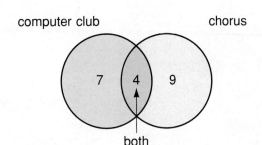

computer club   chorus

both

1. In all, how many students are in the computer club?

2. In all, how many students are in the chorus?

3. How many students will the school need to plan for when it makes schedules for these two groups? How do you know?

Fran used a Venn diagram to show how many students play basketball and bowl. She had one more number to fill in. She knew that a total of 18 students bowl, including those that also play basketball.

4. Of the 18 students, how many just bowl?

5. What numbers did you subtract to find the answer?

6. How many students in all play one or both of these sports?

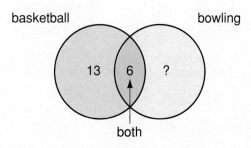

basketball   bowling

both

Solve. Draw a Venn diagram.

7. Everyone in the Winter Sports Club can skate or ski. 14 people ski only, 16 people skate only, and 11 people do both.
   a. How many skate?

   b. How many ski?

   c. How many are in the club?

8. All the people in a survey liked cereal X, cereal Y, or both. 48 liked cereal Y, 31 liked cereal Y only, and 24 liked cereal X only.
   a. How many liked cereal X?

   b. How many liked both?

   c. How many were surveyed?

Using Addition and Subtraction: Whole Numbers and Decimals **89**

ENRICHMENT FOR ALL

Although the ways in which people of various cultures express numbers may be different, the idea of a system of numbers is the same.

THE YORUBA NUMBER

AFRICA

Nigeria

THE GRANGER COLLECTION

The Yoruba [YOR-uh-buh], who live in southwestern Nigeria, in Africa, use a system based on 20. This system uses addition, subtraction, and multiplication to express numbers. To say 35, the Yoruba think of the number as "five less than two twenties." In numerals, the Yoruba expression for 35 looks like this:

$$35 = (20 \times 2) - 5$$

The Yoruba people have single words for the numbers 1 through 10 and for the numbers 20, 30, 200, and 400. Other numbers are expressed as combinations of these number words. The Yoruba numbers from 40 to 49 are given below:

40 = (20 x 2)	45 = (20 x 3) - 10 - 5
41 = (20 x 2) + 1	46 = (20 x 3) - 10 - 4
42 = (20 x 2) + 2	47 = (20 x 3) - 10 - 3
43 = (20 x 2) + 3	48 = (20 x 3) - 10 - 2
44 = (20 x 2) + 4	49 = (20 x 3) - 10 - 1

1. Show how you think the Yoruba numbers from 60 to 69 are expressed.

2. Compare the Yoruba number system to a base-ten number system.

SYSTEM

Mental Math: Multiplying

A. The Museum of Natural History sells souvenir arrowheads and bowls. It receives arrowheads in boxes of 25 and bowls in boxes of 8. How many arrowheads are there in 1,000 boxes? How many bowls are there in 2,000 boxes?

You can use patterns to find some products mentally.

$25 \times 1 = 25$	$8 \times 2 = 16$
$25 \times 10 = 250$	$8 \times 20 = 160$
$25 \times 100 = 2,500$	$8 \times 200 = 1,600$
$25 \times 1,000 = 25,000$	$8 \times 2,000 = 16,000$

There are 25,000 arrowheads.   There are 16,000 bowls.

1. Compare the number of 0s in the factors to the number of 0s in each product. What pattern do you see?

2. Use the pattern to multiply $9 \times 10,000$ and 60×700.

B. You can use the properties of multiplication to multiply mentally.

Commutative Property	$3 \times 5 = 5 \times 3$
Associative Property	$(7 \times 4) \times 2 = 7 \times (4 \times 2)$
Distributive Property	$6 \times 27 = (6 \times 20) + (6 \times 7)$

Multiply mentally: $5 \times (45 \times 2)$
Use the commutative and associative properties.

Multiply mentally: 5×24
Use the distributive property.

Think: $5 \times (2 \times 45)$ Commutative property
         $(5 \times 2) \times 45$ Associative property
            $10 \quad \times 45 = 450$

Think: $5 \times 24 = 5 \times (20 + 4)$
$= (5 \times 20) + (5 \times 4)$
$= \quad 100 \quad + \quad 20$
$= \quad\quad 120$

3. Use the properties to multiply $4 \times 13 \times 25$ mentally.

4. Find 8×25 mentally. Which method did you use?

TRY OUT   Write the letter of the correct answer.

b **5.** $9 \times 6,000$ **a.** 45,000   **b.** 54,000   **c.** 450,000   **d.** 540,000

c **6.** $2 \times 14 \times 5$ **a.** 21   **b.** 120   **c.** 140   **d.** 180

d **7.** 5×42 **a.** 47   **b.** 92   **c.** 220   **d.** 210
   $5 \times (40+2)$
92 Lesson 3–1 $(5 \times 40) \; (5 \times 2)$
                    $200 + 10 = 210$

PRACTICE

Multiply mentally.

8. 6 × 800 *4800*   **9.** 9 × 400   **10.** 5 × 7,000   **11.** 6 × 80,000

12. 40 × 500   **13.** 20 × 9,000   **14.** 14 × 20,000   **15.** 38 × 100,000

16. 68 × 5 × 2   **17.** 2 × 57 × 5   **18.** 4 × 9 × 25   **19.** 25 × 23 × 4

20. 25 × 59 × 4   **21.** 50 × 92 × 2   **22.** 2 × 120 × 50   **23.** 5 × 184 × 2

24. 5 × 26   **25.** 18 × 5   **26.** 12 × 50   **27.** 25 × 24

28. 25 × 32   **29.** 48 × 5   **30.** 25 × 48   **31.** 43 × 25

32. 40 × 200   **33.** 50 × 800   **34.** 2 × 67 × 5   **35.** 4 × 48

36. 7 × one ten   **37.** 6 × one hundred

38. 32 × two thousand   **39.** 80 × five thousand

Mixed Applications

40. On Tuesday 1,235 people visited the museum, and on Wednesday 997 visited it. On which day did more people visit the museum? How many more people visited?

41. The planetarium has 16 seats in each row. If there are 25 rows, what is the maximum number of students who can be seated in the planetarium?

42. Of the students in the museum, there are 168 in the dinosaur area, 97 in the rare gems and minerals room, and 32 in the reptile room. How many students are in the museum?

43. Round-trip bus fare to the museum costs $5. How much will it cost 14 students to take the bus to the museum and back?

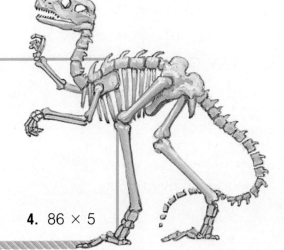

MENTAL MATH

To multiply a number by 5 mentally, you can multiply by 10 and then divide by 2.

$$36 × 5 = (36 × 10) ÷ 2$$
$$= 360 ÷ 2, \text{ or } 180$$

Multiply mentally.

1. 26 × 5   **2.** 44 × 5   **3.** 62 × 5   **4.** 86 × 5

Estimating Products

A round-trip flight on the Midwest Shuttle is 481 miles. In one month there were 37 round-trip flights. About how many miles did the shuttle travel?

An estimate can give you a good idea of the exact answer. Here are two ways to estimate the product.

Front-End Estimation

Use the front digits.

$$37 \times 481$$

Think: $30 \times 400 = 12,000$

Rounding

Round to the greatest place of each factor.

$$37 \times 481$$

Think: $40 \times 500 = 20,000$

The total distance traveled was between 12,000 and 20,000 miles.

1. Is the exact answer greater than or less than the front-end estimate? Is it greater than or less than the estimate by rounding? Why or why not?

2. Estimate $6 \times 1,334$ by using the front digits. Then estimate by rounding. How do the estimates compare?

3. Is 26×193 greater than or less than 2,000? greater than or less than 6,000? Why?

TRY OUT Write the letter of the correct answer.

Estimate by using front-end estimation.

4. 55×467 **a.** 25,000   **b.** 30,000   **c.** 20,000   **d.** 2,000

5. $6 \times 2,732$ **a.** 18,000   **b.** 12,000   **c.** 20,000   **d.** 30,000

Estimate by rounding.

6. 37×566 **a.** 24,000   **b.** 15,000   **c.** 20,000   **d.** 18,000

7. $5 \times 2,159$ **a.** 20,000   **b.** 15,000   **c.** 30,000   **d.** 10,000

PRACTICE

Estimate by using front-end estimation.

8.	948 × 4	9.	8,643 × 9	10.	3,782 × 6	11.	721 × 32	12.	876 × 45

13.	1,249 × 72	14.	4,834 × 29	15.	999 × 92	16.	759 × 27	17.	7,287 × 97

Estimate by rounding.

18.	618 × 8	19.	761 × 5	20.	5,972 × 7	21.	6,294 × 8	22.	674 × 59

23.	304 × 32	24.	531 × 58	25.	843 × 73	26.	4,201 × 64	27.	3,702 × 86

Estimate.

28. 1,623 × 29   **29.** 883 × 94   **30.** 5,329 × 84   **31.** 416 × 8

32. 7,365 × 4   **33.** 8,234 × 99   **34.** 8,537 × 74   **35.** 2,692 × 18

Write the letter of the most reasonable answer.

36. 6 × 417   **a.** 1,902   **b.** 1,962   **c.** 2,502   **d.** 3,102

37. 53 × 648   **a.** 3,434   **b.** 5,184   **c.** 24,344   **d.** 34,344

38. 84 × 735   **a.** 52,112   **b.** 61,740   **c.** 72,004   **d.** 83,615

Mixed Applications

39. John flew his glider a distance of 35 mi one day, 43 mi the next day, and 29 mi the day after that. How far did the glider travel during that period?

40. *Write a problem* involving estimation that uses this information: Jeremy counted 354 planes and 78 helicopters at the local airport.

Mixed Review

Find the answer. Which method did you use?

MENTAL MATH
CALCULATOR
PAPER/PENCIL

41. 8,000 − 5,000   **42.** 15,123,792 + 894,088   **43.** 15,071 − 9,883

44. 8.791 − 3.999   **45.** 236.257 + 197.866   **46.** $3.50 + $1.25

47. 4,693 + 949   **48.** 24 + 9 + 16   **49.** 56,035 − 6,305

Multiplying

A. The Highlander Band is selling tickets for a concert. The band has 124 members. If each member sells 7 tickets, how many tickets will all the members sell?

Multiply: 7 × 124

```
  1 2
  1 2 4
×     7
  8 6 8
```

The band members will sell 868 tickets.

1. Does the answer seem reasonable? How do you know?

2. How could you use the distributive property to multiply 7 × 109 mentally?

B. A band uniform costs $279. How much will 64 uniforms cost?

Multiply: 64 × $279

Step 1	Step 2	Step 3
Multiply by the ones.	**Multiply by the tens.**	**Add the products.**
3 3 $ 2 7 9 ×　　6 4 1 1 1 6 ← 4 × 279	4 5 3 3 $ 2 7 9 ×　　6 4 1 1 1 6 1 6 7 4　← 60 × 279	4 5 3 3 $ 2 7 9 ×　　6 4 1 1 1 6 1 6 7 4 $ 1 7,8 5 6

The uniforms will cost $17,856.

3. For Step 3, Cliff added 1,116 and 1,674 and got an answer of $2,790. What was his mistake?

4. Is $17,856 a reasonable answer? How do you know?

TRY **OUT** Multiply.

5. 7 × 392　　　**6.** 79 × 435　　　**7.** 36 × $8.98　　　**8.** 56 × 804

PRACTICE

Multiply.

9.	377 × 2	10.	409 × 5	11.	514 × 8	12.	628 × 6	13.	$7.05 × 9	14.	813 × 7

15.	739 × 57	16.	827 × 48	17.	298 × 73	18.	507 × 59	19.	$8.02 × 34	20.	$6.79 × 26

21. 5 × 479   22. 4 × $3.06   23. 9 × 862   24. 6 × 307

25. 62 × 178   26. 57 × 603   27. 86 × $7.08   28. 35 × $8.47

Do only those exercises with products greater than 10,000.

29.	345 × 34	30.	989 × 9	31.	415 × 27	32.	674 × 18	33.	281 × 27	34.	423 × 29

Find the missing digits.

35.
```
   5 , ■ 7 ■
 ×       4
 ─────────
  2 0 , 7 1 2
```
36.
```
   ■ , 2 ■ 3
 ×         5
 ─────────
  1 6 , 4 1 5
```
37.
```
   7 , ■ ■ 5
 ×         6
 ─────────
  4 4 , 7 3 0
```
38.
```
     ■ 3 ■
 ×     1 2
 ─────────
  6 , 4 4 4
```

Critical Thinking

The product of 2 two-digit numbers is less than 900. Is the statement always *true*? Give examples to support your answer.

39. Both numbers are less than 30.   40. One number is greater than 30.

Mixed Applications Solve. Which method did you use?

```
ESTIMATION
MENTAL MATH
CALCULATOR
PAPER/PENCIL
```

41. The band has 165 members, and the Art Club has 85 members. If each member of these two groups makes 36 flowers for a float, how many flowers will they make in all?

42. Rita wants to buy a trumpet for $349 and sheet music for $8.95. Would $360 be enough to pay for the items?

43. Joey practices his drums for 20 minutes before school and for 30 minutes after school. For how many minutes does he practice in 5 days?

44. The band's total sales of cassettes was $37.50 from its first concert and $48.25 from its second concert. If the blank cassettes cost a total of $20.35, how much did the band make?

Multiplying Greater Numbers

A. The manager of a video-store chain figures that the chain's profit averages $1,830 per day. At this rate what would the chain's profit be in a year?

Record your estimate.

Anna uses a calculator, and Louanne uses paper and pencil.

Anna	Louanne
365 (×) 1830 (=) **667950.**	$1,830
	× 365
	9150
	10980
	5490
	$667,950

The video-store chain's profit would be $667,950.

1. Does the answer seem reasonable? How do you know?

2. Which method would you use to find 207 × 894? Why? Find the product.

B. When using a calculator you need to be careful about entering digits and signs of operation.

Anna and Louanne use calculators to find 368 × 245.

Anna's answer: **90160.**   Louanne's answer: **156400.**

3. Which answer is more reasonable? How do you know?

TRY OUT
Write the letter of the correct answer.
Use a calculator or paper and pencil.

4. 489 × 217
   a. 4,890
   b. 18,093
   c. 106,113
   d. 1,060,130

5. 602 × 807
   a. 485,814
   b. 426,216
   c. 48,641
   d. 166,242

6. 438 × 3,872
   a. 16,959,360
   b. 1,695,936
   c. 337,080
   d. 302,016

7. 304 × 2,608
   a. 853,024
   b. 7,928,320
   c. 792,832
   d. 1,051,024

PRACTICE

Multiply. Use a calculator or paper and pencil.

8. 524
      × 235

9. 384
      × 106

10. 463
       × 317

11. 719
       × 540

12. 247
       × 358

13. 819
       × 345

14. 576
       × 162

15. 289
       × 380

16. 327
       × 286

17. 763
       × 428

18. 2,817
       ×   157

19. 3,374
       ×   283

20. 1,505
       ×   871

21. 2,267
       ×   904

22. 5,137
       ×   256

23. 1,648
       ×   379

24. 8,216
       ×   321

25. $35.73
       ×   375

26. $52.75
       ×   385

27. $43.59
       ×   105

Compare. Write >, <, or =.

28. 325 × 210 ● 325 × 410

29. 640 × $850 ● 850 × $604

30. 525 × $12.23 ● 515 × $12.33

31. 17 × 9,480 ● 170 × 948

Mixed Applications

32. A video store collects an average of $1,604 each day in rentals. How much does the store collect in a year?

33. Brad rents three videos for $2.99, $1.99, and $.99. How much change does he receive from a $10 bill?

34. *Write a problem* that uses this information: One film class produced 16 videocassettes and another produced 12 videocassettes.

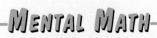

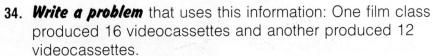

You can multiply two numbers mentally by halving one and doubling the other.

Example: **8 × 15 = 4 × 30 = 2 × 60 = 120**

Multiply mentally by halving and doubling.

  1. 18 × 15   **2.** 16 × 25   **3.** 28 × 50

ACTIVITY Exponents

An amoeba is a one-celled animal that splits in two when it reaches a certain size. How many splittings does it take to have 32 amoebas?

WORKING TOGETHER

Use centimeter cubes to model this problem.

1. Record your results in a table like the one shown. Which splitting has 32 amoebas?

2. At which splitting will there be 64 amoebas? 128 amoebas? Explain.
   See above.

Splitting number	Number of amoebas

One way to find the splitting number for 128 amoebas is to repeatedly multiply 2 by itself until the product is 128. The number of times 2 is used as a factor is the splitting number. You can indicate multiplication using an **exponent**.

Standard Form	**Factor Form**	**Exponent Form**

$$128 = 2 \times 2 \times 2 \times 2 \times 2 \times 2 \times 2 = 2^7$$

exponent ⌐
base ∟

Read as "2 to the 7th power."

3. What does an exponent indicate? Explain what 2^1 means.

4. Add two columns to your table in Problem 1 to show the factor form and exponent form of each splitting.

5. What is the exponent form for the number of amoebas at the 15th splitting? Use your calculator to find the standard form.

Make a table to show the exponent form, factor form, and standard form of 10^1 through 10^7.

6. How many zeros are in 10^8? 10^{12}? 10^{50}?

SHARING IDEAS

7. Is 3^4 the same as 4^3? Why or why not?

8. How are the number of zeros in the product related to the exponent if the base is 10?

PRACTICE

Write in exponent form.

9. $3 \times 3 \times 3 \times 3$ 3^4

10. $10 \times 10 \times 10 \times 10 \times 10 \times 10$ 10^6

11. $a \times a \times a$ a^5

Write in standard form. Use mental math or a calculator.

12. 9^2 $9 \cdot 9$ **13.** 6^3 $6 \cdot 6 \cdot 6$ **14.** 1^4 $1 \cdot 1 \cdot 1 \cdot 1$ **15.** 5^4 $5 \cdot 5 \cdot 5 \cdot 5$ **16.** 3^5 $3 \cdot 3 \cdot 3 \cdot 3 \cdot 3$ **17.** 11^2 $11 \cdot 11$

18. 10^6 $10 \cdot 10 \cdot 10 \cdot 10 \cdot 10 \cdot 10$ **19.** 10^1 10 **20.** 10^{10} $10 \cdot 10 \cdot 10 \cdot 10 \cdot 10 \cdot 10 \cdot 10 \cdot 10 \cdot 10 \cdot 10$ **21.** 18^3 $18 \cdot 18 \cdot 18$ **22.** 29^5 $29 \cdot 29 \cdot 29$ **23.** 86^4 $86 \cdot 86 \cdot 86 \cdot 86$

Use an exponent to write the power of 10.

24. 100,000,000   **25.** 1,000,000,000   **26.** 100,000,000,000

Compare. Write >, <, or =.

27. 2^5 $<$ 5^2 **28.** 3^4 • $3 \times 3 \times 3 \times 4$ $3^3 \cdot 4$ **29.** 30 • 10^3 **30.** 10^4 • $10^3 \times 10$

Critical Thinking

31. How many factors does 2^n have?

32. What do you think 2^0 is? Explain.

Mixed Applications

33. A health official reported 137 cases of measles in May. In April the official reported a total of 89 cases. If the total reaches 300, the official will ask for emergency action. How many more cases will there have to be?

34. A laboratory worker puts 2 oz of yeast in each test tube in a rack that holds 4 rows of tubes. If there are 12 test tubes in each row, how many more racks does he need to hold a total of 100 tubes with yeast samples?

35. A cell of a certain bacterium splits in two every 30 minutes. In 3 hours how many cells will a single cell produce?

36. *Write a paragraph* explaining what you know about exponents.

PROBLEM SOLVING

Strategy: Solving a Multistep Problem

Barbara Sandoval has a flower shop on 8th Street in Miami. She had 8 boxes of orchids with 12 orchids in each box. On the morning of the *Calle Ocho* (CAH-yay OH-cho) festival she sold 11 orchids. During the afternoon and evening, she sold 35 orchids. How many orchids did Barbara have left at closing time?

1. What information do you know?

2. What do you need to find out?

Some problems have to be broken into two or more steps. To solve a problem such as this, you need a plan.

3. What do you need to find out before you can find how many orchids are left?

4. What information do you need to find the answer to solve the problem? What operations can you use?

5. Which operation can you use to get the final answer?

6. How many orchids were left?

PRACTICE

Solve the multistep problem. What steps did you use?

7. Ed has 6 rolls of color film and 8 rolls of black-and-white film. There are 24 exposures on each roll of black-and-white film. There are 12 more exposures on each roll of color film than on the black-and-white. How many exposures does Ed have?

8. The float committee has a carton of screws, nails, and bolts that weighs 25 lb. There are four 3-lb bags of screws. A bag of nails weighs 1.5 lb less than all the screws. How much do the bolts weigh?

9. A stand at the festival had 230 gal of juice. A total of 12 gal of juice was sold in the morning and 15 gal was sold in the afternoon. How many gallons were left?

10. Barbara Sandoval has 6 dozen roses and 9 trays of gardenias with 8 gardenias on each tray. How many flowers are there all together?

Strategies and Skills Review

Solve. Use estimation, mental math, a calculator, or paper and pencil.

11. For a parade picnic, Elisa buys one package of napkins for $.85, peaches for $1.97, and fish for $6.59. Should she overestimate or underestimate to determine if $10 is enough money to buy these items? Why?

12. Music is an important part of the *Calle Ocho* Festival. What kind of music do the students in your class like best? Conduct an experiment. Record the responses of 20 students. Then make a bar graph of the results.

13. Amy bought 10 lb of beads. She bought 3 lb of white beads at $.75 per lb and red beads at $1 per lb. She gave the clerk $10. How much change should she get?

14. Gil bought 2 rolls of crepe paper to decorate a float. Each roll contained 75 yd. He used 3.75 yd that same day. How much crepe paper did Gil have left?

15. A cashier used $159.21 of change on the morning of the festival and $270.25 in the afternoon. Another cashier used $160.09 in the morning and $290 in the afternoon. Which cashier used the most change that day?

16. *Write a problem* that can be solved by using more than one step. Solve your problem. Ask others to solve it.

Using Number Concepts

A. March 15, 1945, was a Great Date. October 7, 1970, was a Great Date. So was May 4, 1920. Can you see why?

Look what happens when you write the dates in numerical form:

    3/15/45   10/7/70   5/4/20

That's right—if you multiply the first two numbers (the month and day) you get the third number (the last two digits of the year).

 1. When was the last Great Date before 1990?

 2. How many Great Dates occurred in 1990?

 3. When will the next four Great Dates occur?

 4. For which years in the 20th century are there the greatest number of Great Dates?

B. Dates can also be palindromes. Remember that a palindrome reads the same either forward or backward.

These years are palindromes: 1551   2002   606

These dates are palindromes: 3/15/13   12/5/21   09/11/90

 5. When was the last palindrome year before 1990? When are the next two after that?

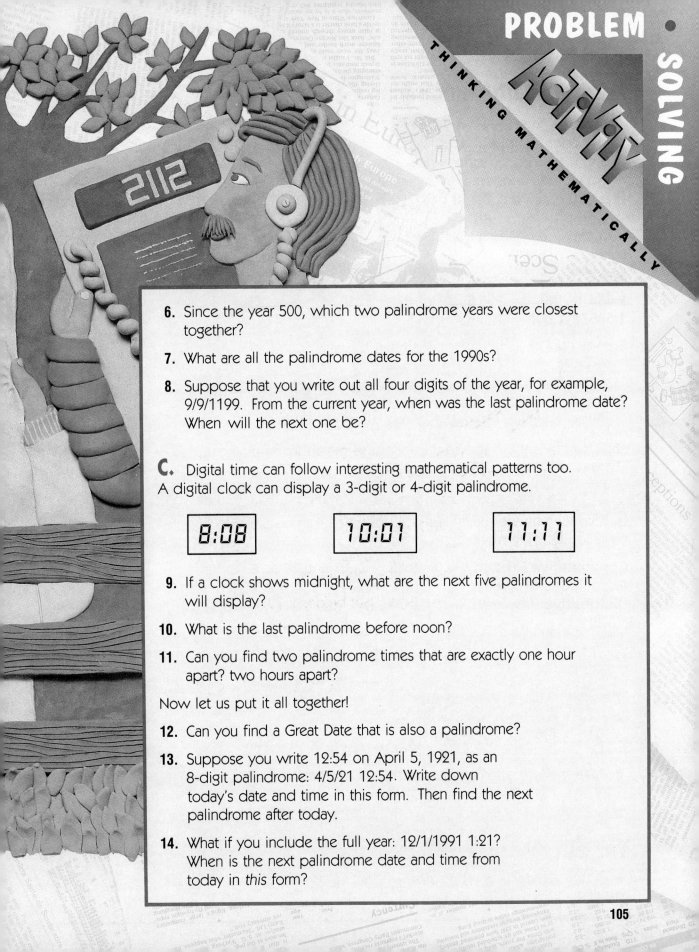

6. Since the year 500, which two palindrome years were closest together?

7. What are all the palindrome dates for the 1990s?

8. Suppose that you write out all four digits of the year, for example, 9/9/1199. From the current year, when was the last palindrome date? When will the next one be?

C. Digital time can follow interesting mathematical patterns too. A digital clock can display a 3-digit or 4-digit palindrome.

8:08   **10:01**   **11:11**

9. If a clock shows midnight, what are the next five palindromes it will display?

10. What is the last palindrome before noon?

11. Can you find two palindrome times that are exactly one hour apart? two hours apart?

Now let us put it all together!

12. Can you find a Great Date that is also a palindrome?

13. Suppose you write 12:54 on April 5, 1921, as an 8-digit palindrome: 4/5/21 12:54. Write down today's date and time in this form. Then find the next palindrome after today.

14. What if you include the full year: 12/1/1991 1:21? When is the next palindrome date and time from today in *this* form?

Mental Math: Multiplying Decimals

A. A pennyweight of gold has a mass of 1.555 g, which is enough to make a small ring. What is the mass of 1,000 pennyweights of gold?

You can use patterns to find the product mentally.

1.555 × 10 = 15.55
1.555 × 100 = 155.5
1.555 × 1,000 = 1,555

So 1,000 pennyweights of gold have a mass of 1,555 g.

1. Compare the position of the decimal point in the first factor to the decimal point in the product. What happens when you multiply by a power of 10?

2. Use the pattern to find the following products mentally: 0.8 × 100 and 0.0067 × 1,000.

B. Sometimes the multiplication properties can be used to help you multiply mentally.

Commutative Property	8.45 × 0.76 = 0.76 × 8.45
Associative Property	(4.2 × 0.6) × 9 = 4.2 × (0.6 × 9)
Distributive Property	8 × 9.5 = (8 × 9) + (8 × 0.5)

Multiply mentally: 2 × (6.8 × 5)
Use the commutative and associative properties.

2 × (5 × 6.8)   Commutative property
(2 × 5) × 6.8   Associative property
   10   × 6.8 = 68

Multiply mentally: 6 × 7.5
Use the distributive property.

6 × 7.5 = (6 × 7) + (6 × 0.5)
      =   42   +   3
      =   45

3. Use multiplication properties to find the product of 4 × 0.73 × 25.

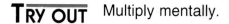

TRY **OUT**   Multiply mentally.

4. 58.72 × 100   **5.** 0.0036 × 1,000   **6.** 2 × 1.95 × 5   **7.** 25 × 0.0356 × 4

PRACTICE

Multiply mentally.

8. 10×2.25

9. 100×0.817

10. $1,000 \times 4.5$

11. 100×0.00725

12. $6.72 \times 1,000$

13. 0.009×100

14. 5.67×10

15. 6.80×100

16. 19.35×10

17. $10,000 \times 6.9$

18. 70.1×100

19. 100×0.08

20. $2 \times 0.46 \times 5$

21. $5 \times 1.076 \times 2$

22. $4 \times 0.0013 \times 25$

23. $25 \times 4.672 \times 4$

24. $2 \times 9.34 \times 5$

25. 4×9.5

26. $4 \times 0.066 \times 25$

27. 6×3.2

28. $4 \times 38.40 \times 25$

29. 8×5.5

30. $5 \times 0.008 \times 2$

31. $50 \times 16.9 \times 2$

32. $10^3 \times 7.112$

33. $10^2 \times 63.8$

34. $10^4 \times 0.0053$

35. 6.8×10^2

36. 0.02×10^3

37. 64.51×10^2

Find the missing number.

38. $3.174 \times \blacksquare = 317.4$

39. $\blacksquare \times 5.125 = 51.25$

40. $2.012 \times \blacksquare = 2012$

41. $\blacksquare \times 10^4 = 596$

42. $10^3 \times \blacksquare = 8.17$

43. $\blacksquare \times 10^2 = 3.2$

Find the answer.

44. What is 1,000 tenths?

45. What is 100 millionths?

Is the number sentence *true* or *false*?

46. 2.325×1 million $= 232,500$

47. $16.82 \times$ ten thousand $= 1,682,000$

48. 0.06×100 thousands $= 60,000$

49. 4.680×1 thousand $= 4,680$

Mixed Applications

50. A bar of pure gold weighs 391.168 troy oz. How much do 10 bars weigh?

51. Kim has 4.445 g of gold. Mark has 6 g. How much more gold does Mark have?

52. A gold coin is 0.508 mm thick. How high would a stack of 100 coins be?

53. Rod bought a gold chain for $165.75 and one for $99.50. How much did he pay in all?

Multiplying Decimals by Whole Numbers

A. When Tanya arrived in France, she exchanged her dollars for francs. She had 8 dollars and received 5.82 francs for each dollar. How many francs did she receive?

Multiply: 8×5.82

Estimate first: $8 \times 5.82 \rightarrow 8 \times 6 = 48$. Then multiply.

Step 1	**Step 2**
Multiply as you would multiply whole numbers.	Place the decimal point in the product.

$$\begin{array}{r} 5.82 \\ \times\ \ \ 8 \\ \hline 4656 \end{array}$$

$$\begin{array}{r} 5.82 \\ \times\ \ \ 8 \\ \hline 46.56 \end{array}$$

Think: The estimate is 48. The decimal point must go before the 5.

Tanya received 46.56 francs for 8 dollars.

1. How many decimal places are there in 5.82? in 46.56?

2. ***What if*** Tanya had exchanged $20 for francs? How many decimal places would she have had in the product? Why?

3. Tell how to place the decimal point in the product of a decimal and a whole number.

B. Some products can be found mentally.

Tanya needs to find 8×6.5.

She thinks: $8 \times 6.5 = (8 \times 6) + (8 \times 0.5) = 48 + 4 = 52$.

So $8 \times 6.5 = 52$..

4. Which property did Tanya use?

TRY OUT Write the letter of the correct answer.

5. 6×4.2 **a.** 252   **b.** 25.2   **c.** 2.52   **d.** 0.252

6. 30×0.25 **a.** 7.5   **b.** 0.75   **c.** 0.075   **d.** 0.0075

7. 27×0.389 **a.** 10.053   **b.** 10.503   **c.** 1.0503   **d.** 0.10503

8. 35×2.5 **a.** 8,755.5   **b.** 875.5   **c.** 87.5   **d.** 8.75

PRACTICE

Multiply.

9.	3.8 × 3	10.	$4.21 × 9	11.	$.23 × 8	12.	0.871 × 2	13.	0.0671 × 5

14.	$2.75 × 25	15.	$.34 × 46	16.	0.067 × 74	17.	0.0172 × 81	18.	2.104 × 33

19. 6 × 0.417

20. 9 × 0.0652

21. 43 × 2.41

22. 52 × 0.1841

23. 65 × 9.73

24. 89 × 7.589

Multiply mentally.

25. 2 × 10.5

26. 4 × 20.5

27. 5 × $3.50

28. 2 × 6.5 × 5

29. 20 × 6.5 × 5

30. 2 × 68.5 × 500

Critical Thinking

31. If you multiply a whole number by a decimal less than 1, will the product be less than or greater than the whole number? Why or why not?

Mixed Applications

Solve. You may need to use the Databank on page 550.

32. From the airport Tanya travels 6.8 km in a taxi that charges 6 francs per kilometer. What is the total cost if she gives the driver a tip of 5 francs?

33. The Ulm Cathedral in West Germany is 528 feet tall. The Eiffel Tower in France is 1.993 times as high as the cathedral. How high is the Eiffel Tower?

34. Lonnie purchases a postcard for 1.45 francs, a magazine for 17.18 francs, and film for 20.31 francs. How much does she spend?

35. How many rubles would you get for $5? for $10? for $25?

Mixed Review

Find the answer. Which method did you use?

MENTAL MATH
CALCULATOR
PAPER/PENCIL

36. 25,321 + 63,824

37. 9,872 − 6,431

38. 8,731 + 582

39. 23 + 30 + 47

40. 679 − 199

41. 5.6678 + 3.012

Estimating Decimal Products

A grandfather clock that gains 0.47 second every hour has been sent to the repair shop to be fixed. Before the clock can be repaired, about how many seconds will it gain in 5.5 hours?

Estimate: 0.47×5.5

Here are two methods you can use.

Front-End Estimation

Use the front digits.

$$0.47 \times 5.5$$

Think: $0.4 \times 5 = 2$

Rounding

Round to the greatest place of each factor.

$$0.47 \times 5.5$$

Think: $0.5 \times 6 = 3$

The clock will gain between 2 and 3 seconds.

1. How can you tell that the exact answer is greater than 2 but less than 3?

2. Estimate: 0.4×7.2. Use both methods. How do the estimates compare?

3. Estimate: 7.8×8.2. Use both methods. Between which two numbers does the exact answer lie?

TRY **OUT**   Write the letter of the correct answer.

Estimate by using front-end estimation.

4. 0.68×3.9 **a.** 2.8   **b.** 2.1   **c.** 1.8   **d.** 2.4

5. 0.9×7.1 **a.** 6.3   **b.** 7   **c.** 71   **d.** 0

Estimate by rounding.

6. 0.59×4.8 **a.** 2   **b.** 2.5   **c.** 25   **d.** 3

7. 6.6×9.4 **a.** 54   **b.** 63   **c.** 72   **d.** 66

PRACTICE

Estimate by using front-end estimation.

8.	8.1 × 0.51	9.	3.91 × 0.4	10.	0.49 × 4.2	11.	12.3 × 0.6	12.	21.04 × 0.74

13.	8.45 × 0.78	14.	0.395 × 9.45	15.	23.929 × 0.23	16.	24.43 × 0.67	17.	0.832 × 33.5

Estimate by rounding.

18.	3.5 × 0.91	19.	5.49 × 0.62	20.	0.28 × 3.1	21.	25.2 × 0.54	22.	32.4 × 0.756

23.	4.72 × 0.32	24.	4.821 × 0.75	25.	34.92 × 3.65	26.	75.1 × 2.39	27.	99.9 × 0.98

Estimate.

28. 0.467 × 9.45 **29.** 5.43 × 6.14 **30.** 7.754 × 0.368 **31.** 24.35 × 0.76

32. 7.43 × 64.23 **33.** 9.56 × 8.321 **34.** 0.35 × 94.45 **35.** 12.921 × 0.937

Write the letter of the better estimate.

36. 0.86 × 5.73   **a.** less than 6   **b.** greater than 6

37. 0.42 × 8.33   **a.** less than 3.2   **b.** greater than 3.2

38. 2.7 × 8.9   **a.** less than 16   **b.** greater than 16

Mixed Applications

39. A watch loses about 0.26 seconds every hour. How many seconds will it lose after 100 hours? How long will it take for the watch to lose 52 seconds?

40. Michael's watch loses 4.75 seconds every hour. After 48 hours, he adjusts the second hand forward by 250 seconds. Did Michael add too much time or not enough?

Multiplying Decimals

A. Mario is riding in a 7.5-km bicycle race. He has already raced 0.82 of the distance. How far has he raced?

Multiply: 0.82 × 7.5

Estimate first: 0.82 × 7.5 →0.8 × 8 = 6.4. Then multiply.

Step 1	Step 2
Multiply as you would multiply whole numbers.	Place the decimal point in the product.

$$\begin{array}{r} 7.5 \\ \times\,0.82 \\ \hline 150 \\ 600 \\ \hline 6150 \end{array}$$

$$\begin{array}{r} 7.5 \\ \times\,0.82 \\ \hline 150 \\ 6000 \\ \hline 6.150 \end{array}$$

Think: The estimate is 6.4. The decimal point must go before the 1.

Mario has already raced 6.15 km.

1. How many decimal places are there in the factors and the product?

2. What rule could you use to place the decimal point in the product of two decimals?

B. Sometimes you may need to round a product.

Multiply: 3.5 × $1.25

Step 1	Step 2	Step 3
Multiply as you would multiply whole numbers.	Place the decimal point in the product.	Round to the nearest cent.

$$\begin{array}{r} \$1.25 \\ \times\quad 3.5 \\ \hline 625 \\ 375 \\ \hline \$4375 \end{array}$$

$$\begin{array}{r} \$1.25 \\ \times\quad 3.5 \\ \hline 625 \\ 375 \\ \hline \$4.375 \end{array}$$

Think:
2 decimal places
+ 1 decimal place
_____
3 decimal places

$$\begin{array}{r} \$1.25 \\ \times\quad 3.5 \\ \hline 625 \\ 375 \\ \hline \$4.375 \rightarrow \$4.38 \end{array}$$

So 3.5 × $1.25 = $4.38.

3. **What if** you wanted to know the product of 2.5 × 8.758? What would be the answer to the nearest hundredth?

4. 3.7 × 8.72   **a.** 32.264   **b.** 322.64   **c.** 3,226.4   **d.** 32,264

5. 0.06 × $4.25   **a.** $.0255   **b.** $.255   **c.** $2.55   **d.** $25.50

PRACTICE

Multiply.

6. 5.2
      × 3.8

7. 2.4
      × 4.6

8. 5.7
      × 9.2

9. $2.75
      ×   2.4

10. 4.21
       × 1.3

11. 2.1
       × 0.37

12. 4.8
       × 0.129

13. 5.12
       × 0.067

14. 7.0142
       ×   6.1

15. 3.812
       × 5.21

16. 8.32 × 4.7

17. 4.32 × 3.78

18. 5.37 × 0.316

19. 6.7 × 0.3 × 0.05

20. 7.2 × 0.3 × 0.2

21. 3.8 × 0.04 × 0.9

Multiply. Round to the nearest cent or to the nearest hundredth.

22. $3.75
       ×   4.5

23. 3.12
       × 2.7

24. $3.49
       × 0.055

25. $9.98
       × 0.0856

26. 6.7
       × 2.171

27. $6.98
       ×   6.6

28. 4.56
       × 0.19

29. 9.12
       × 2.2

30. 5.3
       × 0.28

31. $1.79
       ×   0.5

32. 17.29 × 0.125

33. 5.3 × $8.25

34. 0.08 × $25.39

35. $4.54 × 2.335

36. 6.6 × 0.147

37. 15.2 × 2.1 × 0.04

Critical Thinking

38. Barbara wrote the following problem: 8.03 × 11.18 = 8.97754.
Without multiplying, explain the error in her answer.

Mixed Applications

39. Pedaling, Inc. rents tandem bicycles for $6.95 an hour. They round to the nearest cent when necessary. How much will it cost Shira and John to rent a bicycle for 3.5 hours?

40. The bicycle club traveled 59.8 km on Saturday and 42.25 km on Sunday. On Monday they rode 12.9 km less than they rode on Saturday. How far did the club travel in the three days?

More Multiplying Decimals

A. A bag of cherries weighs 4.8 lb. Sam and Cassie used 0.5 of a bag for pies. How many pounds of cherries did they use?

Sam uses a calculator, and Cassie uses paper and pencil.

Sam	Cassie
0.5 ⊗ 4.8 ⊜ $\boxed{2.4}$	$\begin{array}{r} 4.8 \\ \times\,0.5 \\ \hline 2.40 \end{array}$

Sam says 2.4 lb, and Cassie says 2.40 lb.

1. Do Sam's and Cassie's answers agree? How do you know?

2. Are their answers reasonable? How do you know?

3. What does Cassie have to do to place the decimal point?

4. Why does Sam's calculator show only one digit to the right of the decimal point?

B. Sometimes you have to write one or more 0s to the left of the product to place the decimal point.

Multiply: 0.05 × $1.40

Step 1

Multiply as you would multiply whole numbers.

$$\begin{array}{r} \$1.40 \\ \times\ \ 0.05 \\ \hline 7\ 00 \end{array}$$

Step 2

Place the decimal point in the product.

$$\begin{array}{r} \$1.40 \\ \times\ \ 0.05 \\ \hline \$.07\ 00 \end{array}$$

Think:
2 decimal places
+ 2 decimal places
4 decimal places

So 0.05 × $1.40 is $0.07.

5. Why is it necessary to place an additional 0 in the product?

6. How many decimal places will be in the product if you multiply 0.17 × 0.069? What is the product?

TRY OUT Write the letter of the correct answer.
Use mental math, a calculator, or paper and pencil.

7. 0.3 × 0.7
   a. 21   **c.** 2.1
   b. 210   **d.** 0.21

8. 1.47 × 0.003
   a. 0.00441   **c.** 0.441
   b. 0.0441   **d.** 4.41

9. 4.21 × 6.78
   a. 285.438   **c.** 2.85438
   b. 28.5438   **d.** 0.285438

10. 0.04 × 8.55
   a. 0.342   **c.** 34.2
   b. 3.42   **d.** 342

PRACTICE

Multiply. Use mental math, a calculator, or paper and pencil.

11.   0.15
   × 0.05

12.   0.034
   × 0.07

13. $3.20
   × 0.15

14.   0.0025
   × 0.65

15.   2.312
   × 3.06

16.   0.006
   × 0.009

17.   0.003
   × 0.3

18.   0.052
   × 3.2

19.   0.018
   × 0.12

20. $24.08
   × 0.5

21.   7.08
   × 1.05

22.   0.125
   × 0.8

23.   23.1
   × 0.09

24.   7.63
   × 0.6

25.   0.005
   × 0.18

26. 21.2 × 0.0076

27. 0.87 × 0.023

28. 0.25 × $6,000

29. 0.03 × 0.03 × 0.3

30. 0.07 × 0.006 × 3

31. 0.08 × 0.001 × 0.5

32. 3.2 × 10 × 0.0065

33. 0.072 × $100 × 0.05

34. 0.003 × 2.3 × 0.02

Mixed Applications

Solve. Which method did you use?

35. Giant cashews are priced at $8.15 per lb. Sam wants to buy 0.75 lb. Will $5 be enough for what he wants to buy?

36. The sales tax on a $300 television is 0.05 of the price. What is the total price of the set with the tax included?

37. Victor bought 3 loaves of day-old bread for $.99 each. If he paid with a $10 bill, how much change did he receive?

38. Slacks are on sale for $16.25, sweaters for $15.75, and sneakers for $10.80. Mrs. Washington bought 2 pairs of sneakers and 1 sweater. If she has $50, will she also be able to buy slacks?

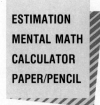

ESTIMATION
MENTAL MATH
CALCULATOR
PAPER/PENCIL

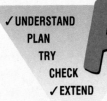

PROBLEM SOLVING

✓UNDERSTAND
PLAN
TRY
CHECK
✓EXTEND

Finding Needed Information

Marion has a book about the planets that contains the following table.

Planet	Diameter at Equator (in miles)	Time for a Revolution Around Sun (in years)
Mercury	3,100	0.24
Venus	7,520	0.62
Earth	7,926	1.00
Mars	4,200	1.88
Jupiter	88,000	11.86

For a science report Marion wants to answer two questions:

- Which of the planets listed in the table is closest in size to Earth?

- About how many days does it take Mercury to revolve around the Sun?

Sometimes you have more information than you need to solve a problem. Then you must select the information you need. Sometimes you do not have enough information. To solve the problem you need to find more information.

1. Does the table provide enough information for Marion to answer the first question?

2. Which part of the table can Marion use to answer the first question? Does she need to use *all* of the information in that part of the table?

3. Which part of the table can she use to help answer the second question?

4. To answer the second question, what information does Marion need that is not in the table?

5. Which of the other planets in the table is closest in size to Earth?

6. About how many days does it take Mercury to make a revolution around the Sun?

PRACTICE

Solve the problem if possible. If there is extra information, tell what it is. If there is not enough information, tell what more you need to solve the problem. Use the table on page 116.

7. Which planet has a diameter of about 22 times that of Mars?

8. Which planet takes about 3 times as long as Venus to revolve around the Sun?

9. A large canyon on the planet Mars is about 10 times longer and 3 times deeper than the Grand Canyon. About how many miles long is the canyon on Mars?

10. The Russian's *Soyuz* 7 mission made 79 orbits and lasted 118 hours and 42 minutes. *Soyuz* 19 completed 96 orbits in a flight that lasted 143 hours and 31 minutes. How many more orbits did *Soyuz* 19 make than *Soyuz* 7?

11. The lunar month is about 29.5 days. It takes the Moon 27.3 Earth days to orbit Earth. How many Earth days will it take for the Moon to complete 8 orbits of Earth?

12. Maxwell Montes is a mountain found on Venus. It is 1.2 mi higher than Mount Everest. How tall is Maxwell Montes?

Strategies and Skills Review

Solve. Use estimation, mental math, a calculator, or paper and pencil.

13. Ricky has a set of space construction blocks. He has 4 packages with 18 space links in each, 5 packages with 12 connectors in each, and 10 transformer parts. How many pieces are in the set?

14. Juan is buying a book about the solar system for $3.95, a mobile for $4.50, and some rocket stickers for $2.50. Is $10 enough to cover the cost of the items? Why or why not?

15. A Martian day is about 24 hours and 37 minutes long. Mars has 2 moons, Phobos and Deimos. Deimos revolves around Mars in about 31 hours. Phobos goes around Mars in a little over 7 hours. How many full trips around Mars can Phobos make in the time it takes Deimos to make one?

16. *Write a problem* that contains more information than is needed to solve the problem. Solve your problem. Ask others to solve it.

Using Multiplication: Whole Numbers and Decimals   **117**

ACTIVITY
Areas of Rectangles

The **area** of a figure is the number of square units that it covers. Some of the units that area is measured in are **square centimeters (cm²)** and **square meters (m²).** You can find the area of a rectangle by either of these two ways:

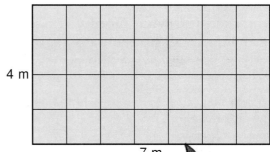

4 m

7 m

- counting the number of squares.

- multiplying the number of rows by the number of units in each row.

Area = length × width

$$A = \ell \times w$$
$$= 7 \times 4$$
$$= 28 \text{ m}^2$$

WORKING TOGETHER

Suppose you have 24 m of fencing to enclose a rectangular garden and you want the garden to have the greatest possible area.

You can solve the problem by drawing a model of the garden using graph paper.

1. Make drawings of all the possible gardens.

2. Label the sides of each drawing.

3. Find the area of each rectangle. Record your results in a table like this.

Length	Width	Area

4. Which type of rectangle has the greatest area?

SHARING IDEAS

5. Compare your results with those of other students. Did all of you get the same result for Problem 4?

6. **What if** you had 20 m of fencing? Which garden would have the greatest area? What would be its dimensions?

7. Do you think this result is always true?

$A = l \times w$

PRACTICE

Find the area.

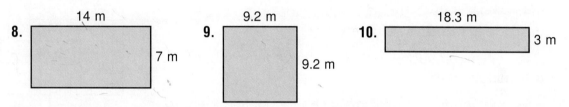

8. 14 m / 7 m

9. 9.2 m / 9.2 m

10. 18.3 m / 3 m

11. rectangle
$\ell = 13$ cm
$w = 5$ cm

12. rectangle
$\ell = 25$ m
$w = 5.3$ m

13. square
$s = 32$ mm

14. square
$s = 12.5$ m

Find the dimensions of the rectangle with the greatest area that can be made using the given perimeter.

15. 36 cm

16. 48 m

17. 56 m

18. 80 mm

19. 64 m

20. 40 mm

21. 7.2 m

22. 8.4 m

Critical Thinking

23. How does the area of a rectangle change when one side is doubled? Give some examples to justify your answer.

Mixed Applications

24. Joy has a garden with a perimeter of 8 m, and Nick's has a perimeter of 12 m. Each garden has the greatest possible area. How much greater is the area of Nick's garden?

25. How many square meters of carpeting are needed to cover a floor 5.4 m by 6.4 m? At $21 per square meter, what will be the cost of the carpeting?

26. How many square meters of wallpaper are needed to cover a wall that measures 12.5 m by 15.8 m?

27. **Write a problem** that involves finding the area of a rectangular fenced pen. Solve your problem. Ask others to solve it.

Activity

Volumes of Rectangular Prisms

The **volume**, or **capacity**, of a container is the number of cubic units the container will hold. A box with rectangular sides, top, and bottom is called a **rectangular prism**. You can measure the volume of a rectangular prism in cubic units, such as **cubic centimeters (cm³)**.

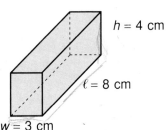

$h = 4$ cm

$\ell = 8$ cm

$w = 3$ cm

WORKING TOGETHER

1. Make a model of the rectangular prism without its top. Use the pattern at the right and centimeter graph paper. Estimate the prism's volume.

2. Use centimeter cubes to find out how many cubes will fit in the model.

3. How can you find the volume without counting the cubes?

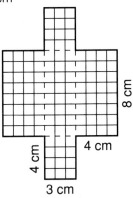

8 cm

4 cm

4 cm

3 cm

Here are two ways to think of the number of centimeter cubes that will fit inside the container.

Think: The bottom layer has 3 × 8, or 24 cubes. There are 4 layers.

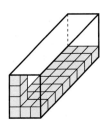

Total amount:
4 × 24 = 96 cubes

Volume = cubes per layer × height
    = (length × width) × height
    = 8 × 3 × 4 = 96 cm³

Think: Each slice has 3 × 4, or 12 cubes. There are 8 slices.

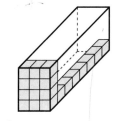

Total amount:
8 × 12 = 96 cubes

Volume = cubes per slice × length
    = (width × height) × length
    = 3 × 4 × 8 = 96 cm³

Both methods show that you can find the volume of a rectangular prism using this formula:

Volume = length × width × height   or $V = \ell \times w \times h$

SHARING IDEAS

4. ***What if*** you had to find the volume of a cube whose sides have a length of *s*? How would you rewrite the formula using an exponent?

5. If two rectangular prisms have different heights, can they have the same volume? Give examples to support your answer.

PRACTICE

Estimate the volume. Then compute it.

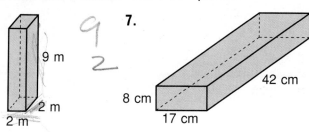

6.

9 m

2 m

2 m

7.

42 cm

8 cm

17 cm

8.

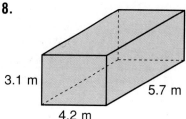

3.1 m

5.7 m

4.2 m

9. cube
s = 8 m

10. rectangular prism
ℓ = 16 m
w = 8 m
h = 4 m

11. rectangular prism
ℓ = 12.1 cm
w = 4.2 cm
h = 7.9 cm

Find the total volume.

12.

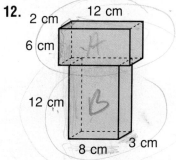

2 cm   12 cm

6 cm

12 cm

8 cm   3 cm

13.

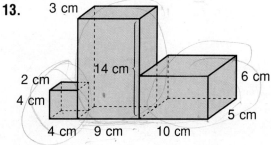

3 cm

14 cm

2 cm

4 cm

6 cm

5 cm

4 cm   9 cm   10 cm

Critical Thinking

14. Joshua found the volume of a cube that measures 4 m on each side by thinking $(4 m)^3 = 4^3 m^3$. Was he correct? Will this method always work? Give some examples.

15. If you double the length of the side of a cube, how will its volume change? Give some examples to justify your answer.

Mixed Applications

16. A rectangular poster measures 60 cm by 35 cm. How much border tape do you need to frame it?

17. A window box is 20 cm wide, 20 cm high, and 60 cm long. How much soil will it hold?

18. A fish tank shaped like a rectangular prism has a volume of 60,000 cm³. What are some possible dimensions for the tank?

19. How much carpeting do you need for a room that measures 7.5 m by 2.6 m? At $17.50 per square meter, how much will you spend?

DECISION MAKING

Problem Solving: Choosing a Pizza Vendor

SITUATION

The class is planning a pizza party after the play. Thirty people are expected to come.

PROBLEM

How many pizzas should the students buy? Where should they buy the pizzas?

DATA

The pizzas will be cut into 6 slices. An average of 2 slices per person will be needed.

GINO'S

- Cheese pizza: $9.25
- Extra toppings, cost per pizza:
- One topping $ .75
- Two toppings $1.25
- Three toppings $1.75
- Four toppings $2.25
- Five toppings $2.50
- Delivery per pizza: $.50

Take $1 off the price of each pizza over 8 pies; pay the regular price for the first 8 pies.

PAPA'S PIZZA

- Cheese pizza: $8.95
- Each extra topping per pizza: $.50
- Delivery: $3.00

For orders of 15 or more pizzas, take $1.50 off the price of each pie.

MARIA'S PIZZA

One cheese pizza $9.75

Free Delivery

Extra toppings, Cost per pizza

One topping
$1.00
Two toppings
$1.25
Three toppings
$1.50
Four toppings
$1.75
Five toppings
$2.00

Take $.50 off the price of each pizza you buy if you buy 10 or more.

USING THE DATA

1. How many slices of pizza does the class need?

2. How many pizzas should the class buy?

What is the cost if the class buys all cheese pizzas and picks the pizzas up?

3. Gino's Pizzeria   **4.** Papa's Pizza Parlor   **5.** Maria's Pizza

What is the cost of the cheese pizzas, if they have the pizzas delivered?

6. Gino's Pizzeria   **7.** Papa's Pizza Parlor   **8.** Maria's Pizza

What is the cost of the cheese pizzas, with 3 toppings, with no delivery?

9. Gino's Pizzeria   **10.** Papa's Pizza Parlor   **11.** Maria's Pizza

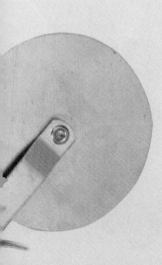

MAKING DECISIONS

12. From which place should the class buy the pizzas if they want cheese pies with no extra toppings and will pick them up?

13. From which place should the class buy the pizzas if they want delivery of cheese pies with no extra toppings?

14. From which place should the class buy the pizzas if they want cheese pies with 3 extra toppings and will pick them up?

15. **What if** the class wanted delivery of pizzas, half with 2 toppings and half with 4 toppings? At which store would they cost the least—Papa's Pizzeria or Maria's Pizza?

16. **Write a list** of other factors the class should consider.

17. Which pizza store would you choose? Why?

Math and Science

The heart is a hard-working organ that pumps blood through about 100,000 miles of blood vessels. The *heart rate* is the number of times the heart pumps, or beats, each minute. The average heart rate of adult men and women ranges from 60 to 80 beats each minute. These figures reflect the resting heart rate, when the person has not been exerting physical effort.

To find your heart rate put your fingers on your neck just below the place where your jaw curves up to your ear. Press gently. You will feel the beat. Count the beats for 10 seconds and then multiply by six to find the beats per minute.

Aerobic exercise strengthens your heart by making it pump harder. Doctors think people should get their heart rate to its optimum rate three times a week for 20 minutes.

You can figure your optimum heart rate this way:

- Subtract your age from 220.
- Divide the difference by 2.
- Multiply the difference by 3 and then divide by 4.

The optimum rate is between these two figures.

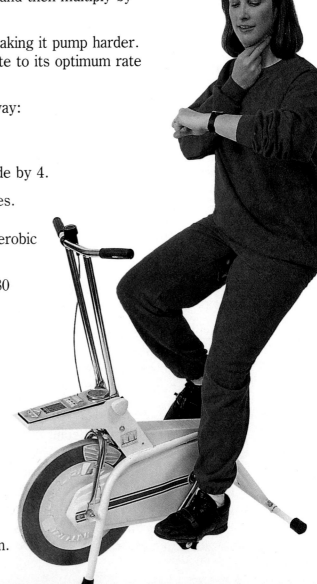

What if a 40-year-old wants to benefit from aerobic exercise? What is the optimum heart rate?

Think: Subtract age from 220: 220 − 40 = 180
Divide by 2:   180 ÷ 2 = 90
Multiply by 3:   180 × 3 = 540
Then divide by 4:   540 ÷ 4 = 135

The optimum heart rate for a 40-year-old is from 90 to 135 beats per minute.

ACTIVITIES

1. Find the optimum heart rate of two people in your family.

2. Research the health practices of your favorite athlete. Write a brief report about how he or she stays in top condition.

Computer Spreadsheet: Income and Expenses

The fundraising square dance is over. Wen, the chairperson, is using a computer spreadsheet to study the income and expenses. He wants to see how much money was earned and to help next year's chairperson plan ahead. Here are the results for this year.

Income

160 tickets @ $30	$4,800
Donations	800

Expenses

Refreshments	$1,290
Band	440
Gym rental	300
Caller	225
Invitations	280

You can use the computer spreadsheet program FUNDRAISING to explore how varying the income and expenses can change the amount of money earned.

AT THE COMPUTER

1. Using the information given, enter the expenses in the correct categories. Then enter the income in the correct categories.

2. The computer will calculate the total income, total expenses, and total money earned. Is the income greater than the expenses? How is the total money earned computed? How much money did the square dance earn this year?

3. Wen discovered that only $635 of the $800 pledged for donations was collected. What is the total money earned now?

4. Next year Wen hopes to sell 60 additional tickets (at the same price) and to collect $900 in donations. He estimates spending $8 on refreshments for each additional person. If he is correct, how much money will the dance earn next year?

5. Wen estimates that reducing the ticket price to $26 may result in as many as 120 more people attending next year than attended this year. However, a larger gym costing $400 would be needed, the cost of the invitations would rise to $320, and refreshments would cost $8 per additional person. Suppose the committee sets $5,000 as its goal for next year's earnings. What are some combinations of ticket sales and donations that can help reach this goal?

EXTRA PRACTICE

Mental Math: Multiplying, page 93

Multiply mentally.

1. 50 × 80
2. 11 × 5,000
3. 25 × 100
4. 13 × 3,000
5. 2 × 79 × 5
6. 4 × 7 × 25
7. 50 × 13 × 2
8. 25 × 35 × 4
9. 38 × 5
10. 28 × 25
11. 18 × 50
12. 60 × 25
13. 8 × 61
14. 6 × 57
15. 5 × 84
16. 4 × 58

Estimating Products, page 95

Estimate.

1. 8 × 62
2. 7 × 532
3. 6 × 7,146
4. 9 × 3,872
5. 33 × 685
6. 58 × 307
7. 42 × 6,875
8. 29 × 7,179

9. 729
    × 7

10. 3,819
     × 6

11. 417
     × 12

12. 5,874
     × 52

13. 6,125
     × 78

Multiplying, page 97

Multiply.

1. 628
    × 7

2. 706
    × 8

3. 187
    × 9

4. 925
    × 36

5. $4.03
    × 65

6. 702
    × 74

7. 248
    × 3

8. 519
    × 16

9. 855
    × 56

10. 627
     × 9

11. 406
     × 38

12. 932
     × 24

13. 6 × 357
14. 4 × $2.05
15. 5 × 892
16. 7 × 654
17. 89 × 715
18. 45 × 708
19. 73 × 236
20. 56 × $1.46

Multiplying Greater Numbers, page 99

Multiply.

1. 517
    × 273

2. 605
    × 178

3. 276
    × 390

4. 814
    × 356

5. $5.08
    × 624

6. 903
    × 714

7. 3,980
    × 245

8. 2,207
    × 468

9. 4,521
    × 217

10. $62.75
     × 308

11. 5,762
     × 492

12. 7,098
     × 721

EXTRA PRACTICE

Exponents, page 101

Write in exponent form.

1. $9 \times 9 \times 9 \times 9 \times 9 \times 9$ **2.** $5 \times 5 \times 5 \times 5$ **3.** $2 \times 2 \times 2 \times 2 \times 2 \times 2 \times 2$

Write the standard form.

4. 2^9 **5.** 10^{11} **6.** 1^5 **7.** 30^2 **8.** 9^3 **9.** 4^4

10. 5^1 **11.** 3^6 **12.** 6^4 **13.** 11^5 **14.** 8^7 **15.** 50^3

Use an exponent to write the power of 10.

16. 10,000,000   **17.** 10,000   **18.** 1,000,000,000,000

19. 100,000   **20.** 1,000,000   **21.** 10,000,000,000

Problem Solving Strategy: Solving a Multistep Problem, page 103

Plan how to solve the multi-step problem. Then solve.

1. There are 6 shelves of books with 22 books on each shelf in one section of a bookstore. In the morning the store sold 28 books. In the evening they sold 14 books. How many books were left in the section at closing?

2. For a bake sale, Mrs. Terzo buys four 5-lb bags of flour and 7 lb of butter. She needs 8 lb of sugar. How much do all the ingredients weigh?

Mental Math: Multiplying Decimals, page 107

Multiply mentally.

1. 10×3.25 **2.** 100×0.91 **3.** $1,000 \times 2.8$

4. $1,000 \times 0.07$ **5.** 100×0.084 **6.** $\$8.80 \times 100$

7. $10^3 \times 0.1$ **8.** 23.5×10^4 **9.** $10^2 \times 6.741$

10. $10^4 \times 0.67$ **11.** 0.002×10^2 **12.** 34.7×10^3

13. 1.485×10 **14.** $10^3 \times 0.018$ **15.** 60.38×10^2

16. $1,000 \times 0.05$ **17.** 2.004×10^1 **18.** $\$3.49 \times 100$

19. $2 \times 0.006 \times 50$ **20.** $5 \times 19.8 \times 20$ **21.** $25 \times 2.09 \times 40$

22. $4 \times 5.4 \times 25$ **23.** $2 \times \$7.89 \times 50$ **24.** $5 \times 3.871 \times 2$

EXTRA PRACTICE

Multiplying Decimals by Whole Numbers, page 109
Multiply.

1.	4.9	2.	$5.32	3.	$.61	4.	0.985	5.	0.0781
	× 4		× 8		× 9		× 5		× 3

6.	$4.55	7.	$.26	8.	0.079	9.	0.0293	10.	3.016
	× 35		× 67		× 86		× 29		× 41

Estimating Decimal Products, page 111
Estimate.

1.	7.86	2.	2.57	3.	5.03	4.	13.2	5.	31.87
	× 0.49		× 0.092		× 2.9		× 0.78		× 0.28

6.	4.856	7.	19.67	8.	827.8	9.	30.1	10.	12.321
	× 0.4		× 3.8		× 0.89		× 5.2		× 0.046

11. 2.17×8.01 **12.** 3.895×0.48 **13.** 7.96×0.081

Multiplying Decimals, page 113
Multiply.

1.	8.6	2.	$3.85	3.	5.7	4.	6.21	5.	9.5032
	× 2.3		× 3.4		× 0.238		× 2.176		× 9.3

6.	2.68	7.	9.734	8.	6.278	9.	5.1	10.	4.192
	× 3.27		× 0.19		× 4.9		× 3.583		× 5.23

11. $5.8 \times 0.4 \times 0.06$ **12.** $8.3 \times 0.9 \times 0.7$ **13.** $9.2 \times 0.03 \times 0.4$

More Multiplying Decimals, page 115
Multiply.

1.	0.0075	2.	0.008	3.	0.063	4.	0.019	5.	9.04
	× 0.35		× 0.007		× 4.2		× 0.15		× 2.05

6. 0.64×0.007 **7.** 3.008×0.95 **8.** 0.0026×0.0032

9. $0.06 \times 0.001 \times 0.5$ **10.** $5.2 \times 100 \times 0.0025$ **11.** $0.007 \times 3.2 \times 0.04$

Problem Solving: Finding Needed Information, page 117 . . . .

Solve if possible. If there is extra information, tell what it is.
If there is not enough information, tell what more you need to
solve the problem.

1. Ranger 7, an unpiloted spacecraft
sent 4,316 pictures back to Earth
from the Moon in 1964. Mariner 9
sent back 2,984 more pictures
than Ranger 7 from Mars in 1971.
How many pictures did Mariner 9
send?

2. The temperature of the surface of
Venus is 800 degrees.
Temperatures on Jupiter are
greater than on Venus. What is the
temperature of Jupiter?

Areas of Rectangles, page 119 . . . .

Find the area.

1.

18 m
18 m

2.
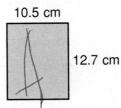
10.5 cm
12.7 cm

3.
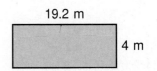
19.2 m
4 m

4. square
s = 45 mm

5. rectangle
ℓ = 12 cm
w = 8 cm

6. rectangle
ℓ = 18 m
w = 7.5 m

7. square
s = 11.5 m

Volumes of Rectangular Prisms, page 121 . . . .

Find the volume.

1.
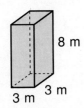
8 m
3 m
3 m

2.
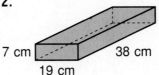
7 cm
38 cm
19 cm

3.
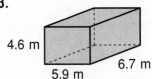
4.6 m
6.7 m
5.9 m

4. rectangular prism
ℓ = 18 m
w = 8 m
h = 5 m

5. cube
s = 5 m

6. rectangular prism
ℓ = 14.7 cm
w = 5.3 cm
h = 8.6 cm

Practice *PLUS*

KEY SKILL: Multiplying Greater Numbers (Use after page 99.)

Level A

Multiply.

1. 4,153 × 34	**2.** 6,871 × 52	**3.** 5,349 × 26	**4.** 8,162 × 91	**5.** 7,648 × 83
6. 234 × 520	**7.** 817 × 436	**8.** 5,863 × 730	**9.** $37.14 × 27	**10.** $25.92 × 360

11. There are 1,152 seats in each section of a stadium. If there are 25 sections, how many seats are in the stadium?

Level B

Multiply.

12. 526 × 314	**13.** 786 × 562	**14.** 2,345 × 625	**15.** 1,618 × 531	**16.** 2,347 × 610
17. 4,367 × 553	**18.** 3,971 × 460	**19.** 9,324 × 658	**20.** $76.85 × 349	**21.** $67.30 × 813

22. A theater can seat 1,275 people. Last year, the theater was filled 128 times. How many tickets were sold?

Level C

Multiply.

23. 4,512 × 304	**24.** 5,786 × 284	**25.** 5,203 × 931	**26.** 8,643 × 236	**27.** 2,046 × 875
28. 8,796 × 675	**29.** 9,078 × 206	**30.** 3,775 × 965	**31.** $87.19 × 705	**32.** $70.16 × 509

33. It costs $96.78 for a band uniform. There are 208 band members. How much will the uniforms cost?

PRACTICE *PLUS*

KEY SKILL: More Multiplying Decimals (Use after page 115.)

Level A

Multiply.

1. $\begin{array}{r} 0.25 \\ \times\, 0.07 \\ \hline \end{array}$	**2.** $\begin{array}{r} 0.053 \\ \times\ \ \ 0.2 \\ \hline \end{array}$	**3.** $\begin{array}{r} 42.19 \\ \times\ \ \ 0.05 \\ \hline \end{array}$	**4.** $\begin{array}{r} 0.0035 \\ \times\ \ \ \ \ 0.3 \\ \hline \end{array}$
5. $\begin{array}{r} 5.03 \\ \times\ \ 2.7 \\ \hline \end{array}$	**6.** $\begin{array}{r} 0.225 \\ \times\ \ \ 0.8 \\ \hline \end{array}$	**7.** $\begin{array}{r} \$25.80 \\ \times\ \ \ 0.15 \\ \hline \end{array}$	**8.** $\begin{array}{r} 0.029 \\ \times\ \ \ 0.8 \\ \hline \end{array}$

9. A truck averaged 58.5 miles per hour. How far did it go in 1.8 hours?

Level B

Multiply.

10. $\begin{array}{r} 3.07 \\ \times\, 2.06 \\ \hline \end{array}$	**11.** $\begin{array}{r} 0.815 \\ \times\ \ \ 0.6 \\ \hline \end{array}$	**12.** $\begin{array}{r} 0.0872 \\ \times\ \ \ \ 0.08 \\ \hline \end{array}$	**13.** $\begin{array}{r} 3.87 \\ \times\ \ 0.5 \\ \hline \end{array}$
14. $\begin{array}{r} 0.009 \\ \times\ \ \ 0.28 \\ \hline \end{array}$	**15.** $\begin{array}{r} 30.5 \\ \times\, 0.75 \\ \hline \end{array}$	**16.** $\begin{array}{r} 0.0008 \\ \times\ \ \ 0.015 \\ \hline \end{array}$	**17.** $\begin{array}{r} 0.5327 \\ \times\ \ \ \ 0.14 \\ \hline \end{array}$

18. A pen costs $1.50. The sales tax is 0.06 of the price. What is the tax on the pen?

Level C

Multiply.

19. $\begin{array}{r} 25.08 \\ \times\ \ \ 0.05 \\ \hline \end{array}$	**20.** $\begin{array}{r} 0.0875 \\ \times\ \ \ \ \ 0.6 \\ \hline \end{array}$	**21.** $\begin{array}{r} 0.094 \\ \times\, 0.015 \\ \hline \end{array}$	**22.** $\begin{array}{r} 0.38 \\ \times\, 0.0077 \\ \hline \end{array}$

23. $0.07 \times 0.07 \times 0.7$

24. $0.75 \times \$20 \times 0.06$

25. $0.008 \times 0.01 \times 0.7$

26. $0.08 \times 1.5 \times 3.7$

27. $8.5 \times 10 \times 0.5$

28. $0.25 \times \$5.60 \times 0.05$

29. A gallon of gas costs $1.05. How much will 18.8 gallons cost?

CHAPTER REVIEW/TEST

LANGUAGE AND MATHEMATICS

Complete the sentences. Use the words in the chart on the right.

1. The ■ of two numbers is found by multiplication.

2. The ■ is the number that tells how many times a number is used as a factor.

3. The ■ is the number of cubic units a container can hold.

4. The number of square units that a figure covers is called the ■.

> **VOCABULARY**
>
> exponent
> area
> product
> volume
> expanded form

CONCEPTS AND SKILLS

Estimate by using front-end estimation or rounding.

5. 8 x 52   **6.** 48 x 7,305   **7.** 6 x 4,325   **8.** 26 x 35.22

Multiply.

9. 32 x 47   **10.** 0.005 x 0.02   **11.** 757 x 1,348

12. 26 x 0.0427   **13.** 834 x 16   **14.** 23.62 x 1.7

Write in standard form.

15. 5^4 **16.** 4^6 **17.** 7^5 **18.** 10^6

Write in exponent form.

19. 5 x 5   **20.** 2 x 2 x 2 x 2   **21.** 7 x 7 x 7   **22.** 4 x 4 x 4 x 4 x 4

Find the area.

23. a rectangle: 41 m by 47.6 m   **24.** a square with sides = 16.4 cm

25. 7 cm — 7 cm

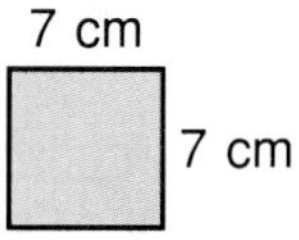

26. 6 m — 2 m

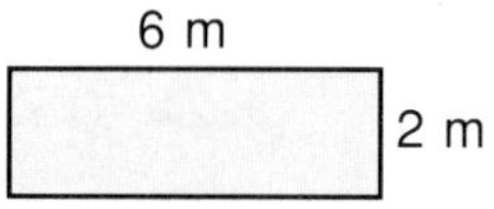

Find the volume.

27. $l = 7$ m, $w = 10$ m, $h = 4$ m

28. 4 m long, 3 m wide, 10 m high

29.

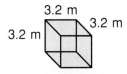

3.2 m

3.2 m

3.2 m

30.

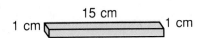

15 cm

1 cm   1 cm

Critical Thinking

31. If only the height of a rectangular prism is doubled, what would happen to the volume? Give an example.

Mixed Applications

32. Mr. Bell is paid $10 an hour. He is also paid $15 for each hour he works over 8 hours. On Monday he worked 11 hours. If he spends $63 of his day's earnings, how much will he have left?

33. A box is 25 cm long and 20 cm wide. Sue has 250 cubes that are 5 cm on a side. What information do you need to find out if all the cubes will fit in the box?

PERFORMANCE ASSESSMENT

Work together with your group to solve this problem.

Suppose you want to carpet the floor of your classroom that is *not* covered by desks and tables. Find the area (in square meters) of the floor space that you are going to carpet.

1. ***Think about:***
   - the total area of the classroom floor
   - the area of the floor covered by each desk and table

2. Write an explanation of the steps you used to solve this problem. Include a diagram to show how your group determined the floor area that is not covered by desks and tables.

CUMULATIVE REVIEW

Choose the letter of the correct answer.

1. Round 0.659 to the nearest tenth.
   a. 0.66
   b. 1.0
   c. 0.7
   d. not given

2. Estimate by rounding to the greatest place of the greatest number: 91,964 + 463,106 + 137
   a. 600,000
   b. 900,000
   c. 500,000
   d. not given

3. 0.6 × 9.1
   a. 546
   b. 54.6
   c. 5.46
   d. not given

4. In which year did D sell less than J?

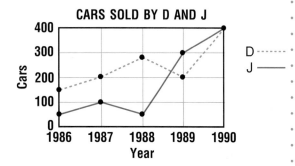

CARS SOLD BY D AND J

   a. 1986
   b. 1987
   c. 1988
   d. not given

5. Estimate by rounding:
   7,532 × 65
   a. 560,000
   b. 490,000
   c. 420,000
   d. not given

6. 13.2 × 0.39
   a. 51.48
   b. 514.80
   c. 0.05148
   d. not given

7. Find the volume of a box 6 m high, 2 m wide, and 7 m long.
   a. 15 m³
   b. 252 m³
   c. 84 m³
   d. not given

8. Which is greater than 0.72?
   a. 0.095
   b. 0.18
   c. 0.75
   d. not given

9. Find the perimeter of a square each side of which is 8.2 m.
   a. 16.4 m
   b. 32.8 m
   c. 67.24 m
   d. not given

10. Choose the standard form for 6².
    a. 12
    b. 600
    c. 6 × 6
    d. not given

11. 278 × 143
    a. 29,789
    b. 39,754
    c. 2,089
    d. not given

12. A total of 3,841 boys voted for X or Y. If 952 chose X, about how many chose Y?
    a. 2,000
    b. < 2,000
    c. < 3,000
    d. 4,000

13. Find the area of a rectangle 5.8 cm by 6 cm.
    a. 23.6 cm²
    b. 34.8 cm²
    c. 11.8 cm²
    d. not given

14. Admission to the fair is $1.50. Each ride is $.75. Ed went on 6 rides. How much did he spend?
    a. $8.25
    b. $6.00
    c. $4.50
    d. not given

RELATING PERIMETER AND AREA

Recall that perimeter is the distance around a figure and area is the amount of space covered by a figure.

Figure A and figure B both have the same perimeter.

1. What is the perimeter?

2. What is the area of figure A? figure B?

3. Do figures with the same perimeter always have the same area? Why or why not?

4. Draw two other figures with the same perimeter but different areas.

A

B

Look at figures C, D, E, and F below.

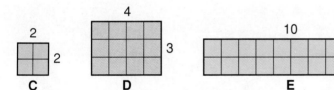

C   D   E

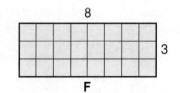

F

5. Find the perimeter and the area of each figure. Copy and complete the table.

Measure	Figure C	Figure D	Figure E	Figure F
perimeter (units)				
area (square units)				

6. Find two figures in which one has the lesser perimeter but the greater area.

7. Does a greater perimeter always mean a greater area?

8. Find the figure in which the number for the area is greater than the number for the perimeter.

Draw your own figure in which:

9. the number for the area is greater than the number for the perimeter.

10. the number for the perimeter is the same as the number for the area.

THE MAYA CALENDAR

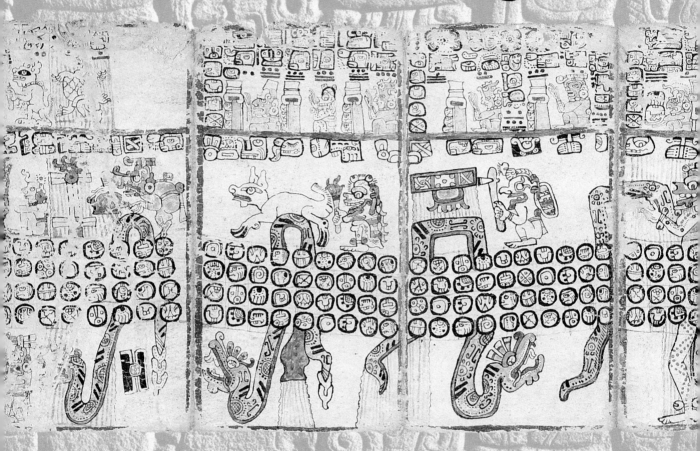

The Maya calendar was based on a number of different cycles. One cycle is the *vague year*, made up of eighteen 20-day periods plus 5 days, for a total of 365 days. It is called "vague" because the earth actually takes about $365\frac{1}{4}$ days to make one revolution around the sun. Over a long period of time, the extra $\frac{1}{4}$ day throws off the cycle. Eventually the seasons occur in a different part of the cycle.

Another cycle in the Maya calendar is called the *ritual almanac*. This cycle contained 260 days. For the most part it was used to keep track of rituals and ceremonies. With this cycle, a new year might begin in the summer months in some years and in the winter months in other years.

Every 18,980 days the cycles of the vague year and the ritual almanac coincided. At that time, great festivals and celebrations were held.

CHAPTER

4

DIVIDING WHOLE NUMBERS

MATH CONNECTIONS: Algebra • Time

1. How many cycles of the vague year and how many cycles of the ritual almanac does 18,980 days represent? Explain how you determined the answer.

2. Compare the Maya calendar with the 12-month solar calendar that we use now. How are they similar? How are they different?

Algebra: Relating Multiplication and Division

A. Caribou are being transported to a national park. There are 48 caribou, but they can only be transported 6 at a time. How many trips will it take to transport all of them?

You can divide to solve the problem.

Divide: $48 \div 6$

Because multiplication and division are **inverse operations**, you can use a related multiplication fact to help you divide.

Think: $n \times 6 = 48$
$8 \times 6 = 48,$ so $\mathbf{48 \div 6 = 8}$ ←quotient

                 dividend   divisor

It will take 8 trips to transport all the caribou.

1. What is $48 \div 8$? How do you know?

2. Use a related multiplication fact to find $63 \div 7$.

B. One and zero have special properties in division. Related sentences help to show these properties.

A number divided by 1 is that number. $8 \div 1 = 8$ **since** $8 \times 1 = 8$

A number, other than zero, divided by itself is 1. $8 \div 8 = 1$ **since** $1 \times 8 = 8$

Zero divided by any number other than zero is zero. $0 \div 8 = 0$ **since** $0 \times 8 = 0$

3. Write the related multiplication sentence for $8 \div 0$. Can a number be divided by zero? Why or why not?

4. Write the related multiplication sentence for $0 \div 0$. Is it possible to divide $0 \div 0$? Why or why not?

TRY OUT   Solve for *n*.

5. $54 \div 9 = n$ **6.** $39 \div 3 = n$ **7.** $120 \div 1 = n$ **8.** $0 \div 298 = n$

PRACTICE

Solve for n.

9. $28 \div 4 = n$ **10.** $21 \div 3 = n$ **11.** $56 \div 7 = n$ **12.** $81 \div 9 = n$

13. $18 \div 1 = n$ **14.** $42 \div 42 = n$ **15.** $0 \div 456 = n$ **16.** $n \div 6 = 0$

17. $n \div 6 = 4$ **18.** $64 \div n = 8$ **19.** $27 \div n = 3$ **20.** $n \div 25 = 5$

Find the answer.

21. The divisor is 3. The dividend is 9. Find the quotient.

22. The divisor is 4. The quotient is 8. Find the dividend.

23. Which of these division problems cannot be solved?
    a. $5 \div 0$ **b.** $0 \div 5$ **c.** $0 \div 0$ **d.** $0 \div 1$ **e.** $5 \div 5$

Critical Thinking

24. Solve for n. How did you find the answer?

    $16 \div 4 = n$ and $m \div n = 16$

Mixed Applications

Solve. You may need to use the
Databank on page 550.

25. Kwan walks 24 dogs after school.
He walks 6 dogs at a time. How
many walks does he take?

26. A chimpanzee eats 3 bunches of
bananas. Each bunch has 9
bananas. How many bananas
does the chimp eat?

27. Which animal can run faster, a
spider or a giant tortoise? a zebra
or a greyhound?

28. Which animal can run twice as
fast as a rabbit?

29. The Flying A Stables has 49
horses. There are 7 exercise
riders who ride the same number
of horses. How many horses does
each rider exercise?

Mental Math: Division Patterns

Each week, 33,000 bottles of soda are equally distributed among 100 stores, while 24,000 cans of soda are distributed among 600 vending machines. How many bottles are distributed to each store? How many cans are distributed to each machine?

You can use patterns to help you divide mentally.

Divide by 10, 100, 1,000	Divide by multiples of 10, 100, 1,000
33,000 ÷ 1 = 33,000	24,000 ÷ 6 = 4,000
33,000 ÷ 10 = 3,300	24,000 ÷ 60 = 400
33,000 ÷ 100 = 330	24,000 ÷ 600 = 40
33,000 ÷ 1,000 = 33	24,000 ÷ 6,000 = 4

Each store receives 330 bottles. Each machine receives 40 cans.

1. Compare the number of zeros in each quotient to the number of zeros in the dividend and the divisor. What is the pattern?

2. Does the pattern work for 30,000 ÷ 60? Why or why not?

3. Use the pattern to find the following quotients: 5,600 ÷ 80 and 720,000 ÷ 900.

TRY OUT Write the letter of the correct answer. Find the quotient mentally.

4. 50,000 ÷ 10   a. 5,000   b. 500   c. 50   d. 5

5. 240,000 ÷ 100   a. 240   b. 2,400   c. 24,000   d. 240,000

6. 4,000 ÷ 5   a. 80   b. 800   c. 8,000   d. 8,800

7. 60,000 ÷ 2,000   a. 30,000   b. 3,000   c. 300   d. 30

PRACTICE

Find the quotient mentally.

8. 9,000 ÷ 10 **9.** 80,000 ÷ 100 **10.** 50,000 ÷ 1,000 **11.** 7,000 ÷ 10

12. 2,700 ÷ 30 **13.** 45,000 ÷ 900 **14.** 63,000 ÷ 7,000 **15.** 2,500 ÷ 50

16. 420 ÷ 70 **17.** 21,000 ÷ 30 **18.** 3,000 ÷ 500 **19.** 4,800 ÷ 80

20. 1,000 ÷ 1,000 **21.** 30,000 ÷ 600 **22.** 54,000 ÷ 900 **23.** 64,000 ÷ 80

24. 720,000 ÷ 90 **25.** 150,000 ÷ 500 **26.** 49,000 ÷ 7,000 **27.** 36,000 ÷ 40

28. 7 thousand ÷ ten **29.** 28 thousand ÷ 7 thousand

30. five thousand ÷ two hundred **31.** thirty-six thousand ÷ ninety

Find the missing number.

32. 30,000 ÷ 20 = ■ **33.** 50,000 ÷ ■ = 50 **34.** ■ ÷ 100 = 800

35. 2,400 ÷ ■ = 8 **36.** ■ ÷ 700 = 90 **37.** ■ ÷ 400 = 300

38. 25,000 ÷ ■ = 5 **39.** 18,000 ÷ ■ = 300 **40.** ■ ÷ 200 = 1,000

Are the quotients the same? Write *yes* or *no*.

41. 7,000 ÷ 1,000 **42.** 40,000 ÷ 800 **43.** 32,000 ÷ 40 **44.** 2,400 ÷ 8
    700 ÷ 100   400 ÷ 80   3,200 ÷ 4   24,000 ÷ 80

Mixed Applications

45. There were 4 showings of the movie *Tarantula* on Saturday. The number of people at each showing was 177, 163, 379, and 528. Estimate the total number of people that saw it on Saturday.

46. There are 10 theaters in a chain of movie theaters. If about 3,500 people go to each theater in a week, about how many people go to the movies in that theater chain in one week?

47. A theater has 1,000 seats. Each section of the theater has 100 seats. How many sections does the theater have?

48. *Write a problem* involving division that can be solved mentally. Solve your problem. Then ask others to solve it.

Mixed Review

Find the answer. Which method did you use?

49. 385 + 999 **50.** 1,000 − 679 **51.** 679 × 3,278

52. 125 − 99 **53.** 1.2678 + 45.375 **54.** 4 × $25

MENTAL MATH
CALCULATOR
PAPER/PENCIL

Estimating Quotients

A. In 1986 Dick Rutan and Jeana Yeager circled the Earth in a small aircraft called *Voyager.* They flew 25,012 mi in 9 days without having to land for refueling. About how many miles did they travel per day?

You can estimate the quotient by using compatible numbers.

Estimate: 25,012 ÷ 9

Change the dividend so that you can use a basic fact to estimate the quotient.

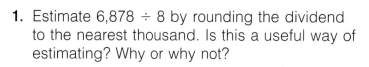

Think: 27,000 ÷ 9 = 3,000

Voyager flew about 3,000 miles per day.

1. Estimate 6,878 ÷ 8 by rounding the dividend to the nearest thousand. Is this a useful way of estimating? Why or why not?

B. To estimate with a 2-digit divisor, round the divisor to the nearest ten, then use compatible numbers.

Estimate: 24,325 ÷ 45

Think: 25,000 ÷ 50 = 500

2. Estimate 37,609 ÷ 48. Which compatible numbers did you use? Is there more than one possible estimate? Why?

TRY OUT Write the letter of the best estimate.

3. 193 ÷ 5   **a.** 4   **b.** 40   **c.** 400   **d.** 30

4. 9,176 ÷ 34   **a.** 200   **b.** 30   **c.** 300   **d.** 3,000

PRACTICE

Estimate the quotient.

5. $317 \div 6$	**6.** $623 \div 7$	**7.** $3,782 \div 2$	**8.** $5,432 \div 8$
9. $65,419 \div 8$	**10.** $23,927 \div 7$	**11.** $449,883 \div 5$	**12.** $191,035 \div 6$
13. $3,872 \div 91$	**14.** $6,017 \div 28$	**15.** $6,243 \div 25$	**16.** $3,582 \div 77$
17. $24,317 \div 52$	**18.** $37,821 \div 88$	**19.** $45,302 \div 59$	**20.** $18,119 \div 24$
21. $47,427 \div 9$	**22.** $581 \div 32$	**23.** $40,172 \div 72$	**24.** $623,717 \div 8$
25. $301,724 \div 47$	**26.** $61,345 \div 91$	**27.** $55,206 \div 86$	**28.** $3,312 \div 84$
29. $78,382 \div 84$	**30.** $124,932 \div 4$	**31.** $737,411 \div 77$	**32.** $541,189 \div 73$
33. $742 \div 78$	**34.** $16,007 \div 9$	**35.** $39,258 \div 84$	**36.** $623,326 \div 67$

Mixed Applications

37. Magellan's ship the *Victoria* returned to Spain after sailing around the world for 155 weeks. About how many years did the voyage take?

38. The passenger ship *Queen Mary* crossed the Atlantic in 4 days in 1938. It sailed about 845 mi per day. About how many miles is it across the Atlantic?

39. It took the Pilgrims 66 days to cross the Atlantic Ocean on the *Mayflower*. About how many weeks is that?

40. **Write a problem** involving division about a long journey you would like to take. Solve your problem. Ask others to solve it by using estimation.

MENTAL MATH

An easy way to divide by 5 mentally is to divide by 10 and double the quotient.

Recall: Multiplying by 5 can be done by first multiplying by 10 and then dividing by 2.

Example: $8,000 \div 5 = (8,000 \div 10) \times 2$
$= 800 \times 2 = 1,600$

Divide mentally.

1. $420 \div 5$	**2.** $1,300 \div 5$	**3.** $26,000 \div 5$
4. $6,900 \div 5$	**5.** $340 \div 5$	**6.** $52,000 \div 5$

The Granger Collection

Dividing by One-Digit Numbers

Amanda Quill, a famous author of children's books, donated 527 books to the Alcott School. The books were divided equally among 6 classes. How many books did each class get? Were any books left over?

Divide: 527 ÷ 6

Step 1

Decide where to place the first digit of the quotient.

$$6\overline{)527}$$

Think:
6 > 5   Not enough hundreds
6 < 52 There are enough tens to divide.

Step 2

Divide the tens.

$$\begin{array}{r} 8 \\ 6\overline{)527} \\ -48 \\ \hline 4 \end{array}$$

Think: $6\overline{)52}^{\,8}$
Multiply.   8 × 6 = 48
Subtract.   52 − 48 = 4
Compare.   4 < 6

Step 3

Bring down the ones.
Divide the ones.
Write the remainder.

$$\begin{array}{r} 87 \text{ R5} \\ 6\overline{)527} \\ 48\!\downarrow \\ \hline 47 \\ 42 \\ \hline 5 \end{array}$$

Think: $6\overline{)47}^{\,7}$
Multiply.   7 × 6 = 42
Subtract.   47 − 42 = 5
Compare.   5 < 6

Check:
Multiply, then add.

$$\begin{array}{r} 87 \\ \times\ 6 \\ \hline 522 \\ +\ \ 5 \\ \hline 527 \end{array}$$

Each class got 87 books, with 5 left over.

1. Divide 408 by 4. What did you do to the quotient to continue dividing?

2. **What if** you were dividing $54.63 by 9? How would you find the quotient?

TRY OUT   Divide.

3. $4\overline{)6,111}$ 4. $3\overline{)18,272}$ 5. $7\overline{)\$3.64}$ 6. $5\overline{)\$213.75}$

PRACTICE

Divide.

7. 5)937 **8.** 7)917 **9.** 3)138 **10.** 4)373 **11.** 6)543

12. 2)7,150 **13.** 4)6,037 **14.** 8)2,306 **15.** 4)52,023 **16.** 7)39,087

17. 3)$2.19 **18.** 9)$3.06 **19.** 6)$8.22 **20.** 5)$9.30 **21.** 8)$9.92

22. 8)$12.56 **23.** 7)$28.14 **24.** 5)$88.95 **25.** 3)$80.76 **26.** 4)$618.32

27. 456 ÷ 7 **28.** 8,021 ÷ 9 **29.** $3.57 ÷ 7 **30.** 16,438 ÷ 8

31. $31.02 ÷ 6 **32.** 832 ÷ 3 **33.** 5,100 ÷ 4 **34.** $414.60 ÷ 6

35. 3,494 divided by 9 **36.** $16,072 divided by 4

Mixed Applications

Solve. Which method did you use?

ESTIMATION
MENTAL MATH
CALCULATOR
PAPER/PENCIL

37. At the beginning of the school year, the teacher passed out 6 textbooks to each student in the class. If she passed out 162 books, about how many students are there in the class?

38. The book *Where the Red Fern Grows* has 249 pages. Juanita read it in 3 weeks. If she read the same number of pages each week, how many pages was that?

39. A school bought 24 copies of *Robinson Crusoe* at $2.95 per copy. How much was the bill?

MENTAL MATH

When dividing by a 1-digit number, you can use **short division** and do some of the steps mentally.

Step 1
5
5)2,6¹7 3

Think: 26 ÷ 5 = 5 R1

Step 2
5 3
5)2,6¹7²3

Think: 17 ÷ 5 = 3 R2

Step 3
5 3 4 R3
5)2,6¹7²3

Think: 23 ÷ 5 = 4 R3

Use short division to divide.

1. 7)468 **2.** 8)7,137 **3.** 28,104 ÷ 9 **4.** $3,178.14 ÷ 6

Dividing by Two-Digit Numbers

Volunteers are putting campaign brochures into packages. There are 998 brochures. If each package holds 24 brochures, how many packages can be filled? How many brochures will be left over?

Divide: $998 \div 24$

Step 1

Decide where to place the first digit of the quotient.

$$24)\overline{998} \quad 24 > 9$$
$$24 < 99$$

Think: Not enough hundreds
Divide the tens.

Step 2

Divide the tens. Estimate.

$$\begin{array}{r} 4 \\ 24)\overline{998} \\ 96 \\ \hline 3 \end{array}$$

Think: $2)\overline{9}$ → 4
Try 4.
Multiply. $4 \times 24 = 96$
Compare. $96 < 99$ Use 4
Subtract. $99 - 96 = 3$

Step 3

Divide the ones. Estimate.

$$\begin{array}{r} 41 \text{ R}14 \\ 24)\overline{998} \\ 96\downarrow \\ \hline 38 \\ 24 \\ \hline 14 \end{array}$$

Think: $2)\overline{3}$ → 1
Try 1.
Multiply. $1 \times 24 = 24$
Compare. $24 < 38$ Use 1
Subtract. $38 - 24 = 14$

Forty-one packages will be filled, with 14 brochures left over.

1. How many brochures would be needed to fill 42 packages? How do you know?

TRY OUT Write the letter of the correct answer.

2. $89)\overline{678}$ **a.** 706 R48   **b.** 75 R11   **c.** 7 R55   **d.** 76 R21

3. $22)\overline{\$814}$ **a.** \$37   **b.** \$3.70   **c.** \$3.07   **d.** \$33.70

PRACTICE

Divide.

4. 64)455 **5.** 43)358 **6.** 81)603 **7.** 32)160 **8.** 48)450

9. 21)549 **10.** 57)812 **11.** 92)936 **12.** 74)888 **13.** 35)983

14. 33)743 **15.** 45)937 **16.** 16)$9.76 **17.** 53)270 **18.** 24)742

19. 12)899 **20.** 74)$518 **21.** 60)800 **22.** 35)$1.75 **23.** 22)117

24. $644 ÷ $23 **25.** 839 ÷ 77 **26.** 413 ÷ 43 **27.** 918 ÷ 51 **28.** $952 ÷ 68

29. 300 divided by 18 **30.** 816 divided by 15 **31.** $315 divided by $45

Critical Thinking

If you divide a 3-digit number by a 2-digit number:

32. What is the greatest number of digits the quotient can have? What is the least number of digits?

33. What is the greatest number of digits the remainder can have? What is the greatest 2-digit remainder?

Mixed Applications

Solve. You may need to use the Databank on page 550.

34. How many more people cast a vote for President of the United States in 1984 than in 1988?

35. Five packages, each with 150 campaign buttons, are to be stored in boxes. Each box can hold 65 buttons. How many boxes are needed?

36. A total of $682.50 was donated to a candidate's campaign by 65 people. What was the average donation per person?

37. The 3 candidates running for treasurer received a total of 86,541 votes. Brown got 28,546 votes, and Smith got 29,872 votes. How many votes did the third candidate, Jones, get? Who won?

Dividing: Changing Estimates

A. The class is making up Paul Bunyan tall-tale problems. Sue makes up this one: "Even as a baby, Paul Bunyan had a huge appetite. It took 192 cows to supply him with milk each day, and he was fed 24 times a day. How many cows were needed for each feeding?"

Divide: 192 ÷ 24

Step 1

Decide where to place the first digit of the quotient.

$$24\overline{)192}$$

Think: 24 > 1   Not enough hundreds
24 > 19   Not enough tens
24 < 192 Divide the ones.

Step 2

Estimate. Change the estimate if necessary. Divide the ones.

$$24\overline{)192} \\ \underline{192} \\ 0$$

8

Think: $2\overline{)19}$ 9

Try 9.
Multiply. 9 × 24 = 216
Compare. 216 > 192 Too much

Try 8
Multiply. 8 × 24 = 192
Compare. 192 = 192 Use 8
Subtract. 192 − 192 = 0

Paul Bunyan needed 8 cows for each feeding.

1. Why did you need to adjust the estimate?

B. Sometimes there are 2 digits in a quotient.

Denzell divided 816 by 27.

2. How can you tell that his answer is wrong without doing the problem?

3. What mistake did he make?

4. What is the correct answer?

$$27\overline{)816} \\ \underline{54} \\ 276 \\ \underline{243} \\ 33$$

29 R33

TRY OUT   Divide.

5. $73\overline{)359}$ **6.** $17\overline{)\$6.29}$ **7.** 218 ÷ 23   **8.** 619 ÷ 39

PRACTICE

Divide.

9. 77)478   6.2
10. 43)675   15.4
11. 32)924   28.8
12. 34)903   26.5
13. 68)488   7.17

14. 47)876   18.4
15. 24)619   25.7
16. 47)912   19.4
17. 26)762   29.3
18. 15)702   46.8

19. 45)925   20.5
20. 76)648   8.5
21. 57)409   7.17
22. 23)710   30.8
23. 75)645   8.6

24. 613 ÷ 67   25. 513 ÷ 53   26. 600 ÷ 75   27. $1.56 ÷ 39   28. $6.38 ÷ 22

29. $8.64 divided by 54   30. 624 divided by 34   31. 372 divided by 59

Do only those problems that have a quotient of less than 20.

32. 26)641   33. 46)829   34. 912 ÷ 37   35. 49)206   36. 315 ÷ 63

37. 575 divided by 78   38. 657 divided by 88   39. 657 divided by 18

Critical Thinking

40. The dividend is 812. The quotient is 40. The remainder is 12. What is the divisor?

41. Estimate 1,125 ÷ 35. First round the divisor up and then round it down. Which estimate is closer to the exact answer?

Mixed Applications

42. Paul Bunyan's bookkeeper, Johnny Inkslinger, had a fountain pen that held 12 gal of red ink. The pen had to be refilled every 2 days. How many days did it take to use 972 gal of ink?

43. One winter it got so cold that words froze as soon as they were spoken. They had to be stored behind the stove. If each word was 28 in. thick, how many words were there in a pile 784 in. tall?

44. When Paul Bunyan was born, he was 12 ft tall. On his first birthday he was 432 ft tall. How much did he grow during his first year?

45. *Write a problem* involving a tall tale. Solve it. Ask others to solve the problem.

Mixed Review

Find the answer. Which method did you use?

MENTAL MATH
CALCULATOR
PAPER/PENCIL

46. 81,000 ÷ 900   47. 629 × 389   48. 6.0172 − 3.8767

49. 125 + 375   50. 3⁴   51. $5.25 − $3.89

EXTRA PRACTICE, page 169; PRACTICE *PLUS*, page 173

PROBLEM SOLVING

Strategy: Making a Table

At the House and Garden Center, 10 tulip bulbs cost $1.99 and 10 daffodil bulbs cost $2.99. Martina wants to plant an equal number of tulip bulbs and daffodil bulbs. How many of each kind of bulb can she buy for $25?

You can make a table to help you solve this problem.

1. Copy and complete the table.

	Number of Bulbs					
	10	20	30	40	50	60
Cost of Tulip Bulbs	$1.99	$3.98				
Cost of Daffodil Bulbs	$2.99	$5.98				
Total of Both Kinds of Bulbs	$4.98					

2. How many of each kind of bulb can Martina buy? How much will the bulbs cost?

3. **What if** Martina wants to plant 50 daffodils and 40 tulips? How much would the bulbs cost?

4. Can Martina buy 30 daffodil bulbs and 40 tulip bulbs if she has $15 to spend? How do you know?

PRACTICE

Make a table to solve the problem.

5. Mr. Nabonsky estimates that 10 boxwood bushes will grow into a hedge about 3.3 m long. About how many boxwood bushes should Mr. Nabonsky buy if he wants a hedge that is 25 m long?

6. Boris mixes 2 cans of white paint with 1 can of brown paint to get beige. White paint costs $10.99 a can, and brown paint costs $8.99 a can. How much does it cost to mix 12 cans of beige paint?

7. Craig wants to build a wall with alternating rows of red and white bricks. The red bricks are 18 cm long, and the white bricks are 24 cm long. The length of the wall can measure between 100 and 150 cm. At what length will the rows of red and white bricks be the same?

8. It takes 2 bags of fertilizer and 3 bags of grass seed to cover about 1,200 m² of lawn. How many bags o each would you need to buy for a lawn that is about 4,800 m² in area?

Strategies and Skills Review

Solve the problem if possible. If there is extra information, tell what it is. If there is not enough information, tell what more you need to solve the problem.

9. Picket fence is sold in 3.5-m sections. Each section costs $9.99. How much will 12 sections cost?

10. Martina wants to buy a broom that costs $6.66, a ladder for $24.98, and a lawn mower for $47.87. Is $90 enough to purchase these items? Did you overestimate or underestimate to solve the problem? Why?

11. Boris works on the lawn 0.7 of an hour for every 0.6 of an hour that Martina works. When Boris has worked 3.5 hours, how many hours will Martina have worked?

12. Hannah bought 5 bottles of plant food and a bag of soil for 30 pots of plants. The soil cost $10.25, and the plant food was $2.10 for each bottle. How much in all did she spend?

13. Anna wants to plant shoots that grew from some leaves she rooted. She has 24 shoots to plant and 3 planter boxes. Does Anna have enough boxes?

14. **Write a problem** that can be solved by making a table. Solve your problem. Ask others to solve it.

COUNT OFF

Algebra: Investigating Patterns

A. Five friends play a counting game. They stand in a circle. They choose a target number and count off. Each time someone says the target number, that person is dropped from the circle. The next person starts over with "1."

For example, if 4 is the target number, the game goes like this:

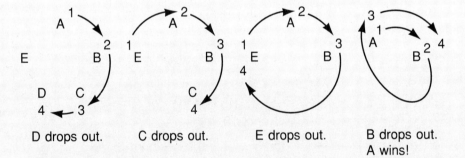

D drops out.   C drops out.   E drops out.   B drops out.
                                                          A wins!

Suppose the five friends play several games. The same friend always begins counting and they always count in the same order. They take turns picking a target number.

1. What target numbers between 2 and 10 should the first player pick in order to win?

You can solve this problem by making an organized table:

Target Number	2	3	4	5	6	7	8	9	10
Winner									

2. What target numbers should the other players choose in order to win? Which player cannot win with a target number between 2 and 10? Which player has the best chance of winning if a number between 2 and 10 is drawn, without looking, from numbered slips in a hat?

B. Now suppose that the number of players changes. Do you think the results will be the same?

3. Suppose 6 players choose a target number of 7. Which position is the winner?

4. Copy and complete this table showing all of the winners for 6 players, using target numbers between 2 and 10.

Number of Players	Target Number								
	2	3	4	5	6	7	8	9	10

5. Add a line to your table, showing the results for 7 players and target numbers between 2 and 10.

6. Now suppose that 25 students in a class are going to play Count Off with their teacher. The last student in the circle will win a prize. If they choose a target number of 2, which position will win? Guess and then check your answer.

Dividing Greater Numbers

A. The world record for domino toppling was set in 1984 by Klaus Friedrich. It took about 13 minutes for 281,581 dominoes to fall. How many dominoes fell per minute?

Jean and William each use a calculator to find 281,581 ÷ 13.

Jean's answer: | *21660.076* |

William's answer: | *2167.7692* |

1. Whose answer is not reasonable? Why?

B. You can use a calculator to find remainders.

The sixth-grade class is using 1,000 wooden cubes. They will put away the cubes, 72 to a box. How many boxes will be filled completely? How many cubes will be left?

First divide: 1000  72 (=) | *13.888888* |

Think: 13 boxes are full. The *0.888888* shows that there will be cubes left. The 13 boxes have 13 × 72 cubes. There are 936 cubes. Subtract 936 from 1,000, to find out how many cubes will be left.

13 (×) 72 (=)		*936.*	—Product of 13 and 72
(M+)		*M 936.*	—Stores 936 in memory
1000 (−) (MR) (=)		*M 64.*	—Calls 936 from memory and subtracts it from 1,000

There will be 64 cubes left.

2. Dominoes come in boxes of 28. How many boxes would you need for 281,581 dominoes? How many dominoes would go into the last box?

TRY OUT Divide. Write the quotient and remainder.

3. 13,642 ÷ 16   **4.** 318,600 ÷ 525   **5.** 42,398 ÷ 46

PRACTICE

Estimate to find the number of digits in the whole-number part of the quotient. Check your answer with a calculator.

6. 8,124 ÷ 45   **7.** 25,637 ÷ 68   **8.** 762,974 ÷ 847   **9.** 789,624 ÷ 389

Write the quotient with a remainder.

10. 1,409 ÷ 36   **11.** 2,586 ÷ 28   **12.** 43,876 ÷ 85   **13.** 12,852 ÷ 75

14. $255,600 ÷ 60   **15.** 145,623 ÷ 93   **16.** 2,077 ÷ 114   **17.** 6,895 ÷ 621

18. 72,831 ÷ 125   **19.** $25,025 ÷ 325 **20.** 162,113 ÷ 649   **21.** 232,105 ÷ 987

Critical Thinking

22. ***What if*** the division key on your calculator is broken? How could you use the broken calculator to find 9,406 ÷ 829?

Mixed Applications

Solve. Which method did you use?

ESTIMATION
MENTAL MATH
CALCULATOR
PAPER/PENCIL

23. The world tap-dancing record is held by Roy Castle. He did about 1 million taps in 23 hours and 44 minutes. About how many taps was that per hour?

24. A 15-year-old boy used 15,714 cards to build a 13-ft house of cards. How many decks of 52 cards did he need?

25. Maxwell Black's entire body was covered by about 100,000 bees. The bees weighed about 27 lb. About how many bees per pound was that?

26. The tallest column of coins ever stacked on the edge of a coin was 205 quarters. What was the value of the 205 quarters?

╴LOGICAL REASONING╴

You can use patterns to divide. The following show multiples of 1,001.

354 × 1,001 = 354,354   565 × 1,001 = 565,565

1. What pattern do you notice?

2. How could you use this pattern to divide these numbers?
   a. 623,623 ÷ 1,001   **b.** 204,204 ÷ 1,001

3. Would this pattern work for 623,457 ÷ 1,001? Tell why or why not.

Multiplication and Division Equations

Mr. Abeyto's class has made 27 posters for a Save-the-Dolphins fundraiser. An equal number of posters will be placed in the elementary, junior high, and high school. How many posters will be in each school?

You can solve this problem by using a multiplication or division equation. If n represents the number of posters in each school, then

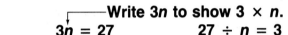
Write 3n to show 3 × n.

$$3n = 27 \qquad\qquad 27 \div n = 3$$

Think: $3 \times 9 = 27$ *Think:* $27 \div 9 = 3$

$$n = 9 \qquad\qquad\qquad n = 9$$

WORKING TOGETHER

Sometimes, it may not be possible to solve equations mentally.

1. ***What if*** the total number of posters is 45? Write a multiplication equation to illustrate this problem.

Use a balance scale, centimeter cubes, and paper bags to solve the equation.

Step 1 Put three empty bags and 45 cubes in the right pan of the balance. Write n on three bags and place them in the left pan.

Step 2 Place equal number of cubes in each bag on the left until the scale is balanced.

2. Without looking in the bag, how can you find the value of n? What is the value of n? How many posters will be placed in each school?

3. Check your answer by looking in the bag and by using the original equation.

4. What operation did you use to solve the equation? How does this operation relate to the one in the original equation? Write a related equation using this operation.

5. What operation would you use to solve $n \div 17 = 68$? Why? Write a related equation and solve it. Check your answer.

6. Solve and check. Do as many as you can mentally.

    a. $12n = 156$ **b.** $n \div 17 = 5$

Explain why you chose each related equation.

PRACTICE

Solve and check.

7. $n \times 7 = 63$ **8.** $6n = 48$ **9.** $n \times 4 = 36$ **10.** $117 = 13 \times n$

11. $7n = 126$ **12.** $84 = 28n$ **13.** $35 \times n = 105$ **14.** $24n = 168$

15. $17n = 136$ **16.** $n \times 90 = 540$ **17.** $n \div 4 = 52$ **18.** $25 = n \div 6$

19. $n \div 5 = 9$ **20.** $n \div 80 = 40$ **21.** $n \div 8 = 7$ **22.** $72 \div n = 8$

23. $64 \div n = 8$ **24.** $42 \div n = 7$ **25.** $144 \div n = 12$ **26.** $121 \div n = 11$

Write the equation and find the number.

27. The product of a number and 12 is 216.

28. If a number is divided by 13, the quotient is 11.

29. The quotient of a number divided by 16 is 22.

30. The product of a number and 32 is 128.

Critical Thinking

31. Explain how you would solve for n in the following:

    a. $a \times n = b$ **b.** $x \div n = y$

Mixed Applications

32. Which is the largest dolphin shown on the graph? the smallest?

33. The killer whale is three times as large as the white-sided dolphin. Write and solve an equation for the length of the white-sided dolphin.

34. Bottle-nosed dolphins live in family groups of about a dozen. If a school of dolphins has 100 members, about how many families are in a school?

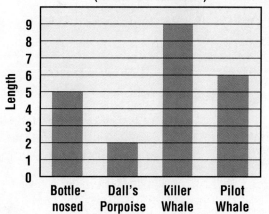

Types of Dolphins and Their Lengths (to the nearest meter)

PROBLEM SOLVING

Strategy: Using Algebraic Equations

A. Linda Chung works at her grandparents' hotel, the Kyongju (kyawng-joo) Hotel named after the Kyongju Valley in Korea. The hotel charges $75 a night for a room. It needs to take in at least $3,300 a day to meet expenses. How many rooms must be occupied each day for the hotel to take in this amount?

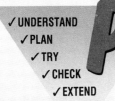

Linda plans to solve this problem by writing and solving an equation. She is going to let n represent the number of rooms that must be occupied for the hotel to take in $3,300. Here is the equation Linda decides to write: $n \times \$75 = \$3,300$.

1. What does $n \times \$75$ represent in this problem?

2. How can you solve the equation that Linda wrote?

3. How many rooms must be occupied for the hotel to take in $3,300 a day?

B. On October 9, the hotel is sponsoring a calligraphy contest in honor of *Hangul Nal* (HONG-ol nahl), Alphabet Day in Korea. Almost 550 years ago King Sejong (say-jong) was responsible for the creation of the Korean alphabet, *hangul*. So far, the hotel has received 64 entries for the contest. When Linda has recorded 12 more entries, she will have recorded all 64. How many entries has she already recorded?

4. What kind of equation could Linda use to solve this problem?

5. How many entries has she already recorded?

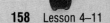

PRACTICE

Write and solve an equation for the problem.

6. Linda is in charge of setting up the contest room. They have set up 75 tables. They have placed 4 chairs at each table for the contestants. How many chairs are there in all?

7. Linda has 25 pictures of temples, tombs, shrines, and pagodas from the Kyongju Valley to hang in the contest room. She has hung 18 of them. How many more pictures does she need to hang?

8. Ms. Mori, a teacher, buys a number of books on *hangul* to share with her students. Each book costs $20. How many books does Ms. Mori buy if she pays $140?

9. Sally is practicing 12 different letters of the *hangul*. She writes each letter the same number of times. She writes 132 letters in all. How many times does Sally write each different letter?

Strategies and Skills Review

Use estimation, mental math, a calculator, or paper and pencil.

10. The hotel received a total of 1,095 entries for the calligraphy contest over the last 5 years. There were 185 entries in each of the first 3 years. There were 262 entries in the fourth year. How many people entered in the fifth year?

11. This year the hotel can accept 300 contestants for the contest. On Monday morning 168 people entered the contest, and that afternoon another 103 entered. That evening another 65 people wanted to enter the contest. Will all 65 people be able to enter? Should you overestimate or underestimate? Why?

12. Jane wakes up at 7:30 A.M. The contest begins at 10 A.M. She has breakfast at 8:10 A.M., and it takes her 25 minutes to eat. After breakfast how long does Jane have until the contest begins? If you have too much or too little information, tell what it is or what more you need.

13. Room service charges $5.15 for a pitcher that holds 3 glasses of juice and $4.80 for the same amount of milk. Ms. Mori wants to order equal amounts of milk and juice before the contest for her students. How many glasses of each can she order for $35?

14. The gift shop has 40 paintings of scenes from the Kyongju Valley. Eighteen paintings cost $60 each. The rest of the paintings cost $45. How much will the gift shop collect if it sells all the paintings?

15. *Write a problem* that involves using an equation. Solve your problem. Ask others to solve it.

Dividing Whole Numbers **159**

Adding and Subtracting Units of Time

A. The Lawndale Civic League is flagpole sitting for charity. Lee Wu sat for 2 hours and 35 minutes. Lisa Rone sat for 220 minutes. Who sat for the longer amount of time?

1 minute (min) = 60 seconds (s)
1 hour (h) = 60 minutes
1 year (y) = 12 months (mo)
1 week (wk) = 7 days (d)
1 day = 24 hours

Convert Lee's time to minutes.

2 h = 2 × 60 min = 120 min
2 h 35 min = 120 min + 35 min
120 min + 35 min = 155 min

Since 220 min > 155 min, Lisa sat for a longer period of time.

1. How could you have compared the times using hours and minutes?

B. You can also add units of time using paper and pencil or mental math.

Add: 3 h 40 min + 2 h 35 min

Paper and Pencil		Mental Math	
3 h 40 min		Start with:	**3 h 40 min**
+ 2 h 35 min		Add 3 h.	**6 h 40 min**
5 h 75 min = 5 h + 1 h 15 min		Subtract 25 min.	**6 h 15 min**
= **6 h 15 min**			

2. In the mental math method, why does adding 3 hours and subtracting 25 minutes give the correct answer?

C. You can also subtract units of time.

Subtract: 3 h 5 min − 2 h 35 min

Paper and Pencil

```
   2   65
   3 h  5 min
 − 2 h 35 min
   0 h 30 min
```

Mental Math

Count from:	Add:
2 h 35 min to 3 h =	25 min
3 h to 3 h 5 min =	5 min
Total =	30 min

3. In the paper-and-pencil method, why was 3 hours 5 minutes changed to 2 hours 65 minutes?

Write the letter of the correct answer.

4. 5 min = ■ s   *300 seconds*

   a. 3,000
   (b.) 300
   c. 120
   d. 35

5. 6 wk = ■ d   *42 days*

   (a.) 42
   b. 72
   c. 144
   d. 420

6.   1 h 50 min
      + 3 h 55 min
      5:05

   a. 4 h 105 min
   b. 4 h 45 min
   c. 5 h 45 min
   (d.) 5 h 5 min

7.   8 h 27 min
      − 2 h 44 min
      6.43

   a. 5 h 43 min
   b. 6 h 83 min
   c. 5 h 83 min
   (d.) 6 h 43 min

PRACTICE

Complete.

8. 144 h = ■ d *6 days*

9. 540 min = ■ h *9 hours*

10. 25 d = ■ wk ■ d *3 wk 4 d*

11. 600 s = ■ min *10*

12. 20 min 5 s = ■ s *1,205 s*

13. 3 h 35 min = ■ min *215*

14. 3 y 2 mo = ■ mo *38*

15. 96 mo = ■ y *8 years*

16. 51 wk = ■ d *357 days*

Add or subtract.

17.   3 h 35 min
       + 2 h 30 min
       6 h 0 5 min

18.   5 d 8 h
       + 2 d 16 h

19.   4 wk 5 d
       + 2 wk 3 d

20.   12 h 5 min
          2 h
       + 4 h 58 min

21.   8 min 20 s
       −   55 s

22.   10 h
       − 2 h 13 min

23.   5 y 2 mo
       − 2 y 7 mo

24.   3 wk 2 d
       −   6 d

Mixed Applications

25. A swim-in was held to buy library books. Sponsors pledged 25 cents per lap. If Jody swam 23 laps; Julio, 27 laps; and Maureen, 35 laps; how much did their sponsors pay in all?

26. Bruce took part in a three-day wheel-a-thon for the disabled. He traveled by wheelchair for 3 h 25 min on the first day, 4 h 40 min on the second, and 2 h 55 min on the third. What was his total time?

27. The public radio station had a membership drive. It cost $45 to become a new member. If the station collected $78,885, how many new members joined?

28. The telethon to benefit leukemia research was on the air for 65 h. For how many days and hours was it on the air?

Elapsed Time

A. Dance practice starts at 1:40 P.M. and lasts for 2 hours 35 minutes. At what time does it end?

Ray thinks: "2 hours after 1:40 is 3:40.
35 minutes after 3:40 is 4:15.
So practice ends at 4:15 P.M."

1. How could you have solved this problem another way?

2. At what time would practice end if it lasted 1 hour 55 minutes?

B. Darlene wants to be at school by 8:15 A.M. It takes her 1 hour 45 minutes to have breakfast, to dress, and to walk to school. At what time should she get up?

She thinks: "1 hour before 8:15 is 7:15, and 45 minutes before that is 6:30.
So I had better get up at 6:30 A.M."

3. How could you have solved this problem another way?

C. School starts at 8:30 A.M. and ends at 3:15 P.M. How long does Darlene spend in school?

She thinks: "From 8:30 A.M. to 2:30 P.M. is 6 hours.
From 2:30 P.M. to 3:15 P.M. is another 45 minutes.
So I spend 6 hours 45 minutes in school."

4. How else could you have solved this problem?

5. How long would school last if it started at 8:15 A.M. and ended at 3:05 P.M.?

Try Out

6. What time is it 2 hours 25 minutes before 1:45 P.M.?

7. What time is it 3 hours 25 minutes after 4:15 A.M.?

8. How much time is there between 8:35 A.M. and 4:25 P.M.?

PRACTICE

What time is it?

9. 3 h 30 min before 8:00 A.M.

10. 2 h 50 min after 1:10 P.M.

11. 7 h 15 min after 11:40 A.M.

12. 4 h 35 min before 12:15 A.M.

Find the answer.

13. The dance auditions began at 11:30 A.M. and ended at 5:05 P.M. How long did the auditions last?

14. Roberto mowed the lawn from 11:35 A.M. to 1:25 P.M. How long did he mow?

15. Rosa left home 2 hours 30 minutes before dance practice began. The practice began at 2:15 P.M. What time did Rosa leave her home?

16. Penny baby-sat from 3:45 P.M. to 10:30 P.M. How long did she baby-sit?

Critical Thinking

17. A leap year occurs every 4 years. The digits of the year form a multiple of 4. Which of these are leap years?
  a. 1991 **b.** 1992 **c.** 1996 **d.** 2000

18. A leap year can begin a century only if the digits of the year form a multiple of 400. Which of these are leap years?
  a. 1500 **b.** 1600 **c.** 1800 **d.** 2400

Mixed Applications

19. Reb slept 9 hours 15 minutes. Louann slept 8 hours 50 minutes. Who slept longer? How much longer?

20. Maya takes a tap-dancing class after school. Each class costs $3.50. How much does Maya pay for 26 classes?

21. Matt started reading at 6:10 P.M. and stopped at 8:40 P.M. He started again at 9:10 P.M. and stopped at 11:30 P.M. How long did he read?

22. So far this year Reb has read 569 pages, Matt has read 708 pages, and Maya has read 632 pages. How many pages have they read in all?

Mixed Review

Find the answer. Which method did you use?

		MENTAL MATH
		CALCULATOR
		PAPER/PENCIL

23. 6.21748 + 2.8767

24. 2,732 − 899

25. 36 × 25

26. 387 ÷ 24

27. 4 × 189 × 25

28. 2,389 × 489

Dividing Whole Numbers **163**

DECISION MAKING

Problem Solving: Choosing a Mode of Transportation

SITUATION

The Stendel family is traveling to a family reunion 450 miles away. There are 2 adults and 2 children in the family. One child is under 12. They will be away for 8 days.

PROBLEM

How should they get to the reunion?

DATA

Cross Country Air

$98
One way

$148
Round trip

Children under 12 fly at half price if with parents.

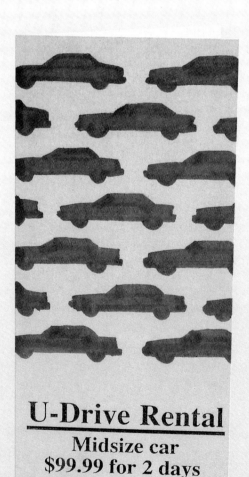

U-Drive Rental
Midsize car
$99.99 for 2 days
Unlimited free miles!

The car gets about 25 miles per gallon. Gas costs about $1.30 a gallon.

Taxi from home to the airport and back is $60. We'll be picked up at the reunion.

USING THE DATA

What is the round-trip cost?

1. car rental only

2. plane tickets only

What is the total round-trip cost, including all expenses?

3. car rental and gasoline

4. plane and taxi

The plane flies at an average speed of 550 mi per hour. The Stendels would average 50 mi per hour by car. About how many hours would it take to get to the reunion?

5. by car

6. by plane

7. How much would it cost for the Stendels to fly to the reunion and come back in one day by car?

MAKING DECISIONS

8. Which is the least expensive round-trip method of travel for the Stendels?

9. Which mode of transportation should the Stendels choose if they want to spend as much time as possible at the reunion?

10. *What if* the Stendels got a car that averaged 30 mi per gal? How much money would they save for the round trip?

11. *What if* the Stendels will have the use of a relative's car when they arrive? How much money would they save by renting a car for 2 days on the way to the reunion and for 2 days on the way home?

12. Why might the Stendels choose the car instead of the plane?

13. *Write a list* of other factors the Stendels should consider.

14. Which method of travel would you choose? Why?

Math and Geography

On a map or globe, the earth is measured by two sets of imaginary lines.

The lines of one set are *parallels*, or lines of *latitude*. They parallel the equator and form whole circles. Parallels measure distances from either side of the equator toward the poles. The equator is 0 degrees (0°). There are 90 parallels from the equator to the North Pole and 90 parallels from the equator to the South Pole. Usually maps and globes do not show every parallel.

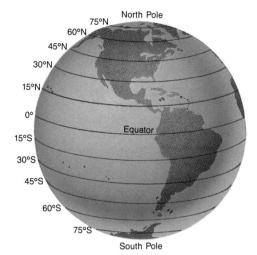

Lines of *longitude*, or *meridians*, are drawn from the North Pole to the South Pole. These lines are also measured in degrees, starting from the *prime meridian*, which runs through Greenwich, England. The degrees are counted both east and west from the prime meridian. Halfway around the world is the 180° meridian. This and the prime meridian form a full circle and divide the world into two halves.

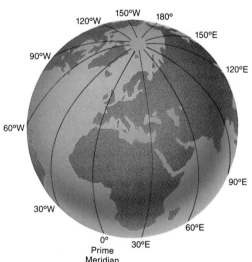

What if you are at 45°S? How many degrees away is 30°N?

Think: From 45°S to the equator is 45 degrees. It is another 30 degrees to 30°N. Add 45 and 30. You are 75 degrees away.

ACTIVITIES

1. On a globe find the place where you live. Note the latitude and longitude. Follow the meridian halfway around the globe to find the place that is directly opposite you. Give a brief report to your class.

2. Work with a partner and a map or globe. Have one person give the location of a place by longitude and latitude. Have the other person find and name the place. Play several rounds.

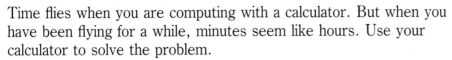
Calculator: Up in the Air

Time flies when you are computing with a calculator. But when you have been flying for a while, minutes seem like hours. Use your calculator to solve the problem.

USING THE CALCULATOR

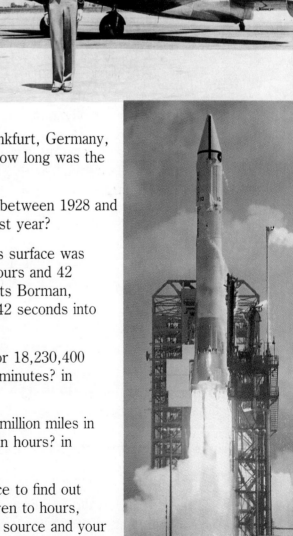

1. In 1927, Charles Lindbergh flew solo across the Atlantic in 33 hours, 29 minutes, and 30 seconds. How long was the flight in minutes?

2. In 1932, Amelia Earhart flew solo from Newfoundland to Ireland in 14 hours and 56 minutes. How long was her flight in minutes? in seconds?

3. In 1936 the *Hindenburg* zeppelin flew from Frankfurt, Germany, to Lakehurst, New Jersey, in 3,077 minutes. How long was the flight to the nearest hour?

4. Max Conrad flew 52,929 hours and 40 minutes between 1928 and 1974. How long was Max airborne to the nearest year?

5. During the *Apollo 8* mission in 1968, the moon's surface was first televised to earth. That flight lasted 147 hours and 42 seconds. For how many minutes were astronauts Borman, Lovell, and Anders in flight? (*Hint:* To change 42 seconds into minutes, divide 42 seconds by 60.)

6. Soviet cosmonaut Valentin Lebedev was aloft for 18,230,400 seconds in 1983. How long did his flight last in minutes? in hours? in days?

7. In 1987 three Soviet cosmonauts covered 98.1 million miles in their 326-day flight. How long did this trip last in hours? in minutes? in seconds?

8. Use an encyclopedia or another reference source to find out about an interesting flight. Convert the time given to hours, minutes, or seconds. Then give your reference source and your converted data to others. Challenge them to use the data to identify the flight.

EXTRA PRACTICE

Relating Multiplication and Division, page 139

Solve for n.

1. $24 \div 6 = n$ **2.** $27 \div 3 = n$ **3.** $35 \div 7 = n$ **4.** $64 \div 8 = n$

5. $45 \div n = 9$ **6.** $16 \div n = 4$ **7.** $n \div 9 = 4$ **8.** $n \div 7 = 9$

9. $56 \div 7 = n$ **10.** $n \div 5 = 5$ **11.** $72 \div n = 8$ **12.** $42 \div 6 = n$

Find the answer.

13. The divisor is 2. The dividend is 8. Find the quotient.

14. The divisor is 3. The quotient is 6. Find the dividend.

15. The dividend is 63. The quotient is 7. Find the divisor.

Mental Math: Division Patterns, page 141

Find the quotient mentally.

1. $90,000 \div 10$ **2.** $70,000 \div 100$ **3.** $30,000 \div 1,000$

4. $72,000 \div 90$ **5.** $36,000 \div 400$ **6.** $4,000 \div 800$

7. $8,000 \div 8,000$ **8.** $48,000 \div 100$ **9.** $63,000 \div 9,000$

10. 5 thousand ÷ ten   **11.** 24 thousand ÷ 6 thousand

12. 3 thousand divided by 5 hundred   **13.** 42 thousand divided by 7 tens

Find the missing number.

14. $4,200 \div \blacksquare = 7$ **15.** $\blacksquare \div 300 = 70$ **16.** $28,000 \div 40 = \blacksquare$

17. $\blacksquare \div 1,000 = 90$ **18.** $35,000 \div \blacksquare = 50$ **19.** $16,000 \div \blacksquare = 800$

Estimating Quotients, page 143

Estimate the quotient.

1. $633 \div 8$ **2.** $3,512 \div 3$ **3.** $612 \div 11$ **4.** $3,962 \div 45$

5. $48,201 \div 69$ **6.** $643,815 \div 9$ **7.** $48,621 \div 7$ **8.** $14,324 \div 22$

9. $41,714 \div 62$ **10.** $248,614 \div 51$ **11.** $53,012 \div 92$ **12.** $797,014 \div 83$

13. $34,574 \div 48$ **14.** $65,104 \div 78$ **15.** $3,507 \div 38$ **16.** $54,382 \div 72$

17. $64,509 \div 87$ **18.** $50,124 \div 58$ **19.** $430,157 \div 71$ **20.** $4,724 \div 58$

EXTRA PRACTICE

Dividing by One-Digit Numbers, page 145

Divide.

1. 8)267
2. 8)346
3. 7)504
4. 5)2,781
5. 4)21,425

6. 9)5,672
7. 7)5,782
8. 4)28,014
9. 3)18,619
10. 6)14,527

11. 8)$6.48
12. 7)$2.31
13. 6)$68.16
14. 5)$12.05
15. 6)$30.12

16. 414 ÷ 5
17. 9,741 ÷ 3
18. 736 ÷ 9
19. 20,417 ÷ 5
20. 49,128 ÷ 8

21. $35.70 ÷ 7
22. $47.10 ÷ 6
23. $81.72 ÷ 9
24. $20.64 ÷ 4
25. $278.19 ÷ 9

26. 7,142 divided by 8
27. $18,074 divided by 7

Dividing by Two-Digit Numbers, page 147

Divide.

1. 53)438
2. 31)187
3. 84)764
4. 62)379
5. 72)654

6. 21)926
7. 78)812
8. 55)389
9. 84)992
10. 42)$504

11. 72)541
12. 65)586
13. 24)$9.84
14. 36)$828
15. 37)779

16. 21)694
17. 35)$7.70
18. 67)812
19. 78)550
20. 84)691

21. 824 ÷ 68
22. 738 ÷ 22
23. 908 ÷ 41
24. 38)883
25. $192 ÷ 32

26. 244 divided by 54
27. 278 divided by 12
28. $768 divided by 24

Dividing: Changing Estimates, page 149

Divide.

1. 78)545
2. 53)896
3. 47)812
4. 64)189
5. 48)918

6. 36)953
7. 94)832
8. 23)806
9. 82)641
10. 58)525

11. 72)561
12. 65)576
13. 14)$9.66
14. 46)$828
15. 37)674

16. 28)614
17. 35)$6.30
18. 67)612
19. 78)570
20. 84)651

21. $8.36 ÷ 44
22. 695 ÷ 38
23. $8.25 ÷ 25
24. 126 ÷ 33
25. 499 ÷ 18

26. 204 divided by 54
27. 125 divided by 24
28. 916 divided by 36

EXTRA PRACTICE

Problem Solving Strategy: Making a Table, page 151

1. Delbert and Alexis ordered 3 sandwiches for $7.50, 3 desserts for $4.50, and 3 glasses of milk for $2.40. Alexis ate 2 sandwiches, 1 dessert, and 2 glasses of milk. How much should he pay?

2. The state sales tax in Pennsylvania is 6¢ on a dollar. The tax in Ohio is 5¢ on a dollar. What are the taxes on items costing $10, $15, $25, $50, $75, $100?

3. It takes 3 quarts of orange juice, 1 quart of pineapple juice, and 2 quarts of club soda to make punch. A quart of orange juice is $.89, a quart of pineapple juice is $1.59, and club soda is $.79 a quart. How much does it cost to make 18 quarts of punch?

4. It takes 2 gallons of white paint and 1 gallon of red paint to cover 1,200 ft² with pink paint. How many gallons of each are needed to cover 3,600 ft²?

Dividing Greater Numbers, page 155

Estimate to find the number of digits in the whole-number part of the quotient. Check your answer with a calculator.

1. $7,541 \div 35$ 2. $65,483 \div 78$ 3. $842,369 \div 782$ 4. $289,632 \div 439$

Use a calculator to find the quotient and the remainder.

5. $3,617 \div 46$ 6. $2,896 \div 38$ 7. $56,617 \div 74$ 8. $46,782 \div 87$

9. $38,758 \div 50$ 10. $264,382 \div 92$ 11. $4,084 \div 154$ 12. $5,875 \div 287$

13. $98,157 \div 376$ 14. $32,085 \div 415$ 15. $194,624 \div 629$ 16. $254,675 \div 832$

Multiplication and Division Equations, page 157

Solve and check.

1. $8n = 56$ 2. $n \times 9 = 54$ 3. $7n = 49$ 4. $n \times 5 = 25$

5. $n \times 17 = 136$ 6. $4n = 64$ 7. $26n = 130$ 8. $45 \times n = 135$

9. $6 \times n = 42$ 10. $34n = 272$ 11. $19n = 76$ 12. $n \times 80 = 720$

13. $n \div 8 = 96$ 14. $n \div 9 = 15$ 15. $169 \div n = 13$ 16. $150 \div n = 6$

17. $n \div 5 = 260$ 18. $n \div 40 = 70$ 19. $375 \div n = 75$ 20. $165 \div n = 33$

21. $n \div 6 = 8$ 22. $n \div 7 = 9$ 23. $81 \div n = 9$ 24. $36 \div n = 6$

EXTRA PRACTICE

Problem Solving Strategy: Write and Solve an Equation, page 159 ....

Write an equation to solve the problem.

1. The Night's Inn charges $85 a night for a room. How many rooms must be occupied to take in $3,570?

2. The Towers Hotel charges $250 a night for a room. How much will it cost for 5 nights?

3. The Park Hotel has 225 rooms. So far 108 have been reserved. How many rooms are left?

4. The dining room manager is setting up tables for 336 people. Each table seats 8 people. How many tables need to be set up?

Adding and Subtracting Units of Time, page 161 ....

Complete.

1. 96 h = ■ d

2. 360 s = ■ min

3. 28 mo = ■ y ■ mo

4. 3 h 10 min = ■ min

5. 4 wk 2 d = ■ d

6. 84 mo = ■

Add or subtract.

7.   4 h 25 min
     + 2 h 55 min

8.   7 d 9 h
     + 3 d 23 h

9.   5 wk 5 d
     + 4 wk 6 d

10.   15 h 6 min
        3 h 12 min
     + 4 h 59 min

11.   7 min 10 s
     −   45 s

12.   8 h
     − 3 h 27 min

13.   3 y 1 mo
     − 1 y 11 mo

14.   4 wk 1 d
     − 2 wk 5 d

Elapsed Time, page 163 ....

What time is it?

1. 2 h 40 min before 7:00 P.M.

2. 4 h 50 min after 2:20 A.M.

3. 5 h 55 min after 11:00 A.M.

4. 3 h 45 min before 2:30 P.M.

5. 3 h 45 min after 11:25 A.M.

6. 9 h 15 min before 3:05 P.M.

How long is it?

7. between 3:55 P.M. and 10:55 P.M.

8. between 6:40 A.M. and 8:10 A.M.

9. between 8:45 P.M. and 9:20 P.M.

10. between 7:20 A.M. and 1:15 P.M.

11. between 9:45 P.M. and 2:05 A.M.

12. between 11:50 P.M. and 10:30 A.M.

Dividing Whole Numbers   **171**

Practice PLUS

KEY SKILL: Dividing by One-Digit Numbers (Use after page 145.)

Level A

Divide.

1. 7)384   **2.** 4)328   **3.** 5)152   **4.** 6)2,803   **5.** 9)5,416

6. 9)$1.98   **7.** 3)$9.63   **8.** 6)$4.32   **9.** 8)$8.24   **10.** 7)$57.12

11. 407 ÷ 5   **12.** 2,873 ÷ 4   **13.** $21.27 ÷ 3   **14.** $81.99 ÷ 9

15. 1,916 ÷ 7   **16.** 852 ÷ 4   **17.** 2,629 ÷ 3   **18.** $42.55 ÷ 5

19. A factory made 5,682 model cars. They are packed in boxes of 6. How many packing boxes did they use?

Level B

Divide.

20. 6)354   **21.** 4)829   **22.** 6)3,854   **23.** 6)9,742   **24.** 7)17,841

25. 5)$86.50   **26.** 9)$27.18   **27.** 8)$81.60   **28.** 7)$15.61   **29.** 6)$491.52

30. 2,071 ÷ 8   **31.** 24,484 ÷ 6   **32.** $46.35 ÷ 5   **33.** $374.22 ÷ 9

34. 32,279 ÷ 4   **35.** $656.91 ÷ 9   **36.** 9,261 ÷ 8   **37.** $76.74 ÷ 3

38. A factory made 12,184 tables in 8 weeks. They made the same number of tables each week. How many did they make each week?

Level C

Divide.

39. 9)2,843   **40.** 7)14,028   **41.** 6)9,615   **42.** 9)8,214   **43.** 7)60,254

44. 8)$97.44   **45.** 6)$10.32   **46.** 9)$198.09   **47.** 7)$125.65   **48.** 8)$12.48

49. 56,018 ÷ 8   **50.** 32,545 ÷ 7   **51.** $469.26 ÷ 6   **52.** $540.45 ÷ 9

53. 44,029 ÷ 9   **54.** 5,778 ÷ 8   **55.** $13.32 ÷ 6   **56.** 76,809 ÷ 7

57. Dora bought 8 chairs for $405.12. Each chair cost the same amount. What was the price of each chair?

KEY SKILL: Dividing: Changing Estimates (Use after page 149.)

Level A

Divide.

1. 34)276 **2.** 28)834 **3.** 42)582 **4.** 58)466 **5.** 62)741

6. 27)581 **7.** 54)259 **8.** 38)758 **9.** 63)816 **10.** 49)$7.84

11. 531 ÷ 38 **12.** 676 ÷ 27 **13.** 290 ÷ 59 **14.** $2.88 ÷ 48

15. 449 ÷ 66 **16.** 818 ÷ 45 **17.** $6.08 ÷ 32 **18.** 472 ÷ 29

19. Georgia has $456 to spend on shoes for her shop. Each pair costs $24. How many pairs can she buy?

Level B

Divide.

20. 39)193 **21.** 66)432 **22.** 46)588 **23.** 34)624 **24.** 28)199

25. 84)580 **26.** 48)763 **27.** 76)448 **28.** 63)875 **29.** 32)937

30. 12)$75.00 **31.** 24)$82.08 **32.** 56)$83.44 **33.** 67)$55.61 **34.** 83)$64.74

35. 499 ÷ 74 **36.** 800 ÷ 54 **37.** $58.38 ÷ 42 **38.** 662 ÷ 85

39. Jack has $682 to spend on shirts for his shop. Each shirt costs $15. How many shirts can he buy?

Level C

Divide.

40. 26)628 **41.** 38)822 **42.** 72)425 **43.** 55)406 **44.** 89)262

45. 35)230 **46.** 16)684 **47.** 77)657 **48.** 92)548 **49.** 13)400

50. 94)$63.92 **51.** 51)$45.39 **52.** 48)$83.04 **53.** 27)$13.77 **54.** 58)$15.66

55. 576 ÷ 83 **56.** 948 ÷ 36 **57.** 705 ÷ 59 **58.** 363 ÷ 96

59. Susan sold 35 skirts at the same price. She received $582.40. What was the price of each skirt?

CHAPTER REVIEW/TEST

LANGUAGE AND MATHEMATICS

Complete the sentences. Use the words in the chart on the right.

1. A number divided by itself has a ■ of 1.

2. The quotient of any number with a ■ of 1 is the number itself.

3. The number which is divided by another number is the ■.

4. The number left over after a division is a ■.

CONCEPTS AND SKILLS

Choose the closest estimate.

5. $43,627 \div 52$ **a.** 80   **b.** 800   **c.** 8,000   **d.** 80,000

6. $336,105 \div 71$ **a.** 50   **b.** 500   **c.** 5,000   **d.** 50,000

7. $542,816 \div 8$ **a.** 70   **b.** 700   **c.** 7,000   **d.** 70,000

Estimate using compatible numbers.

8. $53,621 \div 9$ 9. $1,096 \div 43$ 10. $786,359 \div 19$ 11. $420,868 \div 49$

Divide.

12. $4\overline{)4,472}$ 13. $2\overline{)6,187}$ 14. $5\overline{)446,391}$

15. $3\overline{)6,206}$ 16. $9\overline{)5,155}$ 17. $58\overline{)145}$

18. $3,596 \div 2$ 19. $2,406 \div 8$ 20. $204,282 \div 6$

Solve the equation for n.

21. $12n = 96$ 22. $n \times 9 = 27$ 23. $305 \div n = 61$ 24. $n \div 4 = 13$

Complete.

25. 31 d = ■ wk ■ d   26. 5 min 10 s = ■ s   27. 453 s = ■ min ■ s

28. What time is 1 h 30 min after 10:35 A.M.?

29. What time is it 25 min after 4:40 P.M.?

30. Joan left home at 8:15 A.M. and came home 7 h 15 min later. What time did she return home?

Critical Thinking

31. If a quotient is 46, the divisor is 12, and the remainder is 10, what is the dividend? How do you know?

Mixed Applications

Use a table to solve.

32. Day camp begins Monday, August 5. Each session lasts 1 week (not including weekends). Matt will attend the first and third sessions. If art is taught on Thursdays, on which dates will Matt have art?

Write an equation. Then solve it.

33. Tennis balls come 3 to a can. If you need 42 balls, how many cans must you buy?

PERFORMANCE ASSESSMENT

Work with your group to solve this problem.

Suppose that your school is planning to have an outdoor awards ceremony and you are responsible for arranging chairs on the lawn. The school wants to set up 640 chairs in rows, with an equal number of chairs in each row and an aisle down the center. How would you arrange the 640 chairs for the ceremony?

1. *Think about:*
   - the number of chairs in each row
   - the number of rows on each side of the aisle

2. Write a multiplication equation and a division equation that you can use to find the solution. Then write a paragraph explaining how you determined the arrangement of the chairs on the lawn.

CUMULATIVE REVIEW

1. Which whole number comes between 7.1 and 8.1?

   a. 8
   b. 7
   c. 1
   d. not given

2. Which is the standard form of the number one and six hundredths?

   a. 106
   b. 1.60
   c. 1.06
   d. not given

3. $64.9 + 7.56 + 0.054$

   a. 72.514
   b. 14.590
   c. 145.9
   d. not given

4. Solve: $n - 66 = 95$

   a. 151
   b. 39
   c. 29
   d. not given

5. Which would you use to measure a pencil?

   a. meters
   b. centimeters
   c. kilometers
   d. not given

6. 7.35×64.3

   a. 4,726.05
   b. 472.605
   c. 95.55
   d. not given

7. Choose the exponent form for $4 \times 4 \times 4$.

   a. 3^4
   b. 3×4
   c. 4^3
   d. not given

8. What is the area of a rectangle with a length = 52 cm and a width = 8 cm?

   a. 416 cm²
   b. 3,600 cm²
   c. 120 cm²
   d. not given

9. Estimate by rounding: 472×84

   a. 32,000
   b. 40,000
   c. 45,000
   d. not given

10. Estimate: $31,234 \div 62$

    a. 5
    b. 50
    c. 500
    d. not given

11. $4\overline{)16,315}$

    a. 4,078 R3
    b. 478 R3
    c. 4,001 R1
    d. not given

12. $7,963 \div 56$

    a. 141 R67
    b. 142 R1
    c. 142 R11
    d. not given

13.   2 minutes 43 seconds
    + 5 minutes 31 seconds

    a. 8 min 12 s
    b. 8 min 14 s
    c. 7 min 14 s
    d. not given

14. Kate put 150 pennies in 6 equal stacks. How many pennies were in each stack?

    a. 25
    b. 144
    c. 900
    d. not given

THE 24-HOUR CLOCK

Most people in the United States use a 12-hour clock. Some people, such as scientists and Armed Forces personnel, use 24-hour clocks. This helps avoid confusion between A.M. and P.M. times. In other parts of the world, use of the 24-hour clock is quite common.

In 24-hour time midnight is written as 0000 and noon is written as 1200. The time between 0000 and 1200 is A.M. on the 12-hour clock, and the time between 1200 and 0000 is P.M.

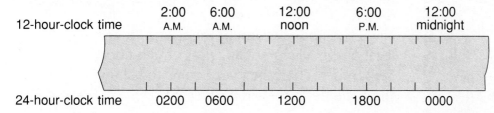

Use the train schedule at the right to solve the problems. For Problems 1–3 write *A.M.* or *P.M.* next to your answer.

BRITISH RAILWAY SYSTEM

	101	102	103	104
London Lv.	0930	1230	1730	2130
Peterborough	1019	1319	1819	2219
Doncaster	1039	1339	1839	2239
York	1129	1429	1929	2329
Darlington	1200	1500	2000	0000
Newcastle	1223	1523	2023	0023
Edinburgh Ar.	1403	1703	2203	0203

1. What time does train 101 leave York?

2. What time does train 101 arrive in Edinburgh?

3. What time does train 104 arrive in Edinburgh?

4. Which train arrives in Darlington at noon?

5. Which train arrives in Newcastle at 12:23 A.M.?

6. If you wanted to arrive in Edinburgh at about 10:00 P.M., which train would you take?

7. How long does it take train 102 to go from London to Edinburgh?

8. What number should you add to a P.M. time to change it to a 24-hour time?

9. What number should you subtract from a 24-hour time to change it to a P.M. time?

10. Make up a problem for which it is easier to use 24-hour time than 12-hour time to find elapsed time.

MEASURING THE NILE

Egypt
B. Nile
W. Nile

AFRICA

On the banks of the Nile River in Egypt, there is a large stone scored with markings that may have been made as many as 5,000 years ago. It is believed that the markings measured the Nile's rise and fall. During the spring, the water level of the Nile gradually rises until it floods in September. Then the river begins to fall until the cycle begins again in the spring.

Shown below are the units of distance used on the stone, which are based on a decimal system—that is, grouping by tens.

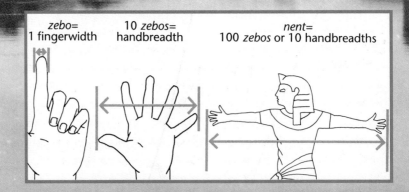

zebo= 1 fingerwidth | 10 *zebos=* handbreadth | *nent=* 100 *zebos* or 10 handbreadths

DIVIDING DECIMALS

MATH *CONNECTIONS*: Algebra • Measurement • Statistics

1

If you lived along the Nile, why might the increase of the water level above or below expected amounts be important to you?

2

What are the advantages and disadvantages of using these ancient Egyptian units for measuring?

Mental Math: Patterns with Powers of 10

Professor Penny invented the Penny Counter, a rack 1.5 m long. When the rack is full, there are 1,000 pennies. What is the length of each section if he divides the rack into 10 equal sections? 100 equal sections? 1,000 equal sections?

Divide the total length by 10, by 100, and by 1,000 to find the lengths of the sections.

Professor Penny used a calculator to find the quotients.

1.5 ⊕ 10 = $\boxed{0.15}$ **1.5 ⊕ 100 =** $\boxed{0.015}$ **1.5 ⊕ 1000 =** $\boxed{0.0015}$

Each of the 10 equal sections will be 0.15 m long.

Each of the 100 equal sections will be 0.015 m long.

Each of the 1,000 equal sections will be 0.0015 m long.

1. Compare the position of the decimal point in the dividend to the position of the decimal point in the quotient. What happens when you divide by 10? by 100? by 1,000?

2. How does this pattern compare with the pattern for multiplying decimals by powers of 10?

3. What happens when there are not enough places to move the decimal point as far to the left as needed?

TRY OUT   Write the letter of the correct answer.
Find the quotient mentally.

4. $86.2 \div 1,000$ **a.** 86,200   **b.** 8,620   **c.** 0.862   **d.** 0.0862

5. $487 \div 100$ **a.** 4.87   **b.** 48,700   **c.** 48.7   **d.** 0.487

6. $10\overline{)6.3}$ **a.** 0.063   **b.** 0.63   **c.** 6.3   **d.** 63

7. $1,000\overline{)0.4}$ **a.** 0.0004   **b.** 0.004   **c.** 0.04   **d.** 0.4

PRACTICE

Find the quotient mentally.

8. $82.7 \div 100$ **9.** $93.1 \div 100$ **10.** $39 \div 10$ **11.** $3.29 \div 10$ **12.** $6.41 \div 100$

13. $14.46 \div 10$ **14.** $0.108 \div 100$ **15.** $5 \div 100$ **16.** $29.2 \div 10$ **17.** $2.6 \div 1{,}000$

18. $10\overline{)14}$ **19.** $1{,}000\overline{)5.69}$ **20.** $100\overline{)805}$ **21.** $10\overline{)6.25}$ **22.** $100\overline{)62}$

23. $10\overline{)0.0012}$ **24.** $1{,}000\overline{)47.3}$ **25.** $10\overline{)93.7}$ **26.** $100\overline{)7.2}$ **27.** $10\overline{)0.473}$

28. $100\overline{)0.005}$ **29.** $100\overline{)296.7}$ **30.** $10\overline{)88}$ **31.** $100\overline{)11.2}$ **32.** $1{,}000\overline{)620}$

33. $1{,}000\overline{)16}$ **34.** $100\overline{)381.8}$ **35.** $100\overline{)1.26}$ **36.** $10\overline{)0.504}$ **37.** $100\overline{)0.06}$

38. $231.7 \div 1$ thousand   **39.** $3.32 \div 1$ hundred   **40.** $0.13 \div 1$ ten

41. $8 \div 1$ thousand   **42.** $118.6 \div 1$ hundred   **43.** $16.8 \div 1$ ten

Find the missing number.

44. $29.5 \div \blacksquare = 2.95$ **45.** $123 \div 100 = \blacksquare$ **46.** $617.4 \div 100 = \blacksquare$

47. $57{,}800 \div \blacksquare = 57.8$ **48.** $\blacksquare \div 10 = 0.00217$ **49.** $0.0861 \times 1{,}000 = \blacksquare$

Mixed Applications

50. Professor Paper invented the Paper Counter to count 1,000 sheets of paper. If 1,000 sheets are 10.2 cm thick, how thick is 1 sheet?

51. Professor Penny's assistant bought 10 boards. If each board cost $5.10, what was the total cost for all the boards?

MENTAL MATH

You can use a shortcut when multiplying a number with the digits 2 and 5 by any number that has a factor of 4. The factor, 4, is used to get a power of 10.

Examples:

25×36	2.5×48	0.25×24
$25 \times 4 \times 9$	$2.5 \times 4 \times 12$	$0.25 \times 4 \times 6$
$100 \times 9 = 900$	$10.0 \times 12 = 120$	$1.00 \times 6 = 6$

Multiply using the shortcut.

1. 25×28 **2.** 2.5×120 **3.** $0.25 \times 2{,}400$ **4.** $0.025 \times 16{,}000$

Dividing Decimals by Whole Numbers

A. It is 25 blocks to the zoo. If this is a total distance of 4.75 km, how long is each block?

Divide: 4.75 ÷ 25

Step 1

Place the decimal point of the quotient above the decimal point of the dividend.

```
   .
25)4.75
```

Step 2

Divide as you would divide whole numbers.

```
   0.19
25)4.75
   2 5↓
   2 25
   2 25
      0
```

Each block is 0.19 km long.

1. How would you divide \$4.75 by 25? What is the quotient?

B. You can also estimate decimal quotients.

Estimate: 3.68 ÷ 5

Rounding	Compatible Numbers
Round the dividend to its greatest place.	**Use a basic fact.**
Think: 3.68 rounds to 4.0.	***Think:*** 3.68 is close to 3.5.
4.0 ÷ 5 = 0.8	**3.5 ÷ 5 = 0.7**

2. Which estimate is greater than the exact answer? Which estimate is less? How can you tell?
3. Estimate 6.54 ÷ 18. Which method would be more useful? Why?

TRY OUT

Estimate. Then find the exact answer.

4. 5)247.75
5. 32)6.08
6. \$49.50 ÷ 9
7. 26.64 ÷ 36

PRACTICE

Estimate. Then find the exact answer.

8. $8\overline{)1.4288}$ **9.** $9\overline{)32.22}$ **10.** $7\overline{)2.2274}$ **11.** $4\overline{)25.6}$

12. $4\overline{)1.036}$ **13.** $31\overline{)4.34}$ **14.** $22\overline{)\$7.92}$ **15.** $26\overline{)83.2}$

16. $53\overline{)143.1}$ **17.** $92\overline{)36.8}$ **18.** $17\overline{)\$60.18}$ **19.** $37\overline{)104.34}$

20. $69\overline{)165.6}$ **21.** $54\overline{)18.36}$ **22.** $18\overline{)136.8}$ **23.** $43\overline{)\$78.26}$

24. $72\overline{)973.44}$ **25.** $53\overline{)58.8883}$ **26.** $64\overline{)2{,}707.84}$ **27.** $74\overline{)20.72}$

28. $15.81 \div 3$ **29.** $39.072 \div 6$ **30.** $499.8 \div 51$ **31.** $86.2875 \div 25$

Compare. Write $>$, $<$, or $=$.

32. $15 \times 5.8 \bullet 850 \div 10$ **33.** $6 \times 25 \bullet 450 \div 3.2$ **34.** $8.4 \div 21 \bullet 7 \times 0.06$

35. $88.6 \div 4.43 \bullet 8 \times 2.5$ **36.** $53.29 \div 7.3 \bullet 0.00733 \times 1{,}000$

Critical Thinking   Use the examples below to answer Problems 37 and 38.

$$79.2 \div 22 = 3.6 \qquad 62.4 \div 26 = 2.4$$

Will the estimate be greater than or less than the exact answer:

37. if the divisor is rounded down and the dividend is rounded up?

38. if the divisor is rounded up and the dividend is rounded down?

Mixed Applications

Solve. You may need to use the Databank on page 551.

39. A polar bear is fed 2.3 kg of food 3 times each day. How much is the bear fed daily?

40. How many kilograms of food does the animal eat daily?
a. elephant   **b.** giraffe

41. About how many times heavier is a polar bear than a gorilla?

42. *Write a problem* involving decimal quotients. Have another student solve it.

Mixed Review ∿∿∿∿∿∿∿∿∿∿∿∿∿∿∿∿∿∿∿∿∿∿∿∿∿∿∿∿∿∿∿∿

Find the answer. Which method did you use?

MENTAL MATH
CALCULATOR
PAPER/PENCIL

43. 9×65 **44.** $68 \times 1{,}000$ **45.** $324\overline{)287{,}064}$ **46.** $81{,}000 \div 9$

47. $4{,}893 + 1{,}562$ **48.** 3×0.005 **49.** $25.78 - 1.039$ **50.** $1{,}292 - 47$

Zeros in the Quotient and the Dividend

A. Ron used the data in the table for his report on people's eating habits. What was a person's average monthly consumption of meat in 1987?

YEARLY CONSUMPTION PER PERSON (kg)

Food Group	1985	1986	1987
Meats	65.35	63.59	61.08
Poultry	31.62	32.66	35.29
Fruits	47.26	50.58	53.34
Vegetables	87.27	87.54	87.18

Divide: 61.08 ÷ 12

```
      5.09
12)61.08
   60 ↓↓
    1 08
    1 08
       0
```

The average consumption was 5.09 kg.

1. Why is it necessary to write 0 in the quotient?

B. Sometimes you need to write a 0 as a placeholder in the dividend.

Divide: 225.4 ÷ 28

Step 1

Divide as far as you can.

```
      8.0
28)225.4
   224 ↓
     1 4
```

Step 2

Add a zero to the dividend and complete the division.

```
      8.05
28)225.40
   224   ↓
     1 40
     1 40
        0
```

So 225.4 divided by 28 is 8.05.

2. Why do you need to add 0 to the dividend in Step 2?

TRY OUT Divide.

3. 45)3.15   **4.** 25)43.5   **5.** 4)8.3   **6.** 16)324.8

PRACTICE

Divide. Remember to estimate first.

7. $4\overline{)3{,}228}$ **8.** $9\overline{)9.945}$ **9.** $6\overline{)5.424}$ **10.** $7\overline{)1.05}$ **11.** $8\overline{)\$40.96}$

12. $4\overline{)0.306}$ **13.** $13\overline{)\$78.26}$ **14.** $39\overline{)79.95}$ **15.** $3\overline{)6.09}$ **16.** $48\overline{)300}$

17. $28\overline{)6.02}$ **18.** $9\overline{)1{,}809}$ **19.** $36\overline{)0.108}$ **20.** $47\overline{)3.76}$ **21.** $25\overline{)\$110}$

22. $36\overline{)0.288}$ **23.** $48\overline{)8{,}016}$ **24.** $21\overline{)\$64.47}$ **25.** $12\overline{)8.808}$ **26.** $16\overline{)1.2}$

27. $4.3 \div 5$ **28.** $0.846 \div 5$ **29.** $\$90.60 \div 15$ **30.** $43.05 \div 21$

31. $6.06 \div 24$ **32.** $9.081 \div 18$ **33.** $0.9108 \div 44$ **34.** $245.7 \div 35$

Critical Thinking

35. Moira decides to divide 9.2 by 3. What will happen if she continues to add zeros to the dividend? Will Moira ever get a remainder of zero?

```
    3.06
3)9.20
  9 ↓↓
  0 20
    18
     2
```

Mixed Applications

Solve. Use the table on page 184.

36. What was a person's total yearly consumption of all four groups of food in 1986?

37. What was a person's average yearly consumption of meats in the three years of 1985–1987?

CALCULATOR

If you divide a number by a second number and multiply the result by the second number, you should get the number you started with.

Example: $8 \div 2 \times 2 = 8$

Use a calculator to find the answer.

1. $1 \div 2 \times 2$ **2.** $1 \div 3 \times 3$ **3.** $1 \div 4 \times 4$ **4.** $1 \div 6 \times 6$

5. For which problems is the calculator display *not* 1?

6. Why do you think the calculator does not display 1?

PROBLEM SOLVING

Strategy: Guess, Test, and Revise

The Community Center is giving a party. Mikhail bought 12 toys for the party. Some cost $8.88 each. Others cost $7.99 each. The total cost was $99.44. How many toys of each kind did Mikhail buy?

You can guess, test, and revise your guess to solve this problem.

1. Did Mikhail buy 6 toys at $8.88 each and 6 toys at $7.99 each? How do you know?

   Guess: 6 at $8.88 each   **Test:** 6 × $8.88 = $53.28
               and   6 × $7.99 = + 47.94
            6 at $7.99 each   Total cost =   ■

2. Revise your guess. Should you try fewer $8.88 toys? Why or why not?

3. Try 5 toys at $8.88 each and 7 toys at $7.99 each. Test to see whether the total is $99.44.

   Guess: 5 at $8.88 each   **Test:** 5 × $8.88 =   ■
               and   7 × $7.99 = + ■
            7 at $7.99 each   Total cost =   ■

4. Do you need to revise your guess again? Why or why not?

5. How many toys of each kind did Mikhail buy?

PRACTICE

Use the Guess, Test, and Revise strategy to solve the problem.

6. Carlos bought a camera and a camera case for $50.98. The camera cost $29 more than the case. How much did the camera cost?

7. There were 15 cycles parked outside of the Community Center. Some were bicycles, and the rest were tricycles. There were 34 wheels all together. How many bicycles and how many tricycles were there?

8. Carlos also bought 9 rolls of film to take a total of 180 pictures at the party. Some rolls had 12 exposures on each roll, and the rest had 36 exposures on each roll. How many 12-exposure rolls and how many 36-exposure rolls of film did Carlos buy?

9. In a game at the Community Center, Rosa won some red game pieces and some blue ones. The reds were worth 7 points each, and the blues were worth 5 points each. She had a total of 31 points. How many of each did Rosa win?

Strategies and Skills Review

Solve. Use estimation, mental math, a calculator, or paper and pencil.

10. Joe is fencing a part of the Center's property. The fence is to go from a point on the road 40 m due east, then 25 m due south, then 8 m due east, then 30 m due north, then 48 m due west, and then back to the starting point. How much fencing does Joe need?

11. Last month the Center used 2,385 kilowatt-hours of electricity. The electric bill was $310.15. The month before that the bill had been only $293.00. How much less was the bill two months ago? Identify the extra information.

12. The kitchen at the Center is rectangular. Its length is 2 m more than its width and its area is 48 m². What are the length and width of the room?

13. In the Community Center, 5 of the lights burned out last week. There were 32 lights that still worked. How many lights are there in the building?

14. Mikhail arranged apples and pears for the party. There were 3 dozen apples. There were 4 more pears than apples. How many apples and pears were there all together?

15. **_Write a problem_** using the Guess, Test, and Revise strategy. Solve your problem. Ask others to solve it.

ACTIVITY Dividing Decimals by Decimals

A 1-km racetrack has flags posted every 0.2 km. How many flags are there around the track?

WORKING TOGETHER

Solve the problem using a model. Then answer the questions.

How does your model show:

1. the total length of the track?

2. the location of the flags?

3. the distance between the flags?

4. the total number of flags?

Here is one way to solve the problem using a paper-and-pencil model.

Step 1 Draw a number line to represent the racetrack. Label the starting line "0" and the finish line "1."

Step 2 Starting at 0, count by 0.2 and make marks. Label the marks 0.2, 0.4, 0.6, and so on.

Beginning at 0.2, each mark represents a flag.

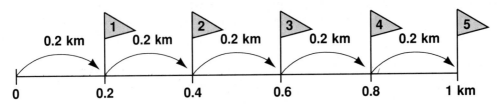

The number-line model shows one way to divide 1 by 0.2.

$$1 \div 0.2 = 5$$

5. How does your model compare with the number-line model?

6. Copy the table. Use models to complete it.

Length of Track	Distance Between Flags	Number of Flags
1 km	0.2 km	5
4.2 km	0.7 km	
3 km	1.5 km	
4 km	0.6 km	
5.2 km	1.2 km	
2 km	2.5 km	

SHARING IDEAS

7. On which tracks is the last flag posted right at the finish line?

8. On which tracks is the last flag posted before the finish line? For each of these tracks, what is the distance from the last flag to the finish line? How long would the track have to be if you wanted to post one more flag?

9. Which track has no flags? How long would the track have to be to have one flag?

10. Study your table. How could you have answered Problems 7–9 using inverse operations?

ON YOUR OWN

Solve the problem using a model.

11. A roll of crepe paper is 3.5 m long. How many pieces 0.5 m in length can be cut from one roll?

12. Jean bought several pieces of oak tag of the same size to make cards. Each piece of oak tag cost $.39. If Jean spent $2.73 on the pieces, how many did she buy?

13. Diana has 4 square sheets of cardboard, all the same size. She wants to cut pieces 0.5 the size of the originals to make signs. How many pieces will she have?

14. Jack bought 3.75 yd of fabric to make some collages. How many collages can he make if each requires 1.25 yd?

15. *Write a problem* involving division of decimals. Solve your problem. Then ask others to solve it.

Dividing Decimals by Decimals

A. Mr. Ali is building a fence 7.2 m long. Starting at one side of his house, he digs holes for fence posts every 0.8 m. How many lengths of fencing does he use?

Divide: $0.8\overline{)7.2}$

You can use a number-line model to solve this division problem.

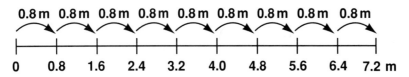

Think: There are 9 segments 0.8 m long.

$7.2 \div 0.8 = 9$

Mr. Ali uses 9 lengths of fencing.

Notice that dividing 7.2 by 0.8 is the same as dividing 72 by 8. Each has a quotient of 9.

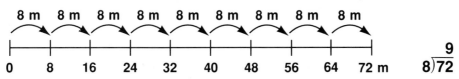

$$8\overline{)72}^{\,9}$$

B. When you divide by a decimal, it is easier to rewrite the problem so that the divisor is a whole number. To do this, multiply both the divisor and the dividend by a power of 10.

Examples: $1.4\overline{)4.27}$ —— × 10 ——→ $14\overline{)42.7}^{\,3.05}$

$0.65\overline{)1.3}$ —— × 100 ——→ $65\overline{)130}^{\,2}$

$0.025\overline{)5}$ —— × 1,000 ——→ $25\overline{)5,000}^{\,200}$

You can use arrows to show how the decimal point is moved to get a whole-number divisor.

By what number are the divisor and dividend being multiplied?

  1. $1.8\overline{)12.9.6}$ **2.** $0.75\overline{)45.75}$ **3.** $2.620\overline{)15.72}$

4. $2.1\overline{)7.581}$ **a.** 36.1   **b.** 3.61   **c.** 0.361   **d.** 0.0361

5. $0.25\overline{)7.5}$ **a.** 0.3   **b.** 3   **c.** 30   **d.** 300

6. $0.004\overline{)0.0016}$ **a.** 4   **b.** 0.4   **c.** 0.04   **d.** 0.004

PRACTICE

Divide.

7. $0.5\overline{)6.25}$ **8.** $0.009\overline{)0.4518}$ **9.** $0.096\overline{)4.86}$ **10.** $3.5\overline{)31.22}$

11. $0.8\overline{)0.16}$ **12.** $0.07\overline{)49}$ **13.** $0.14\overline{)0.056}$ **14.** $0.035\overline{)0.0245}$

15. $0.04\overline{)0.116}$ **16.** $0.62\overline{)1.736}$ **17.** $0.057\overline{)456}$ **18.** $2.3\overline{)5.98}$

19. $0.007\overline{)0.469}$ **20.** $0.065\overline{)13.845}$ **21.** $0.15\overline{)0.4905}$ **22.** $0.66\overline{)0.1914}$

23. $37 \div 29.6$ **24.** $13.63 \div 2.9$ **25.** $0.6006 \div 1.43$ **26.** $1.232 \div 0.056$

Find the quotient mentally.

27. $0.6\overline{)0.54}$ **28.** $0.75 \div 0.25$ **29.** $0.08\overline{)7.2}$ **30.** $0.22\overline{)0.088}$

31. $63 \div 2.1$ **32.** $0.7\overline{)0.0014}$ **33.** $0.8\overline{)0.04}$ **34.** $0.06 \div 1.2$

Find the missing divisor or dividend.

35. $\blacksquare \div 3.3 = 5$ **36.** $8.24 \div \blacksquare = 2.06$ **37.** $2.8\overline{)\blacksquare}^{0.76}$ **38.** $0.7\overline{)43.75}^{\blacksquare}$

Critical Thinking Solve. Give an example to support your answer.

Is the quotient less than or greater than one:

39. if the dividend is greater than the divisor?

40. if the dividend is less than the divisor?

Mixed Applications

41. Mr. Ali is shingling the roof of his shed. Each shingle is 0.15 m wide. If the roof is 6.45 m wide, how many shingles will there be in each row?

42. Gary wants to tile his kitchen floor with square tiles 1 ft on each side. The kitchen measures 12 ft by 10 ft. How many tiles does Gary need?

Zeros in the Quotient and the Dividend

A. The mass of a goldfish is 0.00336 kg. That is 5.6 times the mass of a guppy. What is the mass of a guppy?

Divide: 0.00336 ÷ 5.6

```
              0.0 0 0 6
5 . 6 ) 0 . 0 0 3 3 6
                3 3 6
                    0
```

The mass of a guppy is 0.0006 kg.

1. Why were 0s added to the quotient as placeholders?

B. Sometimes you may need to write additional 0s in the dividend.

Divide: 0.032 ÷ 0.64

```
              0.0 5
0 . 6 4 ) 0 . 0 3 2
              3 2 0
                  0
```

2. Why was an additional 0 needed in the dividend?

TRY OUT Write the letter of the correct answer.

3. 3.2)0.0064   **a.** 2   **b.** 0.2   **c.** 0.02   **d.** 0.002

4. 1.5)3   **a.** 2   **b.** 0.2   **c.** 0.02   **d.** 0.002

5. 0.81)1.944   **a.** 0.24   **b.** 2.04   **c.** 2.4   **d.** 24

6. 0.032)1.07   **a.** 0.334375 **b.** 3.34375 **c.** 33.4375 **d.** 334.375

PRACTICE

Divide.

7. $0.8\overline{)4}$ **8.** $0.7\overline{)0.056}$ **9.** $0.2\overline{)0.0024}$ **10.** $2.5\overline{)6}$

11. $1.4\overline{)0.042}$ **12.** $1.6\overline{)8}$ **13.** $2\overline{)7}$ **14.** $9\overline{)0.0063}$

15. $0.4\overline{)0.2}$ **16.** $1.6\overline{)0.064}$ **17.** $1.3\overline{)0.091}$ **18.** $3.5\overline{)0.021}$

19. $75\overline{)0.165}$ **20.** $0.09\overline{)9}$ **21.** $0.25\overline{)\$8}$ **22.** $0.75\overline{)0.00225}$

23. $0.23\overline{)0.2461}$ **24.** $55\overline{)0.594}$ **25.** $0.12\overline{)\$3}$ **26.** $0.12\overline{)0.00102}$

27. $0.011\overline{)66}$ **28.** $0.057\overline{)0.0798}$ **29.** $0.015\overline{)0.45}$ **30.** $0.009\overline{)0.000315}$

31. $\$91 \div 6.5$ **32.** $0.0115 \div 0.5$ **33.** $0.0126 \div 1.8$ **34.** $0.002047 \div 0.089$

Critical Thinking

Suppose you were dividing a whole number greater than 1 by a decimal greater than 1. Is the statement *true* or *false*?

35. The quotient is always greater than 1.

36. The quotient is sometimes greater than 1.

37. The quotient is never greater than 1.

Mixed Applications

38. Sally's aquarium holds 31.5 L of water. The container she uses to fill the aquarium holds 1.5 L. How many *full* containers of water does it take to fill the aquarium?

39. A stack of unfolded cardboard containers used for carrying fish is 100 mm high. The thickness of each container is 2.5 mm. How many containers are in the stack?

40. A liter of purified water costs $.20. How much will it cost to fill a 40.3-L tank?

41. *Write a problem* that involves dividing decimals. Ask others to solve it.

LOGICAL REASONING

Brad caught a trout, a perch, and a bass. The mass of the trout is 7.5 times that of the perch. The mass of the bass is 0.4 times that of the trout. The mass of the trout is 0.5 kg less than 11 kg. What is the mass of each fish?

Rounding Decimal Quotients

Steve and Karen want to buy cat food. At Animal City a case of 24 cans sells for $11.26. What is the price per can to the nearest cent?

Karen uses a calculator and Steve uses paper and pencil.

Karen

11.26 ÷ 24 = | 0.4691666 |

Steve

```
$    .4 6 9
24)$11.260
    9 6
    1 66
    1 44
      2 2 0
      2 1 6
          4
```

0.4691666 → $.47 $.469 → $.47

Both Steve and Karen find the cost to be $.47 per can.

1. Why did Karen's calculator display seven decimal places?

2. Why did Steve divide to three decimal places?

3. Compare Steve's calculated quotient with Karen's calculator display. How are they the same? How are they different?

4. **What if** you want to find a quotient to the nearest thousandth? To how many places will you need to divide?

TRY OUT
Write the letter of the correct answer.
Use mental math, a calculator, or paper and pencil.

5. 0.2365 ÷ 0.5 to the nearest hundredth
   a. 0.47   c. 0.473
   b. 0.48   d. 4.73

6. 5 ÷ 16 to the nearest thousandth
   a. 0.312   c. 3.125
   b. 0.32   d. 0.313

7. $85.36 ÷ 2.5 to the nearest cent
   a. $3.41   c. $34.14
   b. $3.42   d. $34.15

8. 6.34 ÷ 0.07 to the nearest tenth
   a. 9.05   c. 0.90
   b. 90.6   d. 9.056

PRACTICE

Use mental math, a calculator, or paper and pencil.
Divide to the nearest tenth.

9. $8 \div 3$　　　　**10.** $7.4 \div 62$　　　　**11.** $78 \div 45$

Divide to the nearest hundredth.

12. $3.94 \div 5$　　**13.** $0.875 \div 15$　　**14.** $4.028 \div 150$

15. $97 \div 167$　　**16.** $88.6 \div 7.4$　　**17.** $1.4871 \div 1.2$

Divide to the nearest thousandth.

18. $2.71 \div 8$　　**19.** $7.054 \div 3$　　**20.** $0.578 \div 27$

21. $1.806 \div 9.5$　　**22.** $23.7 \div 0.23$　　**23.** $0.042 \div 0.019$

Divide to the nearest cent.

24. $\$8.21 \div 52$　　**25.** $\$70.85 \div 0.55$　　**26.** $\$26.81 \div 2.3$

Solve.

27. Dog food is on sale for $1.48 for a 3-can package. A customer wants to buy just 1 can. What would be the price for 1 can if the store did not round up to the nearest cent?

28. *What if* the store rounded down instead of up? How much would it lose in dollars and cents by selling 3,000 individual cans at the sale price?

Mixed Applications

Solve. Which method did you use? Round unit prices to the nearest cent.

ESTIMATION
MENTAL MATH
CALCULATOR
PAPER/PENCIL

29. The manager of a kennel bought 20 bags of dog food at $9.59 a bag, 15 dishes at $3.49 each, and 35 boxes of dog treats at $1.49 each. What was the total cost of the items?

30. Animal City sells three different sizes of the same brand of dog food: 5 lb for $2.99, 20 lb for $7.49, and 25 lb for $9.19. Which is the best buy?

31. Bette saw 5 cans of cat food for $1 advertised at Animal City. At Pet Fare 3 cans of the same cat food cost $.69. Which is the better buy? How much can she save per can?

32. Jenna wants to buy a 5-lb bag of dog food for $3.89, a collar for $5.79, a leash for $3.59, and a brush for $4.99. Will $20 be enough to pay for the items?

YOUR MIND'S EYE

Visual Reasoning

A. This pattern could be cut out and folded to form a cube:

What would the resulting cube look like? You could copy the pattern to find out, or you can use reasoning and your imagination. You can try to visualize the complete cube. These puzzles will help you learn to "see" with your mind only.

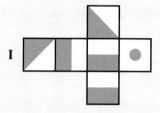

I

1. Imagine pattern I folded into a cube. Which of these views show the cube accurately?

a

b

c

d

2. Now consider folding these patterns into cubes:

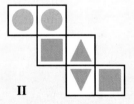
II

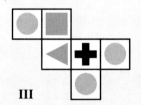
III

Which of the views show the cube from pattern II? from pattern III? Are there any views that could be made from both patterns? Are there any views that could not be made?

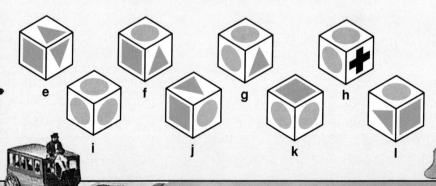

B. Copy and complete the views made from each pattern.

3.

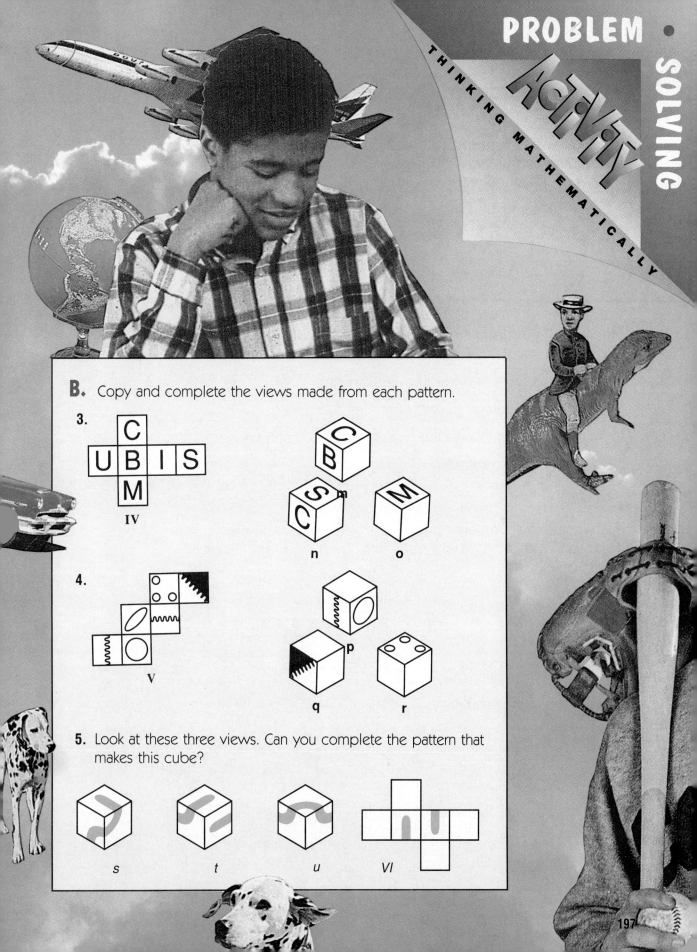

IV

n   o

4.

V

p   q   r

5. Look at these three views. Can you complete the pattern that makes this cube?

s   t   u   VI

197

Algebra: Order of Operations

A. How would you simplify the **expression** $30 \div 5 - 2 \times 2 + 1$?
Depending on the order in which you do the operations, you
will get a different answer.

Method 1	Method 2
$30 \div 5 - 2 \times 2 + 1$	$30 \div 5 - 2 \times 2 + 1$
$\quad 6 \quad - 2 \times 2 + 1$	$\quad 6 \quad - \quad 4 \quad + 1$
$\quad\quad 4 \quad\; \times 2 + 1$	$\quad\quad 2 \quad\quad\; + 1 = 3$
$\quad\quad\quad 8 \quad\quad + 1 = 9$	

To avoid confusion mathematicians have agreed on the
following **order of operations** to simplify expressions.

Multiply and divide in order from left to right.

Then add and subtract in order from left to right.

1. Which method follows the correct order of operations?

2. Simplify the expression.
   a. $6 + 9 \div 3 - 2 \times 4$ **b.** $5 \times 4 + 5 \div 5 - 2$ **c.** $8.5 - 1.8 \times 2.5 \div 3$

B. When there are parentheses in an expression, do the
operations within the parentheses first. Then follow the order of
operations.

Examples:

$8 \times (13 - 7) \div 3$	$27.5 - (2.6 + 4.4) \times 3$
$8 \times \quad 6 \quad \div 3$	$27.5 - \quad 7.0 \quad \times 3$
$\quad\quad 48 \quad\quad \div 3 = 16$	$27.5 - \quad\quad 21.0 \quad = 6.5$

Simplify the expression.

3. **a.** $8 + 3 \times 5 - 2$ 4. **a.** $36 \div 3 + 3 \times 2$ 5. **a.** $42.6 - 8.4 + 2 \times 3.1$

   b. $(8 + 3) \times (5 - 2)$ **b.** $36 \div (3 + 3) \times 2$ **b.** $42.6 - (8.4 + 2) \times 3.1$

TRY OUT   Write the letter of the correct answer. Simplify.

6. $18 \div 2 + 7 \times 4$
   a. 64   **c.** 8
   b. 37   **d.** 2

7. $6 \times (5 - 3) + 8$
   a. 35   **c.** 20
   b. 19   **d.** 60

8. $(8.5 + 7.2) \times (4.7 - 2.8)$
   a. 29.83   **c.** 39.54
   b. 70.99   **d.** 22.18

PRACTICE

Simplify. Do as many as you can mentally.

9. $8 - 3 \times 2 + 6$

10. $12.6 \div 3 + 8 \times 3.2$

11. $9 + 16 \div 2 - 15$

12. $42 \div 6 + 4 \times 9$

13. $5.5 \div 1.1 + 2.3 - 0.4 \times 4$

14. $5.3 + 12.4 - 1.9 \times 6 - 3.1$

15. $4 \times 3.2 - 4.2 \div 3 + 14.1$

16. $18 \times 5 - 44 \times 2$

17. $(8 + 13) \div 7 - 3$

18. $5 \times 6.7 - (16 - 6)$

19. $18 \div (24 - 15) + 5$

20. $(12 + 13) \div (13 - 8)$

21. $13 \times 4 - 8 \times (14 - 8)$

22. $50 \div (37 - 32) - 4 \times 2$

23. $49 - 9 \times (16 - 12) + 32 \div 8$

24. $5 \times (8 + 2) - (23 + 26)$

Write $+$, $-$, $\times$, or $\div$ to make the statement true.

25. $(16 \bullet 3) \bullet 8 \bullet 2 = 3$

26. $22 \bullet (12 \bullet 1) \bullet 18.3 = 36.6$

27. $25 \bullet 5 \bullet (8 \bullet 7) = 6$

28. $(17.9 \bullet 8.9) \bullet (12.3 \bullet 0.3) = 108$

Copy and write parentheses to make the statement true.

29. $28 - 8 \div 7 - 3 = 5$

30. $4 \times 9 - 5 \div 8 = 2$

31. $6 \times 3 \div 12 + 6 = 1$

32. $3 \times 13 - 7 - 11 = 7$

Critical Thinking

33. Are parentheses necessary to simplify the expression $(3 \times 2) + (10 \div 5)$ according to the order of operations?

Mixed Applications

34. Rosalia has number cards from boxes of cereal. To win a prize, she needs numbers that total 1,000. Rosalia has these numbers: 198, 487, 63, and 96. Will she win?

35. Use each of the numbers 2, 3, 4, and 5 exactly once to make up an expression whose value is 9.

36. **_Write a puzzle_** like the one in Problem 35. Ask others to solve it.

Metric Units of Capacity and Mass

A. **Capacity** is the amount that a container can hold. The **liter (L)**, the **milliliter (mL)**, and the **kiloliter (kL)** are common units of capacity in the metric system.

1 L = 1,000 mL   1,000 L = 1 kL

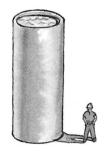

4 raindrops hold about
1 mL of water.

This container holds
1 L of milk.

This water tank holds
1 kL of water.

1. Which unit would be most appropriate to use for measuring very large capacities? very small capacities? Why?

B. **Mass** is the amount of matter in an object. The **gram (g)**, **milligram (mg)**, **kilogram (kg)**, and **metric ton (t)** are common units of mass in the metric system.

1 g = 1,000 mg   1,000 g = 1 kg   1,000 kg = 1 t

The mass of
a small seed
is about **1 mg.**

The mass of
a paper clip
is about **1 g.**

The mass of
this textbook
is about **1 kg.**

The mass of
a compact
car is about **1 t.**

2. Which units would be most appropriate to use for measuring small amounts of mass? for measuring very large amounts of mass? Why?

TRY OUT   Write the letter of the correct answer.
Which is the most appropriate unit to use?

3. capacity of jar   **a.** kg   **b.** mL   **c.** m   **d.** cm

4. mass of a person   **a.** kg   **b.** mL   **c.** m   **d.** cm

PRACTICE

Which is the most appropriate unit to use?

5. A fuel tank of a car holds about 80 ■ of fuel.

6. The amount of water in a small fish pool is about 1 ■.

7. A punchbowl holds about 10 ■ of punch.

8. A bar of soap has a mass of about 120 ■.

9. A new eraser has a mass of about 2 ■.

10. A watermelon has a mass of about 9 ■.

Write the letter of the best estimate.

11. mass of a horse	**a.** 500 kg	**b.** 500 g	**c.** 500 mg
12. mass of a basketball	**a.** 1 kg	**b.** 1 g	**c.** 1 mg
13. mass of a nickel	**a.** 5 kg	**b.** 5 g	**c.** 5 mg
14. mass of an apple	**a.** 150 mg	**b.** 150 kg	**c.** 150 g
15. mass of an ant	**a.** 500 mg	**b.** 5 g	**c.** 5 kg
16. capacity of a teaspoon	**a.** 5 L	**b.** 500 mL	**c.** 5 mL
17. capacity of a swimming pool	**a.** 75 mL	**b.** 75 L	**c.** 75 kL
18. capacity of a home aquarium	**a.** 25 mL	**b.** 25 L	**c.** 25 kL
19. capacity of a large pitcher	**a.** 200 mL	**b.** 20 L	**c.** 2 L
20. capacity of a can of soup	**a.** 300 mL	**b.** 3 mL	**c.** 300 L

Mixed Applications

21. A banana has a mass of about 200 g. What is the mass in kilograms of a bunch with 6 bananas?

22. If 2 kg of cherries cost $9.18, how much does 1 kg cost?

Mixed Review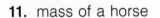

Find the answer. Which method did you use?

23. 387,412 + 973,624

24. 600 ÷ 10

25. 57 − 29

26. 8 × 25

27. 8.105 + 9.996

28. 298 − 128

29. 667 ÷ 23

30. 48.3 ÷ 0.5

31. $1.95 × 32

MENTAL MATH
CALCULATOR
PAPER/PENCIL

Converting Metric Measures

Lara and Frank bought potatoes. Lara chose a 1.2-kg bag of potatoes. Frank weighed his and found that he had 1,400 g of potatoes. Who had the greater amount?

In order to compare measurements, you must express them in the same unit.

Length		
1 km = 1,000 m		
1 m = 100 cm = 1,000 mm		
1 cm = 10 mm		

Mass	Capacity
1 t = 1,000 kg	1 kL = 1,000 L
1 kg = 1,000 g	1 L = 1,000 mL
1 g = 1,000 mg	

Lara converted kilograms to grams by multiplying.

1.2 kg = ■ g   *Think:* 1 kg = 1,000 g
1.2 kg = (1.2 × 1,000) g
1.2 kg = 1,200 g

Compare: 1,200 g < 1,400 g
So 1.2 kg < 1,400 g.

Frank converted grams to kilograms by dividing.

1,400 g = ■ kg   *Think:* 1 kg = 1,000 g
1,400 g = (1,400 ÷ 1,000) kg
1,400 g = 1.4 kg

Compare: 1.4 kg > 1.2 kg
So 1,400 g > 1.2 kg.

Both found that Frank had the greater amount of potatoes.

1. How do you convert a larger unit to a smaller unit? a smaller unit to a larger unit?

2. What is the relationship between grams and kilograms? between milliliters and liters? between centimeters and meters?

TRY OUT   Write the letter of the correct answer.

3. 42.5 cm = ■ m   **a.** 0.425   **b.** 4.25   **c.** 42.5   **d.** 425

4. 4,000 g = ■ kg   **a.** 0.004   **b.** 0.4   **c.** 4   **d.** 40

5. 0.056 L = ■ mL   **a.** 0.56   **b.** 5.6   **c.** 56   **d.** 560

PRACTICE

Complete.

6. 0.35 m = ■ cm

7. 2 L = ■ kL

8. 3,000 kg = ■ t

9. 1,700 mg = ■ g

10. 0.016 mm = ■ m

11. 10 mL = ■ kL

12. 0.015 km = ■ m

13. 0.5 L = ■ mL

14. 0.64 cm = ■ mm

15. 16 g = ■ mg

16. 0.073 m = ■ cm

17. 0.028 kL = ■ L

18. 8 g = ■ mg

19. 13.52 m = ■ cm

20. 0.3 mL = ■ L

21. 2.4 t = 2,400 ■

22. 4.57 kg = 4,570 ■

23. 6.5 cm = 0.000065 ■

Compare. Write >, <, or =.

24. 400 cm ● 5m

25. 0.008 t ● 8 kg

26. 305 mL ● 0.264 L

27. 0.07 mg ● 95 g

28. 12 m ● 1.2 cm

29. 89 g ● 0.089 kg

Mixed Applications

30. Barbara has a liter of soup. José has 5 containers of soup, each containing 250 mL. Who has more soup? How much more?

31. Ken has 3 kg of grapefruits in a paper bag. If each grapefruit weighs about 500 g, how many grapefruits does he have?

32. Mel has 8 m of ribbon to place around a triangular area. Each of two sides measures 275 cm, and the front measures 3.5 m. Does he have enough ribbon?

33. **Write a problem** that involves converting milliliters to liters. Solve your problem. Then ask others to solve it.

CHALLENGE

A cubic centimeter (1 cm³) holds 1 mL of water. A mL of water has a mass of 1 g. A thousand cubic centimeters holds 1,000 mL, or 1 L, of water and has a mass of 1 kg.

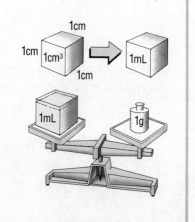

Complete.

1. A container that holds 800 mL will hold ■ cm³ of water.

2. A container that holds 586 g of water will hold ■ L of water.

PROBLEM SOLVING

Strategy: Using Estimation

The owners of Five-Mile Mall are deciding whether or not to add additional spaces in the parking lot. They ask store owners in the mall about the number of shoppers the stores have each month.

Lenny runs a food market called Shelf Stocker in the mall. The table to the right shows the number of shoppers in the market during the month of March.

SHOPPERS AT SHELF STOCKER

Week	Number
1	804
2	917
3	678
4	833

What number should Lenny give to the mall owners? Sometimes you do not need to find an exact answer.

Lenny decides to estimate the total number of shoppers in March. He rounds each week's figure to the nearest hundred. Then he adds.

$$804 \rightarrow 800$$
$$917 \rightarrow 900$$
$$678 \rightarrow 700$$
$$833 \rightarrow + 800$$
$$\overline{3{,}200}$$

Lenny tells the owners that about 3,200 people shopped in his market during March.

1. How many more people shopped during the fourth week than during the first week? Did you estimate or find an exact answer?

2. About how many people shopped during each of the 4 weeks that month? Did you estimate or find an exact answer?

3. What if you want to predict how many people might shop at the Shelf Stocker for the entire year? How can you use Lenny's information to do so?

PRACTICE

Write whether you would estimate or find an exact answer. Then solve.

4. Lenny sold 94 gal of milk last week. How many gallons might he sell in a year?

5. Lenny has 29 chickens in a freezer and sells 7 of them. How many chickens does he have left?

6. This week Lenny sold 116 daily newspapers. He also sold 32 newspapers on Sunday. Predict how many newspapers Lenny can expect to sell in a month.

7. During the first three months of the year, Lenny used 3,876; 4,922; and 5,716 grocery bags. He wants to order bags for the rest of the year. How many should he order?

Strategies and Skills Review

Use estimation, mental math, a calculator, or paper and pencil.

8. A large roll of aluminum foil contains 25 yd more than the next smaller size of foil. One of the large rolls and two of the smaller ones contain a total of 250 yd of foil. How many yards of foil are in the smaller roll?

9. Roberta buys 3 cans of tomato paste at $.37 a can, 2 boxes of spaghetti at $.57 a box, and a carton of mushrooms for $1.19. She gives the clerk a five-dollar bill. How much change should she receive?

10. Lenny's Market ended the week with 42 lb of bananas not sold. The market began the week with 150 lb of bananas. How many pounds of bananas were sold during the week?

11. Marcos has $20 to buy groceries. In the shopping cart he has $3.25 worth of cheese, $8.90 worth of meat, and $4.65 worth of cleaning products. Will he get more than $5 change?

12. Lenny's Market has 86 bottles of orange juice and grape juice. There is a total of 12 cartons of orange and grape juice. The orange juice cartons contain 6 bottles each, and the grape juice cartons contain 8 bottles each. How many bottles of each kind of juice are there?

13. *Write a problem* that can be solved using exact numbers and either addition or subtraction. Write another problem that can be solved using estimation and either multiplication or division. Solve your problems. Ask others to solve them.

MORE PRACTICE, page 217

Mean, Median, Mode, and Range

A. Ms. Johnson has a set of test scores for her geography class:

85, 85, 98, 100, 94, 90.

Mean, median, mode, and range are four statistics that can be used to describe data.

Here is how to find the **mean,** or average, of the scores.

Step 1 Add the scores.   **85 + 94 + 98 + 100 + 85 + 90**

Step 2 Divide by the number   **552 ÷ 6 = 92**
of scores.

The mean of the scores is 92.

B. The **median** is the middle number when the set of data is arranged in order. When the number of items in the set of data is even, the median is the mean of the two middle numbers.

100   98   94   90   85   85

$$\frac{94 + 90}{2} = 92$$ The median is 92.

C. The **mode** is the number or numbers that occur most often in the set of data.

85 85 98 100 94 90

There is one mode in the test scores: 85.

1. Is it possible for a set of data not to have a mode? Why?

2. What if the test scores were 90, 94, 85, 100, 85, and 94? What would be the mode?

D. The **range** is the difference between the greatest and the least numbers in a set of data.

100 − 85 = 15

The range of the data is 15.

TRY OUT   Find the mean, median, mode, and range for the set of data.

3. 20, 15, 12, 18, 17

4. 62, 44, 78, 57, 59

5. $1.50, $1.45, $2.50, $1.50, $3.45

6. 416, 302, 416, 547, 194

PRACTICE

Find the mean, median, mode, and range for the set of data.

7. 4, 11, 3, 6, 9, 10, 7, 6, 6, 4

8. 2, 6, 0, 7, 6, 4, 6, 7, 7

9. 78, 52, 80, 84, 67, 83, 60

10. 83, 104, 85, 79, 76, 89, 111, 87

11. $2.03, $2.35, $2.46, $2.91, $2.35

12. 837, 261, 817, 859, 522

13. $6.29, $5.54, $5.03, $6.49, $4.87, $5.26

14. 312, 655, 126, 240, 175, 916

Critical Thinking

15. Here is a set of data: 75, 88, 88, 89, 90, 90, 91, 91, 92, 105. Nam noticed that most of the numbers in this set of data clustered around 90, so he estimated the mean to be about 90. The exact mean is 89.9. Will his method always work? Why or why not?

16. Jeanne thought that a good way to estimate the mean would be to add the greatest and least numbers in the set of data and divide by 2. Do you agree or disagree? Give an example to support your answer.

Mixed Applications

17. The mean attendance this season for a junior high soccer game was 200. About how many tickets were sold if the team played 9 games?

18. On science tests Jon scored 82 one time, 85 six times, 90 seven times, 95 four times. Find the mean and the median.

19. Jill found her batting average by dividing her number of hits by the number of times she was at bat. She had 10 hits and was at bat 36 times. To the nearest thousandth, what was her batting average?

20. *Write a problem* about how the school could use statistics to plan its budget for the next year. Solve your problem. Ask others to solve it.

Activity

Effects of Changes on Data

Several people in Miguel's neighborhood are forming a kite-flying club. Miguel is keeping a record of their ages.

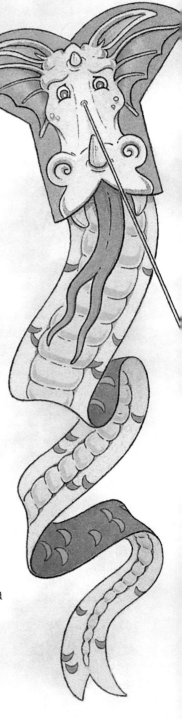

> ## WOODALE KITE-FLYING CLUB
> Age of members: 11, 12, 12, 14, 15, 18, 23
> Mean: 15 Median: 14 Mode: 12 Range: 12

WORKING TOGETHER

Find the mean, median, mode, and range for each of these situations. Record your answers as Miguel did above.

1. The same members are in the club 10 years from now.

2. A 7-year-old joins the club.

3. A 35-year-old joins the club.

4. The 14-year-old moves to another town and a 21-year-old joins the club.

SHARING IDEAS

Compare what you found out about changing data.

5. What happens to the four statistics if the same number is added to each number in the set of data?

6. What happens to the mean and the range when a number greater than the others is added to the set of data? when a lesser number is added?

7. *What if* one new member joins? How old is she if the median remains the same? How old could she be if the median increases? if the median decreases?

8. *What if* two new members join? How old could they be if the median remains the same? if the median increases? if the median decreases?

9. How can you change the mode by adding two numbers to the set of data?

PRACTICE

Solve.

10. Here are the ages of the members of a travel club:
78, 55, 55, 62, 59, 61, 53, 51, 50, 56.
A travel agency is offering a special rate to any group of 10 or more that has a mean age of 60. Can the club get the special rate? If the club increases its membership, how can the members be sure they will qualify for the special rate?

The table shows the 1986 sales quotas for the representatives of a small company. The business grew over the next four years, and in 1990 all of their quotas were 3 times as great as in 1986.

11. Find the four statistics for the sales quota data in 1986.

12. Find the four statistics for the sales quota data in 1990.

1986 SALES QUOTAS (in thousands of dollars)			
Abrams	$80	Martinez	$88
Decker	71	Nardi	74
Harman	97	Pons	62
Kim	64	Rabner	104

13. How does each statistic for 1990 compare with the same statistic for 1986?

14. *What if* all numbers in a set of data are multiplied by the same number (other than 0)? How do you think the new statistics will compare with the original ones?

The frequency diagram shows how many people of certain ages are studying to be dental assistants.

15. What is the mean age of the students to the nearest tenth?

16. What is the median age of the students?

17. Tell how you can use the graph to find the mode. What is the mode?

18. What is the range of the ages?

19. *What if* all the students continue in their studies and no new students enroll in the school? What will the four statistics be exactly one year later?

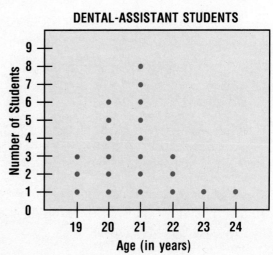

DENTAL-ASSISTANT STUDENTS

Dividing Decimals **209**

Problem Solving: Choosing a Breakfast Cereal

SITUATION

Antonia and Ben, the editors of the school newspaper, are writing a report on cereals. They look at three brands.

PROBLEM

Which cereal should they recommend?

DATA

NUTRITION INFORMATION PER SERVING
SERVING SIZE 1 OUNCE (APPROX. 1 CUP)

	1 oz Total
CALORIES	100
PROTEIN, g	3
CARBOHYDRATE, g	23
FAT, g	1
SODIUM, mg	240

PERCENTAGE OF U.S. RECOMMENDED
DAILY ALLOWANCES (U.S. RDA)

PROTEIN	4
VITAMIN A	100
VITAMIN C	100
THIAMIN	100
RIBOFLAVIN	100
NIACIN	100
CALCIUM	20
IRON	100
VITAMIN D	10
VITAMIN E	100

INGREDIENTS: WHOLE WHEAT, SUGAR, TRICALCIUM AND DICALCIUM PHOSPHATE (PROVIDES CALCIUM), SALT, MALT SYRUP

NUTRITION INFORMATION
SERVING SIZE: 1.4 OZ (1 OZ BRAN FLAKES WITH 0.4 OZ RAISINS; 40.5 g, ABOUT 3/4 CUP)

CALORIES	120
PROTEIN	3 g
CARBOHYDRATE	31 g
FAT	1 g
SODIUM	230 mg

PERCENTAGE OF U.S. RECOMMENDED
DAILY ALLOWANCES (U.S. RDA)

PROTEIN	6
VITAMIN A	15
VITAMIN C	**
THIAMIN	25
RIBOFLAVIN	25
NIACIN	25
CALCIUM	2
IRON	100
VITAMIN D	10

**CONTAINS LESS THAN 2% OF THE U.S. RDA OF THE NUTRIENT

INGREDIENTS: WHEAT BRAN WITH OTHER PARTS OF WHEAT, RAISINS, SUGAR, CORN SYRUP, SALT, MALT FLAVORING

NUTRITION INFORMATION PER SERVING

SERVING SIZE	1 OZ (1 CUP)
CALORIES	110
PROTEIN	1 g
CARBOHYDRATE	25 g
FAT	1 g
SODIUM	190 mg

PERCENTAGE OF U.S. RECOMMENDED
DAILY ALLOWANCES (U.S. RDA)

PROTEIN	2
VITAMIN A	*
VITAMIN C	*
THIAMIN	*
RIBOFLAVIN	15
NIACIN	25
CALCIUM	*
IRON	25
VITAMIN D	*
VITAMIN E	25
FOLIC ACID	25

*CONTAINS LESS THAN 2% OF THE U.S. RDA OF THE NUTRIENT.

INGREDIENTS
CORN, RICE, WHEAT, AND OAT FLOUR; COCONUT OIL; DRIED APPLES; SALT; COCOA; ARTIFICIAL FLAVOR; PARTIALLY HYDROGENATED VEGETABLE OIL. CONTAINS ONE OR MORE OF THE FOLLOWING: COTTON SEED, SOYBEAN; COLOR ADDED (CONTAINING YELLOW)

18 OZ $4.19   15 OZ $2.79   11 OZ $3.09

TASTE REPORT

Raisins 'n' Flakes is not the best tasting, but neither is it the worst. We liked eating the raisins from the box.

Wheat Complete doesn't taste very good. The flakes become mushy and stick to the sides of the bowl.

Cocoa Crunch has a dynamite flavor with a hint of chocolate chip. It looks like little cookies, but it contains no sugar. It even tastes a little too sweet for us.

USING THE DATA

About how much does each cereal cost per ounce?

1. Raisins 'n' Flakes   **2.** Wheat Complete   **3.** Cocoa Crunch

About how much does each cereal cost per serving?

4. Raisins 'n' Flakes   **5.** Wheat Complete   **6.** Cocoa Crunch

About how many servings are there in each box?

7. Raisins 'n' Flakes   **8.** Wheat Complete   **9.** Cocoa Crunch

MAKING DECISIONS

10. Which cereal costs the least per serving?

11. Which cereal has the least number of calories per serving?

12. *What if* someone is on a low-sodium diet? Which cereal should Ben recommend? (Sodium is found in salt.)

13. Which cereal has the highest percent of required vitamins?

14. Which cereal would Antonia and Ben recommend on the basis of taste?

15. *What if* someone were allergic to food coloring? Which cereal should they avoid?

16. *Write a list* of the other factors they should consider.

17. Which cereal would you recommend? Why?

Math and Science

Firewood is usually sold by the cord. A cord is a stack of firewood measuring $8 \times 4 \times 4$ or $8 \times 8 \times 2$ feet, which equals 128 cubic feet. Since different kinds of wood weigh different amounts, the weight of a cord will vary.

If you heat your home by burning wood, you need to know how much heat the wood will produce. The amount of heat put out per pound of wood is about the same for all wood. If you know the weight per cubic foot of the wood, you can find the cost per pound.

What if you get prices for two kinds of wood? Each cord costs $100. Redwood weighs 26 pounds per cubic foot. White oak weighs 47 pounds per cubic foot. Which is the better buy? How much money would you save?

Think: A cord has 128 cubic feet and costs $100.

$100 \div 128 = \$0.78125 \rightarrow \$0.78$/cubic ft

Redwood weighs 26 pounds per cubic foot, and white oak weighs 47 pounds per cubic foot.

Redwood	White Oak
$0.78 \div 26 = \$0.03$/lb	$0.78 \div 47 = \$0.016 \rightarrow \$0.02$/lb

White oak costs one cent less per pound than redwood.

ACTIVITIES

1. Find the weights of some other kinds of wood. How much does a cord of each kind of wood cost in your area? What is the best buy in terms of heat output? Share your findings with the class.

2. Work together in a small group. Find out how much heat other energy sources produce. Compare the sources and prepare a chart for the classroom bulletin board.

Computer Spreadsheet: Mean, Median, Mode, and Range

Many operations performed in mathematics can be accomplished quickly and accurately by a computer. The computer follows the same steps as you do to reach an answer. When there are a lot of steps in a calculation, a computer can be a fast and useful assistant.

In this activity you will use the computer spreadsheet program MEAN MACHINE to find the mean of a set of data. The program calculates the sum of the quantities and divides it by the number of quantities in the set. The program also displays the median, mode, and range of the data.

AT THE COMPUTER

1. Pedro's bowling scores for his last five games were 172, 176, 181, 185, and 176. First estimate his mean score for the five games. Then enter the scores on the computer screen and compare the mean shown with your estimate. Were you close?

2. What is Pedro's median score? What is the mode for Pedro's scores?

3. The maximum score for a perfect game is 300. If he bowls one more game, can Pedro raise his mean score to 200? Enter a perfect score for the sixth game and have the computer find Pedro's new mean score.

4. After the sixth game Pedro's actual mean score was 179. Try entering various scores on the sixth line until the mean is 179. What was Pedro's score for game six?

5. Did the range for Pedro's scores change after the sixth game? Explain.

6. Maria, the league champion, is determined to achieve a mean score of at least 240 for the six games. So far her scores are 258, 219, 224, 237, and 242. Use the computer to find the lowest score that Maria must get in the sixth game to achieve her goal.

EXTRA PRACTICE

Mental Math: Patterns with Powers of 10, page 181

Find the quotient mentally.

1. $25.3 \div 10$ **2.** $342.8 \div 100$ **3.** $127 \div 1{,}000$ **4.** $8.16 \div 100$

5. $0.17 \div 100$ **6.** $3 \div 10$ **7.** $0.29 \div 1{,}000$ **8.** $16 \div 100$

9. $100\overline{)8.2}$ **10.** $10\overline{)15.7}$ **11.** $1{,}000\overline{)3.89}$ **12.** $100\overline{)0.735}$

13. $10\overline{)79}$ **14.** $1{,}000\overline{)62.5}$ **15.** $100\overline{)5.3}$ **16.** $10\overline{)0.672}$

17. $100\overline{)980}$ **18.** $1{,}000\overline{)12.01}$ **19.** $10\overline{)0.678}$ **20.** $100\overline{)874}$

21. $7 \div 1$ ten   **22.** $162 \div 1$ thousand   **23.** $6.3 \div 1$ hundred

Dividing Decimals by Whole Numbers, page 183

Estimate. Then find the exact answer.

1. $7\overline{)1.6338}$ **2.** $8\overline{)25.68}$ **3.** $9\overline{)2.8143}$ **4.** $6\overline{)388.86}$

5. $21\overline{)5.25}$ 0.25   **6.** $32\overline{)\$8.64}$ **7.** $43\overline{)96.32}$ **8.** $52\overline{)145.6}$

9. $74\overline{)\$161.32}$ **10.** $85\overline{)\$264.35}$ **11.** $91\overline{)386.75}$ **12.** $19\overline{)17.67}$

13. $36\overline{)87.48}$ **14.** $47\overline{)\$764.22}$ **15.** $18\overline{)74.4426}$ **16.** $58\overline{)3{,}408.08}$

17. $79\overline{)\$259.91}$ **18.** $82\overline{)154.16}$ **19.** $65\overline{)229.45}$ **20.** $87\overline{)3{,}407.79}$

21. $19.74 \div 7$ **22.** $37.014 \div 6$ **23.** $298.9 \div 61$ **24.** $97.335 \div 45$

Zeros in the Quotient and the Dividend, page 185

Divide. Remember to estimate first.

1. $5\overline{)4{,}017}$ **2.** $8\overline{)8.84}$ **3.** $7\overline{)4.914}$ **4.** $6\overline{)18.24}$ **5.** $9\overline{)\$45.27}$

6. $4\overline{)0.338}$ **7.** $3\overline{)\$21.09}$ **8.** $12\overline{)\$36.72}$ **9.** $38\overline{)0.76}$ **10.** $48\overline{)600}$

11. $52\overline{)3.12}$ **12.** $15\overline{)45.15}$ **13.** $9\overline{)9.81}$ **14.** $35\overline{)2.45}$ **15.** $29\overline{)3.074}$

16. $61\overline{)0.366}$ **17.** $47\overline{)4.935}$ **18.** $33\overline{)68.64}$ **19.** $26\overline{)20.93}$ **20.** $18\overline{)1.17}$

21. $3.83 \div 4$ **22.** $0.346 \div 5$ **23.** $80.88 \div 16$ **24.** $\$155.04 \div 51$

25. $7.07 \div 35$ **26.** $9.696 \div 48$ **27.** $0.732 \div 24$ **28.** $271.8 \div 45$

Problem Solving Strategy: Guess, Test, and Revise, page 187

Guess, test, and revise to solve the problem.

1. Sally read 16 books. She read 3 times as many novels as mysteries. How many novels did she read?

2. Kate and John read a total of 22 books. Kate read 6 more books than John. How many books did each of them read?

3. Kristen bought puzzle books that cost $2 and picture books that cost $3. She spent $28. How many of each type of book did she buy?

4. Bill read 3 more books than Jan. Jan read 5 more books than Hank. Together Bill and Hank read 18 books. How many books did each person read?

Dividing Decimals by Decimals, page 191

Divide.

1. $0.9\overline{)7.38}$ 2. $0.06\overline{)48}$ 3. $0.12\overline{)0.072}$ 4. $0.025\overline{)0.0575}$

5. $0.07\overline{)0.217}$ 6. $0.81\overline{)2.592}$ 7. $0.059\overline{)236}$ 8. $3.4\overline{)7.48}$

9. $0.008\overline{)0.496}$ 10. $0.072\overline{)17.352}$ 11. $0.16\overline{)0.5536}$ 12. $0.55\overline{)0.2695}$

13. $15.6\overline{)39}$ 14. $2.8\overline{)18.76}$ 15. $3.41\overline{)0.7161}$ 16. $0.023\overline{)1.886}$

17. $0.15 \div 0.5$ 18. $56 \div 0.08$ 19. $54.9 \div 0.061$ 20. $29.25 \div 0.75$

21. $10.08 \div 25.2$ 22. $17.68 \div 2.6$ 23. $4.68 \div 0.015$ 24. $1.155 \div 0.035$

Zeros in the Quotient and the Dividend, page 193

Divide.

1. $0.6\overline{)3}$ 2. $0.8\overline{)0.048}$ 3. $0.3\overline{)0.0018}$ 4. $3.5\overline{)7}$

5. $2.4\overline{)0.048}$ 6. $1.2\overline{)6}$ 7. $2\overline{)9}$ 8. $7\overline{)0.0056}$

9. $0.5\overline{)0.3}$ 10. $1.5\overline{)0.075}$ 11. $2.3\overline{)0.069}$ 12. $4.5\overline{)0.054}$

13. $85\overline{)0.374}$ 14. $0.07\overline{)7}$ 15. $0.65\overline{)\$26}$ 16. $0.35\overline{)0.00245}$

17. $0.06624 \div 3.2$ 18. $0.00693 \div 0.66$ 19. $\$9 \div 0.18$ 20. $0.00105 \div 0.15$

21. $0.0705 \div 0.047$ 22. $0.0002 \div 0.008$ 23. $88 \div 0.011$ 24. $0.00075 \div 0.25$

EXTRA PRACTICE

Rounding Decimal Quotients, page 195 ....

Divide to the nearest tenth.

1. $8 \div 6$ **2.** $8.4 \div 52$

Divide to the nearest hundredth.

3. $3.89 \div 7$ **4.** $5.019 \div 250$

Divide to the nearest thousandth.

5. $9.013 \div 4$ **6.** $0.546 \div 16$

7. $2.704 \div 8.7$ **8.** $4 \div 23$

Divide to the nearest cent.

9. $\$80.95 \div 65$ **10.** $\$36.95 \div 3.2$

11. $\$6.89 \div 1.6$ **12.** $\$56 \div 0.42$

Order of Operations, page 199 ....

Simplify. Do as many as you can mentally.

1. $(8 + 19) \div 9 - 2$ **2.** $10.6 - 5 \times (16 - 14)$ **3.** $6 \times 3.5 - (17 - 7)$

4. $400 \div (5 \times 16) \div 5 - 1$ **5.** $16 \div 4 + 5 \times 8 \div 4$ **6.** $9.4 - 3.4 + 5 \times 9$

7. $8 - 9.6 \div 4 \times 2$ **8.** $28 - 2 \times (15 - 2) \div 2$ **9.** $3 + 7.2 \div 8 + 6.5$

10. $4.8 \times 5 - 6.2 \times 3 + 2.6$ **11.** $14 - 3 + 7 \times 15 \div 3$ **12.** $10 \times 4 + 36 \div 6$

13. $12 \div 4 \times 7 - (7 + 8)$ **14.** $54 \div 6 - 0.3 \times 7 + 1$ **15.** $5 + (36 - 24) \times 5$

Metric Units of Capacity and Mass, page 201 ....

Which is the most appropriate unit to use?

1. A milk glass holds about 200 ■ of milk.

2. A bowling ball has a mass of 5 ■.

3. A sink holds 15 ■ of water.

4. A tennis ball has a mass of 50 ■.

5. The amount of water in a lake is 5,000 ■.

6. A rhinoceros has a mass of 2 ■.

Write the letter of the best estimate.

7. mass of a leaf   **a.** 1 kg   **b.** 1 mg   **c.** 1 g

8. mass of an orange   **a.** 250 mg   **b.** 250 g   **c.** 250 kg

9. mass of a person   **a.** 50 kg   **b.** 50 t   **c.** 50 g

10. capacity of an eyedropper   **a.** 1 L   **b.** 1 kL   **c.** 1 mL

11. capacity of a cup   **a.** 250 kL   **b.** 250 mL   **c.** 250 L

Converting Metric Measures, page 203

Complete.

1. $3 L = \blacksquare kL = \blacksquare mL$ 2. $1,500 mg = \blacksquare g = \blacksquare kg$ 3. $0.5 m = \blacksquare cm = \blacksquare mm$

4. $0.3 km = \blacksquare m$ 5. $0.025 L = \blacksquare mL$ 6. $0.75 cm = \blacksquare mm$

7. $12 g = \blacksquare mg$ 8. $0.085 m = \blacksquare cm$ 9. $0.035 kL = \blacksquare L$

10. $9 g = \blacksquare mg$ 11. $126 mm = \blacksquare cm$ 12. $0.8 mL = \blacksquare L$

Problem Solving Strategy: Using Estimation, page 205

Write whether you would estimate or find an exact answer. Then solve.

1. Early in the season, attendance at the Tiger's home basketball games averaged 892 fans per game. How many people might be expected to attend during the entire season if the Tigers play 10 home games?

2. During the first three games of a basketball tournament, 462 boxes of popcorn were sold. If 135 boxes were sold during the first game and 156 boxes were sold during the third game, how many boxes were sold during the second game?

Mean, Median, Mode, and Range, page 207

Find the mean, median, mode, and range for the set of data.

1. 2, 3, 4, 8, 8, 8, 9

2. 9, 14, 6, 4, 2, 6, 15, 16, 9

3. 38, 37, 38, 65, 11, 59, 38, 32

4. 17, 25, 23, 22, 19, 21, 20, 18

5. 945, 101, 612, 774, 101

6. $8.40, $8.60, $8.80, $8.40, $8.10

7. $3.05, $3.50, $3.85, $3.40, $3.90

8. $26.02, $24.56, $24.56, $28.18

Effects of Changes on Data, page 209

The table shows the number of people enrolled in art classes at the community center during the spring. In the summer the center had 2 times as many people enrolled in each class.

SPRING ART CLASSES	
Painting	16
Ceramics	20
Drawing	13
Stained Glass	15
Batik	11
Print Making	15

1. Find the four statistics for the spring enrollment.

2. Find the four statistics for the summer enrollment.

3. How does each statistic for the summer compare with the same statistic for the spring?

Practice *PLUS*

KEY SKILL: Zeros in the Quotient and the Dividend (Use after page 185.)

Level A

Divide. Remember to estimate first.

1. $5\overline{)4.525}$ **2.** $8\overline{)8.864}$ **3.** $7\overline{)4.228}$ **4.** $9\overline{)1.827}$ **5.** $6\overline{)\$30.30}$

6. $8\overline{)0.204}$ **7.** $7\overline{)1.407}$ **8.** $2\overline{)8.04}$ **9.** $14\overline{)\$70.28}$ **10.** $49\overline{)\$51.45}$

11. $60.9 \div 58$ **12.** $5.74 \div 28$ **13.** $0.104 \div 26$ **14.** $4.23 \div 47$

15. $204 \div 8$ **16.** $\$49.44 \div 24$ **17.** $2.34 \div 39$ **18.** $5.434 \div 52$

19. A board is 5.2 meters long. It will be cut into 5 equal-length pieces for shelves. How long will each piece be?

Level B

Divide. Remember to estimate first.

20. $8\overline{)0.404}$ **21.** $4\overline{)8.04}$ **22.** $6\overline{)1.206}$ **23.** $5\overline{)4.02}$ **24.** $7\overline{)\$42.49}$

25. $16\overline{)48.8}$ **26.** $17\overline{)\$35.53}$ **27.** $18\overline{)54.9}$ **28.** $12\overline{)0.288}$ **29.** $44\overline{)3.08}$

30. $0.322 \div 46$ **31.** $94.55 \div 31$ **32.** $66.88 \div 22$ **33.** $1.3905 \div 45$

34. $7.619 \div 19$ **35.** $0.68 \div 85$ **36.** $\$28.08 \div 27$ **37.** $8.282 \div 41$

38. A bolt of material is 18 yards long. The whole bolt of material costs $108.90. How much does one yard of material cost?

Level C

Divide. Remember to estimate first.

39. $46\overline{)0.414}$ **40.** $58\overline{)609}$ **41.** $22\overline{)0.55}$ **42.** $25\overline{)1.4}$ **43.** $61\overline{)\$65.27}$

44. $13\overline{)9.178}$ **45.** $25\overline{)98}$ **46.** $15\overline{)120.3}$ **47.** $18\overline{)17.1}$ **48.** $79\overline{)\$82.95}$

49. $8.08 \div 25$ **50.** $8.048 \div 16$ **51.** $0.6105 \div 33$ **52.** $315.9 \div 45$

53. $3.9546 \div 78$ **54.** $66.24 \div 32$ **55.** $0.979 \div 89$ **56.** $\$8.55 \div 95$

57. A roll of ribbon is 187.6 centimeters long. It is cut into 25 pieces. How long is each piece?

Practice PLUS

KEY SKILL: Zeros in the Quotient and the Dividend (Use after page 193.)

Level A

Divide.

1. $0.6\overline{)3}$ **2.** $0.8\overline{)0.048}$ **3.** $0.3\overline{)0.0012}$ **4.** $3.5\overline{)7}$

5. $1.6\overline{)0.048}$ **6.** $1.5\overline{)6}$ **7.** $2\overline{)5}$ **8.** $8\overline{)0.0056}$

9. $0.4 \div 0.8$ **10.** $0.072 \div 1.8$ **11.** $0.036 \div 4.5$ **12.** $\$4 \div 0.25$

13. $0.0138 \div 2.3$ **14.** $9 \div 4.5$ **15.** $0.072 \div 0.8$ **16.** $0.092 \div 0.4$

17. A stack of papers is 6.14 inches high. If each sheet is 0.02 inches thick, how many sheets of paper are in the stack?

Level B

Divide.

18. $0.5\overline{)0.3}$ **19.** $1.4\overline{)0.084}$ **20.** $4\overline{)9}$ **21.** $3\overline{)0.027}$

22. $75\overline{)0.3}$ **23.** $0.08\overline{)8}$ **24.** $0.25\overline{)\$6}$ **25.** $0.65\overline{)0.00455}$

26. $0.47601 \div 0.43$ **27.** $0.7085 \div 65$ **28.** $\$6 \div 0.15$ **29.** $0.00117 \div 0.18$

30. $0.12768 \div 0.42$ **31.** $\$14 \div 0.5$ **32.** $0.0051 \div 1.7$ **33.** $0.4444 \div 22$

34. The heart pumps 7.6 liters of blood in 1.6 minutes. How many liters does it pump per minute?

Level C

Divide.

35. $0.32\overline{)2.4}$ **36.** $75\overline{)1.545}$ **37.** $0.18\overline{)8.1}$ **38.** $0.15\overline{)0.0897}$

39. $8.7\overline{)0.2001}$ **40.** $0.007\overline{)0.000455}$ **41.** $0.022\overline{)44}$ **42.** $0.012\overline{)0.6}$

43. $\$90 \div 4.5$ **44.** $0.0256 \div 8$ **45.** $0.0234 \div 2.6$ **46.** $0.004108 \div 0.079$

47. $1.53 \div 4.5$ **48.** $7.95 \div 0.0265$ **49.** $0.0462 \div 6$ **50.** $\$10 \div 0.25$

51. Gas sells for $.96 a gallon. How many gallons can be purchased for $21?

CHAPTER REVIEW/TEST

LANGUAGE AND MATHEMATICS

Complete the sentences. Use the words in the chart on the right.

1. The amount of matter in an object is its ■.

2. The difference between the highest and lowest numbers in a set is the ■.

3. The middle number in a set when the numbers are in order is the ■.

4. The amount that a container can hold is its ■.

VOCABULARY
median
capacity
mode
mass
range

CONCEPTS AND SKILLS

Estimate the quotient.

5. $4.37 ÷ 7   **6.** 82.08 ÷ 18   **7.** 14.68 ÷ 32   **8.** 489.7 ÷ 52

Divide.

9. 80.96 ÷ 8   **10.** 25.52 ÷ 22   **11.** 92)$1.84   **12.** 0.05)0.074

Simplify.

13. 6 + 3 x 6 ÷ 2 − 5   **14.** 7 + 6 x (5 + 2) − 3   **15.** 48 ÷ 4 x (3 + 7)

Choose the most reasonable measure.

16. weight of a cat   **a.** 1 mg   **b.** 1 g   **c.** 1 kg

17. water in a bathtub   **a.** 400 mL   **b.** 400 L   **c.** 40 L

Complete.

18. 50 cm = ■ m   **19.** 6,000 L = ■ kL   **20.** 0.056 km = ■ m

Find the mean, median, mode, and range for each set of data.

21. $.68, $.82, $1.02, $1.02, $.81

22. 502, 897, 246, 247, 611, 707, 822

Critical Thinking

23. Place parentheses in the expression
$36 \div 6 \times 3 = 7$ to get these answers. **a.** 9 **b.** 25 **c.** 60

Mixed Applications

24. Frank is paid $14.65 an hour. He started work at 8:10 A.M. and finished at 11:20 A.M. About how much money did he earn?

25. Alex has 14 coins in quarters, pennies, and dimes. He has twice as many dimes as quarters and 2 more pennies than quarters. How many of each coin does he have?

PERFORMANCE ASSESSMENT

Work with your group to solve this problem.

The Bowen family has a yearly budget of $494.04 for electricity. They pay $.12 per kilowatt hour of usage. This table shows their monthly electric bills for January through November.

Determine the Bowens' electric bill for December. Then make a table showing the number of kilowatt hours of electricity they used each month. Find the average (mean) monthly electric bill and the average (mean) kilowatt hours used per month.

Electric Bills			
Jan.	$43.44	Jul.	$37.92
Feb.	$44.88	Aug.	$38.64
Mar.	$42.96	Sep.	$39.84
Apr.	$42.00	Oct.	$41.76
May	$38.88	Nov.	$42.48
Jun.	$37.44	Dec.	■

1. *Think about:*
  - the total cost of electricity per kilowatt hour
  - how to determine the cost of electricity for December
  - how to find the mean of the electric bills and kilowatt hours used per month

2. Write statements explaining how you determined the cost of electricity for December, and how you found the mean of the electric bills and kilowatt hours used per month.

CUMULATIVE REVIEW

Choose the letter of the correct answer.

1. Laura bought a book for $7.85 plus tax. Estimate her change from $10.

    a. $3.00   **c.** $.50
    b. $1.00   **d.** not given

2. 568 + 83 + 967 + 458

    a. 2,156   **c.** 2,046
    b. 2,076   **d.** not given

3. Find the volume of a rectangular prism 2 mm by 6.2 mm by 7.54 mm.

    a. 31.48 mm³   **c.** 62.96 mm³
    b. 93.496 mm³   **d.** not given

4. Choose the standard form for 5⁴.

    a. 625   **c.** 20
    b. 5 × 5 × 5 × 5   **d.** not given

5.   7,151
    ×   319

    a. 2,280,269   **c.** 2,281,169
    b. 286,040   **d.** not given

6. Estimate: 92,365 ÷ 34

    a. 30   **c.** 3,000
    b. 300   **d.** not given

7. 85,015 ÷ 7

    a. 12,140 R5   **c.** 12,102 R1
    b. 12,145   **d.** not given

8. 258)43,261

    a. 167 R175
    b. 169
    c. 167 R171
    d. not given

9. What time is it 6 hours 35 minutes after 8:20 A.M.?

    a. 4:15 P.M.
    b. 4:55 P.M.
    c. 2:15 P.M.
    d. not given

10. 631.962 ÷ 9

    a. 70.218   **c.** 72.18
    b. 702.18   **d.** not given

11. 0.067)36.247

    a. 5,410
    b. 541
    c. 0.541
    d. not given

12. Simplify: 45 ÷ (5 × 3) − 2

    a. 25   **c.** 1
    b. 9   **d.** not given

13. Complete: 2,000 g = ■ kg

    a. 0.2   **c.** 2
    b. 20   **d.** not given

14. Find the mean: 87, 71, 94, 79, 94

    a. 94   **c.** 87
    b. 85   **d.** not given

MAGIC SQUARES

For thousands of years *magic squares* have fascinated people of different cultures. According to Chinese myth, the first record of a magic square appeared during the reign of Emperor Yii. The sum of the numbers in each row, column, or diagonal is the same, and is called the *magic sum*.

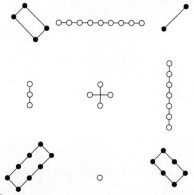

1. What is the magic sum for square A?

2. Is square B a magic square? Tell why your answer is correct.

You can use one magic square to make others.

3. Use square A at the top of the page. Add 5 to each number. Draw the new square of numbers. Is it a magic square? If so, how does the new magic sum compare with the magic sum for the original square?

4. **What if** you start with a magic square and subtract the same number from each number to get a new square? Is the new square also a magic square?

5. Does multiplying each number in a magic square by the same number always produce a new magic square.

A

4	9	2
3	5	7
8	1	6

B

3	2	1
2	1	3
1	3	2

This magic square contains decimals.

1.1	1.3	1.2
1.3	1.2	1.1
1.2	1.1	1.3

6. **What if** you add 0.2 to each number? Do you get a magic square. What happens if you subtract 0.2?

7. What happens if you multiply each number by 0.2? What happens if you divide by 0.2?

8. Draw a new three-by-three square. Fill in the square with digits 1, 2, and 3. Write one digit in each square. Do this so that each digit is used exactly once in each row, each column, and each diagonal. There is more than one way to do this. Find one that gives a magic square.

9. Draw a four-by-four square. Do the same thing you did for the square in Problem 8, but use the four digits 1, 2, 3, and 4. Make a magic square.

The Egyptian city of Alexandria was one of the ancient world's greatest centers of learning. Around 225 B.C., a well-known North African poet, scientist, historian, astronomer, and mathematician named Eratosthenes (air-uh-TOSS-thuh-neez) became the director of the city's huge university library. Eratosthenes also found a way to measure the circumference of the earth.

Alexandria
Syene
(Aswan)
AFRICA

ERATOSTHENES' TALE OF TWO CITIES

In 240 B.C., observations were made of the sun at noon in both Alexandria and another city, Syene (sigh-EE-nee), about 500 miles away. Syene was directly south of Alexandria. The sun's rays pointed straight down at Syene at noon but hit Alexandria at an angle. The angle of the sun over Alexandria was one-fiftieth of a circle. Eratosthenes concluded that Alexandria and Syene were one-fiftieth of a circle apart. He then was able to calculate the circumference of the earth.

1 The angle of the sun over Alexandria was one-fiftieth of a circle. Using what you know about geometry, express the size of that angle in degrees.

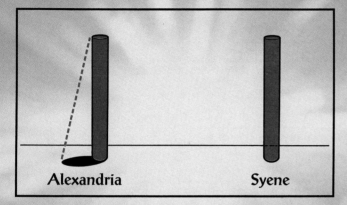

Alexandria   Syene

2 Using Eratosthenes' angle measurement, what is the approximate circumference of the earth in miles?

3 The library in Alexandria reportedly contained 700,000 papyrus and parchment manuscripts. They represented all areas of Greek knowledge. The library was destroyed about A.D. 390. Why was this a great loss for the modern study of mathematics and other subjects?

Mental Math: Divisibility

A. Shelley and Marty are planning the ticket sales for the Wheel-a-thon at Johnson School. They have 1,638 tickets, which they want to divide evenly among the school's 9 classrooms. Will they have any tickets left over?

If 1,638 **is divisible by** 9, there will not be any tickets left over.

Shelley recalls that a number is divisible by 9 if the sum of its digits is divisible by 9.

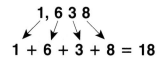

1, 6 3 8

1 + 6 + 3 + 8 = 18

Since 18 is divisible by 9, so is 1,638.

Marty uses a calculator to divide.

1,638 (÷) **9** (=) $\boxed{182.}$

Shelley and Marty find that they will not have any tickets left over.

1. Use Shelley's **divisibility rule** to test if these numbers are divisible by 9. Check with a calculator.
   a. 727   **b.** 6,948   **c.** 5,030,100   **d.** 81,003

2. For each number in Problem 1 that is not divisible by 9, find the two closest numbers that are divisible by 9.

B. Here are a few more divisibility rules.

A number is divisible by:			
2	if the ones digit is 0, 2, 4, 6, or 8.	5	if the ones digit is 0 or 5.
3	if the sum of its digits is divisible by 3.	6	if it is divisible by 2 and by 3.
4	if the last two digits are divisible by 4.	10	if the ones digit is 0.

TRY OUT   Write the letter of the correct answer.

3. Which number is divisible by 9?
   a. 3,499   **c.** 1,070,001
   b. 191,919   **d.** 578

4. Which number is divisible by 6?
   a. 427,616   **c.** 636,363
   b. 12,408   **d.** 38,517

5. Which number is divisible by 5?
   a. 17,340   **c.** 275,396
   b. 5,508   **d.** 515,151

6. Which number is divisible by 4?
   a. 434   **c.** 173,636
   b. 45,405   **d.** 9,462

PRACTICE

Complete the table. Write *yes* or *no*.

Divisible:	37	275	309	1,008	26,453	47,205	8,220
by 2?	7.■	8.■	9.■	10.■	11.■	12.■	13.■
by 3?	14.■	15.■	Yes	16.■	17.■	18.■	19.■
by 4?	20.■	21.■	22.■	23.■	24.■	25.■	26.■
by 5?	27.■	28.■	29.■	30.■	31.■	32.■	33.■
by 6?	34.■	35.■	36.■	37.■	38.■	39.■	40.■
by 9?	No	41.■	42.■	43.■	44.■	45.■	46.■
by 10?	47.■	48.■	49.■	50.■	51.■	52.■	53.■

Critical Thinking

Is the statement *true* or *false*? Give examples to support
your answer.

54. All even numbers are divisible by 4.

55. All numbers that are divisible by 9 are also divisible by 3.

56. All numbers that are divisible by 3 are divisible by 9.

Mixed Applications

Solve. Which method did you use? You may need to use the
Databank on page 551.

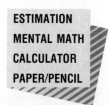

ESTIMATION
MENTAL MATH
CALCULATOR
PAPER/PENCIL

57. How much greater is the seating capacity
of the Kingdome than that of Madison
Square Garden?

58. What is the difference in seating capacity
between the basketball arena with the
greatest capacity and the one with the
least capacity?

59. Bill noticed that the number on his ticket
to the game is the least number that is
divisible by 2, 3, 4, 5 and 6. What is the
number on Bill's ticket?

60. There are 80 people in a marching band.
Can they march in rows of 2? in rows of
3? 4? 5? 6? 9? 10?

Factors and Greatest Common Factor

A. All students who want to play soccer will meet with the coach in Room 4. The room has 24 chairs, and the coach wants to arrange them in rows, putting the same number of chairs in each row.

The coach makes a table and uses multiplication to find all the possible arrangements of chairs.

Number of rows	Chairs in each row
1	24
2	12
3	

1. Copy and complete the table.

2. Can the coach make 5 rows?

Each of the numbers in the table is a **factor** of 24. The factors of 24 are 1, 2, 3, 4, 6, 8, 12, and 24.

3. Find the factors of 36.

B. You can also find **common factors** for two numbers.

Find the factors of 24 and 32.

Factors of 24: 1, 2, 3, 4, 6, 8, 12, 24
Factors of 32: 1, 2, 4, 8, 16, 32

The common factors of both numbers are 1, 2, 4, and 8.

The **greatest common factor (GCF)** of 24 and 32 is 8.

4. What is the greatest common factor of 8 and 12?

TRY OUT Write the letter of the correct answer.

5. Which is a factor of 19?
   a. 9   **b.** 19   **c.** 38   **d.** 18

6. Which is a common factor of 18 and 12?
   a. 3   **b.** 9   **c.** 4   **d.** 36

7. What is the greatest common factor of 16 and 24?
   a. 16   **b.** 48   **c.** 4   **d.** 8

PRACTICE

Find all the factors of the number.

8. 12   **9.** 28   **10.** 30   **11.** 18   **12.** 13   **13.** 50

14. 48   **15.** 49   **16.** 25   **17.** 52   **18.** 56   **19.** 45

Find the greatest common factor of the numbers.

20. 12 and 28   **21.** 20 and 30   **22.** 6 and 18   **23.** 27 and 15

24. 6, 8, and 12   **25.** 10, 20, and 25   **26.** 16, 20, and 28   **27.** 8, 12, 20, and 24

Find the answer.

28. The GCF of two numbers is 3. The greater number is 9. What could the other number be?

29. The GCF of two numbers is 2. The greater number is 6. What could the other number be?

Critical Thinking

30. Which number between 1 and 25 has the greatest number of factors?

Mixed Applications

31. Thirty-six students are to be divided equally into teams with at least 2 players each. What are all the possible numbers of players that could be on a team?

32. Last year 35,670 people attended the big soccer game. This year 37,201 people attended. How many more people came to the game this year?

CHALLENGE

What happens if you add all the factors of a number *except the number itself*? If the sum is:

- less than the number, the number is called a **deficient number.**
- greater than the number, the number is called an **abundant number.**
- equal to the number, the number is called a **perfect number.**

1. Identify all the numbers through 15 as **deficient, abundant,** or **perfect.**

2. What do all abundant numbers have in common?

 **P**rime and Composite Numbers

WORKING TOGETHER

Work in groups. Make a set of number cards from 2 through 30. Shuffle them and place them face down. One student chooses a card and then takes that many centimeter cubes and follows these rules:

- Try to place the cubes into one or more groups with an equal number of cubes in each group.

- Record your results in a table and write the factors represented by the cubes.

Total Number of cubes	Number of groups	Number in each group	Factors
20	1	20	1, 20
20	5	4	5, 4
20	10	2	10, 2
7	1	7	1, 7

- Another student then tries to use the cubes to show two different factors.

- Take turns until no new factors can be found.

- Continue until ten cards have been chosen.

1. Which numbers in your tables can be put only into one group? How many factors other than itself and 1 does each of these numbers have?

A number that is greater than 1 and has exactly two factors, 1 and the number itself, is called a **prime number**.

2. Which numbers can be put into more than one group? How many factors does each of these numbers have?

A number that is greater than 1 and has more than two factors is called a **composite number**.

3. What are the prime and composite numbers in your tables?

Composite numbers can always be written as the product of prime numbers. The product is called the **prime factorization** of the number. One way to find this product is to make a factor tree.

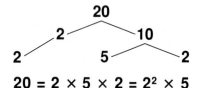

$20 = 2 \times 5 \times 2 = 2^2 \times 5$

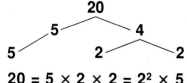

$20 = 5 \times 2 \times 2 = 2^2 \times 5$

4. Make factor trees for 24. How are your factor trees similar? How are they different?

Notice that, even though there may be several ways to start a factor tree, you always end up with the same prime factors.

SHARING IDEAS

Make a class chart listing the numbers from 2 through 30.

5. Use the lists from all the groups to label the prime numbers (*P*) and the composite numbers (*C*).

6. Identify any unlabeled numbers as prime or composite.

PRACTICE

7. 45	**8.** 23	**9.** 56	**10.** 13	**11.** 91	**12.** 55
13. 61	**14.** 19	**15.** 99	**16.** 72	**17.** 89	**18.** 39

Make a factor tree and write the prime factorization.

19. 18	**20.** 54	**21.** 48	**22.** 96	**23.** 100	**24.** 87

Solve. Use your calculator.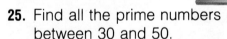

25. Find all the prime numbers between 30 and 50.

26. Find all the prime numbers between 50 and 100.

Critical Thinking

27. List the numbers less than 20 that have exactly three factors. Find two other numbers greater than 20 that have exactly three factors. Look for a pattern.

Mixed Applications

28. Marie buys 3 birthday cards for 95 cents each. The tax is 24 cents. How much does she pay?

29. Gerry scores a total of 456 points in bowling 3 games. What is her average score per game?

30. Bill's score is a 2-digit number. Both digits are prime numbers. The difference between the two digits is 1. What could Bill's score be?

31. *Write a problem* involving prime numbers. Solve. Ask others to solve it.

EXTRA PRACTICE, page 262

Multiples and Least Common Multiple

A. Esther and Harold are preparing the track for the school's field day. Counting from the starting line, they put a green flag every 6 yd along the track.

To figure out where to put the flags, they make a list of the **multiples** of 6.

So 0, 6, 12, 18, and 24 are the first five multiples of 6.

$$6 \times 0 = 0$$
$$6 \times 1 = 6$$
$$6 \times 2 = 12$$
$$6 \times 3 = 18$$
$$6 \times 4 = 24$$

1. What are the next four multiples of 6?

B. You can also find **common multiples** of two numbers. To get the track ready for a different game, Esther and Harold count from the starting line and put a red flag every 4 yd. At which points are there both green and red flags?

Find the multiples of 6 and 4. Do not include 0.

Multiples of 6: 6, 12, 18, 24
Multiples of 4: 4, 8, 12, 16, 20, 24

So 12 and 24 are called common multiples of 6 and 4. These are the points where there are both red and green flags.

The **least common multiple (LCM)** of 6 and 4 is 12. It is the first point after the starting line where there is both a red and a green flag.

2. ***What if*** Esther and Harold had put a red flag every 10 yd and a green flag every 6 yd? Which would be the first point to have both a green and a red flag?

TRY OUT Find the multiples and least common multiples.

3. List the first six multiples of 8.

4. Find the least common multiple of 6 and 8.

PRACTICE

Find the first six multiples of the number.

5. 5   **6.** 7   **7.** 11   **8.** 20   **9.** 25   **10.** 12

Find the least common multiple of the numbers.

11. 2 and 5   **12.** 20 and 5   **13.** 6 and 9   **14.** 12 and 8   **15.** 3 and 6

16. 4 and 10   **17.** 5 and 7   **18.** 12 and 18   **19.** 12 and 16   **20.** 10 and 15

21. 2, 3, and 5   **22.** 6, 10, and 12   **23.** 3, 5, and 10   **24.** 8, 12, and 16

Critical Thinking

25. Write any five multiples of 100 and any five multiples of 1,000. Is every multiple of 100 also a multiple of 1,000? Give an example.

Mixed Applications

26. The fifth graders sit in every third row of the stands. The sixth graders sit in every other row, starting with the second row. What is the first row in which both fifth and sixth graders may sit?

27. Riva and Sam enter a softball-throwing contest. Riva throws the ball 17.6 m. Sam throws it 21.2 m. How much farther does Sam throw the ball than Riva?

28. The school buys 15 dozen hot dogs. If one hot dog costs 12 cents, how much does the school pay for all the hot dogs?

29. A total of 137 students take part in field day. There are 15 more girls than boys. How many girls and how many boys take part?

LOGICAL REASONING

The product of the GCF and the LCM of two numbers is equal to the product of the two numbers.

Example: The product of 6 and 8 is 48.

GCF of 6 and 8 = 2   LCM of 6 and 8 = 24   GCF × LCM = 2 × 24 = 48

1. How could you use this idea to find the LCM of two numbers?

Use this method to find the LCM of the following numbers.

2. 6 and 4   **3.** 4 and 10   **4.** 10 and 25   **5.** 20 and 50

PROBLEM SOLVING

Strategy: Finding a Pattern

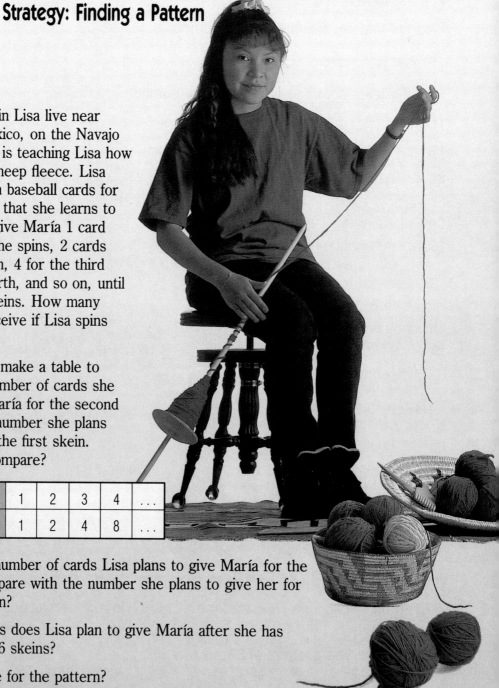

María and her cousin Lisa live near Shiprock, New Mexico, on the Navajo Reservation. María is teaching Lisa how to spin yarn from sheep fleece. Lisa wants to give María baseball cards for every skein of yarn that she learns to spin. She plans to give María 1 card for the first skein she spins, 2 cards for the second skein, 4 for the third skein, 8 for the fourth, and so on, until she has spun 10 skeins. How many cards will María receive if Lisa spins 10 skeins?

1. Lisa decides to make a table to compare the number of cards she plans to give María for the second skein with the number she plans to give her for the first skein. How do they compare?

Number of Skeins	1	2	3	4	...
Number of Cards	1	2	4	8	...

2. How does the number of cards Lisa plans to give María for the third skein compare with the number she plans to give her for the second skein?

3. How many cards does Lisa plan to give María after she has spun 5 skeins? 6 skeins?

4. What is the rule for the pattern?

5. Copy and extend the table to show how many cards Lisa plans to give María for spinning the rest of the skeins.

6. How many cards does Lisa plan to give María for spinning the tenth skein?

7. How many cards in all does Lisa plan to give María?

PRACTICE

Find a pattern to solve the problem.

8. Lisa is designing a pattern like the one to the right to go on the back of her jeans jacket. The dots represent stars. She plans to enlarge the design to follow the pattern and include two larger squares. How many stars will she sew in the largest square?

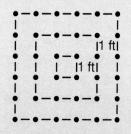

9. A rug that Lisa is weaving from the yarn she has spun and dyed has a striped pattern. The pattern starts with red, red, green, blue, and yellow and then repeats. What color is the 37th stripe?

10. Lisa and her brother Tom are helping their neighbors build a fence around the sheep pen near their *hogan* (traditional Navajo home). On the first day they put in 6 fence posts, on the second they put in 9, on the third they put in 12, and so on. How many posts did they put in on the tenth and final day? How many fence posts did they put in all together?

11. For her father's birthday, Lisa has decided to make him a blanket from the yarn she has spun. Her design calls for a red stripe in the following positions: first row, fourth row, seventh row, and so on. Out of the first 30 rows, how many rows are red?

Strategies and Skills Review

Solve. Use estimation, mental math, a calculator, or paper and pencil.

12. A shop in Sedona sells yarn that María has spun for $24.50 a skein. On Saturday the shop collected slightly under $200 from the sale of that yarn. How many skeins did the shop sell?

13. Another type of yarn sells for $19.80 a skein. A customer bought 5 of those skeins, 3 packages of a yellow dye for $1.35 each, and 12 packages of a blue dye for $1.10 each. How much did he spend?

14. Tom and Lisa added 30 feet of fencing to the sheep pen. They placed a post every 4 feet from the beginning of the fence and had a few feet of fencing left over. How many posts did they place?

15. Lisa and her neighbors are shearing 16 sheep. It will take them $1\frac{1}{4}$ hours to do the shearing. They have 9 sheep left to shear. How many sheep have they shorn so far?

16. María's mother sold 5 pounds of fleece for $17.50. How much did the fleece cost per pound?

17. **Write a problem** that can be solved by finding and using a pattern. Solve your problem. Ask others to solve it.

Fractions and Equivalent Fractions

A. Alicia is looking at a list of the ribbons to be awarded at the school science fair. She thinks: "Plant projects won $\frac{5}{9}$ of the ribbons." Alicia knows that a **fraction** can be used to name part of a group.

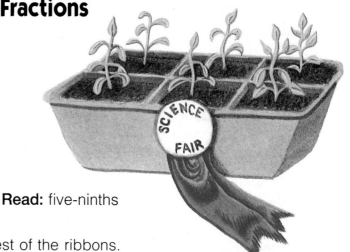

5 ribbons for plant projects → $\frac{5}{9}$ ← **numerator**
9 ribbons in the group → ← **denominator**

Read: five-ninths

1. Write a fraction describing the rest of the ribbons.

B. A fraction can name part of a region. This region is divided into 10 equal parts; $\frac{7}{10}$ of the region is shaded.

2. What part of the region is not shaded?

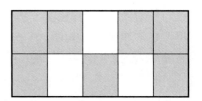

C. Fractions that name the same part are called **equivalent fractions**.

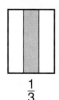 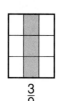 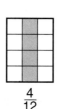

$\frac{1}{3}$ = $\frac{2}{6}$ = $\frac{3}{9}$ = $\frac{4}{12}$

So $\frac{1}{3}$, $\frac{2}{6}$, $\frac{3}{9}$, and $\frac{4}{12}$ are equivalent fractions.

To find equivalent fractions, multiply or divide the numerator and the denominator by the same nonzero number.

$$\frac{2}{6} = \frac{2 \times 2}{6 \times 2} = \frac{4}{12} \qquad \frac{3}{9} = \frac{3 \div 3}{9 \div 3} = \frac{1}{3}$$

You can use equivalent fractions to find missing numerators and denominators.

$\frac{2}{5} = \frac{\blacksquare}{15}$ *Think:* $5 \times \blacksquare = 15$ $\frac{6}{8} = \frac{\blacksquare}{4}$ *Think:* $8 \div \blacksquare = 4$

$\frac{2 \times 3}{5 \times 3} = \frac{6}{15}$ $\frac{6 \div 2}{8 \div 2} = \frac{3}{4}$

3. Which fraction represents the shaded part of the region?

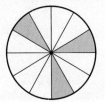

   a. $\frac{3}{5}$ **b.** $\frac{2}{5}$ **c.** $\frac{5}{3}$ **d.** $\frac{2}{3}$

4. Which is equivalent to $\frac{9}{12}$?   **a.** $\frac{18}{10}$ **b.** $\frac{1}{2}$ **c.** $\frac{2}{3}$ **d.** $\frac{3}{4}$

PRACTICE

What fraction of the region is shaded?

5.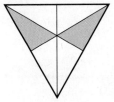
   6.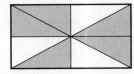
   7.

Find three equivalent fractions.

8. $\frac{2}{3}$ **9.** $\frac{3}{4}$ **10.** $\frac{2}{9}$ **11.** $\frac{6}{7}$ **12.** $\frac{5}{8}$ **13.** $\frac{2}{5}$

14. $\frac{5}{6}$ **15.** $\frac{1}{2}$ **16.** $\frac{1}{3}$ **17.** $\frac{4}{5}$ **18.** $\frac{3}{7}$ **19.** $\frac{4}{11}$

Complete.

20. $\frac{6}{8} = \frac{\blacksquare}{16}$ **21.** $\frac{2}{3} = \frac{\blacksquare}{15}$ **22.** $\frac{1}{2} = \frac{\blacksquare}{20}$ **23.** $\frac{6}{8} = \frac{3}{\blacksquare}$ **24.** $\frac{12}{15} = \frac{\blacksquare}{5}$

25. $\frac{4}{5} = \frac{\blacksquare}{10}$ **26.** $\frac{12}{16} = \frac{3}{\blacksquare}$ **27.** $\frac{2}{3} = \frac{\blacksquare}{15}$ **28.** $\frac{5}{20} = \frac{1}{\blacksquare}$ **29.** $\frac{3}{7} = \frac{\blacksquare}{21}$

30. $\frac{2}{5} = \frac{4}{\blacksquare}$ **31.** $\frac{20}{30} = \frac{\blacksquare}{6}$ **32.** $\frac{2}{5} = \frac{\blacksquare}{25}$ **33.** $\frac{9}{12} = \frac{\blacksquare}{4}$ **34.** $\frac{3}{5} = \frac{9}{\blacksquare}$

Critical Thinking

35. This region is divided into 5 parts. Is $\frac{3}{5}$ of the region shaded? Why or why not?

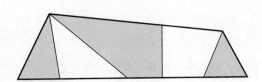

Mixed Applications

36. In the state finals of the science fair, the winner receives $1,000. The next 8 winners receive $750 each. What fraction of the total prize money is the winner's share?

37. The winner of the science fair spent 115 hours on her project. The 8 second-place winners spent a total of 767 hours on theirs. What is the average of hours?

Fractions in Simplest Form

SAW THE SHOW	DIDN'T SEE THE SHOW
卌 卌 卌 卌	卌 卌

Mr. Ortega's class rated a new TV show. They also recorded the number of students who did not watch the show. Their results showed that $\frac{10}{30}$ of the class did not see the show.

Find the **simplest form** of $\frac{10}{30}$.

To find the simplest form of a fraction, divide the numerator and the denominator by common factors until the only common factor is 1. Here are two methods:

Dividing by Common Factors

$$\frac{10}{30} = \frac{10 \div 5}{30 \div 5} = \frac{2}{6} = \frac{2 \div 2}{6 \div 2} = \frac{1}{3}$$

Dividing by the GCF

$$\frac{10}{30} = \frac{10 \div 10}{30 \div 10} = \frac{1}{3}$$

So $\frac{10}{30}$ in simplest form is $\frac{1}{3}$.

1. How would you simplify $\frac{32}{40}$? Which method did you use?

TRY OUT   Write the letter of the correct answer.

2. Which fraction is in simplest form?   **a.** $\frac{4}{6}$ **b.** $\frac{4}{7}$ **c.** $\frac{4}{8}$ **d.** $\frac{4}{10}$

3. Which fraction is *not* in simplest form?   **a.** $\frac{4}{12}$ **b.** $\frac{5}{6}$ **c.** $\frac{27}{100}$ **d.** $\frac{2}{5}$

4. Which fraction is the simplest form of $\frac{24}{30}$?   **a.** $\frac{3}{4}$ **b.** $\frac{4}{5}$ **c.** $\frac{8}{10}$ **d.** $\frac{12}{15}$

5. Which fraction is the simplest form of $\frac{75}{100}$?   **a.** $\frac{1}{4}$ **b.** $\frac{1}{2}$ **c.** $\frac{3}{4}$ **d.** $\frac{7}{10}$

PRACTICE

Write the fraction in simplest form.

6. $\frac{6}{8}$ 7. $\frac{4}{12}$ 8. $\frac{4}{6}$ 9. $\frac{10}{12}$ 10. $\frac{6}{15}$ 11. $\frac{10}{25}$

12. $\frac{25}{100}$ 13. $\frac{6}{50}$ 14. $\frac{9}{27}$ 15. $\frac{27}{36}$ 16. $\frac{3}{18}$ 17. $\frac{6}{24}$

18. $\frac{18}{48}$ 19. $\frac{10}{15}$ 20. $\frac{3}{6}$ 21. $\frac{2}{5}$ 22. $\frac{8}{10}$ 23. $\frac{21}{49}$

24. $\frac{4}{9}$ 25. $\frac{15}{18}$ 26. $\frac{16}{64}$ 27. $\frac{25}{45}$ 28. $\frac{8}{13}$ 29. $\frac{27}{81}$

30. $\frac{24}{48}$ 31. $\frac{64}{72}$ 32. $\frac{21}{25}$ 33. $\frac{49}{63}$ 34. $\frac{42}{75}$ 35. $\frac{18}{26}$

36. $\frac{65}{100}$ 37. $\frac{30}{150}$ 38. $\frac{5}{5}$ 39. $\frac{10}{10}$ 40. $\frac{20}{10}$ 41. $\frac{75}{25}$

Critical Thinking

Tell whether the fraction is in simplest form.
Give examples to support your answer.

42. The GCF of the numerator and the denominator is a prime number.

43. The numerator and the denominator are both prime numbers.

Mixed Applications

44. Five of Mr. Ortega's students who were absent the day the TV show was rated are in class today. They all had watched the show. Now, what is the fraction of the class that did not watch the show? Write your answer in simplest form.

45. All 5 students who had been absent from Mr. Ortega's class gave the television show a rating of "Poor." Did this change the survey? What fraction now represents the part of the class that gave the show a rating of "Poor"? Write your answer in simplest form.

46. Joanne studied nature video tapes from 6:15 P.M. to 10 P.M. on each of 3 nights. How long did she study the tapes altogether?

Mixed Review

Find the answer. Which method did you use?

MENTAL MATH
CALCULATOR
PAPER/PENCIL

47. $450,027 + 5,105 + 536,824$ 48. $\$8,432 + \$685 + \$1,917$

49. 2^5 50. $738 \div 9$ 51. $1.05 \times \$9.80$ 52. $\$18.97 - \$6.27$

EXTRA PRACTICE, page 263

STRETCHING the LIMITS

Visual Reasoning

A. Do these drawings look alike to you?

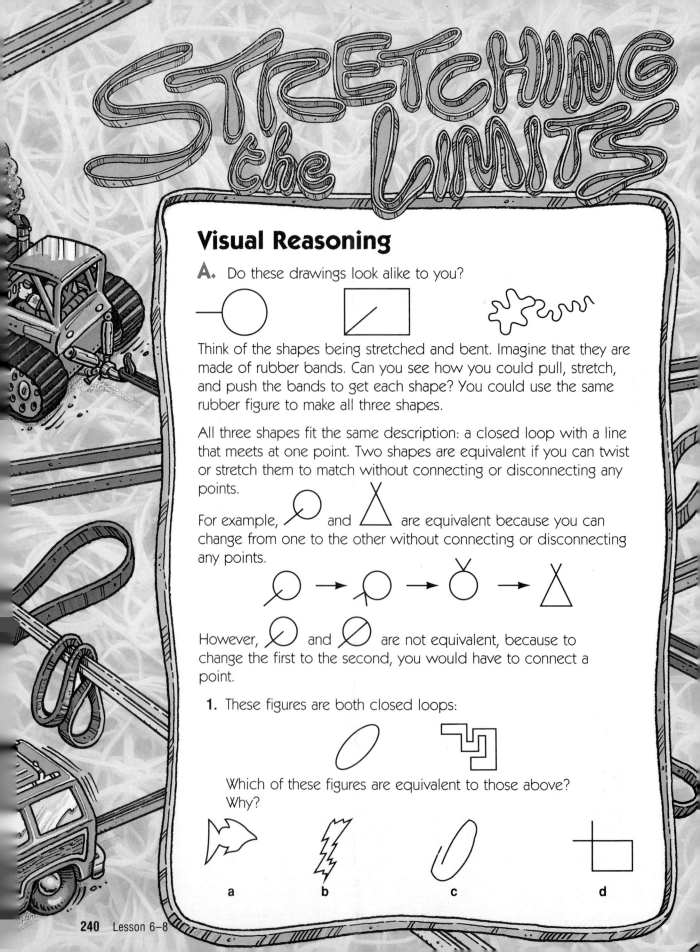

Think of the shapes being stretched and bent. Imagine that they are made of rubber bands. Can you see how you could pull, stretch, and push the bands to get each shape? You could use the same rubber figure to make all three shapes.

All three shapes fit the same description: a closed loop with a line that meets at one point. Two shapes are equivalent if you can twist or stretch them to match without connecting or disconnecting any points.

For example,   and   are equivalent because you can change from one to the other without connecting or disconnecting any points.

However,   and   are not equivalent, because to change the first to the second, you would have to connect a point.

1. These figures are both closed loops:

   Which of these figures are equivalent to those above? Why?

   a   b   c   d

2. Look at this figure:
Which of the figures below
could be made from it?

e. f. g. h.

B. Now look at the set of shapes below.

3. Which shapes are equivalent? To help you find matching
shapes, try describing each shape. For example, shape j is
two closed loops that meet at one point.

i. j. k. l.

m. n. o. p.

q. r. s. t.

u. v. w. x.

4. Now look at the set of letters below.

A B C D E F G H I J K L M N
O P Q R S T U V W X Y Z

Many letters are equivalent to each other. For example,
F is equivalent to G.

F → ⊓ → T → J → G

What other letters are equivalent? Which letters are not
like any others? Can you find letters that are equivalent to
each of the letters of your name?

241

Mixed Numbers

A. Tasha is playing with a puzzle. She is putting pieces into circular frames. Each piece is one-fourth of the circle.

Tasha has eleven quarter circles, or $\frac{11}{4}$. She fills 2 whole circles with 8 pieces and three-fourths of another circle with 3 pieces that are left. So she has covered $2\frac{3}{4}$ circles.

$$\underset{\substack{\uparrow \\ \text{improper} \\ \text{fraction}}}{\frac{11}{4}} \text{ circles} = \underset{\substack{\uparrow \\ \text{mixed} \\ \text{number}}}{2\frac{3}{4}} \text{ circles}$$

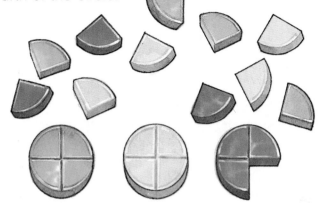

B. You can rename an improper fraction as a mixed number.

Step 1	Step 2	Step 3
Divide the numerator by the denominator.	Write the remainder in the quotient as a fraction.	Write the quotient in simplest form.
$\frac{14}{6} \rightarrow 6\overline{)\begin{array}{r} 2 \\ 14 \\ \underline{12} \\ 2 \end{array}}$	$6\overline{)\begin{array}{r} 2\frac{2}{6} \\ 14 \\ \underline{12} \\ 2 \end{array}}$ $\leftarrow$ remainder $\leftarrow$ divisor	$2\frac{2}{6} = 2\frac{1}{3}$

1. **What if** you had first written $\frac{14}{6}$ in simplest form before dividing? How would the division have been different?

C. You can also rename a mixed number as an improper fraction.

Step 1	Step 2	Step 3
Multiply the whole number by the denominator.	Add the numerator to the product.	Write the sum over the denominator.
$3\frac{1}{4}$ $4 \times 3 = 12$	$3\frac{1}{4}$ $12 + 1 = 13$	$3\frac{1}{4} = \frac{13}{4}$

2. Rename the number 4 as an improper fraction with a denominator of 6.

TRY OUT

Write the letter of the correct answer.

3. $\frac{9}{4} = \blacksquare$ **a.** $\frac{4}{9}$ **b.** $4\frac{1}{9}$ **c.** $2\frac{1}{4}$ **d.** $2\frac{1}{9}$

4. $5\frac{3}{4} = \blacksquare$ **a.** $\frac{20}{4}$ **b.** $\frac{23}{4}$ **c.** $\frac{19}{3}$ **d.** $\frac{15}{4}$

PRACTICE

Write a fraction and a mixed number or a whole number for the picture.

5.   **6.** 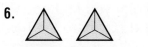   **7.**

Rename the fraction as a mixed number or as a whole number.

8. $\frac{47}{5}$ **9.** $\frac{25}{3}$ **10.** $\frac{17}{4}$ **11.** $\frac{29}{6}$ **12.** $\frac{45}{8}$ **13.** $\frac{85}{9}$

14. $\frac{10}{6}$ **15.** $\frac{48}{10}$ **16.** $\frac{20}{6}$ **17.** $\frac{42}{7}$ **18.** $\frac{24}{6}$ **19.** $\frac{63}{7}$

20. $\frac{18}{7}$ **21.** $\frac{21}{3}$ **22.** $\frac{18}{4}$ **23.** $\frac{36}{8}$ **24.** $\frac{54}{9}$ **25.** $\frac{39}{6}$

Rename the mixed number as a fraction.

26. $8\frac{1}{2}$ **27.** $6\frac{2}{3}$ **28.** $4\frac{3}{4}$ **29.** $3\frac{3}{10}$ **30.** $2\frac{4}{7}$ **31.** $8\frac{3}{4}$

32. $2\frac{7}{9}$ **33.** $5\frac{7}{10}$ **34.** $3\frac{5}{8}$ **35.** $1\frac{2}{3}$ **36.** $9\frac{4}{9}$ **37.** $6\frac{7}{8}$

38. $6\frac{3}{5}$ **39.** $8\frac{11}{12}$ **40.** $5\frac{7}{12}$ **41.** $10\frac{9}{10}$ **42.** $10\frac{7}{8}$ **43.** $10\frac{4}{7}$

Complete.

44. $5 = 4\frac{\blacksquare}{4}$ **45.** $2 = 1\frac{\blacksquare}{5}$ **46.** $5\frac{8}{5} = 6\frac{\blacksquare}{5}$ **47.** $8\frac{7}{8} = 7\frac{\blacksquare}{8}$ **48.** $3\frac{3}{2} = 4\frac{\blacksquare}{2}$

Mixed Applications

49. Tasha makes a puzzle. She cuts out a square piece of cardboard $\frac{45}{8}$ in. on a side. Express the length of a side as a mixed number of inches.

50. Teresa has saved $14 to buy an outfit. The pants cost $8.75, and the shirt costs $5.35. Has she saved enough money?

51. Tina is making a birthday cake. The recipe calls for $4\frac{1}{2}$ c of flour. She has only a $\frac{1}{2}$-c measure. How many times will she need to use the measuring cup?

Comparing and Ordering

A. In Mrs. Teale's class, $\frac{5}{6}$ of the students met their goal in the ticket contest. In Mr. Gordon's class, $\frac{3}{4}$ of the students met their goal. Whose class did better?

Compare $\frac{5}{6}$ and $\frac{3}{4}$.

When fractions have different denominators, you find equivalent fractions with a common denominator and compare the numerators.

Find equivalent fractions.

$$\frac{5}{6} = \frac{5 \times 2}{6 \times 2} = \frac{10}{12} \qquad \frac{3}{4} = \frac{3 \times 3}{4 \times 3} = \frac{9}{12}$$

Compare.

$$\frac{10}{12} > \frac{9}{12}, \text{ so } \frac{5}{6} > \frac{3}{4}$$

Since $\frac{5}{6} > \frac{3}{4}$, Mrs. Teale's class did better than Mr. Gordon's.

The **least common denominator** of $\frac{5}{6}$ and $\frac{3}{4}$ is 12. It is the least common multiple of the two denominators.

1. What is the least common denominator of $\frac{2}{3}$ and $\frac{1}{6}$?

B. You can order fractions by comparing.

On which day did the smallest fraction of students turn in money?

Order $\frac{2}{5}$, $\frac{1}{6}$, $\frac{8}{15}$, and $\frac{3}{10}$ from least to greatest.

Students turning in money:			
Monday	$\frac{2}{5}$	Wednesday	$\frac{8}{15}$
Tuesday	$\frac{1}{6}$	Thursday	$\frac{3}{10}$

First write all the fractions with a common denominator. Use the least common denominator, 30.

$$\frac{2}{5} = \frac{12}{30} \qquad \frac{1}{6} = \frac{5}{30} \qquad \frac{8}{15} = \frac{16}{30} \qquad \frac{3}{10} = \frac{9}{30}$$

The order from least to greatest is $\frac{1}{6}, \frac{3}{10}, \frac{2}{5}, \frac{8}{15}$.

The smallest fraction of students turned in money on Tuesday.

TRY OUT

Which is greater?

2. $\frac{1}{2}$ or $\frac{3}{5}$

3. $\frac{3}{8}$ or $\frac{1}{6}$

4. $\frac{2}{3}$ or $\frac{3}{4}$

5. $\frac{5}{6}$ or $\frac{5}{18}$

Order from least to greatest.

6. $\frac{1}{2}, \frac{2}{3}, \frac{1}{6}$

7. $\frac{4}{5}, \frac{1}{7}, \frac{4}{9}$

8. $\frac{7}{10}, \frac{5}{6}, \frac{3}{5}$

9. $\frac{1}{2}, \frac{1}{3}, \frac{3}{8}$

PRACTICE

Compare. Write >, <, or =.

10. $\frac{1}{4} \bullet \frac{1}{3}$ **11.** $\frac{1}{5} \bullet \frac{3}{15}$ **12.** $\frac{7}{3} \bullet \frac{1}{2}$ **13.** $\frac{4}{5} \bullet \frac{8}{11}$ **14.** $\frac{3}{10} \bullet \frac{1}{4}$

15. $5\frac{5}{6} \bullet 5\frac{3}{4}$ **16.** $2\frac{1}{2} \bullet 2\frac{4}{8}$ **17.** $4\frac{3}{7} \bullet 3\frac{2}{5}$ **18.** $5 \bullet 6\frac{2}{3}$ **19.** $7\frac{1}{2} \bullet 7\frac{4}{5}$

20. $\frac{2}{5} \bullet \frac{1}{3}$ **21.** $4\frac{7}{8} \bullet 5\frac{1}{8}$ **22.** $5\frac{1}{2} \bullet 5$ **23.** $\frac{20}{2} \bullet 10\frac{3}{8}$ **24.** $\frac{2}{3} \bullet \frac{6}{9}$

Order from least to greatest.

25. $\frac{3}{4}, \frac{2}{3}, \frac{1}{2}$ **26.** $\frac{1}{6}, \frac{5}{3}, \frac{2}{9}$ **27.** $\frac{1}{3}, \frac{4}{5}, \frac{5}{6}$ **28.** $\frac{2}{5}, \frac{3}{10}, \frac{2}{3}$ **29.** $\frac{5}{6}, \frac{2}{3}, \frac{4}{9}$

30. $6\frac{2}{9}, 3\frac{3}{7}, 6\frac{1}{8}$ **31.** $2\frac{3}{4}, 3\frac{2}{3}, 2\frac{4}{5}$ **32.** $4\frac{1}{2}, 4\frac{1}{8}, 4\frac{1}{4}$ **33.** $9\frac{1}{5}, 7\frac{1}{3}, 7\frac{2}{5}$ **34.** $12\frac{6}{7}, 7\frac{4}{5}, 1\frac{2}{3}$

35. $8\frac{2}{3}, 5\frac{5}{6}, 8\frac{7}{9}$ **36.** $\frac{4}{5}, 2\frac{2}{3}, 2\frac{3}{8}$ **37.** $5\frac{5}{8}, 8, 5\frac{7}{12}$ **38.** $7\frac{7}{8}, 7\frac{1}{6}, \frac{17}{3}$ **39.** $5\frac{1}{3}, \frac{5}{6}, 6$

Critical Thinking

Fractions with 1 in the numerator are called **unit fractions**.

40. Which is greater, $\frac{1}{2}$ or $\frac{1}{3}$? $\frac{1}{10}$ or $\frac{1}{12}$?

41. Make up a rule for ordering fractions with the same numerator.

Mixed Applications

42. Margaret spends $3\frac{2}{3}$ hours selling tickets on Saturday. Clifton spends $3\frac{7}{12}$ hours. Who spends more time selling tickets?

43. Adult tickets cost $2.75, and student tickets cost 85¢. If you buy 3 tickets, what are all the possible amounts you can spend?

44. Whoever sells the most tickets earns free passes to the fair. Richard has reached $\frac{11}{8}$ of his quota, and Karen has reached $\frac{7}{5}$ of hers. Who is ahead?

45. The serial number printed on the first ticket sold is 00805. The serial number on the last ticket is 01621. How many tickets were sold?

LOGICAL REASONING

A blue beacon flashes every $\frac{1}{3}$ minute. A green beacon flashes every $\frac{1}{4}$ minute. They flash at the same time at 10:00 P.M. What is the next time that the beacons will flash together again?

Rounding Fractions and Mixed Numbers

A. Ben is planting flowers in his garden. He works for 50 minutes on Tuesday, and 25 minutes on Thursday. On Saturday he works for 5 minutes before it starts to rain. On each day, does Ben work about 0 hours, $\frac{1}{2}$ hour or 1 hour?

Think: On Tuesday, Ben works $\frac{50}{60}$, or $\frac{5}{6}$ hour. $\frac{5}{6}$ h close to 1 h

On Thursday, Ben works $\frac{25}{60}$, or $\frac{5}{12}$ hour. $\frac{5}{12}$ h close to $\frac{1}{2}$ h

On Saturday, Ben works $\frac{5}{60}$, or $\frac{1}{12}$ hour. $\frac{1}{12}$ h close to 0 h

Is the fraction described below closest to 0, $\frac{1}{2}$, or 1?

1. The numerator is very small compared with the denominator.

2. The denominator is about twice as great as the numerator.

3. The numerator and denominator are almost equal.

B. You can round mixed numbers to the nearest half or whole number.

Rounding to the Nearest Half

Think: Is the fractional part closest to 0, to $\frac{1}{2}$, or to 1?

Round $2\frac{2}{3}$: $\frac{2}{3}$ is closest to $\frac{1}{2}$, so $2\frac{2}{3}$ rounds to $2\frac{1}{2}$.

Round $5\frac{7}{8}$: $\frac{7}{8}$ is closest to 1, so $5\frac{7}{8}$ rounds up to 6.

Round $8\frac{1}{9}$: $\frac{1}{9}$ is closest to 0, so $8\frac{1}{9}$ rounds down to 8.

Rounding to the Nearest Whole Number

Look at the fractional part of the mixed number.

If it is less than $\frac{1}{2}$, round down. $7\frac{3}{8}$ rounds down to 7

If it is equal to or greater than $\frac{1}{2}$, round up. $2\frac{5}{9}$ rounds up to 3

TRY OUT   Write the letter of the correct answer.

4. Which fraction is closest to $\frac{1}{2}$?   **a.** $\frac{9}{5}$ **b.** $\frac{8}{9}$ **c.** $\frac{5}{9}$ **d.** $\frac{1}{5}$

5. Which fraction is closest to 1?   **a.** $\frac{8}{7}$ **b.** $\frac{7}{1}$ **c.** $\frac{1}{7}$ **d.** $\frac{3}{7}$

6. Round $15\frac{2}{5}$ to the nearest whole number.   **a.** 16   **b.** 20   **c.** 15   **d.** 10

7. Round $63\frac{8}{9}$ to the nearest half.   **a.** 60   **b.** $63\frac{1}{2}$ **c.** 63   **d.** 64

PRACTICE

Is the fraction closest to 0, to $\frac{1}{2}$, or to 1?

8. $\frac{7}{8}$ 9. $\frac{3}{142}$ 10. $\frac{6}{7}$ 11. $\frac{6}{11}$ 12. $\frac{39}{37}$ 13. $\frac{15}{99}$

14. $\frac{1}{10}$ 15. $\frac{4}{10}$ 16. $\frac{10}{21}$ 17. $\frac{98}{100}$ 18. $\frac{3}{100}$ 19. $\frac{8}{9}$

20. $\frac{9}{19}$ 21. $\frac{24}{47}$ 22. $\frac{1}{5}$ 23. $\frac{13}{15}$ 24. $\frac{719}{800}$ 25. $\frac{4}{73}$

Round to the nearest whole number and to the nearest half.

26. $3\frac{7}{8}$ 27. $2\frac{6}{13}$ 28. $8\frac{5}{10}$ 29. $4\frac{1}{10}$ 30. $8\frac{5}{9}$ 31. $6\frac{2}{5}$

32. $10\frac{1}{12}$ 33. $6\frac{8}{9}$ 34. $99\frac{44}{100}$ 35. $5\frac{4}{5}$ 36. $4\frac{8}{16}$ 37. $28\frac{9}{15}$

38. $2\frac{4}{7}$ 39. $16\frac{3}{16}$ 40. $9\frac{9}{11}$ 41. $4\frac{23}{50}$ 42. $10\frac{8}{9}$ 43. $1\frac{19}{35}$

Use a whole number or a mixed number, rounded to the nearest half, to express the information in the statement.

44. Jill runs $3\frac{1}{8}$ miles before school. About how many miles does she run?

45. At the bakery Jack uses 29 eggs in making cakes. About how many dozen eggs does he use?

46. Jason practices for his piano lesson for 4 hours and 34 minutes. About how many hours does he practice?

47. Wilma makes 19 quarter-pound burgers in her job after school. About how many pounds does she make?

Mixed Applications

Solve. Which method did you use?

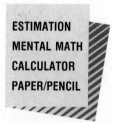

ESTIMATION
MENTAL MATH
CALCULATOR
PAPER/PENCIL

48. Ben pulls weeds for 45 minutes, then trims hedges for 55 minutes. About how long does he work? Round your answer to the nearest half hour.

49. Paul is planting seeds in a row for a science experiment. He plants 1 seed at one end of the row and 1 seed every 3.5 cm along the row. How many seeds will he plant if the row is 70 cm long?

50. Mrs. Loren buys 5 saplings that cost $39.95 each. There is no tax. How much does she pay for the saplings?

51. Gail has $3\frac{1}{4}$ quarts of plant food. She needs 7 quarts. About how many more quarts does Gail need?

Customary Units of Length

A. These pictures show some customary units of length.

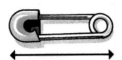

The safety pin has
a length of about
1 inch (in.).

The rain boot has
a height of about
1 foot (ft).

The window has
a width of about
1 yard (yd).

It takes about
20 minutes to walk
1 mile (mi).

These are the relationships among
the common units of length in the
customary system.

1 ft = 12 in.	1 mi = 5,280 ft
1 yd = 3 ft	1 mi = 1,760 yd

B. You can use an inch ruler to measure objects.

The length of the rectangle is:

- 2 in. to the nearest inch.
- $2\frac{1}{2}$ in. to the nearest $\frac{1}{2}$ in.
- $2\frac{1}{4}$ in. to the nearest $\frac{1}{4}$ in.
- $2\frac{3}{8}$ in. to the nearest $\frac{1}{8}$ in.
- $2\frac{5}{16}$ in. to the nearest $\frac{1}{16}$ in.

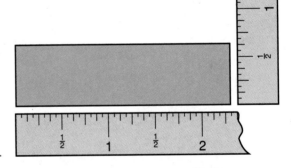

1. What is the width of the rectangle to the nearest inch?
$\frac{1}{2}$ in.? $\frac{1}{4}$ in.? $\frac{1}{8}$ in.? $\frac{1}{16}$ in.?

TRY OUT

Use *in., ft, yd,* or *mi* to complete.

2. The length of your arm is about 18 ■.

3. The width of a living room is about 19 ■.

Measure the line segment to the nearest:

4. inch.   5. $\frac{1}{2}$ in.   6. $\frac{1}{4}$ in.   7. $\frac{1}{8}$ in.   8. $\frac{1}{16}$ in.

PRACTICE

Match. Select the answer that seems reasonable.

9. height of a dog
10. length of a pencil
11. width of a teacher's desk
12. distance between two lines on a football field
13. length of the equator
14. distance from home plate to first base

a. 7 in.
b. 25,000 mi
c. 35 in.
d. 5 ft
e. 10 yd
f. 30 yd

Measure the line segment to the nearest:

15. inch.   16. $\frac{1}{2}$ in.   17. $\frac{1}{4}$ in.   18. $\frac{1}{8}$ in.   19. $\frac{1}{16}$ in.

20. inch.   21. $\frac{1}{2}$ in.   22. $\frac{1}{4}$ in.   23. $\frac{1}{8}$ in.   24. $\frac{1}{16}$ in.

Use a ruler to draw a line segment to the given measure.

25. $1\frac{1}{8}$ in.   26. $\frac{15}{16}$ in.   27. $5\frac{3}{4}$ in.   28. $4\frac{3}{8}$ in.   29. $8\frac{7}{16}$ in.

Estimate:

30. your height.   31. the length of your classroom.   32. the height of a flagpole.

Mixed Applications

33. For 12 weeks in the summer, Alexander mows his lawn every 6 days. How many times does he mow his lawn during the summer?

34. To advertise the opening of a new store, a garden-supply dealer is giving away a car. The dealer says the car is worth a stack of pennies 1 mile high. A roll of 50 pennies is about 3 inches high. How much is the giveaway car worth?

35. Carlotta worked in her garden for 1 hour and 10 minutes on Monday, for 3 hours and 25 minutes on Tuesday, and for 2 hours and 45 minutes on Thursday. How long did she work in her garden during the week?

36. **Write a problem** that involves finding perimeter to the nearest inch. Then solve your problem. Ask others to solve it.

Customary Units of Capacity and Weight

A. Recall that **capacity** is the amount that a container can hold.

The measuring cup holds about **8 fluid ounces (fl oz),** or **1 cup (c).**

The container of yogurt holds about **1 pint (pt).**

The container of milk holds about **1 quart (qt).**

The jug of apple juice holds about **1 gallon (gal).**

These are the relationships among the units of capacity in the customary system.

1 c = 8 fl oz	1 qt = 2 pt
1 pt = 2 c	1 gal = 4 qt

1. Which unit would be the most appropriate for measuring large capacities? very small capacities? Give examples.

B. Recall that **weight** can be used to describe how heavy an object is.

The weight of the letter is about **1 ounce (oz).**

The weight of the butter is about **1 pound (lb).**

The weight of the elephant is about **1 ton (T).**

These are the relationships among the units of weight in the customary system.

1 lb = 16 oz
1 T = 2,000 lb

2. Which unit would be the most appropriate for measuring very heavy weights? very light weights? Give examples.

TRY OUT Write the letter of the correct answer.
Which is the most appropriate unit to measure the:

3. capacity of an ice cube? **a.** fl oz **b.** oz **c.** pt **d.** qt

4. capacity of a kitchen sink? **a.** c **b.** pt **c.** lb **d.** gal

5. weight of a dog? **a.** fl oz **b.** oz **c.** lb **d.** T

6. weight of a tennis ball? **a.** oz **b.** lb **c.** gal **d.** T

PRACTICE

Complete. Write the most appropriate unit.

7. A drinking glass holds about 8 ■.

8. A bucket holds about 2 ■ of water.

9. A small thermos holds about 4 ■.

10. A brick weighs about 2 ■.

11. A baseball weighs about 5 ■.

12. A trailer truck weighs about 8 ■.

Write the letter of the best estimate.

13. capacity of a bottle of hand lotion   **a.** 12 fl oz   **b.** 12 pt   **c.** 12 gal

14. capacity of a large pitcher   **a.** 2 pt   **b.** 2 qt   **c.** 2 gal

15. capacity of a saucepan   **a.** 2 fl oz   **b.** 2 c   **c.** 2 qt

16. capacity of a bathtub   **a.** 45 c   **b.** 45 pt   **c.** 45 gal

17. capacity of a car's gas tank   **a.** 50 pt   **b.** 50 qt   **c.** 50 gal

18. weight of a jar of peanut butter   **a.** 20 oz   **b.** 20 lb   **c.** 20 T

19. weight of a stick of butter   **a.** 4 oz   **b.** 4 lb   **c.** 4 T

20. weight of a man   **a.** 175 oz   **b.** 175 lb   **c.** 175 T

21. weight of a car   **a.** 1 oz   **b.** 1 lb   **c.** 1 T

Mixed Applications

Solve. You may need to use the Databank on page 549.

22. Which passenger ship is about 25,000 deadweight tons heavier than *Onana*?

23. A 1-gal jug is filled halfway with water. How many quarts of water are there in the jug?

24. The maximum weight that a certain elevator can hold is 1,500 lb. About how many 150-lb persons is that?

25. How much heavier is the *Norway* than the *Rotterdam*?

EXTRA PRACTICE, page 265

Number Theory and Fractions **251**

ACTIVITY

Fractions, Mixed Numbers, and Decimals

Helene and Tom measured the same object. Tom used fractions and Helene used decimals. How can they compare their measurements?

WORKING TOGETHER

Here is one way of comparing fractions and decimals. You will need ruled notebook paper.

Step 1 Cut out a blank strip of paper.

Step 2 Write the numbers from 10 down to 0 on a sheet of ruled notebook paper, as shown. Carefully place your blank strip of paper diagonally, one end at the 0 line and the other end at the 10 line. Mark each point where the lines touch the paper strip. Then label each mark with a decimal, as shown. This is your decimal ruler.

Step 3 Take another piece of paper the same length as your decimal ruler and fold it into sixths. Label: $\frac{1}{6}, \frac{2}{6}, \frac{3}{6}, \frac{4}{6}, \frac{5}{6}, \frac{6}{6}$.

Step 4 Measure the fractions using your decimal ruler. Enter your results in a table like the one shown at the right. Record your measurements in the "Estimate" column.

You can use a calculator to check the accuracy of your measurements. To rename a fraction as a decimal, divide the numerator by the denominator.

Example: $\frac{1}{6} = 1 \div 6 = 0.1666666$

1. Use a calculator to find the decimal value of each fraction in your table. Record the results.

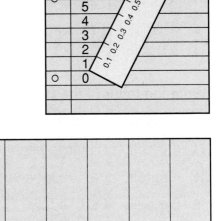

Fraction	Estimate	Decimal Value
$\frac{1}{6}$	0.15	
$\frac{2}{6}$		

SHARING IDEAS

2. Compare your measurements to the decimal values. Are they close?

3. Which estimates are exactly right?

4. Which fractions have an exact decimal value? Can you predict whether $\frac{5}{25}$ is one of those?

5. Which fractions have a decimal value with an unending string of 3s or 6s?

ON YOUR OWN

6. Memorize the decimal equivalents of the following fractions: $\frac{1}{2}, \frac{1}{3}, \frac{2}{3}, \frac{1}{4}, \frac{3}{4}$.

7. Make a "Concentration" game to match fraction and decimal equivalents. Have one student be the moderator, while two other students play the game.

Fractions, Mixed Numbers, and Decimals

A. Jan has a .250 batting average. What fraction of her times at bat does she get a hit?

Rename the decimal 0.250 as a fraction.

Think of the short word name for 0.250:

$$250 \text{ thousandths} = \frac{250}{1,000} = \frac{1}{4}$$

Jan gets a hit $\frac{1}{4}$ of the times she comes to bat.

1. Rename the decimal as a fraction or as a mixed number in simplest form.
   a. 0.6   **b.** 1.25   **c.** 0.005   **d.** 5.36

B. Joe gets a hit $\frac{2}{5}$ of the times he comes to bat. What is his batting average?

Rename $\frac{2}{5}$ as a decimal.

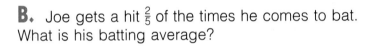

Using Equivalent Fractions

$$\frac{2}{5} = \frac{2 \times 2}{5 \times 2} = \frac{4}{10} = 0.4$$

By Dividing

$$\begin{array}{r} 0.4 \\ 5\overline{)2.0} \\ -2\,0 \\ \hline 0 \end{array}$$

Joe has a .400 batting average.

2. Rename the fraction or the mixed number as a decimal.
   a. $\frac{3}{4}$ **b.** $\frac{6}{5}$ **c.** $3\frac{1}{2}$ **d.** $6\frac{3}{8}$ **e.** $9\frac{7}{10}$

TRY OUT   Write the letter of the correct answer.

3. $0.24 = \blacksquare$ **a.** $\frac{6}{25}$ **b.** $\frac{24}{10}$ **c.** $2\frac{2}{5}$ **d.** $\frac{24}{1,000}$

4. $3.025 = \blacksquare$ **a.** $3\frac{1}{4}$ **b.** $3\frac{1}{40}$ **c.** $\frac{1}{4}$ **d.** $3\frac{1}{25}$

5. $\frac{5}{8} = \blacksquare$ **a.** 1.6   **b.** 0.625   **c.** 0.6   **d.** 6.25

6. $8\frac{1}{5} = \blacksquare$ **a.** 8.02   **b.** 8.5   **c.** 8.2   **d.** 0.82

PRACTICE

Rename the decimal as a fraction or as a mixed number in simplest form.

7. 0.7   **8.** 0.4   **9.** 0.25   **10.** 0.63   **11.** 0.08   **12.** 6.5

13. 0.375   **14.** 2.75   **15.** 25.48   **16.** 0.032   **17.** 0.006   **18.** 2.8

19. 0.05   **20.** 4.625   **21.** 8.35   **22.** 21.064   **23.** 12.225   **24.** 7.72

Rename the fraction or the mixed number as a decimal.

25. $6\frac{3}{4}$ **26.** $\frac{9}{10}$ **27.** $\frac{1}{4}$ **28.** $2\frac{4}{5}$ **29.** $9\frac{1}{8}$ **30.** $\frac{7}{40}$

31. $3\frac{33}{50}$ **32.** $6\frac{9}{25}$ **33.** $5\frac{7}{8}$ **34.** $12\frac{13}{20}$ **35.** $\frac{21}{50}$ **36.** $\frac{5}{2}$

Critical Thinking

Consider all the fractions in simplest form that have denominators of 2, 3, 4, 5, 6, 8, or 10.

37. What are the denominators of those fractions that have a one-place decimal equivalent? a two-place decimal equivalent? Can you find a pattern in the denominators?

Mixed Applications

38. Midge swims 20 laps in 5.72 minutes. Jhin swims the same distance in $5\frac{3}{4}$ minutes. Who wins the race?

39. O'Donnell made 0.65 of the shots he took during a basketball game. What fraction of the shots taken did he make?

40. Larisa ran for 3.6 km on Saturday and twice that far on Sunday. On Monday she ran twice as far as she did on Saturday and Sunday. How far did she run during the three days?

41. Joan and Henry are having an argument. Joan says that 0.01 minute is less than a second. Henry says it is more. Who is right?

Mixed Review

Find the answer. Which method did you use?

> MENTAL MATH
> CALCULATOR
> PAPER/PENCIL

42.
$$\begin{array}{r} 85.2 \\ \times\ \ 16 \\ \hline \end{array}$$

43.
$$\begin{array}{r} 35{,}006 \\ -\ 23{,}042 \\ \hline \end{array}$$

44. $23.7 + 6 + 0.43$

45. What is the greatest common factor of 42 and 54?

EXTRA PRACTICE, page 265

PROBLEM SOLVING

Strategy: Using Different Strategies

At the dog show Joan exhibits her dog, Chichi, on a red velvet carpet. This carpet is a rectangle 2 ft longer than it is wide. Its perimeter is 16 ft. How long and how wide is the carpet?

You can often use different strategies to solve the same problem.

A. Angela decides that making a table will help her solve the problem.

	Possible Dimensions of Rectangle		
Width	1	2	3
Length	3	4	5
Perimeter	8	12	16

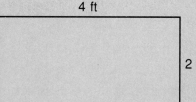

1. How did Angela choose the numbers for the length and the width?

2. Using these numbers, how did Angela find the perimeter?

3. What is the width of the carpet? What is its length?

B. Grant uses a different strategy to solve the same problem. He decides to use the Guess, Test, and Revise strategy.

4 ft

2 ft

4. Test Grant's guess to see if he is correct. Does his guess work? How do you know?

5. If Grant's guess is wrong, revise his guess and test again. Do your results agree with Angela's answers?

PRACTICE

Solve. Use a different strategy to check your work.

6. Mrs. Kranert pays $9.75 to have her dog groomed. She budgets $50 a year for grooming the dog. How many times a year can she have her dog groomed?

7. Mrs. Cooper's dog eats a bag of dog biscuits in 10 days. If you count a month as 30 days, how many bags of biscuits does her dog eat in 6 months?

8. The pet store sells both goldfish and snails in pairs. Mr. Cooper can buy 2 goldfish for $2.85 and 2 snails for $1.10. He wants twice as many goldfish as snails and does not want to spend more than $20. What is the greatest number of goldfish he can buy?

9. Mrs. Katz keeps her collie on a rope that is 10 ft long. She also keeps her dachshund on a rope that is 8 ft long. The stakes the ropes are tied to in the backyard are 20 ft apart. What is the closest the dogs can come to each other?

Strategies and Skills Review

Use estimation, mental math, a calculator, or paper and pencil.

10. The Lancaster County Kennel Club's dogs have taken 166 best-in-show awards, 232 group awards, and 215 specialty awards. Have the club's dogs won at least 500 awards? Did you overestimate or underestimate?

11. The dog show has 21 rings with 40,000 ft² of tenting and 31 judges from 16 states. About how much tenting is there for each ring? Identify the extra information. Then solve the problem.

12. Which kind of pets—cats, dogs, or fish—do sixth graders like best? Conduct a survey in your class to find out. Display your results in a frequency diagram.

13. The animal shelter plans to add space for 8 more stray dogs each year for the next 6 years. They will be able to handle 10 more cats each year for the next 5 years. How many years will it be before the shelter will have added space for 70 or more animals than it has now?

14. **Write a problem** and solve it. Then ask others to solve it by using a different strategy. See if your results are the same.

DECISION MAKING

Problem Solving: Choosing a Doghouse

SITUATION

The Arroyos need a doghouse. They can buy one that is already built, buy a kit, or build one themselves.

PROBLEM

Which doghouse should they choose?

DATA

	Pre-Built	Kit	Do-it-yourself
Basic Cost	$189	$148	60 ft of 1-in. by 8-in. lumber at $.55 per ft 20 ft of 2-in. by 4-in. lumber at $.33 per ft 2 bundles of shingles at $6.29 a bundle 1 lb of nails for $5.27 2 gal of paint at $6.95 per gallon how-to book for $6.85
Construction Time	none	3 hours	14 hours
Tools Needed	none	flat-head screwdriver ($3.95) Phillips screwdriver ($3.95)	hammer ($8.95) saw ($14.50) level ($5.75) tape measure ($3.80) T-square ($9.20) paintbrush ($2.78)

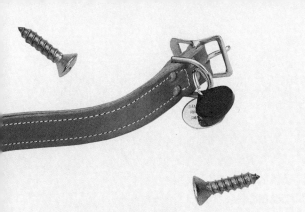

USING THE DATA

What is the total cost of the doghouse including tools?

1. pre-built   **2.** kit   **3.** do it yourself

If they already own the tools, how much money will the Arroyos save on the doghouse?

4. pre-built   **5.** kit   **6.** do it yourself

If they hire a worker who has tools to build the doghouse, the Arroyos will pay the worker $5 an hour. What will be the total cost?

7. kit   **8.** do it yourself

MAKING DECISIONS

9. For which doghouse is the basic cost the least?

10. If the Arroyos choose to build the doghouse themselves, will it be less expensive for them to hire the worker or to buy the tools and do the work themselves?

11. *What if* the Arroyos hire a worker to build the house, but they paint it themselves? The worker has tools and takes 12 hours to build the house without painting it. How much would the Arroyos save if they painted it themselves?

12. What are some of the advantages and disadvantages of buying a pre-built doghouse?

13. What are some of the advantages and disadvantages of buying a kit?

14. What are some of the advantages and disadvantages of building the doghouse themselves?

15. *Write a list* of the other factors the Arroyos should consider.

16. Which doghouse would you choose? Tell why.

Math and Music

The violin is a stringed instrument. Strings are stretched tightly across the hollow body and neck of the instrument. Sound is produced by plucking the strings or drawing a bow across them.

There are four strings. Each string is tuned to a different pitch. To play other pitches, the violinist shortens the length of a string by pressing it against the fingerboard with a finger. The shorter the length of the string, the faster it vibrates. Faster vibrations produce a higher pitch.

The Greek mathematician Pythagoras (582–507 B.C.) discovered the relationship between the length of a string and the pitch it produces.

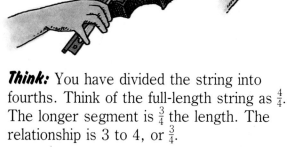

Plucking a string produces a pitch. Pressing a finger at the halfway point changes the pitch. A string half as long vibrates twice as fast. When you pluck a segment one-half the length, the pitch sounds an octave higher. The relationship of the shorter length to the whole length is 1 to 2, or $\frac{1}{2}$.

Pressing a finger at one-third the length of the string also changes the pitch. When you pluck the longer, or $\frac{2}{3}$, segment, the pitch sounds 5 notes higher. It is called a fifth. The relationship of the plucked segment to the whole string is 2 to 3, or $\frac{2}{3}$.

What if you depress a string at the $\frac{1}{4}$ point and pluck the longer segment? What is the relationship of the pitches?

Think: You have divided the string into fourths. Think of the full-length string as $\frac{4}{4}$. The longer segment is $\frac{3}{4}$ the length. The relationship is 3 to 4, or $\frac{3}{4}$.

ACTIVITIES

1. The four strings of a violin produce the pitches G, D, A, and E when they are not pressed down by the violinist. Find out the following things about guitars: the number of strings, the pitches of the strings, and what a guitarist does to produce the sound.

2. Read about other stringed instruments. Share your findings with the class.

Computer Exploration: Prime Numbers

One method that can be used to find primes is called the *sieve of Eratosthenes*. Eratosthenes was a mathematician who studied in Egypt in the third century B.C. Begin with a set of consecutive numbers. Cross out 1 because it is neither prime nor composite. Circle 2 and cross out all numbers having 2 as a factor. Circle 3 and cross out all numbers having 3 as a factor (unless they have already been crossed out). Continue this pattern with 5, 7, 11, and so on. The numbers left are prime.

~~1~~ (2) (3) ~~4~~ (5) ~~6~~ (7) ~~8~~ ~~9~~ ~~10~~
(11) ~~12~~ (13) ~~14~~ ~~15~~ ~~16~~ (17) ~~18~~ (19) ~~20~~

You can use the computer program SIEVE to watch Eratosthenes' method work before your very eyes. The computer will display the set of consecutive numbers you request, show each prime factor as it is used, and make the composite numbers disappear.

AT THE COMPUTER

1. Enter 1 and 100 as the FROM and TO values. Watch as the computer removes the composite numbers. What was the greatest prime factor used? Why was it unnecessary to use any greater prime factors?

2. Copy the primes from 1 to 100. How many are there?

3. Repeat the procedure for 101 to 200. What are the primes in this set? How many are there?

4. Repeat the procedure for 201 to 300 and 301 to 400. Copy and count the primes each time.

5. What conclusions can you reach? Do the primes seem to be getting fewer and farther apart? What patterns do you see?

6. The sequence 32, 33, 34, 35, 36 contains no prime number. It has length 5. What is the longest sequence of consecutive numbers without a prime you can find?

7. Primes such as 3 and 5 or 11 and 13 are twin primes. Find other twin primes on your lists. Can you draw any conclusions?

EXTRA PRACTICE

Mental Math: Divisibility, page 227

Complete the table. Write *yes* or *no.*

Divisible:	29	325	609	2,655	38,364	48,180	7,515
by 3?	1.■	2.■	3.■	4.■	5.■	6.■	7.■
by 4?	8.■	9.■	10.■	11.■	12.■	13.■	14.■
by 5?	15.■	16.■	17.■	18.■	19.■	20.■	21.■
by 6?	22.■	23.■	24.■	25.■	26.■	27.■	28.■
by 9?	29.■	30.■	31.■	32.■	33.■	34.■	35.■

Factors and Greatest Common Factor, page 229

Find all the factors of the number.

1. 14　　**2.** 32　　**3.** 11　　**4.** 26　　**5.** 36　　**6.** 81

Find the greatest common factor of the numbers.

7. 12 and 48　　**8.** 4 and 10　　**9.** 36 and 30　　**10.** 9 and 27　　**11.** 25 and 39

12. 12, 16, and 24　　**13.** 8, 36, and 48 **14.** 27, 36, and 54　　**15.** 14, 42, and 49

Prime and Composite Numbers, page 231

Is the number *prime* or *composite*?

1. 77　　**2.** 31　　**3.** 27　　**4.** 51　　**5.** 59　　**6.** 73

Make a factor tree and write the prime factorization.

7. 36　　**8.** 32　　**9.** 28　　**10.** 105　　**11.** 55　　**12.** 78

13. 85　　**14.** 92　　**15.** 150　　**16.** 24　　**17.** 45　　**18.** 144

Multiples and Least Common Multiple, page 233

Find the first six multiples of the number.

1. 4　　**2.** 8　　**3.** 15　　**4.** 6　　**5.** 16　　**6.** 30

Find the least common multiple of the numbers.

7. 3 and 4　　**8.** 8 and 20　　**9.** 6 and 10　　**10.** 5 and 9　　**11.** 5 and 25

12. 4, 8, and 12　　**13.** 3, 5, and 6　　**14.** 6, 5, and 20　　**15.** 8, 16, and 24

Problem Solving Strategy: Finding a Pattern, page 235

Describe a pattern for the problem. Use it to solve the problem.

1. Tia is planting flowers in a triangular pattern like the one below. Each dot represents a plant.

She plans to enlarge the flower bed to 10 rows. How many flowers will be in the 10th row?

2. John is planting flowers in a circular pattern like the one below. Each dot represents a plant.

The first circle has 2 plants, the second circle has 4 plants, the third circle has 6 plants. How many plants are in the 5th circle?

3. Kim planted rosebushes in this pattern: red, white, pink, red—and then repeated the pattern. What color will the 30th rosebush be?

4. Dee is planting different types of pine trees. Scotch pine has been used for the 1st, 5th, 8th, and so on. In all there are 20 trees. How many are Scotch pine?

Fractions and Equivalent Fractions, page 237

What fraction of the region is shaded?

1.

2.

3.

4.

Complete.

5. $\frac{5}{8} = \frac{\blacksquare}{24}$ **6.** $\frac{1}{2} = \frac{\blacksquare}{10}$ **7.** $\frac{3}{5} = \frac{12}{\blacksquare}$ **8.** $\frac{5}{7} = \frac{10}{\blacksquare}$ **9.** $\frac{2}{3} = \frac{\blacksquare}{12}$ **10.** $\frac{12}{36} = \frac{1}{\blacksquare}$

11. $\frac{12}{15} = \frac{\blacksquare}{5}$ **12.** $\frac{8}{12} = \frac{2}{\blacksquare}$ **13.** $\frac{4}{16} = \frac{\blacksquare}{4}$ **14.** $\frac{18}{24} = \frac{\blacksquare}{4}$ **15.** $\frac{20}{50} = \frac{2}{\blacksquare}$ **16.** $\frac{5}{7} = \frac{20}{\blacksquare}$

Fractions in Simplest Form, page 239

Write the fraction in simplest form.

1. $\frac{2}{4}$ **2.** $\frac{12}{18}$ **3.** $\frac{15}{24}$ **4.** $\frac{7}{35}$ **5.** $\frac{8}{40}$ **6.** $\frac{6}{15}$

7. $\frac{9}{24}$ **8.** $\frac{8}{10}$ **9.** $\frac{20}{25}$ **10.** $\frac{14}{28}$ **11.** $\frac{35}{50}$ **12.** $\frac{18}{45}$

EXTRA PRACTICE

Mixed Numbers, page 243

Rename the fraction as a mixed number or as a whole number.

1. $\frac{42}{5}$
2. $\frac{19}{3}$
3. $\frac{28}{7}$
4. $\frac{61}{9}$
5. $\frac{63}{8}$
6. $\frac{39}{4}$

7. $\frac{22}{6}$
8. $\frac{56}{10}$
9. $\frac{30}{8}$
10. $\frac{26}{4}$
11. $\frac{48}{6}$
12. $\frac{78}{9}$

Rename the mixed number as a fraction.

13. $5\frac{1}{2}$
14. $4\frac{2}{3}$
15. $6\frac{3}{4}$
16. $7\frac{2}{5}$
17. $3\frac{7}{10}$
18. $10\frac{3}{5}$

Comparing and Ordering, page 245

Compare. Write >, <, or =.

1. $\frac{1}{5}$ ● $\frac{1}{6}$
2. $\frac{3}{4}$ ● $\frac{12}{16}$
3. $\frac{8}{5}$ ● $\frac{3}{4}$
4. $\frac{7}{10}$ ● $\frac{3}{4}$
5. $\frac{5}{12}$ ● $\frac{1}{5}$

6. $4\frac{7}{8}$ ● $4\frac{5}{6}$
7. $3\frac{2}{3}$ ● $3\frac{8}{12}$
8. $7\frac{7}{9}$ ● $7\frac{5}{6}$
9. $\frac{30}{5}$ ● $6\frac{1}{8}$
10. $3\frac{7}{9}$ ● $4\frac{1}{9}$

Order from least to greatest.

11. $\frac{5}{6}, \frac{3}{8}, \frac{1}{4}$
12. $\frac{5}{8}, \frac{1}{2}, \frac{3}{5}$
13. $\frac{2}{3}, \frac{1}{6}, \frac{5}{4}$
14. $3\frac{4}{5}, 3\frac{9}{10}, 2\frac{7}{8}$
15. $5\frac{1}{2}, \frac{11}{12}, 5\frac{5}{12}$

Rounding Fractions and Mixed Numbers, page 247

Is the fraction closest to 0, to $\frac{1}{2}$, or to 1?

1. $\frac{19}{40}$
2. $\frac{3}{59}$
3. $\frac{51}{49}$
4. $\frac{15}{31}$
5. $\frac{2}{77}$
6. $\frac{75}{98}$

7. $\frac{79}{100}$
8. $\frac{3}{7}$
9. $\frac{39}{50}$
10. $\frac{4}{97}$
11. $\frac{51}{100}$
12. $\frac{1}{9}$

Round to the nearest whole number and to the nearest half.

13. $2\frac{5}{6}$
14. $5\frac{1}{5}$
15. $6\frac{3}{7}$
16. $8\frac{7}{13}$
17. $5\frac{7}{16}$
18. $9\frac{27}{50}$

19. $1\frac{1}{8}$
20. $4\frac{7}{10}$
21. $7\frac{2}{5}$
22. $2\frac{11}{23}$
23. $1\frac{9}{98}$
24. $3\frac{1}{6}$

Customary Units of Length, page 249

Match. Select the answer that seems reasonable.

1. height of a person   **a.** 9 in.

2. length of a room   **b.** 2,000 mi

3. width of a math book   **c.** 5 ft

4. distance from New York to Los Angeles   **d.** 8 yd

EXTRA PRACTICE

Customary Units of Capacity and Weight, page 251

Write the letter of the best estimate.

1. capacity of a drinking glass   **a.** 1 c   **b.** 1 qt   **c.** 1 gal

2. capacity of a bottle of shampoo   **a.** 15 gal   **b.** 15 pt   **c.** 15 fl oz

3. capacity of a paint can   **a.** 1 gal   **b.** 1 pt   **c.** 1 c

4. weight of a horse   **a.** 1 T   **b.** 1 oz   **c.** 1 lb

5. weight of a bag of flour   **a.** 5 oz   **b.** 5 lb   **c.** 5 T

6. weight of a robin   **a.** 6 lb   **b.** 6 T   **c.** 6 oz

Fractions, Mixed Numbers, and Decimals, page 255

Rename the fraction or the mixed number as a decimal.

1. $2\frac{3}{5}$ 2. $\frac{7}{10}$ 3. $\frac{3}{8}$ 4. $6\frac{2}{5}$ 5. $4\frac{13}{25}$ 6. $5\frac{11}{20}$

7. $3\frac{9}{40}$ 8. $8\frac{11}{25}$ 9. $4\frac{17}{20}$ 10. $3\frac{5}{8}$ 11. $\frac{27}{50}$ 12. $\frac{7}{2}$

Rename the decimal as a fraction or as a mixed number in simplest form.

13. 0.9   14. 0.8   15. 0.75   16. 0.53   17. 9.04   18. 5.25

19. 0.875   20. 0.008   21. 7.45   22. 8.048   23. 6.02   24. 12.68

Problem Solving Strategy: Using Different Strategies, page 257

Solve. Use a different strategy to check your work.

1. Mrs. Williams pays $12.95 to have her car waxed. She budgets $75 a year for the job. How many times a year can she have it waxed?

2. Mrs. Robb uses a tank of gas in 8 days. If you count a month of 30 days, about how many tanks does she use in 6 months?

3. A car mat is 2 in. longer than it is wide. Its perimeter is 68 in. How long and how wide is the mat?

4. Mr. Johnson can buy 2 cans of wax for $3.99 and 2 cans of tire cleaner for $2.98. He wants twice as many cans of wax as tire cleaner. He does not want to spend more than $35. What is the greatest number of cans of wax he can buy?

PRACTICE PLUS

KEY SKILL: Fractions and Equivalent Fractions (Use after page 237.)

Level A

What fraction of the region is shaded?

1.  **2.**   **3.** [square with X crossing it] **4.**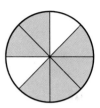

Complete.

5. $\frac{7}{8} = \frac{\blacksquare}{16}$ **6.** $\frac{1}{2} = \frac{\blacksquare}{8}$ **7.** $\frac{3}{4} = \frac{6}{\blacksquare}$ **8.** $\frac{15}{20} = \frac{\blacksquare}{4}$ **9.** $\frac{8}{12} = \frac{2}{\blacksquare}$

10. Seven people were asked to name their favorite sport. Four chose basketball as their favorite sport. What fraction of the group chose basketball?

Level B

Find three equivalent fractions.

11. $\frac{3}{5}$ **12.** $\frac{2}{3}$ **13.** $\frac{4}{9}$ **14.** $\frac{1}{4}$ **15.** $\frac{3}{8}$ **16.** $\frac{5}{7}$

Complete.

17. $\frac{9}{10} = \frac{\blacksquare}{20}$ **18.** $\frac{10}{15} = \frac{2}{\blacksquare}$ **19.** $\frac{7}{8} = \frac{\blacksquare}{24}$ **20.** $\frac{6}{24} = \frac{1}{\blacksquare}$ **21.** $\frac{2}{7} = \frac{8}{\blacksquare}$

22. Eighteen people were asked to name their favorite color. Ten said their favorite color was red. What fraction of the group did not choose red?

Level C

Complete.

23. $\frac{36}{48} = \frac{\blacksquare}{4}$ **24.** $\frac{30}{45} = \frac{2}{\blacksquare}$ **25.** $\frac{7}{9} = \frac{\blacksquare}{63}$ **26.** $\frac{5}{6} = \frac{25}{\blacksquare}$ **27.** $\frac{3}{4} = \frac{\blacksquare}{40}$

28. $\frac{8}{9} = \frac{\blacksquare}{45}$ **29.** $\frac{5}{6} = \frac{55}{\blacksquare}$ **30.** $\frac{20}{36} = \frac{5}{\blacksquare}$ **31.** $\frac{80}{100} = \frac{4}{\blacksquare}$ **32.** $\frac{2}{7} = \frac{\blacksquare}{42}$

33. Kara made a design with tiles. Ten of the tiles were red, 5 were white, 15 were yellow, and 20 were blue. What fraction of the total design is each color?

PRACTICE PLUS

KEY SKILL: Comparing and Ordering (Use after page 245.)

Level A

Compare. Write >, <, or =.

1. $\frac{2}{3}$ ● $\frac{3}{4}$ 2. $\frac{5}{8}$ ● $\frac{10}{16}$ 3. $\frac{5}{3}$ ● $\frac{3}{4}$ 4. $6\frac{3}{4}$ ● $7\frac{1}{4}$ 5. 8 ● $7\frac{1}{2}$

Order from least to greatest.

6. $\frac{1}{4}, \frac{2}{3}, \frac{1}{2}$ 7. $\frac{5}{6}, \frac{2}{3}, \frac{10}{9}$ 8. $\frac{1}{4}, \frac{5}{6}, \frac{5}{8}$ 9. $2\frac{2}{3}, 3\frac{2}{5}, 2\frac{3}{4}$ 10. $6\frac{1}{3}, 4\frac{1}{5}, 5\frac{1}{2}$

11. Jeff's group ate $\frac{5}{6}$ of their pizza. Bev's group ate $\frac{5}{8}$ of their pizza. Which group ate more?

Level B

Compare. Write >, <, or =.

12. $\frac{1}{8}$ ● $\frac{1}{7}$ 13. $\frac{5}{3}$ ● $\frac{3}{5}$ 14. $\frac{2}{5}$ ● $\frac{10}{25}$ 15. $5\frac{3}{8}$ ● $4\frac{9}{10}$ 16. $\frac{42}{8}$ ● $5\frac{1}{3}$

Order from least to greatest.

17. $\frac{1}{2}, \frac{3}{5}, \frac{5}{6}$ 18. $\frac{4}{5}, \frac{3}{10}, \frac{1}{4}$ 19. $\frac{5}{9}, \frac{2}{3}, \frac{1}{2}$ 20. $5\frac{3}{4}, 4\frac{7}{8}, 5\frac{5}{8}$ 21. $6\frac{5}{8}, 6\frac{1}{2}, \frac{19}{3}$

22. Claire spent $2\frac{2}{3}$ hours working at the Pizza Palace on Saturday. Jack spent $2\frac{3}{4}$ hours working at the Pizza Palace on Saturday. Who worked longer?

Level C

Compare. Write >, <, or =.

23. $\frac{3}{5}$ ● $\frac{5}{6}$ 24. $\frac{2}{5}$ ● $\frac{4}{15}$ 25. $2\frac{2}{3}$ ● $2\frac{4}{5}$ 26. $\frac{6}{8}$ ● $\frac{9}{12}$ 27. $3\frac{7}{9}$ ● $2\frac{5}{6}$

Order from least to greatest.

28. $\frac{3}{4}, \frac{7}{8}, \frac{5}{6}$ 29. $\frac{2}{5}, \frac{3}{10}, \frac{2}{7}$ 30. $5\frac{3}{4}, 5\frac{7}{10}, 5\frac{4}{5}$ 31. $6\frac{7}{9}, 5\frac{5}{8}, 6\frac{2}{3}$ 32. $8\frac{2}{3}, 8\frac{5}{8}, \frac{53}{6}$

33. At the Pizza Palace, $\frac{5}{12}$ of the pizzas sold were large, $\frac{17}{60}$ were medium, and $\frac{3}{10}$ were small. List the sizes in order from the greatest to least amount sold.

CHAPTER REVIEW/TEST

LANGUAGE AND MATHEMATICS

Complete the sentences. Use the words in the chart on the right.

VOCABULARY
denominator
mixed number
prime number
equivalent
composite number

1. A whole number with exactly 2 factors is a(n) ■.

2. A whole number with more than 2 factors is a(n) ■.

3. A number that has a whole-number part and a fraction part is a(n) ■.

4. Fractions that name the same number are ■ fractions.

CONCEPTS AND SKILLS

5. List all the factors of the number 38.

6. Find the first six multiples of the number 14.

Find the GCF and LCM for each set of numbers.

7. 12 and 30   **8.** 10 and 25   **9.** 18 and 24   **10.** 9 and 27

Use exponents to show the prime factorization.

11. 60   **12.** 56   **13.** 125   **14.** 66

15. List the prime numbers between 40 and 50.

16. Express $\frac{8}{6}$ as a mixed number in simplest form.

Find the equivalent fraction.

17. $\frac{1}{4} = \frac{n}{12}$ **18.** $\frac{12}{15} = \frac{4}{n}$ **19.** $\frac{5}{8} = \frac{n}{40}$ **20.** $2\frac{1}{7} = \frac{n}{14}$

Compare. Use >, <, or =.   Order from least to greatest.

21. $\frac{30}{24}$ ■ $1\frac{1}{2}$ **22.** $\frac{5}{3}$ ■ $\frac{3}{2}$ **23.** $\frac{5}{9}, \frac{2}{3}, \frac{9}{18}$ **24.** $\frac{21}{8}, 2\frac{3}{5}, 2\frac{1}{2}$

25. Rename $\frac{15}{4}$ as a decimal.

26. Rename 0.075 as a fraction.

Measure the line segment to the nearest: |————————————————|

27. $\frac{1}{2}$ in.   **28.** $\frac{1}{16}$ in.

Choose the best estimate:

29. A pen is about ■ in. long.   **a.** 6   **b.** 18   **c.** 2

30. A sink holds about 2 ■ of water.   **a.** pt   **b.** qt   **c.** gal

Critical Thinking

31. If the denominator of a fraction < 1 is a prime number, is the fraction in simplest form? Is this true for numbers > 1?

Mixed Applications

32. Al bought 3 magic pens for $1.50; Bob bought 4 for $2. Kate spent $4 on magic pens. How many more pens did Kate buy than Al and Bob together?

33. Amy walked a part of a mile each day as follows: $\frac{1}{5}$, $\frac{2}{4}$, $\frac{3}{15}$, $\frac{4}{8}$, $\frac{5}{25}$. If this pattern continues, what part of a mile will she walk on day 10?

PERFORMANCE ASSESSMENT

Work with your group to solve this problem.

Measure and record the length of the shoes worn by each student in your group, to the nearest $\frac{1}{16}$ inch. Then make a table listing the shoe lengths from longest to shortest, expressed as improper fractions and mixed numbers in simplest form.

1. *Think about:*
   - the length of each student's shoe expressed in inches
   - the length of each student's shoe expressed in fractions of an inch

2. Write an explanation of how you determined the order of the numbers in your table.

CUMULATIVE REVIEW

Choose the letter of the correct answer.

1. 654.6×0.22

   a. 1,440.12
   b. 26.184
   c. 144.012
   d. not given

2. Choose the exponent form for 1,000.

   a. 10^2
   b. 10^3
   c. 10^4
   d. not given

3. $5,784 \div 8$

   a. 7,230
   b. 72 R4
   c. 72 R24
   d. not given

4. $37\overline{)15,683}$

   a. 423 R32
   b. 424
   c. 424 R5
   d. not given

5. What time is 3 hours 46 minutes after 11:30 P.M.?

   a. 3:16 A.M.
   b. 2:16 A.M.
   c. 7:15 P.M.
   d. not given

6. $0.06\overline{)3.726}$

   a. 0.621
   b. 6.21
   c. 62.1
   d. not given

7. Simplify:
   $28 \div 4 + (6 - 2) \times 5 - 2$

   a. 53
   b. 25
   c. 19
   d. not given

8. 53.5 cm = ■ m

   a. 0.535
   b. 5.35
   c. 535
   d. not given

9. Find the median:
   5.8, 3.5, 6.2, 3.5, 4.5

   a. 4.7
   b. 4.5
   c. 3.5
   d. not given

10. Which is the GCF of 16 and 24?

   a. 48
   b. 8
   c. 4
   d. not given

11. Which is a prime number?

   a. 4
   b. 9
   c. 21
   d. not given

12. Which is the LCM of 9 and 15?

   a. 3
   b. 30
   c. 45
   d. not given

13. Which is equivalent to $\frac{3}{4}$?

   a. $\frac{12}{16}$
   b. $\frac{6}{12}$
   c. $\frac{13}{14}$
   d. not given

14. Compare: $\frac{2}{3} \bullet \frac{5}{8}$

   a. $<$
   b. $>$
   c. $=$
   d. not given

ENRICHMENT FOR ALL

TERMINATING AND REPEATING DECIMALS

The digits in a decimal can have a pattern.

Terminating decimals, such as 0.56 and 0.3589, have a definite number of decimal places.

Repeating decimals, such as 0.333 . . . and 0.13636 . . . , have a pattern that continues indefinitely.

Repeating decimals can be written with a bar over the digit or digits that repeat.

$0.333 \ldots = 0.\overline{3}$
$0.13636 \ldots = 0.1\overline{36}$

Every fraction can be renamed as either a terminating or repeating decimal.

$\frac{3}{4} = 3 \div 4 = 0.75$ $\qquad$ $\frac{5}{8} = 5 \div 8 = 0.625$

$\frac{2}{3} = 2 \div 3 = 0.\overline{6}$ $\qquad$ $\frac{4}{9} = 4 \div 9 = 0.\overline{4}$

1. Use your calculator to rename these fractions as decimals. Which are terminating decimals? repeating decimals?

   a. $\frac{1}{4}$ $\qquad$ **b.** $\frac{3}{5}$ $\qquad$ **c.** $\frac{5}{6}$ $\qquad$ **d.** $\frac{7}{9}$ $\qquad$ **e.** $\frac{4}{11}$ $\qquad$ **f.** $\frac{8}{27}$

2. Use paper and pencil to rename $\frac{1}{2}$, $\frac{2}{5}$, and $\frac{3}{8}$ as decimals. What is the remainder when the decimal terminates?

3. Use your calculator to rename $\frac{1}{9}$ and $\frac{2}{9}$ as decimals.

   a. What pattern have you found in these decimals?
   b. Use the pattern to rename $\frac{3}{9}$, $\frac{4}{9}$, and $\frac{5}{9}$ as decimals.

4. The fraction $\frac{1}{7}$ can be renamed as a repeating decimal.

   a. Use paper and pencil to rename $\frac{1}{7}$ as a decimal.
   b. Use your calculator to rename $\frac{2}{7}$, $\frac{3}{7}$, and $\frac{4}{7}$ as decimals.
   c. What pattern have you found in these decimals?
   d. Use the pattern to rename $\frac{5}{7}$ and $\frac{6}{7}$ as decimals.

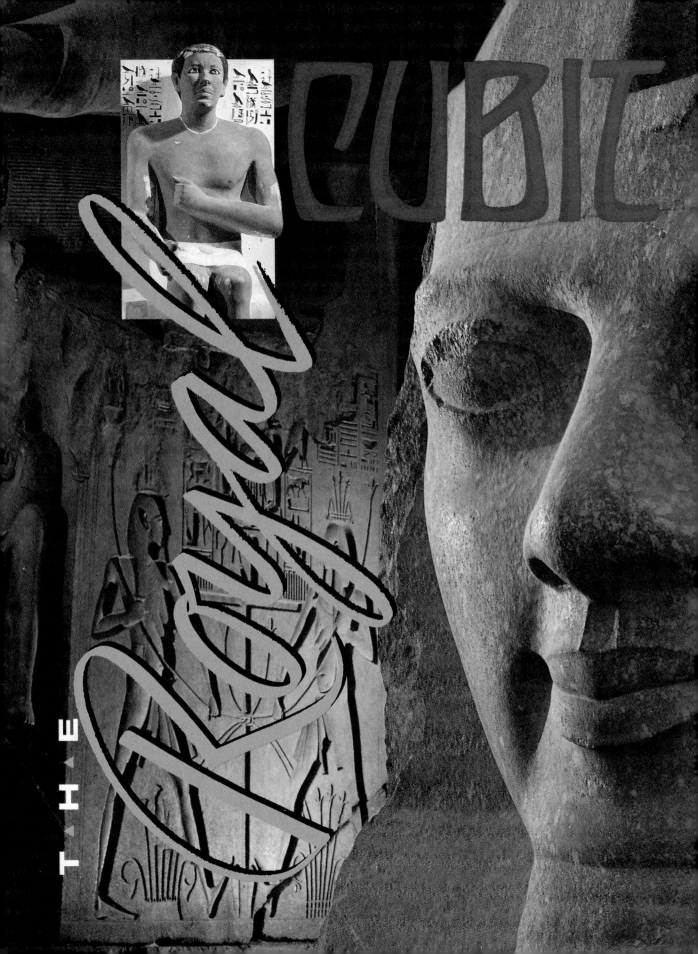

THE Rough CUBIC

ADDING AND SUBTRACTING FRACTIONS AND MIXED NUMBERS

*H*ave you ever measured a room or a part of a yard by counting off steps or foot lengths? Historically, systems of measurement were often based on convenient measures, such as different parts of the body—especially hands, arms, and feet.

▲

At the time when the pyramids were built in Egypt, the *cubit* was used as a unit of measure. The cubit was the length of the arm from fingertip to elbow. The great engineers and architects of Egypt were aware of the importance of accurate measurements in constructing buildings and monuments. But whose measurement should be used?

▲

In this matter, the pharaoh prevailed, and the *royal cubit* was established. The royal cubit used in constructing the Great Pyramid at Giza for the Pharaoh Khufu was about 52 centimeters long.

1. Estimate the height of a person whose royal cubit is 52 centimeters long.

Egypt
AFRICA

2. What fraction of a royal cubit is your personal cubit?

3. About how many personal cubits tall are you?

Estimating Sums and Differences

A. The Mountainside School is collecting pieces of material for a friendship quilt. The sixth-grade class has contributed $\frac{3}{8}$ yd of green velvet, $2\frac{5}{6}$ yd of yellow cotton, and $1\frac{1}{4}$ yd of blue wool. About how much material has the class collected?

You need to estimate the sum of $\frac{3}{8}$, $2\frac{5}{6}$, and $1\frac{1}{4}$.

Rounding	Front-End Estimation
First, round to the nearest whole number. Then add.	First, find the whole-number part. Then add.
$\frac{3}{8} + 2\frac{5}{6} + 1\frac{1}{4}$	$\frac{3}{8} + 2\frac{5}{6} + 1\frac{1}{4}$
↓ ↓ ↓	↓ ↓ ↓
$0 + 3\ + 1 = 4$	$0 + 2\ + 1 = 3$

The class has collected about 3 to 4 yd of material.

1. Why is the rounded estimate greater than the front-end estimate?

B. You can also estimate differences.

Estimate the difference: $6\frac{1}{2} - 2\frac{2}{5}$

Rounding	Front-End Estimation
First, round to the nearest whole number. Then subtract.	First, find the whole-number part. Then subtract.
$6\frac{1}{2} - 2\frac{2}{5}$	$6\frac{1}{2} - 2\frac{2}{5}$
↓ ↓	↓ ↓
$7\ - 2\ = 5$	$6\ - 2 = 4$

The difference of $6\frac{1}{2}$ minus $2\frac{2}{5}$ is about 4 or 5.

2. How does estimating a sum or a difference help you in solving a problem?

TRY OUT   Estimate the sum or difference.

Use rounding.

3. $1\frac{1}{5} + \frac{5}{8}$

4. $\frac{75}{100} - \frac{1}{5}$

Use front-end estimation.

5. $6\frac{7}{10} - 2\frac{8}{9}$

6. $10\frac{2}{9} - 4\frac{7}{10}$

PRACTICE

Estimate the sum or difference. Which method did you use?

7. $1\frac{1}{3} + 2\frac{1}{8}$ **8.** $4\frac{4}{5} + 1\frac{2}{3}$ **9.** $3\frac{3}{10} + 3\frac{7}{9}$ **10.** $1\frac{1}{4} + 1\frac{6}{7}$ **11.** $1\frac{11}{12} + 3\frac{13}{15} + \frac{1}{2}$

12. $3\frac{4}{5} - 2\frac{3}{7}$ **13.** $5\frac{3}{5} - 4\frac{1}{8}$ **14.** $4\frac{5}{6} - 4\frac{5}{12}$ **15.** $4\frac{2}{3} - 2\frac{2}{9}$ **16.** $2\frac{17}{20} - 1\frac{1}{2}$

17. $4\frac{1}{3} + \frac{2}{3}$ **18.** $7\frac{2}{7} - 2\frac{6}{7}$ **19.** $3\frac{9}{16} - \frac{3}{4}$ **20.** $\frac{1}{6} + 1\frac{4}{5} + \frac{5}{8}$ **21.** $2\frac{1}{4} + 5\frac{9}{10}$

22. $1\frac{3}{7} - \frac{3}{8}$ **23.** $\frac{41}{50} + 4\frac{7}{9}$ **24.** $1\frac{17}{18} + \frac{11}{12}$ **25.** $1\frac{4}{5} - 1\frac{1}{8}$ **26.** $\left(5\frac{4}{7} + 2\frac{1}{3}\right) - \frac{4}{15}$

Estimate to compare. Use $>$ or $<$.

27. $1\frac{2}{9} + 3\frac{1}{2}$ ● 5   **28.** $6\frac{7}{10} - 2\frac{2}{3}$ ● 8

29. $\frac{1}{8} + 2\frac{3}{4} + \frac{6}{7}$ ● 2   **30.** $\left(5\frac{5}{6} - 3\frac{1}{2}\right) + 2\frac{1}{4}$ ● 3

Critical Thinking

31. Which estimation method would give a more reasonable estimate to $10\frac{1}{4}$ minus $9\frac{5}{8}$? Why?

Mixed Applications

Solve. Which method did you use?

32. Jesse spent $3\frac{1}{3}$ hours cutting cloth for the quilt and another $1\frac{3}{4}$ hours sewing squares together. About how many hours in all did Jesse work?

33. The class decided to use a square shape for their quilt. Each side of the quilt has 38 squares. How many squares are there in all?

34. Cecilia started with $4\frac{1}{2}$ yd of cloth. After cutting all her squares, she had $\frac{7}{8}$ yd of cloth left. About how much cloth did Cecilia cut into squares?

35. The quilt is bordered in red velvet that cost a total of $21.30. The border required 3 yd of velvet. How much was the price per yard?

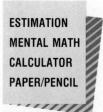

ESTIMATION
MENTAL MATH
CALCULATOR
PAPER/PENCIL

Adding and Subtracting: Like Denominators

A. Elaine worked hard to earn a place on the swim team. When she was training, she wrote down the distance she swam each day. How many miles did she swim all together on the three days?

Day	Monday	Tuesday	Wednesday
Distance	$\frac{3}{10}$ mile	$\frac{7}{10}$ mile	$\frac{8}{10}$ mile

You need to find the sum of $\frac{3}{10}$, $\frac{7}{10}$, and $\frac{8}{10}$.

Step 1

Add the numerators.
Use the common denominator.

$$\frac{3}{10} + \frac{7}{10} + \frac{8}{10} = \frac{18}{10}$$

Step 2

Write the sum in simplest form.

$$\frac{18}{10} = 1\frac{8}{10} = 1\frac{4}{5}$$

Elaine swam a total of $1\frac{4}{5}$ miles on the three days.

1. How can you use the fact that $\frac{3}{10} + \frac{7}{10} = 1$ to find the sum mentally?

B. You can also subtract fractions with common denominators.

Subtract: $\frac{9}{10} - \frac{5}{10}$

Step 1

Subtract the numerators.
Use the common denominator.

$$\frac{9}{10} - \frac{5}{10} = \frac{4}{10}$$

Step 2

Write the difference in simplest form.

$$\frac{4}{10} = \frac{2}{5}$$

2. How does the fact that $1 = \frac{6}{6}$ help you subtract $1 - \frac{5}{6}$?

TRY **OUT** Add or subtract. Write the answer in simplest form.

3. $\frac{3}{8} + \frac{4}{8}$ **4.** $\frac{4}{12} + \frac{5}{12} + \frac{7}{12}$ **5.** $\frac{9}{12} - \frac{4}{12}$ **6.** $\frac{11}{10} - \frac{3}{10}$

PRACTICE

Add or subtract. Write the answer in simplest form.

7. $\frac{1}{5}$
   $+ \frac{3}{5}$

8. $\frac{3}{7}$
   $+ \frac{2}{7}$

9. $\frac{5}{8}$
   $+ \frac{1}{8}$

10. $\frac{5}{12}$
    $+ \frac{8}{12}$

11. $\frac{2}{3}$
    $+ \frac{2}{3}$

12. $\frac{7}{10}$
    $+ \frac{9}{10}$

13. $\frac{3}{4} - \frac{2}{4}$

14. $\frac{5}{6} - \frac{3}{6}$

15. $\frac{7}{12} - \frac{5}{12}$

16. $\frac{7}{8} - \frac{7}{8}$

17. $\frac{18}{13} - \frac{7}{13}$

18. $\frac{10}{10} - \frac{7}{10}$

19. $\frac{6}{8} + \frac{6}{8}$

20. $\frac{8}{15} - \frac{3}{15}$

21. $\frac{9}{9} - \frac{4}{9}$

22. $\frac{16}{25} + \frac{9}{25}$

23. $\frac{11}{12} - \frac{5}{12}$

24. $\frac{6}{10} + \frac{4}{10}$

25. $\frac{6}{10} - \frac{4}{10}$

26. $\frac{15}{12} - \frac{5}{12}$

27. $\frac{11}{15} - \frac{8}{15}$

28. $\frac{3}{10} + \frac{3}{10} + \frac{8}{10}$

29. $\frac{5}{8} + \frac{5}{8} + \frac{5}{8}$

30. $\frac{7}{12} + \frac{6}{12} + \frac{5}{12}$

31. $\frac{3}{9} + \frac{6}{9} + \frac{2}{9}$

32. $\left(\frac{7}{8} - \frac{3}{8}\right) - \frac{1}{8}$

33. $\left(\frac{12}{16} + \frac{2}{16}\right) - \frac{11}{16}$

34. $\left(\frac{8}{8} - \frac{7}{8}\right) + \frac{3}{8}$

35. $\left(\frac{6}{5} - \frac{2}{5}\right) - \frac{3}{5}$

36. three-fourths plus three-fourths

37. nine-fifths minus four-fifths

38. six-tenths minus three-tenths

39. four-sevenths plus one-seventh

Find the missing number.

40. $\frac{7}{10} - \frac{\blacksquare}{10} = \frac{3}{10}$

41. $\frac{3}{7} + \frac{\blacksquare}{7} = \frac{12}{7}$

42. $\frac{\blacksquare}{4} - \frac{3}{4} = \frac{1}{4}$

43. $\frac{7}{6} + \frac{9}{6} = \frac{\blacksquare}{6}$

44. $\frac{9}{15} - \frac{\blacksquare}{15} = \frac{4}{15}$

45. $\frac{\blacksquare}{8} + \frac{3}{8} = \frac{11}{8}$

46. $\frac{12}{13} - \frac{7}{13} = \frac{\blacksquare}{13}$

47. $\frac{\blacksquare}{9} + \frac{8}{9} = \frac{12}{9}$

Mixed Applications

48. Last week Jerry swam for $\frac{3}{4}$ mi on Monday, $\frac{1}{4}$ mi on Tuesday, and $\frac{3}{4}$ mi on Wednesday. How many miles did he swim all together?

49. At a swimming meet each of the 10 swim-team members spent $5.00 for entry fees and $2.85 for food. What is the total amount the team spent?

Mixed Review

Find the answer. Which method did you use?

50. $7.38 + 3.924$

51. $16.35 - 9.8$

52. $6.45 + 7.55$

53. 9.027×26

54. $2.8)\overline{20.72}$

55. $0.7)\overline{0.0245}$

Adding Fractions: Unlike Denominators

Monroe City has plans for a new park. The plans call for $\frac{1}{6}$ of the park to be used for game fields and $\frac{3}{8}$ to be used for playgrounds. How much of the park is to be used for these two sections?

The fractions $\frac{1}{6}$ and $\frac{3}{8}$ have unlike denominators and cannot be added until they have a common denominator. To find a common denominator, find a common multiple of each denominator. The **least common denominator (LCD)** is the least common multiple (LCM) of the denominators.

Add: $\frac{1}{6}$ and $\frac{3}{8}$

Step 1

Write equivalent fractions using the LCD.

$$\frac{1}{6} = \frac{1 \times 4}{6 \times 4} = \frac{4}{24}$$
$$+\frac{3}{8} = \frac{3 \times 3}{8 \times 3} = \frac{9}{24}$$

Think: 24 is the LCD.

Step 2

Add. Write the sum in simplest form if necessary.

$$\frac{1}{6} = \frac{1 \times 4}{6 \times 4} = \frac{4}{24}$$
$$+\frac{3}{8} = \frac{3 \times 3}{8 \times 3} = \frac{9}{24}$$
$$\frac{13}{24}$$

So $\frac{13}{24}$ of the park will be used for the game fields and the playgrounds.

1. Does $\frac{13}{24}$ seem like a reasonable answer? How do you know?

2. **What if** you had used another common denominator instead of the least common denominator? How would your results differ in Step 2? How would they be the same?

Sometimes you can simplify addition by adding fractions that add to 1.

$$\frac{3}{4} + \frac{1}{2} + \frac{1}{4} = 1\frac{1}{2}$$

3. How would you add these mentally?

   a. $\frac{3}{8} + \frac{5}{6} + \frac{5}{8}$

   b. $\frac{1}{4} + \frac{3}{5} + \frac{2}{5} + \frac{3}{4} + \frac{5}{8}$

TRY OUT   Add. Write the answer in simplest form.

4. $\frac{1}{2} + \frac{3}{8}$ **5.** $\frac{5}{6} + \frac{3}{4}$ **6.** $\frac{3}{8} + \frac{2}{9}$ **7.** $\frac{5}{6} + \frac{4}{5} + \frac{1}{6}$

PRACTICE

Add. Write the answer in simplest form.

8. $\begin{array}{r} \frac{2}{3} \\ + \frac{1}{2} \\ \hline \end{array}$ **9.** $\begin{array}{r} \frac{1}{2} \\ + \frac{4}{5} \\ \hline \end{array}$ **10.** $\begin{array}{r} \frac{1}{3} \\ + \frac{3}{5} \\ \hline \end{array}$ **11.** $\begin{array}{r} \frac{3}{4} \\ + \frac{1}{2} \\ \hline \end{array}$ **12.** $\begin{array}{r} \frac{3}{8} \\ + \frac{5}{12} \\ \hline \end{array}$ **13.** $\begin{array}{r} \frac{4}{9} \\ + \frac{8}{15} \\ \hline \end{array}$

14. $\frac{5}{6} + \frac{2}{3}$ **15.** $\frac{3}{8} + \frac{1}{2}$ **16.** $\frac{3}{5} + \frac{1}{2}$ **17.** $\frac{1}{3} + \frac{5}{6}$ **18.** $\frac{3}{4} + \frac{5}{12}$

19. $\frac{1}{8} + \frac{3}{4}$ **20.** $\frac{1}{2} + \frac{5}{8}$ **21.** $\frac{5}{6} + \frac{1}{2}$ **22.** $\frac{9}{10} + \frac{2}{15}$ **23.** $\frac{5}{6} + \frac{7}{10}$

24. $\frac{1}{3} + \frac{3}{4} + \frac{1}{6}$ **25.** $\frac{2}{3} + \frac{1}{10} + \frac{3}{5}$ **26.** $\frac{1}{4} + \frac{2}{3} + \frac{1}{2}$ **27.** $\frac{1}{6} + \frac{1}{2} + \frac{2}{3}$

28. $\frac{4}{5} + \frac{1}{7} + \frac{1}{5}$ **29.** $\frac{5}{6} + \frac{3}{5} + \frac{1}{6}$ **30.** $\frac{7}{12} + \frac{1}{5} + \frac{5}{12}$ **31.** $\frac{3}{8} + \frac{5}{8} + \frac{2}{3}$

32. five-sixths plus one-fourth

33. three-eighths plus five-twelfths

Critical Thinking   Copy and complete the table of least common denominators.

Denominators	2, 3	4, 8	2, 8	3, 5	3, 12	4, 3	4, 7	6, 15
Least Common Denominator	6	8	■	■	■	■	■	■

34. How can you predict when the least common denominator of two fractions will be equal to the product of the denominators?

Mixed Applications   Solve. Which method did you use?

35. Only $\frac{1}{20}$ of the new park will be paved for roads, and $\frac{1}{10}$ will be paved for parking. How much of the park will be used for roads and parking?

36. In the new park 0.44 of the trees will be evergreens, 0.33 will be citrus, and 0.166 will be oak. About what fraction of the trees will include these varieties?

37. The entrance to the new park will be bordered with flowers. There will be 4 long flower beds. Each flower bed will measure 50 ft by 6 ft. In all how many square feet will the flower beds contain?

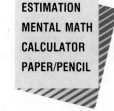

ESTIMATION
MENTAL MATH
CALCULATOR
PAPER/PENCIL

Subtracting Fractions: Unlike Denominators

The mayor of Madison City has a plan to start developing $\frac{5}{6}$ of the new city park. The city council wants to use a plan that develops $\frac{7}{12}$ of the park. Which plan uses more of the park? How much more?

To find these answers, you need to compare the fractions and then subtract.

Think: $\frac{5}{6} \approx 1.$ $\frac{7}{12} \approx \frac{1}{2}.$ $\approx$ means "is about."

So $\frac{5}{6} > \frac{7}{12}.$

Subtract: $\frac{5}{6} - \frac{7}{12}$

Step 1

Write equivalent fractions using the LCD.

$$\frac{5}{6} = \frac{10}{12}$$
$$-\frac{7}{12} = \frac{7}{12}$$

Think: The LCD is 12.

Step 2

Subtract. Write the answer in simplest form.

$$\frac{5}{6} = \frac{10}{12}$$
$$-\frac{7}{12} = \frac{7}{12}$$
$$\frac{3}{12} = \frac{1}{4}$$

The mayor's plan uses $\frac{1}{4}$ more of the park than the city council's plan.

1. How would you subtract $\frac{9}{14} - \frac{11}{21}$? What is the difference?

TRY OUT Write the letter of the correct answer that is in simplest form.

2. $\frac{2}{3} - \frac{1}{2}$ **a.** $\frac{1}{1}$ **b.** $\frac{1}{5}$ **c.** $\frac{1}{6}$ **d.** $\frac{1}{12}$

3. $\frac{11}{12} - \frac{2}{3}$ **a.** $\frac{9}{9}$ **b.** $\frac{9}{12}$ **c.** $\frac{8}{15}$ **d.** $\frac{1}{4}$

4. $\frac{7}{10} - \frac{4}{15}$ **a.** $\frac{3}{5}$ **b.** $\frac{13}{30}$ **c.** $\frac{21}{30}$ **d.** $\frac{8}{15}$

5. $\frac{11}{14} - \frac{3}{4}$ **a.** $\frac{1}{28}$ **b.** $\frac{1}{14}$ **c.** $\frac{3}{28}$ **d.** $\frac{3}{8}$

PRACTICE

Subtract. Write the answer in simplest form.

6. $\dfrac{4}{5}$ $-\dfrac{1}{2}$ **7.** $\dfrac{2}{3}$ $-\dfrac{1}{4}$ **8.** $\dfrac{1}{2}$ $-\dfrac{1}{3}$ **9.** $\dfrac{3}{4}$ $-\dfrac{1}{3}$ **10.** $\dfrac{3}{8}$ $-\dfrac{1}{4}$ **11.** $\dfrac{4}{5}$ $-\dfrac{2}{3}$

12. $\dfrac{3}{5}$ $-\dfrac{1}{4}$ **13.** $\dfrac{2}{3}$ $-\dfrac{1}{5}$ **14.** $\dfrac{5}{8}$ $-\dfrac{1}{4}$ **15.** $\dfrac{3}{4}$ $-\dfrac{5}{8}$ **16.** $\dfrac{5}{6}$ $-\dfrac{1}{3}$ **17.** $\dfrac{2}{3}$ $-\dfrac{5}{12}$

18. $\dfrac{7}{10}$ $-\dfrac{2}{5}$ **19.** $\dfrac{5}{6}$ $-\dfrac{2}{3}$ **20.** $\dfrac{3}{10}$ $-\dfrac{1}{5}$ **21.** $\dfrac{5}{6}$ $-\dfrac{1}{4}$ **22.** $\dfrac{1}{3}$ $-\dfrac{1}{6}$ **23.** $\dfrac{3}{5}$ $-\dfrac{1}{8}$

24. $\dfrac{3}{4} - \dfrac{1}{6}$ **25.** $\dfrac{7}{8} - \dfrac{5}{12}$ **26.** $\dfrac{7}{12} - \dfrac{1}{3}$ **27.** $\dfrac{11}{15} - \dfrac{3}{10}$ **28.** $\dfrac{5}{4} - \dfrac{7}{6}$

Find the difference between the two fractions.

29. $\dfrac{5}{6}, \dfrac{7}{9}$ **30.** $\dfrac{7}{10}, \dfrac{3}{4}$ **31.** $\dfrac{5}{8}, \dfrac{7}{12}$ **32.** $\dfrac{5}{8}, \dfrac{5}{6}$ **33.** $\dfrac{8}{9}, \dfrac{11}{12}$

Add or subtract mentally.

34. $\dfrac{2}{3} + \dfrac{1}{3} - \dfrac{3}{8}$ **35.** $\dfrac{4}{5} + \dfrac{5}{6} - \dfrac{4}{5}$ **36.** $\dfrac{2}{3} - \dfrac{3}{4} + \dfrac{1}{3}$ **37.** $\dfrac{5}{7} - \dfrac{3}{10} + \dfrac{2}{7}$

Mixed Applications

Solve. Which method did you use?

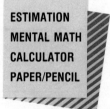

ESTIMATION
MENTAL MATH
CALCULATOR
PAPER/PENCIL

38. Park development funds are 0.05 of the total city budget of $35,654,700. What amount of the budget is for city parks?

39. The goal is to have $\dfrac{5}{6}$ of the park fenced by next year. Only $\dfrac{1}{8}$ has been fenced so far. How much more needs to be fenced?

CHALLENGE

The sum of two squares equals the fraction in the circle between them.

Find the fractions in the squares.

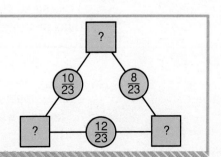

PROBLEM SOLVING

Strategy: Using Number Sense

Maurice walked on the treadmill $\frac{2}{3}$ hour on Monday, $\frac{3}{4}$ hour on Tuesday, and $\frac{1}{2}$ hour on Wednesday. Did Maurice exercise more than $1\frac{1}{2}$ hours?

You can use your number sense to help you solve this problem.

UNDERSTAND

What do I know?

I know that Maurice exercised $\frac{2}{3}$ hour, $\frac{3}{4}$ hour, and $\frac{1}{2}$ hour.

What do I need to find out?

I need to find out whether the sum of $\frac{2}{3}$, $\frac{3}{4}$ and $\frac{1}{2}$ is greater than $1\frac{1}{2}$.

PLAN

What can I do?

I can determine whether $\frac{2}{3} + \frac{3}{4} + \frac{1}{2}$ is greater than $\frac{1}{2} + \frac{1}{2} + \frac{1}{2}$, which is equal to $1\frac{1}{2}$.

TRY

Let me try my plan.

Since both $\frac{2}{3}$ and $\frac{3}{4}$ are greater than $\frac{1}{2}$, the sum of $\frac{2}{3} + \frac{3}{4} + \frac{1}{2}$ is greater than $\frac{1}{2} + \frac{1}{2} + \frac{1}{2}$, or $1\frac{1}{2}$. So Maurice did exercise more than $1\frac{1}{2}$ hours.

CHECK

Have I answered the question?

Yes, Maurice exercised more than $1\frac{1}{2}$ hours.

Is my answer reasonable?

Yes, since the addends $\frac{2}{3}$, $\frac{3}{4}$ and $\frac{1}{2}$ are all greater than or equal to $\frac{1}{2}$, their sum is greater than $1\frac{1}{2}$.

EXTEND

What have I learned?

I have learned that by thinking about the addends I may be able to solve the problem without actually adding.

PRACTICE

Use your number sense to solve the problem.

1. José grew $\frac{7}{12}$ ft one year and $\frac{5}{8}$ ft the next year. Did José grow at least 1 ft in these two years?

2. Joyce wants to make 1 gal of fruit punch. She uses $\frac{1}{4}$ gal of grape juice, $\frac{1}{6}$ gal of lemon juice, and $\frac{1}{3}$ gal of orange juice. Does she have enough punch?

3. Luis wants to prepare about 2 c of salad. He mixes $\frac{1}{2}$ c of cucumber slices, $\frac{1}{4}$ c of bean sprouts, $\frac{3}{8}$ c of shredded lettuce, and $\frac{1}{2}$ c of chopped tomatoes. Will he have less than 2 c of salad or more than 2 c of salad?

4. Penelope makes a health snack mix. She uses $\frac{2}{3}$ lb of dried banana slices, $\frac{5}{8}$ lb of sunflower seeds, $\frac{9}{10}$ lb of almonds, $\frac{3}{4}$ lb of dried apricots, and $\frac{7}{8}$ lb of coconut. Will she have more or less than 3 lb of mix?

> **REMEMBER:**
> **What do you need to find out?**
> **What can you do?**
> **Try your plan.**
> **Check for reasonableness.**

Strategies and Skills Review

Solve. Use estimation, mental math, a calculator, or paper and pencil. You may need to use the Databank on page 552.

5. Conduct an experiment to find out how many times a sixth grader inhales in one minute when at rest. Choose 5 other students. Count the number of times each one inhales in one minute when at rest. Find the average for the 5 students.

6. For lunch Troy chooses $\frac{1}{2}$ c of cottage cheese with 107 calories, $\frac{1}{2}$ of a plain bagel with 90 calories, and 1 c of skim milk with 85 calories. Does Troy's lunch have less than 300 calories? Did you underestimate or overestimate? Why?

7. Margie gives a snack recipe to a friend on Tuesday. Her friend gives the recipe to 2 more friends on Wednesday. Each of these 2 friends gives the recipe to 2 other friends on Thursday. If this pattern continues, how many friends will receive the recipe on Saturday?

8. Claire wants to make a dinner that is between 700 and 800 calories. She plans to eat 4 oz of tuna salad, $3\frac{1}{2}$ oz of string beans, $\frac{1}{2}$ of a potato, 1 c of skim milk, and $\frac{1}{4}$ c of peanuts. Does she stay within her goal?

9. A recipe book is open. The numbers on the facing pages have the product 210. What are the numbers?

10. **Write a problem** that involves using your number sense. Solve your problem. Then ask others to solve it.

Logical Reasoning

Logic can be used to solve many problems. There are many logical strategies you can use. For example, you can:

- use a table to organize information.
- eliminate possibilities.
- solve a simpler problem.
- guess and check.

Try these logic problems about the Podunk Annual Picnic.

1. Petra, Peg, and Penny had a great time at the picnic. But by the end of the fun, they had exchanged clothes by mistake. Each one was wearing someone else's hat and shoes. Peg was wearing Penny's hat and Petra's shoes. Whose hat and shoes was each person wearing?

You may find it useful to organize your information in a table. The table will help you eliminate possibilities. The table at the right shows the information given. Can you complete it?

	Petra	Peg	Penny
Hat		Penny's	
Shoes		Petra's	

2. One of the main events was a pancake-eating contest. The winner ate the greatest number of pancakes.

- Angie ate more pancakes than Dan.
- Only one person ate fewer pancakes than Norm.
- Leah ate more than Steve.
- Steve did not come in last.
- Angie did not win the contest.
- More than one person ate more than Steve.

Can you find the order of winners? Try using a table.

3. Bert asked this riddle about Podunk's famous mayor, Peter Peterson. Can you solve it? Use a calculator to help you. "When Peter Peterson died, his age was $\frac{1}{29}$ of the year of his birth. He was also twice as old as the sum of the digits of the year of his birth and the digits of the year of his death. How old was Peter Peterson in 1900?"

Try breaking the next problem into simpler problems before you begin.

4. The final event at the Podunk Picnic is the Podunk Paddle. It is a boat ride around Lake Pickle in three different kinds of boats. First everyone circles the lake in a dinghy. Then they use a canoe. Finally they circle once more in a rowboat.

- 3 people fit in a dinghy.
- 4 people fit in a canoe.
- 5 people fit in a rowboat.

If 47 boats were used in all, how many people entered the Podunk Paddle?

You can make a guess and check your answer. How will you check your answer?

Adding and Subtracting Mixed Numbers

The sixth-grade classes at Jefferson School need shelving on which to display their poetry books. Room 6A needs $1\frac{3}{4}$ ft of wood, and Room 6B needs $2\frac{5}{8}$ ft of wood. The woodshop has just $2\frac{1}{4}$ ft of wood on hand. How much wood does the woodshop still need?

WORKING TOGETHER

Here is how Tom used fraction strips to find $1\frac{3}{4} + 2\frac{5}{8}$, the amount of wood the sixth graders need.

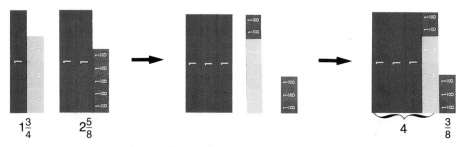

Tom found that $1\frac{3}{4} + 2\frac{5}{8} = 4\frac{3}{8}$.

The woodshop needs a total of $4\frac{3}{8}$ ft of wood.

1. How many unit strips did Tom need for the model? how many fourths? how many eighths?

2. In Tom's model for addition, what fraction strips combined to give one more unit?

Then Tom used his model to find $4\frac{3}{8} - 2\frac{1}{4}$.

He found that $4\frac{3}{8} - 2\frac{1}{4} = 2\frac{1}{8}$. The woodshop still needs $2\frac{1}{8}$ ft of wood.

3. How was $2\frac{1}{4}$ subtracted from $4\frac{3}{8}$?

4. **What if** Tom subtracts $4\frac{1}{2} - 2\frac{1}{4}$? What would he need to do to subtract?

SHARING IDEAS

5. How is adding and subtracting mixed numbers similar to adding fractions?

6. How is adding and subtracting mixed numbers similar to adding whole numbers?

7. *What if* you want to add or subtract two mixed numbers? How could you find the answer without using a model?

ON YOUR OWN

Use your method for adding and subtracting mixed numbers to find the sum or difference.

8. $1\frac{3}{4} + 3\frac{1}{8}$
9. $3\frac{2}{3} + 1\frac{1}{6}$
10. $4\frac{3}{8} + 2\frac{3}{4}$
11. $2\frac{3}{4} + 2\frac{1}{2}$

12. $2\frac{3}{4} - 1\frac{3}{8}$
13. $5\frac{1}{2} - 1\frac{3}{8}$
14. $5\frac{5}{8} - 2\frac{1}{4}$
15. $4\frac{5}{6} - 3\frac{2}{3}$

16. $2\frac{1}{2} + 3\frac{5}{8}$
17. $2\frac{5}{6} - 1\frac{1}{3}$
18. $3\frac{4}{5} + 1\frac{1}{2}$
19. $3\frac{4}{5} - 1\frac{1}{2}$

20. Maria spent $1\frac{2}{3}$ hours writing a poem. It took her $1\frac{3}{4}$ hours to type it perfectly. How much time did Maria spend on the poem in all?

What must you add to or subtract from the number to get 1? to get $3\frac{1}{2}$? Write two equations.

21. $2\frac{1}{2}$
22. $\frac{1}{4}$
23. $2\frac{7}{8}$
24. $1\frac{1}{3}$
25. $2\frac{1}{6}$
26. $3\frac{4}{5}$

Adding Mixed Numbers

A. On Saturday Rico roller skated from his home to the library. The distance is $1\frac{1}{10}$ mi. On the way back home, he stopped by the softball field. This made his return trip $2\frac{3}{10}$ mi longer. How long was his return trip?

To find the exact answer, add $1\frac{1}{10}$ and $2\frac{3}{10}$. Notice that the fractions have a common denominator.

Step 1	Step 2
Add the fractions. Add the whole numbers.	Write the sum in simplest form.

$$1\frac{1}{10}$$
$$+\ 2\frac{3}{10}$$
$$\overline{\ \ 3\frac{4}{10}}$$

$$3\frac{4}{10} = 3\frac{2}{5}$$

Rico's return trip was $3\frac{2}{5}$ mi.

B. You can also add mixed numbers with unlike denominators.

Add: $1\frac{4}{5} + 1\frac{1}{10} + 4\frac{3}{4}$

Step 1	Step 2	Step 3
Write equivalent fractions using the LCD.	Add the fractions. Add the whole numbers.	Write the sum in simplest form.

Step 1:
$$1\frac{4}{5} = 1\frac{16}{20}$$
$$1\frac{1}{10} = 1\frac{2}{20}$$
$$+\ 4\frac{3}{4} = 4\frac{15}{20}$$

Step 2:
$$1\frac{4}{5} = 1\frac{16}{20}$$
$$1\frac{1}{10} = 1\frac{2}{20}$$
$$+\ 4\frac{3}{4} = 4\frac{15}{20}$$
$$\overline{\qquad\quad 6\frac{33}{20}}$$

Step 3:
$$6\frac{33}{20} = 6 + \frac{33}{20}$$
$$= 6 + 1\frac{13}{20}$$
$$= 7\frac{13}{20}$$

1. Find the sum of $3\frac{3}{5} + 4\frac{3}{7} + 2\frac{2}{5}$ mentally.

TRY OUT   Add. Write the answer in simplest form.

2. $3\frac{2}{9} + 2\frac{5}{9}$　　**3.** $1\frac{3}{8} + 3\frac{5}{8}$　　**4.** $2\frac{1}{3} + 5\frac{1}{6}$　　**5.** $2\frac{1}{3} + 2\frac{5}{6} + 2\frac{1}{2}$

PRACTICE

Write your answer in simplest form.

6. $4\frac{1}{8}$ **7.** $2\frac{3}{10}$ **8.** $2\frac{4}{5}$ **9.** $3\frac{6}{8}$ **10.** $3\frac{7}{10}$ **11.** $2\frac{9}{13}$
$+3\frac{3}{8}$ $+1\frac{7}{10}$ $+5\frac{3}{5}$ $+3\frac{6}{8}$ $+4\frac{5}{10}$ $+8\frac{5}{13}$

12. $6\frac{1}{6}$ **13.** $3\frac{1}{3}$ **14.** $6\frac{7}{8}$ **15.** $5\frac{3}{4}$ **16.** $8\frac{2}{9}$ **17.** $7\frac{5}{12}$
$+4\frac{1}{2}$ $+2\frac{5}{9}$ $+3\frac{1}{2}$ $+4\frac{1}{3}$ $+3\frac{1}{6}$ $+5\frac{11}{15}$

18. $1\frac{2}{3} + 2\frac{1}{6}$ **19.** $2\frac{2}{5} + 3\frac{1}{10}$ **20.** $4\frac{1}{8} + 6\frac{1}{2} + 2\frac{3}{4}$ **21.** $6\frac{2}{9} + 4\frac{1}{3} + 5\frac{5}{6}$

22. $3\frac{11}{12} + 2\frac{2}{3}$ **23.** $9\frac{11}{16} + 6\frac{3}{4}$ **24.** $1\frac{2}{7} + 4\frac{5}{7} + 2\frac{7}{8}$ **25.** $9\frac{7}{10} + 6\frac{2}{5} + 3\frac{1}{4}$

26. four and three-tenths plus three and one-half

27. six and eleven-twelfths plus three and one-fifteenth

Find the missing number.

28. $3\frac{1}{2} + 1\frac{1}{2} = \blacksquare$ **29.** $2\frac{1}{3} + 4\frac{2}{3} = \blacksquare$ **30.** $5\frac{1}{3} + 8\frac{1}{2} = \blacksquare$ **31.** $2\frac{1}{3} + 4\frac{1}{2} = \blacksquare$

Mixed Applications

32. George rode his bike around a rectangular garden in the park. The garden is $\frac{3}{8}$ mi long and $\frac{1}{4}$ mi wide. How far did George ride in all?

33. Three bikes had defective tires that had to be replaced. Each tire cost $10.50. How much did it cost to replace all the tires?

34. Miguel rented a bike for $1\frac{3}{4}$ hours on Saturday and $2\frac{1}{4}$ hours on Sunday. The total rent was $26. How much was the rent for each hour?

35. ***Write a problem*** that involves adding three mixed numbers. Solve your problem. Ask others to solve it.

Mixed Review

Find the answer. Which method did you use?

MENTAL MATH CALCULATOR PAPER/PENCIL

36. $7.3 + 19.005 + 608.496$ **37.** $8.6 - 0.982$ **38.** $36.77 - 4.9$

39. 0.07×9.325 **40.** $1.6\overline{)11.272}$ **41.** $6 \times 1.4 \div 0.5$

42. $3 \times 3 \times 3 \times 3$ **43.** $696 + 129$ **44.** $4,842 \div 13$

Subtracting Mixed Numbers

A. Brenda's favorite cereal, Raisin Chewies, contains $4\frac{7}{8}$ oz of raisins in each box. Brian prefers Raisin Flakes, which contains $2\frac{3}{8}$ oz of raisins in each box.

How many more ounces of raisins are in a box of Raisin Chewies than in a box of Raisin Flakes?

Subtract: $4\frac{7}{8} - 2\frac{3}{8}$

Step 1	Step 2
Subtract the fractions. Subtract the whole numbers.	Write the difference in simplest form.
$\begin{array}{r} 4\frac{7}{8} \\ - 2\frac{3}{8} \\ \hline 2\frac{4}{8} \end{array}$	$2\frac{4}{8} = 2\frac{1}{2}$

A box of Raisin Chewies contains $2\frac{1}{2}$ oz more raisins than a box of Raisin Flakes.

1. Is the answer reasonable? How do you know?

B. You can also subtract mixed numbers with unlike denominators.

Subtract: $3\frac{2}{3} - 1\frac{1}{6}$

Step 1	Step 2	Step 3
Write equivalent fractions using the LCD.	Subtract the fractions. Subtract the whole numbers.	Write the difference in simplest form.
$\begin{array}{l} 3\frac{2}{3} = 3\frac{4}{6} \\ - 1\frac{1}{6} = 1\frac{1}{6} \\ \hline \end{array}$	$\begin{array}{l} 3\frac{2}{3} = 3\frac{4}{6} \\ - 1\frac{1}{6} = 1\frac{1}{6} \\ \hline 2\frac{3}{6} \end{array}$	$2\frac{3}{6} = 2\frac{1}{2}$

TRY OUT Subtract. Write the answer in simplest form.

2. $8\frac{5}{6} - 3\frac{1}{6}$ **3.** $6\frac{7}{8} - 6\frac{5}{8}$ **4.** $4\frac{1}{10} - 1\frac{1}{20}$ **5.** $5\frac{5}{8} - 2\frac{1}{2}$

PRACTICE

Subtract. Write the answer in simplest form.

6. $8\frac{7}{8}$
   $- 3\frac{3}{8}$

7. $4\frac{1}{2}$
   $- 2\frac{1}{2}$

8. $4\frac{5}{8}$
   $- 2\frac{1}{8}$

9. $6\frac{5}{6}$
   $- \frac{1}{6}$

10. $11\frac{5}{16}$
   $- 3\frac{1}{16}$

11. $5\frac{2}{3}$
   $- 4$

12. $6\frac{1}{2}$
   $- 2\frac{1}{4}$

13. $10\frac{7}{8}$
   $- 4$

14. $3\frac{5}{6}$
   $- 1\frac{1}{2}$

15. $8\frac{5}{6}$
   $- 5\frac{1}{3}$

16. $11\frac{5}{6}$
   $- \frac{1}{2}$

17. $6\frac{3}{4}$
   $- 1\frac{3}{8}$

18. $16\frac{2}{3}$
   $- 10\frac{1}{6}$

19. $3\frac{7}{8}$
   $- 1\frac{1}{4}$

20. $4\frac{5}{6}$
   $- 1\frac{1}{6}$

21. $9\frac{1}{4}$
   $- \frac{1}{8}$

22. $6\frac{5}{8}$
   $- 1\frac{1}{2}$

23. $8\frac{5}{12}$
   $- 8\frac{1}{3}$

24. $8\frac{4}{5} - 5\frac{1}{10}$

25. $6\frac{2}{3} - 1\frac{2}{9}$

26. $2\frac{3}{4} - 1\frac{1}{3}$

27. $10\frac{3}{5} - 2\frac{3}{10}$

28. $11\frac{5}{12} - 8$

29. $6\frac{5}{6} - 3\frac{2}{9}$

30. $8\frac{7}{10} - \frac{2}{5}$

31. $7\frac{3}{8} - 4\frac{1}{12}$

Compare. Write $>$, $<$, or $=$.

32. $3\frac{1}{3} - 1\frac{1}{6} \bullet 4\frac{1}{2} - 2\frac{1}{4}$

33. $2\frac{3}{4} + 1\frac{1}{6} \bullet 2\frac{2}{3} + 1\frac{1}{4}$

34. $1\frac{7}{8} - \frac{1}{8} \bullet 2\frac{9}{10} - 1\frac{3}{5}$

35. $1\frac{1}{4} + 5\frac{5}{12} \bullet 7\frac{3}{8} - 1\frac{1}{3}$

36. $1\frac{5}{6} + 5\frac{3}{4} \bullet 10\frac{1}{3} - 1\frac{2}{9}$

37. $6\frac{3}{10} - 4\frac{1}{5} \bullet 1\frac{7}{20} + 1\frac{1}{4}$

Mixed Applications

Solve. You may need to use the Databank on page 552.

38. The box of cereal that Chan Wong has says that each serving contains 155 mg of Vitamin C. How much Vitamin C will he get from the cereal by eating one serving each day for a week?

39. On Monday the members of the Costa family ate $\frac{1}{3}$ of a new loaf of bread. On Tuesday they ate another $\frac{1}{2}$ of the loaf. What fraction of the loaf did they have left for Wednesday?

40. Mrs. Lynch said that the price of the breakfast she had in her hotel on vacation was 6 times more than the cost if she had made it at home. The price at the hotel was $4.20. How much less would it have cost her to make the breakfast at home?

41. At breakfast Humberto usually pours a cup of whole milk over one cup of Raisin Flakes cereal, drinks an 8-oz glass of orange juice, and also eats a slice of toast. How many calories does he get from this breakfast?

EXTRA PRACTICE, page 302

Subtract Mixed Numbers with Renaming

A. Mr. Carter took his family on the new interstate from home to Aunt Clea's house. It took $1\frac{3}{4}$ hours to get there. Before the new interstate was built, it used to take $3\frac{1}{4}$ hours. How much less time does it take now than before?

Subtract: $3\frac{1}{4} - 1\frac{3}{4}$

Step 1	Step 2
Rename to subtract the fractions.	**Subtract. Write the answer in simplest form.**
$\begin{array}{r} 3\frac{1}{4} = 2\frac{5}{4} \\ -\ 1\frac{3}{4} = 1\frac{3}{4} \\ \hline \end{array}$	$\begin{array}{r} 3\frac{1}{4} = 2\frac{5}{4} \\ -\ 1\frac{3}{4} = 1\frac{3}{4} \\ \hline 1\frac{2}{4} = 1\frac{1}{2} \end{array}$
Think: $3\frac{1}{4} = 2 + 1\frac{1}{4}$ $= 2\frac{5}{4}$	

On the new interstate it takes $1\frac{1}{2}$ hours less than before.

1. How would you find $6 - 3\frac{5}{8}$? What is the difference?

B. Sometimes you need to rename a mixed number twice.

Subtract: $4\frac{5}{12} - 1\frac{2}{3}$

Step 1	Step 2	Step 3
Write equivalent fractions using the LCD.	**Rename to subtract the fractions.**	**Subtract. Write the answer in simplest form.**
$\begin{array}{r} 4\frac{5}{12} = 4\frac{5}{12} \\ -\ 1\frac{2}{3} = 1\frac{8}{12} \\ \hline \end{array}$	$\begin{array}{r} 4\frac{5}{12} = 3\frac{17}{12} \\ -\ 1\frac{8}{12} = 1\frac{8}{12} \\ \hline \end{array}$	$\begin{array}{r} 4\frac{5}{12} = 3\frac{17}{12} \\ -\ 1\frac{8}{12} = 1\frac{8}{12} \\ \hline 2\frac{9}{12} = 2\frac{3}{4} \end{array}$

2. How would you find $3\frac{1}{4} - 2\frac{1}{3}$? What is the difference?

TRY OUT Subtract. Write the answer in simplest form.

3. $5\frac{1}{8} - 2\frac{7}{8}$ **4.** $4\frac{2}{10} - 2\frac{8}{10}$ **5.** $7\frac{1}{2} - 3\frac{2}{3}$ **6.** $2\frac{1}{3} - 1\frac{3}{5}$

PRACTICE

Subtract. Write the answer in simplest form.

7. $7\frac{1}{8}$ $-\ 4\frac{3}{8}$

8. $3\frac{7}{12}$ $-\ 1\frac{11}{12}$

9. $13\frac{1}{10}$ $-\ 4\frac{3}{10}$

10. $5\frac{3}{8}$ $-\ 2\frac{7}{8}$

11. $10\frac{5}{12}$ $-\ 8\frac{7}{12}$

12. $6\frac{3}{4}$ $-\ 3\frac{3}{4}$

13. $12\frac{1}{8}$ $-\ 8\frac{1}{2}$

14. $10\frac{1}{3}$ $-\ 6\frac{1}{2}$

15. $6\frac{1}{2}$ $-\ 4\frac{2}{3}$

16. $8\frac{1}{3}$ $-\ 2\frac{3}{4}$

17. $5\frac{1}{2}$ $-\ 1\frac{9}{10}$

18. $2\frac{3}{4}$ $-\ 1\frac{5}{6}$

19. $7\frac{1}{10} - \frac{9}{10}$

20. $5 - 1\frac{1}{3}$

21. $12 - 4\frac{4}{9}$

22. $8\frac{1}{5} - \frac{3}{15}$

23. $4\frac{3}{8} - 2\frac{3}{4}$

24. $8 - 3\frac{5}{6}$

25. $6 - 2\frac{3}{8}$

26. $1\frac{5}{12} - \frac{3}{8}$

27. one and seven-twelfths minus five-eighths

28. six and three-tenths less four and three-fifths

29. four and one-third minus two and five-sixths

30. ten and three-fourths less eight and eleven-twelfths

Complete.

31. $\left(3\frac{1}{6} + ■\right) - 2\frac{2}{3} = 2$

32. $5\frac{3}{8} + \left(3\frac{1}{5} - 2\frac{1}{10}\right) = ■$

33. $\left(1\frac{3}{16} + 4\frac{3}{4}\right) - ■ = 3\frac{9}{16}$

Critical Thinking

34. What must be true of two mixed numbers if their difference is a whole number? if their difference is a proper fraction?

Mixed Applications

35. Maria drives a bus between the airport and downtown. One day she made 5 round trips and drove a total of 178 mi. How far is it from the airport to downtown?

36. Mrs. Hood drove downtown from her home in $\frac{3}{4}$ hour. She shopped for $2\frac{3}{4}$ hours. It took her $\frac{4}{5}$ hours to drive home. How much longer was her return trip?

37. Phil drove $1\frac{3}{4}$ mi from his house to the grocery store. When he got back home, he realized he did not buy a roast of beef, so he returned to buy it. In all, how far did he drive to get all the groceries?

38. A truck driver drove from Lincoln to Hammond in $1\frac{1}{2}$ hours and from Hammond to Arlington in $1\frac{3}{4}$ hours. How long did the entire trip take?

PROBLEM SOLVING

Checking for a Reasonable Answer

At the Hillside County Fair, Lucie keeps track of the attendance for the first four days. There were 949 people on the first day, 936 on the second day, 1,019 on the third day, and 1,042 on the fourth day. Lucie uses a calculator to find the total number of people who attended in the four days. She gets a total of 12,370 people. Is Lucie's answer reasonable? You can use estimation to check her answer.

Think: Each of the four numbers is close to 1,000. The total should be close to 4 × 1,000, or 4,000.

$$
\begin{array}{rcl}
949 & \rightarrow & 1,000 \\
936 & \rightarrow & 1,000 \\
1,019 & \rightarrow & 1,000 \\
+\ 1,042 & \rightarrow & +\ 1,000 \\
\hline
& & 4,000
\end{array}
$$

Since 12,370 is *not* close to 4,000, Lucie's answer is *not* reasonable.

1. The exact answer is 3,946 people. What mistake do you think Lucie made with the calculator?

2. **What if** attendance at the fair remains steady? About how many people do you think will attend in a week?

Is the answer reasonable? If it is not, find the correct answer.

3. At the crafts booth Raymond bought a bowl for $19.49, a scarf for $20.25, and a wallet for $19.98. How much did he pay for the three items? Answer: $59.72

4. Mrs. Smith bought $2\frac{1}{2}$ lb of tomatoes, $3\frac{1}{4}$ lb of potatoes, and $1\frac{2}{3}$ lb of cabbage at the fair. How many pounds of vegetables did she buy all together? Answer: $6\frac{11}{12}$ lb

5. Sunshine Farms has a booth at the fair. They are selling 12 oranges for $1.08. How much would 18 oranges cost? Answer: $1.62

6. Mr. Smith exhibits his prize pig in a rectangular pen that is 2.3 m by 1.2 m. What is the area of the pen? Answer: 27.6 m²

Strategies and Skills Review

Solve. Use estimation, mental math, a calculator, or paper and pencil.

7. Tickets of admission to the fair are $3.25 for children and $2.25 more than that for adults. On Saturday 312 children attended the fair. Twice as many adults as children were admitted that day. How much money was collected in admissions on Saturday?

8. Bill wants to be able to spend $10 at the fair. He earns $3.50 for raking leaves, $5.25 for baby-sitting, and $2.15 for running errands. Use estimation to decide whether he has earned enough money. Did you underestimate or overestimate? Why?

9. Roseanne expects to spend $3\frac{1}{2}$ hours at the fair. After spending $1\frac{3}{4}$ hours on the rides, she decides that she has $2\frac{1}{4}$ hours left to spend at the fair. Is Roseanne's answer reasonable? If it is not, find the correct answer.

10. Which is a reasonable measure for the mass of an orange?
    a. 20 g
    b. 200 g
    c. 2,000 g

11. ***Write a problem.*** Give your problem an answer that is *not* reasonable. Then ask others to solve it.

DECISION MAKING

Problem Solving: Choosing a Floor Plan

SITUATION

The student council is planning to buy furniture for its new room. Anne, George, and Gilda each drew a floor plan.

PROBLEM

Which floor plan should the council choose?

DATA

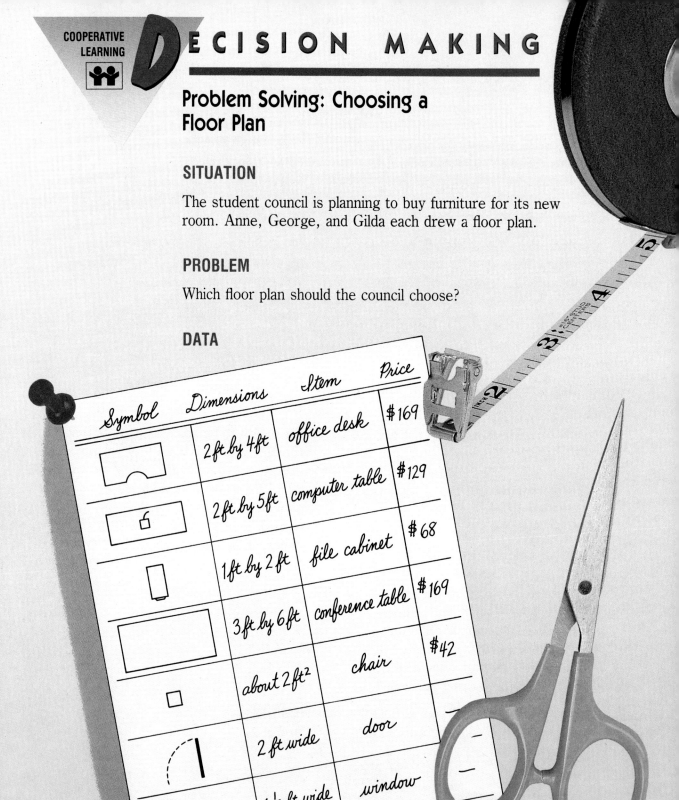

Symbol	Dimensions	Item	Price
	2 ft by 4 ft	office desk	$169
	2 ft by 5 ft	computer table	$129
	1 ft by 2 ft	file cabinet	$68
	3 ft by 6 ft	conference table	$169
	about 2 ft²	chair	$42
	2 ft wide	door	
	1½ ft wide	window	

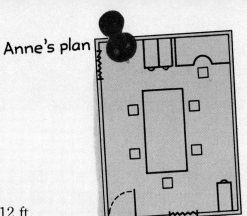

Anne's plan

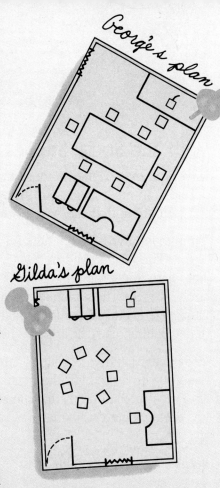

George's plan

The council room measures 9 ft by 12 ft.

USING THE DATA

How much of each type of furniture does the plan contain?

1. Anne's plan   **2.** George's plan   **3.** Gilda's plan

What is the cost of the furniture for the plan?

4. Anne's plan   **5.** George's plan   **6.** Gilda's plan

Gilda's plan

About how many square feet of floor space has no furniture on it?

7. Anne's plan   **8.** George's plan   **9.** Gilda's plan

MAKING DECISIONS

10. Which plan is the least expensive?

11. Which plan should the council choose to have the most empty floor space?

12. Which plan should the council choose to have the most file space?

13. *What if* the council plans to use the room for meetings and presentations? Which plan makes it easier to rearrange the space?

14. *What if* the council could not spend more than $800? Which plan could not be chosen?

15. Use graph paper to draw your own floor plan for the room. Be sure to stay within the budget of $800.

16. *Write a list* of the other factors the council should consider when choosing the furniture and the floor plan.

17. Which floor plan would you choose? Tell why.

Math and Social Studies

Have you ever visited a museum and seen clothing from other time periods? In most cases our style of clothing today is very different. Did you know that the way clothes are sized has also changed?

Until about 1800, men's hats were shaped over a round wooden block. The inside band of a hat was formed into a perfect circle. The diameter—the length across the widest part—of that circle in inches determined the hat's size. After the hats were sized, they were then pushed into a more oval shape that would actually fit a man's head.

Today, hat bands are shaped into ovals, but the measurement is still given as though the band were the diameter of a circle. The most common size for men's hats is $7\frac{1}{8}$. Each larger size is $\frac{1}{8}$ greater and each smaller size is $\frac{1}{8}$ less.

What if Bob's hat size is $7\frac{1}{8}$ and John's is two sizes smaller? What size hat does John wear?

Think: John's hat size is two sizes smaller than Bob's, or $\frac{2}{8}$ less than $7\frac{1}{8}$.

$$7\frac{1}{8} - \frac{2}{8} = 6\frac{9}{8} - \frac{2}{8} = 6\frac{7}{8}$$

John's hat size is $6\frac{7}{8}$.

ACTIVITIES

1. Work in a group. Use a tape measure to find one another's hat size. What is the difference between the largest and smallest sizes? Record the measurements in a chart.

2. Find out how various articles of clothing are sized. You might want to learn about how shoes are sized in the United States and in Europe, and contrast the two methods. Prepare a report for the rest of the class.

Computer Graphing: Line Graphs

Line graphs are often used to study trends. The lines show rising and falling patterns. For this activity you will gather data and enter it into the computer. The computer graphing program SPORTSLINE will draw a double-line graph for you.

To gather your data, use an almanac or a book of sports facts that contains a list of Olympic results. Find the winning time of each swimming event for the years listed in this table.

Year	Women's 100-Meter Freestyle	Men's 100-Meter Freestyle
1924		
1936		
1948		
1960		
1972		
1984		

AT THE COMPUTER

1. Note that some of the winning times are given in minutes and seconds. Express each women's time in seconds, and then round it to the nearest second. For example, the women's time for 1924 is 72 seconds to the nearest second. Enter each time in the correct row and column on the screen.

2. Round each men's winning time to the nearest second. Enter each value in the correct row and column. Then have the computer draw a double-line graph.

3. Use the graphs to decide which twelve-year period has the greatest decrease in the women's time and in the men's time.

4. What patterns do you notice about the changes in men's and women's winning times? At which Olympics were the men's and women's times closest? Do you think times will keep getting closer and closer together? Do you think the men's and women's times will both continue to get faster and faster?

5. Have the computer redraw the graphs using different intervals for the winning-time scale. When would you want to use a scale with a small interval such as 2 seconds? When would you want to use a scale with a greater interval?

EXTRA PRACTICE

Estimating Sums and Differences, page 275

Estimate the sum or difference. Which method did you use?

1. $1\frac{15}{16} + 3\frac{1}{3}$ 2. $\frac{17}{20} + 2\frac{1}{8}$ 3. $4\frac{6}{7} - 1\frac{4}{5}$ 4. $4\frac{2}{3} + \frac{1}{3}$ 5. $3\frac{1}{8} - 1\frac{5}{9}$

6. $3\frac{5}{16} - \frac{11}{12}$ 7. $6\frac{2}{7} - 3\frac{6}{7}$ 8. $\frac{7}{16} + 1\frac{7}{12}$ 9. $\frac{5}{6} + 1\frac{3}{5} + \frac{3}{8}$ 10. $3\frac{2}{3} + 5\frac{9}{10}$

11. $\frac{17}{25} + 3\frac{7}{8}$ 12. $1\frac{15}{16} + \frac{30}{31}$ 13. $6\frac{23}{82} + 2\frac{4}{9}$ 14. $3\frac{4}{15} + 1\frac{1}{2}$ 15. $2\frac{7}{8} + 5\frac{25}{27}$

Adding and Subtracting: Like Denominators, page 277

Add or subtract. Write the answer in simplest form.

1. $\frac{7}{12} + \frac{5}{12}$ 2. $\frac{9}{10} - \frac{4}{10}$ 3. $\frac{14}{15} - \frac{11}{15}$ 4. $\frac{7}{9} + \frac{8}{9}$ 5. $\frac{7}{8} + \frac{7}{8}$ 6. $\frac{15}{18} - \frac{9}{18}$

7. $\frac{3}{4} + \frac{3}{4}$ 8. $\frac{5}{6} + \frac{1}{6}$ 9. $\frac{7}{16} - \frac{3}{16}$ 10. $\frac{2}{9} + \frac{8}{9}$ 11. $\frac{19}{20} - \frac{11}{20}$ 12. $\frac{6}{7} - \frac{4}{7}$

13. $\frac{5}{6} + \frac{2}{6}$ 14. $\frac{2}{7} + \frac{4}{7}$ 15. $\frac{2}{5} + \frac{3}{5}$ 16. $\frac{7}{8} + \frac{6}{8}$ 17. $\frac{11}{12} + \frac{5}{12}$

18. $\frac{5}{8} - \frac{4}{8}$ 19. $\frac{8}{9} - \frac{4}{9}$ 20. $\frac{5}{6} - \frac{5}{6}$ 21. $\frac{10}{10} - \frac{3}{10}$ 22. $\frac{7}{9} - \frac{5}{9}$

23. $\frac{5}{6} + \frac{4}{6} + \frac{5}{6}$ 24. $\frac{11}{12} - \frac{4}{12} - \frac{2}{12}$ 25. $\frac{11}{16} + \frac{3}{16} - \frac{5}{16}$ 26. $\frac{9}{12} + \frac{4}{12} - \frac{3}{12}$

Adding Fractions: Unlike Denominators, page 279

Add. Write the answer in simplest form.

1. $\frac{2}{3} + \frac{3}{4}$ 2. $\frac{1}{2} + \frac{2}{5}$ 3. $\frac{1}{5} + \frac{3}{4}$ 4. $\frac{3}{8} + \frac{5}{6}$ 5. $\frac{5}{6} + \frac{3}{4}$ 6. $\frac{7}{12} + \frac{2}{3}$

7. $\frac{7}{10} + \frac{4}{5}$ 8. $\frac{5}{6} + \frac{2}{3}$ 9. $\frac{7}{8} + \frac{1}{3}$ 10. $\frac{4}{7} + \frac{1}{4}$ 11. $\frac{2}{3} + \frac{9}{10}$ 12. $\frac{1}{2} + \frac{2}{9}$

13. $\frac{1}{6} + \frac{3}{5}$ 14. $\frac{7}{12} + \frac{5}{8}$ 15. $\frac{2}{3} + \frac{1}{6}$ 16. $\frac{5}{6} + \frac{4}{9}$ 17. $\frac{2}{3} + \frac{3}{5}$

18. $\frac{5}{6} + \frac{7}{8} + \frac{3}{4}$ 19. $\frac{3}{4} + \frac{1}{3} + \frac{1}{2}$ 20. $\frac{2}{9} + \frac{5}{6} + \frac{1}{3}$ 21. $\frac{3}{10} + \frac{4}{15} + \frac{3}{5}$ 22. $\frac{3}{8} + \frac{1}{8} + \frac{5}{6}$

Subtracting Fractions: Unlike Denominators, page 281

Subtract. Write the answer in simplest form.

1. $\frac{5}{6} - \frac{3}{4}$
2. $\frac{3}{4} - \frac{2}{3}$
3. $\frac{1}{2} - \frac{2}{5}$
4. $\frac{7}{8} - \frac{1}{2}$
5. $\frac{9}{10} - \frac{2}{5}$
6. $\frac{5}{6} - \frac{3}{8}$

7. $\frac{4}{5} - \frac{1}{3}$
8. $\frac{7}{8} - \frac{1}{4}$
9. $\frac{4}{5} - \frac{1}{4}$
10. $\frac{2}{3} - \frac{1}{6}$
11. $\frac{5}{6} - \frac{1}{2}$
12. $\frac{4}{5} - \frac{2}{15}$

13. $\frac{3}{4} - \frac{5}{12}$
14. $\frac{2}{3} - \frac{7}{15}$
15. $\frac{3}{5} - \frac{7}{20}$
16. $\frac{1}{2} - \frac{1}{6}$
17. $\frac{7}{8} - \frac{11}{24}$
18. $\frac{7}{12} - \frac{1}{4}$

19. $\frac{9}{10} - \frac{2}{5}$
20. $\frac{7}{8} - \frac{1}{4}$
21. $\frac{5}{7} - \frac{1}{2}$
22. $\frac{3}{4} - \frac{3}{8}$
23. $\frac{7}{9} - \frac{1}{6}$
24. $\frac{11}{12} - \frac{2}{3}$

25. $\frac{2}{3} - \frac{2}{5}$
26. $\frac{3}{4} - \frac{1}{6}$
27. $\frac{9}{10} - \frac{1}{2}$
28. $\frac{8}{9} - \frac{1}{3}$
29. $\frac{16}{21} - \frac{3}{7}$

30. $\frac{7}{10} - \frac{1}{4}$
31. $\frac{8}{9} - \frac{1}{6}$
32. $\frac{14}{15} - \frac{3}{5}$
33. $\frac{11}{12} - \frac{5}{8}$
34. $\frac{7}{4} - \frac{5}{3}$

Problem Solving Strategy: Using Number Sense, page 283

Use your number sense to solve.

1. Mr. Goya is building a 40-foot fence around his garden. He bought 80 five-inch-wide slats of wood. Will he have enough wood to build his fence?

2. Jean exercised $\frac{1}{3}$ hour on Monday, $\frac{1}{2}$ hour on Tuesday, $\frac{2}{3}$ hour on Wednesday, and $\frac{3}{4}$ hour on Thursday. Did Jean exercise more than 2 hours in all?

3. Stan wants to make a lemon, lime, and orange juice mix. He uses $\frac{5}{8}$ c lime juice, $\frac{3}{4}$ c lemon juice, and $\frac{1}{2}$ c orange juice. Will there be less than $1\frac{1}{2}$ c or more than $1\frac{1}{2}$ c?

4. Marisa is making a fruit salad. She uses $1\frac{1}{4}$ pounds of apples, $\frac{3}{8}$ pound of bananas, $\frac{1}{4}$ pound of pineapple, $1\frac{1}{2}$ pounds of oranges, and $\frac{9}{10}$ pound of peaches. Does the salad weigh more than 3 lb?

EXTRA PRACTICE

Adding Mixed Numbers, page 289

Add. Write your answer in simplest form.

1. $5\frac{1}{10}$
   $+ 3\frac{3}{10}$

2. $4\frac{3}{8}$
   $+ 2\frac{5}{8}$

3. $2\frac{4}{5}$
   $+ 3\frac{3}{5}$

4. $2\frac{5}{6}$
   $+ 2\frac{5}{6}$

5. $4\frac{7}{12}$
   $+ 6\frac{11}{12}$

6. $3\frac{5}{7}$
   $+ 8\frac{4}{7}$

7. $5\frac{1}{4}$
   $+ 2\frac{1}{3}$

8. $3\frac{2}{3}$
   $+ 7\frac{2}{9}$

9. $6\frac{7}{8}$
   $+ 5\frac{1}{4}$

10. $4\frac{3}{4}$
    $+ 8\frac{5}{6}$

11. $7\frac{7}{9}$
    $+ 5\frac{5}{6}$

12. $4\frac{13}{15}$
    $+ 2\frac{7}{12}$

13. $2\frac{1}{3} + 1\frac{5}{6}$
14. $4\frac{2}{5} + 2\frac{3}{10}$
15. $5\frac{3}{8} + 5\frac{1}{4} + 3\frac{5}{6}$
16. $2\frac{1}{12} + 5\frac{3}{4} + 4\frac{5}{6}$
17. $4\frac{9}{16} + 3\frac{3}{4}$
18. $8\frac{2}{3} + 5\frac{1}{3} + 4\frac{7}{9}$
19. $1\frac{1}{2} + 5\frac{2}{3} + 2\frac{5}{6}$
20. $8\frac{9}{16} + 7\frac{3}{4} + 3\frac{1}{4}$

Subtracting Mixed Numbers, page 291

Subtract. Write your answer in simplest form.

1. $7\frac{5}{8}$
   $- 5\frac{3}{8}$

2. $6\frac{1}{4}$
   $- 2\frac{1}{4}$

3. $5\frac{11}{12}$
   $- 3\frac{5}{12}$

4. $7\frac{11}{16}$
   $- 2\frac{5}{16}$

5. $9\frac{3}{4}$
   $- 7\frac{1}{4}$

6. $11\frac{9}{10}$
   $- 6\frac{3}{10}$

7. $10\frac{1}{2}$
   $- 5\frac{1}{8}$

8. $11\frac{5}{6}$
   $- 3\frac{1}{9}$

9. $15\frac{5}{12}$
   $- 10\frac{1}{4}$

10. $4\frac{5}{6}$
    $- 3\frac{1}{2}$

11. $8\frac{9}{10}$
    $- 8\frac{3}{4}$

12. $7\frac{3}{5}$
    $- 1\frac{4}{15}$

13. $5\frac{2}{3} - 1\frac{1}{4}$
14. $10\frac{11}{12} - 3\frac{2}{3}$
15. $9\frac{2}{5} - 6\frac{3}{10}$
16. $6\frac{5}{6} - 6\frac{2}{3}$
17. $12\frac{9}{10} - 8\frac{1}{6}$
18. $9\frac{7}{10} - 5\frac{1}{2}$
19. $8\frac{2}{3} - 3\frac{5}{12}$
20. $7\frac{20}{21} - 4\frac{2}{7}$

Subtract Mixed Numbers with Renaming, page 293

Subtract. Write the answer in simplest form.

1. $7\frac{2}{5}$
   $-\ 4\frac{4}{5}$

2. $5\frac{1}{10}$
   $-\ 2\frac{9}{10}$

3. $6\frac{2}{5}$
   $-\ 1\frac{4}{5}$

4. $5\frac{1}{7}$
   $-\ 2\frac{3}{7}$

5. $8\frac{1}{4}$
   $-\ 2\frac{3}{4}$

6. 9
   $-\ 3\frac{1}{9}$

7. $7\frac{1}{8}$
   $-\ 1\frac{5}{6}$

8. $11\frac{4}{9}$
   $-\ 7\frac{5}{6}$

9. $12\frac{1}{4}$
   $-\ 9\frac{2}{3}$

10. 5
    $-\ 1\frac{2}{3}$

11. $1\frac{3}{10}$
    $-\ \frac{5}{8}$

12. $9\frac{5}{8}$
    $-\ 8\frac{2}{3}$

13. $7\frac{2}{3}$
    $-\ 4\frac{4}{5}$

14. $6\frac{4}{9}$
    $-\ 3\frac{8}{9}$

15. $5\frac{1}{6}$
    $-\ 2\frac{2}{3}$

16. $4\frac{1}{2}$
    $-\ 1\frac{7}{10}$

17. $7 - 5\frac{3}{4}$

18. $12\frac{3}{10} - 5\frac{4}{5}$

19. $5\frac{7}{10} - 2\frac{9}{10}$

20. $10\frac{1}{2} - 7\frac{5}{6}$

21. $9\frac{1}{4} - 6\frac{1}{2}$

22. $7\frac{3}{8} - 5\frac{3}{4}$

23. $8 - 2\frac{7}{8}$

24. $7\frac{1}{2} - \frac{7}{10}$

Problem Solving: Checking for a Reasonable Answer, page 295

Is the answer reasonable? If it is not, find the correct answer.

1. Mrs. Clark bought $3\frac{1}{2}$ lb oranges, $2\frac{1}{4}$ lb apples, and $1\frac{2}{3}$ lb peaches. How many pounds of fruit did she buy all together? Answer: $6\frac{1}{12}$ lb

2. Mr. Clark wants to build a dog house that is 2.6 meters by 1.3 meters. What is the area of the dog house? Answer: 3.38 square meters.

3. At the market, 6 bananas cost $1.02. How much do 13 bananas cost? Answer: $2.21

4. At the gift store, Gary bought a rose bowl for $26.89, a silk scarf for $32.26, and wool gloves for $16.43. How much did he pay for the three items? Answer: $83.18

Practice PLUS

KEY SKILL: Adding Mixed Numbers (Use after page 289.)

Level A

Write the answer in simplest form.

1. $2\frac{5}{8}$
  $+ 3\frac{1}{8}$

2. $4\frac{2}{10}$
  $+ 1\frac{3}{10}$

3. $3\frac{4}{5}$
  $+ 4\frac{1}{5}$

4. $2\frac{2}{3}$
  $+ 2\frac{2}{3}$

5. $3\frac{6}{7}$
  $+ 2\frac{5}{7}$

6. $5\frac{7}{8}$
  $+ 2\frac{7}{8}$

7. $3\frac{5}{12}$
  $+ 2\frac{1}{4}$

8. $2\frac{1}{2}$
  $+ 1\frac{3}{10}$

9. $5\frac{1}{6}$
  $+ 3\frac{1}{3}$

10. $2\frac{3}{5}$
  $+ 4\frac{3}{10}$

11. $3\frac{7}{8}$
  $+ 1\frac{3}{4}$

12. $4\frac{5}{6}$
  $+ 2\frac{10}{12}$

13. Debbie hiked $1\frac{3}{4}$ miles in the morning and $2\frac{3}{4}$ miles in the afternoon. How far did she hike in all?

Level B

Write the answer in simplest form.

14. $3\frac{1}{6}$
  $+ 2\frac{3}{6}$

15. $4\frac{5}{8}$
  $+ 1\frac{3}{8}$

16. $2\frac{2}{3}$
  $+ 4\frac{5}{6}$

17. $3\frac{7}{8}$
  $+ 4\frac{1}{4}$

18. $2\frac{11}{12}$
  $+ 6\frac{2}{3}$

19. $5\frac{9}{10}$
  $+ 2\frac{1}{2}$

20. $8\frac{1}{4}$
  $+ 7\frac{2}{3}$

21. $3\frac{1}{3}$
  $+ 8\frac{2}{5}$

22. $4\frac{7}{9}$
  $+ 6\frac{5}{6}$

23. $2\frac{3}{4}$
  $+ 9\frac{5}{6}$

24. $6\frac{5}{8}$
  $+ 5\frac{1}{3}$

25. $7\frac{3}{4}$
  $+ 6\frac{3}{5}$

26. Shawn rode his bike $6\frac{5}{8}$ miles in the morning and $7\frac{1}{2}$ miles in the afternoon. How many miles did he ride his bike all together?

Level C

Write the answer in simplest form.

27. $8\frac{3}{4} + 7\frac{5}{12}$

28. $9\frac{7}{9} + 4\frac{5}{6}$

29. $7\frac{5}{6} + 5\frac{3}{4} + 3\frac{7}{12}$

30. $2\frac{3}{5} + 3\frac{2}{5} + 9\frac{2}{3}$

31. $6\frac{3}{4} + 5\frac{1}{2}$

32. $3\frac{1}{4} + 5\frac{7}{10} + 6\frac{4}{5}$

33. $7\frac{5}{6} + 4\frac{7}{10}$

34. $5\frac{2}{3} + 4\frac{5}{6} + 8\frac{7}{9}$

35. $7\frac{3}{4} + 3\frac{7}{12} + 3\frac{3}{8}$

36. $8\frac{4}{9} + 5\frac{8}{15}$

37. $9\frac{5}{6} + 7\frac{3}{5}$

38. $6\frac{3}{4} + 4\frac{1}{2} + 9\frac{4}{7}$

39. Gail worked $4\frac{5}{6}$ hours Friday, $8\frac{3}{4}$ hours Saturday, and $7\frac{2}{5}$ hours Sunday. How long did she work during those three days?

PRACTICE PLUS

KEY SKILL: Subtract Mixed Numbers with Renaming (Use after page 293.)

Level A ....

Subtract. Write the answer in simplest form.

1. $6\frac{1}{3}$
    $-1\frac{2}{3}$

2. $5\frac{2}{5}$
    $-2\frac{4}{5}$

3. $8\frac{3}{7}$
    $-4\frac{5}{7}$

4. $6\frac{5}{8}$
    $-2\frac{7}{8}$

5. 8
    $-2\frac{4}{5}$

6. 7
    $-3\frac{3}{4}$

7. $3\frac{1}{8}$
    $-2\frac{7}{8}$

8. 7
    $-2\frac{2}{3}$

9. $4\frac{4}{9}$
    $-1\frac{7}{9}$

10. $9\frac{1}{5}$
    $-6\frac{4}{5}$

11. $5\frac{1}{4}$
    $-3\frac{3}{4}$

12. 10
    $-7\frac{5}{6}$

13. It is $3\frac{1}{4}$ miles to school from Jake's house. It is $2\frac{3}{4}$ miles from Bill's house to school. How much farther does Jake live from school than Bill?

Level B ....

Subtract. Write the answer in simplest form.

14. $5\frac{3}{8} - 4\frac{7}{8}$

15. $6\frac{2}{7} - 4\frac{6}{7}$

16. $8 - 4\frac{3}{5}$

17. $7\frac{3}{10} - 4\frac{7}{10}$

18. $5 - 1\frac{5}{8}$

19. $9\frac{2}{3} - 7\frac{11}{12}$

20. $10\frac{3}{8} - 2\frac{3}{4}$

21. $11\frac{2}{3} - 8\frac{5}{6}$

22. The library is $7\frac{7}{10}$ miles from Gary's house. It is $8\frac{1}{5}$ miles from Tanya's house. How much closer is Gary's house to the library than Tanya's?

Level C ....

Subtract. Write the answer in simplest form.

23. $6\frac{7}{10} - 4\frac{9}{10}$

24. $7\frac{1}{8} - 2\frac{5}{8}$

25. $9 - 3\frac{7}{10}$

26. $3\frac{5}{8} - 2\frac{3}{4}$

27. $1\frac{1}{5} - \frac{7}{10}$

28. $10\frac{1}{2} - 6\frac{5}{7}$

29. $12\frac{5}{8} - 5\frac{2}{3}$

30. $13\frac{1}{2} - 8\frac{2}{3}$

31. It is $15\frac{1}{6}$ miles to Hamilton from Richmond. It is $9\frac{7}{8}$ miles from Richmond to Hicksburg. How much farther is it to Hamilton than to Hicksburg from Richmond?

CHAPTER REVIEW/TEST

LANGUAGE AND MATHEMATICS

Complete the sentences. Use the words in the chart on the right.

1. The least common multiple of the denominators of two or more fractions is called the ■.

2. To find a common denominator, find a common ■.

3. To add or subtract fractions that have the same denominator, add or subtract the ■.

CONCEPTS AND SKILLS

Estimate the sum or difference by rounding.

4. $\frac{60}{63} + \frac{7}{31}$

5. $\frac{17}{18} - \frac{2}{5}$

6. $3\frac{4}{7} + 4\frac{1}{3} - \frac{2}{15}$

Estimate the sum or difference by the front-end method.

7. $6\frac{5}{7} - 3\frac{7}{9}$

8. $9\frac{3}{4} - 8\frac{2}{5}$

9. $7\frac{11}{12} + 3\frac{1}{2}$

Choose the closest estimate.

10. $1\frac{3}{8} + 2\frac{1}{4}$ **a.** $3\frac{1}{2}$ **b.** 3   **c.** $4\frac{1}{4}$

11. $3\frac{7}{8} - 2\frac{1}{12}$ **a.** 2   **b.** $1\frac{1}{2}$ **c.** $\frac{7}{874}$

12. $5\frac{5}{6} - 2\frac{4}{5}$ **a.** 4   **b.** $3\frac{1}{2}$ **c.** 3

13. $\frac{3}{8} + 9\frac{7}{9}$ **a.** 8   **b.** 10   **c.** $10\frac{3}{8}$

Add or subtract. Write the answer in simplest form.

14. $\frac{15}{16} - \frac{3}{16}$

15. $\frac{2}{12} + \frac{8}{12}$

16. $\frac{1}{18} + \frac{5}{18}$

17. $\frac{2}{5} + \frac{11}{5} - \frac{3}{5}$

18. $\frac{7}{8} - \frac{3}{4}$

19. $\frac{3}{4} + \frac{5}{8} + \frac{7}{12}$

20. $4\frac{5}{6} + 2\frac{1}{3}$

21. $7\frac{1}{6} - 5\frac{3}{4}$

22. $9\frac{8}{9} - 6\frac{5}{9}$

23. $4\frac{1}{6} - 2\frac{2}{3}$

24. $3\frac{1}{2} + 1\frac{4}{5}$

25. $5 - 2\frac{4}{7}$

26. $6\frac{3}{4} + 3\frac{3}{4}$

27. $8\frac{3}{8} - 3\frac{5}{8}$

28. $2\frac{1}{3} + 2\frac{2}{5}$

29. $\frac{9}{10} - \frac{1}{4}$

Critical Thinking

30. If two denominators have 1 as their GCF, their least common denominator will always equal:

   a. the product of their denominators.

   b. the sum of their numerators.

   c. a prime number.

        a

31. Which estimation method would give a more reasonable estimate for these number sentences? Why?

   a. $6\frac{2}{5} - 5\frac{7}{9}$

   b. $7\frac{14}{17} + 2\frac{5}{9}$

   a. Front-end; rounding gives 0

   b. Rounding; both fractions $> \frac{1}{2}$

Mixed Applications

32. Patricia gathered $3\frac{1}{2}$ lb of carrots out of one garden. Her other two gardens produced $2\frac{3}{8}$ lb and $4\frac{3}{4}$ lb of carrots. Did Patricia grow at least 10 lb of carrots in all three of her gardens? **Yes**

33. The area of the earth's surface is 139,660,400 mi². About 40,000,000 mi² is land. About how many square miles of water are there? Answer: about 1,000,000,000 mi². Is the answer reasonable? If not, find the correct answer.

No; about 100,000,000 mi²

PERFORMANCE ASSESSMENT

Work with your group to solve this problem.

Draw a map of your neighborhood. Locate the school and the home of each student in your group on the map. Estimate and label the distance from each student's home to the school, to the nearest fraction of a mile. Determine the distance between the student who lives the farthest from the school and the student who lives the nearest, using your estimated distances.

1. **_Think about:_**
   - how to present and label the map
   - what method to use to find the distance between the students' homes

2. Write a paragraph explaining how you determined the distance between the students' homes and why you chose that method.

CUMULATIVE REVIEW

Choose the letter of the correct answer.

1. $20,475 \div 315$

   a. 64 R305   **c.** 650
   b. 65   **d.** not given

2. What time is it 7 hours 15 minutes after 7:15 P.M.?

   a. 2:30 A.M.
   b. 2:15 A.M.
   c. 12 A.M.
   d. not given

3. $0.07\overline{)0.224}$

   a. 32   **c.** 320
   b. 0.32   **d.** not given

4. Simplify:
   $5 \times 6 - 18 \div (6 - 3) + 3$

   a. 11   **c.** 27
   b. 7   **d.** not given

5. Find the mean:
   14, 17, 17, 15, 12

   a. 5   **c.** 15
   b. 17   **d.** not given

6. Which is the LCM of 9 and 12?

   a. 0   **c.** 36
   b. 3   **d.** not given

7. Which is a prime number?

   a. 101   **c.** 68
   b. 9   **d.** not given

8. Which is equivalent to $1\frac{5}{8}$?

   a. $\frac{14}{18}$ **c.** $\frac{26}{16}$
   b. $\frac{6}{8}$ **d.** not given

9. Choose the decimal form for $\frac{25}{4}$.

   a. 6.25   **c.** 25.4
   b. 4.25   **d.** not given

10. Choose the best estimate:
    $5\frac{4}{5} + 6\frac{5}{18}$

    a. 13   **c.** 12
    b. $12\frac{1}{2}$ **d.** 11

11. Choose the best estimate:
    $1\frac{4}{7} - \frac{4}{5}$

    a. 1   **c.** $\frac{1}{5}$
    b. $1\frac{1}{2}$ **d.** 0

12. $1\frac{3}{4} + 3\frac{1}{2} + 5\frac{3}{8}$

    a. $10\frac{1}{2}$ **c.** $9\frac{5}{8}$
    b. 10.58   **d.** not given

13. $11\frac{1}{2} - 4\frac{4}{5}$

    a. 6.5   **c.** $6\frac{7}{10}$
    b. $7\frac{7}{10}$ **d.** not given

14. Use number sense. If Ben rides 18 miles in $2\frac{1}{4}$ hours, about how many hours would it take him to ride 24 miles?

    a. 2 hours   **c.** 6 hours
    b. 3 hours   **d.** not given

ENRICHMENT FOR ALL

FRACTIONS IN THE EGYPTIAN SYSTEM

The ancient Egyptians used picture symbols to write whole numbers and fractions. They had special basic symbols for certain whole numbers.

Egyptian Symbol	❘	∧	᎒	⃝	⌐
Value	1	10	100	1,000	10,000

To write other whole numbers the Egyptians combined groups of the basic symbols.

Here is how they would have written the number 236:

୨୨∧∧∧⫼⫼

1. How would the Egyptians write 2,306?

To represent fractional numbers the Egyptians almost always used *unit fractions*. These are fractions with a numerator of 1.

Egyptian Symbol	◯ ❘❘	◯ ∧	◯ ∧❘❘	◯ ୨	◯ ᎒
Unit Fraction	$\frac{1}{2}$	$\frac{1}{10}$	$\frac{1}{12}$	$\frac{1}{100}$	$\frac{1}{1,000}$

Write the unit fraction using Egyptian symbols.

2. $\frac{1}{3}$ **3.** $\frac{1}{5}$ **4.** $\frac{1}{13}$ **5.** $\frac{1}{20}$ **6.** $\frac{1}{220}$

The Egyptians wrote some fractions as the sum of two or more unit fractions.

$\frac{3}{8} = \frac{1}{8} + \frac{2}{8} = \frac{1}{8} + \frac{1}{4} \rightarrow$ ◯⫼⫼ + ◯⫼⫼⫼

Rewrite the fraction as the sum of unit fractions in our notation. Then use your results to write the Egyptian symbol.

7. $\frac{5}{8}$ **8.** $\frac{3}{4}$ **9.** $\frac{7}{12}$ **10.** $\frac{4}{9}$

You may need to use more than two unit fractions for Exercises 11–14.

11. $\frac{3}{7}$ **12.** $\frac{4}{5}$ **13.** $\frac{7}{8}$ **14.** $\frac{9}{10}$

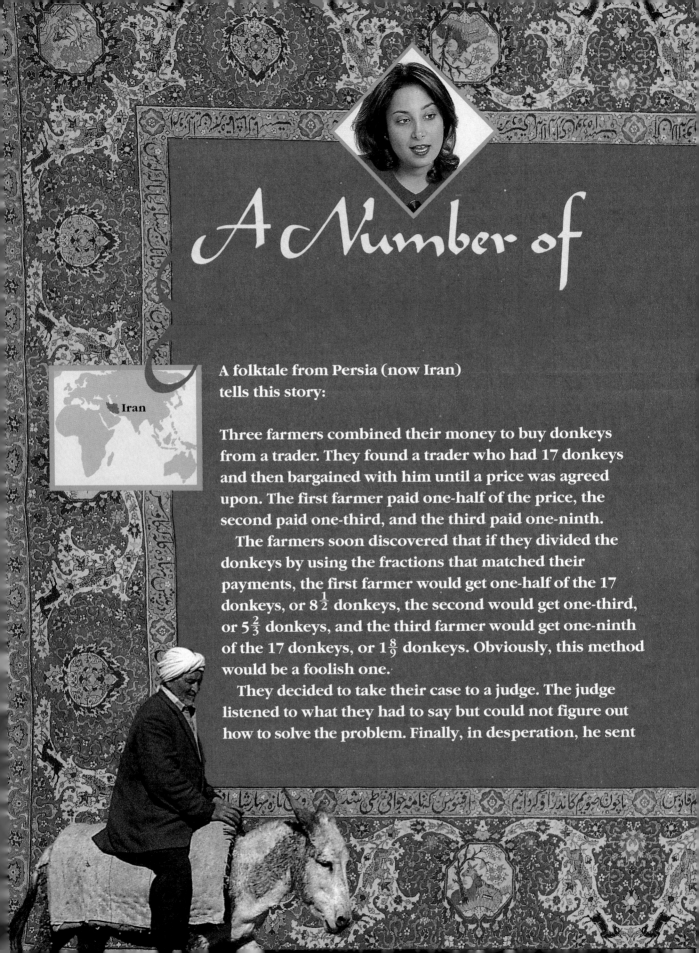

A Number of

A folktale from Persia (now Iran) tells this story:

Three farmers combined their money to buy donkeys from a trader. They found a trader who had 17 donkeys and then bargained with him until a price was agreed upon. The first farmer paid one-half of the price, the second paid one-third, and the third paid one-ninth.

The farmers soon discovered that if they divided the donkeys by using the fractions that matched their payments, the first farmer would get one-half of the 17 donkeys, or $8\frac{1}{2}$ donkeys, the second would get one-third, or $5\frac{2}{3}$ donkeys, and the third farmer would get one-ninth of the 17 donkeys, or $1\frac{8}{9}$ donkeys. Obviously, this method would be a foolish one.

They decided to take their case to a judge. The judge listened to what they had to say but could not figure out how to solve the problem. Finally, in desperation, he sent

Iran

MULTIPLYING AND DIVIDING FRACTIONS AND MIXED NUMBERS

MATH CONNECTIONS: Measurement • Area

for a wise man named Molla Nasreddin. Molla Nasreddin listened to the problem. After thinking for a while, he went and got his own donkey and added it to the 17 others. Then he told each of the three men to take their share.

1 According to Molla Nasreddin's solution, how many donkeys should the farmer who paid one-half the money get? How many donkeys should the second farmer get? How many would the third farmer get? What also needs to happen?

2 Molla Nasreddin found a solution because he saw a mistake in the amount the three men paid the trader. Can you figure out what the mistake was? Who lost out on this deal?

Multiplying Fractions

A. A flower bed was planted with irises. Three-fourths of the flowers in the bed were purple. One-sixth of these purple irises were mixed with yellow irises. What part of the flower bed had a combination of purple and yellow irises?

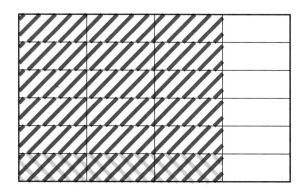

You need to find $\frac{1}{6}$ of $\frac{3}{4}$.

Multiply: $\frac{1}{6} \times \frac{3}{4}$

Step 1	Step 2	Step 3
Multiply the numerators.	**Multiply the denominators.**	**Write the answer in simplest form.**
$\frac{1}{6} \times \frac{3}{4} = \frac{3}{}$	$\frac{1}{6} \times \frac{3}{4} = \frac{3}{24}$	$\frac{3}{24} = \frac{3 \div 3}{24 \div 3} = \frac{1}{8}$

So $\frac{1}{8}$ of the flower bed had a combination of purple and yellow irises.

B. You can also multiply whole numbers by fractions.

Multiply: $\frac{2}{3} \times 18$

Step 1	Step 2	Step 3
Rename the whole number as an improper fraction.	**Multiply the numerators. Multiply the denominators.**	**Write the answer in simplest form.**
$\frac{2}{3} \times 18 = \frac{2}{3} \times \frac{18}{1}$	$\frac{2}{3} \times \frac{18}{1} = \frac{36}{3}$	$\frac{36}{3} = \frac{36 \div 3}{3 \div 3} = \frac{12}{1} = 12$

So $\frac{2}{3} \times 18 = 12$.

C. Two fractions that have a product of 1 are called **reciprocals.**

Look at these examples:

$\frac{1}{8} \times \frac{8}{1} = 1$ $\qquad$ $\frac{6}{1} \times \frac{1}{6} = 1$ $\qquad$ $\frac{5}{6} \times \frac{6}{5} = 1$

1. How would you find the reciprocal of $\frac{1}{10}$?

TRY OUT

Multiply. Write the answer in simplest form.

2. $\frac{2}{3} \times \frac{6}{7}$ **3.** $16 \times \frac{3}{4}$ **4.** $\frac{1}{10} \times 5$ **5.** $\frac{5}{9} \times 1$ **6.** $\frac{2}{3} \times \frac{3}{4}$

Find the reciprocal.

7. $\frac{1}{5}$ **8.** $\frac{1}{3}$ **9.** $\frac{1}{7}$ **10.** 9   **11.** $\frac{10}{11}$ **12.** $\frac{7}{12}$

PRACTICE

Multiply. Write the answer in simplest form.

13. $\frac{1}{4} \times \frac{2}{3}$ **14.** $\frac{2}{5} \times \frac{1}{2}$ **15.** $\frac{1}{3} \times \frac{3}{4}$ **16.** $\frac{2}{3} \times \frac{3}{5}$ **17.** $\frac{2}{5} \times \frac{1}{3}$

18. $\frac{1}{8} \times \frac{1}{2}$ **19.** $\frac{3}{8} \times \frac{3}{4}$ **20.** $\frac{4}{5} \times \frac{3}{4}$ **21.** $\frac{2}{5} \times \frac{2}{3}$ **22.** $\frac{3}{10} \times \frac{5}{6}$

23. $\frac{7}{8} \times \frac{1}{2}$ **24.** $\frac{7}{10} \times \frac{3}{7}$ **25.** $\frac{2}{3} \times 21$ **26.** $\frac{2}{5} \times 20$ **27.** $\frac{1}{8} \times 16$

28. $\frac{5}{6} \times 18$ **29.** $\frac{2}{5} \times 25$ **30.** $\frac{1}{5} \times 15$ **31.** $\frac{3}{4} \times 24$ **32.** $\frac{2}{3} \times 21$

33. $\frac{1}{10} \times \frac{1}{2} \times \frac{1}{3}$ **34.** $\frac{1}{4} \times \frac{1}{5} \times \frac{2}{9}$ **35.** $\frac{2}{3} \times \frac{3}{5} \times 12$ **36.** $\frac{3}{4} \times 8 \times \frac{1}{2}$

Find the reciprocal.

37. $\frac{1}{20}$ **38.** 18   **39.** 1   **40.** $\frac{1}{18}$ **41.** 12   **42.** $\frac{1}{25}$

43. $\frac{2}{3}$ **44.** $\frac{4}{5}$ **45.** 16   **46.** $\frac{2}{9}$ **47.** $\frac{13}{15}$ **48.** 119

Critical Thinking

Is the statement *true, sometimes true,* or *never true*?
Give examples to support your answer.

49. The product of a proper fraction and a whole number is greater than 1.

50. The product of two proper fractions is greater than 1.

Mixed Applications

51. Nathan buys $2\frac{1}{3}$ dozen white rosebushes and $3\frac{2}{3}$ dozen red rosebushes. Each bush costs $12.00. What is the total cost?

52. Katie is going to plant $2\frac{1}{2}$ dozen maple trees and $5\frac{1}{4}$ dozen elm trees. How many dozen trees will Katie plant?

53. Of a $\frac{3}{4}$-mi strip of Main Street, $\frac{1}{2}$ is paved with stones. What fraction of a mile is this?

54. *Write a problem* that involves multiplying two fractions. Ask others to solve it.

Multiplying Fractions: Using a Shortcut

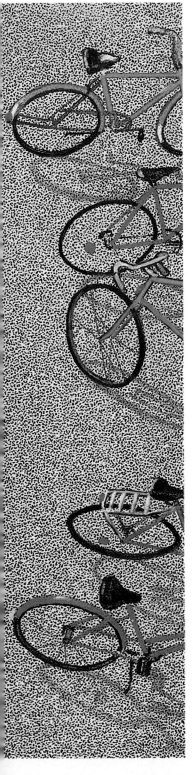

A. Nan and Peter took a safety survey near their school. They found that $\frac{4}{5}$ of the bicycle riders had night reflectors on their bikes. Of these riders $\frac{1}{6}$ wore safety helmets. What fraction of the riders used both reflectors and helmets?

Multiply: $\frac{1}{6} \times \frac{4}{5}$

You learned in the previous lesson how to multiply fractions and then write the answer in simplest form.

$$\frac{1}{6} \times \frac{4}{5} = \frac{\overset{2}{\cancel{4}}}{\underset{15}{\cancel{30}}} = \frac{2}{15}$$

You can also use a shortcut method. Divide a numerator and a denominator by a common factor. Then multiply.

$$\frac{1}{\underset{3}{\cancel{6}}} \times \frac{\overset{2}{\cancel{4}}}{5} = \frac{2}{15}$$

So $\frac{2}{15}$ of the riders used both reflectors and safety helmets.

1. Tell how to use the shortcut method to find the products. Then find the products.

   a. $\frac{1}{3} \times \frac{9}{10}$ **b.** $\frac{5}{8} \times \frac{1}{5}$ **c.** $\frac{1}{4} \times 12$ **d.** $\frac{3}{10} \times \frac{5}{6}$

2. Can the shortcut method always be used? Why or why not?

B. You can often estimate the product of a fraction and a whole number by using compatible numbers.

Estimate: $\frac{1}{3} \times 16$ Estimate: $\frac{3}{5} \times 24$

Think: $\frac{1}{3} \times 15 = 5$ *Think:* $\frac{1}{5} \times 25 = 5$

So $\frac{1}{3} \times 16$ is about 5. $\frac{3}{5} \times 25 = 15$

                                  So $\frac{3}{5} \times 24$ is about 15.

3. How do the estimates compare to the exact answers for the examples above? Why? Find the exact answers and compare.

TRY OUT

Multiply. Use the shortcut if you can.

4. $\frac{1}{2} \times \frac{4}{5}$ **5.** $\frac{2}{9} \times \frac{3}{8}$

6. $\frac{5}{6} \times 12$ **7.** $\frac{1}{8} \times \frac{4}{7}$

Estimate the product.

8. $\frac{1}{3} \times 20$ **9.** $\frac{3}{5} \times 16$

10. $\frac{3}{4} \times 11$ **11.** $\frac{7}{10} \times 22$

PRACTICE

Multiply. Write the answer in simplest form.
Use the shortcut if you can.

12. $\frac{1}{2} \times \frac{8}{9}$ **13.** $\frac{2}{5} \times \frac{1}{2}$ **14.** $\frac{3}{7} \times \frac{1}{9}$ **15.** $\frac{5}{6} \times \frac{7}{10}$ **16.** $\frac{4}{7} \times \frac{21}{28}$

17. $\frac{3}{5} \times \frac{5}{6}$ **18.** $\frac{4}{5} \times \frac{5}{8}$ **19.** $\frac{7}{12} \times 14$ **20.** $25 \times \frac{7}{10}$ **21.** $\frac{2}{3} \times 27$

22. $\frac{2}{5} \times \frac{5}{12}$ **23.** $\frac{3}{4} \times \frac{2}{3}$ **24.** $\frac{3}{8} \times \frac{1}{2}$ **25.** $\frac{3}{10} \times \frac{5}{9}$ **26.** $\frac{4}{11} \times \frac{5}{8}$

27. $\frac{2}{3} \times \frac{3}{8} \times \frac{1}{2}$ **28.** $\frac{4}{5} \times 45 \times \frac{1}{12}$ **29.** $\frac{3}{5} \times \frac{5}{6} \times 120$ **30.** $\frac{1}{4} \times \frac{3}{10} \times 8$

31. three-fourths of two-fifths   **32.** one-third of three-eighths

Estimate the product.

33. $\frac{1}{10} \times 29$ **34.** $\frac{1}{4} \times 13$ **35.** $\frac{1}{9} \times 28$ **36.** $\frac{1}{5} \times 44$ **37.** $\frac{1}{6} \times 38$

38. $\frac{4}{5} \times 36$ **39.** $\frac{2}{3} \times 23$ **40.** $\frac{4}{9} \times 19$ **41.** $\frac{3}{4} \times 45$ **42.** $\frac{5}{8} \times 30$

Critical Thinking

43. Ken multiplied $\frac{3}{4} \times \frac{5}{8}$ as follows: $\frac{3}{\cancel{4}} \times \frac{5}{\cancel{8}} = \frac{15}{2} = 7\frac{1}{2}$. How could

Ken have seen that an answer of $7\frac{1}{2}$ could not be correct?
What error did he make?

Mixed Applications

44. On Tuesday 48 people came into the Bike Shop. Of those people $\frac{3}{8}$ did not buy anything. How many people did make a purchase?

45. Fourteen students bought night reflectors at the Bike Shop. Each reflector cost $8.10. In all, how much did they spend?

46. Al's goal was to cycle 100 mi in 3 days. He rode $27\frac{3}{10}$ mi on Mon., $38\frac{1}{10}$ mi on Tues., and $39\frac{1}{2}$ mi on Wed. By how many miles was he under or over his goal?

47. Four-fifths of the students in a cycling club have reflectors. Two-fifths have helmets. What is the greatest possible fraction that have neither?

ACTIVITY

Multiplying Mixed Numbers

Each can of dog food contains $1\frac{1}{2}$ lb of food. Melissa feeds her dog one-fourth of a can at each meal. What fraction of a pound of food does a serving contain?

WORKING TOGETHER

Solve the problem using a model of your own.

1. How does your model show $1\frac{1}{2}$ lb of dog food?

2. How does your model show that the dog gets $\frac{1}{4}$ of the can?

3. What fraction of a pound of food does the dog receive?

Here is a way to solve the problem using paper and felt-tip pens.

Step 1 Fold a rectangular piece of paper in half vertically. Open it up and then draw a line along the fold. Let each section represent 1 lb of food.

Step 2 Fold the paper vertically into four equal sections. Color three of the sections yellow.

4. How many equal sections do you have? What fraction of 1 lb does each section represent? How many pounds do the three yellow sections represent?

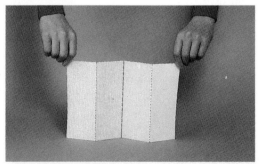

Step 3 Fold the paper in fourths horizontally. Color one of these horizontal sections red. The red and yellow parts will appear orange.

5. How many orange sections are there? What fraction of 1 lb does each orange section represent? How much of 1 lb do all the orange sections represent?

6. How does your model compare with this paper-folding model?

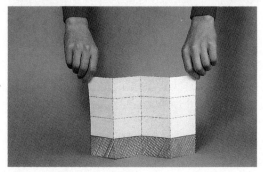

SHARING IDEAS

7. Did you use the same type of model to solve each problem? If not, why did you use different models?

8. Compare your models and results to those of others. How are they different? How are they the same?

ON YOUR OWN

Solve using a model.

9. One day Melissa spent $2\frac{1}{4}$ hours building a scratching post for her cats. She spent $\frac{2}{3}$ of the time cutting carpet pieces. How much time did she spend cutting the carpet pieces?

10. The vet gave Melissa a $2\frac{3}{4}$-oz bottle of medicine to use when her cats were sick. Each cat got $\frac{1}{3}$ of the medicine. How many ounces of the medicine did each cat get?

11. *Write a problem* that involves multiplying a mixed number and a fraction. Solve your problem. Then ask others to model and solve it.

ACTIVITY: Multiplying Fractions and Mixed Numbers

Norma's Advertising Services bought envelopes. Each box had a double set of envelopes, separated by a piece of cardboard. Bob used $4\frac{1}{2}$ boxes of envelopes for mailing ads. Of the ads mailed, $\frac{2}{3}$ were sent to new customers. How many boxes were used for the mailing to new customers?

WORKING TOGETHER

You need to find $\frac{2}{3}$ of $4\frac{1}{2}$, or $\frac{2}{3} \times 4\frac{1}{2}$.
You can use a diagram to help you solve the problem.

Study these diagrams.

1 box   **A** $\frac{1}{2}$ box   **B**

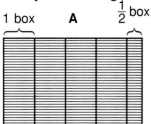
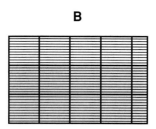

1. What mixed number tells how many boxes of envelopes are in diagram A? What improper fraction tells how many *half* boxes are in $4\frac{1}{2}$ boxes?

2. What fraction of the boxes in diagram B are colored yellow?

3. Find the product of $\frac{2}{3} \times 4\frac{1}{2}$, or $\frac{2}{3} \times \frac{9}{2}$.

4. Record your information in a table like this. Complete the multiplication sentence. Write the product in simplest form.

Fraction	Mixed Number	Multiplication Sentence
$\frac{2}{3}$	$4\frac{1}{2}$	$\frac{2}{3} \times \frac{9}{2} = \blacksquare$

5. How many boxes did Bob use for new customers?

6. Use a multiplication sentence to find out how many boxes of envelopes were not used for the new customer mailing. Write the final answer in simplest form.

SHARING IDEAS

7. Make up some diagrams of your own to show multiplying a mixed number by a fraction. Write the multiplication sentences in the table.

8. Look carefully at the multiplication sentences in your table. Describe a method for multiplying a mixed number by a fraction without using a diagram.

9. How does your method compare with others' methods?

10. Use your method to give examples of multiplying a mixed number by a fraction. Check your answers by drawing diagrams.

PRACTICE

Use your method for multiplying mixed numbers to find the product. Draw a diagram to check your answers in Exercises 11–15.

11. $\frac{2}{3} \times 2\frac{1}{2}$ **12.** $\frac{3}{4} \times 3\frac{1}{3}$ **13.** $\frac{1}{4} \times 1\frac{1}{3}$ **14.** $\frac{1}{5} \times 4\frac{1}{2}$ **15.** $\frac{4}{5} \times 1\frac{2}{3}$

16. $2\frac{1}{2} \times \frac{1}{2}$ **17.** $2\frac{5}{8} \times \frac{3}{7}$ **18.** $2\frac{1}{10} \times \frac{5}{7}$ **19.** $\frac{1}{2} \times 3\frac{1}{4}$ **20.** $6\frac{1}{2} \times \frac{1}{2}$

21. $\frac{3}{4} \times 2\frac{2}{3}$ **22.** $1\frac{7}{8} \times \frac{4}{5}$ **23.** $\frac{3}{7} \times 1\frac{5}{9}$ **24.** $\frac{5}{6} \times 1\frac{4}{5}$ **25.** $\frac{7}{8} \times 4\frac{4}{5}$

Mixed Applications

Solve. Which method did you use?

ESTIMATION
MENTAL MATH
CALCULATOR
PAPER/PENCIL

26. A soap company bought $6\frac{1}{2}$ minutes of advertising time on radio station WZYI. The company used $\frac{2}{3}$ of the time during morning news shows. How many minutes of time was this?

27. Luke worked $2\frac{3}{4}$ hours putting up two billboard signs. He spent $\frac{2}{5}$ of the time on a billboard sign for a restaurant. How much time did he spend on the other billboard?

28. Norma's Advertising Services charged $.25 postage for each one-page advertisement mailed in an envelope. The envelope and stuffing cost $.03. How much did Norma charge for the stuffing and mailing of 500 one-page advertisements?

29. One day Norma received a rush order for 840 ads to be placed in envelopes and mailed out in 3.5 hours. How many envelopes must her staff finish each hour to meet the deadline?

Multiplying Mixed Numbers

A. Susan picks berries every morning during the summer. Yesterday she picked for $2\frac{3}{4}$ hours. She spent $\frac{3}{5}$ of that time gathering strawberries. How many hours did Susan spend picking strawberries?

You have used models, diagrams, and multiplication sentences to develop a method for multiplying fractions.

Here is another method.

Step 1	Step 2	Step 3
Rename the mixed number as an improper fraction.	**Multiply the fractions.**	**Write the answer in simplest form.**
$\frac{3}{5} \times 2\frac{3}{4} = \frac{3}{5} \times \frac{11}{4}$	$\frac{3}{5} \times \frac{11}{4} = \frac{33}{20}$	$\frac{33}{20} = 1\frac{13}{20}$

Susan picked strawberries for $1\frac{13}{20}$ hours.

B. You can use the same method to multiply two mixed numbers.

Multiply: $3\frac{3}{4} \times 2\frac{2}{3}$

Step 1	Step 2	Step 3
Rename the mixed numbers as improper fractions.	**Multiply the fractions.**	**Write the answer in simplest form.**
$1\frac{1}{4} \times 2\frac{2}{3} = \frac{5}{4} \times \frac{8}{3}$	$\frac{5}{\underset{1}{4}} \times \frac{\overset{2}{8}}{3} = \frac{10}{3}$	$\frac{10}{3} = 3\frac{1}{3}$
	Think: $4 \div 4 = 1$ $ 8 \div 4 = 2$	

So $1\frac{1}{4} \times 2\frac{2}{3} = 3\frac{1}{3}$.

1. Is $3\frac{1}{3}$ a reasonable answer? Why?

2. How would you use this method to find $6 \times 8\frac{3}{4}$?

TRY OUT Multiply. Write the answer in simplest form.

3. $\frac{3}{4} \times 1\frac{1}{4}$ 　　　 **4.** $1\frac{1}{5} \times \frac{5}{6}$ 　　　 **5.** $1\frac{1}{3} \times 2\frac{1}{3}$ 　　　 **6.** $4 \times 1\frac{1}{10}$

PRACTICE

Estimate, then multiply to find the exact answer in simplest form.

7. $\frac{3}{4} \times 5\frac{1}{3}$ 　　 **8.** $\frac{2}{3} \times 2\frac{1}{2}$ 　　 **9.** $5\frac{1}{3} \times \frac{1}{2}$ 　　 **10.** $1\frac{3}{7} \times \frac{7}{10}$

11. $6\frac{1}{8} \times 1\frac{1}{7}$ 　　 **12.** $8\frac{1}{6} \times 1\frac{5}{7}$ 　　 **13.** $2\frac{8}{9} \times 1\frac{1}{2}$ 　　 **14.** $2\frac{1}{3} \times 1\frac{1}{8}$

15. $1\frac{2}{3} \times 3$ 　　 **16.** $1\frac{1}{5} \times 1\frac{7}{8}$ 　　 **17.** $2\frac{2}{3} \times 2\frac{2}{5}$ 　　 **18.** $6 \times 4\frac{2}{3}$

19. $3 \times 1\frac{1}{9}$ 　　 **20.** $3\frac{3}{5} \times 2\frac{1}{9}$ 　　 **21.** $7\frac{1}{2} \times 1\frac{1}{5}$ 　　 **22.** $7\frac{1}{5} \times 1\frac{1}{2}$

23. $1\frac{1}{8} \times 2\frac{4}{5}$ 　　 **24.** $5\frac{1}{10} \times 3\frac{3}{10}$ 　　 **25.** $2 \times 1\frac{5}{8}$ 　　 **26.** $3\frac{2}{7} \times 5\frac{1}{4}$

Mixed Applications

Solve. You may need to use the Databank on page 552.

27. Susan picked berries for 4 hours. She picked $3\frac{1}{4}$ long rows each hour. How many rows of berries did she pick?

28. A carton of blackberries sells for $3.85 in the grocery store. Ed picked his own berries and figured he saved $103.95. How many cartons of blackberries did Ed pick?

29. A gardener planted a hedge of Japanese burberry bushes using the recommended distances between bushes. The hedge is 12 bushes long and 4 bushes wide. What is the length and width of the hedge in feet?

30. What is the area of the hedge in Problem 29? What is the perimeter?

MENTAL MATH

You can use the distributive property to multiply mixed numbers mentally.

$10 \times 8\frac{1}{5} = 10 \times (8 + \frac{1}{5}) = (10 \times 8) + (10 \times \frac{1}{5}) = 80 + 2 = 82$

Multiply mentally.

1. $10 \times 4\frac{1}{2}$ 　　 **2.** $12 \times 5\frac{5}{6}$ 　　 **3.** $3\frac{2}{3} \times 15$ 　　 **4.** $7\frac{3}{4} \times 20$

EXTRA PRACTICE, page 343; **PRACTICE PLUS**, page 346

PROBLEM SOLVING

Strategy: Solving a Simpler Problem

The lighting arrangement in a room at the Art Museum has 10 rows of lights. There is 1 light in the first row, and there are 3 lights in the second row. Each row has 2 more lights than the row in front of it. How many lights are there in all 10 rows?

Dan plans to solve a simpler problem. He decides to find the number of lights in the first 2 rows and then the number in the first 3 rows. To understand his data better, Dan organizes his work in a table.

Then he tries his plan.

Number of Rows	Number of Lights
1	1
2	1 + 3 = 4
3	1 + 3 + 5 = 9
4	1 + 3 + 5 + 7 = ■

Dan finds that there are 4 lights in the first 2 rows and 9 lights in the first 3 rows.

He notices a pattern: $1 = 1^2$; $4 = 2^2$; $9 = 3^2$

1. How many lights are in the first 4 rows?

2. Are there 25, or 5^2, lights in the first 5 rows? How do you know?

3. What is the rule for finding the number of lights in this pattern? How many lights are there in the first 6 rows? Check by adding the number of lights in the first 6 rows.

4. Use the rule to find the number of lights in the first 10 rows. You may use a calculator to check your answer by adding.

5. **What if** there were 15 rows of lights following the above pattern? How many lights would there be?

PRACTICE

Use a simpler problem to help you solve the problem.

6. The border design on an antique bureau consists of 24 equilateral triangles arranged in 2 rows to form a parallelogram. The side of each triangle is 1 in. long. What is the perimeter of the design?

7. At the Museum Shop a 30-in. by 30-in. pegboard is used to display postcard-size pictures. The hooks are 2 in. apart and 1 in. from the edges of the pegboard. How many hooks are on the pegboard?

8. In the Appalachian Folk Art display, there is a quilt consisting of squares of the same size. The first section begins with the center square. Around this square is the second section of 8 squares. The third section has 16 squares. The entire quilt has 8 sections. How many squares is it made of?

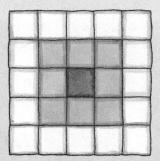

Strategies and Skills Review

Solve. Use estimation, mental math, a calculator, or paper and pencil.

9. The reading room at the museum is a 6-sided polygon in the shape of an *L*. Two carpets cover the entire floor. One carpet is 12 ft by 19 ft, and the other one is 12 ft by 12 ft. What is the perimeter of the room?

10. At the gemstone exhibit, stones are displayed on 24 platforms, with 36 stones on each platform. Are there at least 500 gemstones in the display? Did you underestimate or overestimate? Why?

11. A staircase at the museum has 20 steps. The staircase is made with blocks that look like the three-step staircase shown below. How many blocks are used in the staircase with 20 steps?

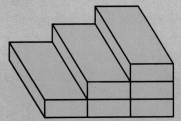

12. Jerome wants to walk from his home (*H*) to the museum (*M*). How many different direct routes can he take?

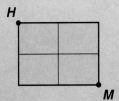

13. ***Write a problem*** that can be solved by first solving a simpler problem. Solve it. Then give it to another student to solve.

ASTOUNDING
Stunts

Measuring

A. Enormous numbers can lead to fascinating conclusions. Do not be afraid of large numbers. All you need to do is take your time and plan your calculations. Just look at some of the amazing conclusions you can draw based on math with massive numbers! Use a calculator to help you.

There are about 1 billion people in China. What if they all marched in a parade? If they lined up 4 to a row and marched past you at a rate of 25 rows per minute, how long would it take the parade to pass?

1. To solve this problem, first you need to find out how many rows there are. Divide 1 billion by 4. It's not hard, but make sure you have the right number of zeros in your answer.

2. Next you can divide your answer by 25 to find out how many minutes it would take for the parade to pass. You have an answer, but it is a very large number in minutes. Your answer will make more sense if you use a larger unit of time. How many minutes in an hour? Convert your answer to hours. How many hours in a day? Convert your answer to days. Now convert the days to years.

B. There are about 5 billion people on earth. What would happen if they all held hands? Suppose that each person takes about 2 yards of space in the hand-holding line. That means the line will be 10 billion yards long!

3. How long is that in miles?

4. The circumference of the earth is about 25,000 miles at the equator. About how many times will the line wrap around the earth?

C. One restaurant chain claims to have sold over 80 billion hamburgers.

5. If a burger is about 1 inch high, would a stack of all the hamburgers sold reach all the way to the moon? (The moon is about 240 million miles away.) About how far would it go?

D.

I'm over a billion seconds old!

I'm over a billion minutes old!

6. Do you believe Pam? Why or why not?

7. Do you believe Sam? Why or why not?

ACTIVITY Dividing Whole Numbers by Fractions

Betty was returning to camp from a backpacking trip. Because the trail was steep and her backpack was heavy, she could hike only $\frac{1}{2}$ mile each hour. Betty knew she was 3 miles from camp. How long did it take her to return to camp?

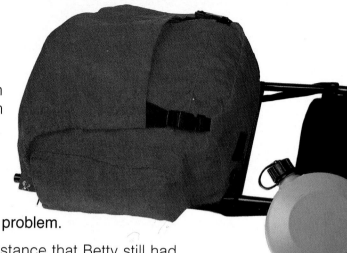

WORKING TOGETHER

Use a model of your own to solve this problem.

1. How does your model show the distance that Betty still had to travel?

2. How does your model show the distance Betty was able to hike each hour?

3. How many hours did it take her to reach the camp?

Here is one way to solve the problem using a model.

Step 1 Let a sheet of paper represent the number of miles to camp. Draw three squares on the paper as shown.

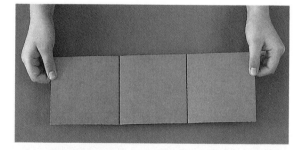

Step 2 Now fold the paper so that each square, or each mile, is divided in half.

4. How many halves are there in all three squares?

5. Since Betty hiked $\frac{1}{2}$ mile each hour, how long did it take her to get to camp? Does this answer agree with your answer to Problem 3?

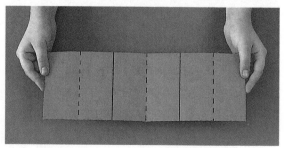

6. How does your model compare with this paper-folding model?

7. What division sentence does the paper-folding model show?

Solve using a model.

8. ***What if*** Betty had hiked only $\frac{1}{3}$ mi each hour? How long would it have taken her?

9. ***What if*** Betty had hiked $\frac{2}{3}$ mi each hour? What is $3 \div \frac{2}{3}$?

10. Cascade Trail is 10 mi long. Bruce plans to hike $\frac{5}{8}$ mi each hour. How long will it take him to hike the entire trail?

11. For night time listening on his camping trip, Victor had 9 hours worth of music. Each cassette had $\frac{3}{4}$ hour of music. How many cassettes did he carry?

SHARING IDEAS

12. Did you use the same type of model to solve each problem? If not, why did you use different models?

13. Compare your models and answers to those of others in the class. How are they different? How are they alike?

14. What division sentences do your models for Problems 10 and 11 illustrate?

ON YOUR OWN

15. ***Write a Problem*** that involves dividing a whole number by a fraction. Solve your problem with a model and write the division sentence.

Activity

Dividing Fractions: Common Denominators

Kadeem has $\frac{8}{9}$ qt of a special natural solution for spraying his tomato plants. The instructions say to use $\frac{1}{9}$ qt each time you spray. How many times can Kadeem spray the plants?

WORKING TOGETHER

You and a partner can use paper, scissors, and colored pencils to model and solve the problem.

Step 1 Fold a sheet of paper into nine equal parts and shade $\frac{8}{9}$ of the paper.

Step 2 Cut off as many $\frac{1}{9}$ sections of the shaded region as you can.

1. How many $\frac{1}{9}$ pieces equal the shaded region? How many times can Kadeem spray the plant? Write a division sentence to illustrate the problem.

2. ***What if*** $\frac{2}{9}$ qt of the solution is needed each time you spray. Model and solve the problem. Write a division sentence to represent your model.

Sometimes the quotient is not a whole number. Look at the following diagram which shows how you can model $\frac{7}{9} \div \frac{2}{9}$.

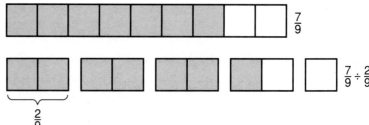

3. How many completely shaded $\frac{2}{9}$ sections were cut off from $\frac{7}{9}$? What part of a $\frac{2}{9}$ section does the partially shaded section represent?

4. Write a division sentence to represent the model.

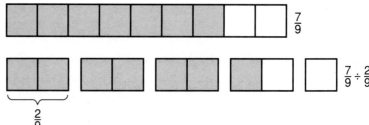

5. Use a model to find the quotient. Write a division sentence to represent each model.

a. $\frac{5}{8} \div \frac{1}{8}$ **b.** $\frac{9}{12} \div \frac{3}{12}$ **c.** $\frac{9}{10} \div \frac{7}{10}$ **d.** $\frac{4}{9} \div \frac{8}{9}$

SHARING IDEAS

Look at your division sentences in Problems 1–4.

6. What do you notice about the denominators? How do the numerators in each division sentence relate to the answer?

7. Use your answers to Problems 6 and 7 to tell how to find the quotient of two fractions that have a common denominator.

PRACTICE

Use your method of dividing fractions to find the quotient. Make a model if you need to.

8. $\frac{3}{5} \div \frac{1}{5}$ **9.** $\frac{2}{3} \div \frac{1}{3}$ **10.** $\frac{6}{8} \div \frac{3}{8}$ **11.** $\frac{8}{10} \div \frac{2}{10}$

12. $\frac{6}{7} \div \frac{2}{7}$ **13.** $\frac{10}{12} \div \frac{5}{12}$ **14.** $\frac{3}{4} \div \frac{2}{4}$ **15.** $\frac{5}{8} \div \frac{2}{8}$

16. $\frac{5}{8} \div \frac{3}{8}$ **17.** $\frac{7}{10} \div \frac{3}{10}$ **18.** $\frac{2}{5} \div \frac{4}{5}$ **19.** $\frac{6}{7} \div \frac{5}{7}$

20. $\frac{11}{12} \div \frac{8}{12}$ **21.** $\frac{12}{20} \div \frac{3}{20}$ **22.** $\frac{3}{20} \div \frac{12}{20}$ **23.** $\frac{8}{9} \div \frac{5}{9}$

Critical Thinking

24. When is the quotient of two fractions a whole number? a mixed number? a fraction less than one?

Mixed Applications

25. George wants to plant apple and pear trees on a $\frac{3}{4}$-acre lot. He will plant the pear trees on $\frac{1}{8}$ acre. How much of the land will be left to plant apple trees?

26. Senga's Tree Farm has a $\frac{6}{10}$-acre plot of land with no trees on it. Ms. Senga decides to divide it into lots of $\frac{3}{10}$ acre each. How many lots can she offer to sell?

27. *Write a problem* that involves dividing two fractions with the same denominator. Solve your problem. Ask others to solve it.

Dividing Fractions: Different Denominators

A. Darius and his sister Daphne each ordered an individual-size pizza for lunch. Darius ate $\frac{1}{2}$ of his pizza, and Daphne ate $\frac{1}{3}$ of hers. They took the rest home. How many times as much pizza did Darius eat as Daphne?

Divide: $\frac{1}{2} \div \frac{1}{3}$

Darius divided using **common denominators.**

$\frac{1}{2} \div \frac{1}{3} = \frac{3}{6} \div \frac{2}{6}$ ***Think:*** $\frac{1}{2} = \frac{1 \times 3}{2 \times 3} = \frac{3}{6}$ $\frac{1}{3} = \frac{1 \times 2}{3 \times 2} = \frac{2}{6}$

$\frac{3}{6} \div \frac{2}{6}$ ***Think:*** $3 \div 2 = \frac{3}{2} = 1\frac{1}{2}$

Darius ate $1\frac{1}{2}$ times as much pizza as Daphne.

B. Another way to divide fractions is to multiply by the reciprocal of the divisor.

Recall that multiplication and division are inverse operations.

Daphne divided using the reciprocal.

$\frac{1}{2} \div \frac{1}{3} = \frac{1}{2} \times 3$ ***Think:*** Dividing by $\frac{1}{3}$ is the same as multiplying by 3.

$\frac{1}{2} \times \frac{3}{1} = \frac{3}{2}$, or $1\frac{1}{2}$

So $\frac{1}{2} \div \frac{1}{3} = 1\frac{1}{2}$.

SHARING IDEAS

1. How did Daphne change the division sentence into a multiplication sentence?

2. How would you use this method to divide $\frac{3}{4} \div \frac{1}{7}$?

3. Use each method to find $\frac{5}{12} \div \frac{1}{10}$. Which method is easier for this problem? Why?

4. Use each method to find $\frac{8}{15} \div \frac{2}{15}$. Which method is easier for this problem? Why?

PRACTICE

Divide. Write the answer in simplest form.

5. $\frac{1}{2} \div \frac{1}{4}$ **6.** $\frac{2}{3} \div \frac{1}{6}$ **7.** $\frac{5}{6} \div \frac{1}{3}$ **8.** $\frac{4}{5} \div \frac{4}{5}$ **9.** $\frac{5}{8} \div \frac{3}{4}$

10. $\frac{1}{2} \div \frac{2}{3}$ **11.** $\frac{1}{3} \div \frac{3}{4}$ **12.** $\frac{1}{2} \div \frac{4}{5}$ **13.** $\frac{1}{8} \div \frac{4}{5}$ **14.** $\frac{3}{4} \div \frac{2}{3}$

15. $\frac{2}{3} \div \frac{1}{8}$ **16.** $\frac{1}{8} \div 3$ **17.** $\frac{5}{12} \div \frac{1}{4}$ **18.** $\frac{1}{3} \div 2$ **19.** $\frac{7}{12} \div \frac{1}{3}$

20. $\frac{4}{5} \div \frac{2}{3}$ **21.** $\frac{3}{4} \div \frac{1}{2}$ **22.** $\frac{3}{8} \div \frac{1}{7}$ **23.** $\frac{3}{4} \div \frac{4}{5}$ **24.** $\frac{1}{3} \div \frac{1}{2}$

25. $\frac{2}{5} \div \frac{3}{10}$ **26.** $8 \div \frac{2}{3}$ **27.** $\frac{1}{2} \div \frac{3}{8}$ **28.** $2 \div \frac{3}{16}$ **29.** $\frac{2}{9} \div \frac{1}{3}$

Critical Thinking

30. *What if* you divide a fraction by a fraction and get a quotient that is greater than 1? What does this tell you about the sizes of the fractions that you divided?

Mixed Applications

31. A large pizza costs $10.00. The pizza is cut into 8 equal pieces and costs $1.50 a slice. How much more is the profit on a large pizza sold by the slice instead of whole?

32. The Pizza Den has 8 tables for 4 people, 6 tables for 2 people, and 10 seats at the counter. How many customers did the Den have last night when it was half full?

33. The cook at Ned's Pizza has $\frac{4}{5}$ lb of mushrooms. He puts $\frac{1}{10}$ lb of mushrooms on each mushroom pizza. How many of these pizzas is the cook able to make with the mushrooms he has?

34. A medium pizza costs $8.50. Extra sausage costs $.75, extra olives cost $.85, and extra green peppers cost $.50. Linda and her friend order a medium pizza with all the extras. How much does their pizza cost?

Mixed Review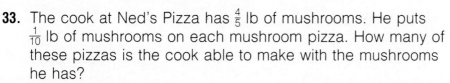

Find the answer. Which method did you use?

35. $1\frac{1}{8} - \frac{7}{16}$ **36.** $\frac{5}{12} + \frac{11}{12}$ **37.** $1\frac{2}{3} + 1\frac{3}{4}$ **38.** $\frac{8}{9} \times 1\frac{1}{8}$

MENTAL MATH
CALCULATOR
PAPER/PENCIL

39. $738 + 987$ **40.** 15×382 **41.** $40,000 \div 80$ **42.** $11.2 - 0.19$

PROBLEM SOLVING

Strategy: Working Backward

Alan has some baseball cards. Bob has twice as many cards as Alan. Cory has 12 cards fewer than Bob. Cory gives $\frac{1}{4}$ of his cards to David, who had none. David now has 13 cards. How many baseball cards does Alan have?

In this problem the final outcome is given, and you are asked to find the beginning number. Plan to solve this kind of problem by working backward.

- Find the original number of cards that Cory had. David has 13 cards. Since David has $\frac{1}{4}$ the number of cards that Cory had, multiply by 4.

$$4 \times 13 = 52$$

- Find the number of cards that Bob has. Since Cory had 12 fewer cards than Bob has, add 12.

$$52 + 12 = 64$$

- Find the number of cards that Alan has. Since Bob has twice as many cards as Alan has, divide by 2.

$$64 \div 2 = 32$$

Alan has 32 baseball cards.

You can check your answer by working forward from Alan to David. If Alan has 32 cards, then Bob has 32 × 2, or 64, cards. If Bob has 64 cards, then Cory had 64 − 12, or 52, cards. If Cory had 52 cards, then David has 52 ÷ 4, or 13, cards.

1. **What if** Cory gave $\frac{1}{6}$ of his cards, instead of $\frac{1}{4}$ of his cards, to David? How many baseball cards would Alan have?

PRACTICE

Work backward to solve the problem.

2. Barbara is treasurer of the Baseball Club. On Monday she withdrew $108.53 from the club's savings account. On Wednesday she deposited $86.43. There is now $193.61 in the account. How much was in the club account before Barbara withdrew the money?

3. In a survey the number of people who liked the Mets best was $\frac{1}{2}$ of the number who liked the Red Sox best. The number who liked the Red Sox best was $\frac{1}{4}$ the number who liked the Indians best. If 32 people liked the Indians best, how many liked the Mets best?

4. During one season Harry played in twice as many games as Max. Max played in 6 more games than Rich. Rich played in $\frac{1}{3}$ as many games as Sam. Sam played in 12 games. How many games did Harry play in?

5. David sold $\frac{1}{4}$ as many tickets to the Baseball Card Show as Cheryl. Cheryl sold 3 times as many as Stu. Stu sold 4 less than Ora. If Ora sold 12 tickets, how many did David sell?

Strategies and Skills Review

Solve. Use estimation, mental math, a calculator, or paper and pencil.

6. Which is a reasonable price for a baseball glove?
   a. $1.15   **b.** $15   **c.** $150

7. Andy buys a baseball cap for $3.95, baseball shoes for $26.95, a bat for $19.95, and a baseball for $2.98. Is $50 enough to buy these items? Why or why not?

8. Joan buys a box of baseball cards and a card holder for $44.96. The baseball cards cost $8 more than the holder. How much does the holder cost?

9. In his career Hank Aaron hit 41 more home runs than Babe Ruth did. How many home runs did Babe Ruth hit? What is missing in order for you to solve the problem?

10. Kim earned $143.78 working at a sporting goods store. She spends $33.41 to fix her bike and $25.91 on baseball cards. How much does she have left?

11. *Write a problem* that can be solved by working backward. Solve your problem. Then ask others to solve it.

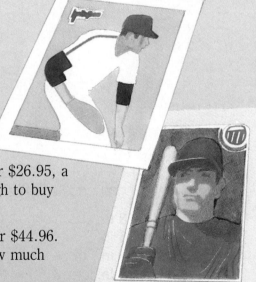

EXTRA PRACTICE, page 344

Converting Customary Measures

A. This table shows the relationship among customary units of measure.

Length	Weight
1 foot (ft) = 12 inches (in.)	**1 pound (lb) = 16 ounces (oz)**
1 yard (yd) = 3 ft	**1 ton (T) = 2,000 pounds**
1 mile (mi) = 5,280 ft or 1,760 yd	

Capacity	
1 cup (c) = 8 fluid ounces (fl oz)	**1 quart = 4 cups**
1 pint (pt) = 2 cups	**1 gallon (gal) = 4 quarts**
1 quart (qt) = 2 pints	

To rename measures with larger units as measures with smaller units, multiply.

2 ft = ■ in.   *Think:* 1 ft = 12 in.
2 ft = (2 × 12) in.
2 ft = 24 in.

To rename measures with smaller units as measures with larger units, divide.

48 fl oz = ■ c   *Think:* 8 fl oz = 1 c
48 fl oz = (48 ÷ 8) c
48 fl oz = 6 c

1. Which operation would you use to find the answer to:
   4 yd = ■ ft? Why?

2. How many tons are in 100,000 pounds?
   How do you know?

B. You can add, subtract, or multiply customary measures.

```
   6 ft   8 in.          8 lb   2 oz          4 qt 1 pt
 + 4 ft   6 in.        − 4 lb   6 oz        ×       5
  10 ft  14 in., or     3 lb  12 oz         20 qt 5 pt, or
  11 ft   2 in.                             22 qt 1 pt
```

Think: 10 ft 14 in. =
10 ft + 1 ft 2 in. =
11 ft 2 in.

Think: 8 lb 2 oz =
7 lb 16 oz + 2 oz =
7 lb 18 oz

Think: 20 qt 5 pt =
20 qt + 2 qt + 1 pt =
22 qt 1 pt

TRY OUT   Complete.

3. $3\frac{1}{2}$ mi = ■ yd

4. 27 qt = ■ gal

5. ```
      10 yd
   −   4 yd 2 ft
   ```

6. ```
      2 lb 3 oz
   ×         6
   ```

PRACTICE

Complete.

7. 72 in. = ■ ft   **8.** $1\frac{1}{2}$ T = ■ lb   **9.** 7 pt = ■ c   **10.** 2 oz = ■ lb

11. 32 lb = ■ oz   **12.** $2\frac{3}{4}$ mi = ■ ft   **13.** 15 c = ■ pt   **14.** $5\frac{2}{3}$ yd = ■ ft

Add, subtract, or multiply.

15.   7 ft
          2 ft 6 in.
        + 5 ft 8 in.

16.   4 lb 10 oz
          5 lb 9 oz
        + 6 lb 11 oz

17.   3 gal 2 qt
          2 gal 2 qt
        + 2 gal 1 qt

18.   2 T 1,000 lb
          1 T 1,500 lb
        + 1 T   700 lb

19.   6 c 9 fl oz
        − 2 c 7 fl oz

20.   5 gal 2 qt
        − 3 gal 3 qt

21.   7 yd 1 ft
        − 3 yd 2 ft

22.   3 lb 7 oz
        − 2 lb 10 oz

23.   3 T 500 lb
        ×   6

24.   1 pt 1 c
        ×   2

25.   4 mi 515 yd
        ×   4

26.   1 ft 3 in.
        ×   9

27.   1 T 800 lb
        −   900 lb

28.   4 gal 3 qt
        ×   5

29.   4 yd 2 ft 2 in.
        + 10 yd 2 ft 10 in.

Mixed Applications

30. Mr. Carson needs fencing for a garden that is 35 ft 10 in. long and 27 ft 8 in. wide. How many feet of fencing does he need?

31. Velma cuts a piece of cloth $3\frac{1}{2}$ yd long from a piece that is 15 yd long. How many yards of material does she have left?

32. Erin has a tablecloth that is 2 yd $1\frac{1}{2}$ ft long. She adds a red border 4 in. wide all the way around the cloth. How many ft long is the tablecloth with the border added?

33. The block where Maurice lives measures 440 yd on each of its four sides. He runs around the block 3 times. How many mi does Maurice run?

Mixed Review

Find the answer. Which method did you use?

MENTAL MATH
CALCULATOR
PAPER/PENCIL

34. 45.2 ÷ 2.5   **35.** 8.5383 ÷ 95.4   **36.** $\frac{1}{3}$ × 693   **37.** 752 × 25

38. $10\frac{1}{3} - 2\frac{2}{5}$ **39.** 515 + 125   **40.** 10 × 3.5   **41.** $2\frac{5}{6} + 3\frac{2}{9}$

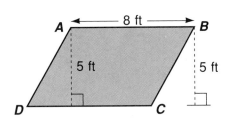

ACTIVITY
Areas of Parallelograms and Triangles

WORKING TOGETHER

You can learn about how to find the area of parallelograms and triangles by doing these activities.

Activity 1: Areas of Parallelograms
Trace the parallelogram shown at the right. Label your figure. Follow these steps.

Step 1	Step 2	Step 3	Step 4
Cut out the tracing you made.	Fold so that point *D* is on side *DC* and so that the fold line goes through point *A*.	Unfold the paper. Cut along the fold line.	Turn over the triangular piece and fit it onto side *BC*.

1. What figure did you form in Step 4?

2. What is the area of the figure formed in Step 4?

3. How does the area of the parallelogram in Step 1 compare with the area of the figure in Step 4?

4. What is the area of the parallelogram?

Activity 2: Areas of Triangles

Step 1	Step 2
Make two tracings of the triangle shown at the right. Cut out both tracings.	Then fit the tracings together to form a four-sided figure.

7 ft
12 ft

7 ft
12 ft

5. Why do both triangles have the same area?

6. What four-sided figure do the two triangles form?

7. What is the area of the parallelogram? of each triangle?

8. Describe a method for finding the area of a parallelogram if you know the length of two opposite sides and the height between them.

9. Tell how to find the area of a parallelogram when the length of two opposite sides is 10 in. and the height is 6 in.

10. Describe a method to find the area of a triangle if you know the length of one side and the height of the triangle.

PRACTICE

Use your method to find the area.

11.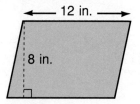

12.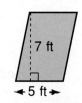

13.

14.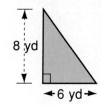

15.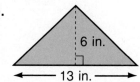

16.

Mixed Applications

Solve. Which method did you use?

17. Mr. Harris is installing triangular-shaped solar panels on the roof of his nursery. If the height of each triangular panel is $2\frac{1}{2}$ ft and the base is 3 ft, what is the area of 10 panels?

18. Jackson spends $\frac{3}{4}$ hour cutting grass, $\frac{1}{2}$ hour spraying bushes, and 11 hours trimming a hedge fence. About how long does he work?

19. Tiles for garden paths are on sale for 75¢ each. Mrs. Harris buys 36 tiles. The tax is 0.05 of the amount of the sale. What is her total bill?

20. Mr. Harris has a square vegetable garden that measures 16 ft on each side. How many square feet does he have in the garden?

ESTIMATION
MENTAL MATH
CALCULATOR
PAPER/PENCIL

DECISION MAKING

COOPERATIVE LEARNING

Problem Solving: Distributing Money to Charity

SITUATION

The class members earned $800 in the walkathon. They must decide how to distribute the money to various charities. There are three plans under consideration.

PROBLEM

Which plan should they choose?

DATA

Charity	Plan A	Plan B	Plan C
Homeless in America	$275	$75	$125
World Childrens' Fund	50	225	300
Local charities	325	100	175
Food Relief for Asia	150	400	200

Hannah Lewis raised $39.00!

USING THE DATA

About what fraction of the money is allocated to the homeless?

1. plan A   **2.** plan B   **3.** plan C

About what fraction of the money is allocated to the World Children's Fund?

4. plan A   **5.** plan B   **6.** plan C

About what fraction of the money is allocated to local charities?

7. plan A   **8.** plan B   **9.** plan C

About what fraction of the money is allocated to Food Relief for Asia?

10. plan A   **11.** plan B   **12.** plan C

MAKING DECISIONS

13. Which plan should the class choose if they want to give $\frac{3}{4}$ of the money to charities in the United States?

14. Which plan should the class choose if they want to give $\frac{5}{8}$ of the money to international charities?

15. Which plan should the class choose if they want to give about $\frac{1}{4}$ of the money to local charities?

16. *What if* a local company matches half of what the class members contribute? How much will each charity get for plan A?

17. *Write a list* of the other factors the class should consider when choosing a plan.

18. Which plan would you choose? Tell why.

Math and Science

Weight is maintained by balancing the number of calories you eat with the number of calories you burn through activity.

A calorie is a measure of energy. Each pound of "you" contains 3,500 calories. To lose one pound, you need to eat 3,500 fewer calories or burn 3,500 more calories by exercising.

The chart shows how many calories are burned if you perform each exercise for one hour.

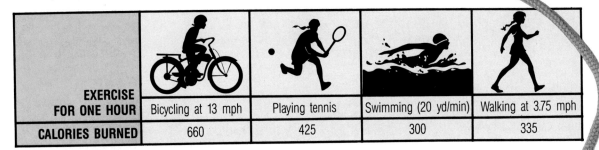

EXERCISE FOR ONE HOUR	Bicycling at 13 mph	Playing tennis	Swimming (20 yd/min)	Walking at 3.75 mph
CALORIES BURNED	660	425	300	335

What if you walk three mornings a week for $\frac{1}{2}$ hour each time and swim three afternoons a week for $\frac{3}{4}$ hour each time? How many calories would you burn by doing these activities for a week?

Walking

Total walking time per week is 3 times $\frac{1}{2}$, or $\frac{3}{2}$.

$$335 \times \frac{3}{2} = 502.5$$

Swimming

Total swimming time per week is 3 times $\frac{3}{4}$, or $\frac{9}{4}$.

$$300 \times \frac{9}{4} = 675$$

$$502.5 \quad + \quad 675 = 1,177.5$$

You would burn 1,177.5 calories a week.

ACTIVITIES

1. Make a chart of your physical activities for a week. Find out how many calories you burned and figure the total for the week.

2. Learn about exercises you can do indoors without special equipment. Draw a poster showing how some of these exercises are done and how many calories they burn. Display your poster in the classroom.

Calculator Algebra: Order of Operations

Use pencil and paper and the correct order of operations to simplify this expression:

$$9 + 2.1 \div 4$$

1. What answer did you get?

2. Now enter the numbers and operations from left to right on a calculator. What does the display show?

A scientific calculator will display 9.525, the correct answer, because it follows the correct order of operations. An arithmetic calculator will display 2.775, an incorrect answer, because it performs operations from left to right as entered.

One way to get the correct answer with an arithmetic calculator is to use the memory keys:

⑨ (M+) ② (.) ① (÷) ④ (=) (+) (MRC) (=)

Here is how you can use a calculator to simplify the expression $8 - 3.4 \times 2$.

Press: ⑧ (M+) ③ (.) ④ (×) ② (=) (M−) (MRC)

The calculator will display 1.2, the correct answer.

USING THE CALCULATOR
Simplify the expression using a calculator.

3. $7 + 21 \div 4.2$

4. $7 + 21 \div 4.2 + 8$

5. $13 - 4 \times 2.1$

6. $13 - 4 \times 2.1 + 7.4$

7. $7 + 21 \div 4.2 - 5$

8. $15 - 3 \times 2.5 - 4.4$

Use a calculator to solve.

9. The floor of the gym has been set up with chairs for a meeting. There are 9 rows of red seats with 15 seats per row and 12 rows of blue seats with 13 seats per row. How many people can be seated?

10. Bologna at the butcher shop sells for $3.50 per pound. Mrs. Davis buys $2\frac{3}{4}$ pounds of bologna for a party. The sales tax on all purchases is 4%. How much is the sales tax and how much is the total cost of her purchase?

EXTRA PRACTICE

Multiplying Fractions, page 313 ....
Multiply. Write the answer in simplest form.

1. $\frac{1}{2} \times \frac{2}{7}$ **2.** $\frac{4}{5} \times \frac{5}{6}$ **3.** $\frac{1}{3} \times 6$ **4.** $\frac{1}{5} \times \frac{2}{3}$ **5.** $\frac{5}{8} \times \frac{2}{3}$

6. $\frac{1}{4} \times \frac{5}{6}$ **7.** $\frac{2}{3} \times \frac{5}{6}$ **8.** $\frac{4}{9} \times \frac{3}{8}$ **9.** $\frac{2}{7} \times 14$ **10.** $\frac{1}{6} \times \frac{6}{7}$

11. $\frac{1}{5} \times 30$ **12.** $\frac{3}{4} \times 16$ **13.** $\frac{5}{8} \times \frac{2}{5}$ **14.** $\frac{7}{8} \times \frac{8}{9}$ **15.** $\frac{2}{5} \times \frac{3}{4}$

16. $\frac{3}{7} \times \frac{1}{3}$ **17.** $\frac{1}{2} \times 12$ **18.** $\frac{7}{8} \times \frac{4}{5}$ **19.** $\frac{3}{10} \times \frac{4}{5}$ **20.** $\frac{4}{9} \times 6$

Find the reciprocal.

21. $\frac{1}{8}$ **22.** $\frac{1}{4}$ **23.** 6 **24.** $\frac{3}{4}$ **25.** $\frac{2}{7}$ **26.** $\frac{7}{8}$

Multiplying Fractions: Using a Shortcut, page 315 ....
Multiply. Write the answer in simplest form.
Use the shortcut method if you can.

1. $\frac{1}{2} \times \frac{2}{3}$ **2.** $\frac{1}{3} \times \frac{3}{7}$ **3.** $\frac{5}{12} \times 24$ **4.** $\frac{7}{10} \times \frac{5}{14}$ **5.** $\frac{4}{9} \times \frac{1}{2}$

6. $\frac{4}{5} \times \frac{5}{4}$ **7.** $\frac{2}{3} \times \frac{9}{10}$ **8.** $\frac{5}{6} \times \frac{6}{7}$ **9.** $\frac{3}{4} \times \frac{8}{15}$ **10.** $\frac{9}{10} \times \frac{5}{18}$

11. $\frac{8}{9} \times \frac{3}{4}$ **12.** $\frac{7}{8} \times \frac{8}{7}$ **13.** $\frac{5}{6} \times \frac{8}{15}$ **14.** $\frac{9}{16} \times \frac{8}{9}$ **15.** $\frac{7}{12} \times \frac{3}{8}$

16. $\frac{5}{16} \times \frac{8}{15} \times \frac{2}{3}$ **17.** $\frac{1}{3} \times \frac{6}{7} \times 35$ **18.** $\frac{9}{25} \times \frac{20}{27} \times \frac{3}{4}$ **19.** $\frac{9}{10} \times \frac{5}{24} \times 32$

Multiplying Fractions and Mixed Numbers, page 319 ....
Multiply.

1. $\frac{2}{3} \times 1\frac{1}{2}$ **2.** $\frac{3}{7} \times 2\frac{1}{3}$ **3.** $\frac{3}{5} \times 1\frac{1}{9}$ **4.** $\frac{2}{3} \times 1\frac{3}{8}$ **5.** $\frac{3}{5} \times 2\frac{1}{4}$

6. $\frac{1}{3} \times 2\frac{1}{4}$ **7.** $3\frac{1}{5} \times \frac{3}{4}$ **8.** $2\frac{1}{3} \times \frac{2}{5}$ **9.** $6\frac{1}{4} \times \frac{3}{5}$ **10.** $\frac{2}{7} \times 4\frac{3}{8}$

11. $2\frac{1}{3} \times \frac{1}{2}$ **12.** $\frac{2}{3} \times 2\frac{1}{2}$ **13.** $2\frac{3}{8} \times \frac{4}{5}$ **14.** $\frac{2}{5} \times 1\frac{2}{3}$ **15.** $3\frac{1}{4} \times \frac{8}{9}$

16. $\frac{6}{7} \times 3\frac{1}{6}$ **17.** $\frac{4}{5} \times 1\frac{1}{8}$ **18.** $4\frac{2}{3} \times \frac{2}{3}$ **19.** $\frac{3}{8} \times 4\frac{8}{9}$ **20.** $\frac{7}{9} \times 1\frac{4}{5}$

Multiplying Mixed Numbers, page 321

Multiply to find the exact answer in simplest form.

1. $\frac{3}{8} \times 2\frac{1}{3}$

2. $1\frac{4}{5} \times \frac{1}{3}$

3. $\frac{1}{3} \times 2\frac{7}{10}$

4. $\frac{4}{5} \times 2\frac{1}{8}$

5. $\frac{2}{3} \times 2\frac{1}{10}$

6. $5\frac{1}{2} \times 2\frac{2}{3}$

7. $2\frac{3}{4} \times 2\frac{2}{3}$

8. $\frac{3}{10} \times 3\frac{1}{3}$

9. $1\frac{2}{3} \times 3\frac{1}{5}$

10. $4\frac{1}{6} \times 1\frac{4}{5}$

11. $3\frac{1}{2} \times 2\frac{2}{3}$

12. $1\frac{1}{8} \times 2\frac{1}{3}$

13. $1\frac{1}{3} \times 4\frac{1}{2}$

14. $1\frac{3}{5} \times 8$

15. $2\frac{2}{3} \times 1\frac{1}{4}$

16. $2\frac{1}{2} \times 3$

17. $3\frac{1}{5} \times 2\frac{1}{4}$

18. $1\frac{1}{2} \times \frac{1}{2}$

19. $10 \times 3\frac{2}{5}$

20. $1\frac{1}{2} \times \frac{2}{3}$

21. $2\frac{1}{8} \times 16$

22. $3\frac{1}{5} \times 9$

23. $4\frac{1}{4} \times 1\frac{3}{5}$

24. $1\frac{1}{5} \times 3\frac{1}{3}$

25. $1\frac{3}{4} \times 2\frac{1}{2}$

26. $3\frac{1}{8} \times 2\frac{3}{5}$

27. $4\frac{1}{2} \times 2\frac{1}{3}$

28. $5\frac{1}{2} \times 4\frac{2}{3}$

29. $1\frac{3}{7} \times 14$

30. $5\frac{1}{3} \times 1\frac{5}{8}$

31. $\frac{3}{5} \times 2\frac{1}{6}$

32. $4 \times \frac{7}{8}$

33. $2\frac{2}{3} \times 3\frac{3}{4}$

34. $1\frac{7}{8} \times 1\frac{1}{6}$

35. $2\frac{2}{9} \times 1\frac{3}{10}$

Problem Solving Strategy: Solving a Simpler Problem, page 323

Use a simpler problem to help you solve the problem.

1. In the supermarket, cans of tuna were arranged in a display as follows: 18 in the bottom row, 17 in the row above it, 16 in the row above that, and so on. How many cans of tuna were in the display?

2. Twenty-four teams are engaged in a single-elimination basketball tournament. This means that a team is eliminated if it loses one game. How many games must be played in order to determine the tournament champion?

3. Mark made a sculpture by stacking plastic foam squares. The largest square, placed on the bottom, has a perimeter of 32 in. Each square in the stack has sides that are 1 in. less than the sides of the square directly beneath it. How many squares are in the stack, and what is the total perimeter of all the squares in the sculpture?

4. How thick, in inches, is a page of your textbook? Use only a ruler to find out. Describe your strategy.

EXTRA PRACTICE

Dividing Fractions: Common Denominators, page 329

Use your method of dividing fractions to find the quotient.

1. $\frac{5}{7} \div \frac{1}{7}$ **2.** $\frac{7}{8} \div \frac{1}{8}$ **3.** $\frac{4}{5} \div \frac{1}{5}$ **4.** $\frac{5}{12} \div \frac{1}{12}$ **5.** $\frac{6}{10} \div \frac{3}{10}$

6. $\frac{9}{12} \div \frac{3}{12}$ **7.** $\frac{6}{9} \div \frac{2}{9}$ **8.** $\frac{15}{20} \div \frac{3}{20}$ **9.** $\frac{8}{15} \div \frac{4}{15}$ **10.** $\frac{2}{4} \div \frac{1}{4}$

11. $\frac{5}{7} \div \frac{3}{7}$ **12.** $\frac{9}{10} \div \frac{7}{10}$ **13.** $\frac{4}{5} \div \frac{2}{5}$ **14.** $\frac{7}{8} \div \frac{5}{8}$ **15.** $\frac{5}{6} \div \frac{3}{6}$

16. $\frac{3}{15} \div \frac{12}{15}$ **17.** $\frac{1}{3} \div \frac{2}{3}$ **18.** $\frac{3}{12} \div \frac{9}{12}$ **19.** $\frac{4}{9} \div \frac{8}{9}$ **20.** $\frac{1}{4} \div \frac{2}{4}$

21. $\frac{5}{6} \div \frac{2}{6}$ **22.** $\frac{3}{10} \div \frac{7}{10}$ **23.** $\frac{14}{20} \div \frac{7}{20}$ **24.** $\frac{4}{5} \div \frac{3}{5}$ **25.** $\frac{5}{12} \div \frac{10}{12}$

Dividing Fractions: Different Denominators, page 331

Divide. Write the answer in simplest form.

1. $\frac{1}{4} \div \frac{1}{8}$ **2.** $\frac{2}{5} \div \frac{1}{10}$ **3.** $\frac{1}{2} \div \frac{5}{6}$ **4.** $\frac{5}{8} \div \frac{1}{4}$ **5.** $4 \div \frac{4}{7}$

6. $\frac{7}{8} \div \frac{1}{5}$ **7.** $\frac{5}{6} \div \frac{3}{4}$ **8.** $\frac{1}{2} \div \frac{5}{9}$ **9.** $7 \div \frac{1}{8}$ **10.** $\frac{7}{12} \div \frac{1}{5}$

11. $\frac{2}{3} \div \frac{1}{4}$ **12.** $3 \div \frac{2}{9}$ **13.** $\frac{11}{12} \div \frac{1}{3}$ **14.** $\frac{1}{4} \div \frac{1}{5}$ **15.** $\frac{7}{9} \div \frac{1}{6}$

16. $\frac{1}{7} \div \frac{1}{8}$ **17.** $\frac{2}{3} \div \frac{1}{2}$ **18.** $\frac{7}{8} \div \frac{1}{6}$ **19.** $\frac{8}{9} \div \frac{2}{5}$ **20.** $5 \div \frac{1}{2}$

21. $\frac{8}{9} \div \frac{2}{3}$ **22.** $\frac{5}{6} \div \frac{1}{2}$ **23.** $\frac{9}{10} \div \frac{4}{5}$ **24.** $14 \div \frac{7}{12}$ **25.** $\frac{5}{16} \div \frac{5}{8}$

Problem Solving Strategy: Working Backward, page 333

Work backward to solve.

1. On Tuesday Sally deposited $210.47 in her savings account. On Friday she withdrew $125.00. There is now $430.66 in her savings account. How much was in the account before Sally deposited money?

2. Jay rode his bicycle twice as many miles as Bob. Bob rode 3 miles more than Ben. Ben rode $\frac{1}{3}$ as many miles as Jeb. Jeb rode his bicycle 15 miles. How many miles did Jay ride his bicycle?

Converting Customary Measures, page 335

Complete.

1. 60 in. = ■ ft   **2.** 16 gal = ■ qt   **3.** 64 fl oz = ■ c   **4.** 3 T = ■ lb

5. 18,480 ft = ■ mi   **6.** 13 lb = ■ oz   **7.** 7 pt = ■ qt   **8.** 108 ft = ■ yd

Add, subtract, or multiply.

9.
```
  3 ft  8 in.
  7 ft  7 in.
+ 2 ft 11 in.
```

10.
```
  3 T 1,000 lb
  4 T 1,600 lb
+ 1 T   800 lb
```

11.
```
  4 yd 2 ft
  3 yd 1 ft
+ 3 yd 1 ft
```

12.
```
  5 gal
  3 gal 3 qt
+ 2 gal 3 qt
```

13.
```
  7 lb 8 oz
- 3 lb 5 oz
```

14.
```
  5 c 5 fl oz
- 3 c 7 fl oz
```

15.
```
  8 yd 1 ft
- 2 yd 2 ft
```

16.
```
  2 mi 1,500 ft
-       2,000 ft
```

17.
```
  2 ft 5 in.
×       6
```

18.
```
  4 yd 2 ft
×       5
```

19.
```
  4 pt 1 c
×      5
```

20.
```
  2 lb 5½ oz
×      3
```

Areas of Parallelograms and Triangles, page 337

Find the area.

1.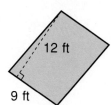
12 ft
9 ft

2.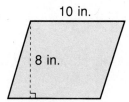
10 in.
8 in.

3.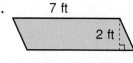
7 ft
2 ft

4.
4 yd
3 yd

5.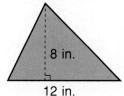
8 in.
12 in.

6.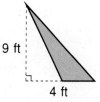
9 ft
4 ft

7.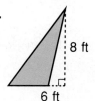
8 ft
6 ft

8.
6 in.
12 in.

9.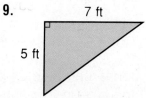
7 ft
5 ft

Practice PLUS

KEY SKILL: Multiplying Mixed Numbers (Use after page 321.)

Level A

Multiply to find the exact answer in simplest form.

1. $1\frac{4}{5} \times \frac{1}{3}$

2. $\frac{7}{10} \times 3\frac{1}{3}$

3. $1\frac{1}{3} \times \frac{3}{5}$

4. $\frac{3}{4} \times 1\frac{2}{3}$

5. $1\frac{3}{5} \times 3$

6. $2\frac{2}{5} \times 5$

7. $1\frac{3}{4} \times 2$

8. $1\frac{2}{3} \times 6$

9. $1\frac{1}{4} \times 1\frac{2}{5}$

10. $2\frac{1}{2} \times 1\frac{1}{3}$

11. $1\frac{1}{3} \times 4\frac{1}{2}$

12. $1\frac{1}{2} \times 1\frac{1}{2}$

13. Jeremy typed for 2 hours. He can type $2\frac{1}{2}$ pages an hour. How many pages did he type?

Level B

Multiply to find the exact answer in simplest form.

14. $2\frac{1}{10} \times \frac{3}{10}$

15. $2\frac{1}{2} \times \frac{4}{5}$

16. $2\frac{1}{3} \times \frac{5}{7}$

17. $2\frac{2}{3} \times 8$

18. $2\frac{1}{4} \times \frac{7}{9}$

19. $1\frac{1}{4} \times \frac{4}{5}$

20. $1\frac{1}{6} \times 4$

21. $1\frac{3}{4} \times 2\frac{1}{2}$

22. $2\frac{1}{5} \times 1\frac{5}{6}$

23. $2\frac{1}{3} \times 1\frac{2}{3}$

24. $3\frac{7}{10} \times 1\frac{3}{7}$

25. $4\frac{4}{5} \times 1\frac{3}{4}$

26. Peter can type $2\frac{1}{3}$ pages an hour. How many can he type in $\frac{3}{4}$ hour?

Level C

Multiply to find the exact answer in simplest form.

27. $3\frac{3}{5} \times \frac{8}{9}$

28. $3\frac{3}{7} \times 3\frac{7}{12}$

29. $4 \times 2\frac{5}{8}$

30. $4\frac{2}{3} \times 1\frac{2}{7}$

31. $2\frac{4}{5} \times 1\frac{2}{3}$

32. $5\frac{5}{8} \times 3\frac{1}{5}$

33. $6\frac{1}{2} \times 1\frac{3}{5}$

34. $2\frac{4}{9} \times 1\frac{1}{2}$

35. $6\frac{1}{10} \times 2\frac{6}{7}$

36. $4\frac{9}{10} \times 2\frac{2}{7}$

37. $7\frac{1}{3} \times 1\frac{2}{11}$

38. $8\frac{3}{4} \times \frac{8}{14}$

39. Jenna can type $2\frac{3}{4}$ pages an hour. How many pages can she type in $2\frac{1}{2}$ hours?

KEY SKILL: Dividing Fractions: Different Denominators (Use after page 331.)

Level A

Divide. Write the answer in simplest form.

1. $\frac{1}{4} \div \frac{1}{8}$ **2.** $\frac{3}{4} \div \frac{7}{8}$ **3.** $4 \div \frac{2}{5}$ **4.** $\frac{9}{10} \div \frac{3}{5}$

5. $\frac{5}{6} \div \frac{2}{3}$ **6.** $\frac{3}{8} \div \frac{3}{4}$ **7.** $2 \div \frac{2}{3}$ **8.** $\frac{5}{8} \div \frac{1}{4}$

9. $3 \div \frac{1}{5}$ **10.** $\frac{1}{2} \div \frac{3}{4}$ **11.** $\frac{3}{4} \div \frac{1}{2}$ **12.** $2 \div \frac{1}{8}$

13. Bert has 12 apples. He uses $\frac{3}{4}$ of an apple to make a dessert. How many desserts can he make?

Level B

Divide. Write the answer in simplest form.

14. $\frac{5}{6} \div \frac{2}{3}$ **15.** $\frac{2}{3} \div \frac{1}{5}$ **16.** $\frac{3}{4} \div \frac{3}{8}$ **17.** $\frac{4}{5} \div \frac{1}{2}$

18. $\frac{7}{12} \div \frac{14}{15}$ **19.** $\frac{2}{3} \div \frac{8}{9}$ **20.** $4 \div \frac{1}{10}$ **21.** $6 \div \frac{1}{2}$

22. $\frac{1}{6} \div \frac{1}{2}$ **23.** $12 \div \frac{1}{7}$ **24.** $\frac{1}{3} \div \frac{5}{6}$ **25.** $\frac{5}{8} \div \frac{5}{12}$

26. Heather has $\frac{7}{8}$ lb of walnuts. She uses $\frac{1}{6}$ lb to make a dessert. How many desserts can she make?

Level C

Divide. Write the answer in simplest form.

27. $\frac{7}{16} \div \frac{7}{8}$ **28.** $\frac{7}{9} \div \frac{5}{6}$ **29.** $8 \div \frac{1}{5}$ **30.** $12 \div \frac{3}{4}$

31. $\frac{5}{6} \div \frac{2}{3}$ **32.** $\frac{5}{9} \div \frac{1}{4}$ **33.** $\frac{3}{4} \div \frac{2}{5}$ **34.** $\frac{7}{12} \div \frac{3}{4}$

35. $4 \div \frac{3}{25}$ **36.** $\frac{2}{5} \div \frac{3}{7}$ **37.** $\frac{3}{4} \div \frac{1}{3}$ **38.** $4 \div \frac{7}{8}$

39. Ben has $5\frac{1}{2}$ cups of milk. He uses $1\frac{1}{4}$ cups to make a loaf of bread. How many loaves can he make?

CHAPTER REVIEW/TEST

LANGUAGE AND MATHEMATICS

Complete the sentences. Use the words in the chart on the right.

1. Two numbers that have a product of 1 are called ■.

2. The area of a(n) ■ is equal to the product of its base times one-half the height.

3. Feet and inches are units of measurement in the ■ system.

4. When a mixed number is a factor in multiplication, rename the mixed number as a(n) ■.

CONCEPTS AND SKILLS

Estimate the product.

5. $\frac{1}{5} \times 17$ **a.** 15   **b.** $\frac{1}{3}$ **c.** 3

6. $\frac{7}{8} \times 25$ **a.** 21   **b.** 14   **c.** 30

7. $\frac{3}{4} \times 7$ **a.** 8   **b.** 6   **c.** 3

8. $4\frac{5}{9} \times \frac{5}{6}$ **a.** 5   **b.** 1   **c.** 4

9. $2\frac{1}{2} \times 1\frac{2}{5}$ **a.** 1   **b.** 2   **c.** 3

10. $3\frac{1}{2} \times 6\frac{3}{4}$ **a.** $9\frac{7}{8}$ **b.** 18   **c.** 28

Multiply. Write the product in simplest form.

11. $\frac{5}{6} \times \frac{9}{10}$ 12. $\frac{7}{8} \times 16$ 13. $\frac{2}{3} \times \frac{2}{3}$ 14. $\frac{2}{5} \times 22$

15. $3\frac{1}{5} \times \frac{1}{2}$ 16. $2\frac{2}{7} \times \frac{5}{8}$ 17. $4\frac{2}{3} \times \frac{6}{7}$ 18. $1\frac{1}{8} \times \frac{16}{21}$

Divide. Write the quotient in simplest form.

19. $\frac{3}{5} \div \frac{1}{5}$ 20. $\frac{4}{7} \div \frac{5}{7}$ 21. $\frac{9}{10} \div \frac{7}{10}$ 22. $\frac{1}{6} \div \frac{5}{6}$

23. $\frac{2}{3} \div \frac{5}{6}$ 24. $\frac{1}{4} \div \frac{5}{8}$ 25. $7 \div \frac{7}{12}$ 26. $5 \div \frac{10}{13}$

Complete.

27. ■ in. = 6 ft 4 in.

28. 3 c 6 fl oz = ■ fl oz

29. 3 ft = ■ yd

30. 4 T   400 lb
− 2 T 1,000 lb

31.   3 yd 1 ft 7 in.
+ 11 yd 2 ft 5 in.

32.   8 gal 2 qt
×   5

Find the area.

33.
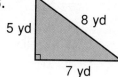
5 yd   8 yd
7 yd

34.
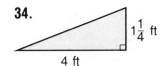
$1\frac{1}{4}$ ft
4 ft

35.
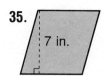
7 in.
7 in.

36.
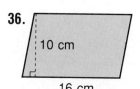
10 cm
16 cm

Critical Thinking

37. A pie was cut into 6 pieces. Gail ate 1 piece. Can you be sure there is $\frac{5}{6}$ of the pie left? Why?

38. If you continue to multiply $\frac{1}{2}$ by itself ($\frac{1}{2} \times \frac{1}{2} \times \frac{1}{2} \times$ . . .), can you reach zero? Why or why not?

Mixed Applications

39. Tim had some balloons, but 5 balloons popped. After he blew up 12 more, he had 24 balloons. How many balloons did Tim have to start?

40. Keychains hang on a board that is 52 in. by 52 in. The hooks are 4 in. apart and 2 in. from the edges of the board. How many hooks are on the board?

PERFORMANCE ASSESSMENT

Work with your group to solve this problem.

Use construction paper, a ruler, and scissors to make a physical model of 9 x $\frac{1}{3}$ and 9 ÷ $\frac{1}{3}$.

1. *Think about:*
- the size of the product when multiplying with fractions
- the size of the quotient when dividing with fractions

2. Write a paragraph explaining how your physical model illustrates 9 x $\frac{1}{3}$ and 9 ÷ $\frac{1}{3}$.

CUMULATIVE REVIEW

Choose the letter of the correct answer.

1. $553.5 \div 4.5$
   a. 123
   b. 1.23
   c. 12.3
   d. not given

2. Simplify:
   $9 - 1 + 48 \div 8 + 2 \times 12$
   a. 192
   b. 38
   c. 108
   d. not given

3. Which is the GCF of 12 and 32?
   a. 2
   b. 4
   c. 8
   d. not given

4. Compare: $\frac{3}{4} \bullet \frac{7}{8}$
   a. $<$
   b. $>$
   c. $=$
   d. not given

5. Measure to the nearest $\frac{1}{8}$ in.

   a. $2\frac{5}{8}$ in.
   b. $2\frac{6}{8}$ in.
   c. $2\frac{3}{8}$ in.
   d. not given

6. Choose the best estimate:
   $(5\frac{1}{5} + 2\frac{7}{8}) - 4\frac{1}{9}$
   a. 7
   b. 5
   c. 4
   d. 2

7. $6\frac{3}{5} + 2\frac{1}{2}$
   a. 8.5
   b. 9.1
   c. $8\frac{9}{10}$
   d. not given

8. $3\frac{1}{8} - 2\frac{5}{12}$
   a. $1\frac{1}{2}$
   b. $1\frac{17}{24}$
   c. $\frac{1}{6}$
   d. not given

9. An empty box weighs $\frac{3}{16}$ lb. When filled with rice, it weighs $2\frac{1}{2}$ lb. How many pounds does the rice weigh?
   a. $2\frac{5}{16}$ lb
   b. $2\frac{11}{6}$ lb
   c. $2\frac{3}{4}$ lb
   d. not given

10. Choose the best estimate:
    $\frac{5}{7} \times 20$
    a. 15
    b. 10
    c. 5
    d. not given

11. $3\frac{1}{5} \times \frac{5}{8}$
    a. $3\frac{1}{2}$
    b. $3\frac{1}{8}$
    c. 2
    d. not given

12. $\frac{5}{6} \div \frac{3}{4}$
    a. $1\frac{1}{9}$
    b. $\frac{5}{8}$
    c. $1\frac{1}{2}$
    d. not given

13. $3\frac{2}{3}$ feet = ■ inches
    a. $108\frac{2}{3}$
    b. 132
    c. $36\frac{2}{3}$
    d. not given

14. Find the area of the triangle.

    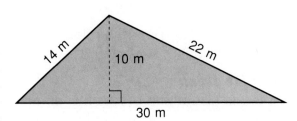

    a. 210 m2
    b. 110 m2
    c. 150 m2
    d. not given

ENRICHMENT FOR ALL

ALGEBRA: FIBONACCI SEQUENCE

A *sequence* is a list of related numbers. The numbers are called *terms*. A famous sequence is the *Fibonacci Sequence*. The sequence begins with two 1s. Every term after that is the sum of the two previous terms.

$$1, \quad 1, \quad 2, \quad 3, \quad 5, \quad 8, \ldots$$

Fibonacci numbers occur in nature. The branches and flowers of the sneezewort plant are an example. From the main stem new branches grow. Other branches grow from those branches.

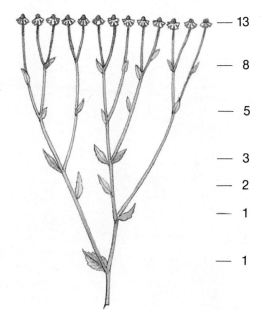

1. Complete the first twelve terms of the Fibonacci Sequence.

   1, 1, 2, 3, 5, 8, ■, ■, ■, ■, ■, ■

Find the sum of the given terms.

2. $1 + 1 + 2 =$ ■

3. $1 + 1 + 2 + 3 =$ ■

4. $1 + 1 + 2 + 3 + 5 =$ ■

5. Find the difference between the sum of the first three terms and the fifth term.

6. Find the difference between the sum of the first four terms and the sixth term.

7. Find the difference between the sum of the first five terms and the seventh term.

8. What pattern do you notice in Problems 5–7?

Use this pattern to find the answer.

9. Find the sum of the first 7 terms.

10. Find the sum of the first 8 terms.

ROYAL PALACE OF KING HASSAN II, MOROCCO

Many of the decorative arts of Islam feature repeated geometric patterns that cover an entire surface.

GEOMETRIC DESIGN IN ISLAMIC ART

Islamic tradition encourages the use of such patterns, which symbolize the belief in a never-ending universe and the unity of all things.

THIS is how to create the popular "star-cross" design, a favorite among Islamic artists. The design relies on the circle, with the radius as the key unit of measure.

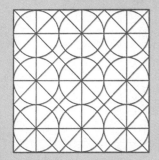

Fill the space with circles that touch. Connect the centers to produce a grid of squares.

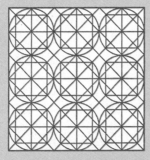

Use the grid to draw two overlapping squares inside each circle.

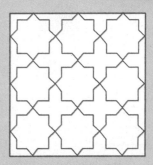

Eliminate unnecessary lines to produce the "star-cross" design.

1 How is the circle an appropriate shape to suggest the idea of a never-ending universe?

2 How is the radius of the circle important in the design above?

3 The circle is the central figure in the designs shown here. What other geometric figures do you see in the designs?

4 Use a straightedge and a compass to create a geometric design inspired by Islamic designs.

MASDJED-É-CHAH, IRAN

Geometric Figures

Everywhere you look, you see objects that suggest **geometric figures.** Most geometric figures are made up of simpler figures, such as points, line segments, and angles.

Geometric Figure	Description	Symbol	Read
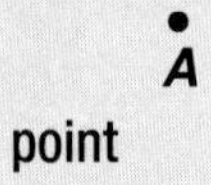 • **A** point	a location in space	point *A*	point *A*
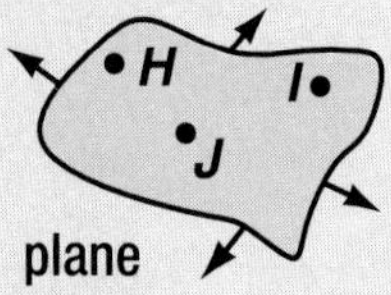 plane	an endless flat surface	plane *HIJ*	plane *HIJ*
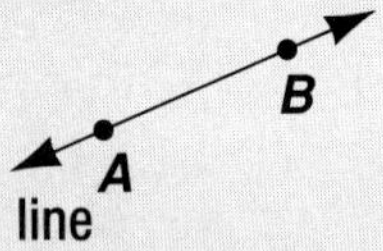 line	an endless straight path	$\overleftrightarrow{AB}$ or $\overleftrightarrow{BA}$	line *AB* or line *BA*
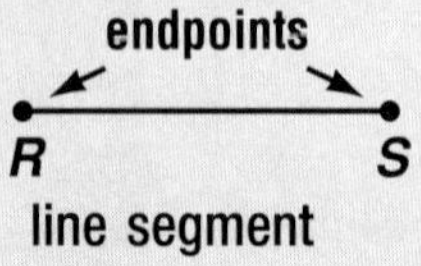 endpoints **R**　　**S** line segment	a straight path from one point to another	$\overline{RS}$ or $\overline{SR}$	line segment *RS* or line segment *SR*
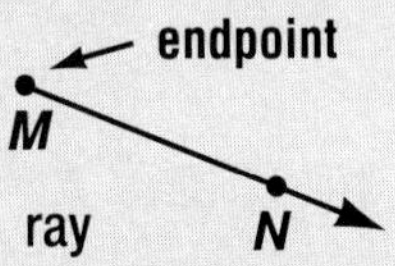 endpoint **M** ray　　**N**	an endless straight path starting at a point	$\overrightarrow{MN}$	ray *MN*
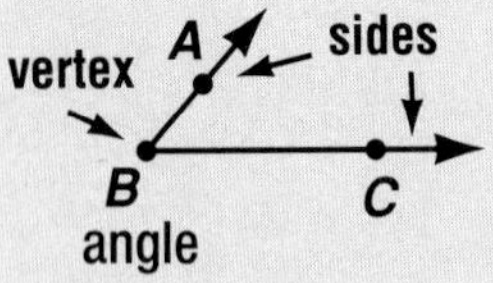 vertex　**A**　sides **B**　**C** angle	two rays with a common endpoint	$\angle ABC$, or $\angle CBA$, or $\angle B$	angle *ABC*, or angle *CBA*, or angle *B*

TRY OUT   Refer to the diagram. Use symbols to name the figure.

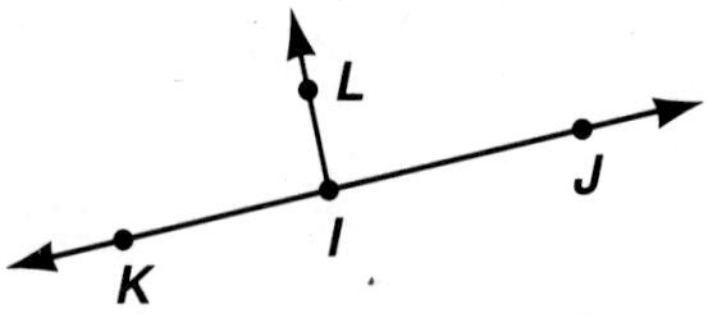

1. Name a line. KJ

2. Name a ray. I L

3. Name a line segment. K I

4. Write a three-letter name for an angle. ray

PRACTICE

Use a symbol to identify the figure.

5.
6.
7.
8.
9.

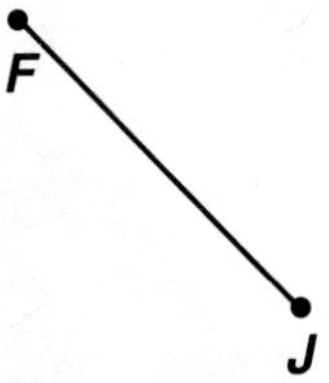

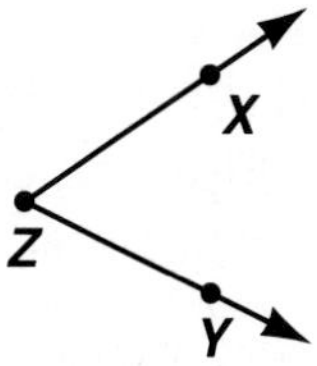

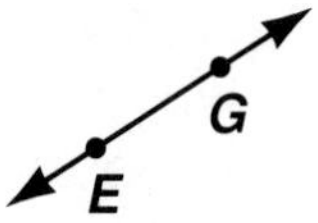

Sketch the figure on dot paper.

10. $\overline{RS}$

11. plane *XYZ*

12. $\overleftrightarrow{MN}$

13. $\overrightarrow{DE}$

14. ∠ *IJK* ∠

15. point *C*

What geometric figure does the description suggest?

16. light from a laser beam

17. the corner of a sheet of paper

18. the edge of a table

19. the ceiling of a room

20. an object that has no line segments and no angles

Critical Thinking

Is the statement *true* or *false?* Why?

21. You can measure the length of a line segment. True

22. You can measure the length of a ray. False

23. The figure at the right is ray *KR*. False

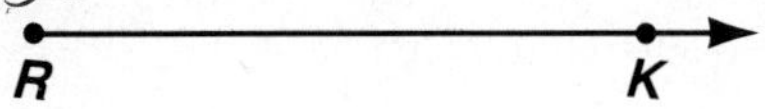

R ————————————→ K

Mixed Applications

24. Gandhi School is building 4 new tennis courts at a total cost of $9,380. What is the cost of building 1 tennis court?

25. What kinds of geometric figures do these parts of a tennis court suggest?
a. the playing surface   **b.** the lines   **c.** the corners

26. The tennis team practices every school day from 3:45 P.M. to 5:15 P.M. How many hours does the team practice in a week?

27. In an international tennis match, the players get a new set of balls every 9 games. How many sets of new balls are used in a 49-game match?

EXTRA PRACTICE, page 384; PRACTICE *PLUS*, page 388

Measuring Angles

A. A sextant measures the angle between a star and the horizon. It can be used by a navigator to determine the position of his or her ship or aircraft.

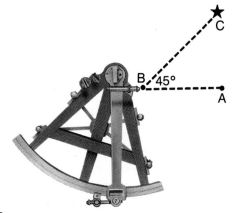

Angles are measured in **degrees** (°). You can use a protractor to measure an angle.

Place the protractor over the angle so that the vertex is at the center and one side of the angle is at 0. Read the measure of the angle along the outer or inner scale. Use the outer scale if the angle opens to the right and the inner scale if it opens to the left.

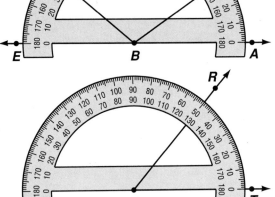

1. What is the measure of ∠ABD? ∠EBD?

B. You can also use a protractor to draw an angle.

Here is how to draw a 50° angle. Draw $\overrightarrow{ST}$. Place the center of the protractor on point S and the 0° mark on $\overrightarrow{ST}$. Mark point R at the 50° mark and then draw $\overrightarrow{SR}$.

C. Angles are named according to their size.

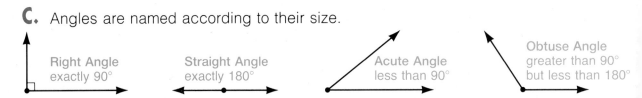

Right Angle
exactly 90°

Straight Angle
exactly 180°

Acute Angle
less than 90°

Obtuse Angle
greater than 90°
but less than 180°

If the sum of the measures of two angles is 90°, the angles are **complementary**. If the sum of the measures of two angles is 180°, the angles are **supplementary**.

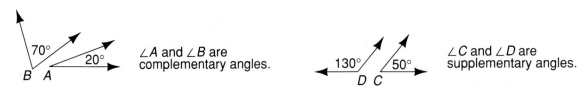

70°
20°
B A
∠A and ∠B are complementary angles.

130° 50°
D C
∠C and ∠D are supplementary angles.

TRY OUT

2. What is the measure of each angle?

3. Which angle is acute? obtuse?

4. Draw an angle with measure 80°.

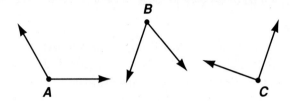

PRACTICE

Estimate the measure of the angle. Then measure the angle.

5. **6.** **7.** **8.**

Without using a protractor, sketch an angle with given measure on dot paper. Then use your protractor to check your estimate.

9. 30°   **10.** 60°   **11.** 45°   **12.** 120°   **13.** 165°   **14.** 100°

Use a protractor to draw the angle with given measure.

15. 45°   **16.** 65°   **17.** 90°   **18.** 110°   **19.** 130°   **20.** 175°

Name the figures.

21. two right angles   **22.** two obtuse angles   **23.** five acute angles

24. two pairs of complementary angles

25. three pairs of supplementary angles

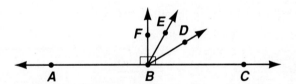

Mixed Applications   Solve. You may need to use the Databank on page 553.

26. How many more travelers use the airport in Atlanta than the airport in Denver?

27. An airplane takes off at 1:00 P.M. and lands at 5:00 P.M. What is the measure of the angle through which the hour hand on a clock has moved while the plane was in the air?

28. If you are looking down from an airplane, what geometric figure is suggested by an airfield? What geometric figure is suggested by an airport control tower?

Perpendicular and Parallel Lines

Roger drew a map of Fantasyland.
The paths on his map suggest several
ways in which lines are related.

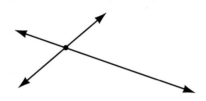

Intersecting lines are lines that meet in a point.

1. Name three pairs of intersecting
   lines in Roger's map.

Perpendicular lines are lines that meet at right angles.

Symbol:	Read:
$\overleftrightarrow{GH} \perp \overleftrightarrow{IJ}$	Line *GH* is perpendicular to line *IJ*.

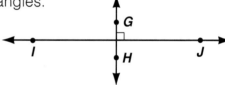

2. Name two pairs of perpendicular lines in Roger's map.

3. How many right angles are formed by two perpendicular lines?

Parallel lines are lines in the same
plane that never meet.

Symbol:	Read:
$\overleftrightarrow{AB} \parallel \overleftrightarrow{CD}$	Line *AB* is parallel to line *CD*.

4. Name two pairs of parallel lines in Roger's map.

TRY OUT Name the lines.

5. intersecting lines

6. parallel lines

7. perpendicular lines

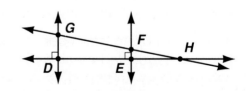

PRACTICE

Write *intersecting, perpendicular,* or *parallel.*

8.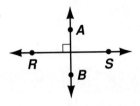

9.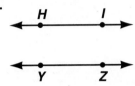

10.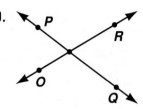

Sketch the figure on dot paper.

11. $\overleftrightarrow{RS} \parallel \overleftrightarrow{TV}$ **12.** $\overleftrightarrow{UP}$ intersects $\overleftrightarrow{YZ}$ **13.** $\overleftrightarrow{DT} \perp \overleftrightarrow{FI}$ **14.** right angle *MNO*

What geometric figure does the description suggest?

15. rails of a railroad track   **16.** a plus sign

Critical Thinking

Is the statement *true* or *false*? Why?

17. You can draw three lines that intersect in one point.

18. Any lines that do not intersect are parallel.

Mixed Applications

19. Roger has gone on 4 rides in 1 hour. If he continues in this way, how many rides will he go on in $3\frac{1}{2}$ hours?

20. Look at Roger's map of Fantasyland on page 358. Suppose that you ride from the Entrance of Fantasyland to the Pirate's Cove and then to the Mile-High Chute. What geometric figure would your path describe?

21. Mia's favorite ride at Fantasyland is the Jupiter Express. The ride lasts $8\frac{1}{2}$ minutes and takes another 5 minutes for loading and unloading. How many rides on the Jupiter Express can Mia possibly take in 1 hour?

Mixed Review

Find the answer. Which method did you use?

MENTAL MATH
CALCULATOR
PAPER/PENCIL

22. $\frac{4}{7} - \frac{2}{7}$ **23.** $3.532 + 0.09$ **24.** $2\frac{4}{15} - \frac{2}{3}$ **25.** $3.4 + 4.3$

26. 9^4 **27.** 0.4×0.09 **28.** $\frac{4}{9}$ of 36   **29.** $3.7\overline{)56.166}$

EXTRA PRACTICE, page 384

Compass Constructions

A. Two figures are **congruent** if they are exactly the same size and shape. You can construct congruent figures by using a compass and a straightedge.

Construct a line segment congruent to $\overline{AB}$.

Step 1	Step 2
Draw a ray with endpoint C.	Open the compass the length of $\overline{AB}$. Mark off point D on the ray so that $\overline{AB}$ is congruent to $\overline{CD}$.

 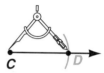

$$\overline{AB} \cong \overline{CD}$$
$\cong$ means "is congruent to"

B. Here is how to construct an angle congruent to another angle.

Construct an angle congruent to $\angle A$.

Step 1	Step 2
Draw $\overrightarrow{DE}$.	Draw an arc that intersects both sides of $\angle A$. Label these points B and C.

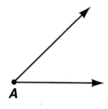

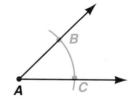

Step 3	Step 4
Using the same compass opening, place the compass point on D. Draw an arc that intersects $\overrightarrow{DE}$ at point F.	Open the compass to the distance between points B and C. Then place the compass point on F and draw an intersecting arc. Label this point G. Draw $\overrightarrow{DG}$.

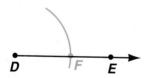

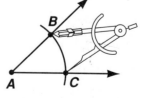 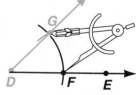

$$\angle A \cong \angle D$$

C. You can also use a compass and a straightedge to **bisect** an angle, or divide an angle into two congruent angles.

Bisect ∠GHI.

Step 1	Step 2	Step 3
Draw an arc with center at *H*. Label points *A* and *B*.	Using the same compass opening, draw an arc with center at *A* and an arc with center at *B*. Label point *J*.	Draw $\overrightarrow{HJ}$.

∠ GHJ is congruent to ∠ JHI. $\overrightarrow{HJ}$ is the bisector of ∠ GHI.

1. Use a protractor to draw a 70° angle. Use a compass to bisect it.

TRY OUT
Use a compass and a straightedge.

2. Draw a line segment. Construct a line segment congruent to it.

3. Draw an 80° angle using a protractor. Construct an angle congruent to it.

4. Construct the bisector of the angle in Problem 4.

PRACTICE

Use a compass and a straightedge.

5. Draw line segment *DE*. Construct a line segment congruent to it.

6. Draw acute angle *ABC*. Construct angle *DEF* congruent to it.

7. Draw obtuse angle *RST*. Construct angle *UVW* congruent to it.

8. Bisect the angles you drew in Problems 6–7.

9. Draw straight angle *XYZ*. Bisect it. Draw a point on the bisector and label it *F*. What kind of an angle is angle *FYZ*?

ACTIVITY Triangles

A **triangle** is a closed plane figure that has three sides. Triangles are named for the lengths of their sides and by the types of their angles. For example, a triangle with all sides of equal length is called an **equilateral triangle.**

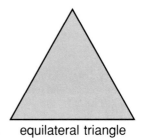

equilateral triangle

WORKING TOGETHER

All triangles, except equilateral triangles, can be made on a geoboard.

1. Make one of each kind of triangle on a geoboard. Then draw several examples of each on dot paper.

   a. obtuse: one obtuse angle

   b. scalene: no two sides of equal length

   c. right: one right angle

   d. isosceles: at least two sides of equal length

   e. acute: all angles acute

SHARING IDEAS

2. Which triangles are described by the lengths of sides?

3. Which triangles are described by the types of angles?

4. Is it possible to have the following types of triangles? If *yes*, support your answer with a drawing. If *no*, give a reason.

   a. equilateral right   **b.** equilateral acute   **c.** equilateral obtuse

   d. isosceles right   **e.** isosceles acute   **f.** isosceles obtuse

   g. scalene right   **h.** scalene acute   **i.** scalene obtuse

5. Measure the angles of a right triangle you drew. What is the sum of the measures of the angles? Measure the angles of other triangles. Are their sums the same? What can you conclude?

6. An **exterior angle** of a triangle is formed by extending a side of the triangle. For each triangle you drew in Problem 1, extend a side and measure the exterior angle that results. Measure the adjacent interior angle. What is their sum? What can you conclude?

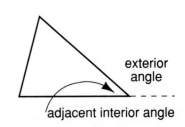

exterior angle

adjacent interior angle

PRACTICE

Give two names for the triangle. Give the measure of an exterior angle at each vertex.

7.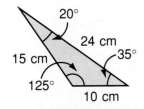

8.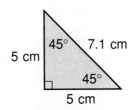

9.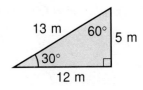

10.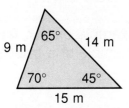

11.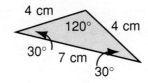

12.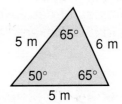

Could the following be the angles of a triangle? Write *yes* or *no*.

13. 40°, 60°, 90°   **14.** 30°, 60°, 90°   **15.** 45°, 55°, 90°   **16.** 35°, 55°, 90°

17. 45°, 45°, 90°   **18.** 130°, 20°, 40°   **19.** 45°, 115°, 20°   **20.** 70°, 60°, 50°

Critical Thinking   Is the statement *true* or *false*? Why?

21. A triangle can have two right angles.

22. A triangle can have two obtuse angles.

23. All scalene triangles are obtuse.

24. Some right triangles are isosceles.

25. Some isosceles triangles are acute.

26. All equilateral triangles are isosceles.

Mixed Applications

Solve. Which method did you use? You may need to use the Databank on page 553.

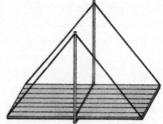

ESTIMATION
MENTAL MATH
CALCULATOR
PAPER/PENCIL

27. The edges of the bridge and the ropes form isosceles triangles. The bridge is 6 ft long. One section of rope is $\frac{2}{3}$ the length of the bridge. How much rope was used to support the bridge?

28. How many feet longer is the longest span of the Golden Gate Bridge than the longest span of the Walt Whitman Bridge?

29. The mean number of cars that travel over a bridge in a day is 29,438. About how many cars travel over the bridge in 1 year?

EXTRA PRACTICE, page 385

Quadrilaterals

A **quadrilateral** is a closed plane figure that has four sides.
Here are several kinds of quadrilaterals.

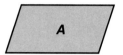 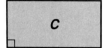 

Figures *A, B, C,* and *D* are all
examples of **parallelograms**. Figures
B and *D* are examples of **rhombuses**.

Figures *C* and *D* are examples of
rectangles.
Figure *D* is an example of a **square**.
Figure *E* is an example of a **trapezoid**.

WORKING TOGETHER

Trace and cut out the quadrilaterals shown above. Label them
with their correct names. Then use your figures, a ruler, and a
protractor to help you with the problems below.

1. Copy and complete the table. Write *must*, *can*, or *cannot* to
complete the description.

Description	Parallelogram	Rhombus	Rectangle	Square	Trapezoid
opposite sides equal in length	must	must	■	■	■
all sides equal in length	■	must	■	■	■
opposite sides are parallel	■	■	■	■	■
only one pair of opposite sides is parallel	■	■	■	■	■
all right angles	■	■	■	■	■

SHARING IDEAS

Write *true* or *false*. Then tell why.

2. All squares are parallelograms.

3. All parallelograms are rectangles.

4. Some rectangles are squares.

5. Some rhombuses are squares.

6. No trapezoids are parallelograms.

7. No trapezoids are squares.

PRACTICE

Give as many quadrilateral names as you can for the figure.

8.

9.

10.

11.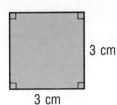

3 cm

3 cm

12.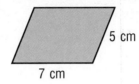

5 cm

7 cm

13.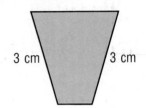

3 cm   3 cm

On dot paper draw a quadrilateral that has:

14. exactly one pair of opposite sides that are parallel.

15. exactly one pair of parallel sides and two right angles.

Mixed Applications

16. Each side of kite A is 16 in. What is its area?

17. Each side of kite B is 22 in. long. What is its perimeter?

18. One of the sticks that forms the side of kite C is broken. The length of the stick is 15 in. If a new stick is $.25 per inch, how much will it cost to repair kite C?

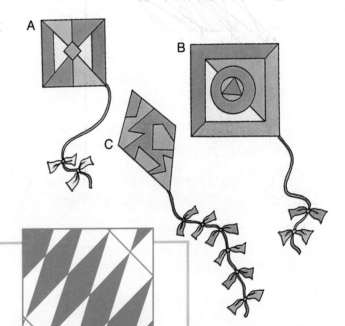

CHALLENGE

Name as many kinds of quadrilaterals as you can find in the design. Combinations of blue and white figures are allowed.

Activity **O**ther Polygons

A **polygon** is a closed plane figure that has three or more sides. Triangles and quadrilaterals are examples of polygons.

Each point at which two sides of a polygon meet is called a **vertex**. A polygon has at least three **vertices.**

Polygons:

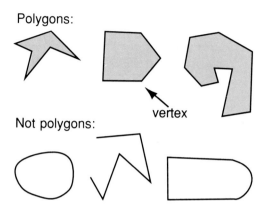

vertex

Not polygons:

Polygons are named by how many sides they have.

Pentagon
5 sides

Hexagon
6 sides

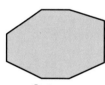

Octagon
8 sides

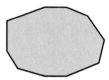

Decagon
10 sides

WORKING TOGETHER

A **diagonal** of a polygon is a line segment joining two vertices. A diagonal cannot be a side of the polygon.

1. Draw a pentagon and all its diagonals. How many diagonals does it have?

diagonal

You can use diagonals to find the sum of the measures of the angles of a polygon.

Step 1 Draw all possible diagonals from a single vertex to divide a polygon into triangles.

Step 2 Count the triangles. Since the sum of the measures of the angles of a triangle is 180°, multiply 180° by the number of triangles.

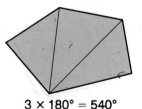

$3 \times 180° = 540°$

2. Draw and divide each of the following polygons into triangles.

    a. quadrilateral   **b.** hexagon

SHARING IDEAS

3. Copy and complete the table.

Polygon	Number of Sides	Number of Triangles	Sum of Measures of Angles
quadrilateral	■	■	■
pentagon	■	■	■
hexagon	■	■	■

4. Look for patterns in your table. What do you notice about the number of sides and the number of triangles?

PRACTICE

Tell into how many triangles you could divide each polygon. Then find the sum of the measures of the angles.

5. octagon

6. decagon

7. heptagon (7 sides)

8. dodecagon (12 sides)

Mixed Applications

A garden is in the shape of a hexagon with congruent sides. It is divided into six equilateral triangles.

9. What is the shape of the part of the garden planted with tulips, carnations, and irises? What is the shape of the part of the garden planted with roses?

10. The cost of a stone wall is $50 per foot. How much will it cost to build a wall around the garden?

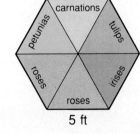

5 ft

11. What is the measure of the angle at each of the six corners of the garden?

12. A rosebush costs $6.99. If there are 12 rosebushes in the garden, what was their total cost?

Mixed Review

Find the answer. Which method did you use?

MENTAL MATH
CALCULATOR
PAPER/PENCIL

13. $\frac{11}{3} + 7\frac{1}{3}$

14. 5.2×41.06

15. $\frac{0.0585}{0.9}$

16. $18 \div 1.8$

EXTRA PRACTICE, page 386; **PRACTICE PLUS**, page 389

PROBLEM SOLVING

Strategy: Making an Organized List

Avi is a computer analyst. He is hooking up computer stations A, B, C, D, and E in groups of 3. Each computer will be hooked to every other computer. How many hookups does he need to make?

Avi plans to make a list to show all the 6 hookups.

He tries his plan.

	Number of Hookups
• First Avi lists all the hookups with computer A. There are 6 hookups.	A, B, C
	A, B, D
	A, B, E
	A, C, D
	A, C, E
	A, D, E 6
• Next he lists all the additional hookups with computer B.	B, C, D
	B, C, E
	B, D, E ?
• Then he lists all the additional hookups with computer C.	C, D, E 1
• He adds to find the total number of hookups.	Total ?

1. How many additional hookups with computer B are there?

2. How many computer hookups does Avi need to make all together?

PRACTICE

Make a list to solve the problem.

3. A scientist is programming a space shuttle to visit three satellites: Aero, Bloy, and Chad. The space shuttle can visit the satellites in any order. In how many different ways can the computer program the space shuttle? What are they?

4. Name the quadrilaterals in the computer wiring diagram.

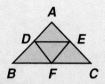

5. The computer store is having a sale. You have a choice of buying a computer with a hard-disk or a floppy-disk drive, a joystick or a mouse, and a color monitor or a black-and-white monitor. How many possible computer choices are there? What are they?

6. The ACE Corporation has 7 offices. Telephone lines are installed so that each office is connected with each of the other offices. How many connections are there all together? What are they?

Strategies and Skills Review

Solve. Use estimation, mental math, a calculator, or paper and pencil.

7. Jay has some computer games. Rose has 2 times as many games as Jay. Howard has 9 less than Rose. Howard gave $\frac{1}{3}$ of his games to Stephen. Stephen has 3 games. How many computer games does Jay have?

8. Luisa is designing a series of figures on the computer. Draw the figure that will come next in the series.

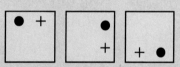

9. Computer disks are sold 10 to a package, and each package costs $8.98. How much do 15 packages cost? What do you *not* need to know to solve this problem?

10. Which is a reasonable amount for the cost of a computer?
    a. $10   **b.** $100   **c.** $1,000

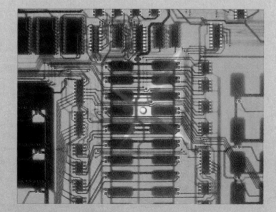

11. Susan spends $39.90 on a box of paper and a ribbon for her computer printer. The paper costs $20 more than the ribbon. How much does the ribbon cost?

12. *Write a problem* that can be solved by making a list. Solve your problem. Then ask others to solve it.

Your Table Is Ready

Visual Reasoning

A. Suppose you are setting up tables for a party. You have 12 square tables. One person may sit on each side.

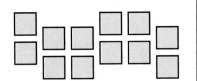

1. If you arrange the tables so that none are touching or connected, how many people can you seat?

2. Suppose you put the tables together to form a large rectangle, 2 tables wide and 6 tables long. How many people can you seat now?

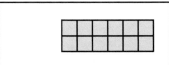

You can do this

but you can't do this

3. If the tables must be connected along at least one full side, what other rectangular arrangements are possible? How many people can you seat each time? Show your results in a table like the one below.

or this.

12-TABLE ARRANGEMENT

Description	Number of People Seated
12 separate tables	
2 tables × 6 tables	

4. What is the greatest number of people you can seat if the tables have to be connected? What is the arrangement?

5. What is the least number of people you can seat? What is the arrangement?

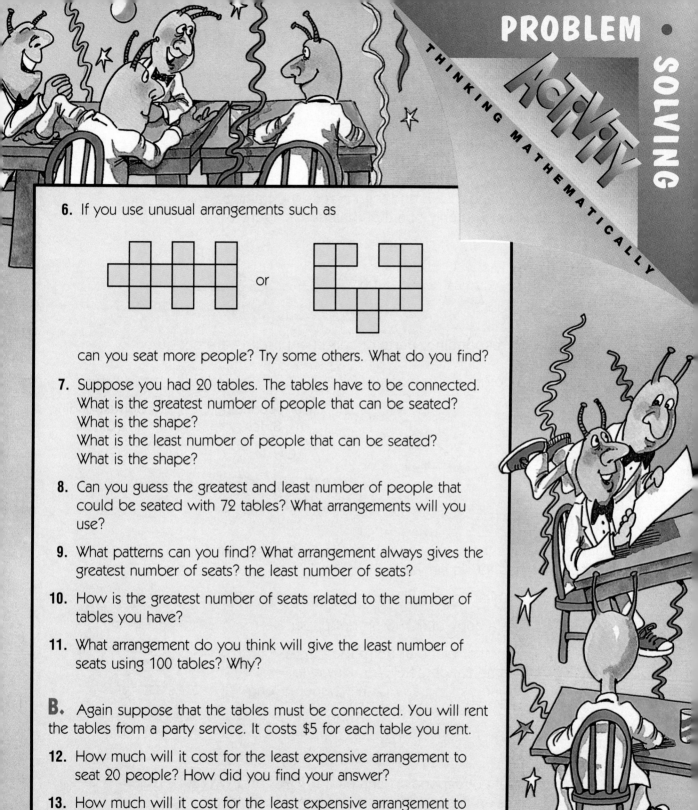

6. If you use unusual arrangements such as

or

can you seat more people? Try some others. What do you find?

7. Suppose you had 20 tables. The tables have to be connected. What is the greatest number of people that can be seated? What is the shape?
What is the least number of people that can be seated? What is the shape?

8. Can you guess the greatest and least number of people that could be seated with 72 tables? What arrangements will you use?

9. What patterns can you find? What arrangement always gives the greatest number of seats? the least number of seats?

10. How is the greatest number of seats related to the number of tables you have?

11. What arrangement do you think will give the least number of seats using 100 tables? Why?

B. Again suppose that the tables must be connected. You will rent the tables from a party service. It costs $5 for each table you rent.

12. How much will it cost for the least expensive arrangement to seat 20 people? How did you find your answer?

13. How much will it cost for the least expensive arrangement to seat 50 people? 64 people?

14. What pattern do you see? Can you use the pattern to find the least expensive arrangement for 300 people?

ACTIVITY Congruence and Similarity

Figures that are the same size and shape are **congruent figures.**

Gina wants to know which triangle is a copy of triangle *DEF*. She traces over triangle *DEF* and then places the tracing over the other triangles. The only one that matches is figure b.

   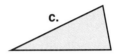

Matching, or **corresponding, parts** of congruent figures are congruent.

Triangle *GHI* is congruent to triangle *JKL.*   △*GHI* ≅ △*JKL*   ≅ "is congruent to"

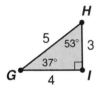   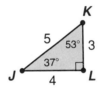

Corresponding Sides	Corresponding Angles
$\overline{GH} \cong \overline{JK}$	$\angle G \cong \angle J$
$\overline{GI} \cong \overline{JL}$	$\angle H \cong \angle K$
$\overline{HI} \cong \overline{KL}$	$\angle I \cong \angle L$

WORKING TOGETHER

Figures that have the same shape are **similar figures.** The symbol ~ stands for "is similar to."

1. Make two similar figures following these steps.

   Step 1 Make a copy of *PQRS* on dot paper.

   Step 2 On another piece of dot paper, make *WXYZ* the same shape as *PQRS*. However, make $\overline{WX}$ twice as long as $\overline{PQ}$, $\overline{WZ}$ twice as long as $\overline{PS}$, and $\overline{ZY}$ twice as long as $\overline{SR}$.

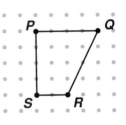

SHARING IDEAS

2. Make a list of corresponding angles for *PQRS* and *WXYZ*. Compare the angles in each pair on your list by placing each angle of one figure over the corresponding angle of the other figure.

3. What rule can you write about the corresponding angles of similar figures?

PRACTICE

Use a compass, a ruler, and a protractor to draw a congruent figure.

4.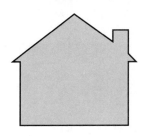

5.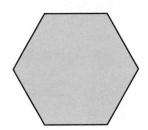

6.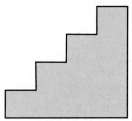

$\triangle ABC \cong \triangle DEF.$ Complete.

7. $\angle ABC \cong$ ■

8. $\angle BCA \cong$ ■

9. $\angle CAB \cong$ ■

10. $\overline{AB} \cong$ ■

11. $\overline{BC} \cong$ ■

12. $\overline{CA} \cong$ ■

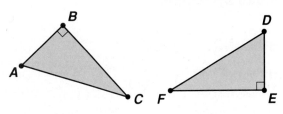

Complete. $\triangle ABC \sim \triangle DEF.$

13. $\angle ABC \cong \angle$ ■

14. $\angle ACB \cong \angle$ ■

15. $\angle FDE \cong \angle$ ■

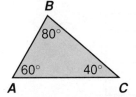

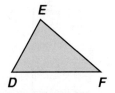

Mixed Applications

16. Look at the diagram. If $\triangle CBZ \cong \triangle XBY$, what is the distance across the stream?

17. How much will it cost to fence in the campground area if the cost of fencing is $8.99 per yard?

18. Leonard's goal is to walk a total of 20 miles by the end of the weekend. He walked 6.5 miles on Friday and 6.7 miles on Saturday. How many more miles does Leonard need to walk on Sunday to reach his goal?

19. *Write a problem* comparing two of the areas in the diagram. Solve your problem. Ask others to solve it.

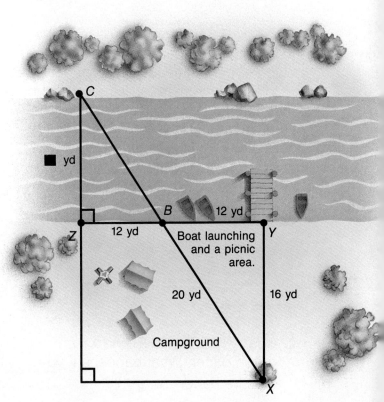

EXTRA PRACTICE, page 386

ACTIVITY Symmetry and Reflections

If you fold a sheet of paper and cut a design into the fold, the shape on one side of the fold will exactly match the shape on the other side. The cut-out shape, when unfolded, is **symmetrical** about the fold line. The fold line is the **line of symmetry**.

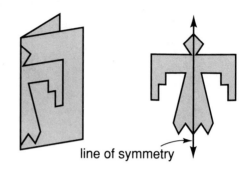

line of symmetry

WORKING TOGETHER

1. Work with a partner. Trace the following figures and cut them out. Draw all lines of symmetry. Fold along your lines of symmetry as a check. How many lines of symmetry does each figure have?

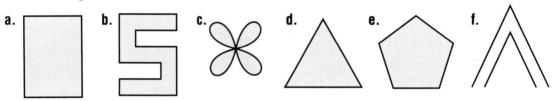

a.   b.   c.   d.   e.   f.

If you draw a figure and place a mirror behind it, perpendicular to the paper, the image in the mirror will be congruent to the figure in front of the mirror. The image in the mirror is a **reflection** of the figure about the line formed where the mirror meets the paper.

$\triangle DFE$ is a reflection of $\triangle ABC$ line XY: $\overleftrightarrow{XY}$ is the line of symmetry.

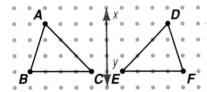

2. Copy $\triangle ABC$, $\triangle DFE$, and $\overleftrightarrow{XY}$ on graph paper. What happens if you fold the paper along $\overleftrightarrow{XY}$?

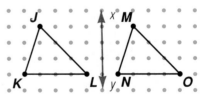

3. Is $\triangle MNO$ a reflection of $\triangle JKL$ about $\overleftrightarrow{XY}$? How can you determine this?

SHARING IDEAS

4. Describe some figures that have no lines of symmetry; exactly 2 lines of symmetry; exactly 4 lines of symmetry.

5. Which letters of the alphabet are reflections about a horizontal line of symmetry? a vertical line of symmetry? Explain your reasoning.

PRACTICE

Is the figure symmetrical about a line? Write *yes* or *no*. If *yes*, trace the figure and draw all its lines of symmetry.

6. 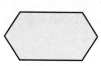 **7.** 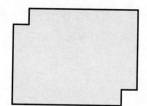 **8.**   **9.**

Copy the figure and the line on dot paper. Complete the figure so that the line is a line of symmetry.

10. 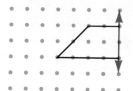 **11.** 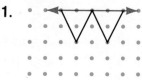 **12.**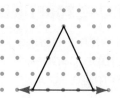

13. Draw any other lines of symmetry in the figures for Exercises 10–12.

Copy the figure and the line on graph paper. Draw the reflection of the figure about the red line. **Check students' work.**

14. 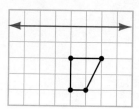 **15.** 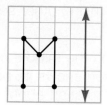 **16.**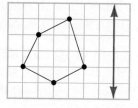

Critical Thinking

17. How many lines of symmetry does a circle have?

EXTRA PRACTICE, page 387

Activity

Translations and Rotations

A package, moving on a conveyor belt proceeds in a straight path. This motion is an example of a **slide**, or **translation**.

A windmill has a turning motion about a point. The motion of a windmill is a **turn**, or **rotation**.

Triangle A has been translated 5 units to the right. The arrow shows the direction. The length of the arrow shows the distance.

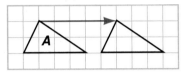

Trapezoid B has been rotated a quarter turn clockwise about vertex X.

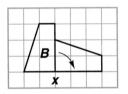

WORKING TOGETHER

Work with a partner. Make a copy of triangle A and trapezoid B on graph paper and cut them out. Use the cutout figures to learn more about translations and rotations.

1. Each of you traces triangle A in the middle of another sheet of graph paper. One person shows each step of this sequence of translations: 6 units left, then 4 units down. The other person shows each step of this sequence of translations: 4 units down, then 6 units left. How do your results compare?

2. Repeat the activity in Problem 1 using other sequences of translations.

3. Each of you traces trapezoid B in the middle of another sheet of graph paper. One person shows its position after a quarter-turn counterclockwise rotation about X. The other person shows its position after a three-quarter turn clockwise rotation about X. How do your results compare?

4. Repeat the activity in Problem 3 using other vertices of trapezoid B.

5. Explain how translations and rotations are alike; different.

6. Will different sequences of translations produce the same result? Explain.

PRACTICE

Copy the figure on graph paper. Draw it in its new position after the translation described.

7.

4 units right

8.

3 units left, then 3 units up

9.

5 units down

10.

2 units left, then 4 units down

Draw each figure on graph paper as it would appear after the rotation about Point C.

11. a quarter-turn clockwise

12. a half-turn counterclockwise

13. a three-quarter turn clockwise

Mixed Applications

14. The hour hand of this clock has rotated a quarter turn about the center of the clock face. What would be its position if it had rotated a half turn? three-quarters of a turn? two full turns?

quarter turn

15. Brian watched TV from 6:45 to 8:05. Write the number of turns of the minute hand on Brian's clock in that time as a mixed number.

16. At 12:15, is the angle formed by the hour hand and the minute hand exactly 90°? Why?

17. *Write a paragraph* about translations, rotations, and reflections.

PROBLEM SOLVING

✓UNDERSTAND
✓PLAN
✓TRY
✓CHECK
✓EXTEND

Strategies Review

You have used the following strategies to solve problems.

- Conducting an Experiment
- Drawing a Diagram
- Finding Needed Information
- Guess, Test, and Revise
- Finding a Pattern
- Making an Organized List
- Making a Table

- Solving a Multistep Problem
- Solving a Simpler Problem
- Using Estimation
- Using Number Sense
- Working Backward
- Writing and Solving an Equation

Solve. Tell which strategy you used to solve the problem.

1. Cinderella had to work a total of 40 hours on Thursday, Friday, Saturday, and Sunday. She worked 12 hours on Friday and 6 hours on Sunday. She worked the same number of hours on Thursday and Saturday. How many hours did she work on Thursday?

2. One of the three little pigs has a rectangular yard that is 21 m by 27 m. He wants to enclose the yard with the back of the house, which is 21 m wide, and with a fence on the other 3 sides. The fence will have posts that are 3 m apart. How many posts will he need?

3. A group of 41 children followed the Pied Piper. There were 7 more boys in the group than there were girls. How many boys followed the Pied Piper?

4. When Ali Baba entered the cave of the 40 thieves, he saw 5 bags of jewelry. There were twice as many bags of silver as bags of gold. There was 1 bag less of silk brocade than bags of silver. The number of bags of jewelry was $\frac{1}{3}$ the number of bags of silk brocade. How many bags of gold were there?

5. Jack is climbing the beanstalk. He climbed 32 ft in the first minute, 16 ft in the second minute, and 8 ft in the third minute. If Jack continues this pattern, how far will he climb in the sixth minute?

6. Five of the seven dwarfs always watch over Snow White. How many different groups of five dwarfs are possible?

7. Little Jack Horner sat in 6 different corners. He sat for 15 minutes in the first corner, for 30 minutes in the second corner, for 45 minutes in the third corner, and so on. For how many minutes did he sit in the 6 corners?

8. The Beast gave Beauty a trunk filled with gold. The trunk weighed 45 lb. Each gold coin weighed $\frac{3}{4}$ oz. How many coins did the trunk contain?

9. A book of fairy tales has 34 stories. Each story is 9 pages long. Nineteen of the stories have 3 picture pages each, 11 of them have 2 picture pages each, and the rest have 1 picture page each. There is 1 title page and 1 page for the table of contents. How many pages are in the book?

10. In the prince's castle is a 9-in. by 12-in. family portrait. It is mounted on a rectangular frame so that there is a 1-in. silver border on all sides. What is the area of the border?

11. Thirty-two giants are having an elimination tennis tournament. Anyone who loses one game is out of the tournament. How many matches must they schedule?

12. Which of the Seven Dwarfs does your class like best? Survey 20 students in your class to find out. Record your results. Then draw a graph. Which character does your class like best?

DECISION MAKING

Problem Solving: Choosing a Sound System

SITUATION

Mr. Lapham, a music teacher, is going to choose a sound system for his classroom. He also wants to buy some recorded music. He is interested in three types of systems.

PROBLEM

Which type of system should Mr. Lapham choose?

DATA

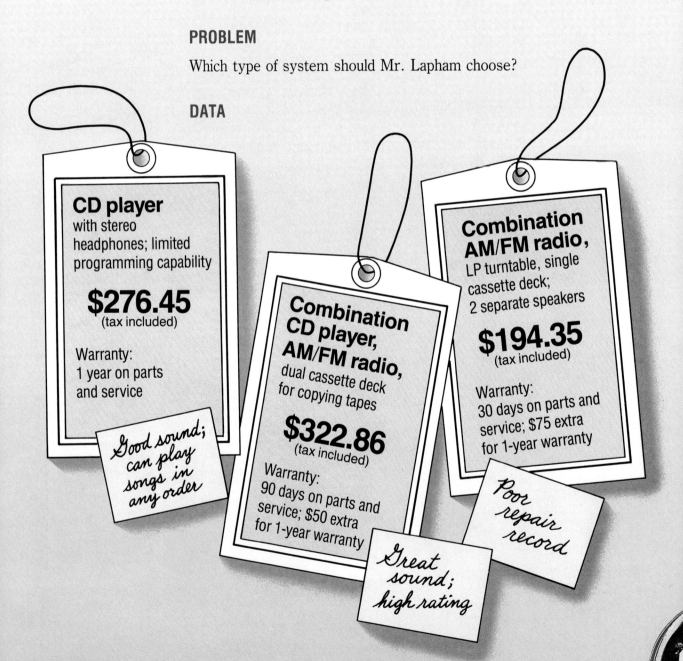

CD player
with stereo headphones; limited programming capability

$276.45
(tax included)

Warranty:
1 year on parts and service

Good sound; can play songs in any order

Combination CD player, AM/FM radio,
dual cassette deck for copying tapes

$322.86
(tax included)

Warranty:
90 days on parts and service; $50 extra for 1-year warranty

Great sound; high rating

Combination AM/FM radio,
LP turntable, single cassette deck; 2 separate speakers

$194.35
(tax included)

Warranty:
30 days on parts and service; $75 extra for 1-year warranty

Poor repair record

USING THE DATA

What is the least amount Mr. Lapham would pay
for the sound system?

1. CD player 2. CD/radio/tape 3. radio/tape/LP player

What is the greatest amount he would pay for the sound
system, including a 1-year warranty?

4. CD player 5. CD/radio/tape 6. radio/tape/LP player

MAKING DECISIONS

7. Which system should Mr. Lapham buy if he wants to spend as
little as possible?

8. Which system should Mr. Lapham buy if he wants to copy tapes
of music recitals for the students?

9. Which system should Mr. Lapham buy if quality
is his main concern?

10. *What if* Mr. Lapham expects to buy 50 recordings over
the next year? How could he save money by buying
the CD/radio/tape player over the CD player?

11. *Write a list* of the other factors Mr. Lapham
should consider.

12. Which system would you choose? Tell why.

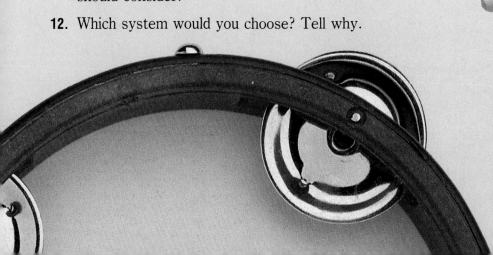

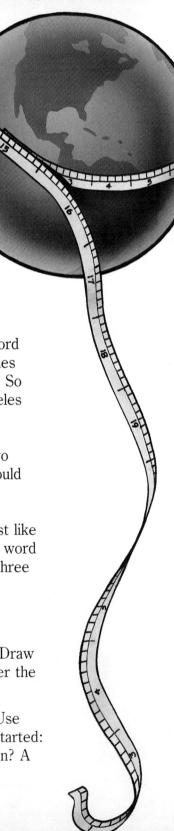

CURRICULUM CONNECTION

Math and Language

Many mathematical terms have come from other languages. *Algorithm* and *algebra* are two terms that were derived from the name of an Arabic mathematician, al-Khowarizmi (al-kwahr-IS-me), and the title of his book, *Al-jabr wa'l muqābalah.*

Other terms have roots in other languages. Knowing the meaning of these roots can help you understand the meaning of the whole word. For example, in *geometry, geo-* means "earth" and *-metry* comes from a word meaning "measure." For *triangle, tri-* means "three" and *-angle* is related to many words, such as the Old English word for fishhook.

You can use roots to help find the meaning of *isosceles.* The word part *iso-* means "same or identical." The word part *-sceles* comes from a word meaning "bent part of the body, such as the leg." So the word *isosceles* means "having two identical legs." An isosceles triangle has two identical legs.

What if you know that the word *bilingual* means "speaking two languages?" Tell what the word part *bi-* means. What word would mean "speaking three languages"?

Think: In the word *bilingual* the word part *-lingual* seems most like the word *language.* The word part *bi-* means "two." Since the word part *tri-* means "three," the word *trilingual* means "speaking three languages."

ACTIVITIES

1. Find examples of geometric shapes in your surroundings. Draw and name the shapes. Use a dictionary to help you discover the roots and word meanings of the names.

2. Make up a silly riddle whose answer is a made-up word. Use the word part *tri-, quad-,* or *pent-.* Here is one to get you started: What do you call someone who takes care of three children? A "trisitter."

Computer: Translations, Rotations, and Reflections

You can use Logo commands to explore the transformation of plane figures.

AT THE COMPUTER

Enter the procedure given below. Then enter POINTER. The computer will run the program and draw the figure shown below.

```
TO POINTER
FD 40 RT 30
FD 40 RT 120
FD 40 RT 30
FD 40 RT 90
FD 40 RT 90
END
```

To draw a translation, or a slide, of the figure 50 steps to the right of the original figure, enter PU RT 90 FD 50 LT 90 PD POINTER.

Remember to clear the screen after completing each problem below.

1. Draw the original figure and slide it 60 steps to the left. What commands did you enter?

2. Draw the original figure and slide it 55 steps to the right *and* 15 steps up. What commands did you enter?

Recall that a rotation is a turning motion about a point.
To redraw the original figure and rotate it a quarter turn (90°), enter POINTER RT 90 POINTER.

3. Draw the original figure and rotate it a half turn (180°) clockwise. What commands did you enter?

4. Draw the original figure and rotate it a quarter turn (90°) counterclockwise. What commands did you enter?

5. Draw the original figure and slide it 40 steps to the right *and* rotate it a half turn (180°) clockwise. What commands did you enter? What do you notice about the relationship between the original figure and the figure after you have completed moving it?

EXTRA PRACTICE

Geometric Figures, page 355 ....

Use a symbol to identify the figure.

1.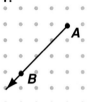

2.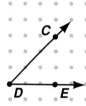

3.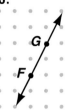

4.

5.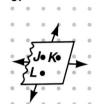

Sketch the figure on dot paper.

6. point K **7.** $\overline{CD}$ **8.** plane ABC **9.** $\overrightarrow{FG}$ **10.** $\angle HIJ$ **11.** $\overleftrightarrow{DE}$

Measuring Angles, page 357 ....

Find the measure of the angle.

1.

2.

3.

4.

5.

Use a protractor to draw the angle.

6. 50°   **7.** 90°   **8.** 75°   **9.** 120°   **10.** 135°   **11.** 170°

Perpendicular and Parallel Lines, page 359 ....

Write *intersecting, perpendicular,* or *parallel.*

1.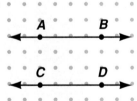

2.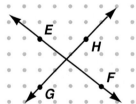

3.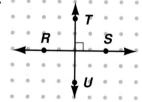

Sketch the figures on dot paper.

4. $\overleftrightarrow{AB}$ intersects $\overleftrightarrow{CD}$ **5.** $\overleftrightarrow{EF} \parallel \overleftrightarrow{GH}$ **6.** right angle RST **7.** $\overleftrightarrow{MN} \perp \overrightarrow{OP}$

EXTRA PRACTICE

EXTRA PRACTICE

Compass Constructions, page 361

Use a compass and a straightedge.

1. Draw line segment *AB*. Construct a line segment congruent to line segment *AB*.

2. Draw obtuse angle *DEF*. Construct angle *GHI* congruent to *DEF*.

3. Bisect angle *DEF* which you drew in Question 2.

Triangles, page 363

Give two names for each triangle.

1.
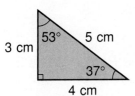
3 cm 53° 5 cm
37°
4 cm

2.
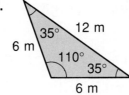
35° 12 m
6 m
110°
35°
6 m

3.
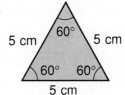
5 cm 60° 5 cm
60° 60°
5 cm

4.
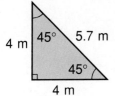
4 m 45° 5.7 m
45°
4 m

5.
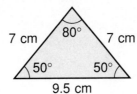
7 cm 80° 7 cm
50° 50°
9.5 cm

6.
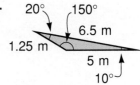
20° 150°
6.5 m
1.25 m
5 m
10°

Quadrilaterals, page 365

Give as many quadrilateral names as you can for the figure.

1.
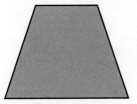

2.
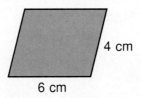
4 cm
6 cm

3.
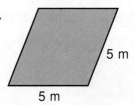
5 m
5 m

4.
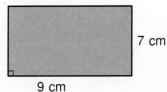
7 cm
9 cm

5.
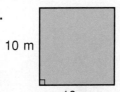
10 m
10 m

EXTRA PRACTICE

Other Polygons, page 367

Name the polygon.

1.

2.

3.

4.

5. Into how many triangles can each polygon in Questions 1–4 be divided? What is the sum of the measures of the angles of each of these polygons?

Problem Solving Strategy: Making an Organized List, page 369

Make a list to solve the problem.

1. How many quadrilaterals are there in the diagram below?

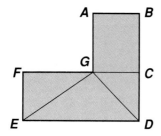

2. In a dart game Paula throws 3 darts. Each dart hits the target. What are Paula's possible scores?

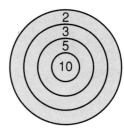

Congruence and Similarity, page 373

Use a compass, a ruler, and a protractor to draw a congruent figure.

1.

2.

Are the figures similar? Write *yes* or *no*.

3.

Complete. △JKL ≅ △MNO

4. ∠JKL ≅ ■

5. ∠KLJ ≅ ■

6. ∠LJK ≅ ■

7. $\overline{JK}$ ≅ ■

8. $\overline{KL}$ ≅ ■

9. $\overline{JL}$ ≅ ■

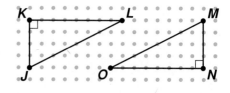

EXTRA PRACTICE

Symmetry and Reflections, page 375

Copy the figure and the line on dot paper. Complete the figure so that the line is a line of symmetry.

1.

2.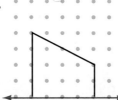

3.

Copy the figure and the line on graph paper. Draw the reflection of the figure about the red line.

4.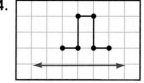

5.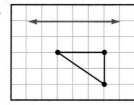

6.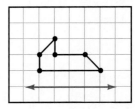

Translations and Rotations, page 377

Copy the figure on graph paper. Draw the translation described.

1.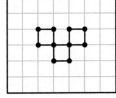

5 units left

2.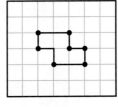

4 units right, then 4 units down

3.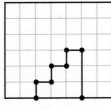

3 units up

4.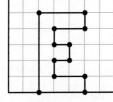

6 units up, then 2 units right

Problem Solving: Strategies Review, page 379

Solve. Tell which strategy you used to solve the problem.

1. Mel typed a total of 42 pages on Monday, Tuesday, Wednesday, and Thursday. He typed 10 pages on Monday and twice as many on Tuesday. He typed the same number of pages on Wednesday and Thursday. How many pages did he type on Thursday?

2. The Greystone Restaurant served 8 dinners on opening day. The second day 15 dinners were served. On the third day 22 were served. If this pattern continues, how many dinners will the Greystone serve on the sixth day after its opening?

Practice PLUS

KEY SKILL: Geometric Figures (Use after page 355.)

Level A

Use a symbol to identify the figure.

1.
2.
3.
4.
5.

Sketch the figure on dot paper.

6. $\overleftrightarrow{CD}$ **7.** $\overline{AB}$ **8.** $\overrightarrow{GH}$ **9.** plane *DEF* **10.** ∠*LMN*

Level B

Use a symbol to identify the figure.

11.
12.
13.
14.
15.

Sketch and label the figure on dot paper.

16. $\overrightarrow{AB}$ **17.** ray *CD* **18.** angle *E* **19.** $\overline{BC}$ **20.** plane *DEF*

Level C

Use as many symbols as you can to identify the figure.

21.
22.
23.
24.
25.

Sketch, label, and write a symbol to identify the figure on dot paper.

26. a line **27.** a segment **28.** an angle **29.** a plane **30.** a ray

Practice PLUS

KEY SKILL: Other Polygons (Use after page 367.)

Level A

Draw these figures. Divide into triangles. How many triangles are there?

1. quadrilateral　　**2.** pentagon　　**3.** octagon　　**4.** decagon

5. What is the sum of the measures of the angles in each figure above?

6. A garden has 8 equal sides. What shape is the garden?

Level B

Copy and complete the table.

Polygon	Quadrilateral	Pentagon	Hexagon	Heptagon	Octagon	Decagon
Number of sides	**7.** ■	**8.** ■	**9.** ■	**10.** ■	**11.** ■	**12.** ■
Sum of measures of angles	**13.** ■	**14.** ■	**15.** ■	**16.** ■	**17.** ■	**18.** ■

19. A garden is in the shape of an octagon. What is the measure of the angle at each of the corners?

Level C

Make a table to compare the number of sides, the number of diagonals, the number of triangles, and the sum of the measures of the angles of these figures.

20. quadrilateral　　**21.** pentagon　　**22.** hexagon

23. heptagon　　**24.** octagon　　**25.** decagon

Look for patterns in your table. Use the patterns you discovered to make a table like the one you made above for polygons with these numbers of sides:

26. 12 sides　　**27.** 15 sides　　**28.** 16 sides　　**29.** 18 sides　　**30.** 20 sides

31. A garden is in the shape of a decagon with a stone wall around the outside. Paths connect the vertices. How many paths are there?

LANGUAGE AND MATHEMATICS

Match each definition with the correct term in the box.

1. an endless flat surface

2. two rays with a common endpoint

3. lines that meet at right angles

4. a closed figure with three or more sides

5. lines in the same plane that never meet

6. two figures that are exactly the same size and shape

VOCABULARY
perpendicular lines
congruent
angle
plane
parallel lines
polygon

CONCEPTS AND SKILLS

Identify the figure.

7.    8.   9. 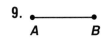   10.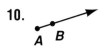

Use the diagram for Questions 11–15.

11. Name 2 right angles.

12. Name 3 obtuse angles.

13. Name 4 acute angles.

14. Name 1 straight angle.

15. Give the measurements of ∠QPU.

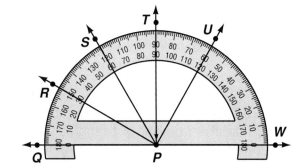

Use a compass and straightedge.

16. Construct an angle congruent to ∠BD.

17. Give the measurement of ∠BDF.

18. Construct the bisector of ∠BDF.

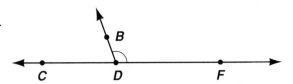

Choose the figure that matches the name.

19. rhombus

20. obtuse triangle

   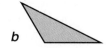

21. Are the figures congruent or similar?

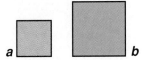

a   *b*

22. Copy this figure and rotate it a half turn about point *A*.

Critical Thinking

23. How many lines of symmetry do the figures have?

   a. equilateral triangle   **b.** scalene triangle   **c.** isosceles trapezoid

Mixed Applications

24. Bea has a mix-and-match outfit of a skirt, pants, and 2 tops. How many outfits can she make?

25. Tom can go skating or bowling. He can eat pizza, soup, salad, or a burger. How many choices of pairs could he make?

PERFORMANCE ASSESSMENT

Work with your group to solve this problem.

Choose a picture of a building from a book or a magazine. Look for a building that has geometric designs, then trace the picture onto a sheet of graph paper. Find as many examples of congruence, similarity, and symmetry in the designs of the building as you can. Copy one of the geometric designs on another sheet of graph paper and rotate it clockwise one-half turn.

1. ***Think about:***
   ■ what the basic geometric figures in the design of the building are
   ■ the characteristics of these geometric figures
   ■ which geometric figure to copy and rotate

2. Write a statement about the design elements that you like in the building and a statement about the design elements you do not like. Include a description of how you would change the designs you do not like.

CUMULATIVE REVIEW

Choose the letter of the correct answer.

1. Which is equivalent to 0.25?
   a. $\frac{1}{25}$ c. $\frac{1}{4}$
   b. $\frac{2}{5}$ d. not given

2. Compare: $1\frac{2}{5}$ ● $\frac{7}{4}$
   a. > c. =
   b. < d. not given

3. Estimate by rounding: $2\frac{4}{5} + 1\frac{1}{3}$
   a. 2 c. 4
   b. 3 d. not given

4. Express in simplest form:
   $2\frac{4}{5} + 3\frac{7}{10}$
   a. $7\frac{1}{2}$ c. $6\frac{15}{10}$
   b. $6\frac{1}{2}$ d. not given

5. $3\frac{2}{7} - 1\frac{5}{7}$
   a. $2\frac{4}{7}$ c. $2\frac{3}{7}$
   b. $1\frac{4}{7}$ d. not given

6. $\frac{7}{8} \times \frac{5}{16}$
   a. $2\frac{4}{5}$ c. $\frac{70}{16}$
   b. $\frac{35}{128}$ d. not given

7. $6 \div \frac{3}{10}$
   a. $\frac{1}{20}$ c. 20
   b. 18 d. not given

8. 2 yd 1 ft 6 in. = ■ in.
   a. 42 c. 90
   b. 54 d. not given

9. Find the area of a triangle with
   $b = 17$ m and $h = 20$ m.
   a. 170 m² c. 340 m²
   b. 18.5 m² d. not given

10. What is the figure?

    ●━━━━━━━━━●

    a. ray c. line
    b. line segment d. not given

11. Identify the angle.

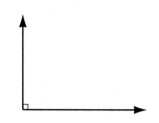

   a. straight c. acute
   b. obtuse d. not given

12. Identify the triangle.

   a. isosceles c. equilateral
   b. scalene d. not given

13. Which figure is symmetrical?

   a.  b.

   c.   d. not given

14. Which diagram shows a
    translation?

   a. 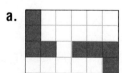 b.

   c. 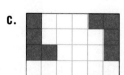 d. not given

BISECTING A LINE SEGMENT

A **bisector** divides a line segment into two congruent line segments. You can construct a bisector using only a straightedge and a compass. Follow these steps.

Step 1 Use your straightedge to draw line segment $\overline{ST}$. Open your compass to greater than half the length of $\overline{ST}$.

Step 2 Place the point of your compass on S and draw an arc.

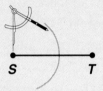

Step 3 Keep your compass opening the same and place the point of your compass on T. Draw an arc that intersects the first arc you drew.

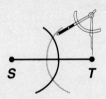

Step 4 Label the points where your arcs intersect P and Q. Use a straightedge to draw $\overline{PQ}$. Use R to label the point where $\overline{PQ}$ intersects $\overline{ST}$.

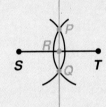

1. Fold your paper along $\overline{PQ}$. What do you notice about $\overline{SR}$ and $\overline{RT}$?

2. Use a protractor to measure the angles formed by the intersection of $\overline{ST}$ and $\overline{PQ}$. What do your notice?

Trace each line segment on your paper. Then construct its bisector. Check your constructions by folding each along its bisector.

3.

4.

5.

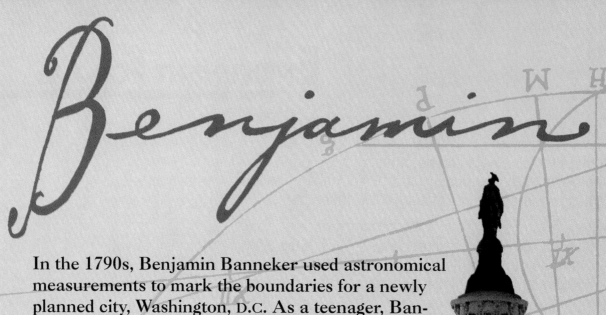

Benjamin

In the 1790s, Benjamin Banneker used astronomical measurements to mark the boundaries for a newly planned city, Washington, D.C. As a teenager, Banneker excelled in math and science. He learned how to use an astronomical clock to pinpoint positions of stars at exact times. By following stars, locations on the ground can be mapped to make straight boundary lines.

Appointed by George Washington, Banneker was the first African American called upon to help with a project of this kind. He worked as a surveyor on a six-person team that mapped boundaries and helped create the plans for Washington, D.C. In addition, Banneker helped to choose sites for several buildings including the U.S. Capitol, the U.S. Treasury, and the White House.

Banneker

During the planning of the city, Pierre L'Enfant, the chairman of the engineering team, suddenly resigned and returned to France, taking all of his plans and drawings with him. It is believed that Benjamin Banneker reproduced the plans completely from memory.

Benjamin Banneker

Black Heritage USA 15c

UNITED STATES

Washington D.C.

1. What kinds of things must be considered when planning a city?

2. Why is mathematics necessary in the planning, surveying, and mapping of a new city?

Ratios and Rates

A. You can use a **ratio** to compare two quantities. The ratio of blue jays to robins is 2 to 3, which can also be written as 2:3 or $\frac{2}{3}$. You read each of these ratios as "2 to 3."

   1. What is the ratio of red-winged blackbirds to all the birds?

B. You can also use a ratio to compare two different quantities. This kind of comparison is called a **rate**.

Here are some examples of rates:

$\frac{30 \text{ miles}}{1 \text{ hour}}$ or 30 miles/hour or 30 miles per hour

$\frac{10 \text{ miles}}{1 \text{ gallon}}$ or 10 miles/gallon or 10 miles per gallon

$\frac{\$5.00}{1 \text{ pound}}$ or $5.00/pound or $5.00 per pound

TRY OUT   Write the letter of the correct answer.

   2. Miriam has 13 balloons. Of these, 6 are red, and 7 are green. What is the ratio of green balloons to all the balloons?

   a. 13:6   **b.** 13 to 7   **c.** 7 to 13   **d.** $\frac{6}{7}$

   3. Sasha read 4 pages in 1 hour. The rate is:

   a. 4 to 1.   **b.** $\frac{4 \text{ pages}}{1 \text{ hour}}$.   **c.** 1 hour: 4 pages.   **d.** $\frac{1 \text{ page}}{2 \text{ hours}}$.

PRACTICE

Write the ratio in three different ways.

4. blue circles to yellow circles

5. yellow circles to blue circles

6. squares to all figures

7. all figures to red squares

8. yellow circles to blue squares

9. all circles to squares

10. stars to squares

11. blue circles to stars

12. all squares to blue circles

13. stars to red squares

Write the rate in two different ways.

14. 4 people per car

15. 8 apples in 1 pie

16. 3 miles/hour

17. 10 books per person

18. $\frac{6 \text{ lemons}}{\$2.00}$

19. $\frac{18 \text{ cassette tapes}}{3 \text{ boxes}}$

20. 4 stamps/$1.00

21. 12 pages in 60 minutes

Mixed Applications

22. On his bird-watching trip, Peter saw 32 sparrows, 16 chickadees, and 2 gold-finches. What was the ratio of sparrows to all the birds?

23. The bird-watching club has 14 members who share 9 pairs of binoculars. What is the rate of binoculars to club members?

24. The zoo has a large population of birds. Last week 35 parakeets were hatched. Most of the new parakeets are green, but $\frac{2}{7}$ are blue. What is the number of blue parakeets?

25. Yesterday morning there were 25 unhatched ostrich eggs. By the afternoon 0.8 of the eggs had hatched. How many eggs still hadn't hatched?

Mixed Review

Find the answer. Which method did you use?

| MENTAL MATH |
| CALCULATOR |
| PAPER/PENCIL |

26. $\begin{array}{r} 0.538 \\ \times\, 0.001 \end{array}$

27. $1{,}000\overline{)3.9}$

28. 300×18.05

29. $0.01\overline{)56}$

30. $\frac{4}{25} + \frac{11}{25}$

31. $\frac{13}{10} - \frac{4}{5}$

32. $\frac{2}{9} \times \frac{3}{8}$

33. $14 \div \frac{3}{4}$

ACTIVITY Equal Ratios

Milagros and Kimi want to know the ratio of students whose parents were born in other countries compared to those born in the United States. In Milagros' class, 12 students have parents born in the United States, and 10 students have parents born in other countries. In Kimi's class, 18 students' parents were born in the United States and 15 students' parents were born in other countries. Do Milagros' and Kimi's classes have **equal ratios**?

WORKING TOGETHER

You and a partner can use two-color counters to model the ratios. Use the red side to represent other countries.

1. Use your model for Milagros' ratio. What is the simplest form of this ratio?

2. Use your counters to find out whether the ratio you found in Problem 1 is the same for Kimi's ratio.

3. Determine whether $\frac{6}{9}$ and $\frac{20}{36}$ are equal ratios by using counters. Explain.

You can use equivalent fractions to find equal ratios.

$$\frac{8 \times 3}{12 \times 3} = \frac{24}{26} \qquad \frac{8 \div 4}{12 \div 4} = \frac{2}{3} \qquad \frac{2}{3}, \frac{8}{12}, \text{ and } \frac{24}{36} \text{ are equal ratios.}$$

4. Show how you would use equivalent fractions to check if $\frac{5}{18}$ and $\frac{15}{36}$ are equal ratios.

Another way to check if ratios are equal is to use **cross products**.

$$\frac{8}{12} \overset{?}{=} \frac{28}{42} \qquad \qquad 8 \times 42 \overset{?}{=} 12 \times 28$$
$$336 = 336$$

Since the cross products are equal, the ratios are equal.

5. What are some other equal ratios that you can find for Milagros' and Kimi's ratios? Check your answers.

SHARING IDEAS

6. Create a class chart listing Milagros' and Kimi's ratios as well as all the equal ratios that were found. Describe any similarities or differences you can find among the ratios in your chart.

7. What other equal ratios can be made from the data Milagros and Kimi collected?

PRACTICE

Are the ratios equal? Write *yes* or *no*.

8. $\frac{5}{8} \overset{?}{=} \frac{10}{18}$ **9.** $\frac{5}{6} \overset{?}{=} \frac{10}{12}$ **10.** $\frac{9}{15} \overset{?}{=} \frac{3}{5}$ **11.** $\frac{35}{21} \overset{?}{=} \frac{5}{4}$ **12.** $\frac{12}{8} \overset{?}{=} \frac{3}{4}$

13. $\frac{4}{9} \overset{?}{=} \frac{14}{19}$ **14.** $\frac{3}{21} \overset{?}{=} \frac{2}{14}$ **15.** $\frac{100}{175} \overset{?}{=} \frac{20}{35}$ **16.** $\frac{7}{16} \overset{?}{=} \frac{3}{7}$ **17.** $\frac{18}{48} \overset{?}{=} \frac{3}{8}$

Find an equal ratio by multiplying and by dividing.

18. $\frac{5}{15}$ **19.** $\frac{7}{14}$ **20.** $\frac{3}{9}$ **21.** $\frac{10}{22}$ **22.** $\frac{20}{50}$

23. $\frac{6}{16}$ **24.** $\frac{9}{21}$ **25.** $\frac{39}{52}$ **26.** $\frac{18}{24}$ **27.** $\frac{90}{150}$

Critical Thinking

28. Use several methods to determine if the ratios are equal. For each, which method did you prefer? Why?

     a. $\frac{12}{40} \overset{?}{=} \frac{15}{50}$ **b.** $\frac{15}{35} \overset{?}{=} \frac{12}{26}$

29. Do equal ratios when expressed as fractions have to have both numerators and denominators that are multiples of each other? Explain.

Mixed Applications

30. Milagros wants to buy seven banners marked "¡Feliz Cumpleaños!" for a surprise birthday party. If each banner costs $1.03, how much change will she get back from $20.00?

31. Mufaro and his cousins have 28 kofis, a traditional African headdress. Three of them are gold, nine are green, four are blue, and twelve are red. Find as many pairs of equal ratios as you can.

Algebra: Proportions

A. Joan and David made a model of their treehouse. The width and the length of one wall of the actual treehouse are 60 in. and 108 in. The corresponding length of the model is 18 in. What is the corresponding width of the model?

You can use a proportion to solve problems.

A **proportion** is a statement that two ratios are equal.

To find the model's width, you can solve the proportion by using cross products:

$$\text{treehouse width} \longrightarrow \frac{60}{108} = \frac{n}{18} \longleftarrow \text{model width}$$
$$\text{treehouse length} \longrightarrow \qquad\quad \longleftarrow \text{model length}$$

$$60 \times 18 = 108 \times n$$
$$1{,}080 = 108 \times n \qquad \textit{Think: What number times}$$
$$n = 10 \qquad\qquad \text{108 is equal to 1,080?}$$

The width of the model of the treehouse is 10 in.

B. You can also solve some proportions using equivalent fractions.

If one cup of corn meal makes 12 muffins, how many muffins does 4 cups make?

Write: $\frac{1}{12} = \frac{4}{n}$ ***Think:*** $\overset{\times 4}{\overbrace{\frac{1}{12} = \frac{4}{48}}}_{\times 4}$

You need 4 cups of corn meal for 48 muffins.

1. Solve the proportion $\frac{9}{12} = \frac{n}{4}$. Which method did you use?

2. Which method would you use to solve the proportion $\frac{8}{15} = \frac{n}{21}$? Why?

TRY OUT Solve the proportion.

3. $\frac{1}{4} = \frac{n}{16}$ **4.** $\frac{2}{3} = \frac{n}{12}$ **5.** $\frac{3}{7} = \frac{15}{n}$ **6.** $\frac{4}{5} = \frac{7.2}{n}$ **7.** $\frac{10}{24} = \frac{n}{36}$

PRACTICE

Solve the proportion.

8. $\frac{1}{6} = \frac{n}{36}$ **9.** $\frac{3}{2} = \frac{n}{4}$ **10.** $\frac{5}{11} = \frac{n}{44}$ **11.** $\frac{1}{7} = \frac{5}{n}$ **12.** $\frac{4}{18} = \frac{2}{n}$

13. $\frac{n}{3} = \frac{21}{9}$ **14.** $\frac{10}{n} = \frac{5}{6}$ **15.** $\frac{2}{n} = \frac{3}{9}$ **16.** $\frac{n}{5} = \frac{24}{30}$ **17.** $\frac{9}{3} = \frac{n}{7}$

18. $\frac{18}{3} = \frac{12}{n}$ **19.** $\frac{n}{54} = \frac{3}{2}$ **20.** $\frac{48}{n} = \frac{3}{2}$ **21.** $\frac{55}{11} = \frac{n}{2}$ **22.** $\frac{7}{n} = \frac{42}{45}$

23. $\frac{14}{n} = \frac{49}{7}$ **24.** $\frac{12}{8} = \frac{21}{n}$ **25.** $\frac{22}{9} = \frac{198}{n}$ **26.** $\frac{24}{75} = \frac{6}{n}$ **27.** $\frac{n}{66} = \frac{7}{3}$

28. $\frac{2.1}{11} = \frac{n}{44}$ **29.** $\frac{4}{1.2} = \frac{3}{n}$ **30.** $\frac{6.2}{3.1} = \frac{n}{3}$ **31.** $\frac{n}{2.8} = \frac{0.6}{0.7}$ **32.** $\frac{0.3}{0.5} = \frac{n}{2.5}$

33. 2 bags of popcorn for 10 people = 4 bags for n people

34. 5 yd of fabric for $10.00 = 1 yd for n

35. 5 gal for 125 mi = n gal for 375 mi

36. 25 copies in 5 minutes = 625 in n minutes

37. 4 packages for $8.20 = n packages for $4.10

38. 30 mi in 20 minutes = n mi in 30 minutes

39. 32 chairs for 8 tables = n chairs for 1 table

Mixed Applications

40. One wall of Joan and David's model treehouse is 14 in. wide and 18 in. long. The length of the actual wall of the treehouse is 108 in. What is the width of the actual wall of the treehouse?

41. Joan put a second floor in the treehouse. It is $\frac{2}{3}$ of the way up from the floor of the treehouse. The treehouse is 108 in. high. How far above the first floor is the second?

42. Joan and David painted their treehouse with 2 cans of white paint and 5 cans of green paint. Their brother painted the garage with 3 cans of white paint and 8 cans of green paint. Did Joan and David and their brother use equal ratios of paint?

43. The garage also needed a new roof. Joan and David's mother priced shingles. A bundle of roofing shingles cost $5.60 for 25 ft². The area of the garage roof is 72 ft². How much will it cost to cover the garage roof with new shingles?

EXTRA PRACTICE, page 424; **PRACTICE PLUS,** page 428   Ratio, Proportion, and Percent

SCALE: 1"=3'

ACTIVITY

Algebra: Scale Drawings

Scale drawings can be used to represent objects. The drawings and actual objects are similar. They have the same shape but not the same size. The ratio of a length in the drawing to an actual length gives the **scale**.

WORKING TOGETHER

Work with a partner. Use two sheets of paper and a tape measure.

Step 1 One partner measures the top of a student desk to the nearest inch and writes the measurements.

Step 2 The second partner makes a sketch of the same desktop without measuring its dimensions and writes the dimensions of the drawing in inches.

1. Is the second student's drawing a scale drawing? Why or why not?

You can use a proportion to find actual lengths from scale drawings.

The scale drawing above shows the length of a table as 2 in., so

$$\frac{\text{length in drawing (in.)} \rightarrow 1}{\text{actual length (ft)} \rightarrow 3} = \frac{2}{n}$$

$$\frac{1}{3} = \frac{2}{n}$$
$$1 \times n = 2 \times 3$$
$$n = 6$$

The actual length of the table is 6 ft.

You can also find lengths on a scale drawing if you know the size of the actual object.

If the width of the table is 4 ft, then

$$\frac{\text{length in drawing (in.)} \rightarrow 1}{\text{actual length (ft)} \rightarrow 3} = \frac{n}{4}$$

$$\frac{1}{3} = \frac{n}{4}$$
$$3 \times n = 1 \times 4$$
$$3 \times n = 4$$
$$n = \frac{4}{3} = 1\frac{1}{3}$$

The width of the table in the drawing is $1\frac{1}{3}$ in.

2. Use the measurements from Step 1 to make a scale drawing of your desk using the scale 1 in. : 4 ft.

3. How can different scale drawings be created for the same object?

4. Explain how it is possible to have the same scale drawing for different objects?

5. Can scale drawings be larger than the objects that they represent? Why?

PRACTICE

Gary has a map of Denver, Colorado, and several nearby cities. The map scale is 0.5 cm : 20 km.

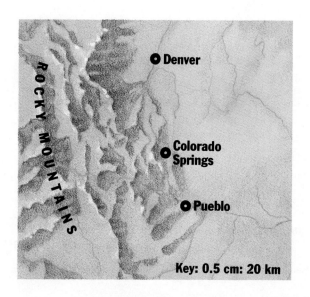

Key: 0.5 cm: 20 km

Use the given map to find the actual distance between two cities.

6. Colorado Springs and Pueblo

7. Denver and Colorado Springs

Use the given actual distance to find the map distance between the two cities.

8. Fort Morgan and Burlington— 160 km

9. Grand Junction and Durango— 205 km

Critical Thinking

10. When are scale drawings used? Why?

Mixed Applications

Solve. Which method did you use?

11. A classroom has a bookcase that is 7 ft long. How much longer or shorter is it than the one in the scale drawing on page 402?

12. The school would like to replace the floor of the classroom. One company charges $9.95 per ft². The second charges $3,000. Which company offers the lower price?

Algebra: Similar Figures

Similar figures are the same shape but not necessarily the same size. The ratios of their corresponding sides are equal.

$$\frac{\text{side } a}{\text{side } d} = \frac{3}{6}$$

$$\frac{\text{side } b}{\text{side } e} = \frac{4}{8}$$

$$\frac{\text{side } c}{\text{side } f} = \frac{5}{10}$$

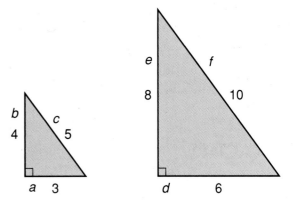

1. What other proportions can you write for these similar triangles?

You can use proportions to find the missing sides of similar figures.

What is the height of the tree?

Think: Use similar triangles formed by the sun's rays and by the lengths of the shadows to find the height of the tree.

$$\frac{\text{boy's shadow} \rightarrow}{\text{tree's shadow} \rightarrow} \quad \frac{4}{12} = \frac{2}{n} \quad \frac{\leftarrow \text{boy's height}}{\leftarrow \text{tree's height}}$$

Use cross products to solve the proportion.

$$\frac{4}{12} = \frac{2}{n}$$

$$4 \times n = 12 \times 2$$
$$4 \times n = 24$$
$$n = 6$$

The height of the tree is 6 m.

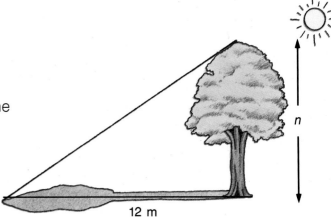

12 m

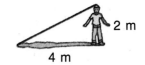

2 m

4 m

TRY OUT Write the letter of the correct answer.
Find the missing length of the similar triangles.

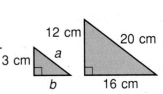

12 cm   20 cm

3 cm   *a*

b   16 cm

2. *b*   **a.** 2 cm   **b.** 4 cm   **c.** 6 cm   **d.** 8 cm

3. *a*   **a.** 5 cm   **b.** 6 cm   **c.** 7 cm   **d.** 8 cm

PRACTICE

Find the missing side for the pair of similar figures.

4.

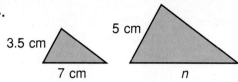

3.5 cm   5 cm   7 cm n

5.

n 9 m   2 m   3 m

6.

2 m   3 m n 6 m

7.

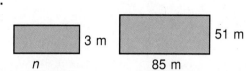

3 m n 51 m   85 m

8.

n 12.5 m   0.5 m   1 m

9.

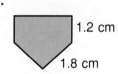

1.2 cm   1.8 cm   1.5 cm n

10.

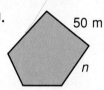

50 m n 5 m   7.5 m

11.

2.3 m   6.9 m   4.1 m n

Mixed Applications

12. A flagpole that is 3 m high casts a shadow 5.5 m long. At the same time of day, a toolshed casts a shadow 22 m long. How high is the toolshed?

13. A window washer starts cleaning windows 3.8 m below the roof of a building and lowers his platform 3.8 m each time he moves to a lower floor. The roof is 95 m above the ground. How many floors does the building have?

14. *Write a problem* involving the indirect measurement of a height by using similar triangles. Solve your problem. Ask others to solve it.

VISUAL REASONING

Draw a line segment that will divide the figure into two similar figures.

PROBLEM SOLVING

Strategy: Using Algebraic Equations

A. The Golden Goose Amusement Park has a special rate of $22.50 for 5 tickets. Nick, Alice, Linette, Rory, and Jan plan to visit the park together. Each one will pay a part of the special rate of $22.50 and the amount of each ticket will be the same. What will each ticket cost?

Alice plans how to solve this problem.
She decides to write an equation: **$22.50 ÷ 5 = n**

1. What does n represent?

2. How much money will each ticket cost?

B. The 5 friends eat lunch at the park. They each order a hamburger for $2.50 and a cup of milk for $1.25. What was the total cost of the lunch?

3. Which equation could be used to solve the problem?
   a. ($2.50 + $1.25) ÷ 5 = n
   b. 5 × ($2.50 + $1.25) = n
   c. 5 × ($2.50 − $1.25) = n

4. What is the total cost of lunch for the friends?

PRACTICE

Write and solve an equation for the problem.

5. Linette rides the Wild Goose Coaster 5 times. She must pay $1.35 for each ride. How much do the rides cost Linette?

6. All 5 friends ride the Merry-Go-Round twice. The total cost is $9.50. How much does each ride cost?

7. Nick tries the Flying Saucer for $2.25 and the Wild Goose Coaster for $1.35. After paying for the rides, he has $6.40 left. How much did Nick start with?

8. Jan rides the Bumper Cars. The ride costs $1.50. How much change does he receive from $5?

Strategies and Skills Review

Solve. Use estimation, mental math, a calculator, or paper and pencil.

9. There were 958 people at the park on Friday and 1,095 at the park on Saturday. If tickets cost $5 each, how much were the ticket sales for the two days?

10. The park photographer took 576 pictures on Friday. Each roll of film had 36 pictures. How many rolls of film did the photographer use?

11. Linette, Rory, Nick, and Jan visited the Baseball Toss booth. Jan knocked down 2 times as many bottles as Rory did. Rory hit 6 more bottles than Nick did. Nick knocked down 6 bottles. Linette hit 2 bottles less than Jan. How many bottles did each one knock down?

12. Rory spent a total of 135 minutes on his favorite rides at the amusement park. A ride on the Twister lasts 3 minutes and one on the Water Whirl lasts 4.5 minutes. How many times did he go on each ride?

13. On Monday 180 people rode the Wild Goose Coaster, on Tuesday 220 people rode the coaster, and on Wednesday 214 people rode it. Did at least 600 people ride the Wild Goose Coaster in the three days?

14. **Write a problem** that can be solved by writing a number sentence. Then solve your problem. Ask others to solve it.

Investigating Patterns

A. You can play Coin Hop with any equal number of nickels and pennies. To play 2-Coin Hop, use 2 of each. Draw a 5-square board like this:

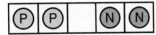

Place 2 pennies on the left and 2 nickels on the right. The object of the game is to switch the order of the coins.

Rules for play:

- Coins may move one square into an open square or jump over *one* coin. They cannot jump over more than one coin.

- Pennies can move only to the right.

- Nickels can move only to the left.

- The first move is always with a penny.

For example, suppose this is your first move:

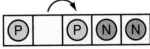

Then there are two possible second moves:

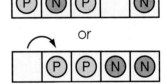

1. Can you find a way to switch the position of the coins? How many moves did it take? What strategy did you use to find your answer?

B. To play Coin Hop with another number of coins, simply draw a larger board. You always need one square for each coin and one empty square in the middle.

To play 3-Coin Hop, begin like this:

| P | P | P | | N | N | N |

2. Can you find the solution to 3-Coin Hop? How many moves did it take?

3. You can find a pattern to help you solve other versions of Coin Hop. Complete the table below. The first row shows information for the very simple game of 1-Coin Hop. Fill in the information you learned playing the 2- and 3-Coin Hop. Can you find the pattern and predict how to solve 4- and 5-Coin Hop?

Number of Each Coin	Solution	Number of Moves
1	p-n-p	3
2		
3		
4		
5		

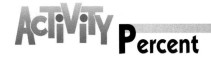

ACTIVITY Percent

How could you express the amount of color in the design below?

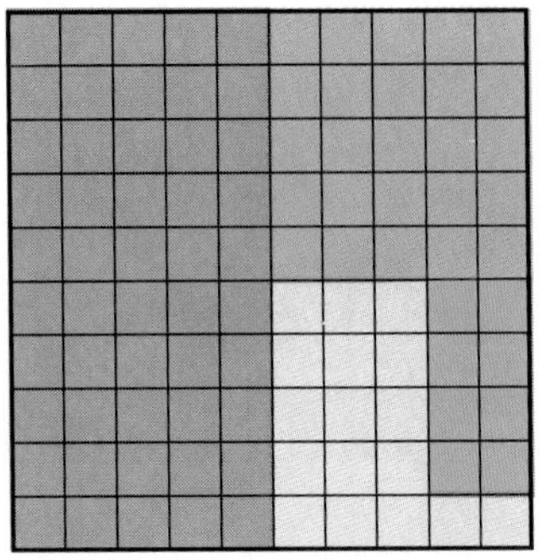

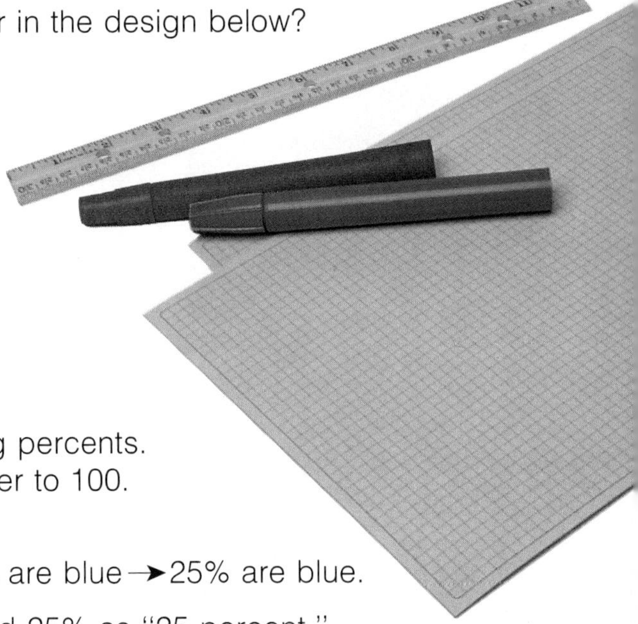

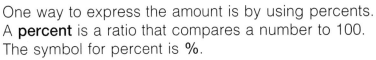

One way to express the amount is by using percents.
A **percent** is a ratio that compares a number to 100.
The symbol for percent is **%**.

In the design 25 out of 100, or $\frac{25}{100}$, squares are blue → 25% are blue.

Since 25% means "25 out of 100," you read 25% as "25 percent."

1. Express the amount of each color using a percent.
a. red **b.** green **c.** yellow

2. Rename each percent in Problem 1 as a ratio of a number compared to 100. Then write each percent as a fraction with a denominator of 100.

WORKING TOGETHER

3. Use graph paper to make a 10-by-10 grid.
Shade the grid to match each of the following percents.

a. 20% green **b.** 30% blue **c.** 5% red **d.** 15% yellow

Here is how Ben shaded the grid.

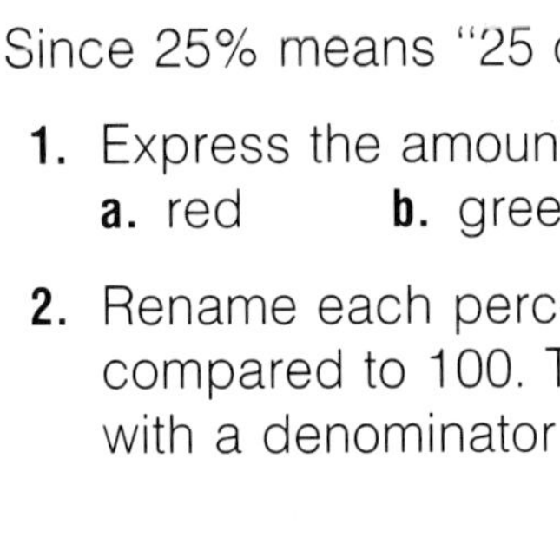

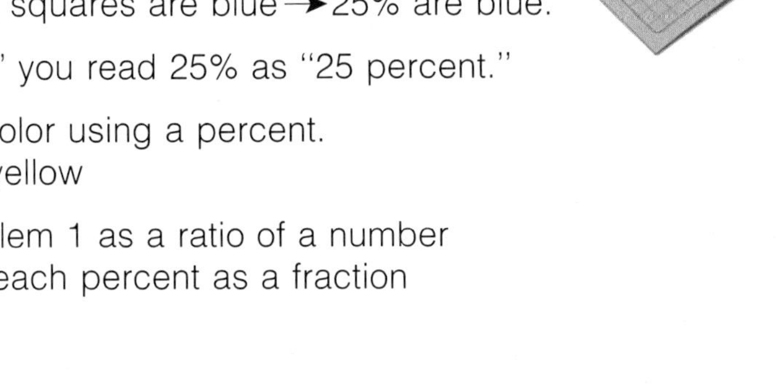

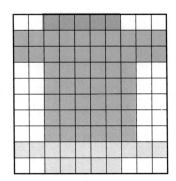

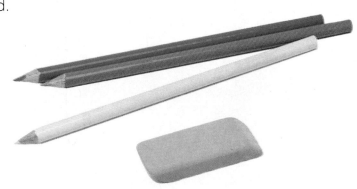

SHARING IDEAS

4. How does your grid compare to Ben's?

5. Compare your grid to those of others. How are they the same? How are they different?

6. What percent of the whole grid is shaded? How do you know?

7. *What if* Ben had shaded 45 out of 100 squares? What percent would he have shaded? What percent would he have left unshaded?

8. What do you think 200% means? How might you show 200% using grids?

ON YOUR OWN

9. *What if* the state sales tax were 6¢ for every dollar? What percent would this be? Why?

10. There were 100 students in a school. Last week 12 students were absent. What percent of the students were absent?

11. Fifty-five students out of 100 voted for pizza to be served in the cafeteria once a week. What percent of the students voted for pizza once a week?

12. Eighty-seven students out of 100 went on the class trip. What percent of the students did not go on the class trip?

13. *Write a problem* involving a percent. Solve your problem. Ask others to solve it.

ACTIVITY Percents and Decimals

A. A farmer planted wheat on 50% of his field, oats on 45%, and barley on 5%. Write the decimal for the part of the field planted with each crop.

W	W	W	W	W	O	O	O	O	O
W	W	W	W	W	O	O	O	O	O
W	W	W	W	W	O	O	O	O	O
W	W	W	W	W	O	O	O	O	O
W	W	W	W	W	O	O	O	O	O
W	W	W	W	W	O	O	O	O	B
W	W	W	W	W	O	O	O	O	B
W	W	W	W	W	O	O	O	O	B
W	W	W	W	W	O	O	O	O	B
W	W	W	W	W	O	O	O	O	B

WORKING TOGETHER

You can use a 10-by-10 grid to represent the different parts of the field.

1. Rename the percent of the field that was planted with each crop as a fraction with a denominator of 100.
   a. wheat   **b.** oats   **c.** barley

2. Rename each fraction in Problem 1 as a decimal.

Here is how the fractions can be renamed as decimals.

Wheat	**Oats**	**Barley**
$50\% = \frac{50}{100} = 0.50$ or 0.5	$45\% = \frac{45}{100} = 0.45$	$5\% = \frac{5}{100} = 0.05$

You can use a shortcut to rename a percent as a decimal.

$50\% \rightarrow 5\,0.\% \rightarrow 0.50$

$45\% \rightarrow 4\,5.\% \rightarrow 0.45$

$5\% \rightarrow 0\,5.\% \rightarrow 0.05$

Think: Move the decimal point two places to the left and remove the percent sign.

Notice that you need to write a zero before the digit 5 to get 0.05.

B. You can rename a decimal as a percent.

Rename 0.09 as a percent. ***Think:*** $0.09 = \frac{9}{100} = 9\%$

3. How can you use a shortcut to rename a decimal as a percent?

SHARING IDEAS

4. When renaming percents as decimals, why do you always move the decimal point two places to the left before dropping the percent sign?

5. When renaming decimals as percents, why do you always move the decimal point two places to the right before adding on the percent sign?

PRACTICE

Write the percent and the decimal equivalent for
the shaded part of the 10-by-10 grid that is:

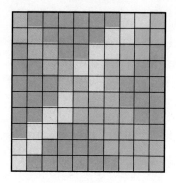

6. red.

7. blue.

8. green.

9. yellow.

10. red and yellow.

11. blue and green.

12. not blue.

13. not green.

Rename the percent as a decimal.

14. 88%   15. 54%   16. 20%   17. 97%   18. 35%   19. 13%

20. 7%   21. 3%   22. 1%   23. 48%   24. 27%   25. 300%

Rename the decimal as a percent.

26. 0.45   27. 0.63   28. 0.15   29. 0.75   30. 0.04   31. 0.09

32. 25 hundredths   33. 85 hundredths   34. 6 hundredths

What percent of a dollar does the amount represent?

35. 25¢   36. 20¢   37. 5¢   38. 50¢   39. 75¢   40. $1.75

Mixed Applications

Solve. You may need to use the Databank on page 553.

41. A farmer planted $\frac{2}{3}$ of his field with
wheat. If his field covered 150
acres, how many acres did he
plant with wheat?

42. A farmer planted soybeans on
40% of his field. He left the rest of
the field unplanted. What percent
of the field remained unplanted?

43. A farmer divided a 10-acre field
into sections of 2.5 acres each. How
many smaller fields did he have?

44. What percent of the world's grain
did the United States produce in
1987?

Percents and Fractions

A. Dan correctly answered 95% of the problems on a math test. How can you rename his score as a fraction in simplest form?

To rename a percent as a fraction in simplest form, use the meaning of percent.

Think: 95% means 95 out of 100.

$$95\% = \frac{95}{100} = \frac{95 \div 5}{100 \div 5} = \frac{19}{20}$$

Dan correctly answered $\frac{19}{20}$ of the problems.

1. What fraction of the math problems did Dan answer incorrectly?

2. Show how to rename 32% as a fraction in simplest form.

B. You can also rename a fraction as a percent.

Rename $\frac{7}{10}$ as a percent.

Step 1	**Step 2**
Write an equivalent fraction with a denominator of 100.	Rename the fraction as a percent.
$\frac{7}{10} = \frac{7 \times 10}{10 \times 10} = \frac{70}{100}$	$\frac{70}{100} = 70\%$

So $\frac{7}{10} = 70\%$.

3. Show how to rename $\frac{3}{25}$ as a percent.

TRY OUT Write the letter of the correct answer.

4. Which fraction in simplest form is equal to 60%?

    a. $\frac{60}{100}$ **b.** $\frac{30}{50}$ **c.** $\frac{3}{5}$ **d.** $\frac{6}{10}$

5. Which percent is equal to $\frac{3}{20}$?

    a. 3%   **b.** 15%   **c.** 3%   **d.** 12%

PRACTICE

Write a fraction and a percent for the indicated part of the square.

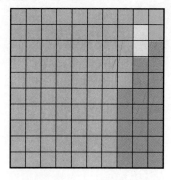

6. orange part
7. purple part

8. gray part
9. aqua part

10. orange and purple part
11. aqua and purple part

Rename the percent as a fraction in simplest form.

12. 5% **13.** 10% **14.** 15% **15.** 4% **16.** 25% **17.** 75%

18. 50% **19.** 95% **20.** 45% **21.** 85% **22.** 6% **23.** 8%

24. 9% **25.** 58% **26.** 12% **27.** 57% **28.** 40% **29.** 30%

30. 60 percent **31.** 16 percent **32.** 55 percent **33.** 14 percent

Rename the fraction as a percent.

34. $\frac{1}{2}$ **35.** $\frac{1}{4}$ **36.** $\frac{1}{5}$ **37.** $\frac{1}{10}$ **38.** $\frac{1}{20}$ **39.** $\frac{1}{50}$

40. $\frac{3}{4}$ **41.** $\frac{4}{5}$ **42.** $\frac{7}{10}$ **43.** $\frac{9}{20}$ **44.** $\frac{3}{50}$ **45.** $\frac{4}{25}$

46. $\frac{9}{10}$ **47.** $\frac{8}{25}$ **48.** $\frac{3}{5}$ **49.** $\frac{17}{50}$ **50.** $\frac{7}{20}$ **51.** $\frac{7}{25}$

Mixed Applications

52. Betsey correctly answered 22 out of 25 questions on a social studies test. What percent did she answer correctly?

53. Mark's scores on the language arts quizzes he took in October were 86, 84, 90, 91, 87, and 96. What was his average score?

54. Paulo correctly answered 8 out of 10 questions on a social studies test and 10 out of 12 on a language arts test. On which test did he do better?

55. Alice has 4 days to study 30 pages for a French test. If she reads the same number of pages each night, how many pages will she read every night?

Mixed Review

Find the answer. Which method did you use?

56. $\frac{3}{4} \div 2$
57. $6\frac{2}{3} \times 6\frac{3}{5}$
58. $22,001 - 1,879$

59. $3,789 + 4,898$
60. $6.001 - 2.897$
61. $314 \div 35$

MENTAL MATH
CALCULATOR
PAPER/PENCIL

ercent of a Number

Mike shot 60 foul shots. He said, "I made a basket from the foul line 75% of the time." How many baskets did he make?

To find the answer to this question, you need to find 75% of 60.

WORKING TOGETHER

You can use graph paper to model the baskets he made. In this model each box represents one foul shot.

1. What percent of the boxes are shaded yellow? What fraction are shaded yellow?

2. How many boxes are shaded yellow?

3. What is 75% of 60?

4. How many baskets did Mike make?

5. **What if** Mike had shot 80 foul shots and had made a basket 90% of the time? Make a model to show the number of baskets Mike would have made.

6. **What if** Mike had shot 120 foul shots and had made a basket 40% of the time? Make a model to show the number of baskets Mike would have made.

SHARING IDEAS

7. How would you rename 80% of 40? 60% of 40? 50% of 40? 40% of 40? 20% of 40?

8. What happens to the percent of a number as the percent decreases?

9. For which percents is the percent of a number less than one half, equal to one half, and greater than one half?

10. Tell how you could find the percent of a number without using a model.

ON YOUR OWN

Write the letter of the correct answer.

11. 40% of 50	**a.** 50	**b.** 40	**c.** 20
12. 60% of 15	**a.** 9	**b.** 15	**c.** 60
13. 86% of 50	**a.** 43	**b.** 50	**c.** 172
14. 25% of 1,000	**a.** 0.25	**b.** 250	**c.** 2,500
15. 75% of 12	**a.** 9	**b.** 12	**c.** 15
16. 100% of 57	**a.** 5.7	**b.** 57	**c.** 570

17. A percent of the ticket sales for home games is budgeted for new equipment. The ticket sales for the year totaled $6,000. If 20% is budgeted for new equipment, what amount will go for new equipment?

18. At a basketball game Barbara had $12 and Jane had $14. Barbara spent 25% of her money on food. Jane spent 50% of her money on food. Who spent more on food? How much more?

P ROBLEM SOLVING

Using Information from a Graph

The members of the Monroe family want to see how they budget their money each month. Mr. Monroe decides to make a circle graph to show how the family income of $3,600 per month is spent.

By using a circle graph, you can see clearly how the money is spent. The parts, or sections, of the graph help you understand where the biggest pieces go. The whole graph is worth $3,600. How much money do the Monroes spend in each category, or what is each section worth?

Plan to solve the problem by looking at the fractions in the circle graph. The fractions must add up to 1.

You can multiply to find the amount of each category.

MONROE FAMILY BUDGET
$3,600 per month

Housing $\frac{1}{2}$

Food $\frac{1}{4}$

Clothing $\frac{1}{10}$

Savings $\frac{1}{20}$

Transportation $\frac{1}{20}$

Travel and Entertainment $\frac{1}{20}$

Housing	Food	Clothing	Transportation	Savings	Travel and Entertainment
$\frac{1}{2} \times \$3,600$	$\frac{1}{4} \times \$3,600$	$\frac{1}{10} \times \$3,600$	$\frac{1}{20} \times \$3,600$	$\frac{1}{20} \times \$3,600$	$\frac{1}{20} \times \$3,600$

1. How much do the Monroes spend on housing?

2. How much do they spend on food?

3. What fraction of the budget is food and housing?

4. For which three categories is the fraction of the budget the same?

5. How much do the Monroes spend on food and clothing each month?

6. **What if** the Monroes have $1,200 to spend on a family vacation? They estimate that they will spend the money as follows: $\frac{1}{2}$ on lodgings, $\frac{1}{4}$ on food, $\frac{1}{8}$ on transportation expenses, and $\frac{1}{8}$ on entertainment. Draw a circle graph that shows how the Monroes will spend the money on their vacation.

PRACTICE

Four hundred students voted on a name for the school's baseball team. The results of the vote were presented in the school newspaper in the form of a circle graph.

Interpret the circle graph.
Then solve the problem.

7. How many students chose *Rangers* as the name?

8. How many chose *Thunderbirds*?

9. Which name was the least favorite? How many students chose it?

10. Two hundred sixth graders voted on a team name. One-fourth chose *Ponies,* $\frac{1}{4}$ chose *Geese,* $\frac{1}{4}$ chose *Surfers,* $\frac{1}{8}$ chose *Trackers,* and $\frac{1}{8}$ chose *Pandas.* Draw a circle graph to show the results.

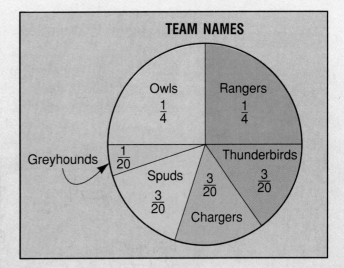

TEAM NAMES

Owls $\frac{1}{4}$ — Rangers $\frac{1}{4}$ — Greyhounds $\frac{1}{20}$ — Spuds $\frac{3}{20}$ — Chargers $\frac{3}{20}$ — Thunderbirds $\frac{3}{20}$

Strategies and Skills Review

Solve. Use estimation, mental math, a calculator, or paper and pencil.

11. A playing field is a square that is 15 m on a side. There is a path 1 m wide going through the center of the field that connects one of the sides with the opposite side. What is the perimeter of this path?

12. Matt earned $25.49 on Monday, $38.50 on Tuesday, and $62.96 on Wednesday. Does he have enough money to buy a new bicycle for $135?

13. A uniform for the school baseball team costs $36. This is twice the cost of a baseball glove. A baseball is half the cost of a baseball glove. How much does a baseball cost?

14. ***Write a problem*** that involves interpreting a circle graph. You may use a circle graph from this lesson or one from a newspaper. Ask others to solve the problem.

DECISION MAKING

Problem Solving: Choosing a Bicycle Tour

SITUATION

The members of the Flying Feet Bicycle Club are planning an all-day bicycle tour. They want to travel between 25 and 35 miles. All the members have helmets, but they need to rent either ten-speed bicycles or mountain bicycles. They find information in a bicycling magazine about three tours.

PROBLEM

Which tour should the bicycle club choose?

DATA

BIKING TOURS

Tour 1

Only **$38** for a 32-mile ride!

Take it easy on a relaxing tour through beautiful countryside. Our guide will do all the work!

Have lunch at a country inn* or bring your own and enjoy the scenery!

We rent:
- 3-speed bikes for **$8**
- 10-speed bikes for **$13**
- Mountain bikes for **$22**

We also rent:
Gloves for **$4**
Helmets for **$7**

Tours run every day of the week!

*$10/per person

Tour 2

We offer a tour through gently rolling hills. We'll stop for lunch at a wayside picnic area ($3.50).

Need equipment? We can provide
- 3-speed bikes **$7**
- 10-speed bikes **$14**
- mountain bikes **$23**

We can also provide gloves ($5) and helmets ($8).

We cover 28 miles. Our charge? $42. Our tours run Thurs. through Sat.

Tour 3

For the more advanced rider— climb the hills and have lunch at one of the most spectacular lookout points in the county!

Miles traveled: 26
Cost of tour: $51
Lunch: Provided
Days of operation:
Friday
Saturday
Sunday

Bicycle rental:
- $7—3 speed
- $16—10 speed
- $28—Mountain

Other rental:
- Gloves—$5
- Helmets—$9

USING THE DATA

What is the total cost for the tour with the rental of a mountain bicycle and including lunch?

1. Tour 1   **2.** Tour 2   **3.** Tour 3

What is the total cost for the tour with the rental of a ten-speed bike and including lunch?

4. Tour 1   **5.** Tour 2   **6.** Tour 3

What is the total cost for the tour with the rental of a ten-speed bike and everyone bringing a lunch?

7. Tour 1   **8.** Tour 2   **9.** Tour 3

What is the total cost for the tour with the rental of a mountain bike and everyone bringing a lunch?

10. Tour 1   **11.** Tour 2   **12.** Tour 3

MAKING DECISIONS

13. Which tour should they choose to spend the least amount with a mountain bike rental?

14. Which tour should they choose to travel between 25 and 30 miles?

15. Which tour should they choose for the most challenging ride?

16. Which tour should they choose if they cannot go on a weekend?

17. *What if* club members decide to rent mountain bikes, helmets, and gloves? Which tour would be the most expensive?

18. *Write a list* of the other factors club members should consider.

19. Which tour would you take? Tell why.

Math and Art

One of the most famous buildings in the world is the Parthenon in Athens, Greece. Completed in 432 B.C., the Parthenon is a graceful building that sits on top of a hill called the Acropolis. This building is so pleasing to the eye because its dimensions conform to a principle of mathematics called the golden rectangle. The ratio of its width to its length forms a golden ratio of 1 to roughly 1.6. Because of this, the Parthenon has been of great interest to mathematicians, engineers, architects, and artists.

What if you wanted to build a picture frame whose dimensions form a golden rectangle? If the shorter dimension of the frame is 16 in., find the length of the other dimension.

Think: The ratio of a golden rectangle is 1 to 1.6. Use equal ratios.

$$\frac{1}{1.6} = \frac{16}{n}$$
$$1 \times n = 1.6 \times 16$$
$$n = 25.6$$

Your finished frame would measure 16 in. by 25.6 in.

ACTIVITIES

1. The ratio of length to width of every American flag is always the same. Measure an American flag. Find the ratio. Then design a flag using the same ratio.

2. Look in art books for reproductions of paintings by Leonardo da Vinci or Piet Mondrian. Use tracing paper to draw any golden rectangles you find in the artists' works. Then measure each rectangle to find the ratio of width to length. Share your findings with your class.

Computer Graphing: Circle Graphs

Patty, the owner of On Wheels Rink, is studying how much her roller-skating rink is used at different times during the weekend. She gathered this data for one weekend.

Time Range	Number of People Skating	
	Saturday	Sunday
8 A.M. to 10 A.M.	45	28
10 A.M. to 12 noon	62	319
12 noon to 2 P.M.	112	357
2 P.M. to 4 P.M.	87	116
4 P.M. to 6 P.M.	192	95
6 P.M. to 8 P.M.	258	84
8 P.M. to 10 P.M.	337	42
10 P.M. to 12 midnight	198	11

Patty wants to organize the data to see how busy the rink is during various parts of the day. The computer program CIRCLE GRAPH computes totals for combined sessions and draws a circle graph based on the data the user enters.

AT THE COMPUTER

1. From the information for Saturday, have the computer find a subtotal for each of these time periods: 8 A.M. to 12 noon, 12 noon to 4 P.M., 4 P.M. to 8 P.M., 8 P.M. to 12 midnight. How many skaters were there in all on Saturday?

2. Instruct the computer to draw the circle graph. Which time period had the most skaters and which had the fewest skaters? Estimate what fractional part of total attendance skated during each time period. Make a sketch of the circle graph to use later.

3. Try the activity again for Sunday. Use the same time periods. Have the computer find each subtotal and the grand total and draw the circle graph.

4. Estimate the size of each sector again. How does the Sunday graph compare with the Saturday graph you sketched in Problem 2?

5. How do you think Patty can use this information? What else do you think Patty might want to know about her business?

Ratio, Proportion, and Percent **423**

EXTRA PRACTICE

Ratios and Rates, page 397

Write the ratio in three different ways.

1. squares to triangles
2. stars to circles
3. triangles to stars
4. circles to stars
5. all the figures to circles
6. all the figures to triangles
7. squares to all the figures
8. stars to all the figures

Write the rate in two different ways.

9. 50 mi/hour

10. 3 cups/loaf

11. 28 mi/gal

12. $2.49 per pound

13. $\frac{6 \text{ oranges}}{\$2.00}$

14. 36 eggs in 3 cartons

Equal Ratios, page 399

Determine whether the ratios are equal.

1. $\frac{3}{4} \stackrel{?}{=} \frac{15}{24}$
2. $\frac{7}{9} \stackrel{?}{=} \frac{42}{63}$
3. $\frac{8}{15} \stackrel{?}{=} \frac{32}{45}$
4. $\frac{16}{6} \stackrel{?}{=} \frac{8}{3}$
5. $\frac{32}{12} \stackrel{?}{=} \frac{8}{2}$

6. $\frac{18}{36} \stackrel{?}{=} \frac{3}{4}$
7. $\frac{27}{18} \stackrel{?}{=} \frac{3}{2}$
8. $\frac{5}{7} \stackrel{?}{=} \frac{25}{42}$
9. $\frac{150}{200} \stackrel{?}{=} \frac{6}{8}$
10. $\frac{200}{500} \stackrel{?}{=} \frac{10}{25}$

Find an equal ratio by multiplying and by dividing.

11. $\frac{6}{9}$
12. $\frac{12}{15}$
13. $\frac{4}{16}$
14. $\frac{11}{22}$
15. $\frac{30}{50}$

16. $\frac{8}{10}$
17. $\frac{9}{12}$
18. $\frac{6}{8}$
19. $\frac{42}{56}$
20. $\frac{90}{120}$

Proportions, page 401

Solve the proportion.

1. $\frac{1}{5} = \frac{n}{45}$
2. $\frac{4}{3} = \frac{n}{6}$
3. $\frac{3}{11} = \frac{n}{55}$
4. $\frac{1}{8} = \frac{5}{n}$
5. $\frac{6}{27} = \frac{2}{n}$

6. $\frac{n}{4} = \frac{27}{12}$
7. $\frac{12}{n} = \frac{4}{5}$
8. $\frac{54}{n} = \frac{3}{2}$
9. $\frac{48}{12} = \frac{n}{2}$
10. $\frac{8}{n} = \frac{48}{33}$

11. $\frac{3.5}{12} = \frac{n}{54}$
12. $\frac{3}{1.5} = \frac{5}{n}$
13. $\frac{2.8}{1.4} = \frac{n}{2}$
14. $\frac{n}{3.6} = \frac{0.8}{0.9}$
15. $\frac{0.4}{0.5} = \frac{n}{3.5}$

EXTRA PRACTICE

Scale Drawings, page 403

Mary has a floor plan. The floor plan's scale is 1 in.:4 ft. What is the actual distance given the scale-drawing measurement?

1. 2 in.   **2.** 5 in.   **3.** $1\frac{1}{4}$ in.   **4.** $2\frac{1}{2}$ in.

5. $\frac{1}{2}$ in.   **6.** $\frac{1}{4}$ in.   **7.** $3\frac{3}{4}$ in.   **8.** 10 in.

A map has a scale 1 cm:50 km. What is the scale-drawing measurement given the actual distance?

9. 100 km   **10.** 250 km   **11.** 300 km   **12.** 25 km

13. 75 km   **14.** 80 km   **15.** 140 km   **16.** 62.5 km

Similar Figures, page 405

Find the missing side for the pair of similar figures.

1.

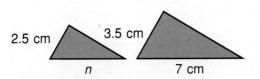

2.

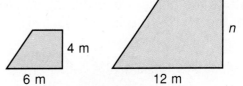

3.

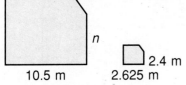

4.

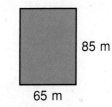

5.

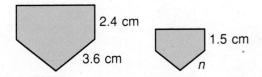

6.

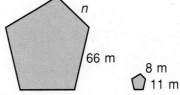

7.

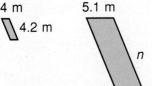

8.

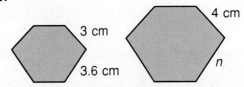

EXTRA PRACTICE

Problem Solving Strategy: Writing and Solving an Equation, page 407

Write an equation to solve the problem.

1. Tracy, Mario, Don, and Jean ride the Carousel 4 times. They pay $.75 for each ride. How much do the rides cost them all together?

2. Jean's favorite ride is the Spider Coaster. She rides the Coaster 5 times and spends $8.75. How much does each ride cost?

3. Mario's favorite ride is the Giant Ant Coaster. He takes 6 rides on the Coaster. Each ride is 264 m long. How many meters did Mario travel?

4. The Carousel offers a special rate of $5.00 for 10 tickets. Mario, Tracy, Don, and Jean buy 20 tickets. How much did each of them pay for their tickets?

Percents and Decimals, page 413

Write the percent and the decimal equivalent for the shaded part of the 10-by-10 grid that is:

1. red.

2. white.

3. blue.

4. yellow.

5. red and white.

6. blue and yellow.

7. not blue.

8. not white.

9. not red or blue.

10. not yellow or white.

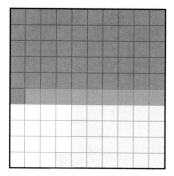

Rename the percent as a decimal.

11. 78% **12.** 32% **13.** 80% **14.** 5% **15.** 200% **16.** 45%

Rename the decimal as a percent.

17. 0.85 **18.** 0.53 **19.** 0.18 **20.** 0.95 **21.** 0.03 **22.** 0.07

What percent of a dollar does the amount represent?

23. 35¢ **24.** 10¢ **25.** 3¢ **26.** 80¢ **27.** 17¢ **28.** $1.50

Percents and Fractions, page 415 ....

Write a fraction and a percent for the indicated part of the square.

1. green part

2. purple part

3. brown part

4. orange part

5. orange and brown part

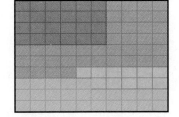

Rename the percent as a fraction in simplest form.

6. 45%   **7.** 20%   **8.** 65%   **9.** 2%   **10.** 35%   **11.** 80%

12. 90%   **13.** 24%   **14.** 6%   **15.** 55%   **16.** 60%   **17.** 7%

Rename the fraction as a percent.

18. $\frac{10}{20}$ **19.** $\frac{2}{4}$ **20.** $\frac{1}{25}$ **21.** $\frac{4}{10}$ **22.** $\frac{3}{20}$ **23.** $\frac{4}{50}$

24. $\frac{15}{20}$ **25.** $\frac{2}{5}$ **26.** $\frac{3}{10}$ **27.** $\frac{17}{20}$ **28.** $\frac{7}{50}$ **29.** $\frac{9}{25}$

Problem Solving: Using Information from a Graph, page 419 ....

Interpret the circle graph. Then solve the problem.

The nutritionist at the school asked some students what flavor bread they liked best. They made a circle graph to show their favorite flavors. There were 300 students surveyed.

1. How many students liked banana the best?

2. How many students liked oat the best?

3. What percent of the circle graph do both white and raisin represent?

4. Which was the least favorite? How many students chose this as their favorite?

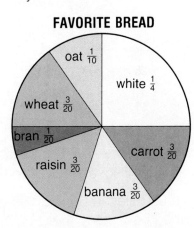

FAVORITE BREAD

oat $\frac{1}{10}$

white $\frac{1}{4}$

wheat $\frac{3}{20}$

bran $\frac{1}{20}$

raisin $\frac{3}{20}$

carrot $\frac{3}{20}$

banana $\frac{3}{20}$

PRACTICE *PLUS*

KEY SKILL: Proportions (Use after page 401.)

Level A

Solve the proportion.

1. $\frac{1}{8} = \frac{n}{32}$ **2.** $\frac{5}{2} = \frac{n}{64}$ **3.** $\frac{5}{7} = \frac{n}{28}$ **4.** $\frac{1}{9} = \frac{6}{n}$ **5.** $\frac{6}{15} = \frac{2}{n}$

6. $\frac{n}{5} = \frac{24}{20}$ **7.** $\frac{20}{n} = \frac{5}{6}$ **8.** $\frac{2}{n} = \frac{3}{12}$ **9.** $\frac{n}{3} = \frac{25}{15}$ **10.** $\frac{8}{2} = \frac{n}{9}$

11. $\frac{16}{4} = \frac{12}{n}$ **12.** $\frac{n}{48} = \frac{5}{4}$ **13.** $\frac{33}{11} = \frac{n}{2}$ **14.** $\frac{24}{n} = \frac{4}{3}$ **15.** $\frac{9}{n} = \frac{27}{15}$

16. 3 shelves for 27 books = 1 shelf for n books

17. Jeff bought 3 yards of fabric for $4.50. What would 6 yards cost?

Level B

Solve the proportion.

18. $\frac{n}{5} = \frac{24}{15}$ **19.** $\frac{16}{n} = \frac{8}{5}$ **20.** $\frac{3}{n} = \frac{4}{8}$ **21.** $\frac{n}{7} = \frac{30}{35}$ **22.** $\frac{8}{2} = \frac{n}{5}$

23. $\frac{21}{7} = \frac{9}{n}$ **24.** $\frac{n}{64} = \frac{5}{4}$ **25.** $\frac{36}{n} = \frac{3}{2}$ **26.** $\frac{66}{11} = \frac{n}{2}$ **27.** $\frac{9}{n} = \frac{54}{21}$

28. $\frac{15}{n} = \frac{35}{21}$ **29.** $\frac{16}{12} = \frac{28}{n}$ **30.** $\frac{22}{5} = \frac{176}{n}$ **31.** $\frac{36}{50} = \frac{9}{n}$ **32.** $\frac{n}{44} = \frac{5}{2}$

33. 14 computers for 56 people = n computers for 72 people

34. Sarah used 6 gallons of gas to travel 125 miles. How many gallons will she use to travel 500 miles?

Level C

Solve the proportion.

35. $\frac{21}{3} = \frac{35}{n}$ **36.** $\frac{n}{68} = \frac{7}{4}$ **37.** $\frac{63}{n} = \frac{21}{7}$ **38.** $\frac{88}{11} = \frac{n}{9}$ **39.** $\frac{9}{n} = \frac{36}{26}$

40. $\frac{28}{n} = \frac{98}{14}$ **41.** $\frac{18}{12} = \frac{21}{n}$ **42.** $\frac{44}{9} = \frac{352}{n}$ **43.** $\frac{64}{125} = \frac{8}{n}$ **44.** $\frac{n}{99} = \frac{2}{3}$

45. $\frac{3.2}{15} = \frac{n}{105}$ **46.** $\frac{5}{2.5} = \frac{7}{n}$ **47.** $\frac{6.9}{2.3} = \frac{n}{4}$ **48.** $\frac{n}{4.9} = \frac{0.5}{0.7}$ **49.** $\frac{0.7}{1.0} = \frac{n}{3.5}$

50. 96 grapefruit in 4 boxes = n grapefruit in 100 boxes

51. Rick drove 55 miles in 60 minutes on an interstate highway. At this speed how many miles could he drive in 90 minutes?

PRACTICE PLUS

KEY SKILL: Percents and Fractions (Use after page 415.)

Level A

Write a fraction and a percent for the indicated part of the square.

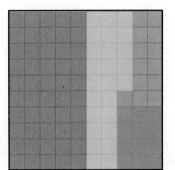

1. red part
2. green part
3. orange part
4. blue part
5. red and green part
6. blue and orange part
7. Annette answered 9 out of 10 questions correctly on a quiz. What percent did she answer correctly?

Level B

Rename the percent as a fraction in simplest form.

8. 16% 9. 82% 10. 45% 11. 60% 12. 90% 13. 32%

Rename the fraction as a percent.

14. $\frac{7}{10}$ 15. $\frac{9}{25}$ 16. $\frac{4}{5}$ 17. $\frac{19}{50}$ 18. $\frac{1}{4}$ 19. $\frac{3}{20}$

20. Julio answered 20 out of 25 questions correctly on a math test and 18 out of 20 on a history test. On which test did he score higher?

Level C

Rename the percent as a fraction in simplest form.

21. 8% 22. 35% 23. 48% 24. 58% 25. 65% 26. 52%

Rename the fraction as a percent.

27. $\frac{19}{20}$ 28. $\frac{27}{50}$ 29. $\frac{15}{25}$ 30. $\frac{3}{10}$ 31. $\frac{24}{25}$ 32. $\frac{39}{50}$

33. Peg scored 42 out of 50 on a science test, 22 out of 25 on a geography test, and 17 out of 20 on a spelling test. List the scores in order by percent from greatest to least.

CHAPTER REVIEW/TEST

LANGUAGE AND MATHEMATICS

Complete the sentences. Use the words in the chart on the right.

1. A ■ is a statement that two ratios are equal.

2. Figures that have the same shape are called ■.

3. The ratio which defines the relationship between map distances and actual distances is called the ■.

4. A ratio that compares a number to 100 is called a ■.

CONCEPTS AND SKILLS

Write the ratio as a fraction in simplest form.

5. 2 to 4   **6.** 10:15   **7.** 20 to 50   **8.** 12:9

Solve for n.

9. $\frac{1}{3} = \frac{6}{n}$ **10.** $\frac{3}{4} = \frac{n}{8}$ **11.** $\frac{5}{10} = \frac{3}{n}$

First write a proportion, then solve for n.

12. 12 oz for 6 people = 36 oz for n people

13. 6 bags for $18 = n$ bags for $24

14. 4 yd for n blouses = 84 yd for 42 blouses

Each pair of figures is similar. Solve for n.

15.

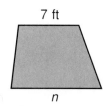

4 ft   7 ft

6 ft

n

16.

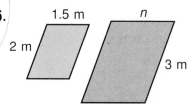

1.5 m n

2 m

3 m

A map scale is 1 cm = 200 km. Solve for n.

17. map distance: 4 cm
actual distance: n

18. map distance: 2.5 cm
actual distance: n

Rename as a decimal.

19. 7%   **20.** 99%

Rename as a fraction in simplest form.

21. 5%   **22.** 80%

Critical Thinking

23. A grape punch has 3 parts juice to 1 part soda. An apple punch has 7 parts juice to 3 parts soda. Which punch has a greater percent of soda?

Mixed Applications

The circle graph shows the number of each type of problem on a math test.

24. What fraction of the problems were *not* multiplication problems?

25. What percent of the problems were addition problems?

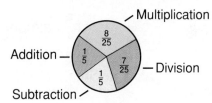

QUESTIONS ON MATH TEST

Multiplication — $\frac{8}{25}$

Addition — $\frac{1}{5}$

$\frac{7}{25}$ — Division

Subtraction — $\frac{1}{5}$

PERFORMANCE ASSESSMENT

Work with your group to solve this problem.

Design a poster showing one wall in a classroom. Make a scale drawing of the wall. Include all the objects in or on a wall such as windows, bookcases, and a bulletin board. Draw each object to scale.

1. *Think about:*
   - the scale you will use in your drawing
   - the length and height of the wall
   - the proportion to determine the length and height of the object in the drawing compared to its actual length and height

2. Write a statement explaining the scale you used in your drawing and why you chose that scale.

CUMULATIVE REVIEW

Choose the letter of the correct answer.

1. 9 to 15 is the same as:
   a. 4 to 5.
   b. 3 to 5.
   c. 15 to 9.
   d. not given

2. Solve: $\frac{8}{12} = \frac{12}{n}$
   a. 1
   b. 8
   c. 18
   d. not given

3. A map scale is 1 cm = 50 km. What is the distance between two places that are 5 cm apart on the map?
   a. 5 km
   b. 10 km
   c. 250 km
   d. not given

4. 7% written as a decimal is:
   a. 0.07.
   b. 0.7.
   c. 7.00.
   d. not given

5. 60% written as a decimal is:
   a. $\frac{1}{60}$.
   b. 0.06.
   c. $\frac{3}{10}$.
   d. not given

6. The angle measures about:

   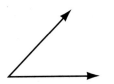

   a. 10°.
   b. 45°.
   c. 80°.
   d. not given

7. One angle of a right triangle measures 24°. What is the measure of the third angle?
   a. 42°
   b. 114°
   c. 66°
   d. not given

8. Which quadrilateral has all equal sides and no right angles?
   a. rhombus
   b. trapezoid
   c. rectangle
   d. not given

9. What is the sum of the measures of the angles of a hexagon?
   a. 180°
   b. 360°
   c. 720°
   d. not given

10. $\frac{3}{8} \times \frac{2}{7}$
    a. $\frac{2}{5}$
    b. $\frac{3}{28}$
    c. $\frac{5}{56}$
    d. not given

11. $18 \div \frac{2}{9}$
    a. 4
    b. 2
    c. 162
    d. not given

12. 72 ft = ■ yd
    a. 2
    b. 24
    c. 216
    d. not given

13. $\frac{3}{7} + \frac{1}{4} + \frac{3}{14}$
    a. $1\frac{5}{14}$
    b. $\frac{25}{28}$
    c. $\frac{7}{25}$
    d. not given

14. $5\frac{3}{5} - 3\frac{1}{2}$
    a. $2\frac{1}{10}$
    b. $2\frac{2}{3}$
    c. $2\frac{1}{5}$
    d. not given

ALGEBRA: MAKING AND USING A HYPSOMETER

A *hypsometer* is a device for finding heights that might be hard to measure directly. By using similar triangles formed by the hypsometer, you can find the heights of objects. You can make your own hypsometer using everyday objects. Make a device like the one pictured at the right. Attach cardboard backing to a yardstick at the 2-ft mark.

The diagram at the right shows how to set up your hypsometer. Place your hypsometer at a specified distance from the object, say 50 ft. Make sure that the yardstick is perpendicular to the ground. Kneel down, look through the straw, and tilt the cardboard till you sight the top of the object.

Find the 50-ft mark on the vertical scale of the hypsometer ("distance from the object"). Locate the point where the string crosses this line. From that point, go down to the horizontal scale ("height of object"). As the red dotted line to that scale shows, the point on the horizontal scale is located at about 23. The distance from *x* to the top of the object is about 23 ft. Add on 2 ft (the height of the hypsometer). The total height of the object is about 25 ft.

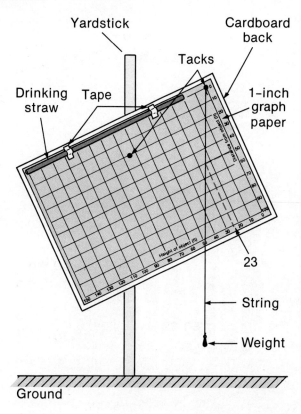

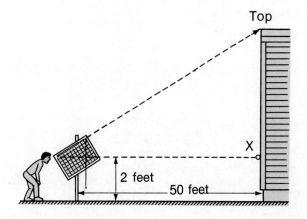

1. Build a hypsometer and use it to measure the heights of three tall objects. Each time, record the distance from the object and the height you get by reading the hypsometer.

2. Could you use your hypsometer to measure heights in yards? in meters? Why?

THE LIFE OF A PERSON IS A CIRCLE

Black Elk, an Oglala Sioux leader, said these words during an interview early in this century. They reflect his feelings at the time long before, when his people were forcibly resettled onto a reservation.

SOUTH DAKOTA

Pine Ridge Indian Reservation

CHAPTER

11

MEASUREMENT: AREA AND VOLUME

MATH *CONNECTION:* Geometry

. . . I came
to live here where I am
now between Wounded Knee
Creek and Grass Creek. Others came
too, and we made these little gray houses of
log, and they are square. It is a bad way to live, for
there can be no power in a square. You have noticed
that everything an Indian does is in a circle, and that is
because the Power of the World always works in circles,
and everything tries to be round. In the old days when we
were a strong and happy people, all our power came to us
from the sacred hoop of the nation, and so long as the hoop
was unbroken, the people flourished. . . . Everything the Power
of the World does is done in a circle. . . . The sun comes forth
and goes down in a circle. The moon does the same, and
both are round. Even the seasons form a great circle in their
changing, and always come back again to where they
were. The life of a man is a circle from childhood to
childhood, and so it is in everything where power
moves. Our tepees were round like the nests
of birds, and these were always set in a
circle, the nation's hoop, a nest
of many nests. . . .

1. WHY DO YOU THINK BLACK ELK CONSIDERED THE CIRCLE TO BE A POWERFUL SHAPE?

2. WHAT GEOMETRIC SHAPES DO YOU SEE IN THE WORLD AROUND YOU?

ACTIVITY
Circles and Circumference

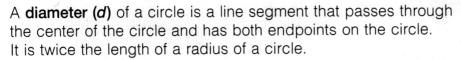

Jack is making a model wagon. He is going to glue a strip of rubber around the outside of each wheel to make a tire. About how long a strip of rubber will he need for each wheel if the wheel measures 12 cm across?

The shape of the tire is a **circle.** All points on a circle are the same distance from one point, called the **center.**

A **radius (r)** of a circle is a line segment with the center and a point on the circle as endpoints.

A **diameter (d)** of a circle is a line segment that passes through the center of the circle and has both endpoints on the circle. It is twice the length of a radius of a circle.

The distance around the circle is called the **circumference (C)** of the circle.

WORKING TOGETHER

You can learn about the relationship between the diameter and circumference of a circle by performing this activity.

Step 1 Use a compass to make a circle with a 12-cm diameter on a piece of cardboard.

Step 2 Cut out the circle. Then use a tape measure to find the distance around the circle to the nearest centimeter.

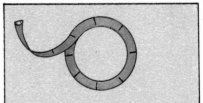

1. About how much rubber will Jack need? (C ≈ ■ cm)

2. Construct circles that have the following diameters and measure to find the circumference.
   a. 15 cm   **b.** 6 cm   **c.** 11 cm   **d.** 8 cm

SHARING IDEAS

3. Copy and complete the table.

Circumference (C)	Diameter (d)	C + d	C – d	C × d	C ÷ d
	12 cm				
	15 cm				
	6 cm				

4. In which column of the table do you see a pattern? What is the pattern?

5. What rule can you write to tell how to find the circumference of a circle if you know the diameter? the radius?

6. What rule can you write to tell how to find the diameter of a circle if you know the circumference?

PRACTICE

What is the diameter of the circle?

7. 3 cm

8. 7 cm

9. 1.5 in.

10. 4.2 m

What is the radius of the circle?

11. 20 cm

12. 5 cm

13. 16 ft

14. $\frac{3}{4}$ yd

Use your rules to find the missing measure.

15. $d = 3$ cm, $C \approx$ ■ cm   **16.** $d = 13$ cm, $C \approx$ ■ cm   **17.** $r = 9$ m, $C \approx$ ■ m

18. $C = 30$ cm, $d \approx$ ■ cm   **19.** $C = 54$ m, $d \approx$ ■ m   **20.** $C = 21$ m, $d \approx$ ■ m

Mixed Applications

21. The diameter of the rim of Jody's unicycle is 24 in. What is the length of a spoke if the center hub has a diameter of 2 in.?

22. A truck traveled 9.42 ft with $\frac{3}{4}$ of a turn of the front wheel. What was the circumference of the front wheel?

EXTRA PRACTICE, page 462   Measurement: Area and Volume   **437**

Finding Circumference

A laser reads the music on a compact disk from the inside to the outside. The diameter of the outside track of music on the disk is 11.6 cm. What is the circumference of the outside track?

In the previous lesson you saw that the ratio of the circumference to the diameter was the same for all circles. This ratio is π **(pi)** and is approximately equal to 3.14 or $3\frac{1}{7}$ or $\frac{22}{7}$.

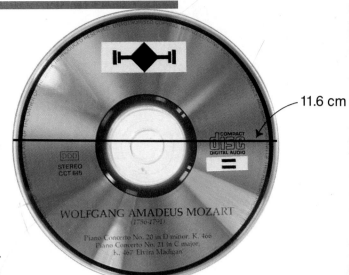

11.6 cm

You can use this fact to find the circumference if you know the diameter.

Think: $C \div d = \pi$ means that $C = \pi \times d$.

If $d = 11.6$ cm, then $C \approx 3.14$ ⊗ 11.6 ⊜ $\boxed{36.424}$.

The circumference of the outside track is approximately 36.4 cm to the nearest tenth of a centimeter.

1. What formula can you use to find the circumference if you know the radius? Use the formula to find the circumference if the radius is $\frac{2}{3}$ ft.

2. What formula can you use to find the diameter if you know the circumference? Use the formula to find the diameter if the circumference is 13.188 m.

3. When might it be more useful to use 3.14 as the approximate value for π? When would $\frac{22}{7}$ be more useful?

4. What number would you use for π to estimate the circumference of a circle? Why?

TRY OUT   Write the letter of the correct answer.
Find the circumference. Use 3.14 or $\frac{22}{7}$ for π.

5. $d = 8.2$ cm   **a.** 12.874 cm   **b.** 16.4 cm   **c.** 25.748 cm   **d.** 51.496 cm

6. $r = 3\frac{1}{2}$ m   **a.** 7 in.   **b.** 11 m   **c.** $18\frac{1}{4}$ m   **d.** 22 m

7. $d = 5\frac{1}{4}$ km   **a.** 33 km   **b.** $16\frac{1}{2}$ km   **c.** $7\frac{6}{7}$ km   **d.** $1\frac{59}{88}$ km

PRACTICE

Find the circumference of the circle. Use 3.14 or $\frac{22}{7}$ for π.

8. $d = 28$ cm

9. $d = 4.5$ km

10. $d = 14$ m

11. $d = 0.5$ km

12. $r = 3.25$ cm

13. $r = 30$ cm

14. $r = 0.5$ m

15. $r = 25$ km

16. $r = 21$ m

17. $d = 8.2$ m

18. $r = 3.55$ m

19. $d = 7$ km

20. $d = 12$ cm

21. $d = 1.4$ m

22. $r = 62$ km

23. $r = 5.6$ m

Estimate the circumference.

24. $d = 2.9$ cm

25. $r = 5.5$ m

26. $r = 6.1$ km

27. $r = 10.4$ cm

28. $d = 12.95$ m

29. $d = 20.03$ m

30. $r = 20.1$ cm

31. $d = 34.9$ m

32. $r = 15.2$ km

33. $d = 8.6$ m

34. $d = 4.54$ km

35. $r = 9.91$ cm

Mixed Applications

Solve. Which method did you use?

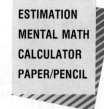

ESTIMATION
MENTAL MATH
CALCULATOR
PAPER/PENCIL

36. The outside groove of a record approximates a circle that has a diameter of 30 cm. What is the circumference of the outside groove?

37. The diameter of the center hole in a record is 3.7 cm. Bill is making a storage case for his records. Will they fit on a wooden peg with a circumference of 11.7 cm?

38. Dr. García wants to buy a compact disk player that costs $689.97, a tape player that costs $349.98, and a turntable for $129.95. She has saved $500. How much will she need to save each week to buy the equipment in 6 weeks?

39. To make room for the stereo equipment Dr. García decides to store 128 record albums in equal-size boxes. Each box holds 18 albums. About how many boxes will Dr. García need?

Mixed Review

Find the answer. Which method did you use?

40.
$$\begin{array}{r} \$149.80 \\ \times \quad 0.25 \end{array}$$

41. $43.89 - $27.38

42. $29.512 \div 6.8$

43. $7\frac{1}{3} + 6\frac{2}{5}$

44. $\frac{9}{16} \div \frac{3}{16}$

45.
$$\begin{array}{r} 2,000 \\ \times \quad 23 \end{array}$$

46. $6\frac{1}{2} - 5\frac{3}{4}$

47. $\frac{2}{3} \times \frac{3}{4}$

Area of a Circle

A plate glass company sells pieces of glass cut to size.
It charges by the square inch. A customer ordered a top
for a circular table that has a radius of 18 in. What area will the
company use in calculating the charge for the glass top?

**Trace around a large paper cup. You can use your drawing to
help you find the area of a circle.**

1. Cut out your drawing. Fold and cut it into eight equal-
   size pieces. Then cut one piece in half.

2. Rearrange the pieces to form a figure that is very
   close to a rectangle.

You can use this construction to develop a formula
for finding the area of a circle.

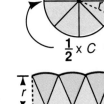

Area (A) = length × width

$$A = \left(\tfrac{1}{2} \times C\right) \times r \qquad \textit{Think: } C = 2 \times \pi \times r$$

$$A = \left(\tfrac{1}{2} \times 2 \times \pi \times r\right) \times r$$

$$A = (\pi \times r) \times r$$

$$A = \pi \times r^2$$

If the radius of the glass tabletop is $r = 18$ in., then:
$$A = \pi \times 18^2 \approx 3.14 \;\text{⊗}\; 18 \;\text{⊗}\; 18 \;\text{⊜}\; \boxed{1017.36}.$$

The area of the glass top is approximately 1,017.36 in.²

3. How would you use the formula to find the area of a circle
   with a diameter of $1\tfrac{1}{4}$ in.? What is the area?

4. Estimate the area of a circle with a radius of 4.9 cm.

TRY OUT

Find the area of the circle. Use 3.14 or $\frac{22}{7}$ for π.

5. 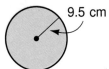 9.5 cm 6. 7 cm 7. 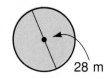 28 m 8. 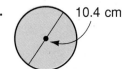 10.4 cm

PRACTICE Find the area of the circle. Use 3.14 or $\frac{22}{7}$ for π.

9. 8 m

10. $1\frac{1}{7}$ m

11. 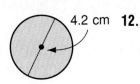 4.2 cm

12. 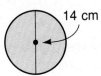 14 cm

13. 20 m

14. 0.9 cm

15. 70 m

16. 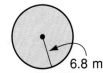 6.8 m

17. a circle whose diameter is 3 m

18. a circle whose radius is 3.2 cm

19. a circle whose diameter is 1.6 km

20. $r = 40$ km

21. $d = 60$ m

22. $d = 7$ cm

23. $r = 77$ m

24. $r = 1$ km

25. $r = 1.6$ m

26. $d = 9$ cm

27. $d = \frac{7}{8}$ cm

Estimate the area.

28. 3.8 km

29. 10.1 m

30. 15.6 cm

31. 9.7 mm

Critical Thinking

32. What is the radius of the largest circle that can fit inside a square with a perimeter of 64 cm? Why?

33. Is this statement *true* or *false*? Why or why not? If you double the radius of a circle, you also double the area of the circle.

Mixed Applications Solve. Use 3.14 or $\frac{22}{7}$ for π. You may need to use the Databank on page 554.

34. A circular piece of glass is to be cut for a picture frame that has a $3\frac{3}{8}$ in. radius. The customer wants an extension of $\frac{1}{8}$ in. on each side. How many square inches of glass will the company use?

35. What two ingredients together make up about $\frac{1}{4}$ of commercial plate glass?

36. If a sheet of glass weighs 3 kg, how much of it is made up of silica?

ACTIVITY

Areas of Irregular Figures

A camera in a high-altitude balloon took a photo of a lake as a part of a mapmaking research project. To measure the area of the lake, a mapmaker put a grid on top of the photo. The sides of each square stand for 1 mi. About what is the area of the lake in square miles?

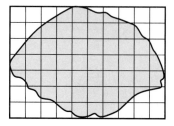

WORKING TOGETHER

1. Trace and shade the lake on a piece of grid paper. Make sure you shade it so you can see the lines on the grid paper.

2. Using the lines of your grid paper, draw the biggest figure you can that lies completely within your lake. Count the squares.

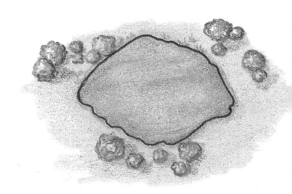

3. Using the lines of your grid paper, enclose your lake in the smallest figure you can. Count the squares between the two figures you drew.

4. How can you use the information in Problems 2 and 3 to approximate the area of the lake?

Here is how Natasha found the area. She counted 29 squares inside the lake. To that number she added one-half of 30, the number of squares between the two figures. So her estimate of the area of the lake is

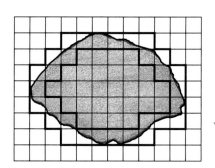

$$29 + \left(\frac{1}{2} \times 30\right) = 29 + 15 = 44 \text{ square miles.}$$

SHARING IDEAS

5. This estimation method uses one-half the number of squares between the two figures. Why do you think this number is used?

6. Find the area of the face of a quarter by tracing it on grid paper and then estimating. Then use the formula on page 440 to find the area. How does your estimate compare with the formula answer?

PRACTICE

Estimate the area of the shaded region. The sides of each square stand for 1 mi.

7.

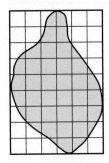

Area is about ■ mi².

8.

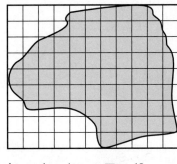

Area is about ■ mi².

9.

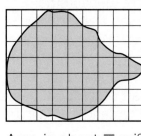

Area is about ■ mi².

10.

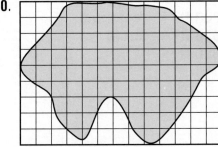

Area is about ■ mi².

11.

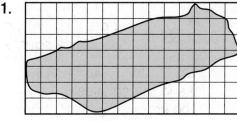

Area is about ■ mi².

Mixed Applications

Solve. You may need to use the Databank on page 554.

12. About how much lower is the surface of Lake Ontario than the surface of Lake Superior?

13. Which of the five Great Lakes is the deepest? Which of the five Great Lakes is the most shallow? What is the difference in their depths at their lowest points?

14. The surface area of Lake Ontario is about 7,540 mi². The surface area of Lake Superior is about 31,820 mi². About how many times greater than the area of Lake Ontario is the area of Lake Superior?

15. *Write a problem* about finding areas of irregular figures. Solve your problem. Ask others to solve it.

EXTRA PRACTICE, page 463; **PRACTICE PLUS**, page 466   Measurement: Area and Volume   **443**

ACTIVITY

Areas of Compound Figures

A. The diagram shows the shape and measurements for a pool that is going to be built in an indoor shopping mall. What is the area of the pool?

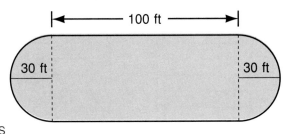

The ends of the pool are half circles. The part of the pool between the half circles is a rectangle 100 ft long and 60 ft wide.

To find the area of the pool, find the area of the rectangle and the area of the full circle you would get if you combined the half circles. Then add.

Rectangle	Circle	Add
$A = \ell \times w$	$A = \pi \times r^2$	6,000 ft² ← rectangle
$= 100 \times 60$	$\approx 3.14 \times 30^2$	+ 2,826 ft² ← circle
$= 6,000$ ft²	$\approx 3.14 \times 900$	8,826 ft²
	$\approx 2,826$ ft²	

The area of the pool is approximately 8,826 ft².

1. Why is the width of the rectangle 60 ft?

B. Judith wants to cement an area around a fish pool in her backyard. To find out about how much it will cost, she estimates the area of the part she plans to cement. About how many square feet does she need to cement?

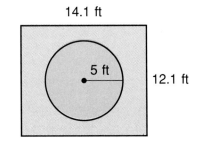

Estimate the area of the rectangle. Then subtract the area of the circle.

Rectangle	Circle	Subtract
$A = \ell \times w$	$A = \pi \times r^2$	168.0 ft² ← rectangle
$A \approx 14 \times 12$, or 168 ft²	$\approx 3.14 \times 5^2$	− 78.5 ft² ← circle
	$\approx 3.14 \times 25$	89.5 ft²
	≈ 78.5 ft²	

The area to be cemented is about 89.5 ft².

2. Is the estimate for the area to be cemented more than or less than the actual area? How do you know?

SHARING IDEAS

Describe a plan for finding the area of the shaded figures at the right. Give the area formulas you would use and tell if you would use addition or subtraction.

3.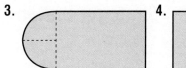

4.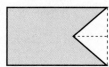

PRACTICE

Find the area of the shaded figure. Assume that parts of circles are half circles.

5.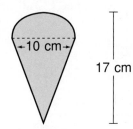

6.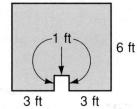

7.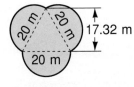

Estimate the area of the figure.

8.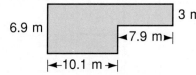

9.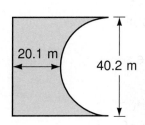

10.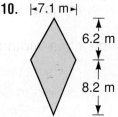

Mixed Applications

11. The shape of a swimming pool is a rectangle with half circles at the ends.

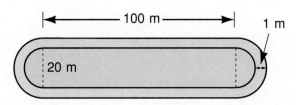

The walk around the swimming pool is 1 meter wide. How far does the lifeguard walk as he goes one time around the outside edge of the walk?

12. A swimming pool has a small, shallow end roped off for beginners.

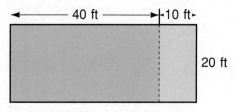

How much greater is the swimming area at the deep end than at the shallow end?

PROBLEM SOLVING

Strategy: Drawing a Diagram

A taxi service connects three railroad stations within a city. The streets run in order from 1st Street through 5th Street. The odd-numbered streets run north. The even-numbered streets run south. The avenues run in an east or west direction. First, Third, and Fifth avenues run west. Second and Fourth avenues run east.

Station A is located at 2nd Street and Second Avenue. Station B is located at 4th Street and Fifth Avenue. Station C is located at 5th Street and Third Avenue. What is the shortest route from Station A to Station B?

One way to plan to solve the problem is to make a diagram and then trace the routes. Here is a diagram you can use.

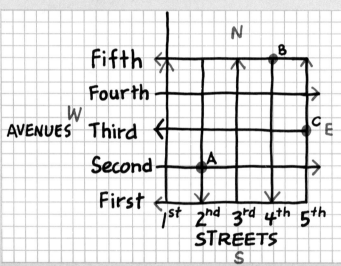

1. What is the shortest route from Station A to Station B?

2. Copy the diagram and trace two different routes from Station A to Station B.

3. Give the direction for each route you chose.

4. *Write a problem* that could be solved with this diagram.

5. Is it easier to get from Station B to Station C or from Station C to Station B? Tell why.

6. *What if* 5th Street were closed between Third and Fourth avenues due to a water-main break? In how many ways could you get from Station C to Station B? What would be the shortest route?

PRACTICE

Draw a diagram to solve the problem.

A water taxi connects the different beaches on the shores of a circular lake. Bright Beach is on the northern shore of the lake. Cove Beach is opposite Bright Beach on the southern shore of the lake. Pine Beach is on the eastern shore opposite Dune Beach, which is on the western shore. The water taxi can travel from beach to beach around the lake or across the lake from one shore to the other.

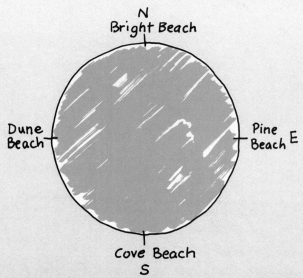

7. In how many ways could the water taxi travel from Pine Beach to Dune Beach? What are they?

8. **What if** there were another beach, Island Beach, on a small island in the middle of the lake? Show two ways the water taxi could travel from Island Beach to Cove Beach.

The Verrazano Narrows Bridge connects Staten Island to Brooklyn. There are three bridges that connect Brooklyn to lower Manhattan—the Brooklyn Bridge, the Manhattan Bridge, and the Williamsburg Bridge. The Staten Island Ferry connects Staten Island with lower Manhattan.

9. Draw a diagram for these routes. In how many ways could you travel from Staten Island to lower Manhattan? What are they?

10. **What if** the Williamsburg Bridge were closed for repairs? In how many ways could you travel from lower Manhattan to Staten Island? What are they?

Strategies and Skills Review

Solve. Use mental math, estimation, a calculator, or paper and pencil. You may need to use the diagram on page 446.

11. Find two possible taxi routes from 2nd Street and Third Avenue to 1st Street and Fifth Avenue.

12. There are 51 bicycles in a shop. Some are mountain bikes, and the rest are racing bikes. There are twice as many mountain bikes as racing bikes. How many racing bikes are there?

13. **Write a problem** that requires the use of a diagram to solve it. Ask others to solve your problem.

Visual Reasoning

A. Some figures have a special relationship between the value of their perimeter and the value of their area. Look at these two figures. Can you find the special relationship?

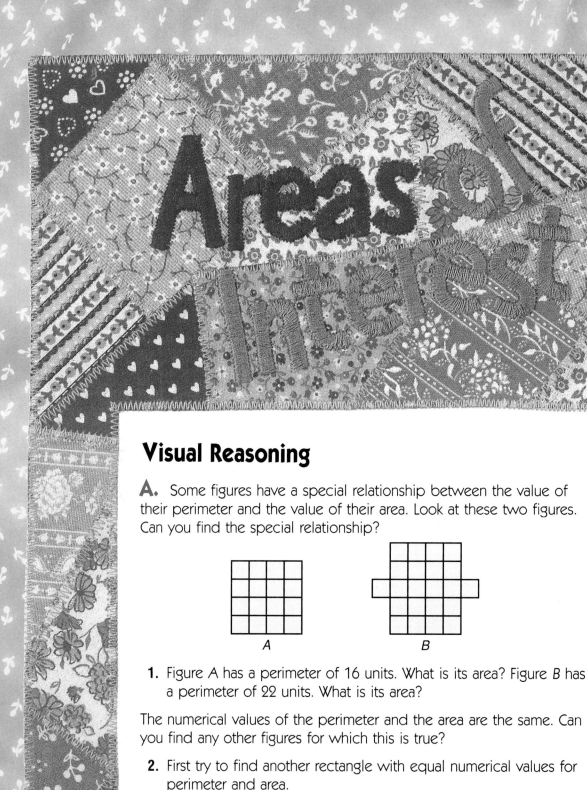

A   B

1. Figure A has a perimeter of 16 units. What is its area? Figure B has a perimeter of 22 units. What is its area?

The numerical values of the perimeter and the area are the same. Can you find any other figures for which this is true?

2. First try to find another rectangle with equal numerical values for perimeter and area.

3. Next try to find a circle whose circumference and area have the same relationship. What numbers might you try for the radius?

4. Which of these right triangles have equal numerical values for perimeter and area?

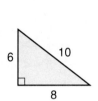
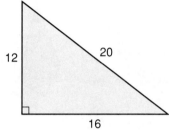

5. Now try to find another shape using square units like Figure B on page 448. Experiment with several different shapes.

B. Now consider this set of shapes:

C   D   E   F

6. Copy and complete this table:

Figure	Perimeter	Area
C		
D		
E		
F		

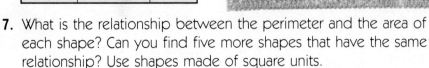

7. What is the relationship between the perimeter and the area of each shape? Can you find five more shapes that have the same relationship? Use shapes made of square units.

8. Now look again at the triangles above. Do any of them have the relationship shown in your chart?

9. Can you find a circle that also shares this relationship?

AcTiViTy **Drawing Space Figures**

Boxes, cans, and other real-world objects suggest **space figures.**
The top row of figures are **polyhedrons** because their flat surfaces,
or **faces,** are in the shape of a polygon. Two faces of a polyhedron
meet at an **edge.** The point where the edges meet is the **vertex.**

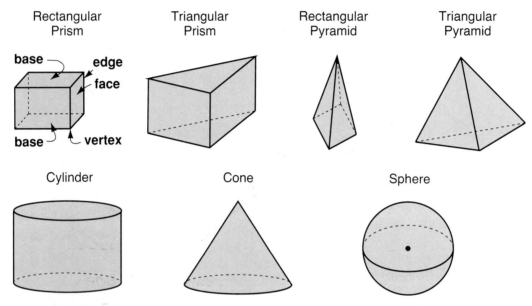

| Rectangular Prism | Triangular Prism | Rectangular Pyramid | Triangular Pyramid |

| Cylinder | Cone | Sphere |

A polyhedron is named by the shape of its **base.** A **prism** has
two congruent bases that are parallel. Its other faces are
parallelograms. A **pyramid** has a polygon for a base. Its other
faces are triangles.

WORKING TOGETHER

Make or find models of the space figures shown above. Then
answer the following questions.

1. Draw what you would see if you were above each of the
   figures and were looking straight down.

2. How are a rectangular pyramid and a triangular pyramid
   different?

3. How is a triangular prism different from a triangular
   pyramid?

4. A cube is a special type of what kind of space figure?

5. Is a cylinder, a cone, or a sphere a polyhedron? Why or
   why not?

SHARING IDEAS

Name the type of space figure that fits the description.

6. A space figure with two congruent, parallel, circular bases

7. A space figure with one circular base

8. A space figure with two congruent, parallel, rectangular bases

9. A space figure that has all its points the same distance from a point inside the figure

PRACTICE

Tell what kind of figure or figures could have a top, bottom, or side view like the one that is shown.

10. Top view

11. Top view

12. Top view

13. Top view

14. Side view

15. Side view

16. Side view

17. Side view

18. Bottom view

19. Bottom view

20. Bottom view

21. Bottom view

Mixed Applications

22. A cube-shaped box is 60 cm on each edge. It will be used for a gift and will be trimmed with gold braid. How much gold braid will be needed?

23. Each edge of a plastic cube is 5 in. long. Marlowe is going to glue a photo of a friend to cover each face. What will be the area of each photo?

EXTRA PRACTICE, page 464

ACTiViTY Volume of a Triangular Prism

Bookends come packaged two to a box. They rest on their triangular bases in the box. Ms. Jensen wants to know how much space the two bookends take up. How can she find the volume of the two bookends?

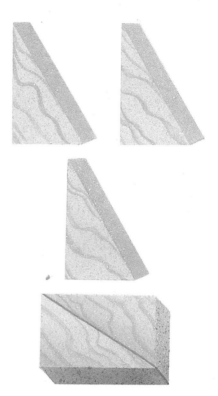

Each of the bookends is a triangular prism. The volume of the two triangular prisms is the same as the volume of the box. The box is a rectangular prism. Recall that the volume of a rectangular prism can be found by multiplying the area of its base by its height.

Volume = Area of base × Height
$$V = B \times h$$

WORKING TOGETHER

Imagine cutting a rectangular prism into two triangular prisms of the same size and shape.

1. How is the area of the base of each triangular prism related to the area of the base of the rectangular prism?

2. How do the heights of the two triangular prisms compare to the height of the rectangular prism?

3. How is the volume of a triangular prism related to the volume of the original rectangular prism?

4. How can you use the formula for the volume of a rectangular prism to find the volume of a triangular prism?

SHARING IDEAS

Here is what Ms. Jensen wrote as a formula to find the volume of *any* prism: Volume = Area of base × Height
$$V = B \times h.$$

5. Do you agree? Why or why not?

6. How can you find the volume of a triangular prism?

7. How can you find the height of a prism if you know its volume and the area of its base?

PRACTICE

Find the volume of the prism.

8.
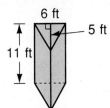
6 ft
5 ft
11 ft

9.
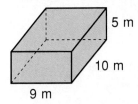
5 m
10 m
9 m

10.
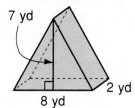
7 yd
2 yd
8 yd

11.
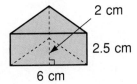
2 cm
2.5 cm
6 cm

12.
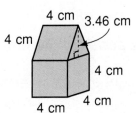
4 cm 3.46 cm
4 cm
4 cm
4 cm 4 cm

13.
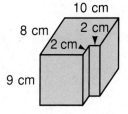
10 cm
8 cm 2 cm
2 cm
9 cm

Critical Thinking

14. The base of a rectangular prism is 15 cm wide and 20 cm long. The height is 10 cm. If a triangular prism has the same volume and the area of its base is 150 cm², what is its height?

Mixed Applications

15. Mrs. Jensen wants to paint one of the triangular walls in her attic. What is the area of the wall that she wants to paint?

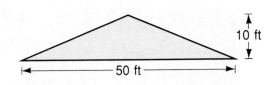
10 ft
50 ft

16. Ms. Jensen has 3 filing cabinets that are each 18 in. wide, 42 in. long, and 36 in. high. How many cubic feet of space will they take up in her attic office?

Volume of a Cylinder

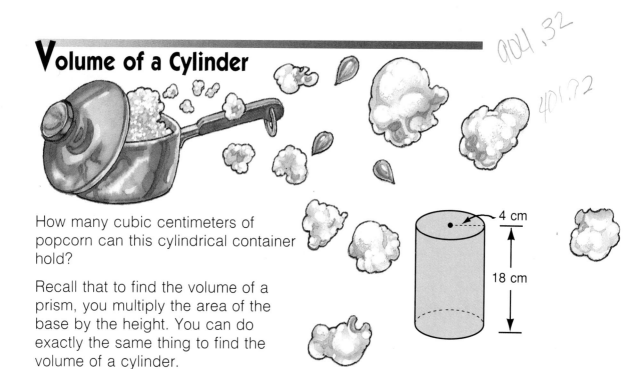

904.32

401.?2

How many cubic centimeters of popcorn can this cylindrical container hold?

Recall that to find the volume of a prism, you multiply the area of the base by the height. You can do exactly the same thing to find the volume of a cylinder.

Volume of cylinder = Area of base × height

$$V = \pi \times r^2 \times h$$
$$V \approx 3.14 \times 4^2 \times 18$$
$$V \approx 3.14 \times 16 \times 18$$
$$V \approx 904.32$$

The volume of the container is about 904.32 cm³.

1. **What if** you double the height of a cylinder but keep the base the same? How will the volume change? Why?

2. **What if** you double the radius of the bases of a cylinder? How will the volume change? Why?

TRY OUT Write the letter of the correct answer. Find the volume of the cylinder. Use 3.14 or $\frac{22}{7}$ for π.

3.

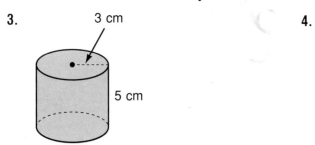

3 cm

5 cm

  a. 9.42 cm³   **c.** 94.2 cm³
  b. 28.26 cm³   **d.** 141.3 cm³

4.

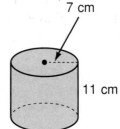

7 cm

11 cm

  a. 44 cm³   **c.** 1,694 cm³
  b. 154 cm³   **d.** 6,776 cm³

PRACTICE

Find the volume to the nearest hundredth. Use 3.14 or $\frac{22}{7}$ for π.

5.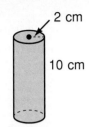
2 cm
10 cm

6.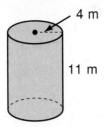
4 m
11 m

7.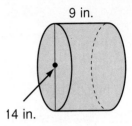
9 in.
14 in.

8.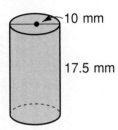
10 mm
17.5 mm

9.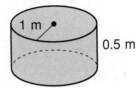
1 m
0.5 m

10.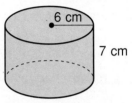
6 cm
7 cm

11.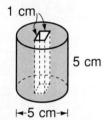
1 cm
5 cm
|←5 cm→|

12.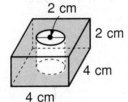
2 cm
2 cm
4 cm
4 cm

13.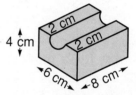
2 cm
2 cm
4 cm
6 cm 8 cm

Mixed Applications

14. A water trough is a half cylinder. The trough is 8 ft long and 2 ft deep. How many cubic feet of water does it hold when it is full to the brim?

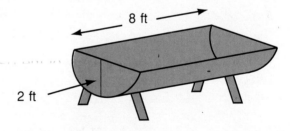
8 ft
2 ft

15. A tin can weighs 20 g. The contents weigh 15 g per in.³. The can has a volume of 55.8 in.³. What is the weight of a full can?

16. *Write a problem* that involves a drum with a diameter of 8 in. Solve your problem. Ask others to solve it.

Mixed Review

Find the answer. Which method did you use?

17. 862 − 794

18. 8 × 8 × 8 × 8

19. 14.3 + 19.91 + 0.6

20. $16\frac{2}{3} \div \frac{2}{5}$

21. 0.072 × 1,000

22. $8\frac{8}{9} + 6\frac{1}{2}$

MENTAL MATH
CALCULATOR
PAPER/PENCIL

***EXTRA* PRACTICE**, page 462

PROBLEM SOLVING

Strategy: Using a Physical Model

Joe Garcia is planning to build a cardboard model of a skyscraper. He is going to stack rectangular prisms and cubes, and then place a square pyramid on top.

Joe begins by drawing patterns for each of the shapes he will use.

First, Joe draws the two patterns shown below on a sheet of paper. He wonders if each pattern will fold to form a cube. To find out, he decides to cut out each pattern and then fold it along the dotted lines.

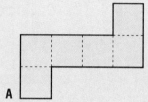

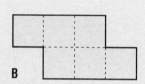

Copy Joe's pattern on a sheet of paper so that each side of a square is 2 in. Then cut out each pattern and fold it along the dotted lines.

1. Which pattern folds to form a cube?

2. Next, Joe draws the pattern shown at the right. What figure do you think the pattern will form if it is cut out and then folded? Copy the pattern on another sheet of paper, then cut it out and fold it. Was your guess correct?

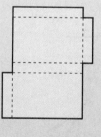

3. To make the top of the skyscraper, Joe needs a square pyramid. He draws the patterns below. Which pattern will fold to make the model Joe wants?

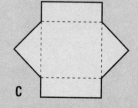

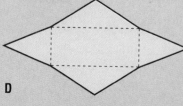

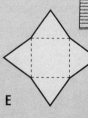

PRACTICE

Solve.

Look at the following patterns. Which do you think can be cut out and folded to form a cube?

4.

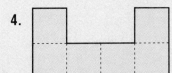

5.

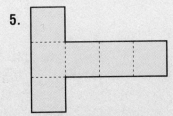

6. Draw two other patterns that can be cut out and folded to form a cube.

7. Draw a pattern for a shoe box without its top.

8. Look at the prism to the right. Draw a pattern that can be cut out and then folded to make a model of the prism.

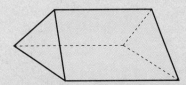

Strategies and Skills Review

Solve. Use estimation, mental math, a calculator, or paper and pencil.

9. On Wednesday the Marlowes had $96 in their entertainment fund. On Thursday they spent $16. On Friday they spent half of what was left. On Saturday Mrs. Marlowe put $25 into the fund. On Sunday they spent $40. How much did they have left?

10. Karen wants to buy a dress that costs $9.18, a coat that costs $53.65, and shoes that cost $29.95. Is $100 enough to purchase these items? Did you overestimate or underestimate to solve the problem? Why?

11. George wants to arrange 6 sports posters on his wall. What is the fewest number of tacks he will need if the four corners of each poster need tacking?

12. *Write a problem* that can be solved by using a physical model. Solve your problem. Ask others to solve it.

DECISION MAKING

Problem Solving: Planning the Shape of a Flower Bed

SITUATION

The sixth-grade science class at Whitman School wants to plant sunflower seeds and keep a record of their growth. Each row of seeds should be 1 ft apart. The seeds in each row should be planted 6 in. apart. There will also be a border of 1 ft all the way around the flower bed. The principal has set aside space for the garden, but there is a flagpole in the middle of the space.

PROBLEM

What shape of flower bed should the class choose?

DATA

A class committee has suggested three different shapes for the sunflower bed.

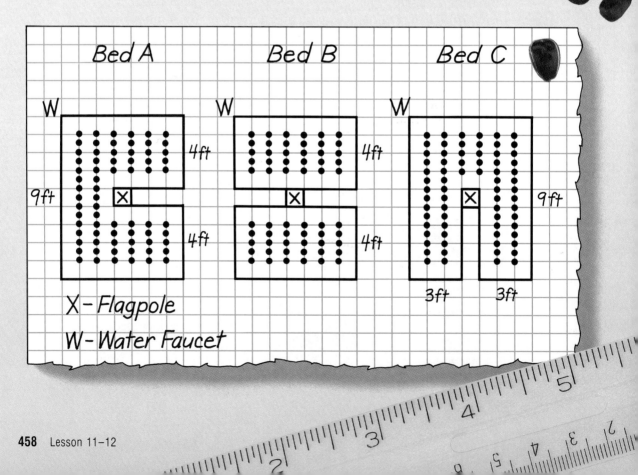

USING THE DATA

What is the area of the flower bed not including the border?

1. Bed A   **2.** Bed B   **3.** Bed C

What is the area of the flower bed including the border?

4. Bed A   **5.** Bed B   **6.** Bed C

How many rows of seeds can the students plant in the flower bed?

7. Bed A   **8.** Bed B   **9.** Bed C

What is the total number of seeds the students can plant in the flower bed?

10. Bed A   **11.** Bed B   **12.** Bed C

MAKING DECISIONS

13. Which flower bed should they choose to have the greatest area for planting?

14. Which flower bed should they choose to plant the least number of rows?

15. Which flower bed should they choose to produce the greatest number of plants?

16. Which flower bed should they choose to have the greatest area?

17. From which flower bed would it be the easiest to raise and take down the flag?

18. Draw your own plan for the flower bed. How did you decide upon your plan?

19. *Write a list* of the other factors the students should consider.

20. Which plan would you choose? Tell why.

Math and Art

Repeated patterns have been used to create designs in many cultures. Examples of this can be found in the mosaic designs in the Alhambra (al-HAM-brah), an Islamic palace in southern Spain built by the Moors in 1248. Some artists use a technique called **tessellation** to create patterns. The surface is covered with repeated flat geometric figures that fit together with no spaces between them. This technique was made famous by a Dutch graphic artist, M. C. Escher (ESH-er).

What if you want to cover a hexagonal surface with equilateral triangles? How many triangles do you need?

Think: A hexagon has 6 equal sides.
You need only 6 equilateral triangles.

ACTIVITIES

1. Make a pattern in the shape of a hexagon. Trace the figure and then cut out several to make a tessellation. Show your results to the class. Try to make a tessellation with a pentagon. Is it possible?

2. Look in books of art reproductions for the works of M.C. Escher. Identify the shapes in his work. Look for examples of symmetry, rotations, reflections, and tessellations. Share your findings with the class.

Computer: Exploring Regular Polygons

You can use Logo commands to explore regular polygons. Recall that regular polygons have angles of equal measure and sides of equal length.

AT THE COMPUTER

The procedure below draws a regular polygon when you enter the number of sides and the length of each side. Enter this procedure:

```
TO POLY :SIDES :LENGTH
REPEAT :SIDES [FD :LENGTH RT 360/:SIDES]
END
```

Notice that the procedure uses a repeat command with as many repetitions as there are sides.

To draw a square with sides of length 10, enter POLY 4 10.

1. Clear the screen and draw a pentagon with sides of length 30. What command did you enter?

2. Clear the screen and draw a hexagon with sides of length 35. Then draw another hexagon with sides of length 45. Continue drawing hexagons and increasing the lengths of the sides by 10 units. How would you describe the drawing?

3. The POLY procedure computes the measure of the turn angle by dividing 360 by the number of sides. What is the measure of the turn angle for a hexagon? for an octagon?

4. In most cases the measure of the turn angle is *not* the same as the angle measure of the polygon. Since the turn angle and the angle of the polygon form a straight angle (with measure 180°), the measure of the angle of the polygon is equal to 180° minus the measure of the turn angle. What is the measure of each angle of an octagon? a decagon? For which regular polygon is the measure of the turn angle equal to the angle measure of the polygon?

5. Use POLY to draw a figure with 20 sides. Experiment with different lengths to get the best drawing. What geometric figure does the figure on the screen resemble? Experiment with larger values for the number of sides. What do you notice?

60°

180° − 60° = 120°

EXTRA PRACTICE

Circles and Circumference, page 437

What is the diameter of the circle?

1.
4 ft

2.
2.3 cm

What is the radius of the circle?

3.
16 m

4.
$\frac{5}{8}$ yd

Find the missing measure.

5. $d = 5$ ft, $C \approx$ ■

6. $d = 12$ m, $C \approx$ ■

7. $r = 7$ cm, $C \approx$ ■

8. $C = 48$ in., $d =$ ■

9. $C = 60$ cm, $d =$ ■

10. $C = 36$ m, $r =$ ■

Finding Circumference, page 439

Find the circumference of the circle. Use 3.14 or $\frac{22}{7}$ for π.

1. $d = 20$ cm

2. $d = 2.5$ km

3. $d = 49$ m

4. $d = 0.8$ km

5. $r = 3.5$ cm

6. $r = 8$ cm

7. $r = 0.4$ m

8. $r = 15$ km

9. $r = 20$ m

10. $d = 5.4$ m

11. $r = 2.8$ m

12. $d = 9$ km

Estimate the circumference.

13. $d = 1.8$ cm

14. $r = 4.6$ m

15. $r = 7.2$ km

16. $r = 11.8$ cm

17. $d = 9.85$ m

18. $d = 30.14$ m

19. $r = 5.9$ cm

20. $d = 19.95$ m

Area of a Circle, page 441

Find the area of the circle. Use 3.14 or $\frac{22}{7}$ for π.

1.
6 m

2.
$1\frac{3}{4}$ yd

3.
5.8 cm

4.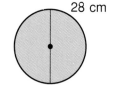
28 cm

5. a circle whose diameter is 5 m

6. a circle whose radius is 4.1 cm

7. a circle whose diameter is 1.4 km

8. $r = 20$ km

9. $d = 80$ m

10. $d = 9$ cm

11. $r = 7$ m

12. $r = 3$ km

13. $r = 2.4$ m

14. $d = 2$ cm

15. $d = \frac{1}{5}$ mi

EXTRA PRACTICE

Areas of Irregular Figures, page 443 ·

Estimate the area of the shaded region. The sides of each
square stand for 1 mi.

1.

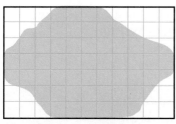

Area is about ■ mi².

2.

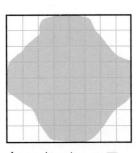

Area is about ■ mi².

3.

Area is about ■ mi².

4.

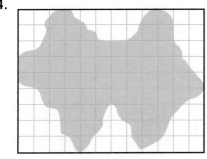

Area is about ■ mi².

5.

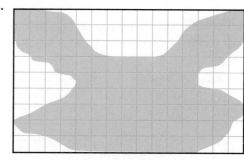

Area is about ■ mi².

Areas of Compound Figures, page 445 ·

Find the area of the shaded figure. Assume that parts of circles
are half circles.

1.

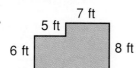

7 ft
5 ft
6 ft
8 ft

2.

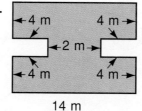

4 m 4 m
2 m
4 m 4 m
14 m

3.

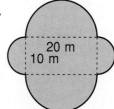

20 m
10 m

4.

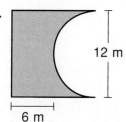

12 m
6 m

5.

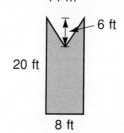

6 ft
20 ft
8 ft

6.

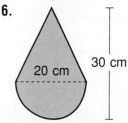

20 cm
30 cm

Measurement: Area and Volume **463**

EXTRA PRACTICE

Problem Solving Strategy: Drawing a Diagram, page 447 . . . .

Draw a diagram to solve the problem.

1. Jay is putting photographs of the school play on the main bulletin board. If he overlaps the corners, he has space to put up 9 photos with 3 in each row. How many tacks will he use?

2. To make a bracelet, Ada separates a long piece of silver into fourths. She keeps one fourth intact, cuts one fourth in half, and another in fourths. Ada cuts the last fourth into eighths. How many pieces of silver does she have?

Drawing Space Figures, page 451 . . . .

Tell what kind of figure or figures could have a top, bottom, or side view like the one that is shown.

1. top view

2. side view

3. bottom view

4. top view

5. side view

6. bottom view

7. top view

8. side view

9. side view

10. bottom view

11. top view

12. top view

Volume of a Triangular Prism, page 453 ·······································

Find the volume.

1.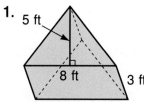
5 ft 8 ft 3 ft

2.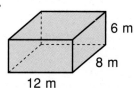
6 m 8 m 12 m

3.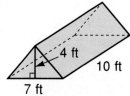
4 ft 10 ft 7 ft

4.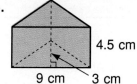
4.5 cm 9 cm 3 cm

5.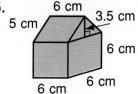
6 cm 5 cm 3.5 cm 6 cm 6 cm 6 cm

6.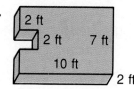
2 ft 2 ft 7 ft 10 ft 2 ft

Volume of a Cylinder, page 455 ···

Find the volume to the nearest hundredth. Use 3.14 or $\frac{22}{7}$ for π.

1.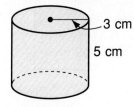
3 cm 5 cm

2.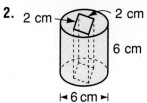
2 cm 2 cm 6 cm 6 cm

3.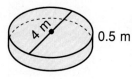
4 m 0.5 m

Problem Solving Strategy: Using a Physical Model, page 457 ··············

Use a physical model to solve the problem.

1. Can the pattern below be folded to form a cube? First guess. Then check your guess by copying the pattern and then cutting it out and folding it along the dotted lines.

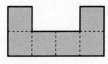

2. What geometric figure will this pattern form?

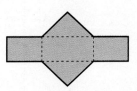

Practice PLUS

KEY SKILL: Areas of Irregular Figures (Use after page 443.)

Level A

Estimate the area of the shaded region. The sides of each square stand for 1 mi.

1.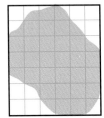

Area is about ■ mi².

2.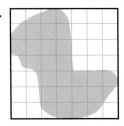

Area is about ■ mi².

3.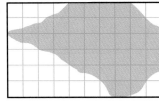

Area is about ■ mi².

Level B

Estimate the area of the shaded region. The sides of each square stand for 1 mi.

4.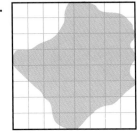

Area is about ■ mi².

5.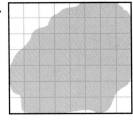

Area is about ■ mi².

6.

Area is about ■ mi².

Level C

Estimate the area of the shaded region. The sides of each square stand for 1 mi.

7.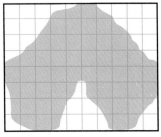

Area is about ■ mi².

8.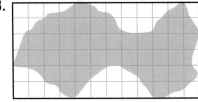

Area is about ■ mi².

KEY SKILL: Areas of Compound Figures (Use after page 445.)

Level A

Find the area of the shaded figure. Parts of circles are half circles.

1.

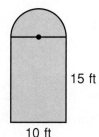

15 ft
10 ft

2.

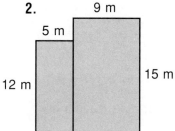

9 m
5 m
12 m
15 m

3.

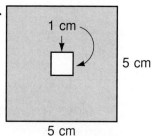

1 cm
5 cm
5 cm

Level B

Find the area of the shaded figure. Parts of circles are half circles.

4.

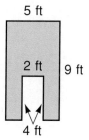

5 ft
2 ft
9 ft
4 ft

5.

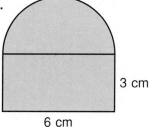

3 cm
6 cm

6.

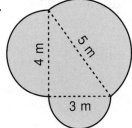

4 m
5 m
3 m

Level C

Find the area of the shaded figure. Parts of circles are half circles.

7.

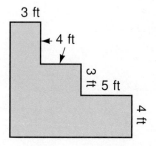

3 ft
4 ft
3 ft 5 ft
4 ft

8.

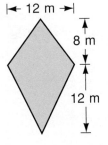

|← 12 m →|
8 m
12 m

9.

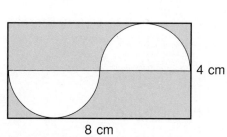

4 cm
8 cm

10. A swimming pool is shaped like a rectangle with a half circle at each end. The rectangular part is 15 ft wide and 30 ft long. There is a 1-ft wide walkway around the pool. What area do the pool and walkway cover?

CHAPTER REVIEW/TEST

LANGUAGE AND MATHEMATICS

Complete the sentences. Use the words in the chart on the right.

1. All points on a circle are the same distance from the ■ of the circle.

2. Prisms and pyramids are named by the shapes of their ■.

3. The distance around a circle is called the ■.

4. The sides and bases of a prism are called ■.

CONCEPTS AND SKILLS

First find the circumference of the circle, then find the area. Use $\pi = 3.14$.

5. $d = 6$ in.   **6.** $d = 7$ m   **7.** $r = 10$ cm   **8.** $r = 5$ m

Find the area. Circle parts are half circles. Use $\pi = 3.14$.

9.
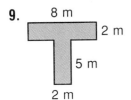

10.
3 in.

6 in.

4 in.

11.
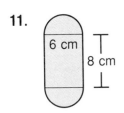

12.
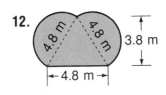

Draw the figure.

13. side view of a cube   **14.** bottom view of a sphere

15. top view of a triangular pyramid   **16.** top view of a rectangular prism

17. side view of a cylinder   **18.** bottom view of a cylinder

Find the volume. Use $\pi = 3.14$.

19.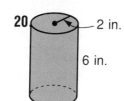
5 ft
10 ft
6 ft

20.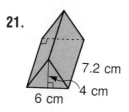
2 in.
6 in.

21.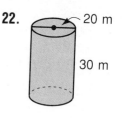
7.2 cm
4 cm
6 cm

22.
20 m
30 m

Critical Thinking

23. What is the volume of the largest cylinder that can fit inside a cube with a volume of 27 cm³?

Mixed Applications

24. A floor is 15 ft by 8 ft. How many square feet would not be covered by a circular rug with a diameter of 8 ft? Use $\pi = 3.14$.

25. A rectangular flower bed is 12 m by 20 m. A sidewalk 4 m wide goes around the bed. What is the area of the sidewalk?

PERFORMANCE ASSESSMENT

Work with your group to solve this problem.

A recreational park is building two swimming pools, one for diving and one for swimming. Both pools will be located in an area that is 125 ft long and 60 ft wide. The diving pool will be circular and the swimming pool will be a rectangle. A deck will be built that goes around the pool area and separates the two pools. Design the new pool area. Determine the size and area of each of the pools and the area of the deck space.

1. *Think about:*
   - the size of the total area
   - how long and wide to make the swimming pool
   - what radius to make the circular pool
   - how to find the area of the deck space

2. Write a paragraph describing how you planned the new pool area. Include statements of how you determined the size of the pools and the deck area.

CUMULATIVE REVIEW

Choose the letter of the correct answer.

1. What is the area of a circle with a radius equal to 6 m?
   a. 9π m²
   b. 12π m²
   c. 36π m²
   d. not given

2. What is the circumference of a circle with a diameter of 8 ft?
   a. 8π ft
   b. 16π ft
   c. 64π ft
   d. not given

3. The top view of a rectangular pyramid looks like a:
   a. triangle.
   b. rectangle.
   c. square.
   d. not given

4. What is the volume of a cylinder with $d = 10$ m and $h = 6$ m?
   a. 50π m³
   b. 60π m³
   c. 600π m³
   d. not given

5. Find the volume.

   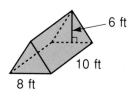

   6 ft
   10 ft
   8 ft

   a. 80 ft³
   b. 240 ft³
   c. 480 ft³
   d. not given

6. 15 to 12 is the same as:
   a. 5 to 4.
   b. 4 to 5.
   c. 3 to 4.
   d. not given

7. Solve: $\frac{4}{7} = \frac{2}{n}$
   a. 8
   b. 14
   c. 35
   d. not given

8. 0.06 written as a percent is:
   a. 0.06%.
   b. 6%.
   c. 60%.
   d. not given

9. $\frac{1}{5}$ written as a percent is:
   a. 2%.
   b. 5%.
   c. 20%.
   d. not given

10. Which is a line segment?
    a. [arrow]
    b. [angle]
    c. [arrow]
    d. not given

11. Two angles of a triangle measure 75° each. What is the measure of the third angle?
    a. 50°
    b. 30°
    c. 75°
    d. not given

12. How many diagonals are in a hexagon?
    a. 3
    b. 5
    c. 6
    d. not given

13. $2\frac{1}{3} \times 3\frac{1}{5}$
    a. $6\frac{1}{15}$
    b. $\frac{35}{48}$
    c. $7\frac{7}{15}$
    d. not given

14. Zita had $204.50 in her savings account. She deposited $12 and $15.50 and withdrew $25. How much did Zita have in her account then?
    a. $207.00
    b. $257.00
    c. $152.00
    d. not given

EXPLORING CROSS SECTIONS

If a plane cuts straight through a three-dimensional figure, the surface of the area that is cut is called a *cross section* of the figure. The size and shape of the cross section depend on how the cut is made. The diagrams below show two cross sections you could get by cutting straight through a cube.

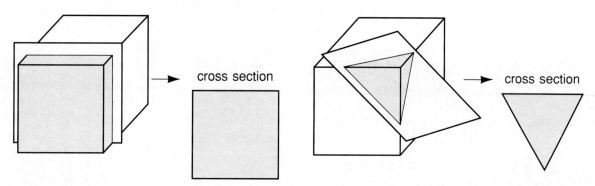

Draw the shape of the cross section you would get for the figure.

1. sphere

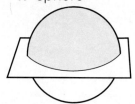

2. cube

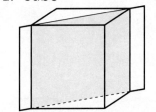

3. cone

4. sphere

5. rectangular prism

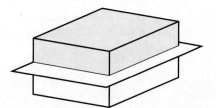

6. triangular pyramid

7. Which of the following could you get if you cut through a cube?
   a. rectangle   **b.** pentagon   **c.** trapezoid   **d.** hexagon
   e. square   **f.** isosceles triangle   **g.** equilateral triangle

8. Which of the following could you get if you cut through a cone?
   a. triangle   **b.** square   **c.** circle   **d.** rectangle

Totolospi [toe-TOE-lahs-pea] is a game of chance that is enjoyed by Hopi adults and children. Many Hopi live in northeastern Arizona in *pueblos* [poo-EBB-lowz]. *Pueblo* is a Spanish word meaning "town."

Totolospi is played with cane sticks from 3 to 6 inches long. The sticks are split so that each has a round side and a flat side. A player holds two or three cane sticks and then drops them on end. The number of spaces a player may move is determined by whether the sticks land on the flat or round sides.

In addition to cane sticks, a counting board is used. Some boards are oval and some are rectangular. Totolospi can be played by two or four players, and the board used depends on the number of players. Players place their counters, which usually represent animals, on a circle called "the house" in the center of the board. The first player to return to the house is the winner.

Hopi Indian
Reservation
ARIZONA

THE
HOPI
GAME
TO

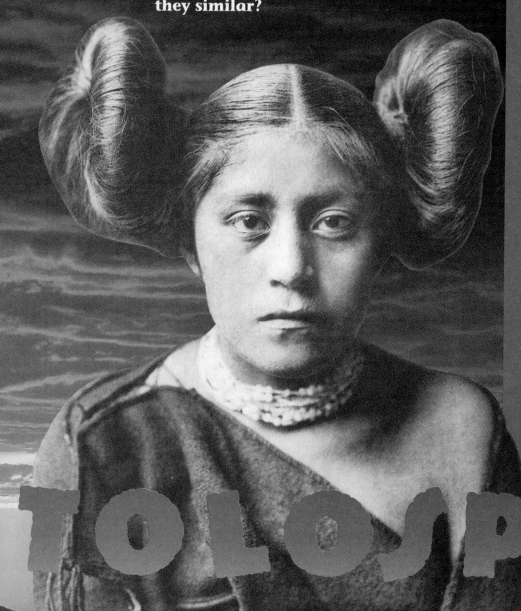

1.

Why is Totolospi considered a game of chance?

2.

What board games have you played that are similar to Totolospi? In what ways are they similar?

TOLOSPI

ACTIVITY

Probability: Modeling an Experiment

Mindy needs to move her game piece exactly five spaces to win. The faces of the number cube she will roll are numbered from 1 through 6. What are her chances of getting a 5?

WORKING TOGETHER

Roll a number cube 60 times. The result of a roll is called the **outcome.** Keep track of the outcomes and record the totals in a chart like the one at the right.

Outcome →	1	2	3	4	5	6
Number of times outcome occurred →						

1. Did you roll some numbers more often than others? If so, which numbers were they? If you repeated the experiment, would you expect the same result?

2. What number did you get least often? If you repeated the experiment, would you expect the same result?

3. Are you as likely to get a 5 as a 2 when you roll a number cube? Are you as likely to get a 1 as a 6? Why?

Here are the results that a pair of students got when they did the experiment.

Outcome →	1	2	3	4	5	6
Number of times outcome occurred →	13	9	10	8	11	9

Notice that:

5 was the outcome 11 out of 60 times, or $\frac{11}{60}$. $\frac{11}{60}$ is close to $\frac{1}{6}$.

3 was the outcome 10 out of 60 times, or $\frac{10}{60}$. $\frac{10}{60}$ is equal to $\frac{1}{6}$.

6 was the outcome 9 out of 60 times, or $\frac{9}{60}$. $\frac{9}{60}$ is close to $\frac{1}{6}$.

Recall that the number cube has 6 numbers on it. Assuming that the cube is fair, you have an equally likely chance of rolling one number as another. The **probability,** or chance, of rolling any one of the numbers is 1 out of 6, or $\frac{1}{6}$.

SHARING IDEAS

4. Combine the experimental results that you or your group got with those of all the groups in the class. For each outcome, do you still get fractions that are close in value to $\frac{1}{6}$?

5. What do you think is the probability of rolling an even number?

ON YOUR OWN

6. Look at these two spinners. Is the probability the same for spinner A as for spinner B that the pointer will stop on green? Why or why not?

Spinner A Spinner B

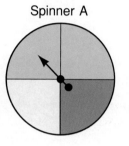 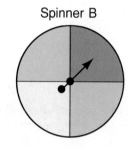

7. Use your numbered spinner. What is the probability that the pointer will stop on 0? on an even number? on an odd number?

8. Write these letters on index cards:

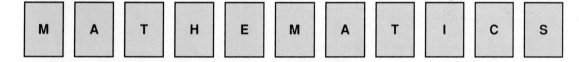

If you were to pick one of the cards without looking, which letters would have a greatest probability of being picked? Why?

Probability

The cubes below are exactly alike except for their color. You put the cubes in the bag, then reach in without looking, and pick a cube. What is the probability that the cube will be red?

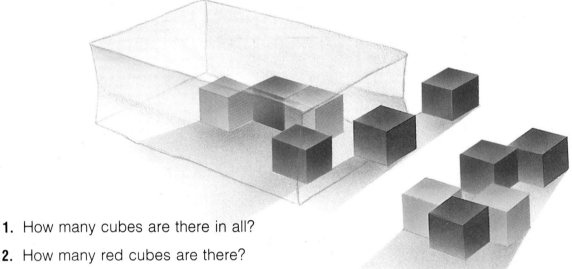

1. How many cubes are there in all?

2. How many red cubes are there?

3. What is the probability of picking a red cube?

The ratio describing the chance that an event will occur is called the probability of the event.

Probability of event = P(event) = $\dfrac{\text{number of favorable outcomes}}{\text{total number of outcomes}}$

The probability that you will pick a red cube is:

$$P(\text{red}) = \frac{\text{number of red cubes}}{\text{total number of cubes}} = \frac{3}{12} = \frac{1}{4}$$

4. What is the probability of picking a green cube? a blue cube?

SHARING IDEAS

5. How could you change the colors of the cubes in the bag to keep the same total but to make it just as likely that you would pick one color as another?

6. **What if** you added 6 more red cubes to the original bag? What would P(red) be?

7. **What if** you added 8 more cubes to the original bag? How many would have to be red to keep $P(\text{red}) = \frac{1}{4}$?

PRACTICE

Suppose you spin the spinner. What is:

8. *P*(red)? **9.** *P*(blue)? **10.** *P*(green)?

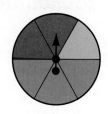

Suppose the cards below are shuffled several times and you pick one without looking.

What is:

11. *P*(■)? **12.** *P*(★)? **13.** *P*(✖)? **14.** *P*(●)?

Mixed Applications

Joanne and Armando did an experiment using a spinner whose sections were red, blue, and yellow.

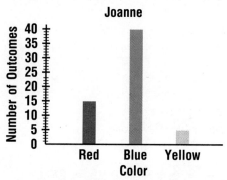 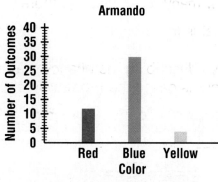

15. How many more times did Joanne spin the spinner than Armando?

16. If they combine their results into one graph, what will be the height of each color bar?

VISUAL REASONING

Trace this figure on graph paper. Show how you can cut this figure into two pieces that are exactly the same size and shape. You must cut only along the grid lines.

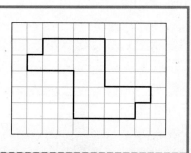

EXTRA PRACTICE, page 502

Probabilities of Events

A. What is the probability that the pointer will land on red or yellow? There are 8 equal-size sections in all. Of these, 4 are red and 2 are yellow. This means that 4 + 2, or 6, favorable outcomes are possible.

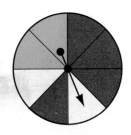

P(red or yellow) =

$$= \frac{4 + 2}{8} = \frac{6}{8} = \frac{3}{4}$$

The probability of the pointer landing on red or yellow is $\frac{3}{4}$.

B. The probability of landing on red or yellow or blue is:

$$\frac{4 + 2 + 2}{8} = \frac{8}{8} = 1$$

The probability of an event that is **certain** to occur is 1.

The probability of landing on purple is:

$$\frac{0}{8} = 0$$

The probability of an **impossible** event is 0.

1. If an event is neither certain nor impossible, between what two numbers is the probability?

C. Since you can rename any fraction as a decimal or as a percent, you can write the probability of an event as a fraction, a decimal, or a percent.

$P(\text{red}) = \frac{4}{8} = \frac{1}{2} = 0.5 = 50\%$ $P(\text{yellow}) = \frac{2}{8} = \frac{1}{4} = 0.25 = 25\%$

2. Write $P(\text{red or blue})$ as a decimal and as a percent.

TRY OUT Write the letter of the correct answer. Use the spinner. What is:

3. $P(\text{yellow})$?
   a. 0   **b.** $\frac{1}{3}$ **c.** $\frac{1}{2}$ **d.** $\frac{2}{3}$

4. $P(\text{purple})$?
   a. 1   **b.** 0.5   **c.** $\frac{1}{3}$ **d.** 25%

5. $P(\text{brown or aqua})$?
   a. 0   **b.** $\frac{1}{3}$ **c.** $\frac{1}{2}$ **d.** 1

6. $P(\text{not aqua})$?
   a. 1   **b.** $\frac{2}{3}$ **c.** $\frac{1}{2}$ **d.** $\frac{1}{3}$

PRACTICE

Use the spinner for Exercises 7–25. Write the probability of the event as a fraction in simplest form or as a whole number.

7. $P(A \text{ or } I)$

8. $P(E \text{ or } O)$

9. $P(I \text{ or } U)$

10. $P(A \text{ or } E \text{ or } O)$

11. $P(O \text{ or } U)$

12. $P(E \text{ or } I)$

13. $P(A \text{ or } E \text{ or } I \text{ or } O \text{ or } U)$

14. $P(\text{not } A)$

15. $P(\text{not } E)$

16. $P(\text{not } O)$

17. $P(\text{not } I)$

18. $P(K)$

19. $P(\text{not } M)$

20. $P(\text{vowel})$

21. $P(\text{consonant})$

Write the probability of the event as a fraction in simplest form, a decimal, and a percent.

22. $P(A)$

23. $P(E)$

24. $P(A \text{ or } E)$

25. $P(\text{not } A)$

A number cube has its faces labeled with numbers from 1 through 6. Find the probability of the event.

26. $P(4)$

27. $P(2 \text{ or } 5)$

28. $P(\text{even})$

29. $P(\text{odd})$

30. $P(7)$

31. $P(1 \text{ or } 5)$

32. $P(\text{number less than } 8)$

33. $P(\text{number greater than } 6)$

34. $P(\text{multiple of } 3)$

Critical Thinking

35. The probability of an event is $\frac{1}{3}$. How can you use this to find the probability of the event not occurring? What is the probability?

Mixed Applications

36. Linda wants to make a spinner with 25 equal sections colored red, blue, and green. She wants $P(\text{green}) = \frac{3}{5}$ and $P(\text{blue}) = \frac{1}{5}$. What must $P(\text{red})$ be?

37. Lynn has a 25% probability of winning a contest, and Adele has a 0.125 probability of winning a different contest. Which person has the better chance of winning?

Mixed Review

Find the answer. Which method did you use?

38. $5 - 3.021$

39. $8\frac{2}{7} \times 17\frac{1}{2}$

40. $49 \div \frac{6}{7}$

41. $71.95 + 843.46$

42. $\frac{2}{13} \times \frac{13}{4}$

43. 100×0.0001

44. $\frac{3}{10} + \frac{4}{15}$

45. $278 \times \frac{1}{278}$

MENTAL MATH
CALCULATOR
PAPER/PENCIL

EXTRA PRACTICE, page 502; **PRACTICE PLUS**, page 506

Activity Probability and Prediction

Without looking you reach in and pick a cube from the bag at the right. You record its color and replace the cube. You shake the bag, pick another cube, and record its color. In 20 draws how many times would you expect to pick a blue cube? a red cube? a green cube?

WORKING TOGETHER

1. Use your centimeter cubes to model the experiment above. Predict how many times you will pick each color in 20 draws. Then actually try it. Record your results.

2. **What if** you were to pick a cube 40 times? What results would you predict for each color? Try it. Are the actual results closer to the prediction this time?

3. Look at your results for 20 picks. What is the ratio of blue cubes picked to the total number of picks? What ratio do you get for red? for green?

4. Answer Problem 3 for 40 picks. Compare the ratios for 40 picks to those for 20 picks. What can you conclude?

These are Eli's results for the experiment. He concluded that the ratios would be about the same no matter how many picks there were.

blue: 20 picks, $\frac{11}{20}$ 40 picks; $\frac{22}{40}$

green: 20 picks, $\frac{3}{20}$ 40 picks, $\frac{7}{40}$

red: 20 picks, $\frac{6}{20}$ 40 picks, $\frac{11}{40}$

SHARING IDEAS

5. In simplest form, what is the probability of picking a blue cube from the bag?

6. Look at Eli's results for 20 picks. Multiply the probability of picking blue by 20. How does this compare to the actual number of times Eli picked blue?

7. Look at Eli's results for 40 picks. Multiply the probability of picking green and of picking red by 40. How do your numbers compare with the actual number of times Eli picked these colors?

8. How can you use the probability of an event to predict the number of favorable outcomes?

PRACTICE

Predict how many times you would pick the color(s) from the bag in 100 picks.

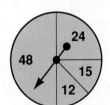

9. red   **10.** blue

11. yellow   **12.** green

13. red or yellow   **14.** blue or red

15. yellow or blue   **16.** red or green   **17.** not red

18. not blue   **19.** not yellow   **20.** not green

Predict the number of favorable outcomes out of 1,000 spins.

21. red   **22.** blue

23. green   **24.** not blue

25. blue or green   **26.** red or yellow

27. neither red nor yellow   **28.** neither red nor green

Suppose you spin this spinner 56 times, predict how many times the pointer will land on:

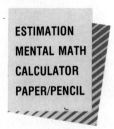

29. a multiple of 5.   **30.** a number divisible by 3.

31. an even number.   **32.** 12.

Mixed Applications

Solve. Which method did you use?

**ESTIMATION
MENTAL MATH
CALCULATOR
PAPER/PENCIL**

33. Marcia wants to make a spinner with 15 equal sections that will be colored red, blue, and green. If $P(\text{red}) = \frac{4}{15}$ and $P(\text{green}) = \frac{4}{15}$, how many blue sections will there be?

34. Hilton has a drawer filled with 12 pairs of socks. There are 4 pairs of blue socks, 3 pairs of black socks, 3 pairs of white socks, and 2 pairs of red socks. If Hilton picks a pair without looking, what is the probability that the socks will be red?

35. A computer randomly prints 1-digit numbers from 5 through 9. If 500,000 of these are printed, about how many times will the number 7 occur?

36. In a contest Phil has a 1 in 500 chance of winning. Ruth has a 2 in 750 chance. Who has the better chance? Why?

ACTIVITY Making Predictions

Lee rolled two number cubes 100 times. Each time he recorded the sum of the numbers on the tops of the cubes. The statistics, or results, are given below.

Sum Rolled	2	3	4	5	6	7	8	9	10	11	12
Number of Occurrences	3	5	8	11	14	17	14	11	8	6	3

Lee invented a game using number cubes. Team A will score a point if a sum of 6, 7, or 8 is rolled. Team B can choose any other three sums that will score them a point. Which team do you predict will win?

WORKING TOGETHER

Divide your group into two teams.

1. Choose any other three sums for Team B. Record your prediction of which team will win. Roll 2 number cubes 100 times. Did the team you predicted win? Explain how you made your prediction.

2. Would you expect the same results if you played the game again?

3. Lee wanted to use his results to make a fairer game. How would you set up a new game so that the teams had the same chance of scoring a point?

This is how Dalia came up with a fairer game.

Team A: $P(2 \text{ to } 6) = \dfrac{3 + 5 + 8 + 11 + 14}{100} = \dfrac{41}{100}$ ⎫
Team B: $P(8 \text{ to } 12) = \dfrac{14 + 11 + 8 + 6 + 3}{100} = \dfrac{42}{100}$ ⎬ roughly equal
⎭

SHARING IDEAS

4. Compare your predictions with the predictions of other groups.

5. How does your new, fairer game compare with those of others?

6. How can you use statistics to make predictions?

PRACTICE

7. Out of 200 light bulbs, 20 were found to be defective. How many would you expect to be defective out of 5,000? Explain how you made your prediction.

8. Look in a telephone book. Record the last digit of each number in one column. How many numbers end in 1? What do you predict you will find if you check the last digit of numbers in another column? If you pick 1,000 numbers at random, how many would you expect to end in 1?

9. Record the weather in your area for a week. By using this record, can you say whether it is likely to be sunny or rainy in your area during this same week next year? Why?

10. Take a survey of left-handedness and right-handedness among the students in your class. How many students out of 1,000 would you predict are left-handed? How sure do you feel about your prediction? Explain your thinking.

Harriet asked a local blood bank about the blood types in her town. They gave her a copy of a graph that showed these statistics.

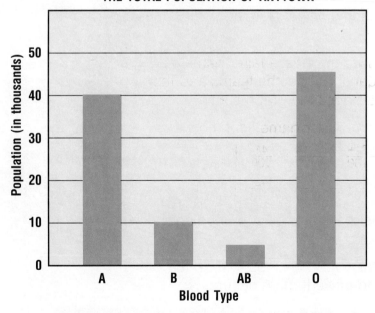

BLOOD TYPES OF THE TOTAL POPULATION OF ANYTOWN

11. When Harriet's company had a blood drive, 250 people donated blood. Predict the number of people with each blood type.

EXTRA PRACTICE, page 503

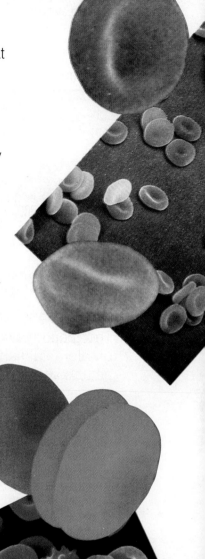

Misleading Statistics

Ms. Smith owns two shoe stores and wants to expand one store. She wants to look at the first six months of sales for each store. The manager of one store prepared a table, and the other prepared a double-bar graph.

MONTHLY SHOE SALES

Month	Shoes Galore	Shoes Plus
Jan.	$22,500	$26,700
Feb.	$29,600	$38,800
Mar.	$40,400	$49,500
Apr.	$40,200	$49,500
May	$45,300	$65,300
June	$28,200	$32,400

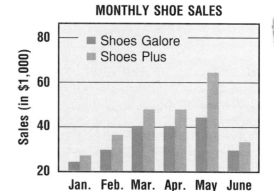

1. What were the total sales for Shoes Galore? for Shoes Plus?

2. The graph makes it look as if Shoes Plus has much greater total sales than Shoes Galore. What is the actual difference in total sales?

The graph above gives a misleading visual impression for some months.

3. According to the table, about how much greater were the sales in May for Shoes Plus than for Shoes Galore? What does the graph show?

4. How does the vertical scale on the graph affect the way in which the data is presented?

SHARING IDEAS

5. For what other months does the graph give misleading data?

6. Ms. Smith asked the manager of Shoes Plus to redo the graph. What should he do to make it more accurate?

7. **What if** Ms. Smith wants to expand both stores? What other information might she need before making expansion plans?

PRACTICE

Use the following graphs and table for Problems 8 and 9.

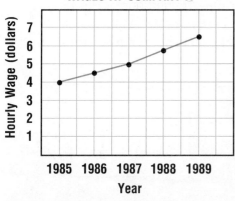

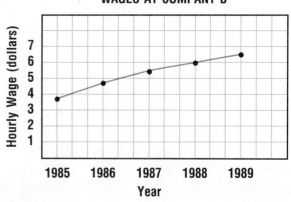

Year	1985	1986	1987	1988	1989
Company A	$4.00	$4.50	$5.00	$5.75	$6.50
Company B	$3.75	$4.75	$5.25	$6.00	$6.50

8. Which company appears to have increased its wages more over the years 1985–1989? Which company actually increased its wages more?

9. Are the graphs misleading? Why?

10. The author of a travel guide used the following temperature table in preparing an article about the town of Lyndon. For the article he averaged the monthly high temperatures. He stated that Lyndon had a mild climate with temperatures around 63°F. Is the statement misleading? Why?

Month	Jan.	Feb.	Mar.	Apr.	May	June	July	Aug.	Sept.	Oct.	Nov.	Dec.
High (°F)	5	10	40	55	98	99	101	100	96	75	65	11
Low (°F)	0	2	10	28	40	78	82	77	76	56	50	2

Mixed Review

Find the answer. Which method did you use?

11. $12.5 \times 803.3 + 26.38$

12. $3\frac{3}{8} \div 1\frac{1}{8}$

13. $30\frac{5}{6} - 26\frac{1}{6}$

14. $(7^3 - 5^3) \times 8$

15. $8,000 \div 20$

16. $\left(\frac{1}{2} \times \frac{1}{2}\right) + 7\frac{3}{4}$

EXTRA PRACTICE, page 503

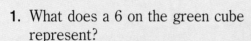

PROBLEM SOLVING

UNDERSTAND
✓ PLAN
✓ TRY
CHECK
✓ EXTEND

Strategy: Conducting a Simulation

Mr. White and Mr. Green are on the ground floor of the Leeman Building, waiting for an elevator. There are six floors above the ground floor. What is the probability that the two men will both get off on the same floor?

You can solve the problem by using **simulation.** Simulate, or imitate, the event by using a white number cube and a green number cube. Let a 2 on the white cube represent Mr. White getting off the elevator on floor 2.

1. What does a 6 on the green cube represent?

When both cubes show a 3, that simulates both men getting off on floor 3. Different numbers on each cube simulate the two men getting off on different floors.

Suppose you simulated the event by rolling the two cubes a total of 50 times and you tallied the results. Look at the results shown at the right.

The cubes simulated the two men getting off on the same floor 8 times out of 50 rolls of the two cubes. Since $\frac{8}{50}$ of the time the cubes showed the same number, it is assumed that $\frac{8}{50}$ of the time the men would have gotten off on the same floor.

SAME FLOOR?

Yes	No
⊣⊦⊦ |||	⊣⊦⊦ ⊣⊦⊦ ⊣⊦⊦ ⊣⊦⊦ ⊣⊦⊦ ⊣⊦⊦ ⊣⊦⊦ ⊣⊦⊦ ||
Total: 8	Total: 42

2. What fraction of the time do you predict that two men who get on the same elevator on the ground floor will *not* get off on the same floor?

3. **What if** there were three men instead of two? How could you use simulation to find the probability that any two of them will get off on the same floor?

PRACTICE

Use simulation to solve the problem. Use coins, spinners, number cubes, or slips of paper that have been numbered.

4. The two teams to play in the World Series are evenly matched. What is the probability that Team A will win the Series by winning the first four games? (*Hint:* Use a coin. Let a head be *Team A wins.* Let a tail be *Team B wins.* Toss the coin four times to represent the playing of the first four games. Do each set of four tosses a total of 50 times.)

5. Find the probability that three of the first five people you meet at any baseball game were born on a Saturday. (*Hint:* Use seven pieces of paper numbered 1, 2, 3, 4, 5, 6, and 7 for the days of the week. Each pick represents the day of the week of a person's birth. Pick and replace the paper five times. Repeat each set of five picks a total of 50 times.)

6. Jimmy is about to take a five-question sports true/false quiz. He says that he can guess the answers correctly more than half the time. What is the probability that he will answer all five questions correctly? (*Hint:* Use a coin. Let a head be a *Correct guess.* Let a tail be an *Incorrect guess.*)

7. Three friends arrange to meet at the Tasty Coffee Shop after their Saturday aerobics classes. It happens that there are three restaurants with that name. What is the probability that all the friends will choose the same restaurant? (*Hint:* Use a spinner with three equal sections. Each spin tells which Tasty Coffee Shop a certain friend picks.)

Strategies and Skills Review

Solve. Use estimation, mental math, a calculator, or paper and pencil.

8. A horseback rider left the stable and rode 4 mi north. She then rode 5 mi east, 8 mi south, 2 mi west, and 4 mi north. How far did she travel from the stable? In what direction will she need to ride to reach the stable?

9. There are two table tennis teams with four players on each team. Before the matches begin, the members of each team will shake hands with each member of the other team. How many handshakes will there be?

10. At the health club Serita earned $48 for cleaning the pool, $24 for running errands, and $37 for stringing tennis rackets. Has she earned enough to buy a tennis racket that costs $125?

11. *Write a problem* that involves doing a simulation. Work together with others to solve the problem.

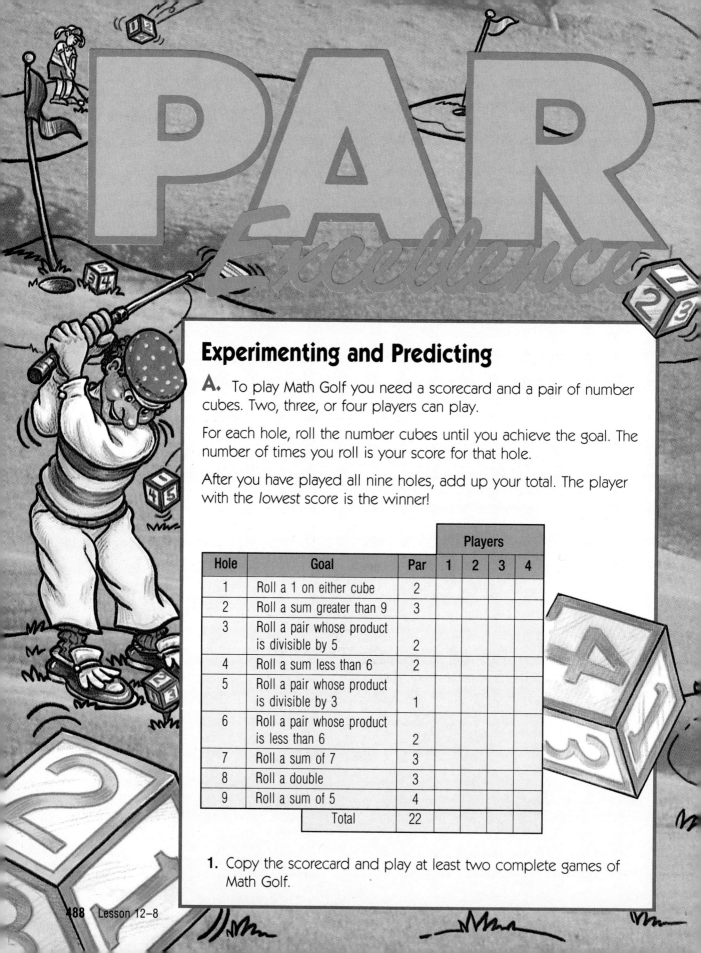

Experimenting and Predicting

A. To play Math Golf you need a scorecard and a pair of number cubes. Two, three, or four players can play.

For each hole, roll the number cubes until you achieve the goal. The number of times you roll is your score for that hole.

After you have played all nine holes, add up your total. The player with the *lowest* score is the winner!

Hole	Goal	Par	Players			
			1	2	3	4
1	Roll a 1 on either cube	2				
2	Roll a sum greater than 9	3				
3	Roll a pair whose product is divisible by 5	2				
4	Roll a sum less than 6	2				
5	Roll a pair whose product is divisible by 3	1				
6	Roll a pair whose product is less than 6	2				
7	Roll a sum of 7	3				
8	Roll a double	3				
9	Roll a sum of 5	4				
	Total	22				

1. Copy the scorecard and play at least two complete games of Math Golf.

B. Now that you have played the game, what do you think the "Par" column tells you? Did you usually score over or under the par score?

Par scores are average scores set for each hole. They are determined by the chances of achieving each goal on any given roll. Thinking about par scores will help you design your own Math Golf course.

2. How many possible pairs of numbers are there for any given roll of the cubes? Make an organized list of the possible pairs. It will help you to determine the chances for each hole on the Math Golf course.

3. This table shows the possible pairs that make the goal for the first two holes. Complete the table for the other holes.

Hole	Possible Rolls	Number of Possible Rolls
1	(1,1), (1,2), (1,3), (1,4), (1,5), (1,6), (2,1), (3,1), (4,1), (5,1), (6,1)	11
2	(4,6), (6,4), (5,5), (6,5), (5,6), (6,6)	6

4. How are par scores determined? Explain your answer.

5. Now design your own 9-hole Math Golf course. You can use any goals you like. Try to include a variety of par scores. How would you invent a par-5 hole?

6. Play the new courses with other students. Are the new courses up to par?

Listing Outcomes

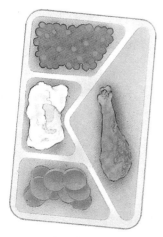

Ken is having lunch at a cafeteria. For the main course he can choose fish or chicken. He can have peas, carrots, or corn for the vegetable. How many possible lunches can Ken have if he chooses one of each item?

Write each of the words *fish, chicken, peas, carrots,* and *corn* on an index card. Arrange the cards for as many different lunches as possible.

1. Make a list of the different possible lunches.

2. How many possible lunches can Ken have?

Another way to find the number of possible lunches is to make a **tree diagram.**

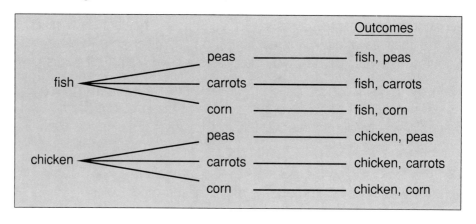

Ken's older sister pointed out a shortcut.

For each of the 2 choices of chicken or fish, there are 3 choices of vegetable: $2 \times 3 = 6$.

There are 6 possible outcomes.

SHARING IDEAS

3. **What if** Ken could also choose between 2 beverages—milk and juice? How many possible meals can he have now? Use a tree diagram and multiplication.

4. If you had to make a list of all the possible meals in Problem 3, would a tree diagram or multiplication be more helpful? Why?

PRACTICE

Find the number of possible outcomes. List the outcomes.

5. You get to select an hour to watch TV (6–7 P.M. or 8–9 P.M.) and a choice of one of four channels: 2, 4, 7, or 11.

6. There are three riders and two horses. Only one person can ride at a time. You are to select the person who rides first and on which horse.

7. You get to select a red, blue, or white shirt and pants that are brown or black.

8. You get to spin twice a spinner with three equal sections. The sections of the spinner are marked 1, 5, and 9. The two numbers you get are the first and the second digit of a number that tells you how much contest money you win. (For example, if you spin 5 first and 1 second, you win $51.)

Find the number of possible outcomes. Use multiplication.

9. On Saturday you are going to the movies and then out to eat. There is a choice of 5 movies and 8 snack shops. How many possible ways can you select a movie and a place to eat?

10. A local arts club offers summer classes in art and music. There are 7 art classes and 9 music classes. How many possible ways are there to pick an art class and a music class?

11. Hilda wants to select a basketball poster, a baseball poster, and a poster of a musical group. The poster shop has posters of 6 basketball players, 10 baseball players, and 5 musical groups. In how many ways can she select the posters?

Mixed Applications Solve. You may need to use the Databank on page 552.

12. At a restaurant, you get to choose between 3 salads, 5 sandwiches, and 4 beverages. In how many possible ways can you have a meal that includes salad, sandwich, and beverage?

13. A restaurant has a minimum charge of $2.50 per table. Three people order milk, which costs $.35 a glass. Have they met the minimum? If not, how much more will they have to pay to sit at a table?

14. Lori wants to have a breakfast of about 400 calories. She decides on toast, cereal, orange juice, and milk. Which kind of milk should she choose?

15. At lunch Lori has a choice between chicken salad and baked potato or tuna salad and string beans. Which meal has the least number of calories?

Probability of Independent Events

A. A number cube has faces numbered 1 through 6, and a letter cube has the letters A through F. What is the probability of rolling a 5 and a C if you roll the cubes together one time?

The outcome from the number cube does not depend on the outcome from the letter cube. The event of rolling a certain number and that of rolling a certain letter are **independent events.**

You can use ordered pairs to make a list of all possible ways the cubes could land when you roll them.

1, A	2, A	3, A	4, A	5, A	6, A
1, B	2, B	3, B	4, B	5, B	6, B
1, C	2, C	3, C	4, C	(5, C)	6, C
1, D	2, D	3, D	4, D	5, D	6, D
1, E	2, E	3, E	4, E	5, E	6, E
1, F	2, F	3, F	4, F	5, F	6, F

Think: There are 36 possible outcomes. The ringed item shows the outcome that has 5 paired with C.

So $P(5 \text{ and } C) = \frac{1}{36}$.

1. What is the probability of rolling an odd number and a vowel?

B. You can also multiply to find the probability of independent events occurring at the same time.

If event X is independent of event Y, then $P(X \text{ and } Y) = P(X) \times P(Y)$.

$$P(5) = \frac{1}{6} \qquad P(C) = \frac{1}{6}$$
$$P(5 \text{ and } C) = \frac{1}{6} \times \frac{1}{6} = \frac{1}{36}$$

2. What is the probability of rolling a 4 and a consonant?

TRY OUT Write the letter of the correct answer.
Use the number cube and letter cube above.

3. $P(\text{odd and consonant})$ **a.** 12   **b.** $\frac{1}{3}$ **c.** $\frac{1}{4}$ **d.** $\frac{1}{36}$

4. $P(3 \text{ and } D)$ **a.** $\frac{1}{3}$ **b.** $\frac{1}{6}$ **c.** $\frac{1}{18}$ **d.** $\frac{1}{36}$

PRACTICE

You spin each spinner once. What is the probability of the event?

5. P(blue and 2)

6. P(blue and even)

7. P(blue and odd)

8. P(red and 4)

9. P(red and even)

10. P(yellow and odd)

11. P(yellow and greater than 1)

12. P(red and less than 3)

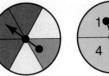

You have a number cube with faces numbered 1 through 6 and a plain cube that is blue on 1 face, yellow on 2 faces, and red on 3 faces. You shake the cubes in a cup and toss them on the floor.

What is the probability of the event occurring?

13. P(1 and blue)

14. P(4 and yellow)

15. P(3 and red)

16. P(odd and yellow)

17. P(even and blue)

18. P(5 and red)

19. P(less than 3 and yellow)

20. P(greater than 1 and red)

21. P(less than 10 and blue)

22. P(less than 1 and yellow)

Mixed Applications

Solve. Which method did you use?

ESTIMATION
MENTAL MATH
CALCULATOR
PAPER/PENCIL

23. You can dial other offices within Kim's company by using 2-digit numbers. You cannot have a number that begins with 0, because dialing 0 first gives you the company operator. How many office numbers can the company have?

24. Nicandro had counters that were green on one side and orange on the other. He had a letter cube with faces lettered A through F. Nicandro shook a counter and the cube in a cup and then tossed them on the floor. What is the probability that he got an E and an orange?

25. Barbara entered a contest that gave her 1 chance in 10,000 of winning. What is the probability that someone else will win?

Mixed Review

Find the answer. Which method did you use?

26. $6 \div \frac{2}{3}$

27. 0.3×0.4

28. 10.7×6.12

29. $6.04 - 5.77$

30. $\frac{84}{90} \div \frac{4}{90}$

31. $7\frac{1}{6} - 1\frac{1}{5}$

32. $(0.05)^2 + 6$

33. $9\frac{3}{5} \times 9\frac{3}{5}$

EXTRA PRACTICE, page 505

ACTIVITY

Counting Outcomes: Arrangements

Karen made three new friends at camp. She wanted a picture of them standing together left to right. She decided to take pictures of them lined up in every possible arrangement. How many pictures did she take?

WORKING TOGETHER

You can use a model to solve this problem.

1. Model this problem using cubes of three different colors.

2. Keep a record of all the arrangements you find. How many are there in all?

3. How many pictures did Karen take?

This is how Eric arranged the cubes.

4. How many choices does Eric have for the color of the first cube? After that, how many choices does he have for the color of the second cube? After that, how many choices does he have for the color of the last cube?

Carla used a shortcut. Each time she made a choice, Carla noticed there was one less choice for the next step.

She multiplied:

	Possibilities for first choice		Possibilities for second choice		Possibilities for last choice
Total number of arrangements =	3	×	2	×	1
Total number of arrangements =	6				

SHARING IDEAS

5. Compare your results for Problem 3 with those of other groups. Did all groups come up with the same total number of arrangements?

6. When you arrange a group of four objects in order from left to right, how many choices do you have for the first place? How many choices do you have left for second place? the third place? the fourth place?

7. **What if** four friends are going to line up for tickets at a movie? In how many different ways can they form the line? How do you know?

ON YOUR OWN

8. A disc jockey has five songs to play. In how many ways can the songs be arranged? How do you know?

9. You have six photographs to hang on your wall. In how many ways can they be arranged?

10. A sick friend asks you to bring her gym shoes from her locker at school. You remember that she gave you the numbers 3, 6, and 8 for her combination lock, but you do not remember the order. In how many orders could you try these numbers?

11. Write a multiplication expression that shows the total number of ways eight friends can sit together in a row at a movie. (You do not have to calculate the product.)

PROBLEM SOLVING

Strategy: Solving a Simpler Problem

Richard tests new bicycles for the Supreme Cycle Shop. On Wednesday he rode one bicycle for $12\frac{1}{3}$ mi. On Thursday he rode another bicycle $3\frac{1}{4}$ times as far. How many miles did Richard ride on Thursday?

Richard decides to solve a simpler, similar problem by using whole numbers instead of mixed numbers.

1. **What if** Richard had ridden 12 mi on Wednesday and 3 times as far on Thursday? Which operation would he use to find out how many miles he would have ridden on Thursday?

   Richard decides to multiply: $12 \times 3 = 36$.
   He would have ridden 36 mi on Thursday.

2. Now solve Richard's original problem. How many miles did he ride on Thursday?

3. How can you check to see whether your answer is reasonable?

PRACTICE

Write and solve a simpler problem. Then solve the original problem.

4. Richard is painting bicycles. He uses $2\frac{1}{4}$ c of paint for each bicycle. He has 27 c of paint. How many bicycles can he paint?

5. In April, Richard worked a total of $134\frac{1}{2}$ hours. In May he worked for $129\frac{3}{4}$ hours. How much longer did he work in April than in May?

6. Last month Richard field-tested 12 bicycles. This month he field-tested $2\frac{1}{2}$ times as many bicycles. How many bicycles did he field-test this month?

7. Last week Richard rode $238\frac{7}{8}$ mi. This week he rode $196\frac{2}{3}$ mi. How many miles did he ride all together?

Strategies and Skills Review

Solve. Use estimation, mental math, a calculator, or paper and pencil.

8. Penny worked on her bicycle for $1\frac{3}{4}$ hours on Tuesday and $\frac{2}{3}$ hour on Wednesday. Did Penny work at least 2 hours on Tuesday and Wednesday?

9. The bicycle-repair manual is open. The page numbers on the facing pages have a product of 420. What are the page numbers?

10. Richard is field-testing a bicycle. He starts at the Cycle Shop and goes $1\frac{1}{2}$ mi east, $\frac{1}{3}$ mi south, $1\frac{3}{4}$ mi west, $\frac{1}{3}$ mi north, and then back to the Cycle Shop. How many miles does he ride the bicycle?

11. At the Cycle Shop, Susan buys a helmet for $34.95, a horn for $14.50, safety reflectors for $2.98, a bike lock for $9.90, and a water bottle for $1.95. Is $60 enough to cover the cost of these items? Did you overestimate or underestimate?

12. Cliff owns the Supreme Cycle Shop. On Thursday he withdrew $919.46 from his store's account. On Friday he deposited $1,001.32. There is now $1,869.77 in the store account. How much was in the store account before Cliff withdrew the money?

13. **Write a problem** that can be solved by using simpler numbers. Solve your problem. Ask others to solve it.

DECISION MAKING

Problem Solving: Planning a School Magazine

SITUATION

This year the Waverly City School has decided to start a school magazine. The student council took a poll to find out what type of magazine the students wanted. All 400 students were polled.

PROBLEM

What type of magazine should the school publish?

DATA

WAVERLY CITY SCHOOL MAGAZINE POLL AND RESULTS

What is your main interest?
A. local events — 142
B. arts — 131
C. sports — 127

What is your main interest in local events?
A. school events — 219
B. neighborhood events — 125
C. city events — 56

What is your main interest in the arts?
A. books — 83
B. music — 168
C. movies — 149

What is your main interest in sports?
A. baseball — 142
B. football — 153
C. tennis — 105

What magazine format do you like best?
A. news stories — 113
B. columns and reviews — 204
C. photos — 83

USING THE DATA

What percent of students were interested in:

1. local events? **2.** arts? **3.** sports?

What percent of students were interested in:

4. school events? **5.** neighborhood events? **6.** city events?

What percent of students were interested in:

7. books? **8.** music? **9.** movies?

What percent of students were interested in:

10. baseball? **11.** football? **12.** tennis?

What percent of students were interested in:

13. news stories? **14.** columns and reviews? **15.** photos?

MAKING DECISIONS

16. Based on the students' response, should the council choose to evenly divide the magazine among local events, the arts, and sports?

17. Within the arts section, about how much of the magazine should be given to books? to music?

18. What kind of format should the council decide to give the magazine?

19. *Write a list* of other factors the council should consider.

20. *What if* you were the editor of the magazine? What kind of content and format would you choose? Tell why.

CURRICULUM CONNECTION

Math and Language

Cryptology is the study of secret communications. One system studied in cryptology is called the *cipher* system. In this system, numbers represent letters. By using a key, a secret message can be *deciphered*.

Imagine that you want to send the message COMING BACK MONDAY. Here is how the cipher system works.

- Use any word as a key. We'll use WHEN.

- Assign a number to each letter in the key word. The assigned number is based on the order in which the letter occurs in the alphabet.

- Write the message in rows beneath the key word and the numbers. Do not include the spaces between the words.

```
W H E N
4 2 1 3
C O M I
N G B A
C K M O
N D A Y
```

- Next the letters are "taken off" by column in numerical order: the letters under the 1, M B M A; then O G K D under the 2, and so forth. The final message reads MBMA OGKD IAOY CNCN.

- Anyone who knows the key word can decipher the message by arranging the letters in the proper order.

What if you receive this message: NEEI OBTA OLAN DTAG? Use the key above to decode the message.

Think:

```
1       2       3       4       W H E N
N       O       O       D       4 2 1 3
E       B       L       T       D O N O
E       T       A       A       T B E L
I       A       N       G       A T E A
                                G A I N
```

ACTIVITIES

1. Go to the library and find books on cryptology. Read about the other codes that are used to send secret messages. Prepare a report for the class.

2. Work with a partner. Choose another key word. Encode messages for each other. Can you think of a way to "crack" this kind of code?

Computer Simulation: Sum Probabilities

Suppose you have two number cubes each with six faces labeled 1, 2, 3, 4, 5, and 6. You toss the cubes and record the sum of the faceup numbers each time. Do you get certain sums more often than others? If so, why?

The computer program CUBE SUM simulates this probability experiment. It will "toss" the cubes as many as 3,000 times. The program keeps track of the sums and indicates how many times each sum occurs.

AT THE COMPUTER

1. Suppose you tossed the cubes 36 times. How many times would you expect to get a sum of 12? How many times would you expect to get a sum of 7? Try it on the computer. Use 36 as the number of tosses for Round 1. Compare your results with your estimates.

2. Run the program four more times. Vary the number of tosses up to 3,000. As the sums are generated, watch to see if there are any patterns in the way the numbers appear. Are the results for a greater number of tosses similar to the results for a smaller number of tosses?

3. Did certain sums always appear more often than others? Which ones? Which sum would you say appeared most often? Which sum appeared least often? Try to explain why this happened.

4. Copy and complete the table at the right to show all the possible sums for tossing two number cubes. How many different outcomes are there in all?

5. Count the number of ways you can get each sum. Then give the probability of each sum.

+	1	2	3	4	5	6
1						
2						
3						
4						
5						
6						

6. Compare the probabilities from Problem 5 with the results of the simulation. Explain your findings.

EXTRA PRACTICE

Probability, page 477

Suppose you choose a marble from a bag that has 8 black marbles, 6 striped marbles, and 2 cat's-eyes. What is:

1. P(black)?　　**2.** P(striped)?　　**3.** P(cat's-eye)?

Suppose you spin the spinner. What is:

4. P(2)?

5. P(1)?

6. P(4)?

7. P(3)?

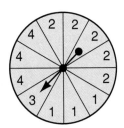

Suppose these names are put in a hat and you pick one without looking. What is:

Sandy	Kipp	Kipp	Tracy
Tracy	Tracy	Tracy	Tracy
Jason	Jason	Jason	Jason

8. P(Jason)?　　　**9.** P(Sandy)?　　　**10.** P(Kipp)?　　　**11.** P(Tracy)?

Probabilities of Events, page 479

Find the probability of the event. Write your answer as a fraction in simplest form.

1. P(+ or •)　　　**2.** P(▲ or ★)　　　**3.** P(+ or ★)　　　**4.** P(+ or ▲)

5. P(• or ★)　　　**6.** P(• or ▲)　　　**7.** P(• or +)　　　**8.** P(+ or ★ or ▲)

9. P(not +)　　　**10.** P(not •)　　　**11.** P(not ★)　　　**12.** P(not ▲)

Write the probability of the event as a fraction, a decimal, and a percent.

13. P(▲)　　　**14.** P(+)　　　**15.** P(▲ or +)　　　**16.** P(not •)

EXTRA PRACTICE

Probability and Prediction, page 481

Predict the number of favorable outcomes out of 1,000 spins.

1. red
2. blue
3. green
4. yellow
5. not red
6. blue or green

Predict how many times you would pick the marble from this bag in 100 picks.

7. black
8. striped
9. cat's-eye
10. white
11. yellow
12. black or striped

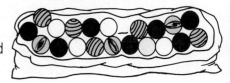

Making Predictions, page 483

Solve.

1. Out of 500 orange trees, 25 did not bear fruit. How many would you expect not to bear fruit out of 5,000? Explain how you made your predictions.

2. Take a survey of the favorite fruit among the students in your class. How many students out of 1,000 would you expect to pick apples? How sure do you feel about your prediction? Explain your thinking.

Misleading Statistics, page 485

Graph 1 and Graph 2 represent the same data.

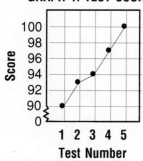

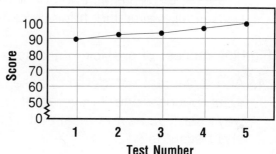

1. Which graph is misleading? Why?

EXTRA PRACTICE

Problem Solving Strategy: Conducting a Simulation, page 487

Solve by using a simulation.

1. Max answered a questionnaire about what kind of magazine the library should carry. There were fifteen questions. Each question had 2 answer choices, *a* or *b*. Jasmine decided to guess how Max answered the questions. She used a coin to represent the 2 answer choices. If Max chose *b* as each answer, what is the probability that Jasmine guessed all of his answers correctly? Do each set of fifteen tosses a total of 10 times.

2. The Twin Valley Marching Band has been asked to march in a parade in another state. To raise money to make the trip, the band members are selling T-shirts. There are 6 different colors of T-shirts. What is the probability that both Marcus and Nelson will buy the same color T-shirt? Use number cubes to conduct the simulation a total of 40 times.

Listing Outcomes, page 491

Find the number of possible outcomes. List the outcomes.

1. You get to select a sandwich with a filling of beef, chicken, fish, ham, or egg and bread that is white, rye, or whole wheat.

2. You get to select a movie from *Back in Time, The Blob, Mountain Adventure,* or *009* and a class from art, dance, music, or drama.

3. You get an hour for a sports activity, either 3–4 P.M., 4–5 P.M., or 5–6 P.M., and you have a choice of baseball, basketball, swimming, track, hockey, or football.

Find the number of possible outcomes. Use multiplication.

4. At a restaurant you get to choose between 2 salads, 4 sandwiches, and 3 beverages. In how many possible ways can you have a meal that includes salad, sandwich, and beverage?

5. You get to choose between 3 pairs of shorts and 7 T-shirts for a running outfit. In how many possible ways can you choose a running outfit?

EXTRA PRACTICE

Probability of Independent Events, page 493

You have a number cube with faces numbered 1 through 6 and this spinner. You roll the cube and spin the spinner. What is the probability of the event?

1. P(1 and A)
2. P(2 and B)
3. P(greater than 3 and C)
4. P(greater than 1 and A)
5. P(less than 4 and B)
6. P(3 and C)
7. P(5 and A or B)
8. P(6 and B or C)

You have 4 red marbles, 3 blue marbles, 2 green marbles, and 1 yellow marble in a bag. You choose a marble and toss a coin. What is the probability of the event?

9. P(red and heads)
10. P(blue and tails)
11. P(green and heads)
12. P(yellow and tails)
13. P(red or blue and heads)
14. P(green or yellow and tails)
15. P(yellow or blue and heads)
16. P(red or yellow and tails)

Problem Solving Strategy: Solving a Simpler Problem, page 497

Write and solve a simpler problem. Then solve the original problem.

1. Mr. Sanchez works $37\frac{1}{2}$ hours a week. Last year he had two weeks of vacation. How many hours did he work last year?

2. During July, Ronnie caught $33\frac{3}{4}$ lb of fish. During August, he caught $41\frac{1}{3}$ lb of fish. How much fish did he catch all together?

3. Mr. Zorba is painting benches at the baseball field. He uses $5\frac{1}{8}$ cups of paint for each bench. He has 82 cups of paint. How many benches can he paint?

4. The B-Healthy Food Store sold $746\frac{1}{4}$ lb of sunflower seeds in May. In June, they sold $739\frac{5}{8}$ lb. How much more did they sell in May than in June?

PRACTICE *PLUS*

KEY SKILL: Probabilities of Events (Use after page 479.)

Level A

Use the spinner. What is:

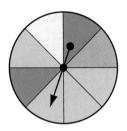

1. P(green or blue)? **2.** P(not purple)? **3.** P(green)?

4. P(blue)? **5.** P(purple)? **6.** P(yellow)?

7. P(purple or green)? **8.** P(blue or purple)? **9.** P(not blue)?

10. There are 10 equal spaces on a spinner. There are 5 red spaces, 4 blue, and 1 yellow. Which color has the greatest chance of the pointer landing on it?

Level B

Use the spinner for Questions 11–19. Find the probability of the event. Write your answer as a fraction in simplest form or as a whole number.

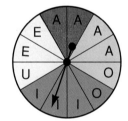

11. P(red A) **12.** P(A, I, or O) **13.** P(not blue)

14. P(consonant) **15.** P(vowel) **16.** P(E or U)

17. P(not E) **18.** P(A, or E, or I, or O) **19.** P(O or yellow)

20. Corey wants to make a spinner with 20 equal sections of red, blue, green, or yellow. She wants the probability to be red $\frac{1}{4}$, blue $\frac{1}{5}$, green $\frac{1}{2}$, and yellow $\frac{1}{20}$. How many sections will each color be?

Level C

A number cube has each of its faces labeled with numbers from 1 to 6. Two sides are red, 3 are blue, and 1 is green. Find the probability of the event.

21. P(5) **22.** P(3 or 4) **23.** P(blue) **24.** P(green)

25. P(number less than 6) **26.** P(number greater than 6) **27.** P(odd number)

28. P(number less than 4) **29.** P(multiple of 2 or 3) **30.** P(blue, red, or green)

PRACTICE PLUS

KEY SKILL: Probability and Prediction (Use after page 481.)

Level A

Predict how many times you would pick the color(s) from the bag in 100 picks.

1. orange

2. aqua

3. brown

4. green

5. orange or brown

6. not aqua

7. not brown

8. not green

9. Five out of the 10 people surveyed chose blue as their favorite color. How many out of 100 people would you expect to pick blue?

Level B

Predict the number of favorable outcomes out of 1,000 spins.

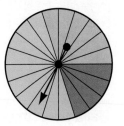

10. orange

11. brown

12. aqua

13. not brown

14. green or aqua

15. not green

16. orange or brown or aqua

17. neither orange nor brown

18. The probability of a marble landing on 2 on a wheel is $\frac{1}{4}$. How many times would you expect 2 to come up on the wheel in 500 spins?

Level C

If you spin this spinner 96 times, how many times would you predict the pointer will land on:

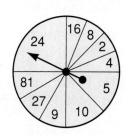

19. a multiple of 9?

20. a multiple of 5?

21. a multiple of 12?

22. a multiple of 8?

23. a multiple of 2 or 5?

24. a multiple of 2 or 3?

25. a multiple of 9 or 10?

26. a multiple of 3?

27. The probability of getting a sum of 7 when two number cubes are rolled is $\frac{6}{36}$. How many times would you expect to get a sum of 7 in 1,200 rolls?

CHAPTER REVIEW/TEST

LANGUAGE AND MATHEMATICS

Complete the sentences. Use the words in the chart on the right.

1. Two events are ■ if the outcome of one does not depend on the other.

2. A tree diagram can be used to list all the possible ■ for two independent events.

3. The probability of a(n) ■ is always zero.

> **VOCABULARY**
>
> certain events
> independent events
> outcomes
> impossible events

CONCEPTS AND SKILLS

These cards were shuffled and laid face down. Write each probability as a fraction, decimal, and percent.

4. $P(\triangle)$

5. $P(\star \text{ or } +)$

6. $P(+)$

Della used the set of cards above and a set of cards numbered from 0–9. She draws a card from each set. What is the probability of the event occurring?

7. $P(\star \text{ and } \triangle)$

8. $P(+ \text{ and odd})$

9. $P(+ \text{ and } 9)$

This graph shows the numbers of two newspapers sold.

10. How many times taller is the *Tribune*'s bar than the *Times'* bar?

11. How many times more papers were sold by the *Tribune* than the *Times*?

12. How could the graph be made more accurate?

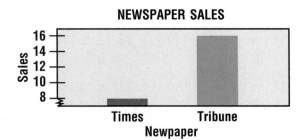

Find the number of possible outcomes. List the possible outcomes.

13. a red or blue shirt with red, white, or blue pants

14. ham or cheese on sesame or wheat bread with milk or soda

The chance of winning Roll-O-Toss is 40%.

15. If Lin plays 40 times, how many times would you expect her to win?

16. Pam won 120 of 500 plays. What is the difference between her number of wins and the expected number of wins?

Critical Thinking

Three pairs of shoes—blue, red, and white—were in a pile. Li picked the left blue shoe and kept it.

17. Without looking, Li picked again. List the possible outcomes.

18. Are the events independent? Why or why not?

Mixed Applications

19. Cheryl calls 4 friends to ask them to help her decide whether to see a movie or to take a walk. What is the probability that all 4 will choose a walk? Use a coin. Let heads be a walk and tails be a movie. Toss the coin 4 times to represent the answers of Cheryl's friends. Do each set of tosses 20 times.

20. Elvis grew a pumpkin that weighs $119\frac{5}{8}$ lb. Jim grew one that weighs $86\frac{3}{4}$ lb. What is the total weight of the pumpkins? Use a simpler problem.

PERFORMANCE ASSESSMENT

Work with your group to solve this problem.

Using two number cubes, each numbered 1 to 6, find the probability of tossing a prime number or a composite number. Then make a table to predict the number of times out of 20, 30, 40, 50, and 60 tosses that the cubes will be a prime or a composite number.

1. ***Think about:***
   - the number of prime and composite numbers on the cubes
   - the possible combinations of numbers that would show prime numbers and composite numbers

2. Write a paragraph explaining how you determined the predictions in your table.

CUMULATIVE REVIEW

Choose the letter of the correct answer.

1. Solve: $\frac{4}{6} = \frac{6}{n}$
   a. 4
   b. 24
   c. 36
   d. not given

2. 0.1 written as a percent is:
   a. 1%.
   b. 10%.
   c. 100%.
   d. not given

3. $\frac{1}{20}$ written as a percent is:
   a. 0.5%.
   b. 2%.
   c. 20%.
   d. not given

Use the spinner for Questions 4–7.

4. P(blue)
   a. 2%
   b. 5%
   c. 20%
   d. not given

5. P(black)
   a. 2
   b. 0.4
   c. 0.2
   d. not given

6. P(yellow or green or black)
   a. $\frac{1}{2}$
   b. $\frac{3}{5}$
   c. $\frac{4}{5}$
   d. not given

7. In 100 spins, how many times would you expect to get black?
   a. 40
   b. 20
   c. 4
   d. not given

8. How many outcomes are there given choices of milk, juice, or soda with pie, cookie, or cake?
   a. 3
   b. 6
   c. 9
   d. not given

9. What is the area of a circle with a diameter of 3 m?
   a. 3π m²
   b. 6π m²
   c. 9π m²
   d. not given

10. What is the circumference of a circle with a diameter of 9 ft?
    a. 9π ft
    b. 18π ft
    c. 81π ft
    d. not given

11. What can the side view of a triangular prism look like?
    a. triangle
    b. square
    c. circle
    d. not given

12. What is the volume of a cylinder with $d = 20$ m and $h = 15$ m?
    a. $1,500\pi$ m³
    b. $3,000\pi$ m³
    c. $6,000\pi$ m³
    d. not given

13. Which triangle has no equal sides?
    a. equilateral
    b. acute
    c. isosceles
    d. not given

14. Which figure has only one pair of parallel sides?
    a. rhombus
    b. trapezoid
    c. parallelogram
    d. not given

DEPENDENT EVENTS

Suppose you have 5 blue cubes and 5 red cubes in a bag. You reach into the bag and choose one of the cubes without looking. You then reach into the bag after replacing the first cube and choose another cube. What is the probability of picking a blue cube, then another blue cube—or
P(blue, then blue) = ?

Think: Since the cube is replaced, choosing the second cube is independent of choosing the first cube. Because the events are independent, you can multiply to find the probability.

P (blue, then blue) = P (blue) $\times$ P (blue)

P (blue) = $\frac{5}{10}$, or $\frac{1}{2}$

P (blue, then blue) = $\frac{1}{2} \times \frac{1}{2} = \frac{1}{4}$

What if you hadn't replaced the blue cube after reaching into the bag the first time? How would this affect the probability of choosing the second blue cube?

Think: Since the cube has not been replaced, choosing the second cube is dependent upon choosing the first cube. This is an example of **dependent events.**

After the first blue cube has been chosen, there are now only 9 cubes in the bag, of which 4 are blue.

The probability of picking the second blue cube would be $\frac{4}{9}$, not $\frac{5}{10}$, or $\frac{1}{2}$.

1. What is P(blue, then blue)?

2. What is P(blue, then red)?

3. ***What if*** Ernesto has 6 red socks and 8 green socks in a drawer? What is the probability that he will reach into the drawer, choose a red sock, not replace the first red sock, then reach in again and pick another red sock?

KABYLE PUZZLE

People in many cultures enjoy using logic to solve puzzles. One popular story that is told is a puzzle about a man crossing a river with three items—usually two animals and some sort of food. In different versions, the man's boat is only big enough for two items, or the man can only carry two items at a time. The problem is how to cross the river without one animal eating the other or eating the food.

One version of this puzzle originated with the Kabyle (ka-BY-uhl) who live in the rugged Djuradjura (JUR-uh-JUR-uh) Mountains on the coast of Algeria. They depend on their grain crops and goat herds, which are at times threatened by jackals. Consequently, the Kabyle puzzle features a man, a goat, a jackal, and a bundle of hay.

The man wants to carry the jackal, goat, and hay across a river. He has no boat, but the river is shallow enough for him to carry one item under each arm. However, the jackal might eat the goat or the goat might eat the hay if he leaves the animals alone together on either bank. The man thinks about the problem and decides on a solution.

1 Find a solution to the puzzle. What strategies did you use? How many times did you have the man cross the river?

2 Compare your solution to those found by other students. Which is the most efficient? Explain.

3 Why do you think this type of puzzle is popular with many cultures?

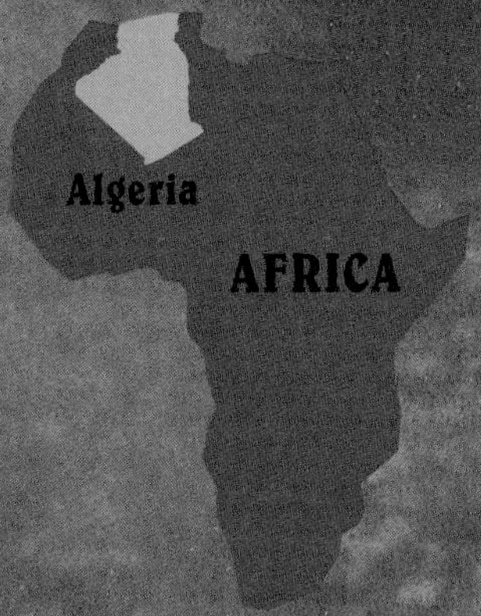

Algeria

AFRICA

Integers

Betty earned $5. She spent $2. You can represent these amounts using yellow and red counters.

Betty earned $5.   **She spent $2.**

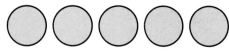

Read: positive 5   negative 2
Write: +5   ‾2

The numbers +5 and ‾2 are **integers.** Integers can be used to represent positive and negative amounts in describing situations such as temperatures above and below zero and heights and depths above and below sea level.

WORKING TOGETHER

Use your two-color counters to model these situations. Let the yellow counters represent positive integers and the red counters represent negative integers. Draw the result and write an integer to label your drawing.

1. 5 degrees below zero

2. lose $2

3. win $3

4. 3 degrees above zero

5. 2 floors up

6. 4 floors down

7. gain 1 kg

8. lose 6 kg

SHARING IDEAS

9. In which situations did you use yellow counters and write a positive integer?

10. In which situations did you use red counters and write a negative integer?

11. Describe two other situations that can be represented by integers.

ON YOUR OWN

Write an integer to describe the situation.

12. The temperature at noon was 21°C above zero.

13. Sue deposited $115 into her savings account.

14. A submarine dove 100 ft.

15. Jill took 3 steps forward.

16. The temperature dropped 6 degrees.

17. Pedro withdrew $25 from his savings account.

18. An airplane climbed 12,000 ft.

19. A jet used up 5,000 lb of fuel.

20. The space shuttle is 6 seconds away from lifting off the launch pad.

Integers and the Number Line

You have learned how to use counters to represent integers. You can also use a **number line** to show points named by integers. Vincent wants to represent ⁺7 and ⁻7 on a number line.

WORKING TOGETHER

1. Draw a number line from 0 to 10. In which direction would you extend the number line to show 0 to ⁻10?

2. Label ⁺7 as *A* and ⁻7 as *B*. How many units from 0 is each integer? What can you say about *A* and *B*?

Here is a number line that Vincent drew.

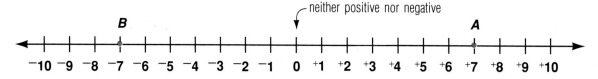

A and *B* are **opposites.** They are the same distance from 0.

SHARING IDEAS

3. How much farther can the number line be extended to the left? to the right?

4. How is the scale of a thermometer like a number line?

5. How would you picture distances above and below sea level?

6. Which integer is the opposite of ⁺6? of ⁻2? of 0?

PRACTICE

Use the number line below. Write the integer that is identified by the letter. Then write the opposite of the integer.

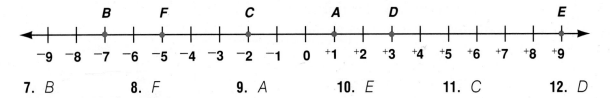

7. *B*   **8.** *F*   **9.** *A*   **10.** *E*   **11.** *C*   **12.** *D*

Write the integer for the points on a number line.

13. 5 units to the left of 0

14. 6 units to the right of 0

15. 13 units to the right of 0

16. 15 units to the left of 0

17. 18 units to the left of 0

18. 20 units to the right of 0

19. opposite of $^+6$

20. 6 units to the left of $^+6$

21. Make your own life time line using integers. Let 0 represent your birth year. Mark as negative integers several points that represent events that happened before you were born. Mark as positive integers points for events that you expect to happen in future years.

Mixed Applications   Solve. Which method did you use?

22. Bert drove 432 mi the first day and 198 mi the second day. How many miles did he drive in the two days?

23. Bonnie drove 252 mi on Monday, 382 mi on Tuesday, 412 mi on Wednesday, and 315 mi on Thursday. About how many miles did she drive in the four days?

24. Bill lives $3\frac{7}{8}$ mi from Don. Carol lives $4\frac{1}{2}$ mi from Don. How much farther from Don does Carol live than Bill?

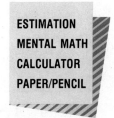

ESTIMATION
MENTAL MATH
CALCULATOR
PAPER/PENCIL

CHALLENGE

The table shows Mr. Alonzo's record of his monthly weight gains and losses. Draw a bar graph to represent the data. Use positive and negative integers.

CHANGES IN WEIGHT (in pounds)

	March	April	May	June	July
Gain	3			1	
Loss		2	4		2

Comparing and Ordering Integers

A. Sally's thermometer showed a temperature of ⁻4°C at 12 noon and ⁻8°C at 12 midnight. Was it colder at 12 noon or at 12 midnight?

Think of a thermometer as a number line. On a number line the number on the left is always less than the number on the right.

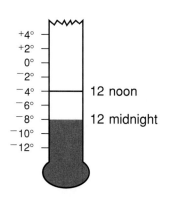

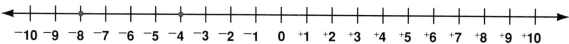

Think: ⁻8 < ⁻4

Since ⁻8 is to the left of ⁻4, it was colder at 12 midnight.

1. Look at the number line to the right. *A* and *B* are two integers. Which integer is less? How can you tell?

2. Why is every positive integer greater than any negative integer?

B. You can also think of a number line when ordering integers.

Order ⁻2, ⁺8, and ⁻5 from least to greatest.

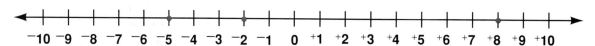

Think: Since ⁻5 is the farthest to the left, it is the least. So ⁻5 < ⁻2 and ⁻5 < ⁺8.
Since ⁻2 is to the left of ⁺8, ⁻2 < ⁺8. So ⁻5 < ⁻2 < ⁺8.

The order from least to greatest is ⁻5, ⁻2, ⁺8.

3. Order ⁺6, ⁻7, and ⁻2 from greatest to least.

TRY OUT   Solve.

4. Which is less, ⁺2 or ⁻5?

5. Which is greater, ⁻10 or 0?

6. Order 0, ⁺6, and ⁻9 from least to greatest.

7. Order ⁻5, ⁺7, and ⁻1 from greatest to least.

PRACTICE

Compare. Write > or <. Think of the integers on a number line.

8. 0 ● $^+$9 **9.** $^+$2 ● $^+$3 **10.** $^-$4 ● $^+$2 **11.** $^-$3 ● 0 **12.** $^-$5 ● $^-$6

13. $^-$3 ● $^+$3 **14.** 0 ● $^-$8 **15.** $^-$7 ● $^-$4 **16.** $^-$12 ● $^+$1 **17.** $^+$7 ● $^-$15

18. opposite of $^+$6 ● $^-$10 **19.** opposite of $^-$12 ● opposite of $^+$24

Write the integers in order from least to greatest.

20. $^+$3, $^-$4, 0, $^+$2, $^-$5 **21.** $^-$8, $^-$1, $^+$5, $^-$10, $^+$2, $^-$4

22. $^+$3, $^+$7, $^-$5, $^-$9, $^-$7 **23.** $^-$1, $^+$1, $^-$6, 0, $^+$6

24. $^+$3, opposite of $^+$7, $^-$2, opposite of $^-$4

Write the integers in order from greatest to least.

25. $^-$12, $^+$13, $^-$14, $^-$19, $^+$15, $^+$21 **26.** $^-$17, $^-$11, $^+$15, $^+$18, $^+$11, $^-$16

27. $^-$22, $^+$22, $^-$25, $^+$27, $^-$28, $^+$29 **28.** $^-$32, $^+$34, $^+$37, $^-$38, $^+$39, $^-$31

29. opposite of $^-$5, $^+$7, opposite of $^+$4, $^-$6

Critical Thinking

30. Is there a greatest positive integer? a greatest negative integer?

31. Is there a least positive integer? a least negative integer?

Mixed Applications Solve. You may need to use the Databank on page 554.

32. The temperature was $^-$2° at 6:00 A.M. At 12 noon it was $^-$5°. At 6:00 P.M. it was $^-$1°. At what time was the temperature highest? At what time was it lowest?

33. Find the mean monthly temperature for Anchorage and San Antonio. About how many times greater is the mean temperature for San Antonio?

34. The temperature is $^-$12° in Freezeburg and $^+$10° in Iceburg. In which is the temperature lower?

35. *Write a problem* that involves ordering integers. Solve it. Ask others to solve it.

Mixed Review ◥◥◥◥◥◥◥◥◥◥◥◥◥◥◥◥◥◥◥◥◥◥◥◥◥◥◥◥◥◥◥◥

MENTAL MATH
CALCULATOR
PAPER/PENCIL

Find the answer. Which method did you use?

36. 6.25 + 4.75 + 7 **37.** 6,001 − 5,999 **38.** 6.04 × 8.247

39. $4\frac{5}{8} - 2\frac{9}{10}$ **40.** 345 + 199 **41.** 380 ÷ 10

EXTRA PRACTICE, page 538; PRACTICE *PLUS*, page 542

ActiVity

Adding Integers

You already know that you can compare and order integers. You can also add integers.

What is $^+5 + ^-5$?

Step 1 Lay out 5 yellow counters to represent $^+5$.

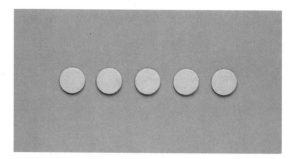

Step 2 Lay out 5 red counters to represent $^-5$.

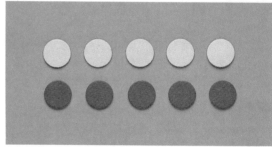

Step 3 Each pair of red and yellow counters is equal to 0.

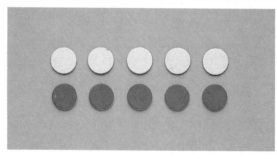

So $^+5 + ^-5$ is equal to 0.

WORKING TOGETHER

Use your yellow and red counters to solve the problem. Remember that an equal number of red and yellow counters represents the number zero.

1. $^+6 + ^+3$ 2. $^+4 + ^+7$

3. $^-2 + ^-4$ 4. $^-3 + ^-3$

5. $^+3 + ^-1$ 6. $^-4 + ^+8$

7. $^+4 + ^-9$ 8. $^-7 + ^+2$

SHARING IDEAS

9. Combine two yellow counters. What is your answer? What does the sum tell you about adding positive integers?

10. Combine two red counters. What is your answer? What does the sum tell you about adding negative integers?

11. Combine 5 yellow counters and 3 red counters. What is your answer? Combine 3 yellow counters and 5 red counters. What do these sums tell you about adding positive and negative integers?

ON YOUR OWN

Write an addition sentence to solve the problem. Use an integer to represent the sum.

12. It was 4 degrees below 0°C. The temperature went up 3 degrees. What was the temperature then?

13. Danny owes his sister $5. He owes his brother $3. How much does he owe in all?

14. In a spelling bee, 1 point is scored for every word correctly spelled and 1 point is lost for every word misspelled. Out of 20 words, June correctly spelled 10. What was her score?

15. A submarine dove 125 ft, then went down another 50 ft. How far below the surface of the water is the submarine?

16. A football team gained 8 yd on one play. On the next play it lost 6 yd. How many yards did the team gain or lose in all on the two plays?

ACTIVITY Subtracting Integers

You have learned to add integers.
You can also subtract integers.

What is $^-6 - ^-2$?

You can use counters to represent
the integers.

Step 1 Set 6 red counters side by
side.

Step 2 Remove 2 red counters. This is
the same as subtracting $^-2$.

So $^-6 - ^-2 = ^-4$.

What is $^-6 - ^+2$?

Step 1 Set 6 red counters side by
side.

Step 2 You need to subtract $^+2$, but
there are no positive integers. Add
two pairs of red and yellow counters.
This is the same as adding zero.

Step 3 Remove 2 yellow counters. This
is the same as subtracting $^+2$.

So $^-6 - ^+2 = ^-8$.

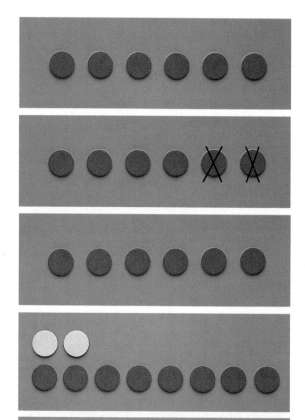

WORKING TOGETHER
Use two-color counters to find the answer.

1. $^+5 - ^+9$ 2. $^-5 - ^+9$ 3. $^-9 - ^-5$ 4. $^+5 - ^-9$

5. $^-5 - ^-9$ 6. $^-9 - ^-5$ 7. $^-5 - ^+5$ 8. $^+5 - ^-5$

SHARING IDEAS

Use your results from Exercises 1–8 to answer the question.

9. If the number being subtracted is greater than the number it is being subtracted from, is the answer a positive or a negative integer?

10. If the number being subtracted is less than the number it is being subtracted from, is the answer a positive or a negative integer?

11. Formulate a rule about subtracting opposites.

ON YOUR OWN

Using integers, write a subtraction sentence to solve the problem. Write an integer to represent the difference. Use counters if you need to.

12. Today the low temperature was ⁻18°F. A year ago today the low was ⁻12°F. How many degrees colder is this year's low temperature?

13. Mel lives 5 blocks north of school. LaDonna lives 7 blocks south of school. What is the distance between Mel's house and LaDonna's?

14. The football team needs 6 yd to make a first down. On the next play the team loses 9 yd. How many yards does it need for a first down now?

15. How many seconds elapse from 7 seconds before lift-off of a rocket to 3 seconds before lift-off?

PROBLEM SOLVING

Strategy: Using More Than One Strategy

Robert Uranga is designing the border for a *serape* (se-RAH-pay), which can be worn around the shoulders like a shawl or a poncho. Robert uses a row of *T*s in alternating colors. The perimeter of each *T* is 10 in. What is the perimeter of a border design of 20 *T*s?

Robert first decides to solve a simpler problem.

- First he draws pictures of border designs that have 2 *T*s, 3 *T*s, and 4 *T*s.

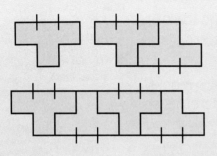

- He finds the perimeter of each design and organizes his results in a table.

Number of *T*s	Perimeter
1	10 in.
2	14 in.
3	18 in.
4	22 in.

- Then Robert looks for a pattern in the table. He sees that the perimeters increase by 4 in. each time he uses an additional *T*. There is always 1 less 4 than the number of *T*s.

$$1 \quad 10$$
$$2 \quad 10 + (1 \times 4)$$
$$3 \quad 10 + (2 \times 4)$$
$$4 \quad 10 + (3 \times 4)$$

1. Guess what the perimeter would be with 5 *T*s. Test your guess. Are you correct?

2. What is the perimeter of a border design of 20 *T*s? Check to see whether you are correct.

3. List all the strategies you used to solve this problem.

PRACTICE

Solve. Which strategy or strategies did you use?

4. On a large poster board Robert has displayed 10 pictures of *serapes*. The pictures are 8 cm squares. They are arranged in 2 rows, 1 cm apart. There is a 2 cm border around the outside of the pictures. What is the area of the posterboard?

5. Robert has also designed 3 woven belts. Each has a different-colored pattern. There are 3 more blue patterns than green patterns and $\frac{1}{2}$ as many red patterns as blue patterns. There are 6 red patterns. How many green patterns are there?

6. A jeans jacket and skirt that Robert is designing require $3\frac{1}{2}$ yards of denim. The jacket requires 1 yard more than the skirt. How many yards does each piece require?

7. Robert has 95 *serapes*, sweaters, and jean jackets. He has $\frac{1}{2}$ as many sweaters as *serapes* and 10 more jean jackets than *serapes*. How many of each does Robert have?

Strategies and Skills Review

Solve. Use estimation, mental math, a calculator, or paper and pencil.

8. In the next 4 weeks Robert plans to work on new designs for at least 160 hours. He works 40 hours the first week, 42 hours the second week, 39 hours the third week, 42 hours the fourth week. Use estimation to decide whether he has reached his goal.

9. Anna, Robert's assistant, kept a record of the number of *serapes* Robert designed over the last year. He designed 95 *serapes* from January to March, 97 from April to September, and 101 from October to December. Using her calculator, she got a total of 1,353 *serapes*. Is her answer reasonable?

10. Anna ships packages to Robert's customers. The charges are $5.25 for the first 5 pounds and $1.50 for each additional pound. If a customer pays $27.75 to ship a package, what does it weigh?

11. Robert makes 7 new *serapes*. He wants to put 5 of them on the wall. How many different selections of 5 can he make?

12. Robert has 25 yd of fabric to make 20 skirts and pairs of slacks. It takes 1 yd to make a skirt and $1\frac{1}{2}$ yd to make a pair of slacks. How many skirts and how many pairs of slacks can he make from the fabric?

13. **Write a problem** that involves using more than one strategy to solve. Then solve your problem. Ask others to solve it.

Investigating Patterns

A. Pietro's Pizza Parlor is having a contest. Contestants will be asked to cut a pizza into the greatest number of pieces using exactly as many cuts as Pietro announces on the day of the contest. Cuts must be straight and go completely across the pie, but pieces do not have to be equal.

You want to win, so you decide to do some investigating before the contest.

If you do not make any cuts in a circle, there is 1 piece:

If you make 1 cut, there will always be 2 pieces:

Suppose you make 2 straight cuts; then you might get 3 pieces: or 4 pieces:

With 2 straight cuts, the greatest number of pieces is 4.

1. Suppose you use 3 straight cuts. How many different ways can you make the cuts? How many pieces are there for each way? What is the greatest number of pieces?

2. Next try to find all the possible ways of making 4 cuts. How many ways are there? What is the greatest number of pieces? How will you know when you have found them all?

B. Now copy and complete this table. Can you find a pattern that will help you predict the greatest number of pieces for 5 cuts? Remember, every cut must be straight and across the pizza, and the pieces do not have to be equal.

Number of Cuts	Drawings of Different Ways	Number of Pieces for Each Way
0	○	1
1	⊘	2
2	⊖ ⊕	3, 4
3		
4		
5		

4. Can you use the pattern to tell what the greatest number of pieces will be for 6 cuts? for 7 cuts?

5. Here is one more cutting problem— but be warned, the answer is tricky! Can you think of a way to cut this cake into 8 *equal* pieces using only three cuts?

527

Graphing Ordered Pairs

A. Mary drew a treasure map on a special grid called a **coordinate grid**. The two number lines on a coordinate grid are its **axes**. The axes intersect at 0. By using the grid Mary is able to describe the location of any point on her map. This is how she describes the location of the Hidden Treasure:

"Start at 0. Count 4 units to the left, then 5 units down."

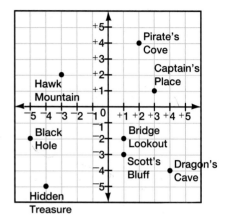

Mary wrote the location using the **ordered pair** ($^-4$, $^-5$). The numbers $^-4$ and $^-5$ are the **coordinates** of the point.

$$(\mathbf{^-4},\ \mathbf{^-5})$$

first coordinate
(distance to the right or left of 0)

second coordinate
(distance above or below 0)

1. What is the ordered pair for Dragon's Cave?

B. You can also graph an ordered pair on a coordinate grid.

Graph the point ($^+1$, $^-3$).

Start at 0. Count 1 unit to the right. Then count 3 units down.

The ordered pair ($^+1$, $^-3$) on Mary's map is the location of Scott's Bluff.

TRY OUT

Write the ordered pair for the point.

2. A   **3.** D

4. F   **5.** I

Name the point for the ordered pair.

6. ($^-1$, $^+4$)   **7.** (0, $^+2$)

8. ($^-3$, $^-3$)   **9.** ($^-1$, 0)

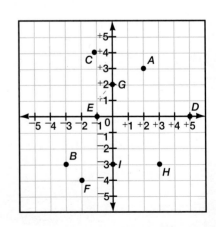

PRACTICE

Write the ordered pair for the point.

10. A   **11.** C   **12.** F   **13.** H

14. J   **15.** L   **16.** M   **17.** O

Name the point for the ordered pair.

18. (⁺2, ⁺2)   **19.** (⁻3, ⁻2)

20. (⁻3, ⁺1)   **21.** (0, ⁻4)

22. (⁻5, ⁻5)   **23.** (⁺5, ⁻2)

24. (⁺4, 0)   **25.** (⁻2, ⁺5)

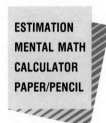

Use graph paper to draw a coordinate grid.
Graph each point.
Then draw line segments to connect the points in order.
What figure have you made?

26. (⁻6, 0)   **27.** (⁻3, ⁺5)   **28.** (⁻2, ⁺7)   **29.** (⁻1, ⁺5)

30. (⁺6, 0)   **31.** (⁺6, ⁻1)   **32.** (⁺5, ⁻2)   **33.** (⁺3, ⁻1)

34. (⁺5, ⁻3)   **35.** (⁺4, ⁻3)   **36.** (⁻1, ⁻1)   **37.** (⁻2, ⁻6)

Mixed Applications

Solve. Which method did you use?

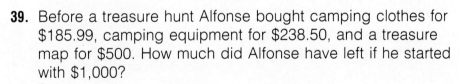

ESTIMATION
MENTAL MATH
CALCULATOR
PAPER/PENCIL

38. To get to Pirate's Cove, Mary had to climb 25 ft above ground level and then descend 50 ft into the cove. How far below ground level is the cove.?

39. Before a treasure hunt Alfonse bought camping clothes for $185.99, camping equipment for $238.50, and a treasure map for $500. How much did Alfonse have left if he started with $1,000?

40. A group of treasure hunters found 200 coins. Each coin is worth about $200 today. About how much are the coins worth?

Mixed Review

Find the answer. Which method did you use?

41. 3.525 + 0.25   **42.** 20 × 399   **43.** 6.172 − 5.89   **44.** $3\frac{2}{3} + 1\frac{3}{5}$

45. 5^3 **46.** 7,081 ÷ 73   **47.** $4\frac{3}{4} - 3\frac{1}{6}$ **48.** 62.75 × 0.009

ACTIVITY

Graphing Transformations

You can use a coordinate grid to graph **transformations,** or movements, of geometric figures.

Translation (slide)
4 units to the right

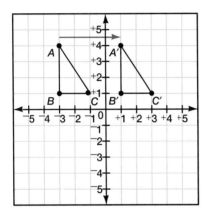

Reflection (flip)
about vertical axis

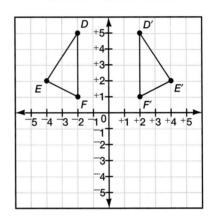

WORKING TOGETHER

1. List the coordinates of the vertices of △ABC.

2. What are the coordinates of its translation, △A'B'C'?

3. Draw △ABC on a coordinate grid. Draw a translation of 5 units down. What are the coordinates of the translation?

4. List the coordinates of the vertices of △DEF.

5. What are the coordinates of its reflection, △D'E'F'?

6. Draw △DEF on a coordinate grid. Draw its reflection about the horizontal axis. What are its coordinates?

SHARING IDEAS

7. What do you notice about the coordinates for the translation along the horizontal axis?

8. What do you notice about the coordinates for the translation along the vertical axis?

9. What do you notice about the coordinates for the reflection about the vertical axis? about the horizontal axis?

PRACTICE

What kind of transformation is shown on the coordinate grid?
List the names and coordinates of each pair of corresponding points.

10.

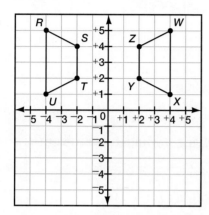

11.

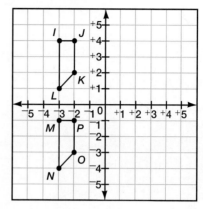

Draw △ABC on a coordinate grid.
Then draw the triangle whose vertices
are given by the ordered pairs below.
Describe the transformation suggested
in each case.

12. (⁻3, ⁻1), (⁻3, ⁻4), (⁻1, ⁻4)

13. (⁻3, ⁻1), (⁻3, ⁻4), (⁻1, ⁻1)

14. (⁺1, ⁺1), (⁺3, ⁺1), (⁺3, ⁺4)

15. (⁺1, ⁺1), (⁺3, ⁺1), (⁺1, ⁺4)

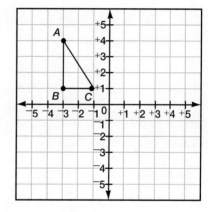

Solve.

16. Draw figure G on a coordinate grid.
Then draw its reflection about the
vertical axis.

17. Draw figure G again. Then translate
the figure 4 units to the right.

18. Draw a geometric shape on a
coordinate grid. Give directions for
translating it. Ask others to draw the
translation.

19. Draw a geometric shape on a
coordinate grid. Give directions for
drawing a reflection. Ask others to
draw the reflection.

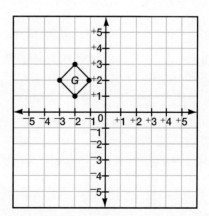

PROBLEM SOLVING

Strategies Review

You have used many strategies to solve problems.

- Conducting an Experiment
- Drawing a Diagram
- Finding a Pattern
- Making an Organized List
- Guess, Test, and Revise

- Making a Table
- Solving a Simpler Problem
- Solving a Multistep Problem
- Conducting a Simulation
- Working Backward

 Solve. Tell which strategy or strategies you used to solve the problem.

1. Victor has a dried-leaf collection. He has 9 maple leaves. The number of oak leaves he has is $\frac{1}{4}$ the number of dogwood leaves. The number of elm leaves he has is 2 more than the number of oak leaves. The number of maple leaves he has is 3 times the number of elm leaves. How many dogwood leaves are in his collection?

2. Davi buys 2 packages of African wildlife notepaper. There are 700 $3\frac{1}{2}$-in. by $3\frac{1}{2}$-in. sheets in each package. What is the area, to the nearest square foot, of the notepaper in the 2 packages?

3. A game of animal cards has 4 different animals on each card. The animals on each card are selected from six animals: elephant, gorilla, bear, lion, leopard, and giraffe. How many different cards are in the set?

4. Raphael's living-room wall is decorated with 8 rows of wooden tropical fish. There is 1 fish in the top row, 2 fish in the second row, 3 fish in the third row, 5 fish in the fourth row, and 8 fish in the fifth row. If the pattern continues, how many fish do you think are in the bottom row?

5. The nature store charges $3.95 to send merchandise that costs less than $30. It charges $1.55 more to send items that cost at least $30 but less than $50 and $1.55 for each additional $20 in merchandise. Nikki pays $8.60 to send a package. How much did the merchandise in the package cost?

6. A frog T-shirt and a frog umbrella cost $41.90. The umbrella costs $10 more than the shirt. How much does the umbrella cost?

7. A framed animal poster measures 25 in. by $35\frac{3}{4}$ in. The frame is $\frac{1}{2}$ in. wide. What is the area of the poster only?

8. How many times have other students visited the zoo in the last two years? Survey 20 students in your class. Record your results in a bar graph.

9. At the nature store Jeffrey buys 2 posters at $3.98 each, a whale mobile for $9.20, and an ant colony for $7.28. He gives the clerk $25. How much change should he get?

10. A circular outdoor thermometer is to be cemented to a square piece of wood so that the circle just touches the four sides of the square. The diameter of the circle is $11\frac{1}{4}$ in. Find the area of the square to the nearest square inch.

11. Abby and Benjy take a nature walk. They walk for 2 hours and travel a total of $4\frac{1}{2}$ mi. Part of the time they walk at a rate of 3 mi an hour. The rest of the time they walk at a rate of 2 mi an hour. How much time do they walk at each rate?

12. John makes a mixture of bird food. He uses 2 lb of sunflower seeds. The amount of corn he uses is $\frac{1}{3}$ the amount of peanuts. The amount of sunflower seeds he uses is $\frac{3}{4}$ lb more than the amount of corn. How many pounds of peanuts does John use in the mix?

13. Valerie and Matthew go apple picking. They get 10 apples from the first tree, 11 apples from the second tree, 13 from the third tree, and 17 from the fourth tree. "It would be great if this pattern continued!" Valerie said. "How many apples would we get from the ninth tree?"

DECISION MAKING

Problem Solving: Choosing a Graph

SITUATION

The Medina Elementary School is celebrating its fiftieth anniversary. On Parents' Day each class will have a display. The sixth-grade class has decided to show the growth of the school's enrollment for each decade over the 50 years.

PROBLEM

Should the class choose a bar graph, a line graph, or a pictograph to display their information?

DATA

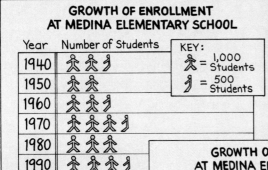

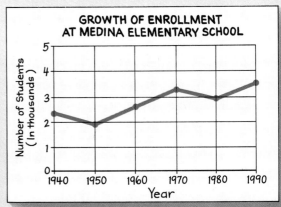

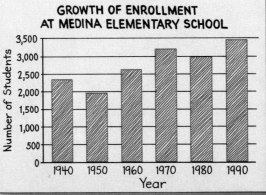

USING THE DATA

What was the difference in enrollment between 1960 and 1990?

1. bar graph   **2.** line graph   **3.** pictograph

Which year had the greatest enrollment?

4. bar graph   **5.** line graph   **6.** pictograph

What was the enrollment in 1950?

7. bar graph   **8.** line graph   **9.** pictograph

What was the total enrollment of Medina Elementary School from 1940 to 1990?

10. bar graph   **11.** line graph   **12.** pictograph

MAKING A DECISION

13. If the class wants to show the change in enrollment over a period of time, which type of graph should they choose?

14. If the class wants to show the comparisons between years, which type of graph should they choose?

15. If the class wants to show the change in school enrollment for the entire United States over the last 50 years, which type of graph should they choose?

16. Can you think of other ways the data could be displayed?

17. *Write a list* of other factors the students should consider.

18. Which type of graph would you choose for the presentation on Parents' Day? Tell why.

CURRICULUM CONNECTION

Math and Science

What is the coldest possible temperature? the hottest? There really is no limit to the highest temperature. For example, the temperature in the middle of the sun can reach hundreds of millions of degrees. But there is a limit to how cold something can get. The coldest possible temperature is called *absolute zero*.

How cold is absolute zero? If you can use the Celsius temperature scale, absolute zero is −273°C. But a more convenient temperature scale was developed by a British physicist, Lord Kelvin.

The Kelvin temperature scale begins at absolute zero. The way to write this is to say that the temperature at absolute zero, in the Kelvin scale, is 0 K. There are no negative temperatures in the Kelvin scale.

How could you convert 50°C to a Kelvin temperature?

Think: Use two number lines to represent each of the temperature scales. Compare the temperature on each scale.

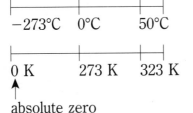

Celsius scale:

$-273°C \quad 0°C \quad 50°C$

Kelvin scale:

$0\text{ K} \quad 273\text{ K} \quad 323\text{ K}$

↑ absolute zero

$50 + 273 = 323$

So 50°C = 323 K

ACTIVITIES

1. Use a reference book to find the lowest and highest temperatures recorded on a Celsius scale. Convert the temperatures to a Kelvin scale. Graph the numbers on each temperature scale. Then compare the results.

2. Research the life of Lord Kelvin. Present your report to the class.

Calculator: Discover the Patterns

There are nine different patterns on this page. You can use your calculator to discover them.

Calculate the first three answers in the exercise. When you discover a pattern, write the remaining answers using the pattern. Then check your answers.

1. $1 \div 0.9$
$2 \div 0.9$
$3 \div 0.9$
$4 \div 0.9$
$5 \div 0.9$
$6 \div 0.9$

2. $1 \div 9$
$2 \div 9$
$3 \div 9$
$4 \div 9$
$5 \div 9$
$6 \div 9$

3. $1 \div 99$
$2 \div 99$
$3 \div 99$
$4 \div 99$
$5 \div 99$
$6 \div 99$

4. $10 \div 9$
$20 \div 9$
$30 \div 9$
$40 \div 9$
$60 \div 9$
$80 \div 9$

5. $10 \div 99$
$20 \div 99$
$30 \div 99$
$50 \div 99$
$70 \div 99$
$90 \div 99$

6. $1 \div 99$
$10 \div 99$
$100 \div 99$
$1,000 \div 99$
$10,000 \div 99$
$100,000 \div 99$

7. What pattern do you notice when a 1-digit number is divided by 9? by 99?

8. Predict the quotient of $2 \div 999$ and of $6 \div 999$.

9. $100 \div 0.9$
$200 \div 0.9$
$300 \div 0.9$
$500 \div 0.9$
$800 \div 0.9$
$1,000 \div 0.9$
$1,100 \div 0.9$
$1,300 \div 0.9$
$1,500 \div 0.9$

10. $100 \div 0.99$
$200 \div 0.99$
$300 \div 0.99$
$400 \div 0.99$
$600 \div 0.99$
$900 \div 0.99$
$1,000 \div 0.99$
$1,200 \div 0.99$
$1,500 \div 0.99$

11. $100 \div 0.999$
$200 \div 0.999$
$300 \div 0.999$
$400 \div 0.999$
$500 \div 0.999$
$800 \div 0.999$
$1,000 \div 0.999$
$1,200 \div 0.999$
$1,500 \div 0.999$

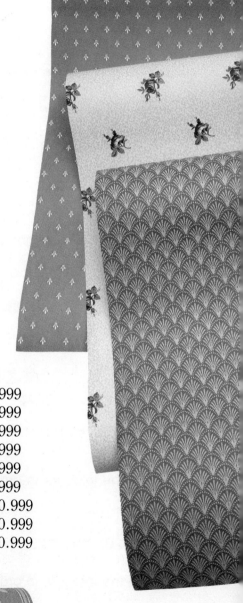

EXTRA PRACTICE

Integers and the Number Line, page 517

Write the integer identified by the letter. Then write the opposite integer.

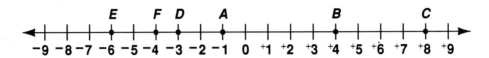

1. *A* **2.** *B* **3.** *E*

4. *D* **5.** *C* **6.** *F*

Write the integer for the point on the number line that is:

7. 15 units to the right of 0. **8.** 17 units to the left of 0.

9. opposite of $^+7$. **10.** 5 units to the left of $^-4$.

11. opposite of $^-12$. **12.** 8 units to the left of $^+8$.

13. 4 units to the right of $^-2$. **14.** 10 units to the right of $^-9$.

15. 6 units to the left of $^-1$. **16.** opposite of $^+15$.

Comparing and Ordering Integers, page 519

Compare. Write > or <. Think of a number line.

1. $^-2$ ● $^+7$ **2.** 0 ● $^-1$ **3.** $^-6$ ● 0 **4.** $^-2$ ● $^-10$ **5.** $^-9$ ● $^-6$

6. opposite of $^+8$ ● $^-12$ **7.** $^-9$ ● opposite of $^-6$

8. opposite of $^-14$ ● opposite of $^+26$ **9.** opposite of $^-93$ ● opposite of $^+2$

Write the integers in order from least to greatest.

10. $^-1$, $^+4$, $^-3$, $^-8$, $^+6$, $^+2$ **11.** $^-16$, $^-10$, $^+16$, $^+19$, $^+12$, $^-15$

12. $^-20$, $^+24$, $^-23$, $^+25$, $^-26$, $^+27$ **13.** opposite of $^-7$, $^+6$, $^-2$, 0, $^-6$

Write the integers in order from greatest to least.

14. $^-25$, $^+29$, $^-28$, $^+30$, $^-31$, $^+32$ **15.** $^-38$, $^+44$, $^+47$, $^-48$, $^+49$, $^-37$

16. $^+5$, opposite of $^+6$, $^-3$, opposite of $^-6$ **17.** $^+12$, opposite of $^+13$, $^-14$, opposite of $^-13$

Problem Solving Strategy: Using More Than One Strategy, page 525 . . . .

Use one or more strategies to solve the problem. Which strategy or strategies did you use?

1. Mr. Rao is decorating a bulletin board with drawings done by 12 of his students. The drawings are 10 in. squares. He wants to arrange them in 3 rows, 2 in. apart. He plans to have a 3-in. border around the outside of the pictures. What is the area of the bulletin board he needs?

2. The sixth-grade civics club is making 6 gourmet baskets for the annual school fair. Each basket contains three kinds of fruit. There are 2 more apples than pears and $\frac{1}{2}$ as many peaches as apples. There are 2 peaches. How many apples are there in all?

3. So far the students in Ms. Wong's class have collected $112.00 for the class barbecue in June. The first week they collected $7.00. From then on, at the end of each week they doubled the amount they collected. How many weeks did it take them to collect the $112.00?

4. The Greenway Garden Center is selling rose bushes for $9.50 each. The azalea bushes are selling for $5.99 each. John wants to plant an equal number of rose and azalea bushes in his garden. He has saved $50.00. How many of each kind of bush can John buy? How much money will be left over?

5. Mr. Clarke owns a local travel agency. He arranges tours to a variety of places. One of the agency's most popular tours is to Yellowstone National Park. The charge for the first day is $75.00. Each day after that is an additional $60.00. A customer paid Mr. Clarke $400, including a $25 tip. How long was the customer's trip?

6. The Barlow family is starting a family exercise program. The one exercise that everyone enjoys is cycling. The first week the family biked 3 mi. They biked 7 mi the second week and 11 mi the third week. If they continue to improve at this rate, how many miles will they bike the sixth week?

7. Barchester County has 5 Little League baseball teams. The teams are playing in a tournament. They will play rounds until each team has played every other team once. How many games will be played in all?

8. Elise is making her costume for the school play. She is using $2\frac{3}{4}$ yd of fabric to make the blouse and skirt. The skirt requires $\frac{3}{4}$ yd more fabric than the blouse. How many yards does each piece require?

EXTRA PRACTICE

Graphing Ordered Pairs, page 529

Write the ordered pair for the point.

1. *B* **2.** *G* **3.** *L* **4.** *M*

5. *F* **6.** *N* **7.** *J* **8.** *D*

Name the point for the ordered pair.

9. ($^+$3, $^+$3) **10.** ($^-$5, $^+$1)

11. ($^-$4, $^-$5) **12.** ($^+$3, $^-$3)

13. ($^+$1, $^+$2) **14.** ($^+$2, $^+$6)

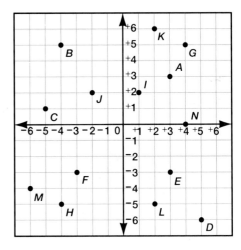

Graphing Transformations, page 531

What kind of transformation is shown on the coordinate grid?
List the names and coordinates of each pair of corresponding
points.

1.

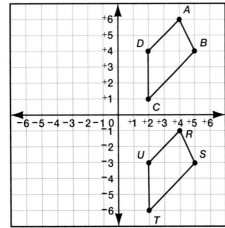

2.

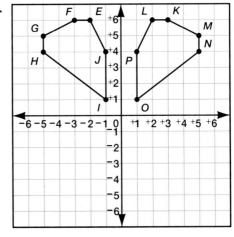

3. Draw a geometric shape on a coordinate grid.
Give directions for translating it. Ask others
to draw the translation.

4. Draw a geometric shape on a coordinate grid.
Give directions for drawing a reflection.
Ask others to draw the reflection.

Problem Solving Strategies Review, page 533 ....

Solve. Tell which strategy you used to solve the problem.

1. The Chesterfield Horse Farm has 25 Arabian horses. They have twice as many ponies as Thoroughbreds. The number of Arabian horses is $\frac{1}{3}$ the number of Thoroughbreds. How many ponies do they have?

2. At the Sav-Mar Department Store, Mrs. Carson buys two bath towels at $7.95 each, two hand towels at $4.25 each, and a set of sheets for $23.88. She gives the clerk $50. How much change does she get?

3. The C & R Leather Store charges $4.25 to send merchandise under $50. They charge an additional $1.70 to send items that cost at least $50 but less than $75, and $1.50 for each additional $25 in merchandise. Mason paid $8.95 to send a package. How much did the merchandise in the package cost?

4. Patrick and Louisa take a walk along the seashore. They walk for $1\frac{1}{2}$ hours and walk a total of 4 mi. Part of the time they walk at a rate of $2\frac{1}{2}$ mi per hour. The rest of the time they walk at the rate of 3 mi per hour. How much time do they walk at each rate?

5. The wallpaper in Sharon's room has rows in the shapes of hearts, diamonds, and squares. The first two rows are hearts, the third row is diamonds, the fourth row is squares, and the seventh row is diamonds. What shape do you think is in the tenth row?

6. The Circle R equestrian team chooses 5 horses to ride at each competition. They have 6 different horses to select from: a calico, a roan, a gray, a black, a white, and a chestnut. How many different combinations of horses are there?

PRACTICE PLUS

KEY SKILL: Comparing and Ordering Integers (Use after page 519.)

Level A ....

Compare. Write > or <. Think of the integers on a number line.

1. 0 ● $^+8$ **2.** $^+4$ ● $^+5$ **3.** $^+3$ ● $^-5$ **4.** $^-4$ ● 0   **5.** $^-6$ ● $^-7$

6. $^-4$ ● $^+4$ **7.** 0 ● $^-7$ **8.** $^-8$ ● $^-5$ **9.** $^-13$ ● $^+2$ **10.** $^+8$ ● $^-16$

Write the integers in order from least to greatest.

11. 0, $^+1$, $^-3$, $^+2$, $^-4$ **12.** $^-3$, $^+1$, $^+3$, $^-2$, $^-7$ **13.** $^-2$, $^+2$, $^-3$, $^+5$, $^-4$

14. Simon has a score of $^-15$, and Mary has a score of $^-16$. Who has the higher score?

Level B ....

Compare. Write > or <. Think of the integers on a number line.

15. $^-8$ ● $^+8$ **16.** $^+5$ ● $^+4$ **17.** $^-7$ ● $^+4$ **18.** $^-9$ ● $^-8$ **19.** $^+6$ ● $^-9$

20. 0 ● $^+10$ **21.** 0 ● $^-9$ **22.** $^-9$ ● $^-5$ **23.** $^-15$ ● $^+4$ **24.** $^+6$ ● $^-17$

Write the integers in order from least to greatest.

25. $^+4$, $^-5$, 0, $^+3$, $^-7$ **26.** $^-9$, $^-1$, $^+5$, $^-11$, $^+3$, $^-5$

27. $^+4$, opposite of $^+8$, $^-3$, opposite of $^-5$ **28.** $^+4$, $^+8$, $^-6$, $^-10$, $^-8$

29. Ben has a score of $^-8$, Tina $^+5$, George $^+1$, and Lara $^-6$. Write the names in order of their scores from least to greatest.

Level C ....

Compare. Write >, or <. Think of the integers on a number line.

30. opposite of $^+6$ ● $^-8$ **31.** opposite of $^+7$ ● opposite of $^-5$

Write the integers in order from greatest to least.

32. $^-2$, opposite of $^-2$, opposite of $^+7$, 0, $^+7$ **33.** opposite of $^-6$, $^+7$, opposite of $^+5$, $^-7$

34. opposite of $^-9$, $^+11$, opposite of $^+9$, $^-10$ **35.** $^+9$, opposite of $^+13$, $^+13$, opposite of $^-11$

36. Pam has a score of $^-7$, Jim has $^+6$, Bill has the opposite of Pam, and Jane has the opposite of Jim. Write the names in order of their scores from greatest to least.

PRACTICE PLUS

KEY SKILL: Graphing Ordered Pairs (Use after page 529.)

Level A

Write the ordered pair for the point.

1. *A*   **2.** *C*   **3.** *E*   **4.** *H*

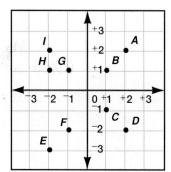

Name the point for the ordered pair.

5. ($^+$1, $^+$1)   **6.** ($^+$2, $^-$2)   **7.** ($^-$1, $^-$2)   **8.** ($^-$1, $^+$1)

9. Suppose you are drawing a map on a coordinate grid. Rockledge is 4 units right and 2 units up from 0. What are the coordinates of Rockledge?

Level B

Write the ordered pair for the point.

10. *B*   **11.** *E*   **12.** *L*   **13.** *Q*

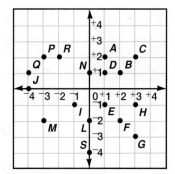

Name the point for the ordered pair.

14. ($^+$3, $^+$2) **15.** ($^+$2, $^-$2) **16.** ($^-$3, $^-$2) **17.** ($^-$4, 0)

18. Suppose you are drawing a map on a coordinate grid. Pine Grove is 3 units left and 4 units up from 0. What are the coordinates of Pine Grove?

Level C

Use graph paper to draw a coordinate grid. Graph each point. Then draw line segments to connect the points in order. What figure have you made?

19. ($^+$3, 0)   **20.** ($^+$3, $^+$3)   **21.** ($^+$2, $^+$4)   **22.** ($^+$1, $^+$3)   **23.** ($^-$1, $^+$3)

24. ($^-$2, $^+$4)   **25.** ($^-$3, 0)   **26.** ($^-$2, $^-$1)   **27.** ($^-$2, $^-$3)   **28.** ($^-$4, $^-$3)

29. ($^-$4, $^-$4)   **30.** ($^+$8, $^-$4)   **31.** ($^+$7, 0)   **32.** ($^+$3, 0)

33. On a map drawn on a coordinate grid, Mosquito Haven is located 3 units left and 4 units down from 0. Swampbrook is located 6 units up from Mosquito Haven. What are the coordinates of Mosquito Haven and Swampbrook?

CHAPTER REVIEW/TEST

LANGUAGE AND MATHEMATICS

Complete the sentences. Use the words in the chart on the right.

1. The opposite of positive seven is ■ seven. *negative*

2. The number lines on a coordinate grid are called ■. *axes*

3. On a coordinate grid, the pair of numbers identifying a point is called its ■. *coordinates*

4. If a figure on a coordinate grid is moved up, the transformation is called a(n) ■. *translation*

> **VOCABULARY**
> integer
> negative
> axes
> translation
> coordinates

CONCEPTS AND SKILLS

Use this line to find the integer described.

⁻10 ⁻9 ⁻8 ⁻7 ⁻6 ⁻5 ⁻4 ⁻3 ⁻2 ⁻1 0 ⁺1 ⁺2 ⁺3 ⁺4 ⁺5 ⁺6 ⁺7 ⁺8 ⁺9 ⁺10

5. 5 units to the right of ⁻5 *0*

6. 8 units to the left of ⁺1 *⁻7*

7. 7 units to the right of ⁺3 *10*

8. 1 unit to the left of ⁻6 *⁻7*

9. opposite of ⁺6 *⁻6*

10. opposite of ⁻8 *8*

Order from the least to the greatest.

11. ⁻10, ⁻20, ⁻15, ⁺2, ⁺3, ⁺4
⁻20, ⁻15, ⁻10, 2, 3, 4

12. ⁺45, ⁺60, ⁻45, ⁻60, ⁺30, ⁻30
⁻60, ⁻45, ⁻30, 30, 45, 60

13. 0, ⁻2, ⁺2, ⁻4, ⁺4
⁻4, ⁻2, 0, 2, 4

14. ⁻10, ⁺12, ⁻13, ⁺14
⁻13, ⁻10, 12, 14

15. 0, ⁺4, ⁻5, ⁻6, ⁻7, ⁺8
⁻7, ⁻6, ⁻5, 0, 4, 8

16. ⁺20, ⁺30, ⁻10, ⁻40, ⁺25
⁻40, ⁻10, 20, 25, 30

Compare using > or <.

17. ⁻86 ■ ⁻85

18. ⁻20 ■ ⁻30

19. opposite of ⁺15 ■ ⁻29

20. ⁻99 ■ ⁺99

21. ⁻82 ■ ⁻92

22. ⁺15 ■ ⁻20

Graph the point on a coordinate grid.

23. (⁺2, ⁺5)

24. (⁻3, ⁻4)

25. (⁻2, ⁺6)

26. (⁺3, ⁻4)

27. (⁺6, 0)

28. (0, ⁺7)

29. (⁻3, 0)

30. (0, ⁻1)

Critical Thinking

31. The first number of the coordinates of each vertex of a square is positive. The second number of each is negative. Describe the sign(s) of the coordinates of the vertices of the reflection about the vertical axis.

32. Both numbers of the coordinates of each vertex of a triangle on a coordinate grid are positive. Describe the sign(s) of the coordinates of the vertices of the reflection about the horizontal axis.

Mixed Applications

33. Lawrence has a collection of seashells. He has shells from the Gulf coast, the Pacific coast, and the Atlantic coast. There are 5 times more shells from the Pacific coast than from the Gulf coast. There are $\frac{3}{5}$ as many shells from the Gulf coast as from the Atlantic coast. Lawrence has 40 shells from the Atlantic coast. How many shells does Lawrence have?

PERFORMANCE ASSESSMENT

Work with your group to solve this problem.

Write a story describing the change in the outside temperature from midnight until noon. Illustrate the rise and fall in the temperature on a number line. Have the temperature drop 3 degrees each hour until 6:00 A.M., and rise 4 degrees each hour until noon. You may wish to start your story like this: At midnight the outside temperature is 14°F.

1. *Think about:*
   - how to show the changes in outside temperature on a number line
   - the greatest and least integers on the number line

2. Write a paragraph explaining how you can use a number line to show the changes in temperature for each hour from midnight to noon.

CUMULATIVE REVIEW

Choose the letter of the correct answer.

1. Which is 3 units to the left of $^-2$ on a number line?
   a. $^-5$
   b. $^-1$
   c. $^+1$
   d. not given

2. Which is 6 units to the right of $^-4$ on a number line?
   a. $^-10$
   b. $^-2$
   c. $^+2$
   d. not given

3. Which statement is true?
   a. $^-8 > ^+4$
   b. $^-6 > 0$
   c. $^+7 > ^-9$
   d. not given

4. Find the coordinates of a point 2 units to the right of $(^-5, ^+2)$.
   a. $(^-3, ^+2)$
   b. $(^-5, ^+5)$
   c. $(^-8, ^+2)$
   d. not given

5. Find the coordinates of a point 3 units up from $(^+4, ^-4)$.
   a. $(^+1, ^-4)$
   b. $(^+4, ^-7)$
   c. $(^+4, ^-1)$
   d. not given

6. Solve: $\frac{5}{6} = \frac{n}{3}$
   a. 2
   b. 24
   c. 25
   d. not given

7. Convert 0.02 to a percent.
   a. 0.02%
   b. 2%
   c. 20%
   d. not given

8. The side view of a cone looks like:
   a. a triangle.
   b. a rectangle.
   c. a circle.
   d. not given

9. What is the volume of a cylinder with $r = 6$ m and $h = 10$ m?
   a. 60π m³
   b. 120π m³
   c. $3{,}600\pi$ m³
   d. not given

10. What is the circumference of a circle with a diameter of 3 ft?
    a. 2.25π ft
    b. 6π ft
    c. 9π ft
    d. not given

11. How many outcomes are there given a black, blue, or red hat with a black, yellow, or red band?
    a. 3
    b. 6
    c. 9
    d. not given

Use the spinner for Questions 12–14.

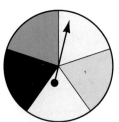

12. P(yellow)
    a. 40%
    b. 4%
    c. 2%
    d. not given

13. P(black)
    a. 0.02
    b. 0.2
    c. 20
    d. not given

14. In 200 spins, how many times would you expect blue?
    a. 4
    b. 20
    c. 40
    d. not given

USING MAPS

Oliver is on his bicycle at intersection 1 and wants to go to intersection 12. Avenue B has two-way traffic, but all the other streets are one-way. He wants to use his map of the city to find the shortest route from one intersection to the other.

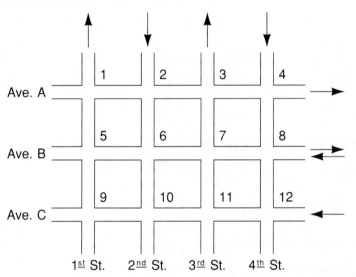

1. Can he use the route 1 → 3 → 7 → 8 → 12? If you answer no, tell why not.

2. Use "arrow routes" like the one in Problem 1 to show what routes he could use to go from 1 to 12. How many routes are there? How many blocks is the shortest route?

3. What is the shortest route from 1 to 9? How many blocks is it?

4. List the routes from 1 to 11. How many blocks is the shortest?

5. List the routes from 9 to 4. How many blocks is the shortest?

6. *What if* Oliver decided to forget about the bike and instead walked from 9 to 4 (the shortest way, of course). List the possible routes. Are they all the same number of blocks?

7. Draw a map of your neighborhood. Show which streets are one-way.

8. Use the map you drew for Problem 7 and trace the route you take from school to your home. Is it the shortest route?

Integers and Coordinate Graphing **547**

DATABANK

The Databank contains statistics and data similar to what can be found in outside reference books. The charts, graphs, menus, and maps contained here provide the real-world information needed to solve problems throughout the Pupil's Edition.

PROJECTIONS OF THE TOTAL UNITED STATES POPULATION BY GENDER AND AGE: 1990 to 2000 (in thousands)

Gender and Age	1990	1995	2000
Total Population	254,122	268,151	281,542
Male	123,698	130,577	137,163
Under 5 years old . .	10,550	10,653	10,508
5–17 years old	23,549	26,074	27,842
18–24 years old	13,283	12,325	12,881
25–44 years old	41,188	42,282	41,581
45–64 years old	22,377	25,518	30,074
65 years old and over	12,751	13,725	14,277
Female	130,424	137,574	144,379
Under 5 years old . .	10,065	10,161	10,022
5–17 years old	22,506	24,915.	26,592
18–24 years old	12,854	11,908	12,445
25–44 years old	41,371	42,262	41,398
45–64 years old	24,390	27,435	31,953
65 years old and over	19,238	20,893	21,969

WORLD'S LARGEST PASSENGER SHIPS

Name	Weight (in deadweight tons)
Norway	70,202
Queen Elizabeth 2	67,139
Canberra	44,807
Royal Princess	44,807
Onana	41,920
Rotterdam	38,644
1 deadweight ton = 1,000 kg or about 2,205 lb	

COMPUTERS R US SALES
(January–June)

Salesperson	Sales
Abrams	$298,871
Cooke	$369,124
Davis	$367,827
Rodriguez	$368,741
Brunelli	$298,962
Rogers	$297,872

DATABANK

FOREIGN EXCHANGE RATES
(VALUE TO $1 U.S.)

Country	Value
Canada	1.23 dollars
France	5.82 francs
Great Britain	0.55 pounds
Japan	125 yen
Italy	1,283 lire
West Germany	1.72 marks
Soviet Union	0.59 rubles

SPEED OF ANIMALS
(miles per hour)

Animal	Speed
Cheetah	70
Lion	50
Quarter Horse	47.5
Zebra	40
Rabbit	35
Greyhound	39.35
Cat	30
Spider	1.17
Giant Tortoise	0.17

MAJOR PARTIES' POPULAR AND ELECTORAL VOTE FOR PRESIDENT

(D) Democrat   (R) Republican

Year	Candidate	Popular Vote	Electoral Vote
1972	Richard M. Nixon (R)	47,165,234	520
	George S. McGovern (D)	29,170,774	17
1976	Jimmy Carter (D)	40,828,929	297
	Gerald R. Ford (R)	39,148,940	240
1980	Ronald Reagan (R)	43,899,248	489
	Jimmy Carter (D)	35,481,435	49
	John B. Anderson (Independent)	5,719,437	--
1984	Ronald Reagan (R)	54,281,858	526
	Walter F. Mondale (D)	37,457,215	13
1988	George Bush (R)	47,545,225	426
	Michael S. Dukakis (D)	40,797,905	112

INFORMATION ABOUT SOME ZOO ANIMALS

	African Elephant	Polar Bear	Giraffe	Gorilla	Hippopotamus
Maximum weight (kilograms)	5,450	725	1,180	200	3,625
Food eaten per day (kilograms)					
Hay	23		7		18
Pellets	1.1		3.2		8.2
Dog food		1.6			
Grain	0.4				
Zoo cakes				1.8	
Fruits and vegetables	1.8	0.9	0.1	4	
Fish		1.4			
Meat		2.1			

PROFESSIONAL BASKETBALL ARENAS

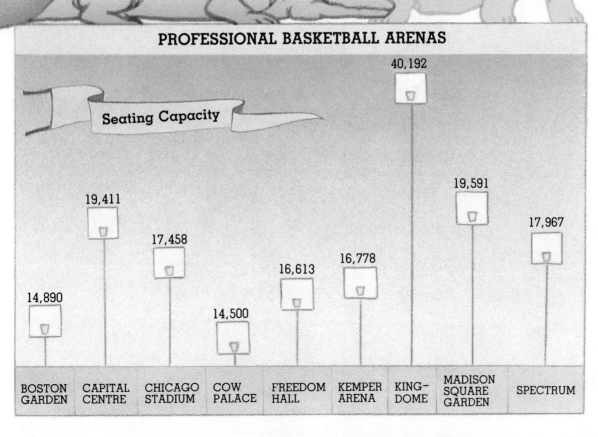

Seating Capacity

BOSTON GARDEN	14,890
CAPITAL CENTRE	19,411
CHICAGO STADIUM	17,458
COW PALACE	14,500
FREEDOM HALL	16,613
KEMPER ARENA	16,778
KINGDOME	40,192
MADISON SQUARE GARDEN	19,591
SPECTRUM	17,967

CALORIC COUNTS OF SOME FOODS

Food	Quantity	Calories
Skim milk	1 cup	85
Whole milk	1 cup	165
Orange juice	8 ounces	110
Toast	1 slice	50
Raisin flakes cereal	1 cup	150
Chicken salad	3 ounces	210
Tuna salad	4 ounces	330
Baked potato	1 medium	150
String beans	$3\frac{1}{2}$ ounces	35
Peanuts, shelled	1 cup	805

PLANTING INSTRUCTIONS

Plant	Distance to be Planted Apart
Anemone	$1\frac{1}{6}$ ft
Castor Bean	$2\frac{1}{2}$ ft
Daisy	$\frac{5}{6}$ ft
Hollyhock	$1\frac{1}{3}$ ft
Japanese Burberry	$1\frac{1}{2}$ ft
Lilac	2 ft
Marigold	$\frac{1}{2}$ ft
Mulberry	3 ft
Peony	4 ft
Petunia	$\frac{2}{3}$ ft

THE BUSIEST UNITED STATES AIRPORTS IN 1987

Airport	Number of Travelers
Atlanta	47,649,470
Chicago O'Hare	57,543,865
Dallas/Ft. Worth	41,875,444
Denver	32,355,000
Los Angeles	44,873,113

NOTABLE SUSPENSION BRIDGES IN NORTH AMERICA

Year	Bridge	Location	Longest Span (in ft)
1964	Verrazano-Narrows	New York, NY	4,260
1937	Golden Gate	San Francisco Bay, CA	4,200
1957	Mackinac	Straits of Mackinac, MI	3,800
1931	George Washington	Hudson River, NY–NJ	3,500
1950	Tacoma Narrows	Tacoma, WA	2,800
1936	Transbay	San Francisco Bay, CA	2,310
1939	Bronx-Whitestone	New York, NY	2,300
1970	Pierre Laporte	Quebec, Canada	2,190
1951	Delaware Memorial	Wilmington, DE	2,150
1968	Delaware Memorial (new)	Wilmington, DE	2,150
1957	Walt Whitman	Philadelphia, PA	2,000

AGRICULTURAL PRODUCTS—UNITED STATES PRODUCTION 1987

Grain	Percent of World Production From United States
Wheat	0.11
Oats	0.12
Corn	0.40
Barley	0.07
Rice	0.01

DATABANK

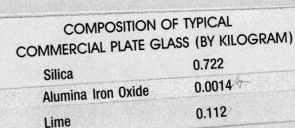

COMPOSITION OF TYPICAL COMMERCIAL PLATE GLASS (BY KILOGRAM)

Silica	0.722
Alumina Iron Oxide	0.0014
Lime	0.112
Magnesia	0.021
Soda	0.137

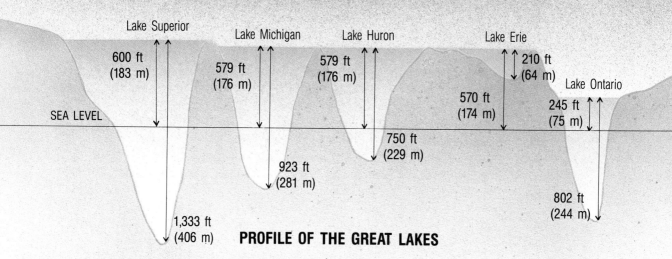

PROFILE OF THE GREAT LAKES

Lake Superior — 600 ft (183 m) — 1,333 ft (406 m)
Lake Michigan — 579 ft (176 m) — 923 ft (281 m)
Lake Huron — 579 ft (176 m) — 750 ft (229 m)
Lake Erie — 210 ft (64 m) — 570 ft (174 m)
Lake Ontario — 245 ft (75 m) — 802 ft (244 m)
SEA LEVEL

MONTHLY NORMAL TEMPERATURE FOR SELECTED CITIES (°F)

	Jan.	Feb.	Mar.	April	May	June	July	Aug.	Sept.	Oct.	Nov.	Dec.
Anchorage, AK	13	18	24	35	46	54	58	56	48	35	22	14
Chicago, IL	21	26	36	49	59	69	73	72	65	54	40	28
Los Angeles, CA	57	59	60	62	65	69	74	75	73	69	63	58
Miami, FL	67	68	72	75	79	81	83	83	82	78	73	69
Phoenix, AZ	52	56	61	68	77	87	92	90	85	73	61	53
San Antonio, TX	50	54	62	70	76	82	85	84	79	70	60	53

A

angle Two *rays* with a common *endpoint*.

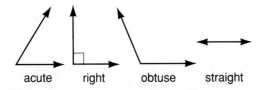

acute   right   obtuse   straight

area The number of square units needed to cover a region.

associative property The way *addends* or *factors* are grouped does not change the *sum* or *product*.

$$3 + (4 + 5) = (3 + 4) + 5$$
$$(3 \times 4) \times 5 = 3 \times (4 \times 5)$$

axes The two number lines on a *coordinate grid*.

B

bisect To divide into two *congruent* parts.

C

capacity The amount of a substance that a container can hold.

certain event An *outcome* that is certain to occur. Its *probability* is 1.

circle A simple closed figure having all points an equal distance from the center.

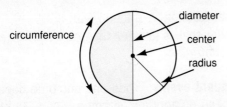

circumference   diameter   center   radius

circumference The distance around a circle.

common denominator A common *multiple* of the *denominators* of two or more fractions.

common factor A *factor* that is shared by two or more numbers.

common multiples A *multiple* that is the same for two or more numbers.

commutative property The order of the *addends* or *factors* does not change the *sum* or *product*.

$$5 + 4 = 4 + 5 \qquad 4 \times 5 = 5 \times 4$$

compatible numbers A number changed to a basic fact to give an estimate. For example, $4.32 \div 6$ becomes $4.2 \div 6 = 0.7$.

compensation Adding and subtracting the same amount to both addends.

composite number A number greater than 1 having more than two *factors*.

congruent figures Figures that have the same size and shape.

coordinate grid The *plane* made by the intersection of two *axes*.

coordinates The numbers in an *ordered pair*.

corresponding parts Matching parts of *congruent* figures.

D

decagon A *polygon* with ten sides.

diagonal A *line segment* other than a side that connects two *vertices* of a *polygon*.

distributive property A redistribution of the numbers which maintains the equality of the equation.

$$4 \times 32 = (4 \times 30) + (4 \times 2)$$

dividend The number to be divided.

divisibility One number is divisible by another if the remainder is 0 after dividing.

divisor The number used to divide another number.

double-bar graph *Data* presented visually using two bars to show comparisons.

double-line graph *Data* presented visually using two lines to show trends and changes over time.

E

endpoint A point at the end of a *ray* or *line segment*.

equal ratios Ratios that make the same comparison.

equation A number sentence with an *is-equal-to* (=) sign.

equivalent decimals Decimals that name the same number.

equivalent fractions Fractions that name the same number.

expanded form A number written as the sum of the value of its digits.

$$4,813 = (4 \times 1,000) + (8 \times 100) + (1 \times 10) + (3 \times 1)$$

exponent form A number expressed using a *base* and an *exponent*.

$$2^3 = 2 \times 2 \times 2 = 8$$

exponent

base   factors

expression A mathematical phrase made up of numbers and operation signs.

F

factors The numbers that are multiplied to give a product.

factor tree A diagram used to find the *prime factors* of a number.

fraction A number that names part of a whole or part of a group.

$\dfrac{2}{3}$ — numerator — denominator

frequency diagram A representation of *data* together with the number of times an item occurs.

frequency table A listing of *data* together with the number of times an item occurs.

G

geometric figures Figures made up of *points, planes, line segments, lines, rays,* or *angles.*

greatest common factor (GCF) The greatest number that is a *factor* of two or more whole numbers.

H

hexagon A *polygon* with six sides.

I

impossible event An *outcome* that has no chance of occurring. Its *probability* is 0.

improper fraction A fraction with a *numerator* that is greater than or equal to the *denominator*.

independent events When one outcome does not depend on another outcome.

integer A positive or negative whole number or zero.

intersecting lines Lines that meet at a point.

inverse operations Operations that "undo" each other.

L

least common denominator (LCD) The *least common multiple* of the *denominators* of two or more fractions.

least common multiple (LCM) The least nonzero number that is a *multiple* of two or more numbers.

line An endless straight path.

line of symmetry A line that divides a figure into two *congruent* parts.

line segment A part of a *line* having two *endpoints*.

M

mass The amount of matter that makes up an object.

mean The sum of a collection of *data* divided by the number of data.

median The middle number when the data is arranged in order.

mixed number The sum of a whole number and a fraction.

mode The number or numbers that occur most often in a collection of *data*.

multiples Products obtained by multiplying a number by 0, 1, 2, 3, . . .

O

octagon A *polygon* with eight sides.

opposite integers Two different integers that are the same distance from 0 on the number line, for example, $^+8$ and $^-8$.

ordered pair Two numbers that name a specific point on a *coordinate plane*.

order of operations The proper sequence of operations: multiply or divide from left to right, then add or subtract from left to right.

outcome The results of an *event*.

P

parallel lines Lines in the same *plane* that never meet.

parallelogram A *quadrilateral* with opposite sides parallel. Each pair of opposite sides and angles is *congruent*.

pentagon A *polygon* with five sides.

percent (%) The *ratio* of a given number to 100.

perimeter The distance around a figure.

perpendicular lines Two lines that *intersect* to form *right angles*.

pi (π) The *ratio* of the *circumference* of a *circle* to its *diameter* (about 3.14 or $\frac{22}{7}$).

place-value chart A chart showing the value of a *digit* by its position in a number.

plane A flat surface that extends in all directions without end.

point An exact location in space.

polygon A closed figure that has three or more sides.

prime factorization A *composite number* written as the product of *prime numbers*.

$$12 = 2 \times 2 \times 3$$

prime number A number greater than 1 that has only two *factors*, itself and 1.

probability The likelihood that an *event* will occur.

product The result when two or more numbers are multiplied.

proportion A statement that two *ratios* are equal.

Q

quadrilateral A four-sided *polygon*.

quotient The result when one number is divided by another number.

R

range The difference between the least and the greatest numbers in a collection of *data*.

ratio A comparison of two quantities.

ray A part of a *line* that has one *endpoint* and continues without end in one direction.

reciprocals Two numbers whose product is 1, for example, $\frac{1}{6}$ and $\frac{6}{1}$.

rectangle A *parallelogram* with four *right angles*.

reflection The mirror image of a figure about a line of symmetry on a plane.

rhombus A *parallelogram* with four *congruent* sides.

Roman numerals A number system using Roman letters as numerals.

rotation The image of a figure moved through an angle about a point on a plane.

rounded numbers Numbers expressed to the nearest ten, hundred, and so on.

S

scale drawing A reduced or enlarged drawing of an actual object.

similar figures Figures with the same shape but not necessarily the same size.

simplest form A fraction in which the *numerator* and *denominator* have no common factors other than 1.

space figures Three-dimensional figures.

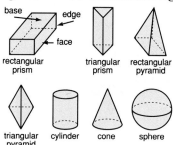

rectangular prism   triangular prism   rectangular pyramid

triangular pyramid   cylinder   cone   sphere

square A rectangle with four *congruent* sides.

statistics The science of collecting, organizing, and analyzing data.

symmetrical When two parts match exactly.

T

translation The *slide* image of a figure on a plane.

trapezoid A *quadrilateral* with exactly one pair of *parallel* sides.

tree diagram A diagram used to show *outcomes* or possibilities.

triangle A three-sided polygon.

V

Venn diagram A special diagram using overlapping circles to show the relationship between groups of objects.

vertex (vertices) The point where two *rays* of an *angle* meet. The point where two sides of a *polygon* meet.

volume The number of *cubic units* needed to fill a *space figure*.

COMPUTER TERMS

cell The way in which one unit of information such as one character, one byte, or one word is stored in a computer. Also, each individual box or square within the coordinate grid of an electronic spreadsheet.

data Information that is put into a computer.

database A group of facts and figures that are related and can be arranged in different ways. For example, the names, addresses, ages, and telephone numbers of every student in your school would be a database.

simulate To use a computer to study the possible solutions to a problem before trying them in real life.

spreadsheet A computer program that arranges data and formulas in a grid of cells.

TABLE OF MEASURES

METRIC UNITS

LENGTH
1 millimeter (mm)	= 0.001 meter (m)
1 centimeter (cm)	= 0.01 meter
1 decimeter (dm)	= 0.1 meter
1 dekameter (dam)	= 10 meters
1 hectometer (hm)	= 100 meters
1 kilometer (km)	= 1,000 meters

MASS/WEIGHT
1 milligram (mg)	= 0.001 gram (g)
1 centigram (cg)	= 0.01 gram
1 decigram (dg)	= 0.1 gram
1 dekagram (dag)	= 10 grams
1 hectogram (hg)	= 100 grams
1 kilogram (kg)	= 1,000 grams
1 metric ton (t)	= 1,000 kilograms

CAPACITY
1 milliliter (mL)	= 0.001 liter (L)
1 centiliter (cL)	= 0.01 liter
1 deciliter (dL)	= 0.1 liter
1 dekaliter (daL)	= 10 liters
1 hectoliter (hL)	= 100 liters
1 kiloliter (kL)	= 1,000 liters

AREA
1 square centimeter (cm²)	= 100 square millimeters (mm²)
1 square meter (m²)	= 10,000 square centimeters
1 hectare (ha)	= 10,000 square meters
1 square kilometer (km²)	= 1,000,000 square meters

CUSTOMARY UNITS

LENGTH
1 foot (ft)	= 12 inches (in.)
1 yard (yd)	= 36 inches
1 yard	= 3 feet
1 mile (mi)	= 5,280 feet
1 mile	= 1,760 yards

WEIGHT
1 pound (lb)	= 16 ounces (oz)
1 ton (T)	= 2,000 pounds

CAPACITY
1 cup (c)	= 8 fluid ounces (fl oz)
1 pint (pt)	= 2 cups
1 quart (qt)	= 2 pints
1 quart	= 4 cups
1 gallon (gal)	= 4 quarts

AREA
1 square foot (ft²)	= 144 square inches (in.²)
1 square yard (yd²)	= 9 square feet
1 acre	= 43,560 square feet
1 square mile (mi²)	= 640 acres

TIME
1 minute (min)	= 60 seconds (s)
1 hour (h)	= 60 minutes
1 day (d)	= 24 hours
1 week (wk)	= 7 days
1 year (y)	= 12 months (mo)
1 year	= 52 weeks
1 year	= 365 days
1 century (c)	= 100 years

FORMULAS

$P = 2(l + w)$	Perimeter of a rectangle
$P = 4s$	Perimeter of a square
$A = l \times w$	Area of a rectangle
$A = s^2$	Area of a square
$A = b \times h$	Area of a parallelogram
$A = \frac{1}{2}(b \times h)$	Area of a triangle
$C = \pi \times d$, or $2 \times \pi \times r$	Circumference of a circle
$A = \pi \times r^2$	Area of a circle
$V = l \times w \times h$	Volume of a rectangular prism
$V = B \times h$	Volume of any prism
$V = \pi \times r^2 \times h$	Volume of a cylinder

SYMBOLS

$=$	is equal to
$\neq$	is not equal to
$>$	is greater than
$<$	is less than
$\geq$	is greater than or equal to
$\leq$	is less than or equal to
$\approx$	is approximately equal to
$\cong$	is congruent to
$\sim$	is similar to
$\ldots$	continues without end
$1.\overline{3}$	repeating decimal 1.333...
%	percent
π	pi (approximately 3.14)
°	degree
°C	degree Celsius
°F	degree Fahrenheit
$\overleftrightarrow{AB}$	line AB
$\overline{AB}$	line segment AB
$\overrightarrow{AB}$	ray AB
$\angle ABC$	angle ABC
$\triangle ABC$	triangle ABC
$\parallel$	is parallel to
$\perp$	is perpendicular to
2:5	ratio of 2 to 5
10^2	ten to the second power
$^+4$	positive 4
$^-4$	negative 4
$|^-4|$	absolute value of $^-4$
$(^+3, ^-4)$	ordered pair 3, $^-4$
$P(E)$	probability of event E

560

Brookland Year   7ᵗʰ grade

20
00
1200
+1200
3
4

1996-1997

Shannon Williams
13
13
36

Cory White

Vann Christian

Ashlee Gary

Ron Hannah

Gavin Mayo-Anderson   Erica Glasper

Anthony Grimes   Dwight

Curry   Terrel

David Harris

Josett Bell

Arnetta Hampton

Erik Trueheart

Tecorious

Rekaira   Domonique

Brian   Tyrone Jackson

Sherree Hatley   Kashonna

Saima Gielani   Natasha Hartley

Gielani Lawrence